AMERICAN
LITERATURE

AMERICAN LITERATURE

As an Expression
of the National
Mind

REVISED  EDITION

RUSSELL BLANKENSHIP

University of Washington

HENRY HOLT AND COMPANY · New York

TO MY CLASSES
IN
AMERICAN LITERATURE

PREFACE TO THE REVISED EDITION

Since 1931 our literature, while not lacking in works of great merit, has been characterized more by confusion than by the quality of the books produced. A grinding depression, a period of political and social reform, and a shattering second world war have kept our writers from proceeding on predictable courses. A rather long new chapter discusses some of the more significant writers of the last two decades. Though the author of the present work disclaims even the most modest prophetic talent, he is willing to suggest that Hemingway, Marquand, and possibly Farrell seem to be permanent additions to our roster of novelists. Most of the others, even John Dos Passos, must be appraised in tentative terms.

Probably the most significant literary event since the recent war is the revival of interest in Henry James. The Jamesian renascence is a belated but wholly laudable atonement for decades of critical and popular neglect.

R. B.

Seattle, Washington
March 28, 1949

BY WAY OF PREFACE—AND APOLOGY

The doleful critic who testified so emphatically to the absence of anything new under the sun would feel that his animadversions were trebly justified could his eyes fall upon any page of this book. And to forestall the all-too-willing echoes of the dour ancient, the author hastens to explain that he planned and wrote the book with never a thought of putting anything new therein. His first aim was to assemble in convenient form the more important facts dredged by the industrious from the dreadful swamp of primary sources; his second aim was to present an interpretation of these facts, along with certain plausible conclusions or theories deduced by our more perspicacious thinkers.

Indeed the habit of authors to invade the preserves of their neighbors and return with booty, the origins of which are but indifferently concealed, is as old as literature itself, and it very likely was that same practice that led the aforesaid ancient to deliver himself of his sweeping reflections on originality. Historians of literature have hardly been exemplars of unquestionable originality. In truth, the accounts of American literature that are notable either for the freshness of their facts or for the newness of their interpretations are only three in number. The first of these is the indispensable survey of our reputed literature from 1607 to 1783 by Moses Coit Tyler, who performed the most unacademic and almost unparalleled feat of reading all the books that he was preparing to discuss. The second is the monumental work by Vernon Louis Parrington on *Main Currents in American Thought*, the originality of which is insured by the author's acquaintance with his material no less than by his daringly liberal point of view. The third history, which cannot be named because of the author's dizzy eminence, is so egregiously lacking in merit that proof of its astounding originality can be detected upon almost every page and in almost every omission. With dozens of histories of our national literature, crowded to repletion with pilfered facts, reposing in utmost respectability upon our shelves, one hesitates not at all to offer another and still maintain a slight claim to ordinary rectitude.

As a matter of fact, in a sketch of our literary history, originality is the last thing either possible or desirable. Within the last few years more or less accurate and illuminating studies of our individual writers have streamed from the hurrying pens of biographers and critics until now there is scarcely a figure in our literature too remote or too obscure to enjoy the distinction of at least a critical essay, while the remains of many not quite illustrious have been embalmed in doctoral dissertations of portentous gravity. For all such works the student should be thankful, and upon each one the author has levied his tribute of assistance.

In addition to the factual work just mentioned, the study of American literature has been vastly expedited of late by the very stimulating criticism done by such men as John Macy, H. L. Mencken, Van Wyck Brooks, Ludwig Lewisohn, Carl Van Doren, Randolph Bourne, Lewis Mumford, Joseph Wood Krutch, Henry S. Canby, William Rose Benét, and many another. Academic folk, taking not at all kindly to the views and personalities of some of these critics, have been disposed to damn the whole group by hinting darkly at "journalistic qualities." Such attempted disparagement is not wholly condemnatory, for the desiderata of competent journalists are accuracy and interest.

The most valuable work done by the "new critics," for such they have been called, has been the linking up of contemporary literature with current problems of social import. Readers who regard literature as something more than the indispensable accompaniment of a hot day and a hammock soon discovered, under the urgings of the new critics, that Messrs. Herrick, Churchill, Dreiser, Lewis, Masters, O'Neill, Sandburg, and Cabell—to name no more—are not positively innocent of all social problems other than those raised by certain recent legislation. Then the more perceptive readers began to entertain the vague suspicion that American literature of the past might not be compounded equally of whiskers, dust, and pious platitudes. Although this suspicion collided violently with most of the ideas retained from the class room, readers and students rediscovered American literature, and one of the most gratifying features of the rediscovery was the realization that such men as Howells, Mark Twain, Whitman, Melville, Emerson, Thoreau, and Cooper did not perpetually immure themselves within splendid ivory towers where they paid incessant worship to that esoteric goddess known as esthetic beauty.

To-day there is none so ignorant as to think that our literature was contrived in the somnolence of the ivory tower. We all know that it came from those workshops, of whatever nature, where the minds and bodies of men were grappling with questions of mundane application. And literature is one in flesh and spirit with those who produce it. No longer should we dispute over the esthetic worth of our letters, nor should we be deeply disquieted lest some of our writers perchance did not bethink themselves to place in their writings those qualities that are the traditional literary insurance against transiency. It suffices to know that there has been a great and disorganizing change in American thinking since 1630 and that our literature makes articulate those long hushed lips whose possessors forwarded the changing of our thought or perhaps resisted innovation as the veritable offspring of depravity. Questions of religion, politics, practical morality, business, and statecraft, whose pallid ghosts hover wanly in lecture halls, again take corporeal form in the pages of our literature. Literature has never been a far remove from life, at least on this continent.

Whether our literature is "great" or not is of comparatively slight importance. It is profoundly expressive of the changing American mind, and that distinction is hardly a minor one among people who value as no paltry thing their cultural heritage and the channels by which that bequest came into their hands. However, it is perhaps correct to say that a conception of the historical and social significance of our national letters was foreign to most people until rather lately. Such a conception entails a reappraisal of our whole literature both in the general and in the specific. And the huge task of putting even intelligent readers into the mood for making this reappraisal was mightily promoted by the new critics. These writers interpreted Dreiser's books, for instance, as products of a mind and art shaped by the modern city and colored by a thought that was strictly contemporary. Now when a man, who has anything more than the most rudimentary reflective powers, gains this idea of Dreiser, he is not to be accounted rash and presumptuous if he speculates on the possibility that Emerson and Cooper were also children of their ages and their localities. It is no disparagement of our erstwhile academic tutors to say that the new critics first showed many of us the inseparable union of literature and the social environment.

In testing whether the literature of the past justly interprets its age, historical studies that emphasize the social environment naturally become very valuable. Indeed if the portions of the present work that are borrowed from historians were to be removed, the mortar would disappear from the structure, and in place of a unified discussion there would be a jumble of short estimates having little relation to each other and none at all to the whole work. Among the histories and interpretations that have been most prolific of assistance are those of Henry Adams, Frederick Jackson Turner, John Bach McMaster, Charles A. Beard, A. M. Schlesinger, James Truslow Adams, Dixon Ryan Fox, Carl Becker, Claude Bowers, Carl Fish, Thomas J. Wertenbaker, Allan Nevins, Ulrich B. Phillips, Solon Buck, and William E. Dodd. The student who wishes to know how fully our literature speaks for its age and how an age is re-created by its literature will find that a knowledge of American social history is probably the most valuable portion of his intellectual equipment.

To conclude, this apology explains both the impulses that animated the author and the methods that he used to write this sketch of American literary development. Like many another man, he had received more than a little college instruction in American history without ever discovering whether *Moby Dick* was a prizefighter or a participant in an obscure slave insurrection. To have suggested to him that Jefferson, Emerson, Whitman, and Lincoln were one in aims and aspirations would only have made him seek refuge in the silence of incredulity. After graduation from college, he began, casually at first, to read some of the new critics. Under the influence of these men he started a somewhat systematic study of American life and letters—a study that is obviously still in its elementary stages. In the course of this task a brief association with the late Vernon Louis Parrington as instructor and friend was by far the strongest and most beneficial influence that he received. The indebtedness to Professor Parrington goes far beyond the limits indicated in either the preface or the body of this book, although the third volume of his extensive work, *The Beginnings of Critical Realism in America,* appeared after the manuscript of this volume was completed.

To be specific, in the preparation of these pages the author found that the following books were of utmost value to him:

Parrington: *Main Currents in American Thought*—Vol. I, The Colonial Mind; Vol. II, The Romantic Revolution.
Tyler: *A History of American Literature* (1607-1765).
A Literary History of the American Revolution.

Beard and Beard: *The Rise of American Civilization.*
Adams: *The Founding of New England.*
Mumford: *Sticks and Stones.*
  The Golden Day.
Riley: *American Thought.*
Jones: *America and French Culture.*
Brooks: *America's Coming-of-Age.*
Van Doren: *The American Novel.*
Schlesinger: *New Viewpoints in American History.*
Macy: *The Spirit of American Literature.*
Turner: *The Significance of the Frontier.*
Hazard: *The Frontier in American Literature.*
Smith: *North America.*
Semple: *American History and Its Geographical Conditions.*
Foerster (ed.): *Reinterpretation of American Literature.*

The author wishes to express his personal thanks to Gertrude Maxwell and Nelly Appy for advice and encouragement when he was planning to make the work something very different from what it eventually became. His colleagues, Ray Lapham and Mark Harris gave generously of their time and counsel during every stage in the making of the book. To them he owes his deepest thanks. To his assistant, Dorothy Hull, he acknowledges a greater debt of gratitude than he can easily express. And finally, without the assistance of Mrs. Harriett L. Carstensen and Ruth Reynolds of the Whitman College library it would have been impossible to collect the material for this book.

For permission to reprint material acknowledgment is hereby given to the following persons and publishing houses:

Willa Cather—for permission to quote from her essay, *The Novel Deméublé.*

Doubleday, Doran and Company—for permission to quote from *John Brown's Body* by Stephen Vincent Benét.

T. S. Eliot—for permission to quote from his poems.

Henry Holt and Company—for permission to quote from *Cornhuskers* and *Chicago Poems* by Carl Sandburg and from *North of Boston, Mountain Interval,* and *New Hampshire* by Robert Frost.

Houghton Mifflin Company—for permission to quote from *Poems and Poetic Dramas* by William Vaughn Moody and from *A Critical Fable* and *Selected Poems* by Amy Lowell.

Horace Liveright—for permission to quote from *The Waste Land* by T. S. Eliot and from various poems by Robinson Jeffers.

Robert McBride and Company—for permission to quote from *Beyond Life* by James Branch Cabell.

The Macmillan Company—for permission to quote from *The Man Against the Sky* by Edwin Arlington Robinson.

CONTENTS

BOOK I: THE BACKGROUND

BOOK II: THE MIND OF COLONIAL AMERICA

CONTENTS

BOOK III: ROMANTICISM IN AMERICA

BOOK I
THE BACKGROUND

CHAPTER I

THE PHYSICAL BACKGROUND

If there is one outstanding fact in American geography, it is the extreme diversity of physical characteristics and climate within the borders of this nation. In soil, surface, drainage, and natural trade routes there is the utmost difference between the various parts of the country, while the climate ranges from the moist, sub-tropical of the Gulf states to that of the upper Mississippi Valley with its great extremes of temperature and that of the semi-arid plains with still greater extremes. So marked is the variation of physical environment within the United States that, if this country had been settled by one homogeneous race, the inhabitants would have developed intellectually along widely different lines. If like-minded Englishmen in Virginia and New York ultimately become unlike in thought and action, how great will the differences become when one colony is settled by Cavaliers, another by the strictest of Puritans, another by Scotch-Irish, and another by Dutch, and still another by the English Quakers. Certainly up to the Civil War we developed sectional differences and peculiarities, but it is a mistake to attribute all the differences to race. Our diversified geography had considerable influence.

Another notable geographical fact is the position of the early settlements on the Atlantic seaboard directly across the ocean from Europe. All portions of the North Atlantic coastal plain are in a very definite sense quite as much the outposts of Europe as they are the beginning of America. Bodies of water are seldom very effectual dividing lines, as the early colonists discovered, and the seaboard towns are always favorite ports of entry for all things foreign, ideas as well as men. But while the Atlantic was far from isolating the English colonies from the mother country, the very distance across the ocean rendered the transmission of detailed orders and close political control almost impossible.

If an aviator flying westward from Europe could approach America at a great enough elevation to allow a view of the country as a whole, he would notice first a strip of level land running along the coast from the rocky hills of New England to the Gulf states, gradually widening toward the south. This is the Atlantic coastal plain, a region of varying fertility that became the home of the first Americans. The plain is divided into two portions by a line parallel to the coast and at an average distance of one hundred miles inland. This dividing mark is named the Fall Line. That portion of the plain to the east of the line is a low-lying level tract known as Tidewater. To the west is a slightly higher region, sometimes referred to as a plateau, called Piedmont. The Tidewater region was settled first and soon became the holding of landed aristocrats, the first families of the colonies. Piedmont was settled by later immigrants who looked upon the older families of the coast with slight favor. Much of the early history of Virginia is written around the disputes between the frontier uplanders and the more pretentious planters of Tidewater.

If our aviator were to continue across the continent, he would see that the coastal plain is bounded on the west by a mountainous region that has a precipitous eastern escarpment with few passes into the interior. Beyond is the great Mississippi Valley, a region of alternating prairie and woodland, bounded on the north by the Great Lakes and Canada and on the south by the Gulf of Mexico. This is the country known as "middle America," and here the nation has reached its most typical development. In this region, much more isolated from Europe than is the seaboard and cut off in early days from easy access to the cities of the coastal plain, the great strength of middle-class America developed. The Valley of Democracy the region has been called, and well it deserves the name. West of the Mississippi Valley, really a part of it, lie the Great Plains, a higher, more arid region than the valley but resembling it in most respects. West of the Great Plains is the plateau of the Rocky Mountains, another barrier with a pronounced eastern escarpment and few passes. Beyond the Rockies lies the diversified Pacific slope.

One peculiarity of the United States is the lack of navigable rivers emptying into the Atlantic. Most of the streams flowing across the coastal plain are small, and all are broken at the Fall Line, where the rivers tumble from the hard rocks of the Piedmont to the soft structure of the plain. The one seeming exception to this statement is the Hudson. The Fall Line reaches the sea below the mouth of this river, but the stream leads to the north and not to the west through the mountain barrier. The entire development of the nation might have been different if a large stream had led from the Atlantic through the mountains into middle America. The lack of such a stream and the scarcity of passes helped to dam up the English settlements in the coastal plain for a century and a half.

NEW ENGLAND

At the northern tip of the coastal plain, but partaking of its character in no respect, lies New England, a region of low hills and narrow valleys that is really an extension of the Appalachian highland. New England is more isolated than any other major division of the United States. To the east and south lies the Atlantic, tempestuous during the long wintry season and capricious at all times. To the north is an almost impenetrable wilderness of lakes and heavy forests, while to the west the hinterland, if not impassable, is far from inviting. In such surroundings it is not surprising that the unique New England mind soon developed. But there were other things favoring the development of a homogeneous people. The soil is generally not very productive, though there are fertile spots, and in all places it is so covered with loose glacial drift that immense labor must be expended in the removal of stones before the land is ready for cultivation. Such conditions favor the development of small holdings worked intensively by the farmer and his family rather than the formation of large landed estates cultivated by hired servants or slaves.

The rather forbidding aspect of the New England hills tended to keep the farmers in the narrow valleys where they naturally congregated in villages. Thus the people developed as village dwellers, dependent upon each other for protection, assistance in labor, and social amusements, a condition that exerts a powerful influence for unity and similarity of thought. Furthermore each Puritan village centered around the church, and the church members in both spiritual and temporal affairs followed the advice of the minister who ordinarily served for life. Among the clergy there was a common aim and unity of ideas, kept alive by frequent ministerial meetings. Geography united with the church to keep down heresies and schismatic divisions among the people and to make for a most pronounced social unity.

Life in early New England was hard. Nature exacted its price. The stony, infertile soil and the long cruel winters combined to in-

culcate in the people a stern sense of duty and responsibility. One
is moved to marvel at the good fortune that brought the Puritans
to New England. They carried thither a crabbed religion that
checked the frivolous nature of man with harsh severity. They
found an environment that tended to foster the virtues that Calvinism prized. Industry, thrift, painstaking care, and unceasing
watchfulness flourished in the New England character under the
vigilant eye of the Puritan church and the relentless pressure of
New England environment.

New England with a great supply of waterpower early turned to
manufacturing, and eastern Massachusetts was the first industrialized
portion of the United States. The very things that made life hard
in rural New England fostered the practice of home manufacturing
and later led to the development of the factory system. The romantic movement that produced writers like Emerson and Thoreau, men
who glowed with enthusiasm for nature and the natural life, was
brought to an end not by the Civil War alone, as is often remarked,
but also by the rising tide of industrialism that ran counter to the
romantic ideal at every point. "Things are in the saddle," wrote
Emerson sadly after visiting one of the early factories, meaning that
material things were in the ascendance over the spiritual. And geography had assisted "things" into the saddle.

Much New England literature is colored by the sea. This is as
it should be. On two sides the land is girt by the ocean, and while
the water is none too inviting it is much more so than the forests
of the hinterland. In early days adventure, romance, and wealth
lay out at sea. Fishing and trade attracted the thrifty, while generation after generation of venturesome New England farm boys answered to the lure of foreign lands and strange peoples halfway
round the globe. Whether the proximity of the powerful, all-con-
quering ocean has given to New Englanders any brooding sense of
inevitability, such as Synge noticed among the Aran islanders, it is
impossible to say. We do know, however, that Melville, who was
half New England in blood, caught perfectly the spirit of the salt-
water in his epic of the sea, *Moby Dick*.

New England geography did more than assist in the creation of a
mass mind, a mind that has left its indelible imprint upon our national development. In our literature the very color of the New
England landscape, the sharp tang of the chilly air, and the sound
of heavy seas dashing upon granite shores have also left their trace

in the writings of a long line of men and women extending from Whittier to Robert Frost and including such names as Harriet Beecher Stowe, Hawthorne, Thoreau, and Sarah Orne Jewett. Most of these writers reveal the mind as well as the appearance of New England.

After the New Englanders had been seasoned in their native home for a century and a half, the surplus population started to find new land. Still they did not escape geography; migrating peoples never do. The one feasible route to the west lay across the Hudson and up the valley of the Mohawk. This valley debouched in northern Ohio. Hence the Mohawk Valley and the Western Reserve, as the region just south of Lake Erie was called, were extensions of New England. From northern Ohio the immigrants pressed on to Illinois, Michigan, Wisconsin, and Minnesota. If it had not been for the outlet afforded New England by the Mohawk Valley, it is quite probable that the politics of the Northwest might have taken on a different color, and this would have been a most serious matter in view of the approaching struggle over slavery. As it was, the Republican party had its birth among the modified Puritans whose ancestors came west through the Mohawk Valley.

THE MIDDLE STATES

If the distinctive feature of New England thinking was unity, the distinctive feature of the middle states' thinking was diversity. In New England a homogeneous people isolated in a harsh but fitting environment produced a type of mind that was like unto nothing else. In the middle states the people were of many bloods, the climate was decidedly more congenial than that of New England, the fertile soil was spread evenly over a level or slightly rolling surface, rather abundant waterpower promised manufacturing, while passage to and from the region was more easy than was the case in the isolated colonies to the north. All these reasons contributed to the variety that has characterized the thinking of the middle states.

The Land and the People.—The people of the mid-Atlantic states came from a variety of sources. New England was settled by English Puritans, who, if they did not comprise all the population, at least held undisputed control of the government and the important social institutions. The middle states had Dutch, English, Scotch-Irish, Swedes, Germans, and other less influential stocks. The people were as divided in church affiliations as in national origins. The

Presbyterian, Lutheran, Catholic, Reformed, and Quaker denominations were only a few of the more important. These diversified peoples came into an environment that at all events did not tend to fuse the population into one uniform mass, as might have been the case in a more compact, isolated homeland.

The congenial and diversified environment before long made its effect felt upon the intellectual life of the region. The inviting farm lands encouraged the people to spread far and wide over the area from central New York to the Potomac. There were many large landholders, especially the patroons of New York, and the great landlords of the Tidewater region, but generally small independent farmers were the dominant element. The congeniality of the climate and the fertility of the soil made the large farming groups ready to accept physiocratic economics, which holds that all wealth comes directly from the soil, while the romantic back-to-nature doctrine also met ready acceptance. Neither doctrine would be gladly received by a people who lived in a repellent environment or who gained a scant livelihood from the soil only with difficulty. Furthermore, the dominance of the small, independent farmer tended to give a distinctive tone to the thinking of the middle colonies that would have been impossible in a society that was regimented into a rigid caste system either by theology or economics.

But all the population of the middle states did not reside on farms. The many good harbors of the coast, coupled with a number of navigable rivers, caused the formation of several seaports that thrived on trade with Europe and with the back country. New York, Philadelphia, and Baltimore early became the homes of a rich and influential commercial class. In the development of the colonies this group usually sided with the patroons or landed aristocrats against the laboring and farming classes. The chief importance of the seaboard cities lies in the fact that they have always been centers of cosmopolitan influence. An amazingly large percentage of foreign ideas imported into the United States have been brought through New York, Philadelphia, or Baltimore. Certainly most of the immigrants have landed in these cities, and large numbers have remained permanently in their port of entry. It is the presence of foreign ideas and recently arrived immigrants that has given New York City its unique place in the intellectual development of this country. From the early eighteenth century to the present the seaports of the middle Atlantic coast have been the first American home of all kinds of new ideas, many of which have profoundly influenced our national development.

The cities have been the site of our most ambitious efforts to assimilate European culture and to create a national art, literature, and music. Some of these efforts have been made possible by the foreign element, to whom art is merely a natural part of life, and some by the wealth in the hands of our commercial class, whose desire to acquaint America with the culture of the old world has been as boundless as their generosity. As a result of these conditions art galleries, symphony orchestras, opera houses, theatrical experiments, and new literary undertakings have flourished in the Atlantic cities. Other cities of the nation, notably Boston and some of the middle-western cities, have not lagged in the providing of cultural opportunities, but not one has surpassed the cities of the middle states.

Literature in the Middle States.—With such a geographical environment and with so many and so diverse influences playing freely among the people, the middle states should have early produced some literature. Since the educated class was not so obsessed with theology as it was in New England, nor with politics as it was in the South, literature was pretty certain to have numerous devotees. As a matter of fact, such was the case. Belletristic literature in America first developed in this region. The earliest American novelist of note was Charles Brockden Brown of Philadelphia, and the first dramatist was Thomas Godfrey of the same city. One of the earliest poets who wrote without a wholly political or religious motive and probably the best poet prior to the romantic era was Philip Freneau of New York and Philadelphia. Before 1830 the middle states were the center of cultural life in the United States. From 1830 to 1860 this center shifted to Boston for a period of great activity in the cultivation of the arts, but since the Civil War the middle states have again won supremacy. At the present time New York lays claim to the musical, literary, theatrical, and artistic leadership of the country. Certainly most of our books are published in that city, most of the interesting new plays are first produced there— and many of them are never seen in other places, the musical opportunities afforded by New York are unsurpassed anywhere in the world, and the largest art collections of America are on or near Manhattan Island.

It would be misleading to attribute the long and energetic cultiva-

tion of the arts to geography alone. As indicated previously, the
mixed blood of the people made for a most helpful clash of ideas.
But behind many of the impulses in the middle states that made
for intellectual effort and a marked cultural life lie the manifold influences of geography. Geography allowed a widespread diffusion
of the people and a consequent feeling of independence. Clerical
domination or political dictatorship of a minority became difficult
if not impossible. The physical environment made it easy to acquire
more than a living, and with the growth in wealth came the growth
of a leisure class with intellectual interests. The physical environment made possible the growth of cities that long have served as
centers of foreign ideas and foreign influence. With such results
to its credit geography can hardly be barred from some consideration
in any study of the development of thought and expression in the
middle Atlantic states.

THE SOUTH

Soil and climate combined in the southern states to foster institutions that were virtually unknown elsewhere in the United States,
and these institutions, created by geography, monopolized the intellectual lives of the people. In almost all portions of the South
the soil was fertile, while in spots it was of surpassing richness.
The climate varied from the mild temperate to the sub-tropical variety, very hot summers being the rule all over this part of the country. All portions of the region had the abundant rainfall required
by the chief crops of tobacco, cotton, rice, and sugar. The large
amount of labor required by such crops led to the extensive use of
slaves for field work. The introduction of slavery was of vast cultural importance, for managing the large servile population, defending slavery through political action, and the making of efforts to
extend the system early monopolized the fine southern mind.

With agriculture in the South early becoming a well-organized business, large estates soon occupied most of the land in southern Tidewater. From the beginning agriculture paid in Virginia and the
Carolinas, while Georgia became prosperous soon after its organization. With the profits from a tobacco, cotton, or sugar crop the
planter could buy more land and more slaves. Again and again
this process would be repeated until estates of baronial proportions
were common in the coastal plain south of the Potomac. Society
was organized in almost feudal fashion. The great landholders and

their families formed the gentry below whom were grouped the servants and slaves. The independent farmer of small holdings, soon finding himself respected by neither gentry nor slave, usually sold out to a prosperous neighbor and migrated to the upland region, commonly called Piedmont. Here he found more like himself who were drawn together by common economic and social interests and by a common dislike of the gentry. But the dominant mind of the South, at least from 1800 to 1860, was developed on the Tidewater and not in the Piedmont plateau. The large estates and slavery lie behind the most typical intellectual product of the South before the Civil War, the ideal of a Greek democracy with a frank recognition of the natural division of mankind into classes.

Literary Life in the South.—The conditions in the South were ideal for the production of belletristic literature. Society was dominated by an aristocracy that was in the best sense an aristocracy of brains. This group had leisure, money, and a rather surprising amount of old-world culture, and its progeny were often men of undoubted ability. Nothing else was needed for the production of literature; with fewer inducements literary men soon appeared in the middle states.

But the fact remains that the South produced little belletristic literature until after the Civil War. Indeed there are those who say that the years immediately before us will see the first flowering of great southern literature. The very things that seemed to make for literary promise before 1860 actually defeated that promise. The South went in for politics and economics. The development and management of large estates, revolutionary and post-revolutionary politics, and the defense of slavery successively engaged the ability of the South. That the southern states had talent of a high order is attested by the distinguished roll of political thinkers who claimed that region as their home. It is conceivable that the wonderfully versatile Jefferson, if he had not been burdened with unremitting political cares, would have been an ornament to American belles-lettres. One can but wonder what our literature and thought lost in the absorption of such men as Calhoun, Augustus Longstreet, or Hugh Legaré in the struggle of politics, law, or the ministry. A few flashes of literary work, like that of Poe, Simms, Timrod, Hayne, and Lanier, show what the southern mind could have done if it had had an intellectual environment congenial to the practice of letters. From 1830 to 1860 while New England was in the golden day of its literature, the South, convulsed by the slavery question, was enlisting its best minds in politics, statecraft, and the army. During those years literature was a neglected by-product. Poe, the greatest genius of his day, found his native region so inhospitable to the belletristic writer that he sought a more congenial home in New York. Ability in great quantity there was in the South, but it was monopolized by the institutions created by the easy environment.

THE OHIO AND MISSISSIPPI VALLEYS

For well over a century the English colonists in North America were dammed up behind the Allegheny Mountains, although west of the barrier lay one of the most inviting regions on the globe. The promising character of the unopened country was well known, but still the settlers lingered east of the highland. The reasons for this delay were various. Until 1763 France claimed the entire Ohio-Mississippi basin, and France was a jealous guardian of her territories, strictly prohibiting English settlements in the regions reserved for the French traders and trappers. From 1763 until the opening of the Revolution England's policy of restricting settlements to the easily controlled areas of the eastern coast again tended to discourage western emigration.

Another constantly operating influence against settling the West was the scarcity of good routes of travel. There were three routes to the West. One was through the Hudson-Mohawk Valley to the region south of the lakes. The second was around the southern tip of the Appalachian highland through what is now Georgia and Alabama. The third was by way of the passes leading west from the middle states through the low but wide highland. At first the northern route was closed to travel by the strong Iroquois confederacy of central New York. Later this route was of great importance and along it poured the New Englanders to their homes in the West. The southern route was also closed by Indians, the fierce Creek and Cherokee tribes successfully withstanding the pressure of their white neighbors until as late as 1820. Hence the only feasible routes lay through the mountain passes. This fact meant that only the middle states were to participate in the first wave of emigration to the West. New England, New York, and the extreme South were disqualified by geography from assisting in the work. Thus the first settlements were made in Kentucky and Tennessee by the restless and the dissatisfied of the middle states.

The restless and the dissatisfied were not from Tidewater. They had slowly collected along the frontier in Piedmont where they lived under conditions of primitive democracy. These people were of mixed blood, English, Scotch-Irish, and German predominating. They held land in small holdings, and worked it usually without slave labor. The lack of transportation prevented a rapid increase in wealth, but what wealth was in the region came as a result of tilling the soil. The remoteness of the region from Tidewater, the home of government, courts, and culture, tended to accent the natural independence of the small farmer on the outskirts of civilization. Upon the ears of the uplanders of Pennsylvania, Virginia, and North Carolina fell pleasingly the first faint whisper of Jeffersonian democracy, with its talk of natural rights, equality, the goodness of living close to nature, and agrarian economics. It was simply a theoretic justification—a glorification—of the lives the frontiersmen were forced to lead.

As the early emigrants poured through the passes and down the rivers of the West, the line of settlements slowly assumed the outline of a rough spearhead pointed westward into the heart of the continent. From the day the first permanent settlement was fixed in Kentucky, the entire mid-section of the continent was fated to be American. There was no turning back. There was nothing to go back for, and geography was constantly forcing the emigrants westward. The rivers were flowing west and south, and the strong current of the Ohio and Mississippi made it easier for the Kentuckian to ship his goods clear to New Orleans than to fight the current of the upper river to Pittsburgh and thence cross the highlands by a wagon road. It is said that it cost the Westerner thirty-three per cent of the value of goods to ship to Philadelphia, while freight could be sent from Illinois to New Orleans for four per cent of its value. Under such conditions it is not strange that the Westerners traveled the easiest routes. Although the emigrants soon lost touch with their old home, speaking vaguely of it as the "back country," they kept untarnished the democratic faith that was theirs when they crossed the mountains.

When the emigrants were across the mountains, they found themselves in a huge area of unknown size, actually embracing, it was later discovered, five-eighths of the United States. Although this area was admirably provided with waterways, soil, rainfall, and a long growing season, the path of the pioneer was far from easy. Sometimes the soil was unfit for the first crops attempted; sometimes a drought came; frequently sickness ravaged frontier communities. The Indians were a constant threat, occasionally breaking out in open warfare. The settlements were usually remote from help, and the highways were always either bad or totally lacking. All these things—a wide extent of country, isolation, and the threat of Indian warfare—welded the western communities into socially minded groups. These groups were wholly possessed by middle-class standards, and as a result the ideals of industry, thrift, and conformity to group thinking to-day characterize much of the United States.

The Bequest of the Pioneer.—The bequest of the pioneer in many respects is most admirable, but in a few it is open to criticism. The distance between the new settlements along the Mississippi and such centers of culture as Boston, Philadelphia, and Charleston, combined with the ideals of the pioneer, made the Westerner contemptuous of leisurely culture and too prone to praise the active and practical. Thus Mark Twain reflects the western spirit in *Innocents Abroad*, when he laughs at Renaissance art which he does not understand. Again, a long conformity to his neighbor's opinions has made the Middle Westerner suspicious of and even hostile to foreign influences. Much of the writing of William Allen White, the Kansas editor and author, exhibits a sharp antipathy to the city as the radiating point of foreign ideas. Among the poets Vachel Lindsay of Illinois wishes to revive the older frontier virtues and to awaken the people to a realization of the beauty around them rather than to introduce European art or thought. Down to 1918 the pioneer spirit reigned almost supreme in the Middle West, and even to-day it is far from disappearing.

In the history of American development the frontier stood for local independence coupled with a strong sense of nationalism, for only by local independence could the prized freedom of the pioneer be enjoyed, while the building of essential improvements such as roads, waterways, and railroads depended largely upon the support of the national government. The highly democratic West opposed the ambitions of the aristocratic, slave-holding South, and in the struggle between the agricultural South and the industrial North, the support given the North by the West was the decisive factor in the Civil War. In its public land policy the West was always in favor of greater concessions to actual settlers, and the adoption of this principle allowed the rapid settlement of the western states. Indeed much of the history of the United States after 1750 can be written in terms of western ideas and actions.

The influence of the West was thus one of diverse aspects. In political and economic affairs it was liberal and progressive, but in the cultural sphere it was much less so, inclining at times to a lamentable narrowness of outlook and a most unfortunate subservience to the "village mind." But the influence of the West, whether for good or for bad, was formed in part by geography. Let those who are prone to criticize this region for its "village mindedness" remember that if it had not been for that keen sense of social solidarity and responsibility, the Great Valley could not have been settled. If the West is reproached for its indifference to leisurely culture, let it be remembered that geography forbade both aristocracy and leisure on the frontier and that a knowledge of Greek and logic was of little "practical use" to a man engaged in plowing the stubborn sod of the western prairie, building a railroad, making fence rails, or navigating a boat through the treacherous currents of the Mississippi River. If Andrew Jackson, Abraham Lincoln, and Mark Twain were victims of anything it was geography, not their wives, or malarial fever, or the lack of training in social etiquette.

THE TRANS-MISSISSIPPI WEST

The settlement of the trans-Mississippi West was a duplication of the migration into the Great Valley with a vastly increased emphasis upon the spectacular and dramatic element. By 1820 the spearhead of western settlement was touching the Missouri River near the site of the present Kansas City. Beyond the river lay a most enticing region. There were stories trickling back from the Rocky Mountains of untold wealth in the fur trade; there was a suspicion of mineral wealth to be found somewhere in the West, a suspicion running back to the days of Coronado and De Soto; and there were unbelievable tales told of the fantastic scenery in the unknown wilderness of plain and mountain. But between the fringe of settlement and the mountains lay a wide trackless plain of so great aridity that settlement seemed to be out of the question while the mere crossing of it was an appalling task. Before this unknown stretch of arid plain and mountain the pioneer halted just as his forefathers had before the Allegheny highlands.

The Pathfinders of the New West.—Then came the golden age of the pathfinder. As George Rogers Clark, Daniel Boone, John Sevier, Callaway, and Kenton had blazed the trails into the first West, so the last frontier had its roll of trail breakers. Lewis and Clark had made the first trip from St. Louis to the Pacific Ocean; Jedediah Smith, Ashley, Jim Bridger, and dozens of other "mountain men" pushed into every valley and plain from the Columbia to the lower Colorado; Kit Carson became another almost legendary figure through his exploits in the Southwest; Jason Lee and Marcus Whitman, missionaries both, established permanent settlements in the Northwest and probably caused others to go to that land of promise; Ewing Young and John C. Frémont found a way to southern California and centered an interest in a part of the West that was augmented by the publication in 1840 of Dana's *Two Years Before the Mast*. These men led lives of spectacular adventures compared with the rather humdrum lives that the pioneers were living in Iowa, Missouri, and Wisconsin, and their exploits kindled the imagination of a nation.

The upshot of the work of the trail makers was to fix in the minds of the American that the routes to the West, though long and arduous, were passable. By 1843 the Oregon Trail was well marked, while the Humboldt-Truckee cut-off to California was discovered shortly. To the southwest from Westport, Missouri, the starting point for western emigration, stretched the Santa Fé Trail with its two branches, the Spanish and the Gila River trails, leading to southern California. The roads to the West were at least known, if not heavily traveled.

As the fringe of settlement halted along the Missouri, momentous events were happening. Urged on by the southern aristocracy, the government fought the Mexican War and took possession of the southwestern states. About the same time gold was discovered in California. At once a tremendous rush of emigrants set out for California, many going overland. It is said that within two years more than one hundred thousand immigrants arrived in San Francisco. The newcomers found that the reports of the gold field were not exaggerated, for wealth was to be had in extravagant quantities at a ludicrously slight exertion compared with the labor expended by the Mississippi Valley farmer to gain a livelihood.

A new world awaited the immigrant from Missouri and Illinois. The physical aspects of the country appeared wild and fantastic to one who was at home in the pleasant but rather monotonous landscape of the Middle West. Huge snow-capped mountains; amazing tangles of deep valleys and precipitous ravines carved by nature into most fantastic or majestic forms; endless deserts, where man and beast might perish from lack of water and where even the pathfinder's sense of direction failed; mammoth trees; roaring geysers, periodically spouting streams of boiling water far into the air—all these things startled the newcomer into a feeling that he was entering a new universe.

The society in California harmonized admirably with its surroundings. The virtuous and the vicious, the roisterer and the steadily industrious, the ruffian and the man of peace, all incongruously consorted on a common ground. The abundance of gold in the new country induced a widespread demoralization which was met by some of the most dramatic and spectacular exploits of early western history. From wealth to poverty and from poverty to wealth were steps so short that the making of them ceased to cause comment. The fantastic and unnatural became the commonplace.

Such conditions were bound to affect any literature that might be produced in that region. The early work of the West abounds in wild extravagances, burlesque, and striking contrasts. Raucous laughter lies in such a book as *Roughing It,* and it is evoked by true western methods. Bret Harte specialized in a study of western society in the manner of Dickens, using sharp contrasts to get his desired effect of laughter and tears. One of the characteristics of Harte is his marked sentimentality, a trait that is apt to be found uppermost in men far removed from their mothers, wives, and children. Primitive western life is also reflected in the work of other men like Artemus Ward and Bill Nye. It is not too much to say that Ward, one of our great social critics, found his method in the West.

Effect of Early Environment.—Long after emigrant times and the chaotic uproar of the "Days of '49" the physical background molded western writing. Physical environment cannot be escaped, but far too much western literature has been concerned with titanic mountains, awe-inspiring canyons, and landscapes of colossal proportions. Too often western poets think that the use of a great mountain as a theme will produce a great poem, or that the selection of a beautiful valley for description will insure a bit of beautiful prose. Western writers are too prone to spend much time and care upon the backgrounds of their works and to neglect the true aspects of human life. Human hands toil and hearts break in the shadow of a snow-capped peak just as they do on a Dakota wheat ranch or in a Kansas corn field or in a city tenement. Western scenery has been too striking for the good of the literature; it has dazzled both the permanent resident and the casual visitor.

It is sometimes predicted that the salubrious climate and the magnificent scenery will attract to parts of the Pacific coast writers and artists who will adequately portray life in those regions. Such predictions may be abundantly fulfilled, but at the present time there is slight reason for thinking that the fulfillment is imminent. The novels of Zane Grey seem rather adequately to measure the capacity of the transplanted writer. Mr. Grey spends the most painstaking care on his background and achieves emphatic success in this work, but his delineation of western life and people in both past and present is hopelessly stereotyped and melodramatic. The scenery has blinded him to perception of the good and bad in humanity. Another purveyor of western romance, the motion picture, has found a prolific source of material in the dramatic days of the old West, but a few minutes with the journal of a "forty-niner" will convince one that the "movie" is more concerned with the spectacular than with the true. It is not improbable that veracious novels, poems, and dramas of the West will be written by realists who take recognition of the influence on man of the environment, both physical and social, but refuse to blink any aspect of truth even though it may be unpleasant.

The surface of western life is merely scratched by the literary craftsman. Entrancing subjects like the immigration of 1849, the opening of new homes, the building of railroads, the development of agriculture, the lumbering industry, all await adequate treatment. Subjects of all varieties are to be found from the grim realism of the wheat ranch to the glowingly romantic figure of Paul Bunyan.

THE PLAINS

In the settlement of the plains the American engaged in his hardest struggle with environment since the days of early New England.

Huge areas of intense aridity, the heat of summer, the blizzards of winter, and the monotonous aspect of the landscape made life on the great plains a hazardous undertaking. The presence of land speculators, the lack of transportation, the demand for irrigation projects, and the constantly hard times on the last frontier created a demand for strong ameliorative measures by the national government and a growing unrest of the people when those measures were not immediately supplied. It was not without geographical significance that agricultural discontent as evidenced in the Greenback, Populist, Free Silver, and Progressive Republican movements received their most enthusiastic support in such states as Kansas, Nebraska, the Dakotas, Texas, and Montana. Aspects of this agricultural unrest are excellently reflected in the early work of Hamlin Garland. His *Main Traveled Roads* is an utterly truthful statement of farm life on the edge of the plains. Ed Howe's *Story of a Country Town* is another grim but accurate account of social conditions on the edge of the arid belt.

The great plains have been so lately settled that it is impossible to discuss with any assurance the effect of their geography upon people's lives and characteristics. Indeed it is doubtful if ever we can do so, for to-day man is growing increasingly independent of his physical environment. Rapid transportation and communication in the shape of automobiles, telephone, and radio are tending to divorce man from the cribbing, confining effects of climate and landscape. If a man can "tune in" on an opera being produced in Chicago, or on a symphony concert played in New York or Los Angeles, the view from his front door and the distance from the nearest neighbor become of less importance than they were ten years ago. But for mechanical invention it would have been possible to see if the depressing landscapes of the Great Plains would have produced in the people a rooted melancholy like that found in other dwellers in monotonous and inhospitable surroundings.

That there were spectacular elements in the opening of the plains region and that these elements have been magnified at the expense of other less interesting but more important factors is not to be questioned. The imaginations of our writers have been entranced by the cowboys, while the plodding, industrious dry-land home-steader and farmer have been utterly slighted. True it is that the cowboy is an interesting fellow, but the cowboy of our present-day story writers resembles the real man as much as a gingerbread man resembles a traffic policeman. The literature of the future may make amends for some of the present-day shortcomings.

SUGGESTED READINGS

The suggested readings are not meant in any degree for a bibliography. They include only a few of the more important and easily accessible references. The lists will include no references to such widely known works as the *Cambridge History of American Literature*, the numerous encyclopedias, and the *Dictionary of American Biography*. The dates indicate an available edition, not necessarily the first.

Adams: *The Founding of New England*. Boston. 1921. pp. 1-13.
  Good brief discussion of New England geography.
Brown: *The Historical Geography of the United States*. New York. 1948.
  A recent and authoritative book. The best in the field.
Jones and Bryan: *North America, an historical, economic, and regional geography*. New York. 1924. pp. 23-45.
  A very excellent, brief discussion of the importance of geography in American development. Best essay on the subject.
Schlesinger: *New Viewpoints in American History*. New York. 1922. pp. 23-44.
Semple: *American History and Its Geographical Conditions*. Boston and New York. 1903.
  A classic work.
Smith & Phillips: *North America*. New York. 1940.
  Interesting and authoritative.
Wertenbaker: *The First Americans*. New York. 1927. pp. 1-21.

CHAPTER II

THE RACIAL BACKGROUND

The question of racial influences and inter-relationships in America is very confused and highly controversial. The complexity of the question has been made appalling by the freedom with which the early European stocks entered this country and the ease with which they moved about in their new home and intermarried. The natural difficulty of the historian in dealing with such a question has hardly been diminished by the publication of reputedly historical studies, which have been written solely for the glorification of the races under discussion. Many such studies are filled with purported facts that are dictated by racial pride or animosity rather than by a desire to tell the results of historical research. This chapter is an attempt to set forth briefly some of the more important elementary facts that have emerged from the haze of controversy.

Americans of the present generation, especially those who are removed from immediate contact with recent immigrants, have been so drilled to think of the "melting pot" aspects of American life that only with genuine difficulty can they think of an America composed of divergent and often opposing racial elements. To many people the term "Americanization" stands for a vaguely understood process that immigrants have always been subjected to and that promptly and completely transforms its subjects from Europeans into Americans. But the indisputable fact remains that a man's method of thinking and his culture cannot be deeply affected by a process of adoption, however loyally attached the man may be to the country that adopts him. Racial characteristics in thinking are as unchanged by naturalization as are physical characteristics. The melting pot merely obscures, it never obliterates traces of racial elements. Our immigrants keep for years or even generations the intellectual traits and outlook that were the product of their old European environment.

Next to the melting pot fallacy, the most common mistake in thinking of racial contributions to our culture is to believe that one

21

race has contributed everything. Partisans of the English frequently point to our use of the English language and our adoption of English institutions as proof of the overwhelming importance of the English race to our culture. True, the English people through certain of their virtues and through certain accidents were enabled to arrive first in this country, take over strategic locations, and assume direction of various institutions, notably the government and the schools, but the numbers in which non-English immigrants have come to this country and the indubitable traces of non-English culture do not warrant us in allowing the English a monopoly of all cultural influence. In the list of our creative writers and critics it is interesting to notice that many names are of non-English origin. Among these names are those of Crèvecœur, Legaré, Freneau, Thoreau, Lafcadio Hearn, Sandburg, Dreiser, Hergesheimer, Cahan, Mencken, Tobenkin, Strunsky, Santayana, Lewisohn, Giovannitti, O'Neill. Furthermore, in the field of practical statecraft where English blood is generally supposed to have had undisputed control, we find that eighteen of our fifty-six signers of the Declaration of Independence were non-English. The theory that American thought is wholly of English origin collapses at the first critical touch.

Certain historians are prone to dispose of the racial problem by saying that America was made by three races each of which brought a particular gift to the new world. These races were the English who contributed the ax, the Scotch-Irish who brought the potato, and the Germans who introduced their new invention, the rifle, to the American frontier before the middle of the eighteenth century. Like many facile generalizations this statement is rather more easily remembered than it deserves to be. It contains a considerable amount of truth, for certainly the three races named contributed much to our cultural history, and undoubtedly a majority of the pioneers in both the old and the new West were of these strains. Surely the three gifts named are not to be despised by any historian of the American people, but each of these gifts was not the exclusive property of the race to whom it is assigned, and each of these races contributed far more than one thing to our development. Furthermore the cultural contributions made by the French, the Scandinavians, the Irish, and the Jews must not be entirely overlooked.

THE ENGLISH

The English were not the first to arrive in North America. When the first permanent English settlement was established in the present United States, the Spanish had been in Mexico for almost a century, while St. Augustine, Florida, was forty years old, and Santa Fé, New Mexico, had been a straggling Spanish outpost for a decade. In 1607 there were many French living in Canada, and Quebec was established the following year. Thus when the English made their first permanent home in the new world, the Spanish had already possessed the southern part of the North American continent, and the French were in process of acquiring the great St. Lawrence and Mississippi valleys. The English came late and took the middle Atlantic seaboard, a region that had not the immediate attractiveness of the portions occupied by the French and Spanish.

Location of the English.—Although the middle Atlantic seaboard may not have been very attractive, in the long run the English were fortunate in gaining it. Both Spain and France had huge and sprawling American holdings of totally undefined extent. The Spanish territories had immense treasures in gold scattered at random over a wide domain, and the French possessions had great potential wealth in the extensive fur trade that soon developed. On the other hand the English found neither gold nor the promise of an extensive fur trade. The physical limitations of their holdings were sharply defined by the Atlantic on the east, the Allegheny Mountains on the west, the French to the north, and the Spanish to the south. The English held the narrow shelf of land on the seaboard within which they were forced to develop such settled occupations as agriculture and lumbering. There were not even rivers and trails leading from the coast into the interior. It was different with the French and Spanish. The presence of easy routes into the interior of their vast possessions, and the prevalence of such nomadic occupations as searching for gold and trafficking in furs sucked the settlers inland and scattered them thinly over large areas. Dammed up between the mountains and the sea, and hemmed in by their enemies, the English developed a solidarity that comes from permanent homes and unromantic occupations. The French and Spanish would traverse a region and lay claim to it; the English would settle in a smaller region and actually possess it. Land into which the Englishman struck a plow became his irrevocably.

Although the Englishman came to America no sooner than his French and Spanish rivals, he did arrive earlier than his competitors who were to settle with him on the Atlantic seaboard. As a result of his arriving early and seizing the strategic locations, all the thirteen colonies, save New York and Delaware, came under the control of the English, and the oversight of allowing the Dutch to settle Manhattan Island and the Hudson Valley was rectified when the Duke of York in 1664 captured New Amsterdam for the English crown. The Swedish colony of Delaware soon came under the control of the Pennsylvania Quakers. Later streams of immigration, finding the English actually in control of the seaboard and all important institutions, went to the frontier where their presence ultimately did much for the American mind. But their passage to the west left the Englishman to mold our institutions and carry on our foreign trade.

The virtual monopoly of our trade by England was made possible because the English seized the strategic locations on the Atlantic seaboard. Boston, Philadelphia, Baltimore, the Virginia estuaries, Charleston, and Savannah, all the first-class harbors except that of New York, were first claimed by the English. Thus trade and commerce fell naturally to the Briton, who carried the trade to British ports, as provided by the Navigation Acts.

The greater prestige of the mother country was another reason for the dominance of the English in the seaboard settlements. England was strong and, even in the early days of settlement, not unmindful of the importance of her transatlantic holdings. France and Spain were busy with their own affairs in the north and south, and no other nation was equipped to dispute supremacy with England in the middle region. The rivalry of Holland ended with the defeat of that gallant but small nation; the Scandinavian powers were incapable of contesting for leadership in America; and Germany was merely a geographical expression until late in the nineteenth century. The other early immigrants were from the British Isles, and when they arrived they found the English ensconced along the seaboard enjoying the trade and directing the government and social institutions of the colonies, for naturally the mother country had entrusted the government of the colonies to her own children, emigrants though they were. The wide diffusion of English ideas in this country was caused in part by the wide dispersion of the English immigrants over the entire nation. While they dominated certain localities, they were strangers in none, and they entered no community in which their presence was not felt. In the westward movement the English were not so conspicuous in the first wave of immigration as were the Scotch-Irish and Germans, but they followed closely on the heels of the other races.

Cultural Contributions of the English.—Among the institutions molded by the English ideas none was more important than the schools. The educational system of America from beginning to end was made what it is by the preëxistence of the schools and colleges of England that stressed the classical curriculum. At first there was no rival educational theory to combat that of the classicists, and all education aimed at the acquisition of classical culture, as exemplified by the Greek and Latin authors. Later under the urging of Franklin and Jefferson there grew up a more practical curriculum that stressed modern language, science, and the fine arts, as well as more practical subjects, but the bent given to early American education by the classical students of Oxford and Cambridge is still plainly discernible. Along with the control of the schools and the government by the English went the direction of the newspapers.

With the English in control of the government, the greater portion of the trade, most of the elementary schools and newspapers, and many of the colleges, and with the English language in common use all over the colonies, it becomes hard not to overestimate the importance of that racial influence. The student of American culture must be on his guard. Our literature, which is a perfectly tangible thing, is written in English, but that fact is no sign that the intangible ideas that went into it were English. English many of them were, but not all. Ideas are the most pervasive things in the world; they are bound by neither the strangeness of the language in which they are first stated, nor the ordinary dividing lines of physical or political geography, nor the antiquity of their origin. America is a great borrower, and not the least notable thing about our borrowing is the fact that new ideas from the four quarters of the globe have been taken over, translated, and adapted by Americans for use in their country. The exact delimitation of the cultural influences exerted by our racial stocks is a matter so sharply controversial that questions in this field can be only approximately answered, but care should be taken not to attribute everything to the English.

It is usually only a presumptuous guess to say that certain of our well-marked national traits, such as our idealism or our spirit of progressive business enterprise, are the exclusive gifts of definite racial stocks, as if America were a husky infant whose red hair and blue eyes were to be traced directly to certain of his immediate ancestors. Speaking very loosely and always subject to check or contradiction, one may say that the English influence seems to have given the nation an innate political conservatism, a marked reluctance to adopt sudden or radical changes in our fundamental laws or our governmental procedure. The same influence has also contributed much of our spirit of commercialism, a spirit that has sometimes tended to hold the rights of property above the rights of man. The English, most ably assisted by their Scotch-Irish neighbors, did much to give Americans a belief that life is too serious a business to be jested about, a conviction that all values can be measured in terms of goodness or badness, and an implicit reliance upon the letter of the law. This contribution might be called Puritanism. Such are a few of the broad gifts of the English.

To come to more specific things, the Anglo-Saxon tradition seems to have been dominant in three great political parties, the Federalist, the Whig, and the Republican, while it was a formidable element in certain aspects of Jeffersonian democracy. Furthermore, English models have formed such governmental institutions as our bicameral legislatures and our powerful courts. England supplied the pattern of many of our most characteristic religious denominations. English thought formulated laissez-faire economics—so dear to American business men—the theory of representative government, and the feeling that government is dependent for its very existence upon the acquiescence of the people. It should not be imagined that these specific ideas have remained unchanged in America. Many have been rendered almost unrecognizable by new world conditions, but if one looks closely enough one can see in contemporary life many of the germinal ideas brought from England.

American literature in its very form and spirit owes more to English authors than to those of any other country, because of the use of a common literary tradition. Among the English authors who have been most influential in determining the direction of our literature are Pope, Wordsworth, Scott, Carlyle, Dickens, Thackeray, and, in recent years, George Bernard Shaw and John Masefield.

THE SCOTCH-IRISH

The Scotch-Irish were a group of English-speaking, lowland Scotch who settled in north Ireland in the early and middle seventeenth century. Here they lived for many years enjoying prosperity and free worship in their national church, the Presbyterian. In the last years of the seventeenth century the hand of the English government was turned against them, and their business and religion were both put under the ban. By 1725 the first of an immense wave of emigration had set out for America. So many came that by the outbreak of the Revolution it is estimated that one-sixth of the three million colonials were of Scotch-Irish blood.

Unlike the English the Scotch-Irish did not remain on Tidewater to become rich planters or in the cities to become wealthy merchants, for when they arrived, the coastal plain was already in possession of earlier immigrants. Therefore they pressed on to the frontier. The movement to the frontier seems to have occurred first in New York and Pennsylvania, a large number settling in the latter region. From these colonies the Scotch-Irish, seeking more and better land, overflowed into the Great Valley and the Piedmont region of Virginia and on into the Carolinas and the new colony of Georgia. They became "uplanders" in all these colonies and systematically opposed the wealthy classes of the seaboard plain, but the great ability, resourcefulness, and ambition of many of these Scotch-Irish led to their adoption by the Tidewater aristocracy. For instance, in South Carolina alone John C. Calhoun, George McDuffie, and William Gilmore Simms were all of Scotch-Irish blood, and the first was the acknowledged political spokesman of the landed aristocrats, while Simms became their most brilliant apologist in the field of letters, even though his adoption by the gentry was rather grudgingly and condescendingly performed.

While a few Scotch-Irish turned from their upland home towards the seacoast to achieve undying fame, more found a way through the Appalachian highland and helped open the West to settlement. They were wholly admirable frontiersmen, not quite so good at settled farming as the Germans, but in performing the herculean tasks and running the imminent dangers incident to the opening of new land, the Scotch-Irish were inferior to none. As trail-breakers they showed intelligence, judgment, and cool foresight, and as frontier fighters they did their work with a zest born of unmistakable liking for the task at hand. It is probable that the West owes more to the Scotch-Irish than to any other racial stock.

Nor did the work of the Scotch-Irish cease when the Indians were dead or driven out and the land was open to development. When the frontier rolled on past a region, all except the most adventuresome and restless settled down to the business of creating the political and economic structures of new states. Scotch-Irishmen practiced law and medicine, preached in the Presbyterian and Congregational churches, taught school, went into politics, and took up the burdens and accepted the profits of large business undertakings. Innumerable Scotch-Irish went to Congress, held governorships, and presided over various courts, while six men of Scotch-Irish lineage went to the White House. These six were Andrew Jackson, James Buchanan, James K. Polk, Chester A. Arthur, William McKinley, and Woodrow Wilson. In politics the Scotch-Irish have not inclined to any one party, though in the early days of the new republic the frontier environment of these people and their dislike of England made many of them Jeffersonians and opponents of the English-loving aristocratic Federalists.

Cultural Contributions of Scotch-Irish.—The religious contribution of the Scotch-Irish was the Presbyterian church with all its branches and its myriad educational and social ramifications. Since the Presbyterians, like the Puritans of New England, thought that every one ought to be able to read and understand the scriptures, they have always maintained schools of all grades, from the primary department to professional schools and seminaries. The colleges founded by Presbyterian influence usually emphasized the classics with a view of preparing their students for theology, law, or an academic career.

In general one can say with safety that the Scotch-Irish have contributed rather little to the purely literary aspect of American culture. The Scotch-Irish mind is philosophical, not poetical. It revels in dialectics, not in imaginative outbursts. For this reason philosophy, theology, and law have always drawn competent and often erudite exponents from our Scotch-Irish population, while poetry, the drama, and fiction have not flourished at the hands of the same group.

In their outlook on life the Scotch-Irish are serious-minded even to the point of melancholy. No English Puritans were ever more God-fearing, determined, and forthright in their efforts to live daily in the "great Task-master's eye." This was natural, for Scotch Presbyterianism in the eighteenth century was unadulterated Calvinism. Naturally one of the chief Scotch-Irish contributions was the strong reënforcement of the Puritanical bent given to our national thought by the New Englanders.

A recent student [1] of the influence of immigration in American history has rightly attributed great importance to the Scotch-Irish in the days immediately preceding the Revolution. He points out that the fierce passion of these people for liberty and their wide diffusion through the country made them serve as an "amalgam to bind together all other racial elements in the population." To this day the Scotch-Irish element is animating many of our characteristic national actions. It is no disparagement of this dynamic people to say that their influence is more often to be found in the practical affairs of every-day life than in the realm of art and belletristic literature.

THE GERMANS

Among all the non-English groups that have come to this country it is probable that the Germans are unique for the unbroken continuity of their immigration and for the early and abiding influence that they have had upon American thought and institutions. Beginning in the early days of colonial settlement and extending down to the present, the Germans have been here in large numbers, and their influence has never been negligible.

When the early German immigrants arrived, they pushed on with the Scotch-Irish to the frontier where the two races became the pioneer trail-breakers and farmers of America. Side by side these two races held the frontier from New York to Georgia, frequently living most amicably in the same communities and often intermarrying. However, in certain districts, notably parts of Pennsylvania, the Germans held exclusive possession of large communities that to this day retain their original language and customs. In the nineteenth century the Teutonic element strongly influenced such communities as Cincinnati, St. Louis, Milwaukee, and Chicago, but the first home of the German was in the rural portion of America, and until shortly before the Civil War his chief rôle was that of a scientific farmer.

It was during the Revolutionary War that German influence first

[1] Schlesinger, *New Viewpoints in American History*, p. 6.

became noticeable. Thousands of Washington's soldiers were of German blood, and Oriskany, one of the important battles of the war, was fought by a force of German farmers under the command of General Herkimer. It was only natural for the Germans to support independence. Like the Scotch-Irish they originally had no love for the English, and the efforts of the king's ministers to check the settlement of the West only added another grievance to the bill against George III. When the Revolution was over and the path open to the West, the Germans with their Scotch-Irish neighbors undertook the task of settling the Ohio and northern Mississippi valleys. They early moved into the upland regions of Virginia and the Carolinas, but they were not so influential in the South as they were in the North and Northwest. The presence of slavery and the rapid spread of the plantation system tended to keep small farmers, like the Germans, north of the cotton kingdom. Later when the Civil War broke out German antipathy to slavery and southern aristocracy was clearly shown by the large numbers of Germans who served in the northern armies.

Although the Germans made enviable records in both the Revolutionary and Civil wars, yet their most valuable contribution to early American development was a practical demonstration of scientific farming. Frontier farmers were notorious for their slapdash and disorderly methods of tilling the soil and for their tumbledown fences and ramshackle buildings. Soil impoverishment should have been unknown in a new country, but the frontier farmer, like the plantation owner of the southern Atlantic states, either did not understand soil conservation or did not take the trouble to practice it. The German kept a model farm. He ditched and drained the swamps and low-lying fields, kept his buildings and fences in good condition, fertilized his exhausted fields, and introduced the practice of crop rotation. Within a few generations the farming methods of the Germans were in general use over the country.

After 1800, incoming Germans poured into the West, settling in every state and giving to certain commonwealths a decided German tone. Into Missouri they swarmed to become successful farmers, orchardists, and business men. They went into Wisconsin, in large numbers, and moved on into Minnesota and the western prairies. In Illinois they became so great a political power that the ambitious young Abraham Lincoln began the study of their language so that he might better court their favor. Incidentally it might be said that in 1860 they supported Lincoln over Douglas in the presidential campaign.

About 1850 the German immigrants began to show signs of changing their character, or at least, there were new elements to be found among them. Before that year the newcomers had been of the ordinary immigrant type. They were farmers, small tradesmen, laborers; few were of the educated class. In 1848 a revolutionary agitation led by intellectuals shook all Germany. The agitation was unsuccessful, and thousands of the leaders and sympathizers were forced to leave their native kingdoms and duchies. Many of these exiles came to America, bringing with them a flaming hatred of tyranny and an ardent idealism that found fruition in every phase of our culture from politics to music, from pure science and philosophy to daily journalism. These "forty-eighters," as they were called, balanced up the interests of our German element as a whole by emphasizing culture rather than the ordinary affairs of everyday life that had attracted the earlier immigrants.

Intellectual Contribution of the Germans.—One can safely say that German influence is to be found in almost every aspect of our national life from the construction of comfortable houses for people and warm, well-built shelters for domestic animals to our most abstruse theories of pure science and metaphysics. However, to the student of American culture the most important influences are to be found in scholarly research, in philosophical thought, and in music. In the nineteenth century American work in the fields of chemistry, physics, history, philosophy, psychology, and linguistics was almost wholly conditioned by German methods and by German scientists. Although that condition does not prevail so completely to-day as it did thirty years ago, German influence is still potent in the laboratories and libraries of our colleges and universities. Not all of this influence has been exerted by scholars and scientists of German blood, for much of it has come from the large number of Americans who did graduate work in the universities of Germany. In the field of philosophy the Germans have again been important. Almost every American college has had at least one teacher of philosophy who was German born or German trained, and it is safe to say that every community in the entire nation has had its German musicmaster. In this field German influence has been indisputably supreme. The great development of American orchestras to-day is largely the result of tireless labor by two German conductors, Theodore Thomas and Leopold Damrosch. Certainly none can deny that our culture shows deep traces of German influence.

In the domain of literature German influence, while not so apparent as in the field of science or music, is still notable. In the early part of the nineteenth century German thought first began to find its way across the Atlantic. Some came in by way of German books and periodicals, some came by way of Carlyle and Coleridge, and some came in the intellectual baggage of American students returning from sojourns in German universities. Unitarianism and transcendentalism were both immensely influenced by contact with German liberal philosophy and theology. Such men as George Ticknor, Emerson, George Ripley, Theodore Parker, Margaret Fuller, Edgar Allan Poe, and probably Hawthorne were all influenced in varying degrees by German literature. Few of the older American writers were of German blood, Joaquin Miller and Henry Timrod being almost the only exceptions. Of contemporary writers many are of German descent. Among these are Theodore Dreiser, Joseph Hergesheimer, and H. L. Mencken.

German influences have not been limited to scientific or literary theories and practices. Collectivism, a social and economic theory that originated largely in Germany, is one of the most influential ideas ever imported into this country. Collectivism is usually known as socialism, but that term is most unsatisfactory, for socialism is only one aspect of a great body of social and economic thinking. The term collectivism includes many widely different forms of economic doctrine. Among these forms are Marxian socialism, the most familiar form of radical economic thought; Fabian socialism, which is a rather less impetuous type than the preceding; guild socialism, which advocates the substitution of government by industrial and economic groups for the present system of political government; and the coöperative movement, which tends to do away with the middleman. These theories have all been greatly affected by German thought, and all have found expression in our recent literature.

A rival theory to that of collectivism has also been imported from Germany. This is Nietzsche's theory of biological aristocracy, with the accompanying doctrine of the will to power. Of course this view is also explicitly contradictory to the Jeffersonian views of equalitarianism and democracy. Nietzsche held that the mass of men are poor spirited because of the poverty of their blood, their poor protoplasm. The leader, superman, as he is frequently called, is simply he who is best endowed by nature with brain and blood and spirit. This view is being spread by many of the doctrines of current psychology. Among writers H. L. Mencken and Theodore Dreiser both represent the Nietzschean temper.

Concerning the more intangible gifts of the Germans one can speak with much less certainty, but surely our much-vaunted American idealism has not suffered from the work of our German immigrants. Many of these newcomers were too idealistic to live comfortably in Germany. They came to America to realize their frustrated dreams, and, while they fell far short of their aspirations, they did not labor entirely in vain.

THE FRENCH

The French element shares honors with the German as the most important non-English influence in America's cultural life. The German influence has been directed quite largely by German immigrants or their descendants, whereas the French influence usually has been exerted by visitors to America, by travelers returned from France, and by books. This is not to deny the existence of influential French immigrants in the United States, for there always have been many such, but the fact remains that the most clearly marked French influence in the country has not been exerted by immigrants.

The first French in what is now the United States were the explorers, trappers, traders, and missionaries who flocked into the St. Lawrence and Mississippi valleys in the wake of Champlain and La Salle until by 1700 France was in possession of all the strategic locations on and near both great waterways. From these trading posts the French *couriers du bois* explored practically all of North America save that portion firmly held by the English and Spanish. To-day virtually the only remaining visible trace of the French is in the very large number of geographical names of French origin that dot our maps from the Appalachian highlands west to Puget Sound. These names are especially numerous in the Mississippi Valley. To the average American the most familiar of these are names such as Detroit, Des Moines, St. Louis, Terre Haute, and Vincennes. However, French names are most frequently met in lists of physical features like rivers and mountains, or in the names of Indian tribes. There is hardly a county in that portion of the country covered by the French explorers that does not contain a French place name. Where the name is applied to a county or city, it will be found that it often was originally attached to a physical feature. Aside from place names the influence of the early French explorers lives on only as a motive for fiction and history. The direct cultural influence is slight.

The next wave of French was composed largely of French Calvinists, ordinarily called Huguenots, who fled their country after Louis XIV outlawed their religion in 1685. These people came to America to make permanent homes, settling largely on the Atlantic seaboard where they exerted deep influence on the culture of that region. A few selected homes in New England, a fact attested by the existence of such family names as those of Faneuil, Freneau, Sigourney, Bowdoin, and Thoreau. In New York the Huguenots founded the town of New Rochelle, and they were rather numerous in Pennsylvania. It was, however, in South Carolina that they were most numerous and influential. Any group must be accounted an important contributor to American life that gives us Francis Marion, Hugh Swinton Legaré, Henry Laurens, Washington Allston, the Ravenels, the Hugers, and the Petigrus. All these were contributions of the French Huguenots of South Carolina. A list of prominent Americans whose names betray French ancestry will include among others Paul Revere, John Sevier, Richard Henry Dana, Audubon, John and Joseph Le Conte, A. W. Tourgée, Senator Soulé, Lucius Q. C. Lamar, and the Grimké sisters.

The Huguenots were joined by other immigrants in large numbers from the outbreak of the French revolution to the middle of the nineteenth century. During the hectic years of the revolution and the Napoleonic era French leaders came to America in especially large numbers, for a political or military defeat usually meant exile for the overthrown chieftains. Although many of these emigrants remained in this country only for short periods and remained largely in New York and Philadelphia, their influence was large. The presence of these French emigrants is partly responsible for the strong cosmopolitan spirit in our two leading cities of the nineteenth century.

For many years New Orleans, the most European of American cities, was the center of French influence in this country. The French determined the culture of that city from its foundation in 1718 until long after the Civil War, and the fact that the French element is still important in Louisiana after all the political, economic, and social vicissitudes of the state is eloquent testimony to the stubborn virility of that strain. George Washington Cable has given us some graceful and pathetic pictures of the Louisiana French in *Old Creole Days*, but more typical and valuable contributions of these people may be found elsewhere. New Orleans introduced grand opera to America as early as 1806, and for more than fifty years thereafter French companies under the direction of French conductors produced the operas and ballets that were the vogue in Paris. In Louisiana theatrical performances were well supported, for wealthy aristocrats from all over the South went to New Orleans each winter to attend the theater and the opera. The cultural effect of these performances could not have been negligible.

However great the personal influence of French-Americans may have been, it is undeniable that the great indebtedness of our country to France is recorded in the field of social, political, and religious thought. In the following pages there will be numerous references to this debt. Here it will be sufficient to say that French thought has been felt in the following movements: deism, or the religious views held by men like Jefferson and Franklin; the democracy and humanitarianism of Jefferson; the religious thinking of Channing and Emerson; Thoreau's "back-to-nature" doctrine; the utopian socialism of Brook Farm; the sociological thinking that sprang from Comte; and some of the radical socialism of recent years. French influence is to be found everywhere in our language, our art, our manners, and our architecture.

THE IRISH

It is so often remarked that the Irish came early to America and immediately assumed charge of our city governments that we are apt to think that the ward politician of dubious value is south Ireland's only contribution to American culture. Such an idea is erroneous, though even a hurried study of our social history will show that in general the Irish have been more interested in politics than in political theory, more engrossed in money-making than in economic doctrines, and far more interested in living than in producing literature. In these interests the Irish immigrant finds himself on common ground with his American neighbor, for Americans have given only a tardy and inattentive ear to the demands of culture.

Our Irish Population.—The Irish came early to America. Just when they began to come in large numbers we do not know, for statistics were not kept in colonial and early national days, but we are certain that there were many Irish in the country at the outbreak of the Revolution. Most of them became ardent patriots, for strong antipathy to England has always characterized our Irish population, and it is probably safe to say that the tendency to oppose England at every turn has been kept alive in this country for the last century by our Irish strain. In 1850 when the first figures were obtained, about one half—forty-two per cent to be exact—of our foreign-born population was of Irish birth. At that time there were here almost one million Irish immigrants, and during the succeeding decades at least 500,000 more arrived. These figures prove a very large Irish strain in our social life.

The Irish population is largely centered in cities like Boston, New York, Philadelphia, Chicago, St. Louis, and San Francisco. Until 1890 the Irish and Germans made up the bulk of city dwellers. The racial percentages have, of course, changed with the recent heavy immigration from southern Europe, but the Irish element in our cities is still large and influential, and it tends to maintain its identity. Two reasons are responsible for this tendency, politics and religion. Irish politicians keep in close touch with their compatriots and encourage the preservation of racial identity so that the vote of the group may be cast as a unit. Furthermore the devotion of the Irish to their national church, the Roman Catholic, has tended to keep them from intermarrying with their American and German Protestant neighbors. With their locations in cities and with their strong race consciousness, the Irish can easily make a unique and highly individualized contribution to American culture.

Irish Contributions to Our Culture.—Such a contribution exists now more in promise than in performance. However, there is some performance. In the field of the drama the Irish have done considerable work. Familiar to the older generation of theater goers are the names of Dion Boucicault, Augustine Daly, and John Drew, and to-day Eugene O'Neill has been acclaimed the leading dramatist produced in this country. Father Ryan, Richard Henry Wilde, Theodore O'Hara, and John Boyle O'Reilly have all produced poetry, small in amount but of fine quality. In art the Irish have had a hand through the work of James Hoban, the architect of the White House, and Augustus St. Gaudens, the leading American sculptor, who was born in Ireland. Donn Byrne, a writer who has given us some of the most beautiful prose of our generation, was a full-blooded

Irishman. The list of those writers who had Irish blood is too long to enumerate. Among the most prominent are Edgar Allan Poe, William Dean Howells, and William and Henry James.

If one can judge by the literature of the mother country, the Irish contribution to American letters will not be lacking in beautiful imagery, wit, the tragic sense, poetry, and a strong feeling for the unity of man with his background. Whatever form it may take, poetry or prose, novel or drama, it will be beautifully phrased with a keen feeling for rhythm. The blood that produced Oscar Wilde, William Butler Yeats, John Millington Synge, and Lord Dunsany may some day find adequate expression in America; and when it does it will be mindful both of its racial inheritance and of the American environment.

THE DUTCH

The fact that the Dutch of New York have always formed a prominent and even aristocratic element in our most wealthy and influential state has somewhat tended to magnify the contribution of those people to American culture. The early burghers of New Amsterdam, so humorously misrepresented in Irving's *History of New York*, had the excellent fortune to light upon a spot that offered unlimited possibilities for trade both with Europe and with the interior. Although not more than ten thousand Dutchmen came to the new world in the seventeenth century, these few devoted themselves so successfully to the exploitation of their location that they soon became extremely prosperous. The prosperity thus inaugurated has always been a most fortunate characteristic of New York, for without a great amount of money freely available for the forwarding of culture many of the recent advances and experiments in education, music, and drama would have been impossible. The accumulation of this money was first started by the Dutch.

As direct contributors to American thought the Dutch were somewhat deficient. They were more interested in commodities that could be bought and sold than in roseate political theories or theological doctrines. Indeed their very indifference to ideas made them extremely tolerant of all shades of belief and opinion. As a result of this easy tolerance in the inhabitants and of the business opportunities offered by the city, people of every race and sect early flocked to the hospitable shelter of Manhattan Island. By the middle of the eighteenth century New York City was a whirlpool of races and ideas. If the city failed to contribute greatly to American culture until another century had passed such failure was caused by the irresistible attraction of commercial and financial ventures rather than by a lack of native ability. Certainly the failure was not caused by any curb on thought or its expression, for one of the most notable events in colonial America was the Zenger trial in New York City, a case which established that the principle of freedom of the press meant that a newspaper was not compelled to stop short of criticizing officials. This decision was in line with the easy tolerance of the Dutch.

In practical politics the Dutch were rather prominent, as became men of wide business interests. More than sixty men of seventeenth century Dutch blood have been elected to Congress from New York alone, and two presidents, Van Buren and Roosevelt, have belonged to this racial element.

With their indifference to ideas as such the Dutch could not be expected to contribute greatly to American literature. Irving was not a Dutchman, although Dutch New York formed the background for some of his most delightful and characteristic work. Among the writers who possessed Dutch blood may be named some of the ornaments of American literature, notably Whitman and Melville, both of whom were sons of Dutch mothers. Bret Harte was also of Dutch descent. Carl Van Vechten and Hendrik Willem Van Loon among contemporary writers, are of Dutch blood, the latter having been born in Holland.

THE SPANISH

There are three points at which Spanish culture might have entered American life: Florida, New Orleans, and the Southwest. That the rather sedate but satisfying Spanish civilization has exerted practically no influence from any of these points is no criticism of the civilization. In Florida Spanish culture never had a secure hold, and under the impact of American enterprise it has completely passed out, leaving behind no traces. In New Orleans the Spanish elements were extinguished or obscured by the more firmly entrenched French life and ways. Very frequently the traveler through southern California, Arizona, New Mexico, or Texas will see a building that shows unmistakable signs of Spanish influence, but it is a question if the Spanish tendencies can persist where the country is being developed with amazing rapidity. Spanish is still heard in the streets, and the curio shops do a thriving business in "Spanish" handiwork, but of the deeper Spanish culture there is scarcely a trace. El Greco, Velázquez, Cervantes, Calderón, Pío Baroja, Azorín, and Unamuno are but little known to even the educated American.

This ignorance of Spanish culture is shown nowhere more conclusively than in our national ignorance of the culture that dominates the western hemisphere from the Rio Grande to Cape Horn. We are prone to look upon Latin America as an area of undefined extent rich in minerals, poor in culture, and excessively prolific of revolutions. That there are universities in Latin-America a century older than Harvard, that these universities have sent forth scientists and writers of international reputation, and that the countries south of the Rio Grande have been interpreted in a worthy and beautiful literature—all these things are matters of almost complete indifference to American readers.

It is true that many young American students are studying the Spanish language, but most of these are either taking the work as a requirement or as a preliminary to the selling of automobiles, hardware, mining machinery, and radio sets to the Spanish-speaking peoples of this hemisphere. It is doubtful if valuable cultural effects will result from such study.

Aside from the collapse of Spanish influence at the points of settlement inside the United States, there is another reason for our failure to absorb anything from Spanish culture and that is the lack of communication between this nation and Spain. Spain has sent us few emigrants, and relatively few American tourists have visited that nation. At least one American thinker and writer is of Spanish birth, and his work is valuable enough to make up for scores of mediocrities; for of all living men none has made a finer contribution to American culture than has George Santayana, poet and thinker, formerly professor of philosophy in Harvard University.

THE SCANDINAVIANS

For more than two generations a nucleus of Scandinavian culture has been germinating in the northern Mississippi Valley. There the Swedes, Norwegians, and Danes, fresh from the mother countries, long labored exclusively at the task of fixing themselves upon the fertile soil that they possessed, and now the children and grandchildren of the immigrants are beginning to interest themselves in a life of culture. With this new interest has arisen a desire for expression, and the first fruits of that desire we now have. The poems of Carl Sandburg and the very significant novels, *Giants in the Earth* and *Peder Victorious*, by O. L. Rolvaag are great portents of the future of American literature in the hands of the Scandinavians.

That the Norsemen can write great novels and dramas is proved by the work of Ibsen, Björnsen, Strindberg, Bojer, Sigrid Undset, Hamsun, Nexö, and others. These authors are distinguished by a fine feeling for the harmony of character and the background, a sense of profound pity at the infinite striving of humanity, and a keen appreciation of the goodness and badness of man. There is no reason for thinking that the Scandinavians in America who attempt writing will abandon any of the characteristics that ennoble the literature of the mother countries. As soon as material conditions make it possible, the northern Mississippi Valley will have its authentic interpreters—interpreters who have neither lost their racial characteristics nor failed to grasp the physical environment and spirit of the new world.

THE ITALIANS

The Italians are another group whose promise far exceeds its present contribution to American culture. Millions of aliens, who live largely in cities and who are concerned intimately with our economic and industrial organizations, would be reasonably certain to add something to our culture, provided that they had even the rudiments of reflective or creative ability. This assurance becomes trebly certain when those aliens are of the blood that produced Dante, Petrarch, Leonardo da Vinci, Michelangelo, Cherubini, Verdi, Mazzini, Leopardi, Croce, and many others. The Italians have too strong a cultural tradition not to make some response when brought into contact with American life.

The exact nature of this response is beyond present knowledge. Will the facts that the Italians are largely city dwellers, and that they are frequently laborers make these people socially minded? Or will they follow their natural bent and become detached individualists? Will they adhere to the fine tradition of their culture and see American life with the impersonal eyes and detached interest of the Latin, or will they brood over their new scene with the personal interest, the subjectivism of the northerner? The one Italian to make for himself a name in current American literature is Arturo Giovannitti, whose book of poems, *Arrows in the Gale,* is one of the most significant social documents ever produced in America. If we may judge from this book the Italian mind will be keenly sensitive to social wrongs and gifted with profound sympathy for the thwarted strivings of humanity. It is not unlikely that Giovannitti's poetry is a forecast of the work of his people.

There are other contributions that Italians may make to our culture. Grand opera is a natural expression of the Italian love of music, and opera in America has been patronized by Italians as well as by Germans and French. To-day many of the singers, conductors, and orchestra players are of Italian blood, while it is apparent to any observer that Italians make up a considerable portion of the audiences. In the field of art Italian influence has been vigorous.

THE JEWS

The Jews are a notable example of an immigrant group that has followed a natural and logical method of throwing its influence into the stream of American culture. The first generation on American soil usually devotes itself to the practical business of getting on in the new world, though few Jews are indifferent to the life of culture and to the deeper significance of liberal education. When a Jewish family is established in a position of relative economic security, the children begin actively to participate in our cultural life. That this participation has not been limited to an unproductive enjoyment is abundantly proved by the large number of interpretative and creative artists now active in our musical, artistic, theatrical, and literary circles. Waldo Frank, Ludwig Lewisohn, Abraham Cahan, Elias Tobenkin, David Pinski, Maxwell Bodenheim, James Oppenheim, Louis Untermeyer, George Gershwin, Ossip Gabrilowitsch, Franklin P. Adams, and Robert Nathan are names that will occur to any one at all familiar with our recent books and music. That many of these men are young is in itself a portent of great things that the future may expect of the Jewish race.

It is a mistake to think of the Jews as a newly arrived immigrant group, unadjusted to the American environment. The first Jews came to America in early colonial days, and with their neighbors shared the vicissitudes of fortune in the new world. Many of the early arrivals were from Spain and Portugal. In the nineteenth century Germany sent us a huge wave of Jewish immigrants, that was reënforced from 1890 to 1914 by a still larger number from Russia and Poland. The long time that Jews have been in America keeps their newly arrived co-religionists from feeling like unattached strangers whose stay in this country is of doubtful duration. The Jews are fixtures in our social fabric, and none realizes that better than they do.

However long the Jews may stay with us, it is unlikely that they will lose their social identity. Nearly all of them live in cities, and city life allows a segregation of people by races and nationalities. If the Jews had scattered to the frontier farms and trading posts, it is probable that their racial identity might have been lost in the "melting pot," but they stayed in cities and did not intermarry with other peoples. So populous are the Jewish communities in our large cities and so self-sufficient are these groups that a permanent feeling of racial identity seems to be assured.

It will be a good thing if the Jews do succeed in maintaining their cultural identity in America, just as it would be a good thing if the Scandinavians, the Italians, and the Germans should keep a firm grip on their old world traditions. This statement does not mean that the immigrant groups should not become good American citizens, but a man may be an exemplary American citizen and still reverence the culture of his race. Indeed our literature will gain immensely if our naturalized Americans will bring their literary traditions to the interpretation of the American scene, and if they will give us the reactions of an old world race to a new world environment. The Jews are doing these very things, and their future contributions to our literature will doubtless be large.

Racial Characteristics of the Jews.—There are certain racial characteristics that forward one's hopes for Jewish writers. In the first place the Jews have a keen social consciousness. This characteristic is due in part to a bitter recollection of age-old suffering from social and religious prejudice and in part to the new world environment. The constant rubbing of elbows by city dwellers never allows those people to forget that social problems exist. Again, the recently aroused prejudice against the Jews in this country is another pinprick to the social-mindedness of the race. For these reasons the Jews have a liking for the scientific study of sociology and allied subjects that develops sometimes into a large amount of ameliorative work, and sometimes into a glowingly idealistic social philosophy.

Along with the sensitive social consciousness of the Jews goes a brilliant and critical mind. Of all alien critics of this country none has viewed the American life and problems with more perception and none has expressed more vigorous and intelligent opinions than has the Jewish critic. But Jewish criticism does not stop short with our institutions; recent American music, art, and literature owe a great debt to those Jewish writers whose brilliant intellects and critical temperaments so illuminate the aims and reveal the shortcomings of our culture. Another hopeful sign in our future intellectual life is the serious intent with which the Jews take up academic work. Philosophy, sociology, literature, history, all are studied as if they were of vital import and not as if they were the leisurely pastimes of college students. With his excellent mind and his interested, vital attitude toward his studies, it will be surprising if the Jew does not contribute more than his share to the intellectual life of America.

Added to his critical mind and his social awareness the Jew has a third trait that is not often found in company with the others. This is the ability to express himself beautifully. Somewhere in the oriental soul of the Jew abides the artistic gift that beautifies literature and enriches life. No better exemplar of this gift can be found than Robert Nathan, whose novels, *The Puppet Master* and *Autumn*, express a pretty consistent philosophy in a delicately poetic prose.

THE NEGRO

Although the contribution of the Negro to American culture has already been far from negligible, no very acute prophet is required to see that this contribution will vastly increase within a very short time. Ten million alien people with a most individual racial background and history could not forever rest contented with the interpretation given them by white humorists and sentimentalists. The Negro race is only now finding its voice, and we may expect that voice to become more confident and fluent. As markedly good as Negro literature is to-day, its high quality is but a portent of the future.

The Negro in Literature.—Although the black race has had its authors since Jupiter Hammon and Phillis Wheatley produced their poetry during Revolutionary days, the Negro's chief function in American literature has been to supply white writers with certain stock figures, usually humorous or pathetic. A Negro minstrel show and Mrs. Stowe's Uncle Tom are typical examples of the habitual treatment of the Negro in earlier days. To-day there is a new tendency. It is inconceivable that the whites will cease writing about the Negroes, but it is perfectly conceivable that they will interpret their subjects in a more original fashion than has been the custom in the past. Indeed, unmistakable signs ot such an interpretation are already to be seen. The methods and aims of such writers as Eugene O'Neill, DuBose Heyward, Mrs. Julia Peterkin, and Dr. Howard W. Odum are as far removed as possible from the methods and aims of Mrs. Stowe, Thomas Nelson Page, and George W. Cable. Whether the new writers are the more accurate and sympathetic interpreters of the Negro is another question, but it is unquestionable that they are writing from a different point of view.

The Negro authors themselves are changing. Some of the older ones were content to let the black man live in American literature as the purveyor of humor and sentiment, expressing himself always in broken English that was the infallible literary sign of the Negro. That the sentiments thus expressed were often as false as the dialect seemed not to trouble these writers. To-day all this is changing. Where dialect is employed, and it is sparingly used, it is more accurate and probably less picturesque, certainly less grotesque than that once used by portrayers of Negro life. But whether the new Negro writers work in dialect or in pure English, they strive first of all to interpret the soul of their race.

The Negro race in art, music, and literature possesses two vast reservoirs of material. These are the African blood and background of the black folk, and, secondly, the American experience of the race. Both white and Negro writers will draw upon both reservoirs. The African blood and background are plainly to be discerned. They are apparent in every shade of Negro temperament, in the humor of the race, in the quickly changeable emotional temper, in the superstitions, in the warm amiability, as well as in the marked illogicality. Among the literary and artistic manifestations of these traits may be mentioned the traditional spirituals and Negro folk lore, including at least part of *Uncle Remus*. Both of these have been the inspiration of much recent literature. The African blood and background have but recently been discovered as incentives of literature. More usual than these themes is the study of the Negro in relation to his American environment. This motive is to be found in our literature in many forms, varying from the songs and stories of the old minstrel show to the productions of men like Paul Laurence Dunbar and Thomas Nelson Page. The prolific "plantation tradition" in our literature has the relation of master and slave as one of its elements, and the same relation exists in thousands of novels and short stories, varying from Poe's *Gold Bug* to the most recent manifestation of mawkish sentiment.

That the Negro is coming to occupy a unique place in American literary life is proved by the considerable number of recent Negro authors. Among these are Dr. W. E. G. Du Bois, whose *Dark Water* is a classic; Booker T. Washington, who gave us another classic in *Up from Slavery;* James Weldon Johnson with his prose and verse; Countee Cullen, who is one of the most promising of America's young poets; and Langston Hughes, interpreter of "the blues" in poetry.

MINOR GROUPS

The specific enumeration of ten or twelve groups does not mean that there are no other elements in American society which are promising to lend a hand in the formation of our future American culture. Just as immigrant groups in the past have made large contributions to our civilization, just so will our higher life in the future be influenced by currents from every quarter and by national elements that we now account negligible in our cultural life.

Among the groups not specifically discussed are the Russians, Poles, Bohemians, Greeks, Gypsies, the Chinese and Japanese, and our American Indians. Because of their colorful and highly individual characteristics these minor groups deserve worthy interpreters. That some of these people are already of some cultural importance is proved by the marked influence of Indian songs upon some of our current poetry and by the impression that Chinese and Japanese art has made upon our artists and craftsmen. Although the Russian immigrants have contributed only slightly to our life, new ideas in the ballet, music, and in the drama have come from Russia. Some of the minor groups are already finding American interpreters. For instance, Willa Cather has given some memorable pictures of the Bohemian immigrants on Nebraska farms. The Indian has been a stock character in our fiction since the day of Cooper, and in 1930 Lafarge's *Laughing Boy,* a story of Indian life, received the Pulitzer Prize as the outstanding novel of the year.

It is probable that some American authors of the future will have about the same connection with this country that Lafcadio Hearn had. This writer, born on an Ægean island, was the son of a Greek mother and an Irish father. He lived in America for a number of years and spent his last days in Japan, where, as an avowed Buddhist, he taught English literature in a Japanese university. Yet he is properly accounted an American writer.

CONCLUSIONS

It is not to be inferred from this chapter that there is no such thing as an American culture. Most emphatically we have a national culture, and the attempt to disentangle the elements woven into it should not be taken as a denial of its existence. Everything that has tended toward an interpretation or an evaluation of American life has contributed to our culture. Crèvecœur, Tom Paine, Carl Schurz, Sandburg, and Giovannitti are contributors to a genuine American literature, just as are such undoubted Americans as Jefferson, Emerson, Whitman, Lincoln, and Mark Twain. The men in the latter group all come of families long established on American soil, hence each has in him more than one racial element and often more than one intellectual strain. The foreign born have a less complex background than many American born have, but it is not quite reasonable to say that, since Jefferson and Emerson, for instance, have very complex racial and intellectual ancestries they are more American than Sandburg and Tom Paine. This action would be equivalent to defining Americanism and American culture merely in terms of complexity as opposed to simplicity. We have a genuinely American literature, but it is our business to discover what it is and how it came into being. To ascertain how literature arose necessitates a close study of our writers' backgrounds and of the intellectual currents that have swept through our nation. There is growing up an American tradition, none the less American because it is compounded of many diverse elements, racial, geographical, and intellectual.

SUGGESTED READINGS

Adams: *Ireland and Irish Immigration to the New World from 1815 to the Famine*. New Haven. 1932.

"The American Negro" (a symposium). *Annals of the American Academy*, Vol. 140. November, 1928.

Faust: *The German Element in the United States*. New York. 1909.
Old but still useful.

Ford: *The Scotch-Irish in America*. Princeton. 1915.

Hanna: *The Scotch-Irish*. New York. 1902.

Hansen: *The Immigrant in American History*. Cambridge. 1940.

Hansen: *The Atlantic Migration, 1607-1860*. Cambridge. 1945.
Both of the works by Hansen are of great value. The first is a sound general discussion. The second is more detailed and thoroughly documented.

Hirsch: *The Huguenots of Colonial South Carolina*. Durham. 1928.

Jones: *America and French Culture*. Chapel Hill. 1927.
An immense amount of research went into the making of this book. An excellent study. The first three chapters are a good introduction to the study of the American mind.

Priestley: *The Coming of the White Man*. New York. 1929.
Good discussions of the Spanish, French, Dutch, and Swedes in America.

Schlesinger: *New Viewpoints in American History*. New York. 1922.
pp. 1-22.
Brief but stimulating discussion.

CHAPTER III

THE INTELLECTUAL BACKGROUND

It is the purpose of this study to stress the importance of American literature as a living illustration of the historical development of the American mind. Assuredly there are many other approaches to the study of our national literature. Some have used it primarily as a museum wherein are exhibited all manner of syntactical oddities and a great display of novel diction. Others have used it because certain of our writers have filled their books with homilies upon the more familiar texts. This use has been called "inspirational teaching." The only possible criticism that can be made of either the practice or the nomenclature is the pertinent observation that too many inspirational teachers usually omit, for sundry reasons, the very writers who deliver the most inspiring messages to the present age.

Still others discuss our literature from the standpoint of the esthetic critic. The very dubious value that many such critics attach to our letters adds weight to the suspicion that most of our authors were more interested in polemics than in esthetics and far more concerned with politics than with beauty. Again, others have applied to the chief ideas in our literature the test of philosophic examination to determine whether or not our writers held opinions that coincide perfectly with truth. The obvious query to direct at the philosophic critic is the unanswered question of Pontius Pilate, but the apposite remark is that American thought and actions have been determined by ideas that were accepted and acted upon as if they were wholly true. For instance, the epistemology and psychology of Puritanism may have been altogether erroneous, but the early inhabitants of New England thought that their ideas were true, and in accordance with their convictions they founded a way of life that has been enormously influential in the current of American thought. Furthermore, it may be that all the ideas promulgated by the romantic school were false, yet America of the early nineteenth century accepted these as if they were of unquestionable validity. Our people have never been renowned for the logic and scientific precision with which they examine ideas and proposals before putting them into practice. As a result, the philosophic critic is constrained to grieve over many things in American life and thought that the historian is forced to record by the inexorable compulsion of facts.

The first task of the historian of literature is to determine what a given writer said. The second task is to discover why he said it. Then, if time, space, and ability have not failed, the historian may speculate on the influence of the writer's work. Usually the historian is far too busy with his primary tasks to devote very much time to a disquisition on what the author should have thought and said. He must delegate to the philosopher and the moralist the task of examining literature for its truth or desirability.

If American literature is to be studied as a tangible result of the American mind in action over a period of three centuries, it must be considered as an entity, a thing continuous in its development. Although it is possible to indicate the chief chronological periods of our development, it is impossible to divide our literature into water-tight compartments. The failure to grasp this fact has led many people to talk about the Colonial Era and the Revolutionary Epoch, the First National Period and the Second National Period, just as if there could be a distinct line drawn between consecutive periods. To read some of our literary histories one would think that our colonial forefathers awoke one morning with a start and impressively remarked to each other that the revolutionary epoch had begun. History and literature do not so develop. In 1825 a man seventy-five years of age could see that during his time great changes had taken place in American life and thought, but even the most acute would have been hard put to it to tell exactly where the line lay that divided the colonial age from the revolutionary period or exactly where and when the Revolution came to an end. Revolutions have a habit of extending far beyond their official limits both in time and influence, so that they profoundly affect the thought of people long before and after the revolutionary period proper. A history of national progress in any field can seldom be fitted into a string of rigidly divided compartments or "periods."

Another objection to the compartment method of treating American literature is to be found in the failure of such treatment to acknowledge the extreme dependence of one age upon another. The thought of one generation always feeds upon the thought of the preceding generations. Books are a visible manifestation of thought, and thought is constantly moving on. Literature develops like a tree, growing year by year from the main trunk and keeping a close connection with what has developed earlier. Some critics talk as if it were a weed that dies down periodically and starts again from the ground.

Rather than seek to divide and sub-divide our literature into rigid chronological epochs, the historian should attempt to ascertain the chief intellectual factors in our development and to trace them through our history, noting how they respond to the modifying influences of time and environment. The development of the American mind has been so natural, so consecutive, and so uninfluenced by the distraction of powerful or fascinating neighbors that the original forces that created American thinking are with us to-day, operating with pristine vigor and fruitfulness.

Dominant Influences in Our Literature.—No two historians agree exactly as to the number or character of the intellectual influences in our development, but for the purposes of this study it will be assumed that there are four well-defined forces. These are, first, the cosmopolitan spirit, which is a convenient term for all phases of foreign thought, chiefly European; second, Puritanism or the spirit of New England Calvinism with all its implications; third, the frontier element; and fourth, mysticism. These four have been abiding influences on American minds and hearts, directing and modifying our thoughts and our feelings. By 1725 all were present on this continent, and two centuries later not one had vanished. Indeed these forces cannot disappear so long as the American mind exists, for they are the warp and woof of that mind. From time to time the pattern of the mind changes, but the elemental stuffs remain constant. Sometimes one element will dominate our whole literary life, sometimes two or more will be found together on terms of equality, sometimes literature is produced by the impact of one force upon another, and sometimes the forces are frankly at war. But whatever may be the relation of the forces to each other, these reciprocal influences have made the American mind.

The same conditions are to be found in our individual writers that we find in our literature at large. In Lincoln and Mark Twain the frontier element is dominant. Both the frontier spirit and cosmopolitanism are to be found in Thomas Jefferson. William Cullen

Bryant represented Puritanism in his poetry and the liberalism of the frontier in his prose, while Joel Barlow started out as a true Puritan and later became wholly cosmopolitan. Hamlin Garland is a blend of frontier thinking and European literary theory. Whitman is a blend of mysticism and the frontier spirit. In fact in the whole stretch of our literature it is very difficult to find an author who cannot be interpreted in terms of one or more of these influences, though it must be admitted that Poe and Melville are not easily accounted for by this or any other method.

THE COSMOPOLITAN SPIRIT

The cosmopolitan spirit in American life means simply the influence of foreign thought. During most of our history we have not been indifferent to foreign ideas, and our years of greatest intellectual and artistic activity are generally the years when we are in closest touch with Europe. European thinking has been a power in all our intellectual activities, and most of our artistic experiments and innovations have been imported from beyond the Atlantic. The cosmopolitan spirit has influenced our religious development, our political theory, our conception of economics, our musical and artistic products, and the theory and practice of literature. Among the more important intellectual movements that developed in America as the direct result of European thought are the deistic conception of religion, the humanitarian impulse that became so marked in the romantic revolution, New England transcendentalism, socialism, the modern biological theory of aristocracy, realism, and literary naturalism. England, France, and Germany have been the originators of most of these movements, and our large cities have been their ports of entry.

Certainly the cosmopolitan spirit in the country has been important—so important that some critics insist that all American thinking is nothing more than European thought appearing in America one or two generations after its birth in the old world. Such commentators overlook the fact that European ideas are usually profoundly affected by their new environment on this side of the Atlantic and, furthermore, that there are many things in American life and thought that are not even remotely European. Walt Whitman, Mark Twain, Abraham Lincoln, and Andrew Jackson are as non-European as are the Mississippi River, Yellowstone Park, Henry

Ford's automobile factory, a Kansas wheat farm, or our innumerable Main Streets. Important though it may be, cosmopolitan thought does not account for all of American intellectual life.

The cosmopolitan spirit came to our shore in a variety of ways. It was imported in books, acquired by American travelers in Europe, scattered by various foreign visitors to this country, brought back by young Americans who were dispatched to Europe to complete their education, and carried into this country by millions of immigrants as a part of their intellectual luggage. In short it came to America just as ideas have always traveled, and thought has a habit of leaping tariff barriers, stealing unseen past political boundaries, and flitting lightly over the most impassable physical dividing lines. Mere differences in race, nationality, and language afford no permanent guarantee that ideas will not travel from one people to another very dissimilar group.

America has not always been hospitable to foreign thought. Frequently "traditional Americanism" has assailed European ideas as dangerous or frivolous. Sometimes it has destroyed the object of its dislike, sometimes it has assimilated the objectionable idea, and sometimes alien thought has conquered traditional Americanism. Yet for every European idea disposed of, there has been a successor generated in some land across the Atlantic, and the successor is always subjected to the same treatment. It is ever thus. Even now the flood of European thought pours into the nation as it did in the beginning. Such a process is a good thing, for it keeps us mentally alert. We reject some ideas, accept others, and thus keep adding to the stock of prejudices and practices that we call "traditional Americanism." Complete subservience to foreign ideas would make us but an echo of Europe. Complete isolation or unrelenting hostility would lead to satisfied but sterile provincialism.

PURITANISM

Puritanism, considered as the name of something in America, is a loose term with at least two distinct meanings, and it is often further used to brand with disapproval almost anything objectionable. Strictly speaking it stands for a religious sect or a moral code. In this last meaning it is sometimes properly called a philosophy of life. As a religion it means that extreme type of Calvinism preached in the churches of New England from 1620 to the opening of the nineteenth century. As such it has considerable interest to the students of American literature, for Puritan philosophy is founded upon the creed developed by Calvinistic theology. This creed will be discussed shortly. However, it is as a moral code growing out of the early Calvinism that Puritanism has had its most enduring influence in American life. The Puritan moralist thinks that the world is a divinely ordered achievement and that man is placed on earth for the primary purpose of glorifying God by faith and obedience. The idea of morality pervades all things, and the final, indeed the only, judgment of everything must be made on the grounds of moral goodness. According to this view every action must have a moral aim, every book must be written for the moral edification of the reader, and life itself must get its meaning from the moral interests of man.

Phases of Puritan Morality.—The moral fervor of Puritanism has passed through three fairly well-marked stages. The first extended through the colonial epoch and lingered on until well into the nineteenth century. The chief aim of the Puritan during this time was to live a life of individual morality. To do this he lived according to the letter of the Scriptures, using as a guide the Old Testament rather than the New. This first stage of Puritanism was a time of great soul-searching and tireless striving for righteousness. The individual subjected himself to a rigorous examination for traces of hidden sin, and sin, when discovered, was repented of with utmost contrition. The only possible objection to this code of morality lies in the fact that the Puritan is so occupied with the question of his own individual sin that he becomes indifferent to the problems of others and especially careless of the obligations and deficiencies of society as a whole. The individualistic Puritan moralist is apt to have no social conscience, no feeling of responsibility for or opposition to such social wrongs as slavery, oppression of the poor, and bad labor conditions. The wrongs and injustices inflicted by society upon the weak and distressed are sometimes lightly dismissed by the Puritan as ordinary and natural things, provided that society is led by men who are personally righteous. This individual Puritan morality gave way slowly to another conception.

During the first part of the nineteenth century the outlook of New England Puritanism became predominantly social. This change was caused by certain outside influences, notably French social and humanitarian thought. Then came the great reform movement in

America when it was believed that all social wrongs like slavery and intemperance could be abolished by appeals to the moral sensibility of mankind. The great reformers like Garrison, Wendell Phillips, Horace Greeley, Lucretia Mott, Elizabeth Cady Stanton, John B. Gough, George H. Evans, Horace Mann, Samuel G. Howe, and Dorothea Dix were all imbued with the new Puritanism, the idea of social responsibility and progress, although many of these people were not New Englanders. As the second stage of Puritanism developed, it became more and more apparent that the motives and aims of its adherents were the exact opposite of those held by earlier Puritans like Cotton Mather and Michael Wigglesworth. The one obvious thing that was transferred from the older generation to the younger was the so-called New England conscience, but the conscience had shifted its emphasis from individual affairs to social concerns. One may say, roughly speaking, that this aspect of Puritanism was closed by the triumph of industrialism, an event that was signalized in our political life by the Civil War.

Since the Civil War and the collapse of moral reform, Puritanism has attempted to effect its desires by the passage of restrictive laws rather than by moral suasion. The early temperance movement in this country, with its program of education and its appeal to the social conscience, is an example of the second stage of Puritanism; the present-day prohibition movement is an example of the third stage. Sometimes this later Puritanism has taken the form of opposition to things that are felt to be distracting to the religious interests of the people. In this approach to religious interests recent Puritanism is closer to the Puritanism of the first stage than to that of the second stage, for many of the reforms of 1830-60 were carried on entirely outside the churches, and very few, if any, of them originated in religious organizations. To-day it is undeniable that there is a tendency to get away from the ideal that ennobled the second stage of Puritanism. That ideal was the greatest possible amount of individual happiness, and it was to be achieved through a program of social well-being.

The Creed of Puritanism.—It is not necessary to make a thorough examination of the creed of the Puritan sect. That familiar creed, which dominated the thinking of New England from 1620 to 1800, helped to create the moral code known as Puritanism and thus affected much of American thought. It contained only three points that are of significance to us. These three are election, bondage of the will, and perseverance of the saints.

Election is sometimes called predestination. It means a belief that all the actions, as well as the eternal fate of every man, have been ordained from the beginning of the world. Election thus divides mankind into two unequal groups, one of which will be saved whatever may befall, and the other will be lost eternally despite personal merit or striving. Sins are fore-ordained, as are virtuous acts, and man has no control over his life. This doctrine has been most influential in Puritan thought, for the theory of predestination or divine determinism, as it is sometimes called, was one of the chief reasons for the Puritan's indifference to social wrongs. It too frequently led our forefathers to look upon oppression and injustice as inevitable occurrences rather than as wrongs that may be abolished. It is obvious that this doctrine had to be modified before the reform movement could gain any headway among the Puritans.

Bondage of the will is the belief that man is not free to make any choice whatever in determining his action. In other words a man's actions are determined for him and not by him. The exact extent of this determinism was a matter of dispute, some holding that man has absolutely no freedom whatever in his actions, while the more liberal Puritans thought that he might be compared to a squirrel in a cage. As the animal has freedom within certain sharply defined limits, so does man have a sharply limited liberty. This belief in the bondage of the will, when joined to the doctrine of election, tended to place man on a low level in the Puritan's view of the universe, for so long as man felt that his will was unfree he would fail to have a very high opinion of himself.

Perseverance of the saints simply means that the elect, those who are chosen to be saved, will endure in their righteousness despite the wiles of the devil who uses every method to cause the chosen to stumble. This doctrine was genuinely comforting to the early Puritans in the bleak, inhospitable New England environment. In fact the environment had a hardening effect upon this belief, for the more hostile man and nature waxed, the closer held the Puritans to this doctrine. It is interesting to speculate upon what would have happened if the early Puritans had landed on a hospitable land in a soft, semi-tropical climate. The intellectual history of America might have been changed.

The most important corollary of the official Calvinistic creed is the doctrine of total depravity. According to this belief all men are totally and hopelessly wicked. Human nature is unspeakably bad. A few may be chosen for salvation, but their election is the result of the grace of God rather than the outcome of good actions by the individuals. This doctrine also had the effect of lowering the position of man in the Puritan's view of the universe.

Election, bondage of the will, perseverance of the saints, and the doctrine of total depravity are in themselves dreary enough, but their implications are more important and even more depressing than the original beliefs.

Official Philosophy of Early Puritanism.—The Puritan thought of God as an omnipotent, all-knowing being of unparalleled perfection and majesty who remains wholly outside the universe. This view made impossible the romantic conception that God manifests himself in nature or in the works of man. Emerson's assertion that he found something of the divine in everything and Walt Whitman's declaration that he found letters from God in every street would have been totally incomprehensible to the early Puritan. The strict Calvinist thought that the gulf between God and man was so vast that it was only betokened and not paralleled by the gulf between man and the spider. To a mind steeped in this philosophy the triumphant pæan of the romantics that they were part and parcel of the divine would have been only presumptuous blasphemy.

The Puritans held that God occasionally interferes with the ordered working of the universe according to the wish or caprice of arbitrary will. These occasional interferences are for the purpose of wreaking immediate punishment upon some sinner, or they are designed to give some striking proof of God's affection for an individual or group of people. Such an interference with the ordinary course of the universe is known as a special providence. This term came to be applied to all coincidences, strokes of good fortune, and the like.

The early Puritan thought of the universe as a static organization. That is to say, the universe is the same to-day that it was in the beginning when God created it, and it will remain the same until God in his own way and own good time brings it to an end. This belief effectually prevented any idea of growth or development, just as it made impossible the belief that mankind slowly approaches the deity and gradually learns the ways of God through man's own strivings and mistakes. Furthermore the Puritan argued that, if the universe is static and everything in it unchanged and unchangeable, all attempts to abolish evil and social maladjustment are futile.

In complete harmony with his other beliefs the Puritan held a theory of knowledge that was anything but inspiring to individual effort. He believed that true knowledge is the result of revelation and not the product of man's endeavors. Much has been written about the logic of Calvinism, but reason was useful to the Puritan only as a means of defending his theological position and reconciling it to Biblical teaching. The position itself was founded on direct revelation as set forth in the Scriptures. At best man's knowledge is dim and fitful, said the Puritan, and in most fields the blackness of ignorance is impenetrable. Faith is the answer to man's desire to understand the universe.

In the popular mind the most important ideas that grew out of the official statements of Calvinism were those of the superlative greatness, majesty, and inscrutable wisdom of God and the contrasting smallness and insignificant status of man. It is with the latter idea that the student of American literature is most concerned. If the Puritan belief that man is totally depraved and worthless had been allowed, this nation could hardly have been founded on the belief in the dignity and worth of the individual. Furthermore, if man bears in him not the spark of divine perfection but the unmistakable signs of depravity, Emerson's triumphant assertion of the divinity of the individual and Whitman's chants of praise for the common man must have been founded upon premises that were far from early Puritanism. It will be interesting to see what intellectual winds blew into Massachusetts to cause Emerson, the most typical product of his time, to take up a position so directly opposed to the Puritan philosophy of early New England.

If God permitted evil and then punished man for sinning, and if all mankind fell into two groups, the elect and damned, and if there could be no passing from one group to another, what was the use to walk uprightly, to strive to live a sinless life? The Puritan admitted readily that the elect could never be lost, and that the non-elect could never be saved, but he still had reasons for living an upright life. According to his belief, the elect never sinned. Hence the man who walked constantly in the path of righteousness had the immense comfort and satisfaction of knowing in his own mind that he had at least a chance at salvation. The flagrant

sinner enjoyed no such chance. Consequently uprightness of conduct was a sign of possible election and not an attempt to gain
salvation. Although it was confidently asserted that not more than
one out of every hundred people could be saved, the Puritan usually
did not have too much trouble in making himself think that he
was the one elect in his circle. If there had not been moments
of optimism granted the Puritan, his stern creed with its accompanying body of thought would have plunged him into the depths
of unbroken pessimism. Even with moments of relative cheerful-
ness, the Puritan thinker was frequently plagued by fits of black
despair.

Political Implications of Puritanism.—In political thought Puritanism had one of its most interesting and characteristic outgrowths,
an outgrowth that paralleled the original body of Puritan theology
in a most striking manner. In a society that was divided into two
groups of unequal size, the smaller containing the elect and the
larger including the eternally lost, the idea of democracy naturally
met with much opposition. It was especially displeasing to the
elect, who were the leaders of society, even if they were a hopelessly small minority, for under a democracy every political election
might mean the domination of the few upright people by the many
sinners. Every defeat of the smaller party would be another triumph
of unrighteousness and another defeat for the Lord's anointed. Such
an occurrence would be more than an offense to the elect; it would
savor strongly of sacrilege. In short, Puritan thought rejected
democracy both as a social theory of equality and as the political
rule of the majority, because democratic theory and practice ran
counter to the divinely established order. Nothing supremely good
could be expected from the great majority composed of totally depraved, eternally lost beings. In the popular mind such distinctions as wealth, ability, and good family were simply marks of divine
favor showered upon the elect, and any attempt to wrest the direction of society and government from the control of these people
was an affront to heaven. Therefore it is only natural that the one
frankly aristocratic political party in American politics should have
had its stronghold in Puritan New England with the ministers as its
strongest supporters. This party was Federalism. It stood frankly
for the control of government by the rich, well-born, and educated,
and before 1800 few except the rich and well-born received college
educations.

Federalism advocated a strongly organized central government, and in this demand it again drew support from the implications of Puritanism. According to Calvinistic theology the government of the universe was a heavenly autocracy with God as the omnipotent ruler. Hence when the Puritan transferred his ideas from the celestial administration to the earthly, he thought of a strongly organized, highly centralized government with ample power to guide the faltering steps of the weak and to punish the misdeeds of the wicked. A paternalistic government, so abhorrent to Jefferson, appealed strongly to minds tempered by Puritanism—so long as the Puritans controlled the government.

In one more respect the Puritan in his political thinking established a parallel to his theological doctrines. Since special providences sometimes meant marks of particular divine favor, it was seemly for earthly governments to bestow special privileges upon the deserving. From this point it is an easy step to the doctrine that governments exist for the benefit of those who do the governing. This theory found a belated echo in the contention of Henry Clay that the government was a cow that was to be milked and the milk distributed among those who supervised the milking. Moreover it is doubtful if this view has entirely disappeared from American politics.

Puritanism Outside New England.—When the New Englander started west, about the close of the eighteenth century, he soon came into contact with frontier conditions which quite materially altered his Puritanism. The aristocratic tendencies of Puritanism disappeared before the irresistible equalitarianism of the frontier; the pessimistic cast of Puritan thought gave way to the abounding hopefulness and buoyant optimism of the pioneer; and the whole Puritan philosophy was displaced by a mode of thinking more in accord with the spirit of the great western country. One characteristic still remained. The New Englander in his new home kept his old habit of judging everything in terms of goodness and badness. Life was still a most serious business, and the wise man was he who kept a firm hold on certain eternal truths. On the frontier the New England emigrant found the Scotch-Irish in large numbers. These people were as serious and as moral as the Puritans, and between the two groups America has been pretty well saturated with a type of morality and moral judgment that deserves the name Puritan. To-day Puritanism as a religious faith has quite largely disappeared from New England as it has from other parts of the country, but it exists all over the nation as a moral force, an influence constantly directing our attention to the fact that life is a most serious business and that everything must be judged in terms of current morality. In this respect Puritanism still is a strong force in American life and thought.

THE FRONTIER

The American frontier is a state of mind rather than a geographical expression, but strictly speaking the term means a moving line of settlement with the uninhabited public domain before it and the settled country behind. This line rolled westward until it hesitated at the Missouri River where it halted before the endless stretch of arid and semi-arid plains and mountains. Soon after the line of settlement reached the Missouri River, gold was discovered in California. A rush of emigration to the gold-fields established another frontier on the Pacific coast, just as the earlier had been started on the Atlantic seaboard. From 1850 to 1890 the two frontiers, one moving west, the other east, slowly closed in upon the disappearing public domain. About forty years ago the two frontiers met not far from the Great Divide, and our pioneering days were over. The visible indication of the passing of the frontier was the disappearance of the last desirable public land. Thus almost all of America was at some time on the frontier, and it is one of the characteristics of the frontier that it influences the customs and thought of a community two or three generations after the rolling line of settlement has passed on. It is not too much to say that the frontier has determined to a very large degree the thinking of our American people.

Double Meaning of "Frontiersmen."—The word "frontiersmen" has a double meaning. In one sense it means those hardy, restless, reckless individuals who felt the irking bonds of society as soon as they could see the smoke from their neighbor's campfire. Such men never waited for the line of settlement to catch up with them. Before the arrival of the plowman and herdsman, these fellows would dash off into the trackless west, fighting Indians, blazing trails, and sending back glowing accounts of El Doradoes just ahead. Such a frontiersman was Daniel Boone. As a man of middle age he did more than any other person to open Kentucky to settlement. When immigrants began to pour into the Blue Grass Region, Boone again plunged into the West, going to Missouri. When the tide of settlement again caught up with him, he yearned to be off once more, and at the age of eighty-four he was deterred only by the pleas of his children and grandchildren from attempting a trip westward to visit the salt mountains, lakes, ponds and those "natural curiosities" that lay about five or six hundred miles west of his home, according to his calculation. The old fellow was also burning with desire to see California. Such men as Boone were of enormous importance in the history of the West, and no one wishes to minimize their worth, but it is a fact that the romantic glow of their dramatic exploits has kept many from appreciating the work of other less spectacular but no less important pioneers belonging to the second group.

It was this second group that established the frontier mind. Following close on the heels of the trail-breakers came the farmers, who methodically took up the onerous task of transforming the frontier into cultivated farms. Those men had a vivid if somewhat primitive interest in economics and politics. They complained vociferously about the prices offered for their products; they wanted more money in circulation; they demanded that the public domain be sold in small lots to actual settlers; they pressed for a homestead act that would give a quarter-section to each settler; they clamored for roads, railroads, and canals; and before long they were sending men to the national capital to voice these demands and to assist in putting into practice the theories of democracy that developed on the small farms of the West. The trail-breaker has disappeared, leaving only a halo of romance about his memory, but the pioneer farmer lives on in his spiritual descendants, who are perplexed to-day by the same social and political questions that gave zest and character to their fathers' thinking. But the frontier mind has something more distinctive and characteristic than the specific questions it raises or the demands it presents. It is distinguished more by peculiar qualities than by its forthright products, more by a manner of thinking than by specific conclusions. Broadly speaking one may say that the frontier mind has a unique color and that it touches nothing that is not immediately suffused with that color.

Causes of the Frontier Mind.—Before proceeding to a consideration of that color it is necessary to look briefly at the reason for the frontier mind. In short the cause was the existence of a huge and seemingly inexhaustible reservoir of open land. The line of settlement moved along at a fairly uniform rate, though it was never mathematically straight, nor was it precise in its movements. Sometimes a portion of the line would come to a halt as it met some physical obstruction, and again a part of the line was thrust out rapidly when an especially inviting region was found. The frontier mind was formed on this line of settlement, but as the line rolled on, the country over which it passed retained frontier characteristics that stubbornly refused to yield to other influences. This trait was caused, at least in part, by the rapid movement of the line of settlement. The Appalachian barrier was not definitely passed until shortly before the Revolution, and within fifty years most of the country east of the Mississippi was settled. So rapidly did the settlers surge forward that the region from the Appalachians to the great river had no time to recover from the shock of frontier conditions. But there were elements in the frontier making for permanence of impression, for Illinois and the old Northwest thought in terms of the frontier for many years after the line of settlement had rolled on westward. Indeed at the present time, after the passage of a hundred years and the influx of many foreign ideas, it is conceivable that the old Northwest still retains the frontier influence as the dominant force in its thinking. Although the frontier was paramount in early Tennessee, the successful introduction of slavery into the Southwest kept this part of the country from exhibiting frontier characteristics so long or so fiercely as did the states to the northward. After the Civil War the frontier reasserted itself in the Southwest, especially in Texas.

The Leveling Tendencies of the Frontier.—The frontier colored the thinking of its inhabitants in almost every conceivable direction. It developed, if not a highly original, at least a distinctive economics; it brought into being the democracy of Jefferson, Jackson, Benton, and Lincoln; it produced a social uniformity unseen probably elsewhere in the world, certainly not in America; and finally it inculcated a mode of thought that is unmistakably born of the soil and the environment.

In social life the frontier was a great leveler. The very rich man seldom penetrated to the line of settlement, and when he did, he discovered that his wealth counted for little and his rank for nothing at all. Frontier social values were not measurable by money or blueness of blood. Strength, rough skill, and courage counted for more than all the aristocratic distinctions. He was the best man who could shoot straighter, plow deeper, swing the ax faster, and fight harder than his companions. By such rude standards were Davy Crockett, Jackson, and Lincoln adjudged community leaders. Nor was nimbleness of wit ever despised, for in the struggles with nature and man the slow-witted frontiersman frequently met death. Since wealth counted for little in establishing one's social status on the frontier, it is not surprising that the wealthy aristocrat preferred to remain in the older sections where he enjoyed certain traditional prerogatives. Some younger sons of the gentry traveled into the West where they either made their way by native ability or sank to an inconspicuous place in society. The pages of western literature hold many accounts of impoverished aristocrats who went West only to find to their infinite disgust that genealogy was one of the least popular subjects of conversation. On the other hand excessive poverty did not set a frontiersman off from his fellows, for all were poor, and all had an equal chance of rising in the economic scale. A man might be excessively poor in wealth and still possess the qualities that would make him a leader of more than local reputation.

Slavery was found on parts of the frontier, even in the extreme Northwest, but it existed in spite of uncongenial surroundings. In general it was unprofitable. The chief slave crops like cotton, rice, and sugar were not raised north of the Ohio, and the close proximity of the Indian country made escape very easy. Add to these economic reasons the fixed aversion of frontier society to any class distinctions, and the reasons for the innate hostility to slavery of such men as Lincoln become apparent. Even Mark Twain, born of a slave-holding family, became a bitter critic of the institution. The submerged classes, along with the aristocrat, never harmonized with the western leveling process. All the West was one class, and that was the middle.

Within the middle class there was a remarkable cohesion and uniformity that was caused partly by the environment. The pioneer's task was to fight Indians, build roads, open streams to navigation, and perform other tasks that required community effort. The man who hung back was not a good citizen. In their sports the Westerners went together. Whether it was a community work-sport like a house raising, or a pure sport like a picnic or horse race, the entire neighborhood joined in. Aristocratic aloofness was sharply frowned upon. Community action dominated the West almost as much as it dominated early New England. Independence there may have been, but it was physical and economic independence. The farmers of the Middle West fled from classification, nor would they admit regimentation into their social structure. They insisted upon the right and even the duty of "getting on" in the world, and they always enjoyed the liberty to move on in hopes of finding a better or at least a newer land. Unfortunately independence of thought was not so highly prized. Indeed the pioneer has generally prided himself on his essential similarity to his fellows in his thinking and his manner of life.

The leveling tendencies of the frontier are quite apparent in the uniformity of life in America. No aspect more profoundly impresses foreign observers than the similarity in every respect of the town and cities of almost our entire country. The towns may vary in the degree of prosperity that they enjoy or in railroad connections, but fundamentally all are alike as peas in a pod. The monotonous uniformity of their newspapers is striking evidence of this fact.

In its political thought the frontier left its indelible mark on American life. This mark is western or Jacksonian democracy. It has about the same relation to Jeffersonian democracy that the broad light of noon has to early dawn. Jefferson was a lifelong fighter for democracy. Beginning with the radical Declaration of Independence, continuing with the abolition in Virginia of entail and primogeniture, and ending his work with the establishment of the University of Virginia, he never failed to strike a blow for democracy. But he worked in a time and in a society that sanctioned slavery and looked upon aristocracy as a natural social and political manifestation. Under these conditions early Jeffersonian democracy had to be somewhat theoretical and not wholly practical. It was upon the frontier, where there was neither aristocracy nor a widespread sanction of slavery that the equalitarianism of Jefferson received its first practical and enthusiastic demonstration. Vulgar the critics of western democracy called it, and even its friends admitted that it was noisy and given to boasting, but it was truly equalitarian. The characteristic that gave it distinction animates the chants of Whitman and the uproarious pages of Mark Twain, while admiration for this wholehearted western democracy finds many an expression in Emerson and Thoreau. In practical politics one of the typical manifestations of democracy was the naïve belief that any man was competent to fill any office within the gift of the people or the elected executives. The quite general application of this belief accounts for some of the most grotesque characters and episodes in American history.

Frontier Economics.—In his economic ideas the pioneer was a true offspring of the middle class which always has as its main aim "getting on" in the world. It is man's duty to work hard and cultivate thrift that he may accumulate property. Indeed it is sometimes more than suggested by middle-class writers that the ability to gain wealth is in itself sufficient proof of the virtue of the individual. The ideals of industry and thrift came to this country from England during the seventeenth century and reached full development among the democrats of the West. They are most congenial economic ideals to a people without wealth who are moving down upon the unexploited treasure of an incredibly rich world. To such people the government has one prime duty; it must assist the exploitation of this wealth, and under no circumstance is it to interfere with any man in his legitimate struggle to acquire property.

In economics the frontier again was sweepingly democratic. Barring the eternal land speculator—and he usually lived in the East—there were at first few men of wealth on the frontier. Land was so cheap, often selling for a dollar an acre, that almost any man could have a farm of his own. Money was scarce, but fortunately not much was needed. A family could almost wholly subsist on goods grown and made on the farm, and surplus crops and animals could be exchanged at the nearest trading point for necessities and such luxuries as the frontier trader provided. In the course of time the increase in the value of the land and the prices received for farm products made those families that kept their holdings accounted fairly well-to-do in even a later and less simple society. Many western farm boys became wealthy through the building of railroads, the exploitation of natural resources, the starting of necessary manufacturing plants in the West, or the emigration to the financial world of a large city—usually New York, Philadelphia, or Chicago. But, however wealthy the Westerner became, he seldom denied his early environment and usually remained to the end, in words at least, a believer in equalitarianism.

Optimism of the Frontier.—Shining through all the thinking and practical work of the pioneer was his ruling philosophy of life, optimism. At first blush it seems that optimism was inevitable all over America. The new immigrants had escaped the fixed and unbreakable bonds of European classification; they had left an unfree economic and political life for one that was relatively free; in short they had traded fixity and stratification for liberty. Crops would grow for all save the most shiftless, cattle waxed fat and multiplied on the rich pasturage of the great western valleys, and there was usually a sale for surplus products of the farms. Hence it may be said that all Americans naturally acquired an abounding optimism.

Such a conclusion overlooks certain historical facts. The new arrivals from Europe were so accustomed to thinking in terms of class that they unwittingly established a society of aristocracy, middle class, and servants. It was but natural that they should do this, since they could imagine no other type. All through Tidewater this society prevailed until after the Revolution. Tidewater was merely an extension of Europe; only the shock of frontier life reduced all classes to a common level. Again, optimism was effectually ruled out of New England by the strongly pessimistic implications of Calvinistic theology. When New England Puritanism crossed the Hudson River, it kept its strong ethical drive, but it soon modified its idea of election and total depravity. This modification was due in part to the influence of the pioneer mind with its strong optimistic philosophy.

The reasons for this optimism are largely physical. Conditions on the frontier were hard enough, to be sure, but they were not beyond hope. To westward lay that ever-alluring body of open land whence came every day most enticing reports sent back by the adventuresome advance guards of civilization. If the crops in a community were poor, the soil unfertile, and the cattle plagued by epidemics, at least there was a chance that another home farther west might be free from those afflictions. The mere chance was sufficient to make a pioneer eternally hopeful. Western history was made by men who started from an eastern state, New York, for instance, settled first in Ohio, moved on to Illinois or Wisconsin, and finally found a last home in the Far West. A favorite route of the Virginians and Kentuckians lay through Missouri, thence northwest over the Oregon Trail to the Willamette Valley. Eternally disillusioned but eternally hopeful the pioneer made his way into every part of the West, seeking El Dorado of his dreams. Without the promise of a new and better home in the vast expanse of public domain such an optimism as his could not have been born.

There were other reasons for the abounding hopefulness of the West. The lack of social stratification, the great economic opportunities, the vast extent of undeveloped natural resources, the constantly promised roads, canals, railroads, and steamship lines—that frequently never materialized—all combined to keep the pioneer in a constant flutter of romantic optimism. Colonel Beriah Sellers in Twain and Warner's *Gilded Age*, is a type of the effervescent pioneer with his high-flown plans for making great wealth.

Drab enough was the actual life of the pioneer with its constant recurrence of malaria, typhoid, drought, crop failure, cattle plague, and the exhausting toil incident to frontier life. When one considers that these depressing conditions were often added to unstimulating social and intellectual life, one immediately sees the immense rôle played by optimism on the frontier. Without a cheerful optimism, a constant faith that to-morrow, or next year, or the next home would bring an end to the perplexing problems, without a trust in the future development and subsequent wealth of a community, it is doubtful if flesh and blood could have endured the grim realities of frontier life. Optimism balanced unpalatable present conditions, just as in Lincoln, a typical pioneer, ready laughter balanced a rooted melancholy. The desire of the Westerner to submerge his troubles in his dreams led to the creation of a highly sugared literature that lives to-day in the pleasant but none-too-realistic novels of such writers as Zane Grey. If there had been nothing but drabness on the frontier, our western national literature might to-day be not unlike that of Russia with its profound melancholy and its unshrinking acceptance of the unpleasant.

Again, the frontier sought a tumultuous escape from humdrum existence in its amusements. Such rustic sports as gander pullings, wrestling matches, fist fights, pitched battles between communities, and especially camp-meetings, and huge political rallies, all served to break the monotony of life. Western leaders not infrequently came to the front at such gatherings, and if the East scoffed at the vulgarity of these leaders, it must not be forgotten that these men were chosen for primitive distinction. The frontier preferred a boisterous but pleasant personality to dignity and evidenced a decided taste for native wit over grave profundity. Davy Crockett's career fully illustrates the tendencies of western political life.

Influence of the Frontier.—The influence of the frontier in American life is beyond computation. There are those who insist that present-day America in its most typical aspect is an inheritance from the pioneer. Certainly these critics are not without arguments. The free competition that has always been the boast and the distinctive characteristic of American business, the rise to power and fame of self-made individuals in finance and in politics, the emotional excesses of our political campaigns and our religion, and the amazing uniformity of our national thought are all certainly not inharmonious with our pioneer heritage, and it may be that they are of it. It is certain that our turgid optimism and our implicit faith in the practicability of the most grandiose schemes for progress are inherited from our frontier ancestors.

In factual history the influence of the frontier is enormous. In 1828 with the election of Jackson the West seized the presidency and except for short intervals, it has not since relinquished its hold. In our religious life the revivalism of Charles G. Finney, our first great evangelist, joined with New School Presbyterianism, the spread of Methodism, the Baptist movement, and the newly founded Disciples of Christ (frequently called the Christian church) to form our distinctive western denominations. When Puritanism crossed the Hudson it met the influence of Finney, and under this influence it espoused such non-Calvinistic doctrines as free will, Christian perfection, and the gospel of love. As New England Calvinism proceeded up the Mohawk Valley and into the western states of Ohio, Illinois, Wisconsin and Minnesota, it changed its temper and its theology. It had met the frontier and had succumbed. The ebullient optimism of the West, economic independence, and the lack of even a rudimentary caste system based on wealth or family, could not tolerate an iron-bound determinism, a belief in the bondage of the will, or a lasting view of man's total depravity. So it was in other fields. Jeffersonian democracy with its theoretical equalitarianism was put to the test, and any good citizen in the West was adjudged the political and social equal of any other, and any man was deemed competent to fill any position under a democracy. From the early thirties to 1890 the social citadels of the East were being stormed by Westerners—Goths, the scornful East called them—and at the end of the assault the last vestiges of aristocracy had disappeared. In business the deliberate and even dignified methods of the early time gave way to the "go-getter" methods of the West. Our pioneer heritage is everywhere; if we would see it, let us look about us.

MYSTICISM

In its broadest sense mysticism is a complete spiritual identification of the individual with another object, usually one infinitely larger and more mysterious in its workings than the individual. Originally mysticism meant a form of religious experience—the knowledge of God by becoming a part of him and by feeling his presence in one's very being. With an identity of self and God, worship becomes direct communion and the conscience becomes the guide of life. Reason abdicates to intuition. Such is the type of mysticism that is usually meant when the term is used. However, there are other varieties.

Religious Mysticism.—The first type of mysticism is the genuinely religious form just mentioned. This kind is exemplified by the Quakers, who originally were pure mystics, feeling an identity with God, communing with him directly without the aid of prayer book, Bible, minister, or church organization, and placing implicit reliance upon the guidance of the inner light. The journal of John Woolman, one of the most precious documents in our literature, illustrates this type of mysticism.

Religious mysticism makes for extreme individualism. If the mystic considers that his union with God is sanctioned by Christ's prayer that "they be one even as Thou and I are one," and if worship is merely a meditative communion directly with the godhead, then the work of clergy and church to bring God and man together becomes an intrusion, an impertinence. With the inner light glowing brightly within one, the assistance of all guides to the better, fuller life becomes quite unnecessary. To the mystic, ever conscious of the indwelling of God, sustained by the knowledge that his will is the will of the deity, every day and hour are times of worship, and every venture becomes a quietly confident walk with God. The mystic recognizes only two beings, himself and God, and they are identical.

So sublime an individualism, so great a concentration in self would be well-nigh unbearable by others if the mystic did not possess certain compensatory traits. These he has. If the mystic wishes spiritually to go his own way, he wishes all other people to order their own affairs in the most satisfying fashion. This complete willingness to allow individual freedom makes the mystic one of the easiest men to live with. Some have called this quality tolerance, but it is more than that. The mystic never thinks he is "tolerating" or allowing anything; he believes that every man has a full and unquestionable right to seek and gain spiritual happiness in any way. Evidence of this assertion is found in the fact that only Rhode Island and Pennsylvania, of all the American colonies, allowed complete freedom of worship, and these commonwealths were guided by two mystics, Roger Williams and William Penn.

Transcendental Mysticism.—Another type of mysticism is that found in Emerson, Thoreau, and other transcendentalists. This variety is broader in scope than the exclusively religious, comprising in its grasp an identity with nature as well as with God. Indeed so pronounced is the preoccupation with nature that this variety might well be called nature mysticism. The transcendentalists thought of God, nature, and man as parts of a great whole, with the same divine spark animating all. The whole creation centered in man, in each individual, who was both human and divine, and who was both a separate entity and a part of a great system. Nature was the soul of man and God made visible. This conception, exalting man and glorifying nature, was the exact opposite of the Puritan view that believed in the utter worthlessness of man and considered nature a mask behind which God worked. The transcendentalist found himself and God both in the natural world, and the most common conception of himself was as a part of nature.

This mystic identification of man with nature and through nature with God had the same effect on Emerson and Thoreau that religious mysticism had on such men as Roger Williams and William Penn. If man is the converging spot of all the universe, and if he enjoys an identity with God, then the individual is of surpassing importance, and his inner promptings, his intuitions, are the voice of God. This idea is the very heart and soul of Emerson's doctrine of the divine and sole sufficiency of the individual

"Trust thyself," Emerson exclaimed, and the self can be trusted because of its communion with nature and with God. "What I must do is all that concerns me, not what other people think," he said again, emphasizing his dependence upon the inner voice. Naturally the transcendentalist gloried in freedom and insisted upon it to the fullest, for anything less than perfect freedom would cramp the activities of the individual and stand in the way of his obedience to the voice of God.

Mysticism of Walt Whitman.—Still a third variety of mysticism is to be found in Whitman's poems. The "poet of democracy," as Whitman is often called, did the perfectly natural thing and identified himself with all humanity. It is true that Whitman, as a transcendentalist of the Emerson school, was far from despising nature, but his great love was all mankind, with whom he felt an utter identity. It is misleading to say that Whitman resented the wrongs done to others as if they were done to him, for any wrong to man was a wrong to the poet.

> The disdain and calmness of martyrs,
> The mother of old, condemn'd for a witch, burnt with dry wood, her
>   children gazing on,
> The hounded slave that flags in the race, leans by the fence, blowing,
>   cover'd with sweat,
> The twinges that sting like needles his legs and neck, the murderous
>   buckshot and the bullets,
>   All these I feel or am.
> I am the hounded slave, I wince at the bite of the dogs. . . .

To Whitman, man and nature had the same elements:

> I swear I think now that every thing without exception has an eternal
>   soul!
> The trees have, rooted in the ground! The weeds of the sea have! The
>   animals!

A more emphatic statement of the divinity of nature would be hard to find.

> I hear and behold God in every object, yet understand God not in the
>   least,
> Nor do I understand who there can be more wonderful than myself.
>   Why should I wish to see God better than this day?
> I see something of God each hour of the twenty-four, and each moment
>   then,

In the faces of men and women I see God, and in my own face in the
      glass,
I find letters from God dropt in the street, and every one is sign'd by
      God's name,
And I leave them where they are, for I know that wheresoe'er I go,
Others will punctually come for ever and ever. . . .

In Whitman there is the same intense love of freedom and the
same individualism that we found in the other type of mystics, and
those qualities are present in *Leaves of Grass* for exactly the
reason that they are present in Emerson's essays or in the writings
of Roger Williams. Whitman saw himself as an epitome of mankind and he called for the identical freedom for all that he wished
for himself. Hence it is not contradictory to say that he is the
poet of individualism and democracy. For once, at least, the problem of maintaining one's individuality in a democracy was solved.

Mystics in American Life.—The roll of mystics in our national
life is a most impressive one. It begins with Roger Williams and
William Penn, fathers of religious freedom in America, friends of
the oppressed, and haters of injustice whatever the source. The
next eminent name on the list is that of Jonathan Edwards, who
needed only a congenial environment to blossom into a mystic of
rare spiritual beauty. As it was, the mysticism of the man was
submerged in a flood of acrid Calvinism, but in his writings there
are hints of other promptings than those of his crabbed theology.
Training and custom made him a preacher of harshest Puritanism;
at heart he was a genuine mystic. Besides Emerson and Thoreau,
the transcendentalists produced one other great mystic in the person
of Theodore Parker, minister and reformer. William Lloyd Garrison, the abolitionist, was one of the most pronounced mystics. Of
Whitman we have already spoken. Again the list is not exhausted.
There are many more, but these are the major figures.

Our national debt to mysticism has not yet been calculated, but
of a few things we are sure. Mystics are among the chief glories
of American life and literature. To them is due much of the
humanitarian effort of our nation, to them we credit much of the insistence upon the rights of the individual that ennobled the literature and politics from 1830 to 1860, and to those men must be
given the honor of putting into noble and expressive words the
hopes and aspirations of the great friends of man. Elusive is the
spirit of mysticism, self-effacing and modest are the mystics in

forwarding their claims, but very precious is the result of their labors. Gazing at the records of our mystics, the beauty of their lives, and the enduring work of their hands, one gains a deeper joy in life, a quickened sense of individual worth, and a renewed faith in the sanctity of human freedom.

The weakness of mysticism is easily detected. It is a tendency to undervalue reason. In many mystics this tendency is not apparent, but in those thoroughgoing "seekers" who carry mystical ideas to the full, the weakness is plainly to be seen. An undervaluation of reason is liable to lead to a despising of "education," and a distrust of "educated people." Education is considered as an obstacle to the revelation of the inner light. However, the weakness of mysticism has never been apparent among the Quakers, the largest body of consistent mystics in this country, for these people have always fostered education and cultivated the reason. The weakness of mysticism becomes an insignificant thing when set beside the good rendered our country by avowed mystics.

SUGGESTED READINGS

Adams: *The Founding of New England*. Boston. 1921. pp. 64-85.
This remains the best brief treatment of early Puritanism.

Bourne: *The History of a Literary Radical*. New York. 1920. pp. 176-187.
Cosmopolitanism.

Brooks: *America's Coming of Age*. New York. 1915.
Stimulating. One of the earliest attempts to trace the broad pattern of our national thinking.

Curti: *The Growth of American Thought*. New York. 1943.
The great amount of detail somewhat obscures the main outline of this work.

De Voto: *Mark Twain's America*. New York. 1940.
An excellent study of Mark Twain's western environment.

Foerster (ed.): *The Reinterpretation of American Literature*. New York. 1928.
Nine essays by as many writers on the general aspects of our national literature. Quite uneven.

Frank: *Our America*. New York. 1919.
An early work which remains stimulating.

Gabriel: *The Course of American Democratic Thought*. New York. 1940.
Begins at 1815. Excellent.

Hazard: *The Frontier in American Literature*. New York. 1927.

Hulbert: *Frontiers*. Boston. 1929.
    Stimulating and suggestive.
Huneker: *Iconoclasts*. New York. 1905.
    Cosmopolitan criticism. Huneker is often overlooked, but he was
    an important critic. See also his autobiography, *Steeplejack*.
Jones: *America and French Culture*. Chapel Hill. 1927.
    Excellent for the early period. Most useful.
Lewisohn: *Upstream*. New York. 1923.
    Autobiography of a cosmopolitan critic.
Mencken: *Prefaces*. New York. 1917.
    A valuable book by one of the important critics of the 1920's.
    Contains essays on Huneker, Dreiser, and Puritanism as a literary
    force.
Miller: *The New England Mind, the Seventeenth Century*. New York.
    1939.
    Not to be overlooked.
Miller and Johnson: *The Puritans*. Cincinnati. 1938.
Mumford: *The Golden Day*. New York. 1926. pp. 11-81.
    A good introduction.
Paxson: *History of the American Frontier*. New York. 1924.
    Sections of this work are of great value.
Perry: *Puritanism and Democracy*. New York. 1944.
    The Puritan social philosophy.
Riegel: *America Moves West*. New York. 1947.
Riley: *American Thought*. New York. 1915.
    Of extreme value, though the author is more interested in class-
    room philosophy than in popular thinking.
Riley: *The Meaning of Mysticism*. New York. 1930.
    This book and Lectures XVI and XVII of William James' *Vari-
    eties of Religious Experience* are the best brief discussions of
    mysticism.
Schneider: *A History of American Philosophy*. New York. 1946.
    This excellent work contains a good bibliography.
Schneider: *The Puritan Mind*. New York. 1930.
    Excellent scholarly survey.
Siegfried: *America Comes of Age*. New York. 1927. pp. 3-146.
    Good criticism by a foreigner, but in the light of recent events the
    author's condescending tone is a trifle irritating.
Turner: *The Frontier in American History*. New York. 1920.
    The first essay in this volume is very likely the most important
    single contribution ever made to the study of American history. It
    is a genuine classic.

BOOK II

THE MIND OF COLONIAL AMERICA

CHAPTER IV

THE BEGINNINGS OF THE AMERICAN MIND

THE MIND OF EARLY NEW ENGLAND

The founders of New England were motivated by a large variety of reasons, but it is undeniable that the officially stated aim of the leaders was to establish an English state in the new world where they and their followers could live under the laws of God as interpreted by themselves. The colonists were Englishmen, and they brought to America English customs and what they conceived to be the true English church. This New England church was founded on the strictest letter of the Bible and fortified by the elaborate theological system of John Calvin. The explicit aim of the leaders as we understand it to-day, was to establish a theocracy, a state under the control of the stewards of God, that is to say the ministers and magistrates. This type of state has also been called a Bible commonwealth.

The Democracy of New England.—It is a common mistake to think that early New England was democratic. With the exception of Rhode Island and Connecticut, no New England community could be called even moderately democratic, and Rhode Island's political and social heresies made that colony the laughingstock of the more conservative communities. The Massachusetts leaders brought to their new domain a deep consideration for rank, precedence, class distinctions, and hereditary social rights. Much of their early legislation had for its aim the perpetuation of old-country distinctions. At the head of society stood the governor followed by the ministers and magistrates. Then, at respectful distance, came the common citizens ranged strictly according to rank. The assignment of seats in the churches, places at the table, and rank in processions all depended upon social status.

When John Winthrop and his associates devised the charter under which they and their followers were to live, they provided for the election of a governor, deputy governor, and magistrates.

These officials were to be named by the "freemen" who were authorized to fill vacancies in their own ranks. Of the 115 freemen named by the charter only 16 came to America and several of these died very soon. Thus the local control of Massachusetts was in the hands of fewer than a dozen men. The mass of the people had little or nothing to say about the government, and could not even appeal legally to the English authorities. This condition lasted for more than half a century, and even then the colony did not become democratic but only a bit less oligarchic. The town meeting was little more democratic than the colonial government. Although all the people might attend and discuss questions, only the freeman could vote except on a few matters. But insignificant as the town meeting was in the beginning, it was the cradle of local self-government and one of the chief contributions of New England to the nation.

The Massachusetts leaders gave no praise to democracy. John Winthrop, first governor of Massachusetts Bay colony, said, "Democracy is amongst civil nations accounted the meanest and worst of all forms of government." He argued against it on the grounds that Israel had no such government and said that, if the freeman allowed it in Massachusetts, their action would be a manifest breach of the fifth commandment. John Cotton, the great Boston preacher, said, "It is better that the commonwealth be fashioned to the setting forth of God's house, which is church; than to accommodate the church frame to the civil state. Democracy, I do not conceive that ever God did ordain as a fit government either for church or commonwealth. If the people be governors, who shall be governed? As for monarchy and aristocracy, they are both of them clearly approved and directed in scripture, yet so as referreth the sovereignty to himself, and setteth up theocracy in both as the best form of government in the commonwealth, as well as in the church."

It is another common mistake to think that the New England leaders came to America to found a colony where each man should have complete religious freedom. To them individual religious freedom would have meant chaos. Furthermore, in a Bible Commonwealth like Massachusetts there could be no question without religious bearings. No intellectual problem could be discussed without reference to the decisions of the magistrates and ministers, and all decisions regarding church doctrine and discipline were enforced by civil authority. Under such a system there could be no intellectual or political freedom, no more than there could be religious freedom. There simply were no non-religious questions. Fashions, business, health, education, and similar interests were all directed by the ministers. The state was governed according to Biblical injunction as interpreted by the rules, and any failure to conform to the standard set by those in authority met with immediate punishment. In a theocracy those who interpret God's word are always highest in authority, and in Massachusetts the place of interpreter was taken by the ministers. No society was ever under a more autocratic clerical domination than that exercised by the ministers of New England from the founding of Massachusetts Bay colony to the end of the seventeenth century. Even after the overthrow of the ministerial oligarchy the clergy long exerted a powerful and sometimes dominant voice in the political and intellectual affairs.

Democratic Elements.—However, there were certain democratic forces at work in New England. The chief of these was the system of holding land in fee simple, which means that each landowner had a deed which gave him the property to have and to hold for himself and his heirs forever. Thus land holding was on a democratic basis. If the land of Massachusetts had been granted to a few great landlords who in turn would have rented small tracts to individual farmers, democracy would have received a tremendous setback. Another democratic influence was the government of each individual church by its members and not by a higher council or assembly. It is true that all had to go to church and that only the very small fraction of the congregation who were members could vote on church questions, but the system adopted had a certain democratic tendency, even if the ministers were slow to admit new members. Another leveling tendency was the establishment of free public schools for boys of every rank. Still another was the slow but stubbornly progressive development of the town meeting that finally brought about a democratic system of local government. These liberalizing tendencies were planted in the shadow of an illiberal theocracy, but they ultimately grew and produced much valuable fruit.

JOHN WINTHROP: PURITAN MAGISTRATE

(1588-1649)

John Winthrop, first governor of Massachusetts Bay colony and staunchest champion of the oligarchy, was born in the county of Suffolk, England, in the year that saw the defeat of the Spanish Armada. His position as landowner and governmental official in his native county lifted him to a place of prominence among his Puritan brethren, few of whom could keep twenty male servants, as he did at one time. But evil days came upon Winthrop. His prosperity sharply declined, though he still possessed a valuable estate; he lost his office; and, worst of all, his affiliation with the Puritan party seemed to be a permanent disability to further political advancement. It was probably he who gave these reasons for coming to America. "His meanes heer are so shortened . . . as he shall not be able to continue in that place and employment where he now is, his ordinary charge being still as great almost as when his meanes was double . . . if he lett pass this opportunitie, that talent which God hath bestowed upon him for publicke service is like to be buried." According to this statement Winthrop came to America because he wished to have a place where he could live up to his former mark and because he wished to exercise his capacity for public service. In the light of subsequent events the last reason means that he wished to found and lead a Bible commonwealth.

Winthrop landed in Massachusetts in 1630, and from the day he arrived until the day of his death he was the leading figure in the colony, serving as governor during most of the time. He was a magistrate in the state and an elder in the church, and never were the two tasks separate in his own mind. In a theocracy like that of Massachusetts to the ordinary duties of the magistrate is added the constant oversight of the church. At the hand of the governor stood the ministers offering advice, and Winthrop seldom rejected that counsel, so thoroughly imbued was he with the idea that the minister was the anointed interpreter of God's word. The relationship of the ministers and the magistrates, as well as the way that the ministers had of effecting their will, is clearly set forth in a short entry in Winthrop's Journal:

After much deliberation and serious advice the Lord directed the teacher Mr. Cotton to make clear by the scripture that the minister's maintenance, as well as all other charges of the church, should be defrayed out of a stock or treasury, which was to be raised out of the weekly contribution: which accordingly was agreed upon.

The executive skill that he displayed as governor of the colony and his zeal as guardian of the church made Winthrop the most conspicuous and successful defender of the theocracy. When the veteran governor died in 1649, it was not yet apparent how completely the Puritan idea was to fail in America. This sorrowful knowledge was reserved for the next generation.

Winthrop's Idea of Government.—Winthrop was an Elizabethan gentleman with all of such a gentleman's prejudices against the idea of democracy, and his devout Puritanism, with its contempt for the non-elect, but hardened the prejudices of his social class against popular government. So complete were these prejudices that he wrote in his Journal his belief that a petition signed by many citizens asking for the repeal of an objectionable law "savors of resisting an ordinance of God." In other words, the few freemen in Massachusetts Bay Colony could elect a permanent group of officials whose laws were as binding and as unquestionable as the laws of God. Again Winthrop wrote: "Whatsoever sentence the magistrate gives, the judgment is the Lord's. . . ." American democracy has developed in spite of such views.

The Puritan idea of political liberty and the abysmal gulf that separates that idea from the one generally held to-day are nowhere better illustrated than by Winthrop's famous speech on liberty and authority which was delivered in the assembly of 1645. The following are a few sentences taken from this address:

The great questions that have troubled the country are about the authority of the magistrates and the liberty of the people. It is yourselves who have called us to this office, and being called by you, we have our authority from God in the way of an ordinance such as hath the image of God eminently stamped upon it, the contempt and violation whereof hath been vindicated with examples of divine vengeance. . . . We account him a good servant who breaks not his covenant. The covenant between you and us [the magistrates] is the oath that you have taken of us, which is to this purpose, that we shall govern you and judge your causes by the rules of God's laws and our own, according to our best skill. . . . When you call one to be a magistrate, he doth not profess nor undertake to have sufficient skill for that office, nor can you furnish him with gifts, etc., therefore you must run the hazard of his skill and ability. But if he fail in faithfulness, which by his oath he is bound unto, that he must answer for. . . . But if the case be doubtful, or the rule doubtful, to men of such understanding and parts as your magistrates are, if your magistrates should err here, yourself must bear it.

Another time he argued:

Now if we should change from a mixed aristocracy to a mere democracy, first, we should have no warrant in scripture for it; there was no such government in Israel. Second, we should hereby voluntarily debase ourselves and deprive ourselves of that dignity which the providence of God hath put upon us, which is a manifest breach of the fifth commandment, for a democracy is among most civil nations accounted the meanest and worst of all forms of government.

Winthrop's ideas of the relationship of church and state are best illustrated in his dealings with Roger Williams and Mrs. Anne Hutchinson. The Williams episode will be related shortly. The Hutchinson case had its origin in minor theological differences that a later age probably would not have either understood or accounted important. Mrs. Hutchinson, a woman of good family and excellent standing in the colony, began the practice of holding Thursday meetings in her house for those women who had not been able to attend church the preceding Sunday. In these meetings the hostess discussed the minister's sermon. Gradually she reached certain convictions that smacked too much of individual liberty to suit the strict magistrates and ministers of the colony. The strongest leaders ranged themselves against the new doctrines, and Mrs. Hutchinson and her adherents were brought to trial. Most of them were ordered to leave the colony. When Mrs. Hutchinson heard her sentence banishing her "as being a woman not fit for our society" she demanded to know why she was being thus punished. Governor Winthrop answered her, "Say no more; the court knows wherefore and is satisfied."

The Hutchinson and Williams cases showed that no person could criticize the civil or church authorities. The colony was wholly under the absolute dominion of the rulers. Church attendance was compulsory, all residents, whether church members or not, were taxed for the support of the church, and non-conformity was made impossible by a law providing that all persons excommunicated by the church should endeavor to have themselves restored to good standing within six months or suffer "fine, imprisonment, banishment, or further." The further evidently meant the death penalty. As a recent historian [1] says, "It is difficult to conceive of a measure more conducive to the rearing of a race of conforming hypocrites." All of these measures received the assent, official or personal, of John Winthrop, whose ideal of a Bible commonwealth was forwarded by each.

Winthrop as Man and Writer.—In his letters Winthrop reveals himself as a highminded, kindly gentleman in whom there was ever something of the dignity and scope that ennobled even the lesser Elizabethans. By nature he had in him little or nothing of the persecutor, but he was so saturated with the idea of ministerial supremacy that he was easily influenced by the illiberal elements in his colony, and chief among the forces of illiberalism were the ministers. The petty and intolerant actions of Winthrop must be assessed against his time and advisers rather than against his generous and upright nature. His mistakes were caused by his zeal for the establishment of a Bible commonwealth.

Winthrop can claim a place in American literature because of his letters and his Journal, but little of his writing is good enough as a literary effort to warrant extended discussion. The letters are direct and sincere expressions of an earnest, admirable man, nor do they lack a flavor of Elizabethan eloquence. The Journal is a record of contemporaneous events from 1630 to 1648. It is a mine of information for the student of early New England life, but the style is not attractive. In the final analysis Winthrop occupies the space given him in this book because of his contribution to the development of American thought. The very fact that our national mind finally developed in the opposite way from that so desired by Winthrop does not nullify the belief that the Puritan governor made a great contribution to American thought. He helped to establish Puritanism in the new world, and Puritanism has been of utmost importance to us all. Its dogged opposition to certain later developments in our national thinking would alone make it of great significance. Winthrop belongs in literary and intellectual history as one of the staunch defenders of early Puritanism.

[1] James Truslow Adams, *The Founding of New England,* p. 172.

JOHN COTTON: PURITAN MINISTER

(1585-1652)

John Cotton was another Elizabethan gentleman who followed his Puritan brethren to the new world and lent abilities of a high order to the establishment of a Bible commonwealth. Although Winthrop may seem to us to-day to have been the most important man in Massachusetts Bay, it is undeniable that the early emigrants assigned first place to John Cotton, the great Boston preacher. Few of Cotton's writings have been reprinted for the use of present-day students, and no adequate biography is in existence. For these reasons Cotton is over-shadowed to-day by his better-known governor.

John Cotton was born in Derby, England, in the year 1585. His good family and his excellent training destined him for leadership of his sect. At the age of thirteen he entered Trinity College, Cambridge, where he devoted himself to a life of scholarship. Upon graduation his studious habits remained, and ever after he was accustomed to spend twelve hours a day in his study. For years he was an esteemed minister of old Boston in England, and when the Puritan migration to Massachusetts Bay set in, he shortly departed for new Boston, where sure honor and preferment awaited him.

Once in New England Cotton went the way of Winthrop. He suffered himself to be led by the illiberal elements in the colony and employed his great ability to defend the doctrine of persecution and the right of banishment. For years his persuasive tongue and his iron logic were used by the magistrates and lesser ministers to expound to the people the distasteful edicts of the government.

Cotton's ideas were those of Winthrop. The great preacher was no friend of democracy, pointing out that, while monarchy and aristocracy were both sanctioned by the Bible, theocracy was undoubtedly the best form of government in the state as in the church and that democracy could not be justified on any basis. Cotton's ideal was a theocracy directed by an aristocracy of the elect. The desire for liberty seemed to him only a mischievous thing, prompted by man's depravity. If democracy and personal liberty were so admirable, would they not have been mentioned in the Bible?

Cotton's belief in the ecclesiastical control of the state is shown by this one sentence:

Now if it be a divine truth that none are to be trusted with public permanent authority but godly men, who are fit materials for church membership, then from the same grounds it will appear that none are so fit to be trusted with the liberties of the commonwealth as church members.

Since very few were admitted to full membership in Puritan churches and those few only after they had satisfied the minister that they were fit, Cotton's scheme simply implied the complete control of the state by a small oligarchy which in turn would be quite subservient to the ministers.

"To found an Hebraic state in which political rights should be subordinate to religious conformity, in which the magistrates should be chosen from a narrow group, with authority beyond reach of the popular will, and with the ministers serving as a court of last resort to interpret the divine law . . . this was the great ambition of John Cotton." Thus a recent student [1] characterizes the minister's aim.

John Cotton is known to-day largely through his defense of persecution against the questioning of Roger Williams, who had suffered because of his non-conformity. In answer to Williams, John Cotton insists that the state has a right to persecute those who differ from the established order. Williams took the ground that a state in forcing a man to worship against his conscience, forced him to commit sin. To this Cotton returned the amazing reply that, if a state had to force a man to conform, the sin was not in the act of conforming against conscience, but was inherent in "his own will that needs to be compelled to a Christian duty." John Cotton and John Winthrop stand in American history as examples of illiberal thought that had to be overcome in Massachusetts before New England could make the contributions to American life that New Englanders are fond of recalling.

NATHANIEL WARD

(1578-1652)

Nathaniel Ward hardly belongs to American literature. He was more than fifty years old when he first put foot on this continent;

[1] Parrington, *The Colonial Mind,* p. 33.

he showed his loyalty to old England by devoting his famous book, *The Simple Cobbler of Aggawam,* to a discussion of English affairs; and late in life he returned to his native land to die. He is given a place in American literature because *The Simple Cobbler* was written in the new world and because it so completely expresses the ideas of New England Puritanism about government, religious toleration, and social questions.

Ward was born in England about 1578. He received an excellent academic training in both law and theology and in his manhood he became intimate with the best and most intellectual society of the old world. After coming to America he served as assistant pastor at Ipswich, Massachusetts, for a few years and then occupied himself with the compiling of a code of law for the colony.

Ward was not a political theorist; he was interested in the practical problems of political administration. The distressing plight of old England during the Civil Wars moved him to write down his views of what was wrong in his native land and what was necessary to end the wrongs. Ward believed in a highly unified state, so dominated by one set of ideas that dissenting views should not be tolerated. His legal training told him that a sure remedy for civil strife was a written law or constitution that would strictly define the powers and privileges of each political group, king, lords, and commons. Just as dissenting views could not be tolerated in the state, neither could they be allowed in religious matters.

In *The Simple Cobbler* Ward disposed promptly of the idea of toleration:

He that is willing to tolerate any religion, or discrepant way of religion, besides his own, unless it be in matters merely indifferent, either doubts of his own or is not sincere in it.

He that is willing to tolerate any unsound opinion, that his own may also be tolerated, though never so sound, will for a need hang God's Bible at the Devil's girdle.

Every toleration of false religions or opinions hath as many errors and sins in it, as all the false religions and opinions it tolerates, and one sound one more.

It is strange to find a man with such views protesting against the loss of liberty, but Ward's protests were made only as a lawyer against the high-handed methods of courts. Dissenters were to be squelched but they must be disposed of according to the accepted rules of law. No lover of liberty was Nathaniel Ward, rather a legalist who hated non-conformity.

After writing *The Simple Cobbler,* Ward compiled a code of laws known as the Body of Liberties. These laws were not wholly mis-named, for they contained certain English safeguards of personal liberty and property against injustice.

"The Simple Cobbler" as Literature.—Since Ward was born only five years later than Ben Jonson and fourteen years later than Shakespeare, his prose might be expected to have some of the Eliza-bethan quality. Nor is this expectation denied, for of all American literature *The Simple Cobbler* is most like the productions that gave distinction to the prose of Queen Elizabeth's time. The vocabulary resembles that of John Lyly, whose *Euphues* set the fashion for quaint conceits of vocabulary and far-fetched language. Ward coined dozens of words and phrases when he could find none in the language to suit his meaning and his ear. In spite of un-familiar diction, the fluent style makes *The Simple Cobbler* easy to read. The following is a fair sample:

It is a more common than convenient saying that nine tailors make a man. It were well if nineteen could make a woman to her mind. If tailors were men indeed, well furnished but with mere moral principles, they would disdain to be led about like Apes by such mimic Marmosets. It is a most unworthy thing for men that have bones in them, to spend their lives in making fiddle-cases for futilous women's fancies; which are the very pettitoes of infirmity, the gibbets of perquisquilian toys.

Occasionally Ward attempted poetry. One of his quatrains reads:

> The upper world shall rule,
>   While the stars will run their race;
> The nether world obey
>   While people keep their place.

It is probable that the basic ideas of Puritanism have never been more accurately stated in so few words.

MICHAEL WIGGLESWORTH: PURITAN LAUREATE

(1631-1705)

While the Puritanism of old England was receiving sonorous ex-pression in the stately organ music of *Paradise Lost,* New England

Puritanism was being put into the unpoetic but highly Calvinistic lines of Michael Wigglesworth's *The Day of Doom*. Nothing better indicates the intellectual and poetic barrenness of New England than the fact that this poem was so popular that it was memorized by children along with the catechism. For a hundred years it retained its place as the best known American poem. To-day it seems ludicrous, but it appealed to the early New Englander as a striking and effective picture of the last judgment.

New England Calvinism had no better interpreter than the Rev. Mr. Wigglesworth. His poem of 1500 lines gives but slight attention to the few elect who are transported to bliss. Most of the work depicts the tortures of the damned. One part, quoted by all anthologies and histories of American literature, gives the conversation between the Almighty and the condemned infants. The infants object to eternal punishment:

> If for our own transgression
>   Or disobedience,
> We here did stand at thy left hand
>   Just were the recompense;
> But Adam's guilt our souls hath spilt,
>   His fault is charg'd on us:
> And that alone hath overthrown
>   And utterly undone us.
>
> Not we, but he ate of the tree,
>   Whose fruit was interdicted;
> Yet on us all of his sad fall
>   The Punishment's inflicted.
> How could we sin that had not been
>   Or how is his sin our,
> Without consent, which to prevent
>   We never had the pow'r?
>
> O great creator, why was our nature
>   Depraved and forlorn?
> Why so defil'd, and made so vil'd
>   Whilst we were yet unborn?
> If it be just, and needs we must
>   Transgressors reck'ned be,
> Thy Mercy Lord, to us afford,
>   Which sinners hath set free.

The Almighty replies:

You sinners are, and such a share
    As sinners may expect
Such you shall have, for I do save
    None but mine own elect.
Yet to compare your sin with their
    Who lived a longer time,
I do confess yours is much less,
    Though every sin's a crime.

A crime it is, therefore in bliss
    You may not hope to dwell;
But unto you I shall allow
    The easiest room in hell.

It requires no argument to prove that readers who are pleased
with such poetry are more interested in theology than in esthetics.

THE MATHER DYNASTY

From the arrival of Richard Mather in Massachusetts in the
year 1635 to the death of his great-grandson exactly a century and
a half elapsed, and in all that time the Mather voice and influence
were powerful in New England councils of both state and church.
There were four ruling members of the dynasty: Richard, founder
of the family in New England, impressive preacher, and ardent
scholar; Increase, preacher-politician and, for a time, the un-
crowned king of Massachusetts; Cotton, whose gigantic literary
labors have been the constant amazement of later generations; and
Samuel, last and least of the line. The golden age of the dynasty
was from 1664, when Increase consented to assume the leadership
of the North Church in Boston, to 1700, by which time it was
clear to all that the star of the New England theocracy was swiftly
declining. And with the theocracy fell the fortunes of the Mather
family, its acknowledged leaders.

The Mathers were not men of superlative ability, nor were tact
and forbearance prime characteristics of the race. Increase and
Cotton came to their leadership by virtue of being admittedly the
leading men of the colony, but to be considered first among the
second generation of New Englanders was not so great a compli-
ment as to be considered first among their contemporaries of old
England or first among such leaders as Winthrop, John Cotton,

Roger Williams, and Thomas Hooker. When one, remembering that Increase and Cotton Mather were undisputed leaders of New England, places those two men beside such contemporary Englishmen as John Milton, John Locke, Sir Isaac Newton, and John Dryden, one begins to suspect that the eminence of the Mathers, as some one has remarked about another man, was due to the excessive flatness of their immediate surroundings.

In every respect the two great Mathers were children of their time and place. When Increase Mather ascended the pulpit of North Church, which he and Cotton occupied for sixty-four consecutive years, the theocracy in Massachusetts was an established fact, and the leaders who had established it had passed on. With none of superior quality to oppose him, Increase was literally given the leadership of church and state in Massachusetts, and with their love for politics and their thirst for power and fame, he and his famous son made the most of their opportunities. The theocracy did not fall because of the Mather family, the Mather family fell because of the overthrow of the theocracy, and the theocracy fell partly because the persecutions of the Quakers and the deplorable witchcraft mania caused a popular revulsion against the clergy. Another powerful force behind the overthrow of the clergy was the king's action in forcing upon Massachusetts a new charter that made citizenship dependent upon the payment of taxes and not upon church membership. This action caused an aristocracy of wealth to succeed the aristocracy of the elect, and wealth always shows a tendency to choose its leaders from the merchants and lawyers and not from the clergy.

In their purely intellectual interests the Mathers were neither far behind nor far in advance of their time. In politics Increase was interested in perpetuating the established order of things; in theology he preached the time-honored doctrines of Calvinism, adding no new interpretation of his own. He was a strong practical man, not a great intellectual leader. Cotton has been extravagantly praised for his belief in inoculation against smallpox and for his interest in science and natural history. For what he has done in scientific endeavor he deserves great praise, but for every line of his writing that shows a scientific interest and temper there is a page filled with grewsome marvels and tales of witchcraft that would have excited the amused skepticism of a medieval peasant. If Cotton surpassed his generation in his minor interests, he certainly agreed with his fellows in his major concerns.

Richard Mather (1596-1669).—In 1634 one Richard Mather, a somewhat inconspicuous Puritan clergyman, was haled before a church court on charges of not conforming to the usages of the Church of England. The evidence was conclusive, and the minister was ordered to betake himself to private life. The following year the same gentleman made his way stealthily and in disguise to a seaport where he took ship for Massachusetts. Upon disembarking at Boston, Richard Mather first achieved eminence among his brethren because his "loud and big voice, uttered with a deliberate vehemency . . . procured unto his ministry an awful and very taking majesty." Moreover he readily achieved a reputation for learning and piety as well as for an irresistible urge to write books. His amazing industry in the reading and writing of books, his commanding pulpit presence, and his love for political intrigue and power, all make Richard Mather very typical of the dynasty that he founded.

If it were not for one thing, Richard Mather would live to-day in American literature only as the author of forgotten sermons and treatises in defense of an order that is long past in church and state. The one thing is his share in the authorship of the Bay Psalm Book, a hymnal for the New England churches and probably the first English book to be published in America. The Bay Psalm Book owes its reputation to its priority and not to the excellence of its poetry. Indeed it is doubtful if worse poetry was ever printed in so large a quantity. Chaotic constructions, tortured rhetoric, unpronounceable combinations of sounds, and approximate rhymes combine to make the poetry very bad.

Richard Mather was one of three men selected to translate the Psalms from the original Hebrew, and to him was delegated the task of writing a preface to the completed work. In this preface he says:

If, therefore, the verses are not always so smooth and elegant as some may desire or expect, let them consider that God's altar needs not our polishings, for we have respected rather a plain translation than to smooth our verses with the sweetness of any paraphrase; and so have attended conscience rather than elegance, fidelity rather than poetry.

Increase Mather (1639-1723).—When Increase Mather began his long ministry in the old North Church of Boston, it must have seemed to many that here was without doubt the divinely appointed leader of New England Puritanism. The young minister was a distinguished graduate of Harvard College and a most promising preacher. He was the son of an eminent divine and the son-in-law of John Cotton, the great preacher of the preceding generation. Withal he had the Mather characteristics,—industry, a love for books, a liking for power, and a voice that he used, according to his son, with "tonitrous cogency," whatever that may mean. It was natural that this man should become the most famous preacher of Boston and the president of Harvard. When Massachusetts was about to be given a new charter against the wishes of the theocracy, it was natural that this man should be chosen to stand before the king to speak for the colony in the diplomatic maneuvers that attended the granting of the new instrument of government. Thus far Increase Mather was the triumphantly successful theocrat.

But evil days were upon the theocracy. The barbarous persecution of the Quakers about 1660 brought about the first defeat of the clergy. The brutality with which the Quakers were whipped, maimed, banished, and hanged, all because they did not conform to Puritan worship, finally caused an influential group in the colony to oppose further persecution and ultimately drew from King Charles II an order forbidding the recurrence of such actions. This first defeat of the theocracy was a momentous thing. For the first time the clergy had been foiled, and they had been foiled while performing an act in the name of religion. The defeat in itself was not a serious one, for it had been effected largely through the intervention of the king, but for the first time the theocrats had not been able to do their will in the internal administration of Massachusetts. Furthermore, they had failed to carry public opinion with them. The defeat, while not decisive, was ominous.

The second rebuff of the theocracy was more important. In 1692 certain children of Salem, Massachusetts, began to exhibit symptoms that were generally regarded in those days as signs of witches' power. The symptoms may have been caused by hysteria or by old-fashioned naughtiness. The people of Salem, disdaining to accept a simple explanation of the malady, could think of nothing short of witchcraft. Soon the colony was in uproar. The ministers, looking upon witchcraft as one of the most abhorrent manifestations of Satan, demanded the execution of these people who had lent themselves to the work of the Evil One. In the persecution mania which overwhelmed the common sense of the colony the Mathers, both Increase and Cotton, did not hold themselves aloof from the wave of hysterical fear which convulsed society, nor did they distinguish themselves by their zeal for blood of witches. They were about on a level with their fellows. Both ministers believed implicitly in witches, both collected and published much evidence of Satan's work, and both declared that the alleged witches were executed under just sentences. After nineteen persons were hanged, the sober common sense of the community returned. Naturally the people were disgusted with the clerical leaders, for if the ministers had advised against persecution of the accused, there would have been no trials. The very conspicuousness of the Mathers in the colony caused much of the wrath of the populace to fall upon them, but they were probably no more or no less to blame than a dozen other ministers and magistrates. The executions at Salem marked the last great triumph of the Massachusetts theocracy.

The new charter that was imposed upon the clergy over the protest of Increase Mather made impossible any reëstablishment of the theocracy. With citizenship dependent upon the payment of taxes and not upon church membership, the ministers were fated soon to lose social and political control of the colony. The loss of religious control was reserved for a later age.

The Mather family went down with the fortunes of the theocracy. Increase and Cotton found themselves on the losing side in politics. The elder man was maneuvered out of the presidency of Harvard, and the two settled down to a fixed policy of querulous and contentious opposition to the new order. When Increase Mather died in 1723, Benjamin Franklin was a runaway apprentice of seventeen, and Franklin belonged to a new age. The day of the Mathers had passed.

Cotton Mather (*1663-1728*).—Cotton Mather's entire life was a feverish endeavor to escape the hand of oblivion. His fear that he might be overshadowed by his famous sire and thus forgotten never led him into a disloyal word or thought against his father, but it did lead him into such unbelievable industry that he became the wonder of his generation and the amazement of later days. Books, sermons, controversial tracts, and essays poured from his desk to the number, we are told, of four hundred titles, though but few of this huge total are ever read. To such advantage did

Cotton Mather labor that his own generation accounted him the greatest of the family, and if later historians are tending to rate Increase higher it is because they think the political labors of the father more significant than the literary endeavors of the son.

Increase and Cotton came as near to being exact contemporaries as father and son can well come. The son was born when the father was only twenty-four, and he outlived his elder only five years. From 1685 to 1723 the two men were very closely associated, and what has been said of Increase applies equally to Cotton. While the father was in England striving to preserve the old order, the son was in New England guarding the fortunes of church and state; the two men went through the witchcraft delusion together; both fell with the theocracy; and finally in the twilight of misfortune each supported the other in vain struggles against adversity.

Increase Mather may belong to American history, but Cotton Mather belongs to our literature. At least three of his books are of extreme value to any student of our colonial life. These books are *Magnalia Christi, Wonders of the Invisible World,* and the diary. The *Magnalia* is one of our chief sources for the early history of New England. It contains a history of the settlement, a sketch of Harvard College, several valuable biographical accounts, and a careful statement of the development of the New England churches, as well as a generous collection of "special providences." *Wonders of the Invisible World* presents the evidence that Mather collected of witchcraft. It has been called a collection of "old wives' tales," and it probably is. As such it is a cruel illustration of the credulity that could exist in what was probably one of the finest minds of the late seventeenth century in Massachusetts. The diary is the gem of the collection. One would declare it impossible if it were not actually in print. It is the unfettered expression of a mind that is egotistical to the point of insanity, morbidly suspicious of every one not wholly in the Mather power, and at the same time abnormal in its delight in self-abasement before the Almighty. The document must be read to be appreciated, and few but abnormal psychologists can read it with approximately full understanding.

Cotton Mather's style is most uneven. At times he writes well, with a genuine eloquence that springs from simplicity and sincerity. At other times his prose is as chaotic as was his grandfather's poetry. When he tried to write in literary fashion he usually spoiled the effect by the use of fantastic and far-fetched comparisons and by the excessive scattering of Latin, Greek, and Hebrew quotations through his pages. He is not an easy man to read, but sometimes the subject matter is worth considerable effort.

It is useless to argue about the final estimate of the Mather family. Our generation is not saying the last word. Although the historians are far from being agreed, the majority of writers to-day look upon the Mathers as the last and most wordy defenders of the theocracy. They represented an order that had to pass before free speculation, political and religious liberty, and social freedom could be accomplished. Roger Williams and Thomas Hooker kept their eyes fastened upon future ages, and future ages have been and will be grateful to the two great apostles of liberty and self-government. The Mathers kept their eyes upon the older day and sought to force the growing ambitions and desires of men into the mold of the past. Subsequent historians have not agreed whether to praise them for their whole-souled devotion to the past or to blame them for their indifference to the future.

SAMUEL SEWALL

(1652-1730)

Samuel Sewall was a great man, could he be judged by only the none too high standards of his generation. His learning was attested by his M.A. from Harvard; his civic worth was proved by his long and honorable service in the councils of the state; and his wealth, according to the general and probably correct belief, exceeded that of any other man in the colony. However, it is doubtful if such attainments impress later generations so profoundly as they do one's contemporaries.

Sewall was born in England, but at the age of nine he was brought to Boston where he lived the remainder of his life. Upon graduation from Harvard he planned to enter the ministry, but circumstances led him into business and the service of the government. It can readily be imagined that the most important event in Sewall's life was his marriage, for he took to wife the only daughter of the wealthy mint-master, John Hull. It is no disparagement of Sewall's ability to say that the man was able to sustain himself at the point to which he was raised by his education and his marriage. Unusual intellectual brilliance certainly was denied Sewall, but just as certainly solid sense, honesty, and courage were his in ample quantities.

For years he served on the Massachusetts court and from 1700 till his death, he was probably the most eminent man in Boston except the Mathers.

Sewall's importance to American literature lies largely in his diary which he kept almost continuously from 1673 to 1729. Cotton Mather's diary is a record of the writer's psychological life, his hopes and fears, his wrestlings with his conscience. Only occasionally does he give us any objective facts. On the other hand Sewall's diary is a factual record of his daily life. What the writer saw while he was walking down the street, what he had to eat and drink, the texts of the innumerable sermons, details of equally innumerable funerals, the births, marriages, and deaths of his children, his second and third courtships and marriages—all these things find a place in this great colonial diary. The value of this document to the social historian is beyond computation. Indeed it is doubtful if a fraction of its worth has yet been extracted. The diary does not read well, but it was not intended as a literary production. It contains a huge accumulation of facts that give us a close insight into the provincialism of Boston and the sharp currents that swept through the Bay Colony after 1690, but it must be taken in large doses to be truly understood and appreciated.

Sewall, the Man.—A more kindly and honest soul never lived than Samuel Sewall. He was a considerate neighbor, a good citizen of Boston, and a notable figure in the administration of Massachusetts, but when these virtues are related there is little more to be said. Cultural interests were totally lacking. He was a graduate of Harvard, and to the end of his life he could summon up his Greek and Latin, but of intellectual curiosity, scientific interest, or free speculation he had not a trace. His favorite study seemed to be the examination of Biblical prophecy with the fixed view that many of the divine promises would be fulfilled in America.

In Sewall and Cotton Mather New England provincialism reached alarming proportions and smugness. The broad world-view brought across the Atlantic by the Elizabethan Englishmen of the first immigration gradually narrowed until the universe was bounded by the confines of Mather's parish or Sewall's judicial circuit. The kindly old judge is always more disturbed over the loss of a cow than over a point of English common law, more concerned with digging a cellar than with political theory. His was essentially a village mind, dominated always by the vexatious round of petty cares that make up village existence. The diary is proof of this statement.

As a member of the ruling class, Sewall had no complaint to register against the old order, but he was not a fanatical adherent of the theocracy. In his diary we see him occasionally opposing a minister and even exchanging high words in public with the redoubtable Cotton Mather. A few years after the Salem witchcraft mania, Sewall became convinced that in his capacity as one of the judges of the special court he had made a mistake in pronouncing sentence upon the accused. Thereupon he expressed his repentance and sorrow in a dignified but sincere statement which the minister read in meeting while Judge Sewall stood before the congregation. To Sewall's credit also is a small tract against slavery. "There is no proportion between twenty pieces of silver and liberty" is probably the judge's most notable saying.

In one passage in Sewall's diary we read that a certain minister, Mr. Willard, was very angry with Sewall because the magistrates preceded the ministers in a procession. Sewall mollified the clergyman with a good dinner, but there is no record that he resigned his place in line. The episode is significant. The old order was passing. No longer were the ministers first in rank. The merchant class was in the ascendant, and that class always gives precedence to the lawyers and judges who are the guardians of property. Sewall lived just at the time when the merchant was displacing the theocrat, and the Puritan was merging into the New England Yankee. He was not quite a Yankee trader nor quite a seventeenth century Puritan, but he had some of both in his make-up.

THOMAS HOOKER: PURITAN LIBERAL

(1586-1647)

Thus far the history of the New England mind has not been the record of a development, for the men discussed were more interested in maintaining a position than in pushing on to new ideas. Liberalizing tendencies there were in plenty between Cape Cod and the Hudson River, and some of these have been named, but it must not be thought that common schools, the system of landholding, the town meeting, and the congregational government of the churches were the sole opponents of illiberalism. Before 1700 these influences were largely only potential forces, though they were exerting a steady, quiet influence against the theocracy. There were human opponents of illiberalism in New England, and they were not quiet. Indeed it was impossible to still them. The chief of these were Thomas Hooker, the founder of Connecticut, Roger Williams, the father of Rhode Island, and John Wise, Massachusetts village preacher.

Thomas Hooker was born in England in 1586. Like so many of the Puritan leaders he was educated at Cambridge and, after years of active preaching, left England to escape prosecution for his non-conformity. After a sojourn in Holland he came to America in the ship that bore John Cotton, chief preacher of the theocrats, but Hooker and Cotton were as different as two Puritans could be. Cotton was of the well-to-do gentry; Hooker sprang from a line of farmers. Cotton liked a government by the people so little that he warmly hated the very name of democracy; Hooker thought that government most satisfactory which rested upon the active consent of all the citizens. Cotton helped establish a state whose officers, chosen by a dozen "freemen," possessed power that could be neither delegated nor removed by the people; Hooker founded a colony whose people committed authority to their officials and insured themselves against a tyrannical government by adopting a written constitution that safeguarded the rights of the individual.

Hooker reached America in 1633 and began preaching in Cambridge, Massachusetts. Soon he and his congregation began to show signs of dissatisfaction, for what reason we are not quite sure. It is probable that Hooker was too democratic and too independent for Massachusetts. At all events in 1636 he led his congregation southwestward to the Connecticut River where he laid out the town of Hartford. Under the leadership of Hooker, Connecticut became the guide and inspiration to liberal political thinkers in all the colonies. To-day our federal government and all the states employ a system of representative democracy, guaranteed by a constitution. This was first devised in America by the Hartford settlers, and the widespread use of this form of government is due in a certain degree to the example of Connecticut.

Hooker's political theory is announced in a letter that he wrote in 1638 to Governor Winthrop:

That in the matter which is referred to the judge, the sentence should lie in his breast, or be left to his discretion, according to which he should go, I am afraid that it is a course which wants both safety and warrant. I must confess, I ever looked at it as a way which leads directly to tyranny, and so to confusion, and must plainly profess, if it was in my liberty, I should choose neither to live nor leave my posterity under such a government.

And we know in other countries, had not the law overruled the lusts of men and the crooked ends of judges, many times, both places and people had been, in reason, past all relief, in many cases of difficulty. You will know what the heathen man said, by the candle-light of common-sense. The law is not subject to passion, nor to be taken aside with self-seeking ends, and therefore ought to have chief rule over the rulers themselves.

It's also a truth, that counsel ought to be sought from counsellors; but the question is, who should those be. Reserving smaller matters, which fall in occasionally in common course, to a lower counsel, in matters of greater consequence, which concern the common good, a general counsel, chosen by all, to transact businesses which concern all, I conceive, under favor, most suitable to rule and most safe for relief of the whole.

The following is a part of an abstract of one of Hooker's sermons delivered at Hartford, May 31, 1638:

Doctrine. I. That the choice of public magistrates belongs unto the people, by God's own allowance.

II. The privilege of election, which belongs to the people, therefore must not be exercised according to their humours, but according to the blessed will and law of God.

III. They who have power to appoint officers and magistrates, it is in their power, also, to set the bounds and limitations of the power and place unto which they call them.

Reasons. I. Because the foundation of authority is laid, firstly, in the free consent of the people.

II. Because by a free choice, the hearts of the people will be more inclined to the love of the persons chosen and more ready to yield obedience.

III. Because of that duty and engagement of the people.

Possessing unbounded authority over his people, Hooker might have made himself priest-king with powers that would have excited Winthrop's and Cotton's envy and admiration, but instead he put his hand to the establishment of a liberal government, not so radically liberal as that of Rhode Island but far more so than that of Massachusetts Bay. Hooker taught that the choice of magistrates "by God's allowance" belongs to the people and that the foundation of authority is laid primarily on the free consent of the governed. The right to vote he considered a political matter to be regulated by the towns. He utterly rejected the idea that the franchise should depend upon church membership or the payment of taxes. In his broad political doctrines Hooker is surprisingly like such later thinkers as Jefferson. He held that a government is formed by an agreement of the governed and that its chief function is to promote the well-being and happiness of its people. These ideas appear more than once in American history, and while Hooker did not originate them, he first put them into practice on this continent. It is certainly something to have been the first in America to state what has long been accepted as the traditional American view of the foundations of government.

ROGER WILLIAMS: REBEL

(c. 1603-1683)

Although Hooker advanced far beyond his Puritan contemporaries in political thought and governmental practice, in religious doctrine he remained a Puritan. It was not thus with Roger Williams. In political thought Williams was as far in advance of Hooker as Hooker surpassed John Cotton, and in religious questions Williams went so far beyond Puritanism that he abandoned all sects and in later life was content to be known as "a seeker," meaning one who seeks God in his own individual fashion and wishes every other man to have the same privilege. The America of the past and present was built of ideas once held by Thomas Hooker; the America of the future may possibly catch up with the ideas of Roger Williams.

Roger Williams was born in England in 1603 and educated at Cambridge. He intended to practice law but in the turmoil of seventeenth century England he found himself irresistibly drawn into the religious and political debates of the time. He entered the ministry and joined the Great Migration to America. Once on these shores he was offered the church afterwards bestowed upon John Cotton, but he refused the proffer and, leaving intolerant Boston, went to Salem. Here he began preaching, but his doctrines were so annoying to his Puritan neighbors that he was ordered banished from the colony. To prevent his being carried back to England he fled to the protection of the Rhode Island Indians. Here he founded a new settlement on the most liberal plan adopted by any colony in America, save Pennsylvania. Williams lived the remainder of his life serving as counselor and friend to the free commonwealth that he established.

It has been truly said that in Roger Williams England gave us of her very best. A more generous, liberal-minded, freedom-loving spirit than that of Williams never came to these shores. To say that the man who believed in the utmost freedom in both religion and government was generations ahead of his time is more of a reflection on the time than on the man.

Williams has two claims upon the grateful memory of America. His ideal of religious liberty was so broad and generous that he made room in his colony for all men, however non-conformist, strange, or even outlandish their religious views might be, and in the realm of government he reached an ideal of freedom, democracy, and happiness that has been equaled only by such advanced political thinkers as Jefferson, Lincoln, Roosevelt, La Follette, or Wilson. Both aspects of Williams's beneficent thinking go back to a fundamental quality within the man's inmost soul. He was a mystic. This attribute colored all his thinking and acting.

As a mystic he placed implicit reliance upon the inner light and its ability to lead man truly. If the inner light is to be trusted, and no mystic ever thinks of questioning its promptings, then every action of the individual must be given the respect and confidence due an act of the divine spirit. The mystic's communion with God is the source of the inner light. Hence any obstacle to the individual's freedom of thought and action is a wrong to the individual and an affront to the divine source. The mystic may see no need for ministers, rituals, creeds, and church organizations, but he is perfectly content to have his fellows invoke all these and other agencies in an attempt to worship in a satisfactory manner. Williams's mysticism had the same general effect upon his political views that it had upon his religious thought. Rhode Island was broadly democratic in its structure, because Williams was a leveler. That is to say he recognized no class distinctions and had no regard for a social structure or government erected upon such a foundation. He believed in the fatherhood of God and the brotherhood of man in the state as well as in the church, and his great contributions to political theory were aimed at the devising of a commonwealth under which a man might enjoy the life, liberty and happiness that are divinely his. Each one of his political ideas was erected on the two propositions that all men are equal and that the state exists for the benefit of the governed.

Political Theory of Williams.—Specifically Roger Williams contributed three ideas to American political theory. He substituted the compact theory of government for that of divine right. The latter view held that the state is established by direct act of God and that the officials are God's stewards on earth. Williams rejected this theory, holding rather that the state is a product of natural law and that the people of a state delegate power and authority to their rulers. Secondly, Williams held that, since a state is the product of social will, all government is merely an instrument or agency of society for the effecting of its desired ends. The last contribution of Williams was the devising of practical machinery for the carrying out of the desires of a democracy like Rhode Island. He was careful to give his state only as much power as is necessary to secure justice for all, specifically forbidding the use of force to influence the thinking or actions of men where those actions worked no injustice upon others. Williams wanted the citizens to make their own laws, in his zeal for direct government foreshadowing even such instruments of direct democracy as the initiative, referendum, and recall. He insisted that the court of last resort in such a state as he proposed must be the people actually assembled or their responsible representatives. Above all, authority should never be delegated to any man as a perpetual gift. Williams feared a written constitution, as Jefferson later did, because he thought that the authority of such a document, becoming more rigid with age, would not be flexible enough to cope with questions that might arise generations after the adoption of the instrument. To give courts the right to declare laws unconstitutional was utterly repugnant to Williams.

Naturally with such a government, Rhode Island was immensely unpopular with the other Puritan colonies—"Rogue's Island," they called it, or the "State of Confusion." All through the colonial period and well into the Revolutionary epoch Rhode Island was despised for its peculiarities, but only in that colony and Pennsylvania would the modern American have felt at home, and the much-ridiculed peculiarities would be the very things creating the congenial atmosphere.

When John Cotton wrote an open letter justifying the course of Massachusetts in banishing non-conformists, Roger Williams answered him in one of the memorable documents in American literature. Williams's answer, *The Bloudy Tenent of Persecution*, is not easy reading, but packed into the crabbed sentences and paragraphs of that book is the most liberal political and religious doctrine enunciated in seventeenth century America. The author's denial of the right to persecute men of opposing opinions is so cogently set forth that Cotton is completely overwhelmed. *The Bloudy Tenent* may not be great literature, but it is great American doctrine—a doctrine originated on the continent by the gentle outcast, who became the strong defender of liberty, Roger Williams.

JOHN WISE: ECCLESIASTICAL DEMOCRAT

(c. 1652-1725)

Although the congregational form of church government was early adopted in principle in Massachusetts Bay colony, the early years of the eighteenth century saw certain clergymen, headed by those energetic schemers, the Mathers, put out a series of questions and suggestions looking toward the establishment of an oligarchic or less democratic form of church control. The suggestion to place direction of the churches in a ministerial association drew fire from John Wise, a village preacher, and a staunch and unterrified democrat. In his two books, *The Churches' Quarrel Espoused* (1710), and *Vindication of the Government of the New England Churches* (1717), Wise gave so convincing an argument for congregational government that it may be said never to have been superseded. Ultimately the cause of democracy triumphed in the New England churches, and no small share of this triumph must be assigned to John Wise.

In the following sentences taken from *The Churches' Quarrel Espoused*, Wise pays his respects to arbitrary power:

Englishmen hate an arbitrary power (politically considered) as they hate the devil.

. . . And though many of their incautelous princes have endeavored to null all their charter rights and immunities, and aggrandize themselves in the servile state of the subjects, by setting up their own separate will for the great standard of government over the nations, yet they have all along paid dear for their attempts, both in the ruin of the nation, and in interrupting the increase of their own grandeur, and their foreign settlements and conquests.

.   .   .   .

The very name of an arbitrary government is ready to put an Englishman's blood into a fermentation; but when it really comes, and shakes its whip over their ears, and tells them it is their master, it makes them stark mad; and being of a mimical genius, they turn arbitrary too.

Wise is of significance in the development of American thought because his argument for church democracy became so implanted in the New England mind that, when the revolutionary fathers half a century later began preaching political democracy, they were not appealing to audiences totally ignorant of all forms of self-government. The preceding struggle for ecclesiastical democracy had accustomed the people to think in terms of popular government. In 1772, just before the outbreak of the Revolution, Wise's *Vindication* was republished in Boston. Two editions of the work were soon exhausted.

EARLY LITERATURE OUTSIDE NEW ENGLAND

It may be that historians have too relentlessly contrasted Cavalier Virginia and Puritan New England, but the differences between the two regions are sufficiently marked to tempt those writers who delight in strong contrasts. Certainly the literature of the two are entirely dissimilar. The literature of New England is the product of that Puritan strain in England that produced Thomas Cartwright and John Bunyan, men whose paramount interests were spiritual and theological. Very little was written in Massachusetts that did not have a strong religious bias. Even a writer like John Wise, who is to-day remembered because of his political theory, wrote his books in the course of a quarrel over church government. The Virginia writers were different. The literary men of that colony, despite the casual interest that many had in literature, were like Raleigh, Hakluyt, and the great names of Elizabethan letters. Virginia authors eschewed theology and politics until well into the eighteenth century. Their theological qualms were easily disposed of by paying an indifferent allegiance to the ceremonies of the established church and by light-heartedly dismissing to the ministers all concern with doctrine, and their political philosophy progressed hardly any farther into the realm of intellectual speculation.

The fundamental aims and philosophies of the two peoples were entirely different. The New Englanders were engaged in a frightfully serious business. They came to America to make this country a fit dwelling place for the Kingdom of God on earth, and in the achievement of their grand aim they were willing to sacrifice ease and temporal pleasures. Literature, like that produced by the poets and dramatists of the Mermaid circle, most assuredly was accounted a temporal pleasure, and the Puritans were so rapt in the contemplation of their grand destiny that they had no time for any distraction. Their literature was valued for its substance; style seems seldom to have been a consideration. It was not thus with the Virginian. He came to America to find an easy life and material prosperity. Never was he indifferent to pleasure, and his literature not indistinctly reveals this characteristic. Although Virginia was decidedly not a literary community, its authors produced geographical descriptions, histories, pamphlets to attract colonists, and an occasional belletristic effort. And one can imagine a Shakespeare, Spenser, or Jonson making a wry face at a knotty Puritan tract and then settling down for a riotous hour of vicarious adventure with Smith or Strachey, and it is indeed quite conceivable that almost any of the Elizabethan poets would have preferred the couplets of Sandys to the pious lucubrations of Michael Wigglesworth or the harsh dissonances of Richard Mather's psalm book. The Virginian was inclined to enjoy his ease in his Zion, taking care only to choose a Zion that was acceptably comfortable. On the other hand the New Englander set out deliberately to make a dwelling place for the Spirit in the most forbidding surroundings, however arduous the task might prove to be. One was concerned with the passing show of life; the other kept his mind upon the rigorous task at hand and the beatific promise of its completion.

But there are other reasons why the literature of Virginia differs from that of New England. The Puritans early established schools and colleges, and shortly after they landed, their printing press was turning out Calvinistic tracts. Virginia discouraged literature by its indifference to education and its hostility to the printing press. Furthermore, a significant difference between the leaders of the two colonies accounts for another difference in their literature. The Virginia leaders were usually men of action, totally oblivious to literary fame. The Puritan ministers were often better acquainted with the atmosphere of their studies than with practical problems, and such men are seldom indifferent to the lure of literary renown.

Notwithstanding its close reasoning and its cacophonous sentences, the literature of New England has been very influential in the development of the American mind, while that of early Virginia was not. Indeed some of the most delightful work of the Cavaliers was not printed until a hundred years after the death of the author. One might almost say that because the literature of Virginia was easy to read, it was uninfluential in the development of American thought. It dwelt too much on pleasant verities. The books and sermons of New England were influential simply because they presented uncertain speculation in the domains of theology and politics, two places where later Americans were to expend an immoderate amount of meditation. Smith wrote to attract settlers; John Wise dedicated his stubborn sentences to the defense of liberty. The one pleased the readers; the other made them think.

JOHN SMITH
(1579-1631)

Although Elizabethan prose of the Lyly tradition was first written in America by Nathaniel Ward, the full flavor of the bluff, hearty Elizabethan spirit, unwarped by artificial diction or affected manners, surged into American literature almost forty years before the euphuistic *Simple Cobbler* saw the light. In his life John Smith embodied a large number of Elizabethan traits and, if we may believe the captain, a full complement of Elizabethan virtues. During his life he was sailor, random wanderer, explorer, geographer, colonizer, fighter, and executive, but above all he was a fellow of infinite zest and genuine ability. Discount as we may his own unauthenticated stories of his youth, there still remains incontrovertible evidence of his amazing energy, pluck, and versatility. His first forty years were one long adventure that moved at a quick-step through a colorful period of history, and Smith's personality was evidently not wholly impervious to the adventures through which the doughty captain passed. Part chivalric knight and part Elizabethan sea-dog, with a considerable dash of braggadocio, Smith remains one of the unquestionably romantic figures of our history, despite the efforts of critical historians to tarnish the glitter.

Smith wrote his books as part and parcel of his energetic and venturesome life. Some were done to acquaint the people of England, especially the proprietors of the colony, with the promise of Virginia, while others were done to encourage emigration to New England. In none of them did the author forget to mention repeatedly the exploits of Captain John Smith. But when Smith picked up the pen, awkwardly enough he himself admits, his personal characteristics, combined with an unfeigned interest in his story, gave his style a straightforward energy, dignity, and interest that the plodding polemics of New England seldom attain.

Smith was born in Lincolnshire in 1579. He went to sea in his youth and, according to his own story, spent ten years in southern Europe, Turkey, and the Near East. Scholars have not yet agreed as to the veracity of Smith's autobiography. However, we do know that he sailed for Virginia with a party of colonists in December, 1606, and landed at Jamestown the following April after a long and very trying voyage. Soon his ability and his decisive nature led to his appointment as governor of the feeble colony precariously perched on the bank of the James. Smith held this post until 1609 when he returned to England, never again to see Virginia. He was on two voyages to New England before the Pilgrims sailed for the new world. His later years seem to have been spent in London where he was evidently accepted as an authority on colonization.

During his residence in Virginia, Smith wrote three pieces of literature. The first was *A True Relation of Virginia*, written probably in 1608 and certainly published in England in the latter part of that year. The book is a simple narrative of the founding of Jamestown. Smith tells of the difficulty of getting enough to eat, of the relations with the Indians, of his exploring tours, and of the prospects for the colony. Nor does he forget to include a number of the gaudy adventures that seemed to dog the writer's footsteps. Withal the book is a good one. If American literature had never seen a worse piece of work, its general level would be considerably higher than it is. Smith's second piece of literary work was a letter to the importunate proprietors. Although not composed for publication, it was later printed. His third attempt was a combination of his work as geographer, observer, and literary man. It was a map of Virginia with a competent description of everything that the proprietor or prospective colonist might be interested in.

Smith's literary style is fairly well represented by these few sentences from his second effort, the letter to the proprietors:

I received your letter wherein you write that our minds are so set upon faction and idle conceits in dividing the country without your consents; and that we feed you but with if's and and's, hopes, and some few proofs, as if we would keep the mystery of the business to ourselves; and that we must expressly follow your instructions sent by Captain Newport, the charge of whose voyage amounts to near two thousand pounds,—the which if we cannot defray by the ship's return, we are alike to remain as banished men. . . . For the charge of this voyage of two or three thousand pounds, we have not received the value of an hundred pounds. . . . From your ship we had not provision in victuals worth twenty pound; and we are more than two hundred to live upon this,—the one half sick the other little better. For the sailors, I confess they daily make good cheer; but our diet is a little meal and water, and not sufficient of that. Though there be fish in the sea, fowls in the air, and beasts in the woods, their bounds are so large, they so wild, and we so weak and ignorant, we cannot much trouble them. . . . When you send again, I entreat you rather send but thirty carpenters, husbandmen, gardeners, fishermen, blacksmiths, masons, and diggers up of tree's roots, well provided, than a thousand of such as we have; for except we be able to lodge them and feed them, the most will consume with want of necessaries, before they can be made good for anything.

After Smith returned to England he wrote a *Description of New England* (1616), *New England's Trials* (1620), *General History of Virginia* (1624), *A Sea Grammar* (1627), and *Advertisement for Unexperienced Planters* (1631). These all have the general characteristics of the earlier books.

Although Smith set a respectable standard for subsequent writers, his books do not fall readily into the stream of American literature. Political and theological argumentation simply do not touch him. He was a man of affairs, tremendously glad to be alive in a world where there was so much to do. Leave theology to the clergy and political theory to the lawyers; he would have none of them. His was the task of mapping Virginia, of colonizing New England, and in general of forwarding the work of carving an English domain out of the new world. To find another like Captain John Smith one must go to his Elizabethan brethren like Sidney and Raleigh. Most like him was Sir Walter Raleigh. But for the misfortune of lowly birth Smith might easily have been one of the greater figures in Elizabethan society. Had the undoubted redness of his blood been tempered by a bit of blue, his executive ability might have been recognized less grudgingly, his tall stories might have been received with less skepticism, and his literary style might conceivably have been benefited by an acquaintance with polite literature. But the advantages of birth and breeding would scarcely have added anything to the rugged energy of the man or to the eager curiosity of his nature. And these two qualities are the charm of Smith's writings and his chief contribution to our national letters.

WILLIAM STRACHEY

The close relationship of English and American literature has usually been signalized by the influence that writers of the mother country frequently exercise upon those of the new world, but, curiously enough, one of the first books written in America is supposed by many to have reversed the usual relationship and to have influenced one of the superb masterpieces of the English tongue. A respectable number of critics argue, with more than a little show of plausibility, that the opening scenes of Shakespeare's *Tempest* were suggested by a description of a storm at sea that was written by William Strachey in his *True Repertory of the Wracke and Redemption of Sir Thomas Gates*. We are not certain that Shakespeare was indebted to the work of Strachey, but it is eminently safe to say that the vivid description of a storm and shipwreck is worthy of the supreme attention that some think it received.

In 1609 a company under the command of Sir Thomas Gates set out for Virginia. A terrific storm wrecked the commander's boat upon the Bermudas. After great hardships the leader and his small company built two small boats out of the wreckage of their ship and reached Jamestown. In Gates's company was a man named William Strachey. Of him virtually nothing is known, except what he tells incidentally in his own writings, and he easily avoided Smith's error of talking too much about himself. Evidently he was a man of some little education, for his style and diction are those of a cultivated man, and soon after his arrival in Jamestown he was elected secretary of the colony. While living in Virginia, Strachey wrote the book that contains an account of the voyage thither and a description of the colony. The popularity of *The True Repertory* is indicated by its republication in Purchas's *Pilgrims*.

The power and vividness of Strachey's work can hardly be indicated in a short excerpt, but the following sentences show something of his style:

For four and twenty hours the storm, in a restless tumult, had blown so exceedingly, as we could not apprehend in our imaginations any possibility of greater violence, yet did we still find it, not only more terrible, but more constant, fury added to fury, and one storm urging a second, more outrageous than the former, whether it so wrought upon our fears, or indeed met with new forces. Sometimes strikes in our ship amongst women, and passengers not used to such hurly and discomforts, made us look one upon the other with troubled hearts and panting bosoms, our clamors drowned in the winds, and the winds in thunder. Prayers might well be in the heart and lips, but drowned in the cries of the officers,— nothing heard that might give comfort, nothing seen that might encourage hope . . . and it now being Friday, the fourth morning, it wanted little but that there had been a general determination, to have shut up hatches and commending our sinful souls to God, committed the ship to the mercy of the sea. Surely that night we must have done it, and that night had we then perished; but see the goodness and sweet introduction of better hope by our merciful God given unto us. Sir George Somers, when no man dreamed of such happiness, had discovered and cried "Land."

After returning to England, Strachey brought out *For the Colony in Virginea Britannia; Laws Divine, Morall, and Martiall*. About 1618 he wrote a *Historie of Travaile into Virginia*. This latter work does not seem to have been published until 1849 when the Hakluyt Society published it from a manuscript in the British Museum.

GEORGE SANDYS

(1578-1644)

Smith, Strachey, John Pory, Alexander Whitaker, and the other Virginia writers were generally men of affairs and only incidentally men of letters. Most of their writings were composed for some utilitarian purpose, to dissuade the proprietors from their wrath, to attract new colonists, or to arouse the interest of the English in the Virginia experiment. Such was not the case with the work of George Sandys, the first poet of America. As the son of an archbishop of York and the younger brother of Sir Edwin Sandys, the prime aversion of James I, George Sandys received a good education and the advantage of foreign travel. His first book was an account of his journey through Europe, Egypt, and Palestine. When he arrived in Virginia in 1621, he already possessed an excellent reputation at home as a poet and scholar. This reputation was based in part upon a translation of the first five books of Ovid's *Metamorphoses*.

As colonial treasurer, Sandys found himself deluged with official cares when a disastrous Indian massacre in 1622 threw Virginia into a panic. In spite of the distractions he applied himself to the task of turning the remainder of the *Metamorphoses* into English couplets, and by the time that he returned to London, probably in 1625, he had his translation ready for the printer. In the dedication to King Charles, the poet speaks of his work as "limned by that unperfect light which was snatched from the hours of night and repose."

Sandys' translation has been called "the first utterance of the conscious literary spirit articulated in America." Just as Smith and Strachey set a high standard for subsequent American prose, Sandys set an immoderately high mark for later poetry. For more than a century his translation of Ovid retained its great popularity. Fuller included him in his *Worthies of England*, and both Dryden and Pope spoke of him with deep respect for his poetical art.

WILLIAM BYRD
(1674-1744)

Whenever a New Englander wrote anything, good or bad, he was pretty sure to see that it was printed and subjected to the hazard of popular favor. This practice gave books at least a chance to influence thought and thus become a part of the national literary tradition. The indifference with which even educated Virginians regarded literary fame and the subsequent failure of the early writers of that colonly to influence our national thinking are excellently illustrated by the case of the Westover Manuscripts, the complete works of an early and certainly not our least accomplished native-born writer. William Byrd, proprietor of the famous Westover estate on the lower James, wrote three sprightly books on his journeys through Virginia and North Carolina. Aside from their historical value, these books can be read to-day with more than a little pleasure, for the author's charming wit, combined with a vein of cutting sarcasm, makes his observations always interesting and sometimes very humorous. Often the wit is of the broad, eighteenth century variety, but no reader can doubt its effectiveness. Yet these writings of Byrd were allowed to remain unpublished for more than a hundred years. Finally in 1841 they were given to the world as the Westover Manuscripts. In the nineteenth century the chief value of these works was historical, but if they had been published at the time that they were written, they would have stood an excellent chance of setting up a literary model for American writers that would have been infinitely closer to the standard of early eighteenth century English writers than were the Calvinistic tracts of New England.

William Byrd, son of one of the prominent and wealthy men of Virginia, was born at Westover in 1674. Educational facilities were so lacking in Virginia that the boy was early entrusted to the care of relatives in England where he was educated. He studied in Holland, visited the court of France, and was called to the bar in the Middle Temple. Upon his return to Virginia, he assumed a prominent place in public life that he never relinquished. In his intellectual tastes and personal life Byrd seems to have been an English gentleman transported from the London of Queen Anne to the banks of the James. Visitors to Westover were charmed by the master's wit no less than by the opulence of his living, while his intellectual interests were indicated by the possession of one of the finest libraries in all the colonies.

The difference between New England and Virginia appears in a glance at the contemporaries, William Byrd and Samuel Sewall. Both men were well educated, both were wealthy and influential, and both held high public office. Yet to turn from the sparkling wit and deft sarcasm of Byrd to the funereal pleasures of the solemn Sewall is like passing from one epoch of literature to another. That the two writers were contemporaries in colonial America is only further evidence of the diverse strains that went into the making of our national mind. It may be conceivably true that a society founded by men like Sewall will be solider and more substantial than one established by men like Byrd; certainly it will be more serious-minded. However, it is not inconceivable that American literature would have benefited if the Puritan strain had been tempered, somewhat earlier than it was, by the insouciant gayety and wit of an antagonistic element.

In 1729 Byrd was a member of the surveying expedition that established the line between Virginia and North Carolina. He left a record of his experiences in *The History of the Dividing Line,* probably the most typical of his works. Three years later he took a trip to his mines in western Virginia that he described in *Progress to the Mines.* The following year he visited his large holdings in North Carolina and left a record of this excursion in *A Journey to the Land of Eden.* These works, known as the Westover Manuscripts, were first published in 1841. Twenty-five years later a better edition appeared, and it was only recently announced that another manuscript of the *History of the Dividing Line* has been discovered that contains portions omitted from the earlier editions.

In 1708 there appeared at London a satirical poem entitled *The Sot-Weed Factor* by Eben. Cook, Gent. Absolutely nothing seems to be known of the author, not even his name, for the signature under which the poem was published is conjectured by many to have been a pseudonym. Sot-weed factor translated into current English means tobacco merchant, and the poem gives a highly humorous account of the experiences of such a businessman in the new colony of Maryland. In its broad humor, wit, and lusty critical slashes the poem invites comparison with Samuel Butler's *Hudibras*. Here is Cook's description of his experience with a Quaker:

> While riding near a sandy bay
> I met a Quaker "Yea" and "Nay";
> A pious conscientious rogue,
> As e'er wore bonnet or a brogue,
> Who neither swore nor kept his word
> But cheated in the fear of God;
> And when his debts he would not pay,
> By light within he ran away.
> With this sly zealot soon I struck
> A bargain for my English truck,
> Agreeing for ten thousand weight
> Of sot-weed good and fit for freight,
> Broad Oronooka bright and sound,
> The growth and product of his ground;
> In cask that should contain complete
> Five hundred of tobacco neat.
> The contract thus betwixt us made,
> Not well acquainted with the trade,
> My goods I trusted to the cheat,
> Whose crop was then aboard the fleet;
> And, going to receive my own,
> I found the bird was newly flown.

ROBERT BEVERLEY

(c. 1673-1722)

Robert Beverley, son of a prominent Virginia gentleman and son-in-law of the opulent William Byrd of Westover, is another man of affairs who turned his hand casually to literature and produced a strikingly good piece of work. Beverley was educated in England and upon his return to the colony assumed the position of a man of wealth and influence. He served for some time in the House of Burgesses and held many official positions. While he was visiting London about 1705 he was asked by a bookseller to criticize a history of Virginia that was then on the market. Beverley became so engrossed in correcting the mistakes of the book that he determined to do one of his own. The resultant work was called *The History and Present State of Virginia*. A French translation appeared in 1707, and the author issued a second edition in 1722.

Beverley's history was written in an easy, almost colloquial style that makes it exceedingly pleasant reading. Historians assure us that there are errors of fact in the work, although some have called the book the "first authoritative history of the colony." Beverley's style is shown by this short description of Virginia hospitality:

> The inhabitants are very courteous to travelers, who need no other recommendation but the being human creatures. A stranger has no more to do, but inquire upon the road where any gentleman or good housekeeper lives, and there he may depend upon being received with hospitality. This good nature is so general among the people, that the gentry, when they go abroad, order their principal servants to entertain all visitors with everything the plantation affords. And the poor planters, who have but one bed, will very often sit up, or lie upon a form or couch all night, to make room for a weary traveler to repose himself after his journey.

SUGGESTED READINGS

Adams, Brooks: *The Emancipation of Massachusetts*. Boston. 1919.

Adams, James T.: *The Founding of New England*. Boston. 1921. pp. 253-277.

Bassett: Biographical sketch in *The Writings of Colonel William Byrd*. New York. 1901.

Boas: *Cotton Mather, Keeper of the Puritan Conscience*. New York. 1928.

Cobb: *The Rise of Religious Liberty in America*. New York. 1902.

Ernst: *The Political Thought of Roger Williams*. Seattle. 1928.

Miller: *The New England Mind; the Seventeenth Century*. New York. 1939.

Miller and Johnson: *The Puritans*. New York. 1938.

Morison: *The Puritan Pronaos; Studies in the Intellectual Life of New England in the Seventeenth Century*. London. 1936.

Morison: *Builders of the Bay Colony*. New York. 1930.

Murdock: *Selections from Cotton Mather*. New York. 1926. Especially pages ix-lx.

Murdock: *Increase Mather, the Foremost American Puritan.* Cambridge. 1925.

Sympathetic treatment. See works by Parrington, Brooks Adams, James Truslow Adams, and Cobb.

Parrington: *The Colonial Mind.* New York. 1927.

A monumental study.

Schneider: *A History of American Philosophy.* New York. 1946. Parts I and II.

Tyler: *A History of American Literature, 1607-1765.* New York. 1878.

Although this work is seventy years old, it is still most useful.

Wendell: *Cotton Mather.* Cambridge. 1891.

CHAPTER V

THE FLOWERING OF THE COLONIAL MIND

The eighteenth was one of the greatest of centuries. The low estimate which it too frequently attracts is caused by the criticisms of nineteenth century writers who despised the preceding age as one addicted to cold reason rather than to human emotion, to form rather than to spirit, to order rather than to unlimited freedom. In many ways Pope is a typical poet of the eighteenth century, and this very finished writer prized the form of his poetry more than the thought, and he cared infinitely more for the thought than for the emotion expressed by his lines. He wrote in most exact and careful fashion, bestowing endless pains upon his meter and rhyme, and taking care always to compose according to the difficult and detailed rules governing the heroic couplet. Later critics have called his lines "hobbyhorse poetry," because of the regular flow of the couplets. It is true that "An Essay on Man" sounds hopelessly stilted and artificial beside such romantic poems as Whitman's "Song of Myself" or even Shelley's "To a Skylark," but it must be remembered that Shelley and Whitman would have been impossible without the great liberalizing work of the eighteenth century, and much of the early part of that century is embodied in Pope.

The Age of Reason.—The great work of the eighteenth century was the application of reason to every human activity, and under the touch of reason many age-old superstitions and irrational institutions crumbled into dust. The seventeenth century was a time of faith. During that period religion, government, and science lived on tradition. The doctrines of extreme Calvinism, the theory of the divine right of kings, and the older conceptions of the universe, though all were sharply challenged, pretty generally managed to survive well through the century even in the minds of the thoughtful and educated. The spirit of the seventeen-hundreds, which began twenty or twenty-five years before the chronological start of the century, changed all such ideas. The acute mathematical mind of Sir Isaac Newton gave such order and reason to the universe that the conception of the Newtonian world-machine was not questioned for two hundred years. The reasoning of John Locke completely demolished the divine right theory of kingship and firmly established in political philosophy the right of a people to rebel against an unjust or tyrannical ruler. With reason working many changes in science and politics, it was certain to enter the great field of theology. Enter it did, and its impact created the very striking religious thought known as deism.

John Locke was one of the most influential thinkers of modern times. He belonged by birth to the mid-seventeenth century, but his ideas did not gain general acceptance until the last decade of that century. In a sense he was the intellectual founder of the Age of Reason, as the eighteenth century is called. His influence was felt in philosophy, psychology, education, and economics, but it was in his political philosophy that he probably achieved his greatest work. Locke thought that all governments must recognize that nature has bestowed certain rights upon every man and that these rights can neither be given away nor removed save as a punishment for crime. Any government that disregards such rights as life, liberty, and the legal possession of property becomes at once unjust and tyrannical, and rebellion against such a government is not only justifiable but laudable. Locke colored all later English political thinking for more than a hundred years, and in France and America his ideas were as well known as they were at home. Voltaire popularized Locke's theories in France, and they were further developed by the whole group of revolutionary thinkers that preceded and accompanied the great French revolution. In America Jefferson, Samuel Adams, Franklin, John Adams and the other promoters of our revolution were deeply read in Locke. Any thinker who becomes the philosophical grandfather of two world-shaking revolutions is entitled to a high place in the history of human thought. Such was John Locke, and his influence was exerted to substitute reason in government for tradition and irrational authority.

Equaling Locke's influence in the field of politics was the work of Sir Isaac Newton in mathematics and astronomy. Copernicus (1473-1543) was the first modern to challenge the old theory that the sun and other heavenly bodies revolve around the earth, though he merely stated his belief that the sun was the center of our system, giving little proof of his views. The observations of Galileo and Kepler confirmed the correctness of the Copernican theory, but it was reserved for Newton to offer a striking and original explanation of the solar system. This system, as explained by Newton's theory of gravitation, was a perfect organization, running according to the changeless laws of nature. It was mathematically exact, complete in every detail, and, in short, absolutely perfect. That man's reason, unaided by divine revelation, could formulate so great a theory appealed mightily to Newton's contemporaries. Here was a most striking proof of the greatness and sole sufficiency of reason.

A universe so perfect as that explained by Newton necessarily bespoke a perfect creator, and if man's unaided reason could grasp the secrets of that universe, unaided reason could reveal and understand that creator. By such a clear bit of argument did the eighteenth century bring reason into the realm of religion. This view of religion that sees a perfect creator as the first cause of a perfect universe, that finds God in nature and not in revelation, is called deism.

To many people deism was a hateful word. To some it meant infidelity or atheism, to others it meant a presumptuous and conceited attempt of man to fathom unsearchable mysteries. Certainly it was not atheism, however much it might tend to minimize the importance of revelation. But assuredly it glorified the power of man's reason. It challenged the right of ministers to pose as the sole interpreters of God's word, and it was indifferent to the ordinary church organization and to traditional worship. To the true deist, God and nature were synonymous, hence the existence of a God could be proved beyond doubt without recourse to the Bible or Christian theology.

In France the new religious thought was popularized by Voltaire and adopted by virtually all the thinkers of the eighteenth century. In America deism aroused the bitter opposition of the New England clergy when it was introduced by Franklin and Jefferson, two of the leading deists of the day, through whose influence it was widely accepted.

The Eighteenth Century in America.—In general the eighteenth century in America was a somewhat belated reflection of English thought and work, though after 1750 certain French influences entered. In the new world there was that complete confidence in the unbounded power of human reason, the same reverence for natural science, and the same insistence upon natural religion that we have found in England. When Franklin went to London as a young man,

Newton was the object of his hearty admiration. Franklin and Jefferson both read Locke more than they read any other political thinker, both praised natural science as the most worthy of all studies, and both spread deism so successfully in this country that Timothy Dwight gloomily reported that the educated people of New England were all on the verge of adopting this new belief. The spirit of the Age of Reason was revered in America, and Franklin and Jefferson were its chief prophets.

In addition to the spirit of rationalism American life received two very influential forces from 1725 to 1775 that were of extreme importance in determining our national mind and life. These two forces were the coming of the Scotch-Irish and the beginning of active frontier influences. Most of the early immigrants to this country were English, but about 1725 the vanguard of the Scotch-Irish immigration appeared in the colonies. These newcomers found the seaboard already occupied, but to the west lay an open empire of unknown extent. The hardy, enterprising Scotch-Irish never hesitated. They became our first genuine Westerners, and through them the frontier first exerted a real influence on the nation. The Scotch-Irish were by nature energetic, independent, democratic, and the frontier accented to a marked degree their native characteristics.

Besides the Scotch-Irish contribution to our democratic way of life, the eighteenth century saw another leveling influence begin its work in America. This was the shipment to this country of thousands of indented servants. Men, women, and children, upon whom old world fortune had frowned, sold themselves for a term of servitude, usually from four to seven years, to any one who would pay for their transportation to the new world. Such persons were common from the earliest days of settlement, but thousands came during the eighteenth century. Many people of fairly good families and moderate education were among this class, though most of the indented servants were a sorry lot in blood, ability, and ambition. Gradually these servants were absorbed by the growing society about them. Some became small landholders, while others slipped away to the frontier where social rank was never thought of. Whatever became of these people we know that their influence must have been exerted toward a leveling process, toward social and political democracy, for the memories of old world injustice and enforced servitude certainly rankled in their hearts for more than a generation. John

Wise, the proponent of liberty in the New England churches, was the son of an indentured servant.

The Commercial Spirit.—Still another influence that developed during the eighteenth century was the spirit of commercialism. This spirit which is to be seen in the growing power of the merchants and traders, appeared in New England very early. It was almost obscured for a time by the strong religious tone of the Puritan colonies, but it appeared plainly in Samuel Sewall and some of his contemporaries. Commercialism was to be found early in the middle colonies, where the rich merchants of New York and Philadelphia soon held great social and political power. By the time of the Revolution the merchants made an influential and aggressive class in almost every colony. Their power was directed, first, against any hampering legislation that might be enacted by England and, second, against the leveling tendencies of the frontier.

JONATHAN EDWARDS AND NEW ENGLAND PURITANISM

By 1725 the defeat of the New England theocracy was so apparent that every one saw the hopelessness of trying to reëstablish the old order. Besides, more pressing tasks were upon the Puritan ministers. The scientific spirit that made for deism in England crossed the Atlantic and began to challenge Puritanism in its very stronghold. This challenge was not aimed at any of the political or social implications of Puritanism; it was directed at the fundamentals—the five points of Calvinism, especially predestination and bondage of the will. Locke had taught that mind is determined by experience. There is nothing in the mind, he said, that is not placed there by some direct experience of the individual. Therefore man is the product of his environment, and, since he has some power over his surroundings, at least to the extent of choosing one environment over another, he is to a degree possessed of free will. Thus at one blow Locke struck at the ideas that man's mind and nature are divinely determined and that man is a creature of fettered will. Furthermore English rationalism by generally holding that human nature is not inherently bad broke with the doctrine of total depravity. Reason challenged the very essence of Puritanism. The challenge was heard in New England before the mid-eighteenth century, and guardians of Calvinistic orthodoxy looked about anxiously for a champion. To relieve the distress of the faithful and to answer once and for all the presumptuous spokesmen of rationalistic science were the gratefully accepted tasks of Jonathan Edwards.

Jonathan Edwards (*1703-1758*).—Jonathan Edwards, the intellectual flower of New England Puritanism and one of the finest minds ever developed on the American continent, was born in East Windsor, Connecticut, in 1703. He came of four generations of religious leaders, and at once proved himself worthy of his ancestry and gave promise of future eminence by entering Yale before his thirteenth birthday. After a college career that amply satisfied all expectations he was graduated and soon thereafter accepted a position as tutor of his college. The careless pranks of the students became annoying to the sedate young instructor, and at the age of twenty-four he became pastor of the church at Northampton, Massachusetts, where his maternal grandfather had served for many years.

At Northampton Edwards developed his very remarkable talents as a preacher, soon becoming one of the most famous speakers in New England. Under the glowing power of his sermons a stirring revival movement, known as the Great Awakening, spread over America and made its existence felt in England, where John Wesley, founder of Methodism, heard the irresistible call to a more deeply religious life. Jonathan Edwards preached the immeasurable majesty and greatness of God, the insignificance of man, and the imperative duty of living a strictly upright and moral life.

Although some of the older Calvinists shrank from the excesses of the Great Awakening, it was the insistence upon practical morality and rectitude in everyday conduct that finally caused trouble for Edwards. The great minister opened a train of critical inquiry into the lives of his parishioners that threatened to touch some of the most important families of Northampton. One of Edwards's indictments of young people specified the reading of demoralizing books. Tradition has it that Samuel Richardson's *Pamela* was one of the objectionable books. Since the expressed aim of *Pamela* is to show that virtue is sure of its reward, and since Edwards later expressed admiration for Richardson's style, the tradition is probably a mere fiction. However that may be, the leaders of the Northampton church refused to follow Edwards in his proceedings against the offenders. The outcome of the quarrel, which was in progress for some time, was the dismissal of the minister from his church—an almost unprecedented event in New England where ministers were seldom discharged from their churches save for flagrant offenses.

In 1750 Edwards went from Northampton to Stockbridge in western Massachusetts where he served as missionary to the Indians and wrote his philosophical treatises. The great preaching days were over. For seven years the missionary labors continued, until finally Princeton recognized the extraordinary talents of the man by calling him to assume the presidency of the institution. Edwards died early in 1758, only three months after accepting the presidency of the New Jersey college.

Significance of Edwards.—No man in America has ever had greater opportunity for diversified development than Jonathan Edwards possessed; no man of his generation, not even Franklin, could have traveled so many roads to intellectual and spiritual eminence; and none went so far along one path, and that, as we think to-day, the wrong one. Edwards is the most melancholy example in American literature of a brilliant and capable man wholly dominated by an environment that was fated soon to disappear. He could have achieved distinction as a natural scientist, an idealistic philosopher, a stern and compelling moralist, or a religious mystic, but he was the product of generations of New England consciences, and he never allowed any distractions to divert him from his main task, the defense of a hard-pressed Puritan theology. Although he never suffered theology to stamp out all of his other interests, religious dogma was first in his mind, as it was first in the minds of his contemporaries. To-day we remember Edwards as a great Puritan mystic, or as a potential scientist in the opening days of the scientific century, but actually the chief work of this great man was to state in iron-clad logic the doctrines of early Calvinism, and by so doing bring all the unlovely features of the harsh system into high relief against the background of contemporary rationalism. Early Calvinism was tottering, it gravely needed a support, but it could not stand a defense based upon an unmistakable restatement of bondage of the will and human depravity. The American environment supplemented by English rationalism had made these doctrines obsolete. The fearless logic of Edwards and his uncompromising allegiance to the old tenets simply served to heighten the disfavor into which Calvinism had fallen.

Before the rising flood of theological controversy submerged

Edwards, he exhibited a keen appreciation of the methods and aims of natural science. The notes that have been preserved report exact observations in a simple and direct style. Moreover, the young man had the ability to reason closely and accurately from the data that he collected. Because he soon forsook scientific observation for theological debate, Edwards is almost never considered in relation to the science of his time, but in gaining its greatest theologian America lost what could have been one of our finest scientific minds, had it developed.

Philosophy of Edwards.—The philosophical work of Edwards is too involved and metaphysical for explanation in a short space. Suffice to say that his major effort, *On the Freedom of the Will,* was a carefully wrought argument proving that the idea of free will is a delusion. The work is so admirably executed that, if the reader goes a step with Edwards, he must go the whole distance. James Boswell, the biographer of Dr. Samuel Johnson, declared that his only relief from the relentless logic of the book was to forget it. No philosopher or theologian accepting Edwards's idea of God has ever successfully attempted to refute *On the Freedom of the Will.* Later writers have avoided the acute Puritan by holding another conception of the deity.

As a popular theologian and preacher Edwards first made his reputation with such sermons as "God Glorified in Man's Dependence," and "Sinners in the Hands of an Angry God." To-day we would gladly forget these sermons, so filled are they with the brimstone and terror of early Calvinism, and to do so would be a kindness to Edwards, but the eighteenth century knew the great preacher through these sermons and it was by such utterances that he most affected his generation. Old-time Calvinism was too far gone for recovery, but so powerfully and clearly did the sermons of Edwards set forth the early creed that all its unlovely features stood revealed. The champion of Puritanism was too strong; a weaker man would have compromised or obscured some of the repellent details. There was neither obscurity nor compromise in the soul of Edwards. New England listened, marveled at the intellect of the man, then turned to more congenial doctrines.

The criticism, directed against many Puritan leaders, that they were more concerned with minute questions of theology than with problems of everyday conduct, cannot be uttered against Edwards. It is true that he did not have the interest in social problems that

John Woolman and Benjamin Franklin possessed, but he devised a set of rules that governed his ordinary conduct in the most strict fashion. Like Milton, Edwards ever felt himself under the eye of the Great Task-master, and never did he allow himself to forget his duties or overlook his personal obligations. The practical morality of the man is best shown in the famous resolutions, seventy in number, most of which were written before the author's twenty-first birthday. Further evidence of his interest in everyday morality can be found in the causes of the Northampton quarrel. If Edwards had not possessed a sensitive conscience, he might have spent his life ministering to the Northampton parish.

Edwards as Mystic.—The phase of Edwards that the twentieth century is coming to admire more and more is the man's unmistakable mysticism. Outwardly the defender of Puritanism was clad in the armor of Calvinism, but in his heart of hearts he was one of the world's great mystics. That his mysticism was almost hidden under Puritanism is not so much a proof of the weakness of the mystic nature as of the strength of the Puritan doctrine and of the current interest in theological battles. Now that the dust of controversy has settled and our interest is no longer in debates on predestination, we are beginning to see and understand the mysticism of Edwards.

Even his contemporaries remarked that Edwards was more eloquent in expounding the love of God than in demonstrating his unpitying punishment of the wicked, though sermons on the latter theme were always popular. One sermon that must have caused some little perplexity among the practical men of Northampton set forth the idea that God communicates His will to man in other ways than through the physical senses. The preacher's favorite text was "I am the rose of Sharon and the lily of the valley," and his favorite words were "sweet and bright." To-day the secret of the man is at least partly revealed. Jonathan Edwards was a thorough mystic, believing in the worth of the inner light and holding that direct converse with God is entirely possible. His favorite text shows a mystic submergence of the self, and his favorite words are the keynotes of mystics everywhere. One finds unmistakable traces of mysticism in Edwards's works with a feeling of profound melancholy. Old-time Puritanism conquered a man who, but for his entanglement in theology, might have stood beside such men as Roger Williams, John Woolman, Emerson, Thoreau, and

Walt Whitman. Puritanism thrust Edwards back into the company of the Mathers and the other theocrats. He does not belong there.

BENJAMIN FRANKLIN—THE EPITOME OF THE EIGHTEENTH CENTURY

In 1777 France was all agog. Some ten years earlier Rousseau had announced his famous doctrine that civilization destroys the fine natural elements in man and that the best people are those who live closest to nature. The whole belief was violently anti-aristocratic. Now there had arrived in Paris an ambassador from the newest and most democratic country in the world. Monsieur Benjamin Franklin, American citizen and no aristocrat either, was at the French court to represent the natural men and women of a new world, uncorrupted by the civilization of centuries. The ambassador was everything that even Rousseau could have asked. He charmed all who met him by the simplicity of his manner, his natural courtesy, his wit, his wisdom, and his love of science. Here was indeed a natural man, a living proof of Rousseau's doctrines. How very exciting!

If the French had only stopped their chorus of admiration long enough to analyze the object of their praise, they would have seen that in entertaining Franklin they were entertaining much more than a natural democrat from America. The witty American was all that the Parisians thought and a great deal more. He was the epitome of the eighteenth century. In an age that was beginning to reverence the idea of equality, he was the representative of farmers and merchants, meeting the aristocrats of the old world only to demonstrate the inferiority of the cultured élite to the natural man. In an age that relied implicitly upon science and reason, he was one of the world's great experimental scientists. Among a people who loved wisdom seasoned with wit, Franklin delighted all with his practical common sense and enchanted his hearers by his sallies of wit. Among the adherents of deism, the American was renowned for his calm and reasoned allegiance to the religion of nature. In a society that was coming to be dominated by the commercial classes, Franklin was a conspicuous example of one who by his own exertion climbed from the deepest obscurity to dizzy eminence. The Boston runaway, the apprentice printer, the thrifty tradesman, the busy man-of-affairs, now stood before kings and lords speaking for a sovereign people who had just declared their separation from the ways of monarchs and titled aristocrats. And in this same Philadelphia tradesman centered most of the currents of the eighteenth century, and from him radiated much of the nineteenth.

Franklin's Career.—No one should be allowed to retell the story of Franklin's early life and struggles, for it has been inimitably told in the *Autobiography,* one of the glories of our literature. This little book contains something valuable for every type of reader, and there are few students of American life or literature who are not thankful to the instructor or friend who first opened for them its pages. If the reader likes a good story well told, the *Autobiography* gives delight by its dramatic passages related in perfect narrative style. If the reader wants inspiration from the reading of successful struggles, there is the story of America's first self-made man, who, like most of his kind, was unwilling to minimize the grimness of the struggle or the completeness of the triumph. To the reader who likes the record of human nature with all its faults and virtues, the autobiography stands as a great human document with few faults omitted and fewer virtues unacknowledged.

Franklin was born in Boston in 1706, three years later than Jonathan Edwards, but aside from chronology there is no parallel in the lives of the two great leaders. Edwards, the crown prince of a ruling Puritan family, was destined by birth to a good education and an influential post in society, whereas Franklin, the youngest son of five generations of youngest sons, was merely one of the seventeen children of an obscure Boston candle-maker. He was destined to have only what he could get for himself, but his ability to get things was limited only by the supply of things to be got. His formal schooling was of the scantiest description, but despite this lack of formal education he read and studied until he alone of all Americans before 1775 was adjudged the equal of the trained scientific and philosophic minds of Europe.

Young Franklin's reading was in well-selected works. His first books were the theological treatises that he found in his father's library, but these he soon discarded for *Pilgrim's Progress, Essays* by Defoe, Locke's work on the human understanding, Plutarch, and, most influential of all, Addison's *Spectator Papers.* Franklin had been early apprenticed to his brother, a Boston printer who was about to start a newspaper, and, as the boy did the innumerable duties about the shop that were a part of a printer's training, he set for himself the task of learning to write in the style of Addison. It was as if an American boy of to-day were to model his style on that of the most capable and successful New York or London journalist. As Franklin learned about type and presses, he gradually developed his skill in writing, and before long he was writing articles for publication.

In the meantime, James Franklin, the brother, was in trouble with the authorities. He had criticized certain things in Boston, and Cotton Mather was thundering at him and his paper. Finally he was clapped into jail, leaving the struggling journal in the keeping of Benjamin. The paper flourished so well in the hands of the youngster that, by the time of James's release, Benjamin was beginning to sense his own ability and importance. Naturally the older Franklin was a bit jealous and somewhat inclined to fault finding, though one may be sure that Benjamin was rather trying to his employer-brother. Soon a break came, and Benjamin, a runaway apprentice, forsook the frigidly intolerant atmosphere of Boston for a more congenial clime.

He went first to New York, but, finding nothing in that town to attract an ambitious young printer, moved on to Philadelphia. He reached the Quaker capital a most bedraggled and forlorn creature without friends and with only a dollar in money. Thus did the seventeen-year-old boy enter unheralded into the city that he was later to dominate for almost fifty years.

Soon Franklin found work, but he quit Philadelphia to go to London on a wild goose chase, being sent thither by a scoundrelly governor to buy equipment for a print shop. When he reached London he found himself again friendless in a strange city and virtually penniless. The governor never had any intention of supplying him with funds. Once more Franklin went to work, this time in a very congenial atmosphere, for intellectual London was under the influence of Newton, the aged scientist. These months in England must be accounted among the most valuable of Franklin's early life. He met new people, absorbed new ideas, and began the scientific and philosophic inquiries that later were to bring him so great honor. After eighteen months in London he returned to Philadelphia.

Back home once more, Franklin entered upon a career of un-checkered success. He soon started a print shop and managed his business with such industry and thrift and so canny a knowledge of human nature that he was able to retire a wealthy man at the early age of forty-two. He pursued his scientific experiments until he became probably the most famous "natural philosopher" in the world. With his leisure and his private means he was the logical man for public service. He began his work in the service of his city and colony, then became postmaster general of all America, repre-sented the colonies at the English court with tact and ability, served in the Continental Congress, went to France as American representative, and at last returned as an old man to have honors and duties heaped upon him until he complained that his fellow citizens "have eaten my flesh and seem resolved to pick my bones." Finally he wound up a most amazingly active and successful public life by serving in the constitutional convention of 1787. He died in 1790, and at the news of his death both the American Congress and the French Assembly adjourned out of respect to the great man.

Franklin the Public-Spirited Citizen.—Franklin was the first citizen of Philadelphia. He was one of the wealthiest men of his city, the most prominent, and beyond question the most useful. Chambers of commerce, civic committees, and service clubs were unknown in Franklin's day, but, if those institutions had existed in eighteenth century Philadelphia, we may be sure that he would have had a leading part in all of them. As it was he always lent a hand in all city improvements. Acting upon an idea gathered in London, he founded the first public library in America. The fire hazard in the town led him to organize a company of fire fighters. A shrewd suggestion of his resulted in the successful financing of a hospital that is still in existence. He helped found an academy that grew into the University of Pennsylvania. The streets of Philadel-phia were unpaved, dirty, and unlighted until Franklin prevailed upon his townsmen to pave the streets, hire them cleaned regularly, and erect street lights of recent and superior design—Franklin's own, by the way—which eliminated smudgy chimneys. All these activi-ties—and the list is not exhausted—show Franklin's determination to be a valuable citizen and to aid in the material progress of his city. It is easy to object that his activities were all materialistic in aim, that Franklin and his work lack the rich spirituality of

Edwards, Emerson, and many another. The charge must be admitted. Franklin was the true son of a materialistic century; he could be none other than a practical man of affairs. If, as a recent writer has said, Franklin was more concerned in the paving of Market Street, Philadelphia, than in the golden paving of the New Jerusalem, not all the fault can be assessed against the man. America and the eighteenth century were both partly to blame.

America as a whole has adopted the Franklin policy and interests. The prevailing characteristic of our country has been a worship of progress, civic betterment and public improvements, and well-housed, efficient school systems. It is easy to see the danger in this practice. A nation devoted to material progress is apt to lose sight of many valuable aspects of life, to measure progress by the money accumulated, and to babble with foolish enthusiasm at every mention of "progress." That there is a danger in Franklin's example should not blind us to the worth of the man's life. Colonial America was a hard place for a home. Life was uncomfortable for the lack of a few mechanical contrivances. Franklin lent his inventive talent and his personal influence toward making this country a more pleasant and convenient home.

Franklin the Scientist.—Reason was the watchword of the eighteenth century, and, since Franklin was wholly a child of his time, reason was his watchword. From his earliest days, irrational ideas had been repulsive to him, and after his stay in the stronghold of English scientific thought, he became consciously a rational philosopher. His interest in physics led him to attempt an experiment that proved the identity of lightning and electricity. The intensely practical mind of Franklin seized upon the significance of this discovery and the invention of the lightning rod was the next step. The experiment he made with a boy's kite was one of the notable events in the history of science, and the application of the abstract knowledge gained thereby to the practical problem of protecting houses from lightning was the portent of America's future inventive genius. The inventor had previously made himself famous among housewives by inventing the Franklin stove, a device that was a vast improvement on the hitherto universal fireplaces. So far did Franklin's scientific fame spread from Philadelphia that Yale and Harvard honored him with honorary degrees and when he went abroad world-famous scientists and philosophers delighted to do him honor. When he and Voltaire met, the French hailed the two old men as the representatives of that philosophy that had rescued mankind from fanaticism.

When a man once accused Franklin of having no religion, a wit answered that Dr. Franklin was a self-made man and like all created beings he worshiped his maker. Surely excessive modesty was not one of his faults, but neither critic even glimpsed the man's true religion. Deism was the prevailing religious tendency of the time, and Franklin never stood far from the rationalistic thought of the century. The best statement of his religion was made by the man himself in a letter written only a few weeks before his death:

You desire to know something of my religion. It is the first time I have been questioned upon it. But I cannot take your curiosity amiss, and shall endeavor in a few words to gratify it. Here is my creed. I believe in one God, creator of the Universe. That he governs it by his providence; that he ought to be worshipped; that the most acceptable service we render to him is doing good to his other children; that the soul of man is immortal, and will be treated in another life respecting its conduct in this; these I take to be the fundamental principles of all sound religion and I regard them as you do in whatever sect I meet with them.

As to Jesus of Nazareth, my opinion of whom you particularly desire, I think the system of morals and his religion, as he left them to us, the best the world ever saw or is likely to see; but I apprehend it has received various corrupting changes, and I have, with most of the present dissenters in England, some doubt as to his divinity; though it is a question I do not dogmatize upon, having never studied it, and I think it needless to busy myself with it now, when I expect soon an opportunity of knowing the truth with less trouble. I see no harm, however, in its being believed, if that belief has the good consequence, as it probably has, of making his doctrines more respected and better observed.

As he wittily remarked, he soon had an opportunity of knowing the truth, for he died only five weeks after writing these words.

In a postscript to the letter from which the foregoing quotation is made, Franklin said: "I have ever let others enjoy their religious sentiments, without reflecting on them for those that appeared to me unsupportable and even absurd." This touches on another fine trait in the man, his tolerance. Benjamin Franklin was ever an easy man to live with, for he fully realized the futility and folly of quarreling with those with whom he had to associate. Our history has no record of a more tolerant and sensible man than the first citizen of Philadelphia.

Franklin: Economist and Politician.—In his economics Franklin broke sharply with mercantilism, the old theory that the state should exercise a sharp control over business and industry, and accepted the views of his friend, Adam Smith, that the best government for business is that which governs as little as possible. This doctrine is the laissez-faire theory that soon became so popular. Franklin's advocacy of laissez-faire was probably caused, in part, by his desire to see American business unhampered by the repressive laws of a distant parliament and king. In his views on the origin of wealth Franklin again accepted certain ideas that were coming to be current. The physiocrats were a school of economic thinkers who believed that all wealth is derived from land. They thought that with wealth originating in the soil, the whole system of economics could be reduced to an exact science like geometry or physics. The laws of nature are the correct economic laws, they said, and it is necessary for man only to discover these laws and then let them take their unimpeded course. Again Franklin, in accepting these views, reflected eighteenth century rationalism and his American environment. In an agricultural country like the new world the view that wealth has its origin in the soil is very apt to prevail. Franklin was openly agrarian in his admiration for agriculture and his distrust of manufacturing and commerce. He once wrote: "There seem to be but three ways for a nation to acquire wealth. The first is by war, as the Romans did in plundering their conquered neighbors. This is robbery. The second by commerce, which is generally cheating. The third by agriculture, the only honest way."

In his political theory Franklin was a good democrat. He was so thoroughly middle class that he could hardly have been anything else. He believed that the best government rested close to the control of the people, and that an elaborate system of checks and balances was "like putting one horse before a cart and the other behind it and whipping them both. If the horses are of equal strength, the wheels of the cart, like the wheels of government, will stand still; and if the horses are strong enough, the cart will be torn to pieces." Franklin was an advanced democrat for his day. He believed in unrestricted manhood suffrage, annual parliaments, and a unicameral legislature subject to the direct will of the voters.

In his political views, as in his economic theory, Franklin reflected the sentiment of the American farmer—agrarianism, this sentiment is called, and many a time shall we meet it between the days of Franklin and the administration of President Hoover. It is a body of doctrine, native to the soil of America and reaching its fullest development among western farmers, both in 1760 and in 1928.

Franklin as a Literary Man.—At scarcely any time in his life was Franklin a conscious man of letters. His autobiography, upon which much of his literary fame rests, was written for the eyes of his son and did not see light in its original form until a century had elapsed. *Poor Richard's Almanac,* the book that made much of Franklin's fortune and contemporary fame, was done as a bit of journalism. His other writings are state papers, letters, articles for the newspapers, and scientific studies. In none of these is literary style the most desirable quality. However, despite the lack of a conscious literary note in Franklin's writings, few authors have been so successful in creating a perfect vehicle for the transmission of their ideas.

Franklin's style in the autobiography is wholly admirable. It is so well adapted to its use that the reader is perfectly unconscious of it, and this is the decisive test of a simple narrative style. The book is gossipy, episodic, and filled with anecdotes, but the elements are so neatly welded together that the finished whole is a complete picture of Benjamin Franklin, the prudent self-made American.

Poor Richard's Almanac is a successful attempt to produce the most popular type of non-theological literature in eighteenth century America. Many almanacs were published, but none was so successful as Franklin's, for none of the other authors or compilers had Poor Richard's native wit or his skill with a pen. The proverbs that were thickly scattered through the almanac are frequently quoted to-day. Some of the commonest are:

Experience keeps a dear school, but fools will learn in no other and scarce in that.
If you will not hear reason she'll surely rap your knuckles.
'Tis hard for an empty bag to stand upright.
Silks and satins, scarlet and velvets put out the kitchen fire.
A ploughman on his legs is higher than a gentleman on his knees.
Fools make feasts, and wise men eat them.
One today is worth two tomorrows.

Sloth, like rust, consumes faster than labor wears, while the used key is always bright.

A word to the wise is enough.

Forewarned, forearmed.

Keep thy shop and thy shop will keep thee.

He that would have a short Lent, let him borrow money to be repaid at Easter.

Lost time is never found again.

Three removes are as bad as a fire.

He that riseth late must trot all day.

These proverbs, used as "fillers" in the almanac, are one of the secrets of Poor Richard's popularity and Franklin's consequent prosperity. They are merely short witty sayings, embodying the chief virtues of the middle class, and appealing mightily to that portion of the American people. Poor Richard praised industry, thrift, honest business enterprise and found opportunity to speak a word for the democratic plowman and to raise his voice in support of reason. Middle-class America first became articulate in the pages of Poor Richard.

Franklin's numerous other works were created for utilitarian purposes. They are political letters and treatises, arguments against the British policy from 1760 to 1775, and scientific speculations. They all embody the qualities that distinguish the autobiography and Poor Richard—shrewd common sense, prudence, and reasonableness. It would probably surprise Franklin if he could know that to-day we regard him as the first typical American and our first great man of letters, but he would be immensely gratified to know that we prize his writings for the expression of the very qualities that he most highly valued in his own life.

Franklin's Significance.—Enough has already been said of Franklin's significance. He did nothing and wrote nothing that was not significant of the man and of the time. The fact that America adopted most of the Franklin characteristics only heightens the importance of this great eighteenth century figure.

The three important traits of Franklin are his rationalism, his utilitarian preferences, and his democracy. The first came from the age in which he lived, the second from the middle class that gave birth to the man, and the third from an acquaintance with the desires and problems of American small farmers—the frontier class. Every proposal submitted to Franklin must stand these three tests: Is it reasonable? Is it useful? Is it in accord with the principle of equality?   Above everything Franklin insisted that nothing be allowed to prevent or impede the steady material progress and welfare of the deserving man.

It is too much to say that practical-minded America has consciously followed the example set by Franklin. It is nearer the truth to say that the shrewd and sensible Franklin of all Americans first trod the path that the entire nation was destined later to travel. With his interest in practical mechanics and invention, his insistence upon progress and public improvements, and his desire to "get along" with his neighbors Franklin was the forerunner of the nation that he helped found.

When all is said, it must be conceded that Franklin was a very great man. Upon the monument erected in Philadelphia over his grave are the words, attributed to Turgot: "He snatched lightning from the clouds and the sceptre from tyrants."   Let it not be forgotten that Franklin did these deeds to make the world a happier, safer, more rational and more prosperous dwelling place for the children of men.

JOHN WOOLMAN: MYSTIC

(1720-1772)

Edwards's laborious theological disputations seem to have for their aim the "justification of the ways of God" to a rebellious and skeptical generation; Franklin's aim was to prove the fundamental worth of such homely virtues as thrift, prudence, and industry; but John Woolman as quietly and resolutely turned his back on theological argument as on the gospel of progress and prosperity. Woolman lived with but one purpose. His aim was to keep his eyes on the inner light until his whole being would be suffused with the love that was God and he would feel himself, body and soul, a part of the Infinite.

John Woolman was born in Northampton, New Jersey, of a Quaker family. After a slight education he became successively a clerk and a tailor. A considerable portion of his time was spent on the road in America as an itinerant preacher and teacher to the Quakers of the middle colonies. In 1772 he went to England where he died at York on October 7 of the same year.

Outwardly Woolman's life is the "short and simple annals of the poor," but inwardly it was one of amazing wealth.   The poor

Quaker tailor was never called to stand before kings or to defend a nation from the rapacity of a corrupt government, as Franklin was; nor did he ever attempt the herculean task of fortifying a decaying theological system, as Edwards did. Woolman's task was more titanic than that of either of his great contemporaries. It was the bringing of his own and other lives into harmony with the divine love, and in the achieving of this harmony it was necessary to call attention to and denounce certain money-begotten practices that made for cruelty, indifference, and unhappiness.

John Woolman was a true Quaker, following the promptings of his conscience and mindful ever of the inner light, but he was no quietist in the face of social wrong. When he was a clerk of twenty-two a request to make out a bill of sale for a slave led him into a way of thinking that soon developed into a rooted aversion to slavery, an institution that was then prevalent among the American Quakers. Four years later he wrote his little pamphlet on the keeping of negroes, in which he argued that black slaves were "of the same spirit with ourselves," that they were endowed with certain natural rights, and that the keeping of these people in bondage was neither righteous nor holy. So earnest were the arguments of Woolman against slavery, and so great was the moral prestige of the man, that within a few years slavery disappeared among the Quakers. The victory of Woolman is a prime example of moral reform unaided by any appeal to fear, prejudice, or economic interest.

Woolman's social teachings did not stop with an interest in the abolition of slavery. Beard and Beard's *The Rise of American Civilization,* says, "In the writings of this simple workman . . . are to be found the roots of American intellectual radicalism." This statement seems to be supported by irrefutable evidence. Woolman wrote and spoke on such topics as labor, the schools, considerations on trade, poverty, and the "Right Use of the Lord's Outward Gifts." He questioned the ethics of private holding of land, saying that the Creator of the earth is the owner of it, and so earnestly did he plead the cause of the poor, beseeching short working hours and good living conditions, that his wealthy co-religionists, alarmed at the radicalism of his social doctrines, managed to prevent the publication of the plea for the poor for full thirty years. Woolman was convinced that the mad passion for wealth was productive of much oppression and war. Hence he warned those who held property to use their wealth in the way that would be most highly approved by heaven. Wherever human wrong existed Woolman attacked it in the simplest and most direct fashion, always fortified by the mystic's faith in the righteousness of his cause and the divinity of his inspiration.

Woolman has a twofold significance. He was one of the few eighteenth century Quakers to leave a full and revealing account of his religious experience and, what is more important, he was the first intellectual radical to question certain established economic institutions, attacking them, like many a later radical reformer, from the vantage point of a religious mystic to whom all lives are sacred and to whom the greatest of blessings is individual liberty.

CRÈVECŒUR: FRONTIERSMAN AND FOREIGN OBSERVER

Hector St. John Crèvecœur (1735-1813) has a double claim to distinction in American literature. First, the man was one of the earliest and also one of the shrewdest of those many foreigners who have come to America for sojourns of varying lengths and produced books describing this land and its people, and, second, he was the first frontiersman in America who clearly recognized the importance of the frontier and set down his opinions where all might read. In both rôles he has had most distinguished successors, but few of these have equaled the early writer in the accuracy and penetrating insight of observation or in the clarity and incisiveness of presentation.

Crèvecœur was a Frenchman from the province of Normandy who came to America about 1760, and after extensive travels over the continent of North America, which he probably knew better than any traveler of his time, he became a frontier farmer in Orange county, New York. Here he led an idyllic life observing nature and society with an inquiring and friendly eye. The Revolution shattered Crèvecœur's peaceful existence. Failing to take either side in the preliminary squabbles, he became suspected by both the patriots and the English. After being confined in New York in a British prison, he was allowed to sail for Europe. In 1781 he reached France. After the Revolution he returned to America to find his wife dead, his family scattered, and his house burnt. For a time he was French consul in New York. He died in France in 1813.

Crèvecœur and the American Frontier.—The frontier is the fundamental fact in Crèvecœur's life. Of all Americans, native and immigrant, he was the first to sense in a broad way the economic and social significance of free land. Crèvecœur thought that a new people was emerging in America, but he attributed rather slight importance to the mixture of blood—the melting pot idea—that seems to many the dominant fact in our national life. He believed that the most significant thing in America was the environment, and to him the environment was literally the frontier. "Men are like plants," said he, "as the goodness and flavor of fruits proceed from the peculiar soil . . . in which they grow. We are nothing but what we derive from the air we breathe, the climate we inhabit, the government we obey, the system of religion we profess, and the mode of our employment." The true American was to be seen on the frontier, where the environment had an unimpeded chance to work its way. "He who would wish to see America in its proper light . . . must visit our extended line of frontiers. . . ."

It was the chance for economic independence that Crèvecœur found so valuable and attractive on the frontier. The poor European or native American could move to the region of cheap or free land and shortly acquire acres of tillable ground, cattle and improvements, ample leisure, and all the things that give stability and independence to the small farmer. A confirmed agrarian was Crèvecœur, for to him the happiest of men and the main supports of any nation are the small farmers. Like all agrarians he had for his basic economic doctrine the belief that all wealth ultimately comes from the soil. This is the chief element in the physiocratic theory. Like all true American frontiersmen, Crèvecœur was cheerfully optimistic. He is continually drawing parallels between the American and the European, always to the disadvantage of the latter. The European is in a stationary society; a man is born into a social level from which death alone removes him. He lacks courage, ambition, restless energy simply because these qualities have no incentive to develop. Society cramps and kills the natural ability of men. Such is not the case in America. The free land, vast economic opportunities, the absence of a hampering population closely crowded together, the strong leveling tendencies of frontier life, all make a new man out of the immigrant—an American out of a European.

French Elements in Crèvecœur.—Some of Crèvecœur's characteristics owe their origin to his French blood and training. In his love for nature and his admiration for the natural man he rivaled Rousseau. In his letters there is no hint of a scientific acquaintance with the ways of nature but there is expressed a constant pleasure in living close to the flowers, woods, and fields. Again Crèvecœur indicates his French origins by his marked humanitarianism. He loved peace and hated war; he was concerned with justice to all and with the welfare of every member of society; he wished to see the spirit of tolerance and independence, characteristic of small farmers, extended to all mankind. In short his chief intellectual interests connect him firmly with French revolutionary philosophy. In elaborating this philosophy on the American frontier Crèvecœur was the forerunner of many other men, notably Jefferson, Benton, and Lincoln.

However clearly Crèvecœur may have written, the man is important to us not as a literary figure but as a great landmark in the development of American thought. In his works we find French philosophy developing in the congenial atmosphere of the American frontier. The man is a close combination of two enormously important elements in American thought, the cosmopolitan and the frontier.

SUGGESTED READINGS

Allen: *Jonathan Edwards*. Boston. 1890.
Beard and Beard: *The Rise of American Civilization*. New York. 1927.
    pp. 122-188.
Faust: *Jonathan Edwards*. New York. 1932.
    This work has a valuable introduction.
Faÿ: *Franklin*. Boston. 1929.
McGiffert: *Jonathan Edwards*. New York. 1932.
    Satisfactory treatment of a difficult subject.
Mitchell: *St. Jean de Crèvecœur*. New York. 1916.
Parkes: *The Fiery Puritan*. New York. 1930.
    Another treatment of Edwards.
Savelle: *Seeds of Liberty*. New York. 1948.
    Eighteenth Century thought. Most valuable.
Van Doren: *Benjamin Franklin*. New York. 1938.
Whitney: *John Woolman: American Quaker*. Boston. 1942.
Winslow: *Jonathan Edwards*. New York. 1941.
    The most useful biography.

CHAPTER VI

REVOLUTION AND REACTION

Influences Making for Revolution.—Historians have so great difficulty in disentangling the causes of our struggle for independence that they usually preface their chapter on the reasons for the Revolution with the declaration made by John Adams in 1818 that "the true history of the revolution can not be recovered." Adams was so active in fomenting the war and so intelligent an observer of all that he saw that his word naturally carries considerable weight with present-day writers.

Although it may be true that the ultimate causes of the Revolution are hopelessly obscure, still it is possible to find a few general and more than a few specific reasons for the break with England. There were causes economic, political, social, and geographic, some operating among the merchants, some among the southern planters, some among the small farmers of the West. The Puritan of New England had one grievance, the Episcopalian tobacco grower of Virginia another, while the New York merchant chafed under restrictions to which other classes were wholly indifferent. So diverse were the reasons for discontent that the chief task of such agitators as Samuel Adams was not to discover excuses for fighting but to keep all sections and classes in the mood to fight all at the same time. It was necessary to combine these divergent reasons in a few easily grasped, general slogans. "Taxation without representation" was such a slogan. It was a cry readily understood all over the colonies, but to the different sections of the country and the different classes in those sections it meant widely different things. To-day the task of historians is to interpret the meaning of this slogan to the various people of the colonies—a very difficult task.

In the first place, geography itself made for the Revolution. Although the Atlantic was by no means an impassable barrier between England and her colonies, still the way was long, and as much as six months elapsed between the sailing and the docking of a vessel. Emigrants could cross with no enormous difficulty, but for the king's government in London to exercise a strict control over America by means of direct and detailed orders was quite an impossibility. But the effect of geography is not exhausted with the Atlantic Ocean. Within the colonies distances were immense, and routes of communication almost totally lacking, save along the few rivers. A farmer on the western frontier in Virginia was far more independent of the king's governor in Williamsburg than the king's governor was of his master in London. Undertaking to hold America in British grasp looks very difficult from the standpoint of geography, even if there had been no other forces making for disunion.

As already pointed out, the people of the colonies were not all of one race. True the English predominated, but not all of them were loyal to the mother country, and the hundreds of thousands of Scotch-Irish and Germans on the frontier were notable for their anti-English prejudices. Scattered through many of the colonies were thousands of unassimilated non-English stock who owed nothing to England save a few grudges and who felt no bonds of affection or loyalty binding them to the British crown. Among the English colonists themselves, thousands were indentured servants or direct descendants of those bound to servitude. Many carried vivid recollections of English jails or workhouses, while others smarted under the recollection of grinding poverty endured in England. These different racial influences made revolution an easier matter than it otherwise would have been.

One very good reason for American restiveness after 1760 was the new spirit of the British government. From the early days of settlement to the accession of George III the English crown was relatively weak. Some of the kings were quarreling with Parliament, some were kept busy with wars and politics on the Continent, and some were frankly not interested in anything at all. Under such conditions it is not surprising that the American colonies developed a certain degree of both self-government and self-reliance. But George III came to the throne with no distractions in England or on the Continent to divert his attention, and he determined to bring the thirteen American colonies into a closer union with the mother country. To effect this aim it was necessary to enforce certain old laws and pass some new regulations. Both steps met with spirited opposition from the Americans.

The mercantile theory was the incentive for England's government of her colonies during the whole colonial period. Under this theory the colonies were looked upon as mere sources of English wealth. Each outpost under British dominion must be productive of wealth to the home government—and to the English merchants. Colonial welfare was never considered; such a question would have been irrelevant to the aim expressed by the mercantile theory. That virtually all the colonists were poor, that many were hopelessly in debt to English merchants meant nothing to the king and his ministers. All colonies existed only for the profit of the home country, and the American group was no exception.

In pursuance of its aims the English government at various times passed certain laws. The oldest and most effective regulations were the navigation acts which provided that all trade with the colonies was to be carried on English-built ships manned by English sailors. In general the colonists were allowed to sell their products in the best market, English or Continental, but there were certain irritating exceptions. Tobacco, shipmasts, turpentine, and certain other articles had to be sent to England. On the other hand, American importers were compelled to buy all their goods from English merchants. Furthermore colonial manufacturing was greatly restricted by the ban on the making of woolen cloth, hats, and steel. To the American business man probably the most objectionable law was that forbidding the colonies to issue paper money. Since England kept America constantly drained of gold and silver, the use of paper currency was almost a necessity. However, the issue of such money was strictly forbidden. All these restrictive laws, although they were probably more lenient than those of any other European colonial power, had the effect of goading the Americans into either sullen acquiescence or active opposition.

American opposition to English wishes was not a new thing in 1775. In general the colonial government was carried on by a governor appointed by the king, a council named by the governor, and the assembly which was elected by the voters of the colony. Breaks between the governor and the assembly were very common occurrences, so very common that a state of chronic disagreement was the ordinary condition. Since the members of the assembly had the power to vote or to withhold appropriations of money, the colonials frequently had the better of the squabbles. These disagreements with their royal governors tended to get the more audacious Americans into the way of thinking that opposition to the

king's representative was not treason and that a victory over roya..
wishes was not impossible.

American Classes and the Revolution.—Broadly speaking there
were three influential groups in the colonies during the Revolutionary agitation. These were the merchants of the northern seaboard towns, the planters south of the Potomac, and the small
farmers of the frontier. The great influence of the frontier will be
discussed shortly.

The wealthy merchants, who were congregated in towns from
Philadelphia north to New Hampshire, were naturally greatly distressed by the navigation and trade laws. They opposed these
regulations in a serious fashion but they were hardly willing to go
the lengths that the laborers and farmers were clamoring to travel.
But the early opposition of the wealthy class to England was of
extreme value to the agitators, for if a merchant-prince opposed the
mother country, that action lent an air of respectability to the
opposition of the propertyless. However, at the outbreak of the
Revolution, many of the merchants refused to join the revolt. It
is reported that two hundred of them left Boston when it was
evacuated by the British army early in the war.

The planters of the South had their own reasons for discontent.
The chief of these was the fact that most planters were perpetually
in debt to London merchants. The southern gentleman lived on a
grand scale, indulging his extravagant tastes with little thought of
the cost. As a result, the debts of the planters were actually
hereditary, being passed on from father to son like the plantation itself. Since the chief crops of the planters were sold in English markets at prices fixed by the Englishman, the colonials saw
little chance to pay their obligations save by the use of paper
money, and such action was forbidden by Parliament. Hence a
revolt from English dominion looked attractive to many planters.

There was another way out of debt, a way glimpsed by such
men as Washington, who was not burdened by his debts, and that
was the opening of the vast western domain beyond the Alleghanies.
Many Virginia planters were planning to recoup their fortunes by
removing to the Ohio country or by speculating in the land, but
the king set aside the entire area west of the mountains as an
Indian reservation and forbade further land grants in this region.
The Quebec Act of 1774 extended the boundaries of Quebec to the
Ohio River and transferred the control of this land to the crown.

Clearly it was the English intention to maintain the Ohio country as an Indian hunting ground and fur-producing region, all to the great enrichment of the Londoner and the impoverishment of the colonies. It is said that this act forbidding western migration did as much as any one thing to make a revolutionist out of George Washington.

The Puritan Spirit and the Revolution.—The New England Puritans were never the meekest and the most dutiful children of the empire. In the beginning only those came to America whose views were too extreme to allow comfortable residence in England, and the very fact that many came under the lash of persecution embittered them and their children's children against the government. Furthermore the New England colonies were allowed to develop according to their bent, and, however undemocratic some of them may have been, all enjoyed a certain measure of self-government that they clung to with utmost stubbornness. These facts alone would hardly have made the Puritans of New England happy to obey King George. But there were other reasons.

If there was anything that the Puritan prided himself on, it was his personal godliness and the extremely moral tone of his whole social order. Now it must be admitted that eighteenth century English society was not notable for its purity. The shocking state of public morality was equaled only by the still more shocking state of private morality among the ruling classes. In public affairs parliamentary seats were bought and sold like merchantable commodities, bribery was the accepted way of getting bills enacted into laws, every official was open to bribes, and English society was tainted by the presence of many whose vulgar extravagances were made possible only by the appalling extortion and misgovernment of the helpless natives of India. One may be sure that the New England guardians of righteousness were not long in discovering the failings of their rulers. That the English lower and middle classes lived pure lives was little satisfaction to the Massachusetts clergyman; those classes had nothing to say about the unspeakably corrupt government. No one would contend that English corruption was a primary cause of the Revolution, but it was merely one of the many things that aggravated the ill-feeling between the colonies and the king's government. A Puritan would have had more hesitation in rebelling against a ruler who was wholly upright than in striking at one whose moral offenses smelled to Heaven.

A more potent cause of trouble in New England than English moral decline was the provision of the Quebec Act which guaranteed the French Catholics of the province free exercise of their religion. By the same act the southern boundary of the province was fixed at the Ohio River. This provision fanned the indignation of New England clergymen to flames. A recent historian has remarked that the reaction of the New Englander to the English toleration of Catholicism was hardly to the credit of those men whose ancestors came to America to worship as they wished. But tolerance was not the chief virtue of the Puritans, and the clergymen and political agitators raved to appreciative audiences about the "menace to Protestantism" and the "growth of popery in America." Revolutionary processions and mobs in New England frequently carried banners calling for "no popery," while the ministers blustered and stormed from every pulpit.

Another contributing cause to revolutionary agitation in New England was the fear of the Episcopal church and more particularly the fear that England was about to set up a bishop in North America. To Americans of to-day such fears are laughable, but to the Puritans who had fled from the Church of England and the domination of bishops the matter was not so humorous. The thought of an established church set up by law in all the colonies, that is, a church supported by taxation just as the state is supported, was highly displeasing to many an American, and to none was it so distasteful as to the Puritans. The creation of a bishop of North America was looked upon as the first step toward the establishment of the Episcopal church, and for many years English churchmen ominously discussed the question of an American bishop.

Although the Puritans were affected by many of the same influences that were felt in various colonies, it is probably safe to say that Puritanism, because of its unique history and temperament, responded to stimuli that were felt slightly or not at all by other classes. At all events the loyalists looked upon the Presbyterian and Congregational clergymen as arrant traitors and preachers of sedition, and on the other hand Revolutionary agitators considered the ministers among their most potent assistants. "Do the ministers preach against oppression?" anxiously inquired John Adams in a letter to his wife, and the answer was that the meeting house resounded every Sunday to the most satisfactory doctrines.

The Cosmopolitan Spirit.—The influence of foreign thought in Revolutionary literature is enormous. The causes of the outbreak were purely American, but when the native agitators sat down to rationalize the Revolution and justify it before the world, they relied largely upon foreign thought to supply the philosophical reasons.

In the early days of Revolutionary agitation colonial spokesmen based their argument against the passage of restrictive laws upon the fact that the colonists as British citizens were entitled to the time-honored privileges of Englishmen. In formulating this argument all English law and constitutional history were raked over for evidence. In this stage of the debate Blackstone, the great commentator on common law, was one of the authors most widely read. "I hear as many Blackstones are sold in America as in England," declared Burke, who, almost alone of all Englishmen, understood America and knew what the Americans were reading and thinking.

When the colonists saw that an appeal to the king based upon the immemorial privileges of Englishmen was of no avail, they shifted their argument to the broader ground of natural rights. For many years it was the custom of historians to speak of the natural rights philosophy as being exclusively French. To-day we realize that such an assumption is totally false. The eighteenth century French thinkers knew this philosophy and wrote of it learnédly and enthusiastically, but they borrowed their original ideas from certain English thinkers, chief of whom was John Locke. This great thinker's works, especially his second treatise on government, were in the library of virtually every American intellectual and Locke was quoted more often than any other writer was.

But the colonial leaders did not stop with Locke. John Adams read and cited such men as Harrington, Hobbes, Hooker, Montesquieu, Rousseau, and Grotius. Franklin knew Sidney, Milton, and Montesquieu in addition to Locke. Samuel Adams and Alexander Hamilton knew all the writers just mentioned, while John Dickinson, "the Pennsylvania farmer," had read Hooker, Hume, Locke, and Montesquieu. Jefferson was widely read in political theory especially that of Locke. Passages from the Declaration of Independence almost exactly parallel sentences from the second treatise on government. To our surprise relatively obscure men like southern planters or New England clergymen had a wide knowledge of European political philosophy.

Any account of the Revolution that slights the cosmopolitan spirit fails to take account of the very force that rationalized and gave coherent unity to the diverse and confused aims of the Americans, that linked the struggle for liberty in the new world with the long struggle in the old, and that gave the American revolutionists a standing in the eyes of European intellectuals.

The Frontier and the Revolution.—If the wealthy merchants entered somewhat gingerly into revolutionary agitation and if many refused to do more than make an academic protest, the frontiersmen suffered from no such hesitancy. The proposal to separate from England drew a prompt and enthusiastic approval from the West, and the frontiersmen with true pioneer spirit began to fight and left philosophizing to the parsons and the politicians. The spirit of the frontier was displayed when the Scotch-Irish farmers of Mecklenburg county, North Carolina, met and declared their independence of Great Britain months before the Continental Congress seriously discussed that momentous step. Still more strikingly was the frontier spirit shown on field after field of the war. Without the battle of Oriskany, fought by General Herkimer and his German farmers, the great victory of Saratoga might have been impossible. In the South one of the decisive conflicts was at King's Mountain, a victory won entirely by Westerners.

Behind the frontiersman and his readiness to fight for independence lay the frontier itself with its leveling tendencies and great physical independence. Class distinctions simply did not exist there, and England was a country of sharp class divisions. Every blow struck at the king's army was in the eyes of the Westerner a blow of democracy against aristocracy. The frontier was restless, even to the point of resistance, under the control of seaboard lawyers and merchants, but such control was infinitely to be preferred to that of a vigilant and harsh English government. From its very psychology the frontier was a hotbed of anti-English feeling for years before the outbreak of the war.

There were certain generalized grievances of the colonists that the frontiersman had no trouble in understanding. Chief among these was the outcry of taxation without representation. For a long time the frontier had considered itself discriminated against by the people of Tidewater. Steadily population had been moving to the western counties of the various colonies, but the representation allowed the West in the assemblies had not been increased, despite the deep disgust of the frontier. Thus when Revolutionary agitators

inveighed against taxation without representation even the most un-
lettered farmer of the West knew exactly what the argument was
all about. His share in the war needed no further rationalizing.

Another cause of western discontent with English rule was the
prohibition of settlement beyond the mountains. For several generations the colonists had been dammed up behind the mountain
barrier, and to have the British king forbid settlement of Kentucky
and Ohio just about the time that the hardiest pioneers were reaching out for the new lands was an injury that the West could not forgive. That the West ardently desired the Ohio country is readily
enough shown by the fact that George Rogers Clark and a band of
intrepid frontiersmen captured the British posts of Cahokia, Kas-
kaskia, and Vincennes, and thus gave the American peace commis-
sioners a strong reason for demanding the captured territory when
making the treaty of peace.

In short the frontier with its democratic, leveling tendencies had
already fully prepared its people for a break with England when
revolutionary agitation was started. The frontiersman needed no
political philosophy to justify his fighting; he already understood
what was meant by taxation without representation. Once in the
fight the backwoodsmen rendered a great service to their cause on
many a battle field and especially in their capture of the Northwest
Territory.

Revolutionary Leaders and Literature.—Like all revolutions the
American revolt was preceded by a war of propaganda. To the
American agitator printed propaganda was an easy and quick way
of scattering his views, unifying colonial aims, and fanning the waning zeal of his fellows. To the Tory—Loyalist, he was sometimes
called—political literature offered the best way of combating the
pernicious ideas of disloyal colonists. Printing presses were busy,
and the land was filled with handbills, pamphlets, sermons, and
more ambitious books in which everything was discussed from the
natural rights of man to the cost of horseshoe nails. That most
of this literature is to-day known only to professional historians
is no reflection upon the literary taste of our generation; much of
it was merely hurried journalistic writing, meant only for the moment and interesting to belated readers neither for its style nor its
content. However, some of the propagandists deserve more than
passing notice.

SAMUEL ADAMS

(1722-1803)

During his lifetime Samuel Adams of Boston was admitted by friend and foe alike to be the firebrand of the American Revolution. Subsequent generations neglected him because his ardent democracy, that was so agreeable to American ears before and during the Revolution, was a trifle too ardent for those guiding the new nation after the successful termination of the war. One of the duties of this age is to reëstablish the fame of Samuel Adams, our staunchest democrat of revolutionary New England and one of the most skillful agitators of America.

Adams was born into a cultured, prosperous family that had in it suspicions of radicalism and a love of political speculation. The father belonged to that large group in Massachusetts which earnestly desired to increase the amount of money in circulation. In other words, he was sympathetic to those who owed money. To effect his aims the elder Adams established a land bank. The decided opposition of the royal governor to the new institution caused the bank to fail, and Adams lost most of his property. In the meantime the son had taken two degrees at Harvard with the idea of entering the ministry. He found that he had small liking for this profession and studied law. Equally distasteful was the new work. Then he followed business in unsuccessful fashion until 1769 when he abandoned his private affairs to give all time to public questions. From then on Adams was a tireless journalist, pamphleteer, and letter-writer. He presided over countless meetings in Boston, served in the Continental Congress, and finished a great career by serving as governor of Massachusetts until age forced his retirement from public life.

Adams the Agitator.—Adams was our first and one of our most successful molders of public opinion. Agitators, we call his like to-day. He found American opinion vaguely discontented, yet cringingly obsequious to royal prerogative and power, and his task was to transform the Americans into a generation of revolutionists and their vague discontent into an articulate protest against specific injustices. In this work he used the ways of all agitators—the press, pulpit, the public platform, personal letters, revolutionary committees, and tireless energy. No one has ever known better than Adams the value of publicity, and if one method of appeal to the public was fruitless, he immediately tried others. That success came to him was due no less to his energy and resourcefulness than to the justice of his cause.

The first task of Adams was to create a revolutionary mood in America—to screw American indignation to the sticking point of rebellion against His Majesty King George III. Quarreling with a royal governor was one thing, but it was quite another thing to flaunt the king by taking up arms against his flag. One might quarrel with a governor and live to conduct other quarrels, but he who took up arms against the king might find himself decorating a gallows. However, it was not fear that Adams had to conquer so much as it was awe of royalty. Even to the colonists who never saw Europe or a crowned head, a king was almost sacrosanct; a divinity hedged about the royal name that made rebellion seem a sin. This psychology Adams set about to destroy. The task required years for completion, but when the first shots were fired at Lexington the work was done.

The second task of Adams, at which he worked contemporaneously with the first, was to unify the American mind and keep it constantly aroused, to keep all parts of the country inflamed over wrongs done to any one class or colony, to combine colonial grievances and state them in language that would appeal to all reading and thinking people, whether on the frontier or at the court of the king. This task was of supreme difficulty. To accomplish it required the knowledge of a mob psychologist, the pen of a persuasive writer, and the brain of a political philosopher. But it too was successfully carried out, and when the other colonies came to the rescue of beleaguered Massachusetts, Adams had a visible sign of success.

Idealism of Adams.—The reasons for Adams's implacable hostility to England are hard for us to discover. Some have thought that the ruin of his fortune permanently embittered him against the government, but this theory is weak, for the man was never greedy for money—never a self-seeker. When King George was informed that Adams was the chief trouble-maker in Massachusetts, he inquired in surprise, "Why has he not been bought off?" The query sheds a vast light at once on the king's ordinary political methods and on his ignorance of the Massachusetts agitator. Still others have thought that Samuel Adams's zeal was caused by his love of power. This theory goes farther than the preceding, but it too has its weakness. Adams may have loved power but he was certainly ready to relinquish it to others. When the war broke and men came into sweeping authority over the lives and property of others, he was willing to recede into the background and relinquish to other men the conspicuous posts. Adams never ran from responsibility, but that fact does not imply that he craved power.

Samuel Adams is best explained by saying that he was a great idealist. He sincerely loved liberty and hated aristocratic tyranny whether it was in Europe or America. He honestly believed that the majority should rule the minority, and he proved his sincerity by the devotion of his best years to the task of organizing the common people to take over governmental functions. Adams was a great democrat, and to be a consistent democrat in the face of popular ignorance, indifference, and vacillation requires a large measure of idealism. But his was an idealism that never wearied and never sacrificed a desirable end to a visionary method. His whole being was imbued with high ideals, and once the aim was stated, however idealistic it was, he pursued it relentlessly. Joseph Galloway, the Loyalist, said of him: "He is equal to most men in popular intrigue and the management of a faction. He eats little, drinks little, sleeps little, thinks much, and is most decisive and indefatigable in the pursuit of his objects." Rarely was so glowing an idealist so practical as a man of affairs.

In his statements of American grievances Adams was vastly influenced by the middle-class political philosophy of John Locke. "The immortal Locke," he called his English guide, and again praises him as "one of the greatest men who ever wrote." Although Locke was a constitutional monarchist and Adams was democratically inclined, the American agitator made telling use of Locke's theory of natural rights. If one wishes to understand the fundamental views of Samuel Adams, one has only to read the pages of Locke.

It may seem strange that so much attention is given to a purely political writer in a history of American literature, but it should not be forgotten that without the work of such writers as Adams, Paine, and Jefferson, the work of later belletristic writers would have been impossible. The work of the political and social philosopher is like the foundation of a beautiful building—not very beautiful in itself but very necessary to the superimposed structure. Our forefathers wrote sermons, political tracts, letters, and newspaper articles; their sons wrote essays, novels, and poetry that reflect the political passions of the time; and now their sons' sons are writing lyric poetry, dramas, and fiction with no other aim than that of the belletristic author.

THOMAS PAINE

(1737-1809)

In 1775 the work of Samuel Adams in creating a Revolutionary psychology was about complete, but although America was ready to take up arms in redress of her grievances, the ultimate aim of the Revolutionary party was not clear. Lexington, Concord, and Bunker Hill were in the past; revolution was in the air. But to what was the war leading?

Independence was thought of by only the most radical and talked by only the admitted extremists. In the spring of 1775 Jefferson "looked with fondness toward a reconciliation" with England. The. Pennsylvania lawmakers passed a resolution that "the idea of unconstitutional independence is utterly abhorrent to our principles." Only three months before he took command of the colonial army, Washington assured his friends with great emphasis that he did not advocate independence. Suddenly large numbers of Americans were demanding independence. While it is manifestly absurd to attribute this quick change in American thinking to any one thing, certainly one of the potent influences was the work of Thomas Paine.

Paine was an English Quaker who supplemented a slight education by systematic reading until he possessed a mind well stored with natural science, philosophy, and political thought. Successful as he was in his education, he had not been so fortunate in his business undertakings, for he had failed in venture after venture until he resolved to begin anew in America. In some manner Paine had made the acquaintance of Benjamin Franklin, then in London as representative of the colonies, and the great American was attracted to the vivacious and intelligent Englishman. When Paine sailed for Philadelphia he carried with him a letter of introduction from Franklin. He landed in December, 1774, and within a year was editor of a Philadelphia magazine.

Paine's Pamphlets.—In 1775 came Lexington, Concord, and Bunker Hill. The country was aflame with war spirit but to what ultimate end none could say. Paine seized upon the white-hot indignation of the colonies and directed it toward independence. In

January, 1776, he published *Common Sense,* probably the most effective piece of propaganda ever written on this continent. Dismissing all previous arguments with England as mere legal and philosophical quibbling, he set forth the case for independence with so great logic, sound sense, and clarity that he converted the Americans to his way of thinking almost overnight. That the publication of this pamphlet was one of the momentous events of the Revolution was attested by men so divergent as Washington and Jefferson. "I find *Common Sense* working a powerful change in the minds of men," reported Washington, in whose mind it had already wrought a great change. Paine cut through the tangle of argument that surrounded the vexatious question of English-American relations and stated the case for independence on the grounds of economics and expediency. He spurned the question of constitutionality as irrelevant and asked the simple question if America would not be better off if it had independence, asserting that the answer to this question was not to be given by lawyers and statesmen but by the people who would speak from the knowledge gained in their everyday business.

That the people read this doctrine is shown by the sale of 120,000 copies of the pamphlet within three months. Half a million were sold within a short time, many of them in England, and the French estimate that they bought more copies than the Americans did. But the effect of the pamphlet was more amazing than its sale. Every literate American read it, and surprisingly large numbers accepted its doctrines. Within six months after its publication, independence was declared with pretty general approval. This would not have been the case at the end of 1775.

Paine's second Revolutionary service was the writing of a series of articles to bolster up American civilian morale. These pamphlets were issued at intervals from December, 1776, to December, 1783, sixteen numbers in all appearing. The value of these brief articles in sustaining American courage during the darkest Revolutionary days is beyond computing. They did the same service during the war that *Common Sense* did at the start.

If Paine had never written another line he would belong in American literature by virtue of *Common Sense* and *The American Crisis* series. In these works the thought is clear, the argument convincing, and the style incomparably smooth and simple. The author had one of the finest journalistic styles ever in America, and the aim of journalism is to present facts with brevity and unmistakable clarity.

Lincoln read Paine with delight, and in the clear, simple style of his great speeches and letters, one can find traces of Paine's influences.

THE DECLARATION OF INDEPENDENCE

The Declaration of Independence is worthy of much more than a careless reading, for it contains both the general political philosophy of the American Revolution and the specific causes of resistance to Great Britain. The document should not be regarded as an instrument by which the Continental Congress first gave notice of our independence, for the resolution declaring our separation from England had already been passed when the Declaration was adopted. It is only a succinct statement to the world of the reasons impelling America to seek its independence.

On June 7, 1776, Richard Henry Lee of Virginia introduced three resolutions in Congress, the first of which said that the colonies "are and of a right ought to be free and independent" of Great Britain. Three days later, while Lee's resolution was pending, Congress voted to appoint a committee that should write a declaration to accompany the resolution of independence. On the following day Thomas Jefferson, John Adams, Benjamin Franklin, Roger Sherman, and Robert Livingston were named as such a committee. On July 2, Congress adopted Lee's resolution and thus declared our independence. The Declaration as submitted by the committee was agreed to on July 4 and signed about a month later by all members of Congress in attendance. A few members signed at other times.

Thomas Jefferson of Virginia was almost wholly responsible for the composition of the Declaration. At the first meeting of the committee the other members insisted that the Virginian do the work, for his peculiar felicity of expression was well known. The document was written, so Jefferson always said, without recourse to any book or pamphlet. It was submitted to Adams and Franklin, each of whom made a very few verbal changes, and then presented to Congress where several changes were made, the most notable being the omission of a fierce indictment of the English for protecting the slave trade. As the Declaration stands in our national literature it is almost wholly the work of Jefferson. In its statement of specific grievances no less than in its philosophy and literary qualities, it unmistakably belongs to the great Virginian.

Structure of the Declaration.—The Declaration is composed of four parts: a preamble, two sections in the body of the document, and a conclusion. The preamble says that the Declaration sets forth the reasons for the separation from Great Britain. It reads:

When, in the course of human events, it becomes necessary for one people to dissolve the political bond, which has connected them with another, and to assume among the powers of the earth, the separate and equal station to which the laws of Nature and of Nature's God entitle them, a decent respect to the opinions of mankind requires that they should declare the causes which impel them to the separation.

The first section of the body sets forth a general political philosophy which asserts the right of a people to set up and overthrow its government. It reads:

We hold these truths to be self evident, that all men are created equal, that they are endowed by their Creator with certain inalienable rights; that among these are life, liberty, and the pursuit of happiness; that to secure these rights governments are instituted among men, deriving their just powers from the consent of the governed; that whenever any form of government becomes destructive to these ends, it is the right of the people to alter or abolish it, and to institute new government, laying its foundation on such principles and organizing its powers in such form as to them shall seem most likely to effect their safety and happiness.

The second section proceeds from a statement that governments "long established should not be changed for light and transient causes" to a list of "repeated injuries and usurpations" of the "present king of Great Britain." This list of injuries was presented as proof of King George's tyrannical indifference to the inalienable rights of man.

The conclusion states that the colonies are free and independent and that they have power to carry on war, conclude peace, make alliances with other nations, establish commerce, and perform the ordinary functions of a state. "And for the support of this declaration, with a firm reliance on the protection of a divine providence, we mutually pledge to each other our lives, our fortunes, and our sacred honor." With that sentence, memorable alike for its sentiment and expression, the Declaration of Independence closes.

The Ideas of the Declaration.—In his later years John Adams, who was always known for his testy temper and sharp tongue, made a few sneering remarks concerning the lack of originality in the Declaration. There was not an idea in it, he declared, which had not been "hackneyed in Congress for two years before." Jefferson freely admitted the truth of the criticism, saying that he did not consider it a part of his business in writing the document "to invent new ideas altogether and to offer no sentiment which had ever been expressed before." His work was "to place before mankind the common sense of the subject, in terms so plain and firm as to command their assent." He aimed at no originality of principles or sentiments, but took ideas as he found them, "whether expressed in conversation, in letters, printed essays or the elementary books of public right, as Aristotle, Cicero, Locke, Sidney, etc."

In making his explanation Jefferson showed that the Declaration was composed with the idea of massing the evidence of English tyranny and placing the decision of Congress to separate from the mother country upon generally accepted premises. If Jefferson had advanced any new argument he would have defeated his aim, for he wished only to collect the arguments already in circulation. So it is with almost any state paper that strikes a responsive popular chord. Jackson's attacks on the United States Bank contained no new arguments; neither did the Emancipation Proclamation, the Gettysburg address, or any of Wilson's utterances during the war with Germany. The essence of a great popular appeal is not to say something new, but to say in memorable fashion what every one is thinking.

Richard Henry Lee said that the Declaration was copied from Locke's treatise on government, and this criticism is certainly nearer the mark than is the one by Adams. The spirit of Locke and even some of his phraseology are clearly apparent in the general justification of revolution. The creation of men as equals, the endowment with life and liberty, the view that government is instituted to secure these rights, and the inalienable right of a people to abolish tyranny are all drawn straight from the pages of Locke. Jefferson only summarized in brilliant form the English philosopher's view of natural rights, the compact theory of government, and the justification of rebellion. It is no criticism of Jefferson to say that he followed Locke closely without referring to book or pamphlet, but it is proof of his intimate acquaintance with the treatise on government. And Jefferson knew Locke little better than did dozens of other American leaders.

At one time it was generally said that Jefferson drew his ideas from Rousseau, the French philosopher. To-day we know that such was not the case. The French and Americans both drew their fundamental ideas from the same source, and that source was John Locke. There is one point where Jefferson deviates sharply from Locke's views, and that is in the statement of our inalienable rights, "life, liberty, and the pursuit of happiness." The first two rights are undeniably Locke's but the English thinker would have completed the trilogy by including "the possession of property." The substitution of the pursuit of happiness gives a fine humanitarian and idealistic tone which appeals as much to the propertyless as to the moneyed classes. Where Jefferson found this right to pursue happiness we do not know for certain, but surely it has a strong flavor of French humanitarian thought.

Whether the Declaration is true or false is of slight concern to the present-day historian; that it was generally considered true in the eighteenth century is sufficient. Better than any other short document it epitomizes the political thought and the particular complaints that brought on the Revolution. Later generations have been trained in schools of thought other than that conducted by John Locke. Jefferson quoted Locke simply because the Englishman had put into political philosophy exactly what every American in 1776 wanted to believe.

FRANCIS HOPKINSON

(1737-1791)

Philadelphia at the outbreak of the Revolution was the center of colonial wit and culture. The town possessed a large number of wealthy merchants whose sons were given the best education available in America and England. When the young men returned from their sojourns abroad they brought with them a taste for music and literature, and not a few set themselves up as town wits, those typical products of London coffee houses. Conspicuous among this younger generation was Francis Hopkinson, eminent lawyer, judge, man of wealth, musician, natural philosopher, painter, and poet. In short he was conspicuous in a refined society for his cultivated tastes and attainments. Francis Hopkinson was of the colonial class that frequently remained loyal to England. He was wealthy, he had friends and relatives in the English ruling caste, he married one of the greatest heiresses of the colonies, and finally he was a lawyer, many of whom remained true to England through regard for strict legality. But Hopkinson turned revolutionist, jeopardized his estates by signing the Declaration of Independence, and freely placed his talents, both legal and literary, at the disposal of his countrymen.

Hopkinson belongs in American literature because of his witty and effective attacks on the British that kept the colonists in good humor during the dark days of the war. The Americans were still in awe of the king's men, and Hopkinson did a great service to his cause by getting the colonists to laugh at the pompous but inefficient British, for no man can stand greatly in awe of one at whose discomfiture he has just laughed heartily. Among the writer's most successful sallies are a skit addressed to General Burgoyne and "The Birds, the Beasts, and the Bat," a fable in verse. But the most popular work that came from his pen was a ballad, worthless as literature, called "The Battle of the Kegs." The poem was occasioned by an attempt of the Americans to send some primitive submarine mines among the English ships in Philadelphia harbor. The plans failed, but the English were so alarmed that they employed rifle and artillery fire against every bit of driftwood that they could spy. Such an occurrence was humorous in itself, and it lost nothing in Hopkinson's telling.

In later years Hopkinson grew mistrustful of revolutions and revolutionists and became very conservative, employing his still abundant wit against Jeffersonian democrats and French revolutionists alike.

JOHN TRUMBULL

(1750-1831)

Trumbull belongs to a group known as the Connecticut or Hartford Wits,[1] but by virtue of his famous mock-epic, *M'Fingal*, he claims notice in any sketch of our Revolutionary literature. Besides his long poem he contributed to the American cause an "Elegy on the Times," which drew enthusiastic praise from John Adams.

The author of *M'Fingal* was related to the powerful Connecticut family of Trumbulls, and on his mother's side he was descended from the grandfather of Jonathan Edwards. With so imposing family connections he was certain of at least respectable eminence in his native colony. Naturally he went to Yale—all young Connecticut men of his class did—and proceeded from college to the law office of John Adams in Boston. There was probably some

[1] P. 185.

revolutionary sentiment in Yale, for the young student of Black-stone entered easily into the agitated atmosphere of Boston, and in the creation of a war psychology in the turning of minds against the Loyalists, Trumbull did valiant revolutionary work with his poetry.

M'Fingal is a burlesque on the misfortunes of a Loyalist who tasted several different kinds of colonial vengeance. The poem contains many humorous episodes and some extremely effective lines, but as a whole it is too stilted and grandiose. Trumbull could not unbend, as Hopkinson did so easily, and as a result, his ambitious effort is valuable to-day chiefly as a historical relic. But whatever we may think of *M'Fingal,* our Revolutionary grandfathers were delighted with it. Thirty editions were printed, and in the number of readers the work was no mean rival of *Common Sense.* But it is to be feared that the patriotic Americans of 1776 read *M'Fingal* for its humorous account of Loyalist misadventures rather than for its poetry. However, it was read, and it helped to mold public opinion. It is probable therefore that the poem fulfilled the chief aim of its author.

JONATHAN ODELL: TORY SATIRIST
(1737-1818)

It is not to be imagined that all the wit and literary skill was on the American side during Revolutionary days. Probably one-third of our colonists were opposed, in greater or less degree, to a separation from England, and since these Tories comprised many men of ability and education, it is not strange that they produced some satirists. To-day we read few of their products, for often the poetry is poor and the opinions positively archaic, but once the authors contributed their share to the war of ideas that swept America more thoroughly if less destructively than did the hostile armies.

There were many Loyalists who essayed literature in various forms, and it must be admitted that the tattered American army officered frequently by small farmers and tradesmen, the wretched condition of colonial finances, and the feebleness of Congress all were themes attractive enough to the satirist. Among the practitioners of Loyalist verse and propaganda were Joseph Stansbury, song writer and satirist; Jonathan Boucher, a minister who had George Washington in his congregation; Samuel Peters, minister and historian; and, most important of all, Jonathan Odell.

Jonathan Odell.—Odell was born in New Jersey in 1737 of a long line of American ancestors, the earliest of whom had assisted in the foundation of Massachusetts. He was educated at Princeton and entered the medical profession, but withdrew to prepare himself for the ministry. He held the parish at Burlington, New Jersey, from 1767 until 1775. During these troubled years he remained loyal to England, though he refrained as a minister from any discussion of political affairs. After the outbreak of hostilities he became the bitterest Tory poet and song writer.

Odell incurred American displeasure in 1776 by writing an ode for the king's birthday that breathed a spirit of fervent devotion to George III. So indignant did his neighbors wax over the poem that, but for the assistance of a friendly Quakeress, the loyal poet would have become acquainted with prison fare or with even harsher treatment. After escaping from his enraged neighbors, Odell went to New York where he had a hand in the Arnold-André conspiracy, officiated as chaplain in the king's army, and wrote verse. Among his poems are "The Congratulation," "The Feu de Joie," and "The American Times."

Odell pays his hottest compliments to all Americans, both in the mass and as individuals, who were guilty of rebellion against the king. This is his salutation to Thomas Paine:

> Others apart in some obscure recess,
> The studied lie for publication dress:
> Prepare the vague report, fallacious tale,
> Invent fresh calumnies, revive the stale,
> Pervert all records sacred and profane,
> And chief among them stands the villain Paine.

> Our hireling author having changed his soil,
> True son of Grub Street, here renewed his toil.
> What cannot ceaseless impudence produce?
> Our Franklin knows its value and its use;
> He caught at Paine, relieved his wretched plight,
> And gave him notes, and set him down to write.
> Fire from the Doctor's hints the miscreant took,
> Discarded truth, and soon produced a book . . .
> A pamphlet, which without the least pretense
> Of reason, bore the name of Common Sense.

> And work, like wildfire, through the country ran,
> And folly bowed the knee to Franklin's plan . . .

And General John Sullivan is thus greeted:

> Amidst ten thousand eminently base,
> Thou, Sullivan, assume the highest place.
> Sailor and farmer, barrister of vogue,
> Each state was thine, and thou in each a rogue.

"The American Times," generally regarded as Odell's best work, continues the agreeable task of flaying the rebels. Some of its passages are of undeniable strength, a strength that came from Odell's personality and his fierce conviction that the Loyalist cause was righteous.

At the conclusion of the war this fiery satirist, refusing to accept the new order, emigrated to Nova Scotia, where he, his son, and his grandson successively entered public life. Odell died as he had lived, thoroughly unreconciled to the American Revolution and subsequent independence.

THE RESULTS OF THE REVOLUTION

Without question the most important result of the Revolution was England's acknowledgment of American independence, but any student of history knows that wars always carry in their train a group of results that are never mentioned in the treaty of peace and seldom by popular historians. Thus it is with the American Revolution. The war had certain social effects that may not seem very important to the political historian, but without these results the later development of the American mind would have been vastly different. It is quite true that our revolutionary forefathers did not aim specifically at these changes at the outset of the war, but a revolution always has a habit of extending its scope in ways that are beyond the understanding or control of those who start it.[1]

Changes in the Social Order.—The Revolution caused the virtual extinction of aristocracy in America. Here and there vestiges of a higher class lingered on, as in New York, but in general the aristocracy disappeared with the withdrawal of British troops from

[1] The social changes of the Revolution are discussed in Dr. J. Franklin Jameson's book: *The American Revolution Considered as a Social Movement.*

American soil. Most of the aristocrats were irreconcilable Loyalists, and at the end of the war they sought a haven in Canada or the British Isles. Those few Tory aristocrats who returned to their homes after 1783 found their property scattered and their influence gone.

Now if the leveling process of Revolution was assisted by bringing the aristocrat down, it was helped no less by the elevation to the ruling class of many hitherto denied the right to vote. The Revolutionary period saw the right of suffrage greatly extended. During that time at least eight of the thirteen colonies adopted new constitutions that greatly increased the number of voters. Many of those newly franchised were so unused to the conduct of government that their incompetence excited much aristocratic mirth, but the new voters wanted to extend the suffrage still more rather than to restrict it, though manhood suffrage was far in the future.

The Revolutionary age also saw a change in the status of slavery. Earlier Americans like Samuel Sewall and John Woolman had spoken and written against the institution, but it was not until 1775 that anti-slavery sentiment became at all organized or effective. Thomas Paine's first writing after he came to America was against African slavery, and almost at the same time an anti-slavery society was formed in Philadelphia. Soon the Quakers took official steps to abolish the system among their members. During the discussion of independence Paine was constantly urging Congress not to forget "the hapless African," and Jefferson's first draft of the Declaration contained a blast against slavery that was stricken out on the demand of extreme southern representatives. In 1774 Rhode Island's lawmakers passed a resolution that slaves thereafter brought into the colony should be free, pointing out that it was not seemly to desire liberty ardently for themselves and refuse to extend it to others. Delaware, Virginia, Maryland, and South Carolina all forbade importation of slaves, the latter state for only a period of years, and Connecticut, Massachusetts, Pennsylvania, and Rhode Island all provided for the gradual extinction of slavery. In 1782 Virginia passed a law allowing the freeing of slaves by their owners. Thus from every angle the status of slavery was much changed during the period from 1774 to the adoption of the constitution in 1789.

Changes in Landholding.—American life, thought, and literature are all based upon the proposition that all men are equal. Without the existence of such a belief our social and political institutions could not have been what they are to-day, and without the social and political patterns our literature would be vastly different from that which we have. Below our governmental and social structure lies the fundamental fact of economic democracy—the equality of economic opportunity. The Revolution gave a swift impetus to this tendency in American life, working chiefly in the system of landholding.

Land was of tremendous importance to our forefathers. They came to this country to get land; nine-tenths of them lived directly on the soil; and any system that prevented the free and equitable distribution of land by settlement, purchase, or inheritance simply blocked the early Americans in their most cherished designs. Although the settlers in the colonies wanted land above all things, they unfortunately imported certain features of the English system of landholding. This system made for inheritance by the oldest son, for the perpetuity of estates, for the holding of vast tracts by one man, and for the payment of rent by many tenant farmers. All these were changed from 1775 to 1795, and American landholding became democratic.

One of the chief economic results of the Revolution was the break-up of large estates. In many colonies, especially New York, Pennsylvania, Maryland, and Virginia huge tracts of land had been granted to individuals. These tracts were held in the same families for generations, and at the outbreak of the Revolution thousands of American farmers were tenants. The Van Rensselaer manor in New York contained more than 430,000 acres. The great Fairfax estate in Virginia at one time contained about six million acres— almost 10,000 square miles, a tract as large as the state of Vermont. The Revolution caused the breaking up of most of these estates and the transfer of the land to many small farmers. We read that 275 men purchased farms on one estate and 250 on each of several others. The Penn holdings in Pennsylvania brought the state five million dollars when it was sold to individuals, and New York realized half as much from the sale of its confiscated property. The estates were confiscated by the Americans because the owners were Loyalists.

The laws of inheritance were also changed during the Revolutionary period. Under the rule of primogeniture an estate could be inherited only by the eldest son, when there was a male descendant. This rule made impossible the division of property upon the death of the owner. Furthermore under the law, an estate, once placed in entail, could never be sold out of the family possession. Thus with primogeniture and entail governing landholding, little democratic progress could be made. These systems were strongest in Virginia, and here Jefferson, attacking them as aristocratic, succeeded in abolishing them. The other states followed Virginia's lead, and soon the right of sale and the right of equal inheritance by all children were universally recognized, though in two states daughters were not placed on a complete equality with sons.

The breaking up of huge estates and the abolition of primogeniture and entail were of great concern to the farmers of Tidewater, but they meant little to the frontiersmen. However, the Westerner realized his great ambition in landholding when King George's edict against western migration was disregarded and the Ohio country opened to settlers. The Quebec Act of 1774 forbade western settlement, but the treaty of peace made this country American. Immediately emigrants began crossing the mountains in a steady stream, and the most momentous fact in American social life was made inevitable. Without the immense reservoir of open land to the west our nation would have been far different in life, thought, and literature.

Other Results of the Revolution.—There were other results of the Revolution, important enough to our development, but none of so great consequence as those just named. For instance, our educational system became less English and more American; the Revolution saw the beginning of a complete democratization of our schools; and a college education was no longer the prerogative of the rich and well-born. Our barbaric codes of criminal law and our unspeakably brutal treatment of prisoners were attacked in the name of reason and common humanity. This attack also was led by Thomas Jefferson. In the realm of religion the Revolution again made itself felt in the abolition of an outgrown law. In 1775 nine colonies had churches supported by taxation. In Massachusetts, Connecticut, and New Hampshire the Congregational church was the official denomination, while the Episcopalians enjoyed the distinction in New York, Maryland, Virginia, North and South Carolina, and Georgia. In all the states save Virginia and those of the New England group the establishment was quickly swept away. In Virginia the opponents of establishment rallied to the leadership of Jefferson, and after ten years of struggle the victory was theirs. The

Congregational body was finally disestablished in New Hampshire in 1817, in Connecticut in 1818, and in Massachusetts in 1838.

One important result of the Revolution was the opening of the country to French influence. As a result of her assistance during the war France became very popular in this nation, and the manners of our late allies, their political thought, and their culture all became models for the intellectuals of America. In view of the French Revolution, which was to break shortly with tremendous reverberations on both sides of the Atlantic, the opening of America to French thought was of great importance.

It can readily be seen that the American Revolution was more than a political upheaval or a military revolt; it was in a profound sense a "social, economic, and intellectual transformation." Without the leveling processes that were introduced into America from 1770 to 1800 the quickening touch of romanticism could never have been felt from 1800 to 1860, and romanticism is the greatest intellectual and literary fact ever experienced by this nation. Romanticism was founded on a belief in the essential equality of man, the fundamental goodness of human nature, and a cheery faith in the permanent possibility of progress. Without the social changes of the American Revolution, the romantic movement would have died an early death in this country.

REACTION: THE CONSTITUTION

During the Revolutionary era such leaders as Samuel Adams, Paine, and Jefferson had gone too rapidly for the taste of certain influential groups. Naturally enough the dispossessed aristocrats were outraged at the indignities heaped upon them; the beneficiaries of the established churches were eager to fly at the party that was trying to thrust them from the public treasuries; the hardly reconciled Loyalists—those who remained in the country after 1783— were ready to join any movement against further disturbance of the old order. Everything was set for a reaction against the powerful liberalizing tendencies in the land.

Moreover a stronger group than any just named was distressed at the trend of affairs. This was the rapidly growing commercial class, the business men. This group was not so much alarmed at what had already been done as it was at the discouraging prospects for a secure and prosperous development of business enterprise in

America. That the bankers and men of affairs had grounds for complaint few would attempt to deny. In the first place the thirteen states were held together in a confederation, that is in a loose union. Congress, the only governing power of the confederation, had insufficient powers to raise money by taxation, regulate commerce between the states and with other nations, remedy national finances, or establish a system of uniform courts and laws. Interest on the public debt was unpaid; the land was filled with worthless currency, issued by Congress and by the various states; those who had debts due them were unable to collect in gold or silver; our diplomatic relations with European powers were hopelessly muddled; business enterprise, especially the more adventurous sort known as speculation, was paralyzed or at best moving but feebly. The commercial class had certain specific remedies for this wholly unsatisfactory condition. They wanted a stronger central government with power to regulate and protect foreign and domestic trade; they demanded uniform currency based upon a visible supply of gold and silver; they wanted national, state, and private debts paid in hard money; furthermore they longed to begin speculation in western lands.

The Critical Period (1783-1789).—The six years from the end of the war to Washington's inauguration are generally referred to as the Critical Period. During this time the nation was going through a readjustment following the war, certain social reforms already mentioned were in progress, and consequently business was not very brisk. For long it was the custom to treat this period as a reign of anarchy that was brought to a close by the adoption of the Constitution just in the nick of time. To-day no one denies that there were grave weaknesses under the confederation, but the fact that a large group consistently opposed the Constitution and demanded only a few amendments to the Articles of Confederation shows that some were fairly well satisfied with conditions during the so-called period of anarchy.

Of the prominent revolutionary leaders only a few were at the Constitutional Convention. Paine was in Europe exhibiting the model of an invention, Jefferson was in France, and Samuel Adams and Patrick Henry were at their homes. Although the latter was elected he refused to attend. Franklin was one of the few revolutionary agitators who was present, and the Constitution that was finally adopted contained almost every feature in government that he disliked. In short the liberal, democratizing party, frequently called the agrarian because it embodied the ideals of the western farmers, was not enthusiastic about a strong federal union with all the powers that business men wished it to have. As a result the Constitution was written by a group of men who were more mindful of business interests than of further agrarian reforms.

The Constitution.—The temper of the Constitutional Convention is well expressed by certain remarks that fortunately have been preserved in the notes of a few members, especially Madison, for the meetings of the delegates were behind closed doors. Hamilton once said that all communities divide themselves into the few and the many. The few are the rich and well-born; the many are the great mass of people who cannot be trusted to think or do the right thing. Gouverneur Morris wanted a senate, representing an aristocracy of wealth, that would be strong enough to put down and keep down the turbulence of democracy. Randolph, with more perception and frankness than later historians have usually possessed, said that the unsatisfactory conditions from 1783 to 1787 were caused by "the turbulence and follies of democracy." Elbridge Gerry, agreeing with Randolph, declared that the evils complained of were caused by "an excess of democracy." Even Madison, a friend of Jefferson, wanted a constitution that would secure public welfare and private rights against majority rule and at the same time preserve the form of popular government. Madison's wish was realized to the full.

The designers of the Constitution were evidently so absorbed in the work nearest their hearts that they neglected to include a bill of rights in the document. When this oversight was revealed to the public, the agrarians almost expired with rage. Jefferson filled the mails from France with letters denunciatory of the omission, finally advising his friends to support the Constitution only when he was assured that a bill of rights would be added in the form of amendments. The constitutional leaders kept faith with Jefferson, and our national bill of rights is to be found in the first ten amendments.

The Constitution was adopted after a spirited campaign in which the losing side was espoused by western farmers, "those who favored the annihilation of debts," and the advocates of paper money. The solid and substantial business interests, the lawyers, the clergy, and creditors of both individuals and the states—all these warmly supported the proposed Constitution. With the Jeffersonian group silenced by the promise of immediate amendments, the instrument of government was adopted.

"The Federalist."—Most of the political pamphlets that poured from the presses of both parties during the ratification campaign have deservedly been forgotten. It is not so with one collection of essays. During the hot fight over ratification Alexander Hamilton and John Jay of New York and Madison, a Virginian, issued a number of explanations and defenses of the Constitution that were later collected under the title of *The Federalist*. The collection has been lavishly praised as the most profound political doctrine enunciated in America, and such praise may not be excessive if one's consideration is limited to conservative political discussion only. Certainly never again was the case for Federalism so strikingly stated. The tone of *The Federalist* is indicated by such a statement as the following: "The preamble to the constitution is a better recognition of popular rights than volumes of those aphorisms which make the principal figure in our state bills of rights, and which would sound much better in a treatise of ethics." The essay from which this statement is taken was written by Hamilton.

The two main contentions of the writers are that a strongly centralized state is highly desirable and that the minority must be protected from the majority when the mass is not actuated by motives strictly in accord with justice and law. These views are the very essence of Federalism and the chief aversions of the Jeffersonian party. The western farmer never saw any value whatever in a strongly centralized government until he reached the Ohio country and beyond where the need of military protection, roads, and canals reconciled him to a powerful national government. Nor did he, accustomed to the leveling process of the frontier and the transaction of all business by a majority vote, have the fear of a rampant majority that so haunted the rich and well-born conservatives. *The Federalist* clearly points out the line of future cleavage in American politics —a cleavage that was to endure for many years.

The significance of the constitutional struggle to the student of literature lies in the fact that the adoption of this Constitution marked a direct check to the liberalizing tendencies of the agrarian party. Federalism was a distinctly aristocratic reaction. That faction won the first battle and began to fashion the government according to its ideals of responsibility and authority in the hands of the rich, well-born, and able. For twelve years the opposition grew stronger and stronger, until in 1800 Jeffersonian democracy swept the Federalists as a party into permanent oblivion. The contest over the Constitution simply indicated the lines of cleavage in the country between the liberals and the conservatives. In the next generation most of the romantic writers were in sympathy with the ideals of the liberals, for romanticism and Jeffersonian democracy had the same intellectual ancestry.

BATTLE OF IDEAS

In the hectic days of political campaigns belletristic literature is usually slighted in favor of heavy-handed but convincing argument or recrimination. So it was in the early days of our republic when the cross-fire of accusation and counter-accusation often made even the placid Washington yearn for the quietness of Mt. Vernon. The leading talent of the country put its best into political argument. Some belletristic literature there was, but virtually all writing was only argument or satire, fashioned for the service of one or the other party.

The French Revolution.—Before proceeding to a discussion of the chief writers of this period it is necessary to notice a European cataclysm that "drew a red-hot plow share through the history of America," not merely dividing parties but molding them. This great event was the French Revolution.

Washington had not been in the presidential chair a week when the first event of the French Revolution occurred across the Atlantic. The revolution started as only a liberalizing influence on the outgrown governmental machinery of France. Soon it developed alarming leveling tendencies in politics, society, and economic life. The motto "Liberty, Fraternity, Equality" was applied with a vengeance. Aristocrats went to the guillotine in droves, estates were confiscated, and the extreme levelers, the Jacobins, ruled France with a bloody hand. America, so lately embroiled in a revolution, watched French affairs with intense interest.

At first American opinion was all with the revolutionists. It took no great imaginative flight to see in the loose and corrupt government of France a fellow to the corrupt and tyrannical English system. When the Bastille fell, the key of the gloomy prison was sent to Washington as a symbol that tyranny had passed from France

All America rejoiced with the French. But soon a more radical group came into control in Paris, and such Federalists as Hamilton and Adams dropped their revolutionary sympathies, sensing that the loosed whirlwind was liable to level all class and property distinctions. The ominous forebodings were justified. The Jacobins seized control of the Revolution and the Reign of Terror was on. The execution of Louis XVI caused a revulsion throughout conservative ranks in America, for that amiable though incompetent and corrupt monarch was regarded in this country with sentimental affection for the aid he lent us in our Revolution. The Federalists became violently anti-Jacobin.

But not all Americans followed Federalist precedent. Among the anti-Federalists or the agrarians the French revolutionists were extravagantly praised. Rapidly the nation split into the two groups indicated previously in the struggle over the Constitution, the one fiercely against French tendencies, the other as enthusiastically for them. When Great Britain declared war on France, the Federalists were solidly pro-English, and the Jeffersonians vociferously pro-French. The French party, under the stimulus of Parisian events, began a frontal assault on such vestiges of the old aristocracy as titles, social distinctions, and the aristocratic wig and short breeches. John Adams, the vice-president, yearned for a pompous title, but he received only an unmerciful lashing from democratic speakers and the open ridicule of the agrarians in the Senate. Even staid Boston succumbed to revolutionary fervor and blossomed forth with a Liberty Square and an Equality Lane. In certain quarters it was all the vogue to follow the French fashion in political and social leveling as well as in clothing.

The fury created by the French Revolution was of great importance to American liberalism. Under the impetus of foreign example the aristocratic tendencies in America, more powerful from 1783 to 1790 than from 1775 to 1783, were finally checked. The period of reaction was at an end, and the way was open for the flood of social democracy and European romanticism.

Naturally theology had to enter the fight, especially in the regions dedicated to Puritanism. The radical French thinkers were Voltaire, Rousseau, d'Alembert, Montesquieu, and many others. Suddenly these men were discovered to be "infidels," "atheists," and "corrupters of youth." Old time Puritanism almost solidly arrayed itself against the "infidel and irreligious philosophy." The democrats came to the rescue of the French thinkers, and even back-woods settlements seriously, if rather too heatedly, discussed some of the great figures in modern thought. To this day a faint odor of impropriety hangs over the most serious arguments of the French philosophers, and this odor was redolent during the 1790's.

JOHN ADAMS
(1735-1826)

If John Adams had written any belletristic literature that reflected his own strong personality, the poetry would have been harsh and crabbed, and the prose shrill and high-pitched beyond belief, but he was too busy helping found and govern this nation to tinker with sonnets or fuss around over the cadence of sentences. Not so liberal as his kinsman Samuel or so commercially minded as Hamilton, John Adams is important in the development of the American mind as our best example of a man who honestly thought that government by a natural aristocracy is the only means of guaranteeing justice to all social classes. "Take away thrones and crowns from among men and there will soon be an end of all dominion or justice," he once wrote with angry indiscretion. Though he admitted that a monarchy might not be essential to good government in the United States, he insisted that the central government was always to be controlled by an aristocracy of "talents and wealth." Despite his occasional lapses into monarchical sentiment, Adams was pretty consistently republican, that is, he believed in a representative government.

Work of Adams.—Born into a good New England family, Adams completed his scholastic training at Harvard and almost immediately took rank as one of Boston's best lawyers. He early lent a hand in stirring up revolutionary sentiment in Massachusetts and became one of the spokesmen for that colony in the Continental Congress. During the Revolutionary period he was always on the side of human rights, but from 1783 to 1790 he shifted over to the conservative view of the superlative value of property, though he never went the full length with Alexander Hamilton.

After serving as minister to Holland, Adams came home to accept the vice-presidency. In this office his pompous vanity and amazing tactlessness stirred up all the democratic opposition in the country and won many converts to Jeffersonianism. When elected to the presidency in 1796, he set about, honestly but blunderingly, to carry on the government according to his unchangeable views. French immigrants were intriguing against the administration, and criticism of the president was running high. Adams put through the Alien and Sedition laws, the second of which allowed the fine and imprisonment of all persons found guilty of opposing any act of government, impeding the administration of any law, or uttering false, scandalous or malicious criticism of the government or its officers. The first act gave the president power to expel or imprison alien enemies in time of war.

The passage of these laws sounded the knell of Adams and the Federalist party. The party never again enjoyed wide power, and Adams was retired permanently from political life, though he lived in studious retirement for twenty-five years.

Adams as a Thinker.—Adams was a hard-headed, practical thinker, devoid of imagination and quite immune to the appeal of "progress." It might be said of him that he fully represented the early eighteenth century whose desire was to seek "tranquillity in an established society sustained by religious sanction." A change in the established order was always to be deplored, unless the evils complained of were very apparent and very clearly capable of being remedied.

No romantic idealist was John Adams, no dreamer of imposing dreams, no seeker after impossible Utopias. He had small faith in the goodness of human nature and no belief that man will do right without energetic direction. The time is out of joint, he argued, and things are hopelessly muddled, but there is no help for conditions. The best policy is to face our problems bravely and wring from a reluctant life what comfort we can. Grandiose dreams of human betterment through political assistance he abominated. When Adams faced the problems of the future, he had two guides, common sense and an excellent knowledge of history. For proof of human futility and imbecility he could cite historical event after event that ended in disaster to the dreamer and exponent of progress. Adams's consistent policy was that of "standing pat" with utmost emphasis. His careful study of history told him that power in the state always went to the possessors of property. Naturally in all societies there were fewer rich men than poor. Hence it was to be expected that the few would hold dominion over the majority. These few were the natural aristocrats, men of family, education, and ability, and the very fact that they were such put them in possession of wealth. Although he would not limit the ballot to these few, he was far from advocating manhood suffrage. Seemingly he thought that voting should be done by the upper and middle classes, with no voice allowed the great mass of laborers, renters, tenant farmers, and small landholders.

But if Adams would not allow the mass a hand in the government, neither would he suffer the rich to grow richer by exploiting the poor. Money was not John Adams's god; his natural aristocracy possessed wealth because it had the important characteristics of breeding and ability. In his refusal to consider the commercial class as the natural aristocracy Adams broke with Hamilton, the frank exponent of government by the financiers.

Adams as a Literary Man.—Although with some reason Adams has been called our most notable political thinker, his writings are not widely read except by serious students. His chief books are a defense of the Constitution and a collection of articles called *Discourses on Davila*. The latter was an intemperate attack on democracy that only added to the author's unpopularity. The first is Adams's chief contribution to political thinking. It has been called a reply to the French liberal philosophers, and such it is in that it defends our conservative Constitution against the attacks of radical leveling democrats. Among our most valuable political writings are the letters of Adams. In the long days of his retirement he conducted a huge correspondence, discussing with friends, admirers, and former enemies every question that could be raised about his teeming activities from 1765 to 1800. In his later life he became reconciled with his old enemy, Thomas Jefferson, and in many a letter they lived again their great days.

John Adams may not have been gifted with tact, diplomacy, or persuasive eloquence, but he had one quality that has been altogether too scarce an article in American public life. That quality was indomitable honesty, fearful of no consequence and trimming the truth for no man.

ALEXANDER HAMILTON

(1757-1804)

American history is full of peculiar things, but one of the most peculiar was the spectacle of Alexander Hamilton, a penniless emigrant from the West Indies, leading the extreme Federalists and becoming our most brilliant champion of the rights of property. Hamilton had one of the finest minds of his or any other generation. Its clearness, preciseness, and cold logic made it the admiration of his followers and the dread of his opponents. He belongs in American intellectual development because of his insistence upon a firmly unified, highly centralized state and for his frank advocacy of government by the commercial and financial interests. He made an effective political and governmental machine of the Federalist party; he placed our national finances upon the foundation that still supports them; and he skillfully repulsed all agrarian attacks on his party until the monumental blundering of John Adams brought down an irresistible avalanche of adverse votes. A more successful public financier or a more effective party leader has never entered American politics. But in this book we are interested in Hamilton's ideas—not his public career.

Hamilton's Political Philosophy.—Hamilton was the most broadly national thinker yet produced in the United States. A recent historian [1] has correctly remarked that his alien origin allowed him to see American problems unblinded by any touch of local interests or prejudices. As a result, Hamilton's primary aim, the establishment of a strong, highly centralized national government, was developed with no regard whatever for the rights of individual states. States' rights, he thought, could lead only to the lamentable consequences of rivalry and bloodshed. The only assurance of peace, prosperity, and the security of property is a federal government that is much stronger in every respect than any or all of its component parts.

Given such a government, the next concern of Hamilton was to secure the control in the hands of the proper class. This class was to be composed of the men of property—the large landowners of the seaboard, the rich merchants and shippers, and the well-to-do professional men. Hamilton's aristocracy would naturally

[1] Parrington, *The Colonial Mind*, p. 293.

be a small minority of the people, and admission to this group depended solely upon the possession of property or the delegated right to speak for those who had wealth. To Hamilton birth into a certain class was incidental; the possession of property was the major consideration. He and Adams differed somewhat on the choosing of a "natural aristocracy," though in the end they agreed upon the specific individuals. Adams looked first for ability and gentility of birth, thinking that property would naturally be found among the able and well-born. Hamilton looked first for wealth, believing full well that ability and good family connections would be found among the wealthy. Both men ardently desired a constitution that would ensure the permanent control of society by this aristocracy of talents and wealth. Adams believed in an elective executive, such as is provided by the Constitution; Hamilton wanted a hereditary executive, with a life tenure of office, in other words, a king. His chief objective was the undemocratic control of government.

Hamilton was actuated no less by his love of the upper classes than by his fear of the masses. His opinion of human nature was notoriously low. Once he broke out with "The people is a great beast"—an indiscretion that Jefferson did not neglect to report. If Adams flung away sentiment and romantic idealism because they did not accord with his idea of common sense, Hamilton also rejected these qualities, because their acceptance would impede the realization of his clear aims. Adams had in him too much of the Puritan to imagine that man is devoid of all depravity. Hamilton accepted an easy but cynical view that every man is a knave, governed wholly by self-interest, and must be ruled accordingly. The love for individual freedom, humanitarian ideals, and the concept of a mild government, productive of progress, happiness, and justice to the majority of its subjects, never entered Hamilton's thinking. His constant desire was to repress and control the majority for the benefit of the few.

Hamilton thought that government is a thing over and beyond the powers of any and all groups of society; it is no created force, he contended, that moves and lives through its own will. Rather it is an instrument to be placed in the hands of the ruling class. But its power is strictly limited to the aiding of business; regulation and control are beyond its jurisdiction. It is needless to remark that this conception of government did not pass away with the death of the Federalist party.

Hamilton never trusted or understood agrarianism. Such instruments of democracy as town meetings, frontier mass assemblies, or state legislatures elected by small farmers and village dwellers aroused only his contemptuous opposition. His ideal was that of an industrialized or commercialized America with the financial classes in secure control and the agrarians in silent oblivion. America had already had too many agrarian reforms from 1775 to 1789 to stand any more. Business needed no more reform but tranquil stability.

Sources of Hamilton's Thought.—Hamilton was America's nearest approach to an original political thinker. In him we find no Locke, Harrington, or French liberal thought. Physiocratic economics with its insistence upon the importance of agriculture never received a passing glance. He found in Adam Smith's *Wealth of Nations* a congenial theory that government should refrain from regulating or controlling industry, and in Hobbes's *Leviathan* he found the idea of a state with huge power, a centralized force with a slight local government. But in general Hamilton thought more than he read, and his thinking was conditioned by his ideals enumerated in the preceding paragraphs and by the peculiar American conditions.

With the exception of his essays in *The Federalist*, Hamilton left little writing that is read to-day. However, he was a prolific pamphleteer and journalist, contributing his share to the great political debate from 1785 to 1800. His letters are of extreme value to students of our early government or American political theory.

THOMAS JEFFERSON

(1743-1826)

On June 24, 1826, just ten days before his death, Thomas Jefferson wrote that he always had believed "that the mass of mankind was not born with saddles on their backs, nor a favored few booted and spurred ready to ride them legitimately, by the grace of God." These unequivocal words afford a succinct and correct explanation of a career that has been attacked numberless times as the epitome of inconstancy and political perfidy. From th' time that he entered Virginia politics as the young spokesman of the upland farmers until he penned the sentence just quoted, Jefferson was motivated in every important action by his love for democratic equality and his hatred for every form of aristocratic privilege. As conditions varied through his public life of more than fifty years, common sense forced him from time to time to shift his immediate policy to meet new situations, but he never changed his great aims to secure justice for the many against the rapacious power of the few, to make government quickly responsive to the majority will, and to "make war on every form of tyranny over the minds of men." The animosity that Jefferson engendered among the apologists of privilege has never disappeared. During his life and for almost a century after his death he was reviled and misrepresented until his unquestionable right to be known as the father of American democracy was almost obscured. To-day an unbiased examination of Jefferson's career and the attacks on him reveals the fact that the animosity of his enemies was caused by his support of the very things that later observers have most valued in American life. Among the actions that made him unpopular with the privileged classes were his successful efforts to abolish the last relics of aristocracy in the social life of Virginia, his insistence upon the separation of church and state, and his efforts to equalize economic, political, and educational opportunities in this country. His activities in these causes excited so great an animosity that a century after his death the true fame of the man was almost forgotten and the causes of the animosity were veiled in the obscurity of age and controversy. Moreover, as an English historian remarked, hostility to Jefferson frequently took the form of writing his life or editing his works. To-day, thanks to the labors of unprejudiced and competent historians, we are gaining a clear view of the great democrat and of the causes of the animosity to him. And the more we read the more clearly we see that the constant aim of the man was to forward the principles of democracy and that the hostility of his opponents was the hatred of privileged men who were disturbed in the exercise of their outmoded, aristocratic privileges.

Jefferson and the Frontier.—The frontier with its democratic tendencies was one of the dominant influences animating Jefferson. In the mid-eighteenth century his birthplace in Albemarle County, Virginia, was on the frontier, and until the boy started to college he had never seen a village of as many as a dozen houses. Thus he received to the full every influence of the frontier, and whatever liberal foreign thought he may have absorbed later served only to strengthen and rationalize his frontier tendencies. With the independent spirit of a true pioneer, he hated and feared an upper class as much for its lordly contempt for the commoner as for its aristocratic habit of living at the expense of the lower orders. In his economics Jefferson again was a true son of the frontier, for he looked upon the farmer as the foundation of society and the creator of all wealth; merchants, commercial men, financiers—townsmen in general—he regarded as parasites on society. On the frontier human nature was pretty well revealed, and Jefferson had seen enough of it to reject alike John Adams's jaundiced view of mankind, which had in it much of the Puritan doctrine of total depravity, and Hamilton's cynical belief that man's scoundrelly qualities can be repressed only by the hand of authority. The boy from Albemarle County early concluded that man has in him both good and bad, and he was not long in deciding that the pressure of society and the hand of government are more apt to bring out the bad than to promote the good. A frontiersman, intimately acquainted with informal yet effective government by backwoods mass-meetings and assemblies, would naturally mistrust a centralized power, far removed from popular control, impersonal in its operation, and expensive in its upkeep. The man who saw social well-being in the West and social misery under aristocratic governments was very apt to want western conditions made universal. Such a man was Jefferson, and wherever one looks in his writings and actions, one finds unmistakable traces of frontier influence.

Jefferson and Foreign Thought.—We have already seen that Jefferson's familiarity with Locke was reflected again and again in both the words and ideas of the Declaration of Independence, and his acquaintance with European thought did not begin and end with Locke.

Jefferson was well educated. The good beginning in the College of William and Mary he supplemented throughout all his subsequent days with unremitting labor in his study. That the lessons of the classroom were not cast off under the pressure of active life, as seems to be the deplorable modern custom, is proved by the existence of the so-called *Jefferson's Bible,* selections from the New Testament in parallel columns of Greek, Latin, French, and

English. In a letter, written when he was almost eighty years old, he discusses the pronunciation of Greek words. Something in the man's nature forced him constantly to be learning new things. On one passage across the Atlantic he mastered Spanish with the aid of a grammar and a copy of *Don Quixote*. And Jefferson acquired languages not as pretty accomplishments but as tools for use. Language opened his way to a new literature and new information.

Jefferson read omnivorously in every language at his command. Besides Locke, he knew all the great English political writers like Hobbes, Harrington, Sidney, and Milton, and in addition was equally at home in the works of Rousseau, Montesquieu, Diderot, and other Continental thinkers. In his political philosophy he began as a student and follower of the English liberals and soon added to his doctrine the leavening humanitarianism of the French. It has been frequently remarked that the enumeration of man's inherent rights as life, liberty, and the pursuit of happiness shows that Jefferson had combined English and French thought, for the first two are English and the last French. To the end of his days he remained a lover of books. He collected and read one of the finest libraries of his time, and shortly before his death his books were purchased by the government to become the nucleus of the great Library of Congress.

But his scholarly activity did not end with the languages, for in scientific interests and the practical application of his knowledge he rivaled Franklin, and on the older man's death succeeded to the leadership of American scientists and inventors. He was deeply interested in aerial navigation, steam engines, machines for coining money, life preservers, metronomes, and chemistry which he regarded as "among the most useful of the sciences and big with future discoveries for the utility and safety of the human race." He invented the plow with a mold-board constructed on his own mathematical formula for securing the least resistance from the soil—a formula that is said to govern the shape of mold-boards to-day. Furthermore he invented the leather top of a buggy, and devised the first swivel chair. For his plow the French institute of agriculture gave him a medal.

In his religious views Jefferson, along with Franklin and many another eighteenth century worthy, accepted without reservation the doctrines of the deistic philosophy. A scientist, a thinker, and a deep student of European thought was very apt to do this, and Jefferson's religion simply followed his temper and the spirit of the time. Upon his election to the presidency the New England ministers ranted about the election of an "infidel" under whose administration churches would become temples of reason, Bibles would be cast into bonfires, and family bonds would be degraded. But nothing of the sort happened. Jefferson's unfailing courtesy and his reliance upon reason made him as respectful of others' beliefs and practices as he wished others to be mindful of his own.

Jefferson's Social Philosophy.—Individual well-being was the keynote of Jefferson's social philosophy. Hamilton seemed to think exclusively in terms of the moneyed class; Adams conceived of society as a whole, divided into its inevitable classes, with never a thought of the individual; Jefferson began every train of thought with the proposition that the rational happiness of the individual is the supreme end to be sought by all governmental and social activities. He never made a move that he later recalled with pride that did not have for its aim the freeing of the individual from some form of law, custom, or superstition which tended to make men unfree and unhappy.

Few men have been so honored by their state and nation as was Jefferson, and few have discharged the obligations incident to those honors with more satisfaction to their fellow countrymen. Yet when Jefferson wrote his own epitaph he indicated therein only that he was "the author of the Declaration of American Independence, of the statute of Virginia for religious freedom, and the father of the University of Virginia." The significance of this epitaph should not be missed by any student of American democracy.

A catalog of Jefferson's principal performances in behalf of individual liberty is most impressive. He wrote the Declaration of Independence to give America's reasons for seeking political independence from England. He led in the movement to abolish primogeniture and entail that destroyed the legal protection of landed aristocracy in Virginia and established the equality of all in the eyes of the law. He started the attack on the established church and wrote the law that guarantees religious freedom in his state. He assisted in the revision of the Virginia criminal code "with an eye single to reason and the good of those for whose government it was framed," and under his direction capital punishment was abandoned for all offenses save murder and treason. He urged greater freedom of the press, more and better schools, and advocated the wider study of science in preference to the intensive study of the classics, for he considered that scientific studies were of greater immediate benefit to mankind. To forward the pursuit of science and to provide an education for young men that would be free from all theological and ministerial domination, as his last great work he established the University of Virginia. Any man who did all these things was making no meaningless gesture when he swore eternal hostility to all forms of tyranny over the minds of men.

In his more formal social philosophy Jefferson was an idealist. The numerous and far-reaching social reforms that he assisted were to him but faint preludes of the golden day that he dreamed of. His ideal was a society that was overwhelmingly agricultural in its composition, for he thought of farming as the basis of all wealth, and tillers of the soil as the repositories of special virtue and happiness. Over this society he would install a government whose power would be limited to that which is sufficient to keep order and to provide for the defense of its subjects. Such a government must be responsive to the people, economical in operation, and totally without the trappings of aristocracy or royalty. Education would be provided for all, and the leaders of society would be selected from those who prepared themselves, regardless of origin. Finally this ideal state would have no slavery or serfdom.

Jefferson thought of the state as a thing different from that described by Adams or Hamilton. He believed that the state becomes a fact through the agreement of the people from whom it derives all its powers. John Adams's solicitude for absolute justice concerned Jefferson not at all. He thought that the people have a right to do anything that they wish. Hence justice becomes merely social expediency and the expression of the majority will. A state in which there are such conceptions of justice and majority rule would be an unspeakable place according to Adams and Hamilton, for the former would be repelled by a government dominated by depraved and inferior men, while the latter would shrink from a state run by knavish fellows each seeking his own gain. Such fears did not disturb Jefferson. He had much of the glowing back-to-nature philosophy of Rousseau, and he contended that in a simple agricultural state, uncontaminated by cities and unspoiled by oppression, man would be virtuous and magnanimous. The Jeffersonian ideal state was one animated by humanitarian motives, and not by fear or villainy. It was to be an instrument in the hands of a rational, merciful majority; not a lash over the bowed backs of laboring humanity.

Not the most dismaying incidents ever dashed Jefferson's faith in the people. The cure for democracy is more democracy, he argued, and the older he grew the more democratic he became. The best government of all is that which is the most responsive to the people. Revolutions he did not fear, saying that a nation ought to have one every twenty years, but he deplored bloodshed and wished that overturns of government might be by ballot.

Jefferson and Democracy.—It is the fashion to-day to sneer at the democracy of a man who owned slaves and a large plantation, lived on a grand scale, and deliberately cultivated aristocratic virtues like independence of mind and a contempt for mass thinking. But Jefferson hated slavery, as did many slaveholders of his day, his plantation was not large when compared with those of his neighbors, and his cultivation of aristocratic virtues made him refuse to follow the old ways of thinking that recognized class distinction as natural and inevitable. Jefferson was an early democrat and laughing at his conception of democracy is like laughing at mankind for creeping before walking.

In an age when the masses of Europe were without education and were regarded as an inferior order of human beings Jefferson declared his belief that man was a rational animal, endowed by nature with rights and with an innate sense of justice; and that he could be restrained from wrong and protected in right by moderate powers confided to persons of his own choice and held to their duties by dependence on his own will.[1]

THE LATER WORK OF THOMAS PAINE

If the ship that bore Paine back to Europe in 1787 had foundered we should look on the author of *Common Sense* and *The American Crisis* as our most effective Revolutionary pamphleteer, worthy of the unalloyed admiration of all Americans of all time without regard to creed or party. But fortunately the tempest was stayed, and Paine lived to become in three nations the storm center of violent debates whose reverberations disturb us even yet.

[1] *The Rise of American Civilization,* Beard and Beard, Vol. I, p. 379.

Only a few years ago Mr. Roosevelt referred to Paine as a "filthy little atheist," and such a characterization was only an echo of other more flaming ones that were flung about recklessly after 1790. To-day we ought to take a more temperate view of the controversy. Indeed as several have already pointed out, Paine was neither little, nor dirty, nor an atheist. But he mortally offended every influential group in England and alienated all those in America who liked class distinction, a landed aristocracy, or orthodox theology. The process by which Paine turned a good reputation into an evil thing is interesting.

"The Rights of Man."—When Paine saw that the American Revolution was accomplished, his constant urge to do something for the betterment of mankind caused him to experiment with different types of bridges that would be more economical and useful than were the older kinds. He produced the model of an iron structure that drew such praise from his friends that he left for Europe in 1787 to exhibit it in France and England. The design was pronounced a success, but before many months had passed the French Revolution broke with a crash, and Paine again found himself in a turmoil of action and discussion. He accepted a seat in the French assembly, for his great fame preceded him to Europe, and for the second time in his life his fearless and vigorous writing presented a brilliant defense of a revolutionary activity.

In 1790 Burke, a former friend of America but no lover of revolution, set forth his alarm over the French situation in a pamphlet called *Reflections on the French Revolution*. In this work the writer took the view that, if government is once established by contract, that is by permission of the governed, such a government cannot be overthrown. In other words the social contract is perpetual. Hence revolutions are moral wrongs. Paine replied to this theory in one of his most telling works, *The Rights of Man*.

The Rights of Man is probably the best statement of radical revolutionary philosophy that we have from the eighteenth century. Burke had admitted that the English people had the right in 1688 to expel their unjust king and install another, but he denied that right to succeeding generations. Paine took the ground that the social contract must be agreeable to or at least silently accepted by every generation, pertinently asking if the sovereignty that belonged to the generation of 1688 was not bequeathed to the next generation just as other things were. He furthermore demanded to know if one generation could bind their descendants to the end of time. According to Paine the power of a government rests upon the immediate consent of those governed. He attributed entire sovereignty to the citizens. "That which a nation chooses to do it has a right to do," he declared, stating the very core of democratic thought from Rousseau to the frontier cracker-box philosopher. There are no permanent rights of classes or vested interests; a majority of the people have the right to revoke any privilege granted by themselves or by any previous generation. The wicked injustice of majorities never alarmed Paine; to him the great mass of people were always just and always motivated by high ideals. He held that increasing knowledge and progress in the arts of civilization would tend to make the state more and more unnecessary. *The Rights of Man* influenced many political thinkers, both European and American, but its chief effect on this side of the Atlantic was to fortify the beliefs of Jefferson and the frontier democrats. To this day the book is widely read and as widely debated.

"Agrarian Justice."—*The Rights of Man* alienated Paine from all conservative political thinkers, and his next little book, *Agrarian Justice,* outraged the feelings of large landowners everywhere. This work appeared in 1796 as an answer to a sermon by an English bishop on "The Wisdom of God in Having Made Both the Rich and the Poor." In his reply Paine boldly attacks the problem of poverty from the point of view of an agrarian democrat with a pronounced physiocratic economics. He takes the same ground that Henry George took a century later by holding that land monopoly is the cause of all poverty and all wealth. Economic equality will come only when "monopoly of the source of wealth is made impossible." He takes the bold ground that, in dealing with land monopoly, property rights are not perpetually sacred but may be revoked if the needs of society demand it. The man who buys land and holds it waiting for an advance in value because of the thrift or energy of his neighbors is entitled only to what he originally invested, Paine argued, for the increase is the work of society and not that of the owner. Thus he disposed of the "unearned increment" exactly as Henry George did in *Progress and Poverty* Furthermore Paine wanted an inheritance tax of ten per cent. The sum created by this tax was to be used to prepare the young for

active life and to pension the old. This plan would be only a form of social insurance.

In *Agrarian Justice* we find the best example of Paine's humanitarianism. He was laboring with a problem of relieving the oldest and most widespread social wrong, and he solved it in the spirit of the French humanitarian who had accepted to the full the principles of democracy. The book was far ahead of its time, but not so far that it was not understood. The rising hosts of democracy hailed it as an attempt to democratize economic opportunity, and the conservative landholders reviled it as the fruits of a mind poisoned with hatred of the propertied class.

"The Age of Reason."—Paine like Jefferson was a confirmed deist, and *The Age of Reason* is a studied attempt to make the reader accept the principles of that belief. The revolution in France swept into excesses that Paine could not countenance. He was thrown into jail and marked for the guillotine, but through either the carelessness or kindness of his keepers he escaped death. While waiting for his fate, he heard that certain agitators were leading the French people into an acceptance of atheism. To combat the tide of irreligion by pointing out the reasonableness of deism he wrote his most widely known book—one that drew down on him all the vindictive hatred of the orthodox, especially in New England. In parts *The Age of Reason* sounds like the devout belief of a religious person. Certainly at no place is it atheistic. The second page of a recent edition begins:

I believe in one God and no more; and I hope for happiness beyond life. I believe in the equality of man, and I believe that religious duties consist in doing justice, loving mercy, and endeavoring to make our fellow-creatures happy.

Obviously a man holding such sentiments is not an atheist. But Paine proceeded to give unmistakable proof of his deism by repudiating the clergy and the Biblical foundation of religion. To the orthodox his views were odious, but he might have escaped total condemnation had he stated them in indirect or conciliatory language. This he did not do. In the most trenchant manner Paine makes a headlong assault on orthodoxy, stating his opinions, as was his custom, in the most vigorous and direct fashion. The orthodox never forgave him, and for a century his reputation was blasted. Successive generations of students knew him only as a dangerous atheist. No atheist was he, but a great revolutionary agitator and pamphleteer, a great American patriot, and a great hater of oppression wherever he found it.

THE LAST CRY OF THE PURITAN FEDERALISTS

The Connecticut Wits.—After 1790 the tide of Jeffersonian democracy rose with amazing speed, appalling it was to the Federalists. The hated doctrines of the French Revolution spread through the land; liberty, fraternity, and equality became the despised slogan of the agrarians; Paine's writings permeated even the precincts of Yale, where, Timothy Dwight despairingly reported, only one Christian was to be discovered in the entire student body; state after state surrendered to the democrats until the reviled leader of the masses swept into the White House and hurried the Federalists into oblivion. But though all was lost, New England struggled against the Jeffersonian revolution, and the Connecticut wits became the last cry of a disappearing order.

Connecticut in 1800 was probably the most conservative state, and her wits were the most reactionary men within her borders. These admirers of an older day were John Trumbull, Timothy Dwight, Lemuel Hopkins, David Humphreys, and several others. This group, trained at Yale in the strictest Puritan doctrine— this was before Paine's day—naturally espoused the social and political views of Adams and Hamilton. Jefferson and his leveling doctrines seemed the essence of all that was wicked and contrary to nature's plan. To the wits the obvious way out of all perplexities, governmental, social, and religious, was a return to the primitive but tranquil order of the early theocracy.

The most eminent of the group was Timothy Dwight, called by his critics "The Pope" because of his unquestioned eminence in Connecticut religious and political life. Dwight was a clergyman, the president of Yale, and the near relative of the most important men in the state. His aims were to keep orthodox Puritanism unpolluted by the heresies of Paine and his crew, to repel Jeffersonian democracy which was knocking imperiously at the door, and to make the youth under his direction efficient leaders in the fight against deism and agrarianism. That he was not wholly successful was in no wise due to his lack of sincerity or to his failing energy. The times were against him. Standing unseen on the threshold of

New England was a mightier force than deism or democracy. The force was romanticism under whose impetus New England's social order, thought, and religious life were renovated. As a state leader Dwight was formidable, but the very qualities that made even the reckless democrat quail before the severe Federalist but ill fitted him for a literary life. Yet he wrote voluminously. Poems, tracts, sermons, travels, streamed from his flying pen. Like many an early writer, he is little known to-day, save to literary antiquarians, but to those who possess hardiness and patience he speaks the plainest Federalist doctrine. All mankind is elect or lost; the saved are few, the wicked are many. How disrespectful to the obvious will of heaven would be the rule of the majority. Besides if the wicked rule, the elect might lose some of the property awarded them for their wisdom and virtue. Plainly democracy would never do. This theme the redoubtable doctor stated again and again with only slight variation. The curious may find it in such works as *The Triumph of Infidelity, The Duty of Americans at the Present Crisis, Nature and Danger of the Infidel Philosophy,* and *Travels in New England and New York.*

Trumbull's work has already been discussed, and the work of Barlow will be mentioned shortly. The other Connecticut wits merely echo Dwight.

PHILIP FRENEAU

(1752-1832)

Philip Freneau is another early writer who has had his just claim to a place in our literature obscured alike by the venom of political opponents and by the misguided praise of friendly but impercep- tive critics. By the one group he has been called "a mere incen- diary," "a barking cur," and "that rascal Freneau," while the other faction has labored to pull the veil of charity over his political activities by extravagantly lauding his nature poetry. As a matter of fact Freneau was the poet of freedom and democracy. In his battle for human rights he was successively an American revolu- tionist, an agrarian, an exponent of French political thought, and a Jeffersonian democrat. In the course of his long contest with his opponents he was both a poet and a fiery editor, but the same ideas are present whether the vehicle be a lyric, a satire, or an editorial.

Freneau's Political Poetry.—Freneau began his literary career in 1771 at Princeton by writing, with the assistance of H. H. Bracken-ridge, a commencement ode breathing so devout a spirit of loyalty to England that it shortly was the source of deep embarrassment to the youthful poets. By 1775 Freneau had revised his ode and espoused the American cause. Sharp lampoons and humorous satires from his pen helped Paine and Samuel Adams in their ef-forts to rid the colonists of the royal bogy, and their twittings helped make Americans cease crooking the knee at the mention of the king. During the war Freneau was captured by the enemy and held on a prison ship for some time. His wretched experi-ences here gave rise to one of his longest and most effective poems, "The Prison Ship." One of his early lyrics, "The Battle of Eutaw Springs" was memorized by Sir Walter Scott as a fine lyrical out-burst. Among his other revolutionary activities was the ratifica-tion of independence in four hundred lines. In short Freneau did his share in the spreading of the American cause by songs and satires.

When the war was over, Freneau moved straight ahead in the democratic path that his feet were treading. For him there was no shrinking from the results of the Revolution, no yearning for the royal state of England. When our national government was established, the poet obtained a post under Jefferson as French translator for the state department. Shortly thereafter he became editor of the *National Gazette,* a violently Anti-Federalist news-paper. In the columns of this journal he began a vigorous warfare on titles, class distinctions, and all the semi-regal trappings that Adams and the Federalists so ardently desired. Those attacked repaid their debts in kind, and the battle waxed furious. To make matters worse Freneau was an ardent friend of the French revolu-tionists. This was too much for respectable Federalists to endure, so they read the poet, in company with Jefferson and Paine, out of the society of decent people by dubbing him an "atheistic edi-tor." To the Federalists Freneau was a democrat, a democrat was a follower of Paine and Jefferson who in turn believed in the "infidel" French philosophy. Therefore a democrat was an atheist. The logic was a trifle weak, but the conclusion eminently satisfied such guardians of righteousness as Timothy Dwight. Thus Fre-neau, like Paine, was saddled with an odium that he did not de-serve.

Freneau's chief work from 1790 to 1800 was to popularize in his usual way the important elements in French social thought. His poetry was democratic, in the full meaning of that word, and it contained the germ of the "back-to-nature" doctrine that we are later to hear about so often.

Freneau a Poet of Nature.—Such poems as "The Wild Honey Suckle," "The Indian Burying Ground," "On a Honey Bee," all show that Freneau had a genuine love for nature, and if he had not been the poet of two revolutions and a busy democratic editor, we might have had many more lyrics of this type. The poems named are just about the first American poetry that to-day we can read without pain or weariness. Freneau will have to go down in our literature as one who loved beauty, but, like so many Americans, he was too busy with other things to set forth his love in adequate words.

JOEL BARLOW
(1754-1812)

Joel Barlow started life as one of the die-hard aristocrats of Connecticut and by a strange turn of fate ended as the trusted friend of Jefferson and one of the extreme democrats of his age. The explanation of this strange transformation is to be found in the fact that his frigid conservatism was blown upon by the hot winds of revolutionary doctrine, and the conservatism melted. As a young man Barlow, just released from the strict discipline of Yale, wrote pretentious but clumsy poetry, preached to the ragged revolutionary soldiers, attempted law and journalism, dabbled in a bit of land speculation, and through all firmly held to respectable political opinions. Entering the employment of a land company, he went abroad for a business trip that lasted from 1787 to 1805. During these years his early opinions gave way to an ardent love for the rights of man as expounded by Paine and the European liberals.

"Advice to the Privileged Orders."—"Tom Paine is not a more worthless fellow," exclaimed John Adams in a typical note of petulance when Barlow was mentioned, and Barlow's "worthlessness" was caused by a little book called *Advice to the Privileged Orders*. Barlow had a mind so receptive that it took him no time at all to drop his Connecticut Puritanism and become a cosmopoli-

tan. He soon became at home in London and Paris, where he thoroughly absorbed the doctrines of European democratic thinkers. As his share of liberal thinking he contributed his *Advice*. The dominant notes in this work are the insistence upon social well-being as the chief end of government and the belief that society is morally responsible for individual happiness and welfare. The first doctrine, rich in humanitarian feeling, demands the constant cultivation of a social conscience. The second, as elaborated by Barlow, demands that society give to all its members equal opportunities, and equal opportunities are possible only if all men receive a chance at the same educational advantages. Barlow placed his finger unerringly upon the chief implication of democracy, universal education, for by no other means can numerical majorities be made wise and just, by no other way can leadership be opened to the able of any class and not only to the sons of the rich and well-born. But to those of aristocratic pretensions the doctrine was more than hateful. That it does not seem so to-day is simply one proof that Barlow saw the way along which the America of the future was to travel.

Our literary chroniclers have refused to do the graceful, kindly thing and allow Barlow's poetry to remain in dusty oblivion. If the *Advice* was nineteenth century in its tone, *The Columbiad*, Barlow's long patriotic poem, was early eighteenth in its form. The sentiments expressed are laudable, but the author's fancy was too heavy and his pen too serious to write easy poetry. When he attempted majesty of style he achieved only artificial grandiosity. "The Hasty Pudding" is better, but it is an insignificant composition compared with some of the author's prose. The kindly thing is to remember Barlow as a lover of freedom and an ardent advocate of universal education and to forget his heavy-handed toying with poetry.

HUGH HENRY BRACKENRIDGE

(1748-1816)

H. H. Brackenridge, Princeton classmate of Madison and Freneau, Pennsylvania judge, Jeffersonian democrat, belongs in our literature by virtue of his work *Modern Chivalry*. This prose satire, a loosely constructed novel, has been variously judged. By some the book has been considered only an attack on democracy, but this judgment is certainly not correct. A more likely appraisal is that it is our "first backwoods book." A good democrat was Brackenridge, and he traveled much on the frontier where he saw democracy in its fullest and most unlovely garb. Faults in the system could not escape his detection, but *Modern Chivalry* never questions the fundamental rightness of democracy. Just as Barlow touched the future strength of democracy, so did Brackenridge point out its future weakness. This weakness is the inevitable tendency of the majority to harken to loud-voiced demagogues who are as short of principles as they are of learning. Brackenridge saw that democracy is liable to choose as its representatives men like Davy Crockett, who can cover their boundless ignorance with a ready homespun wit, a genial disposition, and free-handed readiness to "treat the crowd." If *Modern Chivalry* devotes many of its pages to satirizing such fellows and those who elect them to office, it should not be supposed that the author was hostile to democracy. He was not, but he saw the weaknesses of the order, and, like the friend that he was, called attention to them before it was too late.

Brackenridge has the distinction of having produced in *Modern Chivalry* the most interesting book of fiction during the early Jeffersonian epoch. The satire has survived through more than a century of changing tastes, and to-day it can be had in modern dress provided by a contemporary publisher. Not so much can be said of many of our early attempts at fiction. He also wrote two of our early dramas, *The Battle of Bunker's Hill*, and *The Death of General Montgomery*.

SUGGESTED READINGS

Adams: *The Adams Family*. New York. 1930. pp. 3-115.
    Competent study of John Adams.
Adams: *Revolutionary New England*. Boston. 1923.
    The second book in the series that gives a consecutive account of the history of New England. Like its fellows, it is an excellent study.
Andrews: *The Colonial Background of the American Revolution*. New Haven. 1924.
Beard and Beard: *The Rise of American Civilization*. New York. 1927. Vol. I, pp. 189-335.
Becker: *The Declaration of Independence*. New York. 1922.
    Excellent study of sources.

Best: *Thomas Paine*. New York. 1927.
> A popular work. Not so good as Conway's biography but more easily found.

Bowers: *Jefferson and Hamilton*. Boston. 1925.

Chinard: *Thomas Jefferson*. Boston. 1929.
> Fairly satisfactory. Minimizes Jefferson's relation to his American background.

Conway: *Thomas Paine*. New York. 1892.
> Old but still most useful.

Cunningham: *Timothy Dwight*. New York. 1942.
> Takes issue with many of the critics of Dwight.

Faÿ: *The Revolutionary Spirit in France and America*. New York. 1927.
> "A study of the moral and intellectual relations between France and the United States at the end of the eighteenth century."

Forman: *The Political Activities of Philip Freneau*. Johns Hopkins Studies in History and Political Science. Vol. 20, pp. 473-569.
> Excellent.

Hazen: *Contemporary American Opinion of the French Revolution*. Johns Hopkins Studies in History and Political Science. Extra Volume 16. Baltimore. 1897.

Hirst: *Life and Letters of Thomas Jefferson*. New York. 1926.
> An English interpretation. Should be read with Chinard and Nock.

Howard: *The Connecticut Wits*. Chicago. 1943.
> Definitive study.

Jameson: *The American Revolution Considered as a Social Movement*. Princeton. 1926.
> The best discussion of the subject.

Koch: *Republican Religion*. New York. 1933.

Koch: *The Philosophy of Thomas Jefferson*. New York. 1943.
> Both of the books by Koch are very useful to the serious student.

Leary: *That Rascal Freneau*. New Brunswick. 1941.
> Satisfactory treatment of the subject.

Maclay: *The Journal of William Maclay*. New York. 1927.
> Maclay, Senator from Pennsylvania, gives a vivid account of the beginnings of our national government. Many of his expressed views run counter to those of orthodox historians. Not to be overlooked.

Morais: *Deism in Eighteenth Century America*. New York. 1934.

Mudge: *The Social Philosophy of John Taylor of Caroline*. New York. 1939.
> No student should overlook this work, though the writing is heavy.

Newlon: *The Life and Writings of Hugh Henry Brackenridge*. Princeton. 1932.

Nock: *Jefferson*. New York. 1926.
> Certainly one of the finest books on the subject. Nock was a Jeffersonian and, in addition, a fine stylist. Most important.

Parrington: *The Colonial Mind.* New York. 1927.
  Parrington is always stimulating.

Pattee: *Sidelights on American Literature.* New York. 1922.
  Essay on Freneau.

Peach: *Paine.* New York. 1928.
  A selection of Paine's writings and a good introduction.

Pearson: *Tom Paine: Friend of Mankind.* New York. 1937.

Robinson: *Jeffersonian Democracy in New England.* New Haven. 1916.
  A good account of the clash of liberalism with Puritan-Federalism. Valuable.

Savelle: *Seeds of Liberty.* New York. 1948.
  Should be consulted. Written from the point of view of a liberal.

Tyler: *A Literary History of the American Revolution.* New York. 1897.
  A monumental work. All students are indebted to it.

BOOK III
ROMANTICISM IN AMERICA

CHAPTER VII

AMERICAN ROMANTICISM

The romantic revolution, affecting everything from our verse form to our conception of man's place in the universe, was probably the most influential and widespread intellectual force ever liberated in the United States. The fundamental premises of romanticism were so congenial to the American environment and temper, and the immediate results so harmonized with certain other forces already in this country, notably Jeffersonian democracy and the frontier spirit, that the movement spread rapidly to all parts of America and held on tenaciously even after its main ideas became hopelessly old-fashioned.

What Is Romanticism?—It is quite impossible to give a wholly satisfactory definition of romanticism, just as it is impossible to give a short adequate definition of the medieval spirit, or of the Renaissance, or of Puritanism. Romanticism, like all the influences just mentioned, can best be discussed in terms of its results, for it varied so widely from time to time and from place to place that it is impossible to give a thumb-nail characterization that will do more than indicate a few broad and general features. A short definition of romanticism must be of necessity more notable for its generality than for its preciseness, for when such a definition attempts particulars, it becomes involved in a morass of qualifications, each additional qualification having the tendency to obscure the subject still more. But it is no simple matter to define romanticism in terms of its results, for these are very numerous and extremely diverse. So diverse are they that often one wing of romanticism will flatly contradict the most cherished tenets of another. This is to be seen very clearly in the case of the South Carolina and the Massachusetts romantics. The Southerners visioned a society modeled upon that of ancient Greece with its sharp division into aristocrats, middle class, and slaves. The romantic reformers of Massachusetts gratefully accepted as their chief task the abolition of slavery upon which southern society was founded. The specific characteristics of romanticism of South Carolina bore only the vaguest of resemblances to that of the Mississippi Valley, while one might have to search for long to find much in common between two romantics like Thoreau and Irving. Romanticism was a rapidly shifting, elusive force that defies compact definition.

By and large one can say that romanticism was a protest against the dominant ideas of the mid-eighteenth century. It tended to substitute imagination for logic. It preferred a life governed by feeling and emotion to one of cold reason. Beyond everything it stood for individualism, emphatically rejecting a scrupulous observance of established rules and regulations in favor of a life of individual liberty. Liberty was the first watchword of romanticism; later fraternity and equality were added. In the development of the American mind, the most important product of this adherence to liberty was the liberation of the human imagination from the bonds of outworn conventions. Imagination thus freed created a spirit of fine idealism as opposed to hard practical sense, the spirit of materialism, that had ruled the mind of man for many years. Idealism tempered by humanitarianism, at once made itself felt in the changed conception of individual worth, in political theory and the practical work of government, in religion, in everyday life, and especially in literature, which enjoyed some changes of its own and carefully reflected all the other transformations wrought by the quickening influence.

Jean Jacques Rousseau.—Those who seek easy explanations for the romantic revolution are fond of attributing the entire movement to one man, Jean Jacques Rousseau (1715-1775), a French writer whose two books, *Émile* and *The Social Contract,* are frequently spoken of as the incentives of a sudden and violent overturning of old ideals. No greater amount of misinformation could be collected in a few lines. In the first place the romantic movement was an intellectual development that occupied many years in reaching its height and then as slowly gave way to other ideas and new trends of thought. No intellectual revolution is accomplished overnight, and romanticism is far from an exception to the rule. In the second place Rousseau's works made a profound impression, but like so many books of immense popular appeal, they simply stated what a great many people were thinking. The eighteenth century, well called the Age of Reason, had so wantonly disregarded the feelings of mankind that many were already deeply dissatisfied with the spiritual and intellectual life of the time when Rousseau made his appearance. The French proponent of a life of feeling merely summarized the prevailing unrest in his two notable books, one on education and the other on government.

But though Rousseau is more important as an intellectual and spiritual barometer than as a creative thinker, a short survey of his ideas will show the temper of early romanticism. He felt that man was at heart a good being and that civilized society had corrupted him. The sure cure for all evils that afflict civilized man was to drop all traditional restrictions, all hampering conventionalities, and return to the original state of nature. Such a return will insure justice, liberty, kindness, and universal happiness. Social well-being was Rousseau's aim, and that well-being was to be effected through individual welfare. Man's chief desire, urged Rousseau, is liberty to do what he wishes. The very center of such thinking is concentrated individualism.

Rousseau was forced to recognize the fact that individual liberty frequently runs counter to governmental regulations and to the expressed will of society. His final solution of the problem was to give the greatest liberty to the greatest number. In other words he advocated majority rule, thinking that the innate goodness and wisdom of the natural man would lead the majority to do only the best thing for the general good. He held that the majority can be assisted in their search for wisdom and justice by a judicious education that will carefully cultivate the latent good qualities in man. Once these qualities are cultivated, an enlightened citizenship will result, and social well-being will be accomplished.

For the proper functioning of the democratic majority thus visualized, Rousseau laid down certain definite conditions. He said that a state to function properly ought to be small in size; the people should have "simple manners," that is, agriculture and small business ought to predominate to the exclusion of elaborate commercial ventures with their complex social problems; the citizens ought to have absolute equality of rank and justice, for without this provision equality of rights cannot prevail; and finally society ought not to enjoy luxury, "for luxury either comes of riches or makes them necessary." Given these conditions, the human race has unlimited possibilities of progress, he declared with the jaunty optimism so characteristic of romanticism. Such were the major tenets of Rousseau, and such were some of the major tenets of romanticism.

It is not necessary to point out that many of these ideas reached America in the hands of Franklin, Jefferson, and Paine. At first the new doctrines were felt only in political and social speculation, but after 1800 they received a ready expression in literature.

It is difficult to attach any dates to the romantic movement. It slowly developed during the latter part of the eighteenth century and then as slowly subsided. In America it first appeared in the early 1770's, by 1800 it was something of an influence, and from 1830 to 1860 it was at its height. The opening of the Civil War is fixed as the terminal date of the movement, but its end was caused more by the rise of industrialism than by the war.

MANIFESTATIONS OF ROMANTICISM

As previously remarked, romanticism is best known by its works, but it must always be remembered that not all of the works were visible at any one time or in any one place.

Romanticism and the Status of the Individual.—Romanticism was overwhelmingly individualistic in its tendencies. The eighteenth century had talked much about "Man" but little about men as individuals. Pope wrote his "Essay on Man" that spoke of men as a generic class, but Wordsworth, a genuine romantic, wrote "Michael," a poem about a particular man. Pope sought the qualities common to all men, his was a typical man; Wordsworth sought qualities peculiar to one man, his was an individual, Michael the countryman. In politics Jefferson was concerned with a problem of individual liberty in a social order. Emerson spent a long and fruitful life preaching the doctrine of self-reliance. Thoreau made his life a living proof of the contention that man develops better as an individual when unhampered by the bonds of society and man-made institutions. Whittier burned with indignation when individual freedom was violated by slavery. In the hands of the romantic thinkers and writers the exaltation of the individual and the defense of his specific rights were paramount tasks. The chief of these rights was liberty, the liberty to conduct one's own affairs in one's own way, to enjoy one's own interpretation of religion, and to develop one's own individuality despite governmental and social interference. Preceding generations had relied on the strength of the government or the church to sustain society; the romantic shifted the sanction to himself. "Trust thyself," exclaimed Emerson, "every heart vibrates to that iron string," and again, "What I must do is all that concerns me, not what the people think." Walt Whitman celebrated himself as the center of the universe and took upon his own shoulders the toil and suffering of all humanity. In short the romantic regarded individual human personality as the greatest thing in the world.

Romantic Optimism.—So vivid a conception of the dignity and worth of the individual as that entertained by the romantic must have been founded upon an implicit faith in the goodness of human nature. If all men are not perfect, they have in them the possibility of perfection. This is the fundamental belief upon which the romantic erected his whole social philosophy. As a result, he would suffer no institution to repress or pervert the goodness of man, nor would he tolerate any tradition or belief that conflicted in the slightest with this cheerful faith in the individual. The radiant optimism of the romantics was of immense historical importance, for it was a powerful influence in the work of freeing the mind of the timid inhibitions and repressions imposed by an age that feared the natural man as the child of depravity. At the same time this optimism in the hands of Emerson and Whitman became a stirring trumpet summoning all men to great lives that would be worthy of the divinity within.

The prevailing optimism elevated the idea of progress almost to the position of a national religion. For a hundred years the word "progress" was a wand to transform into realities all kinds of theories, good, bad, and totally indifferent. Even sturdily independent thinkers like Emerson, Thoreau, and Whitman agreed with the national belief in that they emphasized the possibility of spiritual progress and the perfectibility of human nature. Running through all the pages of Emerson and Thoreau there is a constant overtone of optimistic faith, and in the verse of Whitman this overtone is swallowed in a rattle of drums and a blast of trumpets that celebrate the goodness of man and the certain felicity of his fate. Some modern readers find this confident optimism rather annoying, but no other trait is more characteristic of the romantic movement.

Without an optimistic belief in the goodness of human nature much of the romantic doctrine would have been senseless and even dangerous. Emerson's individualism would have been demoralizing had it not been founded on the assumption that the innate goodness of man will suffer the individual to do no wrong so long as he follows the prompting of an enlightened conscience. Certain present-day critics who cavil at the shortcomings of the romantic school forget the very premise upon which romanticism reared its body of teaching.

The Reform Movement.—If man is good and capable of unlimited progress, and if we should look upon all his aspirations in a spirit of tenderness, mercy, and helpfulness, is it not reasonable—is it not our moral duty—to seek to abolish any institution, habit, or tradition that keeps man from developing in the way of liberty and happiness? Thus ran the question, and the obvious answer to this query precipitated the great American reform movement that reached its height from 1830 to 1860.

The reforms suggested were numerous and widely different. To the northern romantic the most glaringly evil of all repressive forces was that of Negro slavery. Second only to that was the drink habit. Then came a huge number of projected reforms from the regulation of diet, supported so ardently by Dr. Graham, inventor of whole-wheat flour, to a sweeping renovation of society which was advocated by any number of ecstatic reformers. The rights of women, including the right to vote, attracted many champions. Horace Mann led in the reform of our elementary schools. Universal peace and internationalism had their advocates. Amelia Bloomer held her opinions about the proper clothing for women. But the climax of reform came when a group of fantastic enthusiasts announced the abolition of sin.

One of the most interesting and significant outgrowths of romanticism was the establishment of a large number of communistic societies in which the members lived on a common footing and devoted themselves to the common welfare. The primary purpose of all these groups was to allow the members to enjoy immediately all the blessings visioned by romantic idealism. Some of the communities were purely religious, some were attempts to achieve at once the golden age of social life, but all grappled at some time with the growing problem of labor and industrialism. The most famous of these societies was Brook Farm, but the most successful and longest lived was the Oneida community of central New York.

There were dozens of these groups scattered throughout the country, although there were very few in the South.

In short, any reform ever proposed had its adherents in the United States during this epoch, and despite much gusty talk and harmless vaporing great social good was effected by the implanting of a keen social conscience in the heart of America. This reform movement is one of the finest fruits of romantic idealism, the habit of dreaming Utopian dreams. That many of the projected reforms have been realized is sufficient proof that not all the leaders were impractical visionaries. In fact the reformers constituted a high-minded, public-spirited group of men and women.

Romanticism and the Humble Life.—Glorifying equality, the simple life, and the innate goodness of every individual as it did, romanticism naturally extolled the humble man, the one who lived close to nature, rather than the man most elevated by artificial society to a place far above his fellows. Romantic writers usually attributed huge importance to feeling or emotion—intuition it was frequently called—and it was thought that man's intuitions function more freely as the individual is more and more released from the conventions of society. Hence the humble were regarded as the keepers of peculiar wisdom and virtue. Of all romantic writers none illustrates this tendency so well as does Wordsworth, but it can be found frequently in America, especially in the Emerson-Thoreau group.

The Romantic Concept of Nature.—Next to human personality the greatest thing in the romantic world was nature, and man and nature were considered as complementary parts of a whole. From nature man received his culture and his knowledge, and to it he must go for inspiration and guidance. The individual heart and soul can most safely be accepted as guides when they have been subjected to the tutelage of nature, the great mother.

Everything about nature appeared good to the adoring eyes of the romantic. Wordsworth spoke of "nature's holy plan," Emerson accepted nature as the guide of his life, and Thoreau literally lived outdoors, not because he was a naturalist, but because he loved nature far more than he liked society. Every true romantic felt that he was drawn by the power of nature into a better understanding of himself, into clearer, more trustful relations with his fellows, and into a closer communion with God. Nature was altogether good, and its teachings were a great, infallible Bible open before the eyes of man. In other words, nature was the mind of God made visible. Man is a part of nature and as a partaker of her calm wisdom becomes a part of the divine. "Standing on the bare ground—my head bathed by the blithe air, and uplifted into infinite space . . . I am part or particle of God," testified Emerson. Again he declared that nature deifies man.

The romantic idea of nature differed widely from the Newtonian conception. Sir Isaac Newton thought of nature as a stringently regulated system, every part of which fitted into an orderly scheme governed by immutable laws. A static nature, ruled by comprehensible regulations, offered the highest example of the application of reason to the ordering of things. Rousseau and the romantics in general had a different idea of the meaning and working of nature. Newton saw in nature the embodiment of reason; the romantics saw the embodiment of freedom. Newton gazed at the heavenly bodies and saw order insured by changeless law; the romantics, looking upon the untrammeled life of wild animals and the "natural man," saw liberty unfettered. Each saw what he looked for, and each drew his own conclusions from his observations. Reason told Newton that he was right; intuition told the romantic that he was right. But whatever the cause may have been for so thinking, the glowing romantic saw in nature the happy effects that would come to man could all repressive laws, customs, and institutions be nullified. Nature was more than the mind of God made visible, it was the spirit of liberty made manifest. And the mind of God and the spirit of liberty were not antagonistic.

Any doctrine that placed so great an emphasis upon nature and the natural man stood an excellent chance of being favorably received in America, for on this continent nature was inescapable. In Europe man had to flee from society and seek nature; in America nature came to a man's door and demanded admittance. The new world was much in the thought of European romantics. Southey and Coleridge planned to establish a communistic society on the Susquehanna River, and nearly every idealist of France or England looked upon America and her "natural" men as living illustrations of romantic ideals. Under such conditions it is no wonder that the new philosophy reached its highest development in this country and lingered on here long after it had virtually disappeared from Europe. Walt Whitman, the last great romantic, was born only four or five years before Shelley and Keats died, and he continued the romantic tradition in America until 1892.

The Romantic Appeal to Imagination and Feelings.—However widely the romantics may have differed in their opinions of man, the reform movement, optimism, or the meaning of nature, they all came together on common ground in attributing great importance to imagination and emotional feeling. Idealism was the mainspring of romantic thought, and idealism always feeds upon imagination. The eighteenth century, with its insistence upon reason and common sense, had too long fettered the fancy of man. By 1790 the race was suffering from a case of suppressed desire—the desire to let the imagination run riot. Romantic idealism in its various forms offered a realization of this desire, and early in the nineteenth century human imagination enjoyed one of its great flowering times.

The true romantic indulged his sense of mystery and wonder. The eighteenth century had banished everything that it could not explain by reason, but the romantic felt that many of man's most valuable experiences cannot be explained by logic and common sense. The romantic doted on mystery and wonder because they give expression to imagination and allowed the fancy to stray without encountering the chilling presence of reality or common sense. Poe's deft stories of the marvelous and the supernatural, Charles Brockden Brown's terrifying mysteries, Irving's "Rip Van Winkle," and some of Hawthorne's fiction all give different expressions of the imagination and the sense of wonder inherent in man. In English literature "The Ancient Mariner" is a great example of romantic supernaturalism.

But there are more ways of appealing to the imagination than by the use of the unreal and the mysterious. Strange lands, alien people, scenes "far away and long ago" all make a mighty appeal. Under the romantic impulse Americans began to travel for the sake of seeing things, and every ruined castle and picturesque landscape in Europe soon had its quota of visiting Americans. Those who stayed at home read Irving's books of travel, Longfellow's *Outre-Mer,* and a bit later Bayard Taylor's description of Europe and the Orient, just as to-day the romantically minded read Richard Halliburton and Harry Franck.

The medieval, too, had its vogue. Whereas the eighteenth century had arched a supercilious eyebrow at the "barbarous" life the "superstitions," and the savage architecture of the middle ages, the romantic mind found a constant delight in the very things that were so contemptuously dismissed by the rationalists of the age of reason. Many of Longfellow's ballads and Lowell's "Sir Launfal" are the American counterparts of Keats's "The Eve of St. Agnes" and "La Belle Dame Sans Merci." The same incentive, a sympathetic feeling for things medieval, gave rise to all these poems, though the English poet far surpassed the Americans in verbal beauty and poetic mastery.

American writers, having no native medievalism to exploit, turned their attention to a consideration of our past history, and, under the influence of Scott's historical novels, discovered rich fields for romantic treatment in the colonial and revolutionary periods and in the dramatic exploits of frontier life. Cooper and Simms produced many a novel in these fields, and Hawthorne placed his delicate psychological study, *The Scarlet Letter*, against the gray background of Puritan New England. Furthermore a deepening interest in our past led to the production of such works as Irving's *Life of Columbus*, and Sparks's *Life of Washington*. Although the latter of these books has since been sharply discredited by modern critical scholarship, at least it told what the Americans of the early nineteenth century wished to believe about one of our national heroes. The romantic age demanded nothing more.

One of the typical products of the romantic imagination was exoticism. Broadly speaking this quality may mean only the element of strangeness that many romantic poets and novelists injected into their characters and backgrounds. As such the term might be applied to the use of the supernatural, the classical element, the medieval, or the merely foreign, but it should be restricted to extremely strange or imaginative materials that were frequently used in romantic literature. Melville's use of the totally unknown South Seas in *Typee* and *Omoo* and the imaginative background in *Mardi* are examples of exoticism. The exotic is a large element in the stories and poems of Edgar Allan Poe.

However much the romantic might enjoy an imaginative reproduction of the past, there was one thing that he would not suffer, and that was the imposition of the traditions and customs of previous ages upon living generations. In *The House of Seven Gables* Hawthorne says that every age should build its own houses, for a structure suits only those who build it. The romantic applied the same idea to government, religion, literature, law, and custom.

Romantic Literary Forms.—The age of reason had its distinctive poetic form in the heroic couplet, two rhyming lines of iambic pentameter verse that completely expressed a thought. In the hands of Pope the couplet became a stanza written according to certain definite rules. The author strove for form and pithiness of expression, and as a result many of our most easily remembered poetic quotations are heroic couplets. This couplet was admirably suited to the needs of the time, for it has a fixed form with recognized rules governing its construction, and it was well adapted to the expression of ideas. However, it was not readily expressive of imaginative flights and deep emotional feeling, for the poet was held to a certain number of syllables for the transmission of each thought. It was the failure of the couplet to provide a flexible form for free expression that caused the romantic age to employ this verse form only occasionally. English poetry since 1800 shows a great variety of meters, rhyme schemes, and stanza forms. Blank verse was again used after a long period of neglect, and Whitman wrote in free verse, a form which discarded both meter and rhyme.

Geography of Romanticism.—Each portion of the country had its peculiar manifestation of the romantic movement. In Virginia, where romanticism fell upon soil already prepared by Jefferson and his followers, the movement was in congenial surroundings from the first. A rural society, almost idyllic in its genteel simplicity, afforded a most promising place for the practicing of the fundamental romantic tenets. Jefferson had brought all Virginia to a sympathetic regard for the worth of the common man, and as the result of his teaching the doctrine of individual liberty was actively practiced and not given lip honor as only a laudable precept. Until economic stringency forced Virginia to join hands with the lower South, the Old Dominion was one with the West and the romantics of the North in paying respect to the political and social principles of Jefferson, and in doing this it also honored the fundamentals of romanticism. Virginia was the fountainhead of romanticism in the country. Many of the strictly foreign elements were brought to that state and naturalized by the Jeffersonian school before they were diffused over the nation. The West felt that in the Virginian it had a sympathetic friend. The exclusive drawing rooms of Philadelphia subjected to the test of polite conversation the accepted principles of Jeffersonian democracy, and as large an impetus as the romantic movement of New England ever received was in the person of William Ellery Channing, who went to Massachusetts fresh from an association with the people and the books that were molding Virginia society. Each of the other portions of the country contributed its distinctive variety of romantic thought. Philadelphia was one of the centers of French and English influence, and ideas radiating from this intellectual center trickled down to even the least literate portions of our people. The South gave its undying fealty to its romantic ideal of a Greek democracy. In New England the movement reached its highest pitch and its most diverse manifestations. Jeffersonian social and political doctrines, the religious revolution that resulted in the Unitarian movement, the most extreme reform movements, communistic societies, and the transcendentalist who elevated the romantic movement into a sublime way of life—all these were found in the New England states, especially in eastern Massachusetts.

Beyond the Appalachians the temper of the frontier was such that the West, acting like a great sounding board, caught the first echoes of romanticism from Europe and flung them back in a mighty reverberation to the awakening romantics of New York and New England. "Pioneering is the romantic movement in action," says Lewis Mumford, and without the ever-present example of a functioning western society, constructed unconsciously on the romantic model, eastern romanticism might easily have lacked some of its unquenchable optimism and vitality. What the exact intellectual relations of the West and the East were we do not yet know, but we do know that Theodore Parker, the great transcendental preacher of Boston, and Abraham Lincoln of Illinois were in almost direct communication. Emerson watched western affairs with eager attention, and Thoreau looked upon western society with somewhat less than his usual asperity.

Each one of the well-known writers of American literature before 1860 belongs to the romantic group by virtue of certain characteristics that place him unmistakably in the great romantic movement. In Virginia Kennedy and Cooke idealized what was already an almost ideal society of marked Jeffersonian flavor. Caruthers represented the broad tolerance and ready sympathies of Virginia thinking. Poe turned his back upon his homeland and feverishly plunged into the exotic lands of his abounding imagination. In Philadelphia Charles Brockden Brown placed between the same covers a Gothic novel and a considerable amount of foreign social philosophy. The southern writers were under the spell of their romantic literary gods, Scott and Byron. William Gilmore Simms was greatly influenced directly and indirectly by Scott. In New England Whittier, Garrison, and Mrs. Stowe were the literary wing of the reform army. Emerson, Parker, Thoreau, and Margaret Fuller were representative of the transcendentalists. Longfellow, Holmes, and Lowell, refusing to venture far enough into the turgid current of romanticism to disturb timid souls, were content with the gentler and more placid manifestations of the great movement. Cooper showed the romantic in him by turning to our early history and to the frontier for his material. Melville was a primitive romantic who made occasional tours into the exotic.

Old-fashioned the premises of romanticism soon became under the impact of the "common sense" of industrialism and the cold dissection of nineteenth century science, but it will be a sorry day for America when Jefferson's love of liberty, Emerson's quickening call to self-reliance, and Walt Whitman's deep love for all humanity fail to impress our people. And liberty, self-reliance, and humanitarianism are the very heartbeats of romanticism.

The next task will be the discussion of romanticism in its various garbs in the different geographical portions of the United States.

SUGGESTED READINGS

Barzun: *Romanticism and the Modern Ego.* Boston. 1943.

Boas (ed.): *Romanticism in America, a Symposium.* Baltimore. 1940.

Brooks: *The Flowering of New England.* New York. 1936. Chapters IV, V, IX.

Colum: *From These Roots.* New York. 1937
    Of considerable value, but some of the pronouncements on American writers should be checked against the facts.

Foerster (ed.): *The Reinterpretation of American Literature.* New York. 1928. pp. 114-138.

Parker: "Theodore Parker's Experience as a Minister."
    A letter written to Parker's church. A most valuable source. To be found in the life of Parker by John Weiss.

Parrington: *The Romantic Revolution.* New York. 1927. pp. iii-x.

CHAPTER VIII

THE ROMANTIC MOVEMENT IN VIRGINIA

For many years the voice of Virginia was potent in national affairs, and in all that time the influence of the Old Dominion was always to be found on the side of high-minded devotion to social welfare, fidelity to public trust, the love of individual liberty, and a generous humanitarianism. The state had taken its politics from Jefferson, and the politics thus received stood for liberalism, with all its implications, adapted to the needs of an agrarian society. The leaders developed by such a political philosophy were worthy of their doctrines. They were as famed for their punctilious courtesy and keen sense of honor, both public and private, as for their democratic dogma. That austere moralist, William Ellery Channing of Massachusetts, who lived in Richmond for a short time about 1800, was charmed by Virginia culture, tolerance, and good breeding, and the characteristics that Channing admired were the very ones that the state attempted to contribute to our national mind.

The heyday of Virginia was passed by 1840. The rapidly developing slave economy of the South and the equally rapidly developing industrialism of the North presented problems that were too knotty for solution by any formula known to Jeffersonian agrarianism. Leadership departed from the hands of the upper South. Although Jefferson long remained a word to conjure with in various quarters, each part of the nation took what it wished from his principles, and none accepted the system as a whole. The extreme South revered him because of his belief in local government—states' rights the famous doctrine soon came to be called—but while praising the author of its favorite political principle, South Carolina bitterly repudiated the "glittering generalities" of the Declaration of Independence. The West came nearest to following in the footsteps of Jefferson, but after the Civil War a combination of sectional bitterness and industrialism pretty generally overwhelmed the earlier agrarian doctrines, though to this day there are occasional flashes of the old fire in parts of the Mississippi Valley.

But from 1800 to 1830 Virginia enjoyed the flowering of a fine civilization. With a free and easy economics, with a patriarchal relation of slaves and masters and an abundance of leisure to acquire and enjoy culture, life on the plantations was not far from ideal. Idyllic, it seemed when viewed from the dark days after the Civil War. Virginia contributed of its very best when it gave to American literature a picture of its plantation life and its controlling spirit, the Virginia gentleman. That both were later idealized was only to have been expected; idealization is the prerogative of romanticism.

JOHN PENDLETON KENNEDY AND THE PLANTATION TRADITION

The "golden age" of Virginia had its earliest and quite likely its best interpretation in the pages of John Pendleton Kennedy (1795-1870), a native of Maryland, whose connection with the Old Dominion came through his mother, Nancy Pendleton. Although Kennedy in his political affiliations was not a Jeffersonian, no one can read his *Swallow Barn* and not see that he loved the gentle ways and the easy agrarian life along the James and Rappahannock.

"Swallow Barn."—In 1832 Kennedy published the book that gives him a lasting place in our literature. *Swallow Barn* is a series of sketches of life on a Virginia plantation. Well written and charming in its delineation of manners and conversation, the book fixes the tone of all future presentations of the plantation. Kennedy was so frankly in love with the life that he described that we are certain that Virginia idealism left one literary bequest in the pages of this book.

Swallow Barn had a wealth of romantic material upon which to draw. The faithful slaves, the motherly matron of the plantation home, the gay and pleasure-seeking young people, the abounding hospitality are all here, and the success of Kennedy's portrayal is attested by the fact that subsequent treatments of the plantation tradition by John Esten Cook, Thomas Nelson Page, and others have utilized the dominant themes of *Swallow Barn*. Some critics have made much of the fact that *Swallow Barn* is modeled on Irving's sketches of English country life in *Bracebridge Hall*, but the fact is of significance to few except professional critics and historians. No one has yet impeached Kennedy's knowledge of Virginia life or his essential truthfulness in setting forth his knowledge. Certainly no one can question the influence of *Swallow Barn* in the development of the plantation tradition in our literature.

Other Books.—Besides *Swallow Barn* Kennedy left three novels. *Horseshoe Robinson* is a typically romantic novel of the Revolution, with a frontiersman for a hero. Tidewater aristocrats and historical personages serve to maintain the Revolutionary atmosphere, while the real action of the book is contributed by the backwoodsmen. The battle of King's Mountain affords a fitting climax to the story. *Rob of the Bowl* is a novel of colonial Maryland in the days of Charles II. Mr. Parrington, a sensitive critic of our literature, places this work first among Kennedy's productions calling it "one of the most finished and delightful of our earlier romances." *Quodlibet* is a witty, rollicking satire on Jacksonian democracy. Original Jeffersonianism was one thing, but frontier democracy with its blatant office-seekers and its noisy boasting was quite another. The West lacked the easy dignity that so characterized Virginia life.

As a writer Kennedy is far above many more renowned figures in our literature. He is a good observer of life, he creates characters that have reality, and he is a competent literary craftsman. To-day he is only slightly read, though we gravely discuss many of his less worthy contemporaries.

WILLIAM ALEXANDER CARUTHERS

Dr. William A. Caruthers is probably to-day the most unjustly neglected novelist in our whole literary history. The South, usually so proud of its writers and so scrupulous in recording the events of their lives, has totally forgotten one of its most deserving sons. To-day Caruthers is simply a name of doubtful spelling, his biography is unwritten, his books are out of print, and even the dates of his birth and death quite conjectural. It is probable that he was born about 1800 and died between the years 1845 and 1850. He was a native of the Virginian Piedmont region, a student at Washington College (now Washington and Lee), and a practicing physician of Savannah, Georgia.

"The Kentuckian in New York."—In 1834 Caruthers published a book by which he deserves to be known. *The Kentuckian in New York,* subtitled "The Adventures of Three Southerners," is a set of sketches, in construction much like *Swallow Barn*. The sketches give the adventures of a young Kentuckian and two Carolinians in

New York City and the experiences of a Virginian in South Carolina. The author knew the North as well as he knew the South, and the book should have contributed much to national understanding and good will. However, it was submerged by the rising tide of the slavery controversy.

Caruthers shows his Jeffersonian sympathies in almost every episode. He could tolerate the system of slavery as he saw it in Virginia tempered by warm humanitarianism, but he bitterly objected to the exploitation of the Negro in Carolina under the lash of white and black overseers. However, his chief criticism of the South arose from the absence of a middle class of landholders, the very basis of agrarian democracy, holding with the Jeffersonians that such a group is necessary to social welfare. In South Carolina he has praise for a community of foreigners who possess "industry, health, and intelligence," without the exalted aristocracy or the debased slave class that he saw all about. Caruthers, seeing that Tidewater Virginia was deserting the ways of Jeffersonian simplicity and democracy, looked with satisfaction upon the rapidly advancing West that was developing upon the repudiated principles of the Old Dominion.

Caruthers produced two more books. *The Cavaliers of Virginia* is a lively historical novel of colonial Virginia with Bacon's Rebellion supplying the motive power of the plot. The hero is a figure that might justly be called Byronic. He is aloof, mysterious, and endowed with a keen sense of the dramatic, just as were Byron himself and all his heroes. *The Knights of the Golden Horse-shoe* is another novel of colonial times with the expedition of Governor Spottswood to western Virginia as a major incident.

Caruthers deserves to be rescued from oblivion by a sympathetic reading of his books and careful research into the facts of his life. He and Kennedy are by far the best interpreters of life in Virginia while the Jeffersonian tradition prevailed.

JOHN ESTEN COOKE

(1830-1886)

John Esten Cooke was the last writer to contribute to the development of the plantation tradition before the local color school deluged it with sentiment. He belonged to a later generation than that of Kennedy or Caruthers, further removed from the Virginia of Jefferson and nearer the aristocratic tradition of the far South. But for all that when he wrote his novels of colonial Virginia, rather stiff with brocade, gold lace, and the stately bows of aristocrats, he allowed the fine humanitarian ideals of Jeffersonian Virginia free circulation under the cover of a courtly society. But Cooke had listened to too many fire-eaters expound the social theory of the Greek democracy, and as a result he had too great an aristocratic element in his books and too little frontier leaven.

The Virginia Comedians (1854) is generally ranked both as Cooke's major work and as one of the best presentations of the old order in Virginia. *Leatherstockings and Silk, The Youth of Jefferson, Henry St. John, Gentleman,* and *The Last of the Foresters* are also among his best known titles. Cooke served during the Civil War on the staffs of Jackson and Stuart. His experiences naturally colored his later work, but the novels after 1865 are not so highly regarded as are the earlier ones. The war made the romantic novel seem a bit out of place. Serious fiction was moving in the direction of realism, and historical romance was surrendering to the dime novel with its oceans of blood and tears.

In addition to his novels Cooke wrote an excellent history of Virginia. By far the greater portion of the book is devoted to colonial life and events.

EDGAR ALLAN POE

(1809-1849)

There was one young writer who turned his back upon the delectable life in Virginia and, using his pen as a magic wand, created a literary kingdom out of place and out of time. Plantation life, the stately society of eighteenth century Williamsburg, the colorful days of Jamestown when Virginia was an outpost of Elizabethan England, the clash of Tidewater and upland—all these had satisfied Kennedy, Caruthers, and Cooke and conceivably could have satisfied many greater novelists, but Poe would have none of them. Indeed his stories and poems give only faint reflections of a life that he must have known.

The Young Poe.—Edgar Poe was born in Boston. His father was of the well-known Baltimore family, and the mother an Englishwoman. Both were actors. When the father died we do not know, but it was early in Poe's infancy. The mother died in Richmond in

1811. The little boy was then taken into the family of John Allan, a well-to-do tobacco merchant of Richmond, but he was never legally adopted, though he added Allan to his name. Poe received a good preparatory education, partly in England, and entered the University of Virginia in 1826. Up to this time he had probably been given too much money. At the end of the first year a large number of unpaid bills so angered Mr. Allan that he refused to allow Poe to enroll a second year. A quarrel ensued, and the boy enlisted in the army under the name Edgar A. Perry. Mr. Allan discovered the whereabouts of the boy, procured his discharge from the army, and gained admission for him to the United States Military Academy. Mrs. Allan was dead, and within a brief time Mr. Allan married again. Poe, despairing of any further assistance from his former home, deliberately neglected his duties in order to bring about his court-martial and dismissal from the academy. Henceforward he was dependent upon his pen for support. Some of these facts are essential for an understanding of Poe's reluctance to employ the Virginia background.

Mr. Allan was not extremely wealthy during Poe's boyhood, though about 1825 he inherited a large fortune. However, the foster-father indulgently supplied the boy's needs and kept him in the society of scions of Virginia's aristocracy. In such a group, where more than a little importance was attached to family and ancestry, the fact that Poe was a son of poor strolling players and that he was not even legally adopted by Mr. and Mrs. Allan must have been a constant source of embarrassment to the super-sensitive boy. Poe says that while he was in the university Mr. Allan did not give him a sufficient allowance. This fact would gall his spirit, especially when he was thrown in with a crowd of extravagant spenders, as most Virginians were.

Again Poe may have felt that he was physically inferior to his companions, and if he did, such a feeling would have been certain to set up a psychological mood of aloofness, a feeling that he was radically out of place in the society of his acquaintances. [This sense of inferiority in rank and fortune and the suspicion of ineradicable differences between him and his fellow men are sufficient to account for Poe's selection of his backgrounds.]

Smarting under the feeling that he was "different," Poe called his very keen intellect and his vivid imagination into play and created a land to his heart's desire, where the annoying spites of his own earthly life would be missing and where the unbelievable would be the normal and the fantastic would be the rule of nature. This kingdom Poe created, and in its creation he probably felt one of his few moments of comparative happiness, for the "misty mid-region of Weir" existed only for the delight of its maker.

In creating his land where the unnatural would be the natural, Poe became one of the last Gothic romancers. The Gothic novelists had relied upon such eerie or supernatural things as ghosts, sleep-walking, birds of ill omen, and mysterious happenings that defied the explanation of common sense. Any one who reads such of Poe's works as "Ulalume," "The Raven," "The Masque of the Red Death," "The Black Cat," "The Pit and the Pendulum," and "The Fall of the House of Usher" will understand what is meant by Gothic romances and by "the misty mid-region of Weir."

Poe as a Poet.—

> Banners yellow, glorious, golden,
>   On its roof did float and flow,
> (This, all this, was in the olden
>   Time, long ago),
> And every gentle air that dallied
>   In that sweet day,
> Along the ramparts plumed and pallid,
>   A winged odor went away.

> Falling in wreaths through many a startled star.

> For the moon never beams, without bringing me dreams
>   Of the beautiful Annabel Lee;
> And the stars never rise, but I feel the bright eyes
>   Of the beautiful Annabel Lee. . . .

These three short quotations are fair examples of Poe's typical poetry. Its crowning glory is a melodiousness of utterance that at times becomes pure music. No American poet, with the possible exception of Lanier, has been able to write poetry so hauntingly beautiful in its liquid melody, and no reader with an ear attuned to the sheer music of English verse ever reads Poe's poetry without feeling increasingly that its author was master of the exact use of descriptive epithets and action words. Poe creates an unforgettable mood in the minimum of words. Indeed his poems are all short lyrics, and they are few in number, but any poet who can achieve eight or nine acknowledged masterpieces in a slender volume of verses must be ranked among the world's great poetic craftsmen.

A frequent criticism of Poe as a poet finds fault with his lack of "content." It is true that "Ulalume" and "The Haunted Palace" do not carry the heavy burden of thought that we find in Emerson or Browning, but still it must be remembered that we do not criticize Shakespeare for failing to put into a sonnet all the effects of a Hamlet or Lear. One of the very first tasks of intelligent criticism is to find out what the artist is trying to do. Poe was trying to write beautiful verse that would create a definite impression in the mind of the reader. Sensitive critics have unanimously agreed that he was successful.

Poe and the Short Story.—Poe bore two relations to the short story. He gave us the first definition of the short story, and in the second place he wrote memorable examples of this type of literature. In his definition he emphasized brevity and unity of impression. The latter is the all-important element, and by unity Poe meant totality or oneness of impression. If an author wishes to give an impression of dreariness and melancholy, that impression must be stressed to the exclusion of all others. If the writer wishes to leave a feeling of horror, every element must be kept out of the story that does not contribute to the dominant impression. Poe stresses brevity because he thought, quite rightly, that unity of impression would be blurred and lost in the mass of details inevitable in a long story or novel. [It will be noted that Poe did not stress the plot or action in his definition of a story. He insisted that the writer must first determine the effect that he wished to produce and then deliberately choose incidents to assist in the creation of such an effect. "The Fall of the House of Usher," one of Poe's most widely read and successful stories, lives up to its author's definition in every respect.]

It has been asserted times without number that Poe invented the short story. The assertion will not stand examination. Before Poe entered the University of Virginia French writers were producing stories that convey a complete totality of effect, and short narratives with marked unity of impression are as old as literature. Hawthorne was writing short stories as early as Poe was. But Poe was the first man, in American literature, at least, to distinguish between a short story and a story that is short. His identification of the short story as a distinct literary form was a part of his review of Hawthorne's *Twice-Told Tales.*

Poe did not invent the short story, but he introduced the detective story to American readers. "The Murders in the Rue Morgue" was his first attempt at a type that has since become amazingly popular. Few later stories have improved upon the skill or effectiveness of Poe's great effort. "The Gold Bug," another of his famous productions, is not a detective story, although it owes its interest, in part at least, to the solution of a mystery. Another very effective mystery story is "The Purloined Letter."

But it is not in the solution of mysteries, eminently successful as he was, that Poe achieved his greatest triumphs. Rather it was with tales of impressionistic effect, where he exploited to the fullest the methods and aims that he glimpsed in his definition of the short story. Some of these stories have been models for all subsequent work in this class. Horror, fear, melancholy, are the chief impressions sought by Poe, and no writer has ever surpassed him in this field.

Poe as Critic.—When Poe came into the literary field, American criticism was feeble, academic, and quite non-committal save in perfunctory praise. Poe gave a new note to discussions of books and authors, vigorously blasting reputations, condemning books and their writers, and indicating weaknesses in otherwise satisfactory performances. In his hands criticism became analytical, because he had a finely analytical mind that refused to accept muddled, pointless performances as a work of art. Furthermore Poe had one more qualification of a good critic; he knew literature. His reading was always wide and intelligent, and when he approached his critical work it was with a well-stored, acute mind that expressed itself in the most incisive fashion. When Poe thought that Longfellow had not sufficiently indicated the sources of some of his ballads, he accused the writer of plagiarism. Naturally Poe made enemies, but offending poor writers is one of the penalties of acute and honest criticism. If American literary criticism later developed into an exchange of compliments by a mutual admiration society, the catastrophe was not the fault of Poe. He had indicated and used another method. To say that Poe was our first great critic is only to say the truth.

Poe's Artistic Conscience.—Poe had that rare thing in American literature, an artistic conscience, so fully developed that he was literally driven to a feverish search for perfection. He was almost our first belletristic writer, almost the first American ever to think of literature in terms of beauty, and for the beautiful to be effectively presented it must be given near-perfect expression. It is this search for perfect artistic form that distinguished Poe from many of his contemporaries and successors. The slap-dash and disorderly, the muddled, the poorly proportioned found no favor with him. He sought the perfect union of meaning and expression, and even though he never found it to his satisfaction, his search resulted in a belletristic literature that has brought pleasure to millions of readers.

Certainly Poe had his weak points, and they have detracted from the appeal of his works. To many the most glaring fault is a total lack of humor. American writers have usually possessed humor, and its absence in so great a genius as Poe is all the more noticeable. Then, he is completely at a loss in the creation of character. His people are mere automatons that aid in the securing of certain preconceived effects. He creates them exactly as he creates incidents— merely to heighten the desired impression. Since he has no sense of character, his action is never deeply motivated. His people do what they do simply because he wants them to, and not because those actions are grounded in the characters of his men and women. Action in the hands of a man like Conrad is a method of showing character. Conrad's men do what they do because they are what they are. Poe's characters are only checkers to be moved around at the will of the author.

What may be regarded as a grave weakness of Poe is his intellectual detachment from his time and environment. The reasons for that detachment have already been indicated. Poe was the victim of personality and circumstances. The reader who goes to American literature for a better understanding of American life, past and present, will not get the enjoyment from Poe that he will from many another, but he who reads literature purely for esthetic enjoyment will gain great pleasure.

As a romantic Poe disregarded such attractions as French revolutionary philosophy, humanitarianism, reform, the new interpretation of nature, or exploration of the past, and devoted himself to the work of exploiting his purely imaginative faculty in the realm of mystery and horror. This was the inevitable course of any man who deliberately turned his back on the spacious life of old Virginia and began the exploration of the "misty mid-region of Weir."

The course of later history has made it seem to many that the natural affiliation of the Virginia writers was with those of the lower South. Such an idea is erroneous. There was no such affiliation until the struggle over slavery and economic considerations combined to push Virginia into a half-hearted alliance with South Carolina. The social philosophies of the two regions were too different before 1850 to allow a complete harmony of thought and aspirations. The philosophers of the cotton kingdom early repudiated every iota of the Jeffersonian teaching except the insistence upon local government, which they transformed into the convenient doctrine of states' rights. It is true that the fire-eater Beverley Tucker advocated an early alliance with Calhoun, but he was years in advance of current Virginia thinking.

The West was the natural ally of Virginia. The Old Dominion sent out thousands of sons who peopled Tennessee, Kentucky, Illinois, Missouri, and other western states, and the Jeffersonian doctrine taken out of Virginia by these men did not go the way of light and transient things. The frontier was congenial to things Jeffersonian, and wherever the principles of Jefferson found hospitable reception there the way of romanticism would be easy. Even after Virginia had repudiated, by implication at least, the ideas of Jefferson, the West remained true to its mentor, and when the aristocratic South had denounced the Declaration of Independence as a tissue of falsehoods, Lincoln and the Young Republicans of the West were solemnly reiterating their sincere belief in the theory that all men are created equal.

However, the writers of Virginia were not influential in the West. Caruthers seems never to have been widely read, and Kennedy and Cooke tilled the rather narrow field of the plantation tradition until their work smacked somewhat of the provincial. The exoticism of Poe pleased many but it attracted no worthy imitators.

SUGGESTED READINGS

Allen: *Israfel.* New York. 1926.
    This book is on the whole the most satisfactory biography of Poe.
Beard: *Economic Origins of Jeffersonian Democracy.* New York. 1915.
    An extremely important study.
Beaty: *John Esten Cooke.* New York. 1928.
    Satisfactory biography of a minor romantic novelist.

Brooks: *The World of Washington Irving*. New York. 1944.
Chapters XV and XIX contain a discussion of Poe.

Campbell: *The Mind of Poe and Other Studies*. Cambridge. 1923.
The work of a distinguished Poe scholar.

Foerster: *American Criticism*. Boston. 1928.
For discussion of Poe see pp. 1-51.

Gaines: *The Southern Plantation*. New York. 1924.
Good discussion of the "plantation tradition."

Gwathmey: *John Pendleton Kennedy*. New York. 1931.

Krutch: *Edgar Allan Poe*. New York. 1926.
Psychological interpretation. A most interesting work, but not necessarily definitive.

Macy: *The Spirit of American Literature*. New York. 1912. Poe, pp. 123-154.

Parrington: *The Romantic Revolution*. New York. 1927.
The author gives a good account of romanticism, but he slights Poe.

Quinn: *Edgar Allan Poe*. New York. 1941.
The work of a capable and industrious scholar. Detailed and accurate, but somewhat inclined to labor trivial points. Not to be overlooked.

Smith: *Forces in American Criticism*. New York. 1939. Poe, pp. 185-202.
Stimulating discussion.

Woodberry: *Life of Poe*. Boston. 1909.
An excellent biography, but considerable material has been discovered since 1909.

CHAPTER IX

THE WEST

It is difficult to over-emphasize the extent to which the principles of Jeffersonian democracy were accepted by the West. So whole-hearted an acceptance was only natural, for Jefferson's dominant ideas of liberty, equality, simplicity of manners, and majority rule were frontier living conditions translated into political theory and agreeably tempered by the warm humanitarian teaching of French revolutionary philosophy. Indeed the West accepted to the full all of Jefferson's principles—and more. As the early settlers possessed Tennessee, Kentucky, the north bank of the Ohio and pushed on into Missouri, the influence of the frontier became more and more emphatic, and the restraining influence of the commercial class and the wealthy landowners correspondingly relaxed. As a result the new West developed Jacksonian democracy, thus called from its first national leader, Andrew Jackson of Tennessee, who was a product of this movement and not its creator. Long after Virginia had begun to desert the major premises of Jeffersonian teaching to cast its lot with the slave economy of the far South, the West still remained true to its agrarian doctrines. As late as 1856, when the Republican party first nominated a national ticket, the western farmers and the laborers of the eastern cities, the two classes that formed the new party, wrote into their platform an affirmation of their allegiance to the principles of Thomas Jefferson.

There is an idea abroad that in 1828 Andrew Jackson, an illiterate frontiersman, led a shouting, unkempt rabble of western Goths into control of the government where they perpetrated hitherto unheard-of practices in administration. Such an idea is erroneous. Jackson was the product of a great democratic movement that was only a fulfillment and a slight extension of the Jeffersonian principles that triumphed in the political revolution of 1800.

There were two forces behind the so-called Jacksonian democracy. These were the western agrarians and the rising laboring class of the eastern cities. Contrary to popular idea, the democracy of the

West represented little that was new. Since the Jacksonians had no political philosophers and few apologists, we must judge the movement solely by its deeds, and in its working it seemed to carry out the unrealized desires of Jefferson. There was very little in Jacksonian democracy that did not exist in germinal form in the writings of Jefferson and his immediate followers. The chief difference in western democracy in 1800 and in 1830 is one of strength and not of ideas. In 1800 there were five million people in the United States, one-twentieth of whom lived west of the Alleghanies; in 1830 there were twenty million, one-third of whom lived in the same region. Again, the eastern portion of the nation was divided into north and south, but in 1830 the West knew no such division. It was a solid block with strength enough to get what it wanted in governmental affairs.

The second influence behind the new democracy was the rapidly increasing class of industrial workers. The factory system had come into its own in this country by 1830, and as a result a new class was clamoring for recognition and assistance. The condition of labor at this time was shocking. Hours were barbarously long, wages were low, and living conditions were unspeakable. To ameliorate these evils labor unions were being formed, but these organizations lacked effective power, for the eastern states, where industry was flourishing most, barred laborers from voting. The demands of the unions were for an extension of the franchise, universal education, election of officials by the people, and the abolition of religious legislation. These were already realities in the western states. Thus a bond of sympathy was cemented between the agrarians and the workers. During the 1820's many of the demands of labor were realized, and the newly enfranchised voters of the cities united with the West to sweep Jackson into the presidency. In 1856 when the Republican party was formed the same classes united again.

Assuredly the new democracy had its weaknesses, nor was it lacking in detractors who made the utmost of these deficiencies. A good writer in 1830 among the Westerners or laborers could conceivably have made much of his opponents' shortcomings, but at that time culture was a possession of the few, and those few were not Jacksonians. As early as 1800 Brackenridge in *Modern Chivalry* pointed out the weaknesses of democracy that Kennedy satirized in 1840 in the pages of *Quodlibet*. These weaknesses were a tendency to follow noisy demagogues, a delight in sonorous buncombe,[1] and the habit of ascribing divine intelligence and powers to the majority vote. Certainly these were weaknesses, but were they any more glaring than the tendency of the pseudo-aristocrats to exploit the lower classes of society for the benefit of their own pocketbooks? The opponents of democracy have made too much of such a character as Davy Crockett, who represented some of the worse features of western democracy, while they have systematically slighted men of deep intelligence and integrity like Jackson, Henry Clay, Thomas Hart Benton, and Abraham Lincoln, who were just as representative of the West as was Crockett. Whatever may be the weaknesses of the Westerners, it must be admitted that western democracy stood unflinchingly for the rights of man when these rights were being trampled under foot by the exploitation of labor, free and slave, in both the North and the South.

AUGUSTUS BALDWIN LONGSTREET

(1790-1870)

It is hard for us to-day to think of a man as a Westerner who spent almost his entire life in Georgia, Mississippi, and South Carolina, but Judge Longstreet, an eminent citizen of the three states just mentioned, stands as an excellent example of the old Southwest before Texas, Oklahoma, Arizona and New Mexico became the frontier. In his later years Longstreet allied himself with his neighbors and became an exponent of extreme southern views, but in his youth he was a true son of the West.

Augustus Longstreet was born in Augusta, Georgia. After completing his education at Yale he became successively a lawyer, politician, editor, author, minister, and college president, and in all his professions he achieved more than average success, despite his constant dabbling in farming and land speculation. When he died he was certainly one of the most distinguished citizens of the old South, but to-day we remember him as the author of a single book, *Georgia Scenes.*

"*Georgia Scenes.*"—When Longstreet began the practice of law in Georgia about 1815 that state had all the characteristics of the frontier. The population was rough, uncultured, and noisy. Dif-

---

[1] So called from Buncombe County, North Carolina. The term is now shortened to bunk.

ferences of opinion were settled in the most primitive fashion. Political questions were red-hot, and religious revivals worked up enthusiasm enough to satisfy even those whose emotions were starved on the slender spiritual diet of the frontier. Longstreet mingled with the people of this frontier, observing their ways with a friendly, humorous eye, and, when he became an editor, wrote a series of sketches descriptive of his earlier experiences. The writing extended over a period of years, but most of the articles date from 1833-1835.

Georgia Scenes contains eighteen sketches, entirely unconnected save for the similarity of background, which is unmistakably frontier. The sketches often contain humor and not a little rough narrative skill, but the most striking characteristic is the extreme realism of the author. The rough edges of frontier society are not smoothed off, for the roistering, drinking, fighting life is set down in all its unlovely colors, just as it actually existed. The reading of one or two of these sketches will knock much of the glamor off our modern idealization of the frontier. The best sketches are "Georgia Theatrics," "The Character of a Native Georgian," "The Fight," "The Gander Pulling," and "The Shooting Match."

Longstreet was not an intellectual, despite his high academic rank. *Georgia Scenes* contributes nothing to our knowledge of western political philosophy, but it does give us invaluable insight into the life of the old Southwest before the frontier crossed the Mississippi. The later writer who worked closest to Longstreet in content and method was Mark Twain, and although the great humorist of the West immeasurably surpassed the earlier man, it was something to have entered first the realm that Mark Twain was later to make gloriously his own.

DAVID CROCKETT
(1786-1836)

Colonel Davy Crockett is another example of a self-made man who had vast reverence for his maker. To-day we are beginning to suspect that Crockett's reputation was made to order by eastern politicians, but Davy himself never doubted that his popularity was the result of his own native shrewdness.

Crockett was a genuine frontiersman. He was born on the fringe of settlement, he lived the life of a wandering hunter, never content to settle down and cultivate the soil, and he died on the extreme frontier, fighting at the Alamo for the independence of Texas. After tasting a bit of authority as rural justice of the peace, Crockett was elected to the Tennessee legislature, achieving success at the polls through his wit and his never-failing willingness to "treat the crowd." After serving two sessions in the legislature he ran for Congress but was defeated by an opponent who assured the people that the high price of cotton was caused by a new tariff that he had just voted for. Two years later the price of cotton was down, and Crockett was triumphantly elected. He served in Congress for six years.

Crockett went to Washington as the friend of Jackson, but before long there came a break between the two backwoodsmen. The opponents of the president quickly capitalized this quarrel; here, they exclaimed, is an authentic Westerner who hates Jackson and all his works. Up and down the country they paraded Crockett, laughing at his witticisms, applauding his ignorance as if it were sublime wisdom, and giving their victim the erroneous impression that he was an extremely clever fellow. But a day of reckoning was at hand. Crockett had quarreled with the idol of Tennessee, and now he had to stand for reëlection. As a result of his openly expressed contempt for Jackson, he was defeated. In a huff he left the United States, joined the Texan revolutionists in their war for independence from Mexico, and fell at the battle of the Alamo.

Crockett, the Westerner.—Crockett shows up the worst side of western democracy more glaringly than it was ever exhibited by any adverse critic. He was a rustic wag, totally lacking in education and wholly ignorant of even the most trivial public affairs, but he had a quick native wit and a clever tongue, and these assets carried him farther than solid qualifications would have taken him. He demonstrated that a good joke is more appealing to a frontier audience than is an hour of logical argument. If he had possessed a few ideas, he would have been a dangerous demagogue, but without them he was thoroughly harmless. If the West had produced only public leaders like Davy Crockett, the sharpest critics of democracy from John Adams and Brackenridge to H. L. Mencken would have been more than justified in their censures.

In private life Crockett again was wholly unadmirable. He was a shiftless squatter, content each year to harvest a straggling crop of corn and then move on, never willing to undertake the sustained labor necessary to develop a farm out of the wilderness. In fact, Crockett prided himself on the fact that he was no farmer. He was a hunter—a veritable "game-hog" of the kind that devastated the richest hunting grounds the temperate zone has seen in recent centuries. In the fifteenth chapter of his autobiography he boasts that he killed 47 bears in one month and 105 in less than a year.

"The Autobiography."—In the course of their exploitation of Crockett's hostility to Jackson, the politicians put out three or four books under the name of the Tennessee hunter. It is almost certain that Crockett wrote only *A Narrative of the Life of David Crockett of the State of Tennessee*. This is a book that no student of American life can afford to miss. In it democracy receives its cruelest presentation by a man who would have been impossible under any society other than that of the backwoods. Democracy has survived in spite of ignorant, demagogic leaders like the bragging joker from Tennessee. To-day the most hopeful sign is the relative scarcity of such officials, though the tribe is even now far from extinct.

ABRAHAM LINCOLN

(1809-1865)

In a letter dated April 6, 1859, Abraham Lincoln wrote the following words:

Soberly it is now no child's play to save the principles of Jefferson from total overthrow in this nation. The principles of Jefferson are the definitions and axioms of free society. And yet they are denied and evaded with no small show of success. One dashingly calls them "glittering generalities." Another bluntly calls them "self-evident lies." And others insidiously agree that they apply only to "superior races." These expressions, differing in form, are identical in object and effect—the supplanting of the principles of free government and restoring those of classification, caste, and legitimacy. They would delight a convocation of crowned heads plotting against the people. They are the vanguard—the miners and sappers of returning despotism. We must repulse them, or they will subjugate us. This is a world of compensation; and he who would be no slave must consent to have no slave. Those who deny freedom to others deserve it not for themselves; and, under a just God, cannot long retain it.

Writing in a year when the defenders of slavery all over the country were most vociferous in their denunciations of the Declaration of Independence, Lincoln thus defiantly took his stand on the principles of equalitarianism expressed by Jefferson. Other men might scoff equally at the rhetoric and the philosophy of the Declaration, but Lincoln would not. And he would not because he so perfectly expressed the age-old democracy of the frontier. The same influence that had touched Jefferson touched him.

The Democracy of Lincoln.—The democracy of Lincoln was founded upon the double basis of economics and humanitarianism. Many of the free-soil men had no conscientious scruples against slavery. They opposed only the extension of slavery, for they well realized that the small farmer of the Northwest could not compete against the large accumulation of land and capital in the hands of wealthy slave owners. If slavery once entered the Northwest, the small farmers would be crushed as were the small landowners in the South. Furthermore the entrance of slavery into the northwest territories would close that area to settlement by the men from Illinois, Ohio, and Wisconsin. Then in the course of a few years the territories would be admitted to the union as slave states, and the slave power would be guaranteed permanent control of the government. It was fear of this eventuality that drove many Westerners to oppose slavery. The idea of the Civil War as a clash of the agrarianism of the Northwest and the slave economy of the South has not been sufficiently emphasized.

In his economic theory Lincoln was altogether western. His thinking was founded upon an acceptance of the farmer as the dominant economic influence, for only late in life did he come to a realization of the importance of industrial organizations. He believed that every man had a right to make progress and accumulate property. Any power that curtailed such a right he looked upon as unjust and unjustifiable. Thus far he was a true free-soil economist, opposed to slavery upon practical grounds.

But there was another basis of Lincoln's opposition to slavery. This was a humanitarian objection, based squarely on the plain words of the Declaration of Independence. All men are created equal, Lincoln insisted, and they have the inalienable rights of life, liberty, and the pursuit of happiness. In his definition of equality he indulged in no logic chopping. He took the typically western attitude that equality did not refer to physical or mental endowment. It referred to equality of opportunity—equality of chance at life, liberty, and happiness. The statements of the Declaration of Independence he cheerfully seconded as "a stumbling-block to tyrants for all time to come."

Inevitably Lincoln was forced to face the question: If the right to make economic progress—to acquire property and "get on in the world"—conflicts with the rights of liberty and pursuit of happiness, what shall be the solution? This question Lincoln answered in the letter already quoted in part: "The Democracy of to-day holds the liberty of one man to be absolutely nothing, when in conflict with another's right of property; Republicans, on the contrary, are for both the man and the dollar, but in case of conflict the man before the dollar." Lincoln's compromise, unlike that of many politicians, was neither muddled nor evasive.

With all his idealism, all his democracy, Lincoln would not pursue the dream until hard realities were covered with a concealing glamor of romantic hope. He saw the situation confronting North and South more clearly than any man of the time saw it, and his calm opinion was memorably stated in a few words:

"A house divided against itself cannot stand." I do not believe that this government can endure permanently half slave and half free. I do not expect the Union to be dissolved—I do not expect the house to fall— but I do expect it will cease to be divided. It will become all one thing, or all the other. Either the opponents of slavery will arrest the further spread of it, and place it where the public mind shall rest in the belief that it is in the course of ultimate extinction; or its advocates will push it forward till it shall become alike lawful in all the states, old as well as new, North as well as South.

Practical common sense and clear political vision never combined to make a truer statement.

In general Lincoln has been hopelessly idealized by our patriotic historians, but of late a few critics have been snarling at his willingness to compromise. Within limits the criticism is just. Lincoln was a popular leader of the political thought and action of his time. He was no fanatical doctrinaire, no mere theorist, intent upon holding to the last letter of his belief and unwilling to stop short of complete realization. He took to-day what he could get and saved the remainder of his platform for another day. Slowly he brought the nation to his way of thinking, and his final, complete triumph should be sufficient proof that he permanently compromised on no vital issue.

Lincoln in American Literature.—As a writer of beautiful prose

Lincoln came slowly to his full stature. His early speeches were notable for their sound sense and good argument and equally distinguished by the lack of rhetorical bombast that was so popular in the early West, but of memorable utterances there were few. Lincoln never set out to charm or dazzle an audience by a burst of glittering, high-sounding words, as is the custom of many orators. As he grew older he developed a style peculiarly his own, and in his last speeches and letters he uttered thoughts and emotions in perfectly cadenced sentences that loosed the great organ music of the best English prose. However, the development of the great style did not keep him from frequently expressing himself in pithy sentences whose sound sense and broad western humor set the nation to chuckling and thinking.

Lincoln will live in literature as the author of the inaugural addresses, the Gettysburg speech, the farewell to his Springfield friends, and such letters as that to Mrs. Bixby. However, a slighting of his early political speeches and the swift, epigrammatic letters that he frequently dashed off during the war will be a wrong to him as a man and as a writer. If Americans all over the country should vote on the historical character who has most fully typified American life, probably the vote would favor Lincoln. He stands for more things to more people than does any other man. And any representative selections from his writings must include examples of his middle-class doctrine of progress, his democracy, his good common sense, his convincing logic, and his humor, as well as the acknowledged masterpieces that he contributed to English prose.

To discuss the West and romanticism is to discuss one and the same thing. The fundamentals of romanticism were the political and social philosophy of the West, and there was scarcely a manifestation of the movement that was not to be found in Middle America during the first half of the nineteenth century. Of course, the western writers did not give us the finished literary products of romanticism that we had from the hands of the English poets or even from the American writers of the Atlantic seaboard, but the deficiency of western literature was not the lack of romantic qualities but the lack of literary finish. The Westerners were busy living romanticism; their literary ability was not equal to the task of writing *Lyrical Ballads, The Prelude,* or *Moby Dick.*

In its romantic strivings the West found a sympathetic fellowship in Virginia and among the romantics—the anti-industrialists of New England. Much of the romantic doctrine of the West had come from Virginia, and much of it was sent on to the transcendentalists of Massachusetts. Jefferson was Lincoln's great guide in social philosophy, and there is in existence a considerable correspondence between W. H. Herndon, Lincoln's law partner, and Theodore Parker, the great Boston preacher, that shows the unity of aims and ideals reached by the western and the New England romantics. The South and the West were always hostile, and this hostility was manifested in opposing political, social, and economic theories. The idea of a Greek democracy was as hateful to the Westerners as the pioneer insistence upon equality was to the aristocrats of South Carolina.

SUGGESTED READINGS

Beveridge: *Abraham Lincoln*, 1809-1858. Boston. 1928.

    A notable piece of work. Especially good for the legal and political aspects of Lincoln's early career. Lays low many a myth.

Bowers: *Party Battles of the Jackson Period*. Boston. 1922.

    Describes the reverberations of western democracy throughout the nation.

Charnwood: *Abraham Lincoln*. New York. 1917.

    One of the very best of the innumerable Lincoln biographies. Written from the English point of view.

Hazard: *The Frontier in American Literature*. New York. 1927. Crockett, pp. 62-69.

Herndon and Weik: *Abraham Lincoln*. New York. 1889.

    The original, unexpurgated biography in three volumes. The Lincoln mythology grew up in spite of this work. Later editions are judiciously pruned. Herndon was Lincoln's law partner.

Lamon: *Recollections of Abraham Lincoln*. Out of print. An edition was published in Washington, D. C., 1911.

    The author was a close personal friend of Lincoln.

Newton: *Lincoln and Herndon*. Cedar Rapids. 1910.

    The title hardly describes this book which gives the correspondence between Herndon and Theodore Parker. This work is clear proof of the close relationship between western democracy and New England transcendentalism.

Nicolay and Hay: *Abraham Lincoln*. New York. 1917.

    The official biography in ten volumes. Relatively little attention is given to the period before 1858.

Parrington: *The Romantic Revolution*. New York. 1927. pp. 137-179.

Rankin: *Intimate Character Sketches of Abraham Lincoln*. Philadelphia. 1924.

    Gives interesting and important glimpses of Lincoln.

Rourke: *David Crockett.* New York. 1934.

By far the best work on the subject.

Sandburg: *Abraham Lincoln: The Prairie Years.* New York. 1926.

A sympathetic and illuminating biography by a poet. Excellent treatment of the frontier environment. The spiritual life of America during the 1940's receives attention. In dealing with the temperament and intellectual life of Lincoln, Sandburg sometimes allows his imagination considerable scope, but he always keeps his subject in character.

Sandburg: *Abraham Lincoln: The War Years.* New York. 1939.

This work has been aptly called by a Lincoln authority "a glowing portrait gallery; a monumental task impressively performed." Not a military biography, and not a discussion of the politics of the time, but the man in the White House receives unrivaled treatment.

Schlesinger: *The Age of Jackson.* Boston. 1946.

A history of the Jacksonian period but very important for an understanding of Lincoln's political background in national affairs.

Tarbell: *Life of Abraham Lincoln.* New York. 1917.

One of the landmarks of Lincoln study.

Wade: *Augustus Longstreet.* New York. 1924.

A satisfactory work, though the frontier characteristics of Longstreet's *Georgia Scenes* are not overemphasized.

The amount of writing on Lincoln is literally stupendous. Titles given above indicate only a few of the longer and more significant books. For a good working bibliography of Lincoln see Randall: *Lincoln the President.* For a complete list of books on the subject see Monaghan: *Lincoln Bibliography, 1839-1939.*

CHAPTER X

CHARLESTON AND SOUTHERN CULTURE

It has always been a favorite occupation of romantics all over the world to conceive an ideal state of society with an accompanying political state to serve its needs. These ideals have taken various forms. The industrialist of the northeastern states wanted a society made up of docile laborers under the domination of their employers. Jefferson visualized an agrarian state founded upon justice and equality. Others, especially in the North, rejecting utterly the idea of exploited human labor or the wage system, actually formed small communistic experiments where manual labor would be subordinated to the common happiness. And the South, not to be outdone, formed the most magnificent conception of all—and came nearest to a realization of its dream. This dream may be called a Greek democracy in America.

Greek Democracy.—Drawing upon their large supply of classical learning, the southern leaders devised the plan of a perfect society modeled closely after that of Athens in the brilliant days of Pericles. Athens in the fifth century before Christ was composed of a rather small number of free citizens of the upper class, a much larger middle class, and a large slave population. The last two groups carried on the labor and trade of the city, while the small leisure class of aristocrats gave heed to government and culture. Such a social order appealed mightily to southern aristocrats from 1830 to 1860.

Before 1830 the South was somewhat Jeffersonian in its thinking, though its agrarianism was always affected by the presence of large plantations and the dependence of agriculture upon a large supply of slave labor. Beginning with 1830 the South rapidly changed. The slave system, pushing out across the old frontier that Longstreet knew, took in all the states as far west as Texas. Agriculture became "big business," with large accumulations of capital in the hands of a few and with a frank recognition of the necessity of the exploitation of slave labor. The upper class was small in number;

231

the slaves were many. Between the two stood the small landowners, white and often of Scotch-Irish blood, who maintained themselves within and upon the edge of the Black Belt. That the southern aristocrats did not wholly desert their earlier Jeffersonianism is shown by their acceptance into the ruling class of promising men who sprang from the small farmers. It is said that Alexander H. Stephens, Jefferson Davis, Robert McDuffie, and even the great John C. Calhoun were not of the aristocracy save by adoption or marriage. But Jeffersonianism, the native philosophy of small farmers, colored southern thinking little save in the argument over states' rights. There Calhoun drew upon Jefferson's belief in local government to justify his own allegiance to the doctrine of nullification. However, Jefferson had espoused states' rights to guarantee and protect majority rule; Calhoun did so to perpetuate minority control.

Idealism and realism were strangely blended in the southern conception of a Greek democracy. Calhoun's ideal was founded solidly upon the plain facts of economics. The Southerners realized that the new age in their country meant a new economics. Business and industrial expansion filled the air. In the North wealth was taking the form of factories and machinery; in the South it was in the shape of land and slaves. In both regions large profits were to be made from the harsh exploitation of labor. Gone alike were the days of home manufacturing and of the patriarchal relations of slave and master. The Southerners examined the living conditions of Massachusetts and English laborers, and decided that the life of southern slaves was infinitely to be preferred. Furthermore they appealed to history and contemporaneous social conditions to prove that natural ability divides mankind into two groups, very unequal in size, the men of marked capacity in the one group and those of mediocre or no ability in the other. The humanitarian argument of such Jeffersonians as Lincoln they opposed with blunt assertion that the rights of man spoken of in the Declaration of Independence were wholly imaginary. The aim of society, they contended, is not to secure the rights of the majority, but to guarantee the minority in their position of supremacy and to keep the lower classes free from avoidable wrongs. The exploitation of labor was an unavoidable thing. Upon this very realistic basis of economics did the southern leaders build their dream of a Greek democracy in America.

Southern Imperialism.—Southern imperialism is simply a convenient name for the attempt of southern leaders to introduce slavery into regions not then occupied by whites and into settled states where slaves were unknown. The desire for expansion had a twofold origin. In the first place, southern economics constantly demanded fresh lands. Slave labor, so notoriously wasteful of the soil, created a steady demand for new land, and furthermore the younger sons of planters often wished to migrate to new regions where they could open up plantations. In the second place national politics forced the South to seek expansion. The southern states had for their prime task the defense of slavery. This institution was being attacked in Washington as a national evil. Hence it was necessary to hold as many votes in Congress as the North had, and these votes could be had only by the admission of new slave states. These were the reasons behind the struggle over Missouri, the Mexican War, the admission of California, and the contest for Kansas. Southern imperialism founded on a slave economics was in a death struggle with the agricultural and industrial states of the North.

Southern Leaders.—If the South had produced no poetry or fiction, it would be perfectly fitting in a sketch of American intellectual development to discuss the works of such southern leaders and political thinkers as John C. Calhoun, Jefferson Davis, Alexander Stephens, Hugh Swinton Legaré, and many another. But the South had its literature. True it is that the finest minds of the Black Belt were devoted to agriculture, military science, law, and politics. As a result the total literary output of the southern states was smaller than that of New York or New England, but in constitutional history and law, oratory, and political theory the South produced far more than its share of acutely reasoned and well written treatises. In the light of the fact that the South had its own fiction and poetry, extended consideration of these treatises should be left to the political scientist and the historian.

John C. Calhoun (1782-1850) dominated the intellectual life of the South from 1830 to 1860. Although Calhoun came from the middle class, his position as unchallenged leader of the southern aristocracy led him to drop from his political and social thought every vestige of his origin. His whole mind was concentrated upon the problem of perpetuating an aristocracy based upon wealth in land and slaves. His task was the defense of southern culture, and never did a culture have a more brilliant apologist. In his defense he ranged the field of political and social philosophy, taking here and there the elements needed for the construction of his ideal. The

Jefferson who feared a strongly centralized government supplied him with certain points; Hamilton and Adams, with their admiration for aristocracies, gave others. From Greek life came the pattern, and all elements were welded with consummate skill by the man's extraordinary mind. For more than twenty years his accurate knowledge and superb logical skill held at bay his opponents and for ten years after his death in 1850 his ideas still dominated southern thinking. In him the far South produced its greatest mind. Aside from his numerous speeches and his voluminous letters and state papers, Calhoun left two treatises on political theory, *A Disquisition on Government,* and *A Discourse on the Government and Constitution of the United States.* The first of these has been called "one of the most logical treatises on political philosophy ever written, and among American works, the most notable systematic study produced during the nineteenth century." [1]

Hugh Swinton Legaré of Charleston excellently bridges the gap between political philosophy and polite literature. His mind was too crammed with learning, too cold and stiff, to unbend to poetry or fiction, but in his leisure moments between rendering erudite legal opinions Legaré wrote some solid criticism and encouraged others to produce novels and lyrics. The man's learning was enormous. Not content with knowing law, philosophy, politics, and history, he learned language after language until Theodore Parker and George Ticknor of Boston were said to be his only linguistic rivals in America. To-day Legaré is remembered as a symbol of southern culture and as the founder of the *Southern Review* of Charleston, a publication that for four years opened a channel for southern literary expression.

Charleston.—South Carolina was the intellectual center of the old South, and Charleston was the heart and soul of South Carolina. In addition to being Calhoun's capital city, the old town boasted a genuine culture, a coterie of literary men, and a gay but decorous society. Legaré pronounced it the most English of all American cities. Certainly of all American cities it was least like a frontier town that preached and practiced the principle of equality. Charleston was proud of its social and cultural domination by a recognized aristocracy, waited upon by a slave population that made up more than half of the town. Each winter the South Carolina gentry from the low country, as the Carolinians called Tidewater, would be

[1] Wright, *Source Book of American Political Theory,* p. 512.

joined in the old town by other aristocrats from all over the South to make up the most brilliant society in America. Dinners, balls, races, the theater, were the chief entertainments, all of which were conducted according to the austere social code of a proud, dignified aristocracy. Charleston would have been an ideal home for a great southern literature had not the talk been everlastingly of politics.

The intellectual taste of Charleston was as aristocratic as were its people. Jeffersonian equalitarianism, agrarian pretensions, and romantic admiration for Rousseau's man of nature found here no echoes. Readers formed their tastes on the classics and the older English writers. Modern literature of all nations was little known. Even so fine a linguist as Legaré learned German after he went abroad at the age of thirty-five. But in its literary taste Charleston made exceptions of two moderns, Byron and Scott—needless to say, the aristocratic writers of the romantic period. Burns, Wordsworth, Shelley, Coleridge, and Keats were almost unknown. Unknown also was the quickening interest in nature that so vivified the thought of Boston. Charleston took its romanticism in the form of its ideal Greek democracy and in the exploitation of its own colorful history. This last work was done by the greatest writer of the far South, who was potentially one of America's greatest novelists.

WILLIAM GILMORE SIMMS

(1806-1870)

William Gilmore Simms, the most talented man of letters of the far South, was Charleston born. Steeped in the history and legends of his native town, loving his people and their ways, he was always distinguished for his intense local patriotism. This warm admiration for Charleston was one-sided, for Simms was not of the gentry, and this shortcoming caused the aristocratic literary circles of the city to treat their one competent novelist with so studied a neglect that it is a wonder he was not lost permanently to Charleston and to literature. Lost to literature he might well have been, had it not been for the generous and hearty encouragement that he received from the North and from other parts of the South.

Simms, the Carolinian.—Simms made every effort to ingratiate himself into the favor of his high-bred townsmen. He who by instinct was certainly a Jeffersonian democrat accepted without question every ideal of the old South. Greek democracy in America never had a more impassioned advocate. Class distinction he declared to be the law of nature, and the southern gentry he hailed as nature's masterpiece. He joined with the extreme Southerners to exalt slavery and defend the cause of states' rights, and even in his private life and manners he approached the southern ideal. By marriage he was connected with a good family of some means, and at his plantation, Woodlands, he dispensed the hospitality for which the South is famous. Still Charleston accepted him but grudgingly, and it was not until just before the Civil War, when a younger generation was in control of the town, that Simms finally established his reputation.

Without question the effort of Simms to be a good Charlestonian and a worthy son of South Carolina cost American literature heavily. With a native talent that has been pronounced greater than that of Cooper, richly gifted with humor and the ability to see and describe, he frittered away his time with politics, oratory, and local literary enterprises. As some critics have pointed out, even when he set himself to the task of writing a novel, he allowed his Charleston tastes to impede his work. By nature Simms was something of a realistic humorist, a bit akin to the Mark Twain of *Roughing It*, but notwithstanding his undoubted success with such low characters as Lieutenant Porgy and Sam Bostwick, he felt that he had to make his novels center about aristocrats who are starched too stiffly to walk or talk like human beings. Without the urge to make aristocrats the "stars" of his novels, Simms might have given us book after book filled with rascals, black comedians, and country bumpkins that would have elevated the author to an undisputed eminence in American fiction. But the aristocrats are there, and every judicious reader must edit and omit as he reads. The Charleston tradition was too strong.

Novels of Simms.—If one must skip judiciously to read a Simms novel with enjoyment, still more must one skip in choosing novels to be read from his long list. It is easy to prove that Simms wrote too much. A bibliography compiled by Professor Trent lists eighty works, of which thirty-five are novels, novelettes, or collections of stories. There are three poetic dramas listed, ten volumes of history and biography, eighteen titles of poems or collections of poems, and twelve miscellaneous works. The strange thing is not that Simms so often failed, but that he succeeded as often as he did. He was a competent historian, a vigorous poet, and, in spots, an excellent novelist.

Critics differ as to the relative excellence of the novels, but there is a fair amount of agreement on the books that should go into the better group. The ones most often chosen are *Guy Rivers*, the story of a Georgia bandit; *The Yemassee*, the best known work, an Indian story with certain elements of greatness; *The Partisans*, a novel of Revolutionary days in Carolina; *Woodcraft*, another Revolutionary story; *The Forayers*, which shows the great Porgy at his best, and *Eutaw*, a sequel to *The Forayers*.

As will be seen Simms dealt largely with the Revolution and the frontier. At his very best he combines these elements and gives us unforgettable pictures of backwoods patriots. He tells us himself of his favorite material for novels:

> Partisan warfare, itself, is that irregular and desultory sort of life, which is an unavoidable suggestion of the deeds and feelings of chivalry— such as gave the peculiar character, and much of the charm to the history of the middle ages. The sudden onslaught—the retreat as sudden—the midnight tramp—the moonlight bivouac—the swift surprise—the desperate defence—the cruel slaughter and the headlong flight—and, amid the fierce and bitter warfare, always like a sweet star shining above the gloom, the faithful love, the constant prayer, the devoted homage and fond allegiance of the maiden heart.

This quotation gives a clew to the author's weaknesses: highly colored melodrama well flavored with sentiment. Murder, mortal combat, flight and pursuit, surprise, and pitched battles were the fare which the readers of the forties and fifties demanded, and Simms gladly supplied the demand. His worst novels are only bloody melodramas, but in his best there is the saving grace of humor and sharp observation.

A comparison of Simms and other American novelists would be out of place here, despite the fact that such a book as *The Yemassee* almost demands comparison with *The Last of the Mohicans*. Suffice it to say that at his best he is surpassed by no novelist of the frontier and Revolution. He has an amazing amount of material in every book, and one of his chief merits is his ability to tell his story in a racy, pungent style, worthy of the best writers of colloquial English. That Simms is no better known is hardly to the credit of our readers or teachers of American literature.

PAUL HAMILTON HAYNE

(1830-1886)

The Civil War wrecked only the end of Simms's life and probably robbed us of few first-rate novels, but the great struggle broke when Paul Hayne was only thirty and took from him his health, his property, and his chance at great eminence.

Hayne was born into the society that Simms had so craved. His father was a naval officer, and his uncle was Robert Y. Hayne, the orator and opponent of Webster. Wealth and influence the family possessed in great measure, and the way to success seemed open to Paul Hayne. He studied law and became one of the literary circle that gathered about Simms from 1850 to 1860. After the war Hayne, broken in health and reduced to bitter poverty, went to Georgia where he lived the remainder of his life.

Hayne's poetry is of a type that is much easier to read than to discuss. He was a true lyric poet, writing frequently of nature and allied objects in verse that is notable for its charm. Ease, grace, and tender feeling give his lines distinction, without elevating them to the rank of great poetry. It is notable, however, that the excellence of Hayne will frequently make one compare his effects with those of men like Wordsworth. It is quite conceivable that the war cheated the South out of a poet of the first rank among Americans.

At his weakest Hayne was an imitator of poets like Keats, William Morris, and Tennyson, but at his best as a poet of the southern countryside he strikes an original note, not strong but true and of the very essence of poetry. Professor Trent says of Hayne: "If he lacked Simms' vigor and powers of varied accomplishment, or Timrod's artistic self-control, his genius was, nevertheless, more receptive, more keenly alive to the beauties of nature and art."

HENRY TIMROD

(1829-1867)

Timrod, a man of even greater talents than Hayne, also belonged to the Simms group in Charleston. He was the son of a mechanic of German blood who wrote poetry that attracted some little attention. The boy inherited little from his father save a poetic faculty, and poverty kept him from receiving a good education. He began writing promising poetry while he was young, but the war and its attendant calamities deepened the feeling of his verses. Probably his finest production is an ode that was sung in 1867 at the dedication of Magnolia cemetery in Charleston. This short poem is a masterpiece of deep but restrained feeling expressed in the most musical and felicitous language. Two more poems animated by the war are "Carolina" and "Ethnogenesis," both excellent in content and execution.

Probably Timrod is better known to-day for his nature poetry. He admirably translated in words the soft dreamy atmosphere of the southern landscape, and as proof of his ability to do so we have the widely known "Spring" and "The Cotton Boll." The first is one of America's most sincere poetic versions of the passing of winter, while the latter includes a colorful description of the South's most typical sight, a cotton field lying white under the semi-tropic sun.

SUGGESTED READINGS

Dodd: *The Cotton Kingdom*. New Haven. 1919.
  Good for social and political background.
Dodd: *Statesmen of the Old South*. New York. 1911.
  Good essays on Jefferson, Calhoun, and Jefferson Davis.
Parrington: *The Romantic Revolution*. New York. 1927. pp. 61-144.
Phillips: *Life and Labor in the Old South*. Boston. 1929.
  Excellent study of the economic background.
Mims: *Sidney Lanier*. Boston. 1905.
  Contains many references to Hayne.
Trent: *William Gilmore Simms*. Boston. 1892.
  One of our most intelligent literary biographies.
Wauchope: *Henry Timrod*. Columbia, S. C. 1915.

CHAPTER XI

PHILADELPHIA

In 1800 Philadelphia was in the vanguard of American culture.
The thrift and industry of the Quaker merchants early brought the
town a marked degree of prosperity. Land speculation had further
enriched certain of its inhabitants, and from 1790 to 1800 it was
the political and financial capital of the new republic. The young
Franklin found the town an agreeable home, and he spent most
of a long life making it more so. Culture the town surely possessed,
if not in the quantity or quality that London did, at least it had
sufficient to put it ahead of any American city. Philadelphia was
the national capital in the days when Jefferson and Hamilton were
waging their memorable duel over domestic politics and the French
Revolution, and this conflict generated an intellectual stimulus that
was felt in every Philadelphia drawing room. Young men heatedly
professed the latest doctrine from France, while their elders gravely
disapproved. English radical doctrines were as freely read and discussed as were those from Paris, and probably the most important
of the foreign influences was that of William Godwin, English political philosopher, novelist, and father-in-law of the poet Shelley.

Ideas of Godwin.—William Godwin, one of the most influential
radical thinkers of the English-speaking race, put his most important
ideas in one large work that he called *Political Justice*. In this
book Godwin did not do so much original thinking, but he combined
and persuasively stated the views of others. Starting with the assumption that human nature is good and that its faults are traceable to the influence of artificial institutions, Godwin proceeded to
the startling view that governmental and all other restrictions on
man are bad and should be abolished. He most attractively sketched
a state of free society which gave its people the greatest happiness
by allowing every man to act according to his own will and reason.
Godwin's importance to-day is twofold. He lives in political philosophy by virtue of this book, and he occupies a considerable place
in literature because of his great influence upon such men as Words-

worth, Coleridge, and Shelley. In addition to his political theory
Godwin left a famous novel, *Caleb Williams,* the very interesting plot
of which frequently keeps the reader from realizing that the book
contains most of the author's political philosophy. On this side of
the Atlantic Charles Brockden Brown eagerly accepted the doctrines
of Godwin.

CHARLES BROCKDEN BROWN
(1770-1810)

Charles Brockden Brown, the first successful American novelist,
combined in a very striking fashion the literary tendencies of England and materials selected from the new world about him. In 1800
the English were still reading the Gothic novel with its emphasis
upon the uncanny and the supernatural, and Brown introduced this
type of romance to America, managing to keep its most grewsome
aspects while giving it an American background.

Early Works.—In *Wieland* (1798), the story turns on a horrible
murder committed by a religious fanatic. The bloody melodrama is
brought about by ventriloquism and completed by a case of spontaneous combustion. In spite of an unnatural narrative style *Wieland* is the first American novel that is still readable. However, its
strictly native elements are limited to the scene which is laid on the
Schuylkill River.

Godwin's influence is plainly seen in *Ormond* (1799) which uses
the plot of *Caleb Williams.* The chief character for whom the book
is named is a helpless woman, over whom a man held power, until
in desperation she killed her tormentor. This book made a strong
appeal to another of Godwin's disciples, Shelley, to whom the young
woman seemed the symbol of pure humanity oppressed by vicious
institutions. It is altogether probable that Brown wrote with such
a symbol in mind, for he was saturated with radical political thought.

Edgar Huntly (1799) marks the first use in fiction of the Indian
and the frontier. The chapters in this book describing details of unpleasant scenes are unforgettable in their stark realism and unpleasant truth. Even in a thoroughly American book like *Edgar Huntly*
Brown could not forget the Gothic. In this novel he utilized sleep-
walking to explain the mystery.

"Arthur Mervyn" (*1799-1800*).—Brown's last novel, *Arthur Mervyn* shows more plainly than do any of his other books the influence

of Godwin. *Caleb Williams* again supplied the plot, only this time the persecuted one is a young man. Mervyn is a high-minded product of a natural environment, intelligent, generous, and easily moved to pity. He loves justice and by nature espouses the cause of right. In short he is Rousseau's natural man in the American environment, just where Rousseau would have expected to find him. Furthermore, he is a brilliant demonstration of the soundness of Godwin's theories. In this work Brown joined hands with English and French romanticism to indicate the future development of the American novel. Since 1800 our native novelists have never long lost touch with European literary currents. Brockden Brown, by either his keen insight or mere chance, is fully entitled to be known as the father of the American novel.

ROBERT MONTGOMERY BIRD

(1805-1854)

Bird has been called the ablest man of letters produced by Philadelphia and one of the best in our early literary history. During his youth Jeffersonian liberalism was coloring our national thinking, and as soon as political romanticism began to express itself in literature Bird was a young man ready to devote his life to the making of romantic literature. He began his writing by producing a number of dramas of so great worth that he stands as one of our earliest successful dramatists. Two of his plays, *The Gladiator* and *The Broker of Bogota*, were enormous successes, the first being an especial favorite of the great tragedian, Edwin Forrest. Bird and Forrest quarreled over royalties, and the dramatist turned to the writing of novels.

"Nick of the Woods."—*Nick of the Woods* is a frontier mystery tale the action of which is determined by the old but popular revenge motive. A frontier Quaker farmer, practicing non-resistance and the spirit of good-will, is attacked by the Indians who murder all his family and leave him for dead. Thereafter the Quaker, now feigning non-resistance, becomes the terror of the border. He relentlessly pursues and mysteriously strikes down his foes in silence. Bird scored a huge success with this figure and with one other in the book, Ralph Stackpole, who provides a bit of comic relief in the shape of a western humorous character. The Indians in *Nick*

of the Woods are neither Rousseau's "natural men" nor Cooper's "noble redskins." Rather they are coarse, brutal savages, richly deserving the fate that the Quaker holds over them. *Nick of the Woods* is one of our better early novels. Since its publication in 1837 it has appeared in twenty American editions and has been translated into three European languages. To-day it is readily accessible in a modern edition.

After 1800 Philadelphia suffered a slow decline from its preëminent position. Philadelphia commerce suffered a stunning blow when the purchase of Louisiana and the opening of the Erie Canal made New Orleans and New York the gateways of the Mississippi and Ohio valleys. Then the removal of the national capital to Washington in 1800 took out of the city its most stimulating intellectual force. Since 1825 or 1830 Philadelphia has never recovered its leadership in American letters.

It seems that the romantic writers of Philadelphia were rather lacking in influence on later men, though this statement may have to be modified if ever we are given adequate studies of Brown and Bird. The lack of influence of the two men may be explained in part by the quiescence of intellectual life in Philadelphia after 1825. Of the two writers Brown is the more obviously romantic in his acceptance of the theories of Godwin and in his adaptation of the Gothic novel to the American scene. Bird is a romantic by virtue of the very materials and methods of his novels.

SUGGESTED READINGS

Parrington: *The Romantic Revolution.* New York. 1927. pp. 185-192.
Van Doren: *The American Novel.* New York. 1921. Brown, pp. 10-15.

CHAPTER XII

NEW YORK, THE COSMOPOLITAN CITY

New York City has always been famous as a meeting-place of races and cultures. Before the end of the Dutch rule many different languages were heard in the streets of the village, and by the middle of the nineteenth century, when the town had become the unquestioned metropolis of America, its cosmopolitan characteristics had but deepened.

New York in 1800.—In the year 1800 New York had not yet become the metropolis of the nation or its literary center, but there were certain influences in and around the town that foretold its future eminence and divergent interests. Not very many miles west of Manhattan Island lay the frontier. Owing to the presence of the Iroquois Indians the settlement of western New York had progressed rather slowly, and by the opening of the century a man in the center of the state was as much on the frontier as he would have been in Kentucky or Tennessee. The Indian and his pioneer-enemy, the vast reservoir of open land, and the aspirations and desires of the frontiersman were all living realities even to those city dwellers who never left the vicinity of Broadway. All the important New York writers like Irving, Cooper, Bryant, Paulding, and Greeley reflect in different ways and to varying degrees the influence of the frontier.

The second large influence in New York was the presence or at least the remains of European feudalism transplanted to America as a system of landholding by patroons along the Hudson River. The aim of the patroons was to establish a feudal relationship of landlord and tenant in New York society. Although many of the huge estates had been broken up by the Revolution, several were still in existence, notably that of the Van Rensselaers, and the example of the patroons along the river was often imitated, however unsuccessfully, by large landowners and speculators on the frontier. Naturally the influence of such men would be exerted against the predilection for leveling, and we are not surprised to find these men and their adherents enrolled with the aristocratic Federalists against the demands of democracy. Cooper is the prime example of a writer influenced by the landlord class. Indeed it is to be questioned if his anti-democratic bias was not the strongest motive in his writing. At all events it should never be forgotten that he was the son of Judge Cooper, the largest landholder in central New York, who lived at Cooperstown in a state of baronial splendor.

The third important influence was that usually connected with New York, commercial enterprise. Beginning with the unimaginative but financially successful Dutch traders, business was always uppermost in the minds of the New Yorkers. By the time of the Revolution the commercial class was prosperous and very influential, and Alexander Hamilton achieved no little of his fame by acting during Washington's administration as the spokesman for this class. Wall Street had its reputation by 1800, and by the middle of the century it was in unquestioned leadership of our national finance. But banking and trade were not the only aspects of business enterprise in New York. The phenomenal rise of manufacturing in America brought to the city scores of large factories with their attendant problems of wages, working hours, and living conditions. From the very beginning of the factory system in America, New York has always been one of the centers of manufacturing and likewise one of the centers of agitation for the rights of labor. Together the financial interests and the factories made New York a great commercially minded city. The death of Stephen Van Rensselaer in 1839 marked the passing of the last of the patroons. Thenceforward commercial enterprise, represented by such men as John Jacob Astor, was the dominant element in New York City. Irving served for a time as the publicity agent for Astor, and in such a capacity wrote *A Tour of the Prairies, Bonneville,* and *Astoria.* These books are often cited as proof of Irving's interest in the frontier, but they are better proof of his interest in the fur-trading enterprises of Astor, the wealthiest man in America. Horace Greeley, with his warm espousal of the rights of labor, represented the influence of the working man and his problems.

The Erie Canal.—Nature endowed New York with a rather restricted hinterland that the city was forced to expand by artificial methods. The Hudson Valley was narrow, and the amount of rich land in the center of the state was limited. As a result, during the eighteenth century Boston, Philadelphia, and Baltimore equaled or surpassed the city in shipping. Early the New York business man saw that leadership would go to the city that could control the trade of the upper Mississippi and Ohio valleys. The Hudson and Mohawk valleys offered an almost level road to the Great Lakes. The Hudson was easily navigable to Albany, and from that city to Buffalo the state constructed the Erie Canal, completing the work in 1820. This was the most important commercial improvement ever undertaken by New Yorkers. Within a few years the products of Middle America were pouring through the canal to New York whence they were exported to Europe. With the huge development of foreign trade the city became the chief port of entry for immigrants and for old world thought, and since 1840 few aliens and fewer foreign ideas have entered the country through any other city. The extreme cosmopolitanism of present-day New York can be traced back to the influence of the Erie Canal, a commercial enterprise designed originally only to open the western hinterland of the city.

As a result of the diverse influences playing upon the intellectual life of the city, New York had no well-defined "school" of writers as Charleston had. To speak of the Knickerbocker School as if all the writers living in and around New York were dominated by the same impulse is to commit a most lamentable error. Place of residence is about all that Irving, Cooper, Paulding, and Greeley had in common. And both Irving and Cooper were very much at home in Europe.

WASHINGTON IRVING

(1783-1859)

Washington Irving has been called the first of American romantics. This enviable distinction might also be claimed by Brockden Brown, for the Philadelphia novelist was twelve years Irving's senior, he wrote his first romantic novel when Irving was only fifteen years old, and furthermore Brown's romanticism was of a deeper grain than that of the better known writer. Although Irving must be awarded a place, and a high one, in the development of American romanticism, it is indisputable that his romantic leanings were few and relatively superficial. No man ever more resolutely turned his back on the present than did Irving during most of his creative years. Turning to the past with genteel disregard for the rights of man, the principles of French revolutionary philosophy, the agitation of labor for the vote and for better working conditions, the transcendental and reform movements of New England, and all the manifestations of romanticism in America, Irving sought the romantic in the far away and long ago, in the life of an eighteenth century English squire, in the lights and shadows of the old Moorish castle of the Alhambra, and in the lives of phlegmatic Dutch villagers in New Amsterdam. The picturesque was Irving's one delight; the sordid affairs of everyday life left him profoundly unmoved.

Irving the Romantic.—After 1800 England and America were sorry places for one who was a confirmed seeker after the picturesque. With its spacious manners, its knee breeches and wigs, its fine ladies and gentlemen born to their ranks, and its well-behaved lower classes, the old life offered something to the leisurely lover of color and quietude. But the old life was passing. Revolutions, political and industrial, were overturning the old institutions, and gentlemen were being shouldered out of their places by sweaty workmen who were clamoring for the right to vote out of existence the last vestiges of the old order. Irving saw all this and was not pleased. He demanded the picturesque, and whatever a literary man with a good imagination demands in the way of material for a book, that will he find.

As a young man Irving had satirized his fellow townsmen with good-natured raillery in *Salamagundi*. A hundred years later he might have found his place as a columnist on a daily newspaper and spent the rest of his life writing humorous quips and light essays, but in 1807 the columnist was unknown, and Irving had to seek another field. He turned to the placid but happy days of old New Amsterdam and created *Knickerbocker's History of New York,* a work so filled with humor and sprightly narrative that it has never lost its appeal. To many people this work stands as the one indubitable masterpiece of Irving's creation. The author's one aim was the presentation in humorous form of the picturesque early life of the colony. Humorous it is. If Irving could not get a laugh by a sly joke, he seized a slap-stick and laid about him. If one of his heroes was not funny enough in the smoke and bloodless mêlée of a burlesque battle, Irving was not above making the worthy fall down in the best fashion of movie comedians. *Knickerbocker* used the whole repertoire of the humorous writer, and as a result readers have laughed with it for a hundred years at the exaggerated foibles of the early Dutch. In excellence of style and freshness of narrative charm Irving never surpassed his first sustained book.

In 1815 Irving went on a business trip to Europe. The next year his firm failed, but still he remained abroad until 1832. It was during this protracted stay in England and on the Continent that he wrote some of the works by which he is best known. Among these are *The Sketch Book, Bracebridge Hall, Life and Voyages of Columbus, The Conquest of Granada,* and *The Alhambra.*

After he had been in England for four or five years, Irving began to compile a volume of sketches that would interpret the most agreeable features of that country and the United States. In the case of this author the agreeable always is synonymous with the picturesque. *The Sketch Book* was the result of this task. The most famous pieces in this book are two American sketches, "The Legend of Sleepy Hollow" and "Rip Van Winkle." The first is an idyllic but highly humorous story of Dutch life in a sheltered little valley beside the Hudson in the days just after the Revolution. The place and the time both would have lent themselves to a simple and sentimental sketch brimming with tears, yet rejoicing in a happy end. But Irving's humor saved the day for better literature. The misadventures of the inept Ichabod Crane, the patron saint of all subsequent pedagogues, form one of the masterpieces of American humor. It took Mark Twain himself to surpass the description of Ichabod and his worthy steed, Gunpowder, as they sallied forth to win the blooming Katrina, and even Twain did not succeed every time he put pen to paper. No humorist of the English tongue would disdain to envy Irving the midnight ride of Ichabod and Gunpowder pursued by the avenging headless horseman. The long popularity of "Rip Van Winkle" has undoubtedly been aided by the superb portrayal of the title character by Joseph Jefferson, who made of Irving's work a memorable piece of sentiment. The sketch is a folk-tale of colonial New York with the central figure of Rip, a shiftless loafer, to whom befell marvelous adventures. Many have commented upon the fact that the ne'er-do-well Rip might be the author himself in a thin disguise. The likeness is heightened at the very end, when Rip is amazed at the change from the placid life of pre-revolutionary days to the bustling, hurrying life of a Yankee village with bedraggled politicians vociferously seeking the votes of the crowd. Rip is slightly bewildered, slightly displeased. So was

Irving. He never was quite reconciled to the change from a picturesque life to one of noise and business.

The Romantic in Europe.—Other memorable pages of *The Sketch Book* describe "Westminster Abbey," "Stratford-on-Avon," and Christmas Eve at an English country house. This last sketch was so successful that the author elaborated it as *Bracebridge Hall,* a delightful study of rural England where the land-owning gentry are kind, considerate, and condescending, and the tenants are happy and obsequious. So lovingly does Irving describe the landlord of England that one is tempted to wonder if he regretted the disappearance of the patroons from New York.

From England Irving went to the Continent, spending most of his time in Spain where he steeped himself in the legends and history of the Moors and prepared for the writing of his biography of Columbus. Probably the finest and certainly the most typical book of the Spanish period is *The Alhambra,* a wholly delightful mixture of fact and tradition. For delicacy and charm there are pages of this book that the author never surpassed. During his stay in Spain Irving held the post of attaché to the American legation in that country. He later became secretary of the legation in England.

It will be noticed that Irving brought back from Europe no heartening doctrines of human equality, no visionary schemes for the regeneration of the human race, no startlingly new literary theories. As a result the cosmopolitan influence in American life owes little to the long European sojourn of our first famous man of letters. Few American authors have been able to remain in Europe for any length of time and not show some intellectual traces of their stay. Irving is among the few. He went to Europe a seeker for the picturesque, and he brought back from Europe only a heightened appreciation of his early love. The only influence that made much change in his literary output was purely American. It was a product of business enterprise and the frontier.

Irving in America (1832-42).—Irving returned to a changed America. The laboring men had been given the ballot, the West had elevated its man to the presidency, and the spirit of big business was in the air. All eyes were on John Jacob Astor, the coming figure of the nation. Irving met the great man and was impressed. Evidently the great man was impressed too, for he saw at once the value that an internationally famous writer could be to him in his economic exploitation of the frontier and the wide open spaces beyond. It took no great amount of argument to make Irving see that the frontiersman, the mountain man, the trapper, and the scout all had elements of the picturesque. The result of Irving's association with Astor was three books, that have been variously estimated but not read half enough, regardless of the judgment of critics.

It is true that Irving wrote these books as the publicity director of the Astor Fur Company, and it is furthermore true that he did not have enough realism about him to show up the hard life of the explorer and trapper without a romantic glamor, but these are minor defects. The worst defect of the books is the persistent presentation of Astor as a finely idealistic figure who is animated in his enterprises by high patriotic motives. Astor was a pretty sordid money grubber, but his author was careful not to let this disconcerting fact leak through his pages. It is true that Irving was never far enough away from a good dinner, a warm fire, and a comfortable bed to be able to visualize the blistering terrors of the desert or the hardships of a winter journey. Granted all these facts—and facts they are—still the western books deserve to be read, for better than any easily available volumes they tell the great story of early pathfinders in the trans-Mississippi West. The skill of the narrative will attract almost any reader, and there are few who will not find here and there through the books more than a few hints as to the significance of these pathfinders. If Irving had not always been trying to find the picturesque he might have produced some true records of the early West. *A Tour of the Prairies* came out in 1835, *Astoria* in 1836, and *The Adventures of Captain Bonneville* in the next year.

Irving was not insensible to further lures of American business, for he made some heavy investments in wild lands. The speculation failed and the author was glad to become minister to Spain in 1842. He remained in Madrid for four years, coming back to America to spend the remainder of his days at his home near New York.

Irving as a Biographer.—In these days of finished psychological and sociological biographical studies it is the fashion to dismiss the biographies wiitten by Irving as rather crude and immature attempts that uniformly resulted in failures. But such procedure is grossly unfair to the writer, for there are three biographies that deserve more than passing notice. These are the *Life and Voyages of Columbus*, *Life of Goldsmith*, and the *Life of Washington*.

The biography of Columbus was based upon a dry but heavily

documented work in Spanish that Irving rewrote in the shape of an easy narrative. It does not say the last word on the great explorer, for a large amount of original material has been discovered in the last hundred years, but the book is so readable that it cannot be lightly dismissed. The art of scientific biography is a recent invention, and it is not fair to compare a work done in 1828 with a recent study by one of the modern writers like Mr. Strachey or Mr. Bradford. Compared with the other productions of its time, Irving's life of Columbus is a distinctly superior work.

The *Life of Washington* is often spoken of as payment of a debt that Irving owed to America and to the great man for whom he was named. If this statement is true, certainly few debts have ever been so completely paid in hard labor. The biography, done in Irving's declining years, lacks the author's customary sparkle and easy style, and it is so long—it appeared in four volumes—that the figure of Washington scarcely emerges from the mass of detail. However, with all its faults it is better than the contemporary lives of our first president, that of Jared Sparks and that of the egregious Parson Weems, who deliberately suppressed facts and falsified history to make Washington a perfect man. Irving avoided this fault, and if he toppled into over-exactness of details, it was the preferable of two evils.

The Life of Goldsmith, the vagabond Bohemian of eighteenth century English literature, is a delightful thing, perfectly true to the spirit of the subject and written with unfailing grace and skill. Of the three biographies it is by far the easiest to read. It deserves to live in literature as a well-written sketch for the average reader who is as much interested in the biographer as in the subject. On the same level is Samuel Johnson's lives of the English poets and Izaak Walton's biographical sketches.

Irving and American Culture.—As a romantic Irving stands too far aloof from the strongly blowing winds of doctrine that swept early nineteenth century America and Europe. To be a champion of ideas, an espouser of noble causes was not his rôle. His was to be the rôle of the genial story-teller who looked at all aspects of contemporary life with the same bland indifference and endeavored to live on terms of smiling amiability with every one. Coming from Europe with no revolutionary ideas, he found that a revolution in America had been effected in his absence, and that the western democrats were in the White House. Although his sympathies were certainly with the old aristocratic party, he called on the backwoods president and at once warmed up to "the game old cock of the woods" as he called Jackson, though he rejected the principles of agrarian democracy. Later he graciously accepted the position of minister to Spain from the hands of Daniel Webster, one of Jackson's chief enemies. Thus Irving kept on good terms with every one, and all delighted to honor him. It was this unvarying geniality that kept him aloof from the conflicts of his time.

A confirmed devotee of the picturesque, Irving could find but little of his material in the party squabbles of everyday life or in feverish agitation for a new order of things. As a result he must remain in our literature as one who contributed little to our thought but much to our merriment. He made few observations on our national life and manners but many shrewd and witty comments on the life of the past. For these sins of omission he stands amply forgiven. The creator of the ageless Ichabod and his one-eyed mount is as sure of immortality as is American literature itself. The man whose scepter called into being Rip Van Winkle and Woulter Van Twiller and repeopled the tenantless courts of the Alhambra with the music and laughter of ages gone is not very apt to become only a name, for despite our intellectual interests we occasionally weary of those writers whose books are bulging with "messages" and turn with positive relief to one who tells a story with the sole aim of holding "children from play and old men from the chimney corner."

JAMES FENIMORE COOPER

(1789-1851)

James Fenimore Cooper is a man of many contradictions. He was at once the most popular novelist and the most unpopular citizen of the United States. He was too democratic for Europe and too aristocratic for America. He hated the noise and vulgarity of Jacksonian democracy no less than he despised the money-making energy of the Whigs. His most celebrated novels are concerned with frontier life, but the author was always a lover of the old landed aristocracy.

It is this last characteristic, a love for the landed gentry, that stands out quite plainly in most of Cooper's books and in some of them constitutes the main theme. Once, comparing society to a marble column, every part of which has a certain fixed place, Cooper wrote: "In New York the great landholders long have, and still do, in a social sense occupy the place of the capital" (of a column). Cooper has best been characterized as an eighteenth century squire, whose broad acres are being invaded on the one hand by a crowd of social levelers, Jacksonian democrats, on the other by a similar crowd of vulgar money grubbers. Neither crowd is welcome. In accepting this generalization it is necessary to bear in mind that the traditional squire was a man devoted to duty, patriotism, honor, and the welfare of his dependents.

Cooper as a Young Man.—Cooper's father was Judge William Cooper of Cooperstown, New York, who gave his full devotion to the Federalist party and to the acquisition of more land. So successful was he in this latter ambition that he could boast that he had brought more acres under cultivation than had any other man of America. His devotion to Federalism was no matter of private information either, for the Judge was once cited to appear in court for having threatened with financial ruin those of his tenants who did not vote for the Federalist candidates. In a state of rude splendor this doughty old aristocrat lived almost on the edge of settlement, repelling the onslaughts of the agrarian rabble as a feudal baron of the Middle Ages repelled the attacks of the barbarians.

In a home dominated by such a father, Cooper spent the impressionable years of his boyhood. In order that the son might receive instruction from another quarter in the ways of aristocratic thinking, the father sent him to an Albany school presided over by a clergyman who was fervent in his devotion to high church principles and thrice fervent in his hatred of democracy and all its ways. From the Albany school Cooper proceeded to Yale which was then in the keeping of the redoubtable Timothy Dwight, iron-clad Puritan and Federalist. But the strait-laced ways of Yale were not for the young chap; the discipline committee functioned, and Cooper's academic career was at an end. A short term of duty on a merchant ship was brought to a close by the father who found an appointment for his son as lieutenant in the navy, an experience that certainly did not tend to make the young man more democratic. His naval service was in turn closed by his marriage to a Miss De Lancey, daughter of one of the old Loyalist families of New York. If there was the slightest latent sympathy with democracy in Cooper this connection with one of the oldest and most aristocratic families of

New York would have been pretty certain to cure it. So far as one can tell, Cooper never lost the impressions gained in his early life and accented by his marriage to a De Lancey.

The Writings of Cooper.—Cooper is one of our most voluminous writers. He published in book form thirty-nine principal works, and the newspapers and magazines of his time are filled with occasional articles, mostly controversial in character. Of this large mass of books only a few are read. Many are known only by name, while some rest in almost utter neglect. The curious misconception of Cooper that is generally accepted as gospel truth is probably caused by a partial knowledge of the man's works.

Cooper's works may be roughly divided into three groups: those that are read, largely the Leatherstocking tales and a few of the sea stories; those that are known by name, including *The Spy, Lionel Lincoln,* and most of the sea tales; last, those that are known only to serious students of American literature. In this group are all of the author's critical work, usually in the form of novels, and three books, *Satanstoe, The Chainbearer,* and *The Redskins* which so discriminating a critic as Professor Parrington has pronounced, with the Leatherstocking tales, the most important works of Cooper. Other books in the critical list are *The Monikins, Homeward Bound,* and *Home as Found.* The student of early American life will do well to read these.

Cooper's Novels: The Leatherstocking Tales.—Cooper deserves a place in world literature as the creator of Natty Bumppo, the first internationally famous character in American fiction. The Leatherstocking tales give the life history of this great figure from his first appearance as the youthful hunter and warrior in *The Deerslayer* to the death of the old man in *The Prairie.* The other members of the group are *The Last of the Mohicans, The Pathfinder,* and *The Pioneers.* These books will never grow old so long as there are youthful minds to feel the thrill of chase and the battle, to glow with pride at the accomplishment of superhuman feats, and to rejoice in the triumph of bravery and the defeat of villainy.

Critics, many of them his fellow novelists, have used Cooper badly in the appraisal of these works. Some have pointed out that the style is hopelessly stilted and out-of-date. Others have commented on the impossibility of the feats described, and still others have attacked the author's ability to depict living characters. It is probable that all the counts in the indictment can be sustained

But despite this fact, the American boy devours every book of the series, judiciously skipping the quite terrible attempts at sentiment and love-making. He cares no more for Cooper's heroines—females, they are called—than does the most sophisticated critic. The boy is interested in the main story, and that story is so constructed that none need feel apologetic over becoming interested in it.

The typical Leatherstocking plot is simplicity in itself. The story opens with some one in danger. There is a rousing battle followed by flight and pursuit. The usual end is another fight that settles all scores. Suspense is the one element of interest that so simple a plot can have, and suspense these books have in plenty. The characters may be wooden, and they may talk together as never men and women conversed, but, covering all defects in its charitable folds, a cleverly contrived major suspense holds the reader in breathless expectancy until the very end of the book. Cooper never fell into the nefarious modern practice of failing to distinguish between the good characters and the villains. He emphasizes the goodness of the good and the badness of the bad. When the two groups take to the warpath, there is blood-letting enough to satisfy the thirstiest, and at every skirmish there is always the possibility that the good may fall before the fire of the villains, though this disheartening catastrophe occurs but seldom. However, there is the frequently realized possibility that the bad may once more escape their just doom. With such possibilities in the air, the reader hastens on, engrossed in the action of the book. Literary sins of omission and commission mean nothing at all to one who is in the grip of a well-contrived suspense.

Cooper's Indians have caused endless debate. Discussion has raged as to whether or not they are "true to life." Inasmuch as some of them are represented as being good, some as bad, and some as quite indifferent, it probably may be safely assumed that they are reasonably close to life. This is a matter for antiquarian research and not for literary discussion. Were Shakespeare's Danes true Danish characters? Or were Milton's demons truly demoniac? Who cares?

Unlike most of the romantics Cooper cared little for scenery. Where most of his contemporaries spent page after page describing the "beauties of nature," evidently for the mere sake of talking about them, Cooper used scenery only when he needed it to forward the action of his plots. In many novelists it is usually advisable to skip the descriptive passages, but such is not the case in the Leather-stocking series. The reader who skips the description of a dark wood is frequently surprised at the appearance of a band of whooping savages coming from nowhere at all. They were lurking in that wood. If they had not been, Cooper would not have mentioned the forest.

The Sea Stories.—Cooper's sea novels are only a bit less interesting than the Leatherstocking series, though they do not have the presence of one unifying character. These books have a suspense that is gained by much the same method employed in the frontier novels, and there is the same deft handling of minor incidents and the same satisfying amount of fighting. In the creation of his characters he shows a little fondness for gloomy Byronic heroes, shrouded in the glamor of mystery or villainy, until the right moment arrives, when they throw off the mystery and reveal themselves as noble and valorous men. That method was much used in Cooper's day, and it has not entirely disappeared to-day, especially among the novelists of sentiment.

Mark Twain once declared that, if the captain of a ship should give the commands used by one of Cooper's characters in the face of a dangerous storm, he would soon have his vessel two miles in-land. It is hard for landsmen to pass judgment on such a criticism. However, since Cooper learned his seamanship on the ocean, while Mark Twain had his on the Mississippi River, it may not be too safe to agree wholly with the critic. Joseph Conrad, master mariner and master of all who have written stories of the sea, pays a warm tribute to the salt-water novels of Cooper. Praise from such a source is praise indeed.

Cooper as a Critic of American Life.—In 1826 when Cooper had six novels to his credit, including two of the Leatherstocking series, he took his family abroad for a visit that was protracted until 1833. Unlike Irving, he was vastly affected by his European trip. Always a truculent, high-tempered man, filled with stubborn prejudices both by training and association, he had until this time evidently done little thinking about the proper constitution of society and the cor-rect form of government. Cooper found Europe in confusion. The high enthusiasms of the French Revolution had expired in the bloody welter of the Napoleonic wars, but still the humanitarian principles of the great upheaval were firmly fixed in the minds and hearts of thinking men. The rise of the factory system on the Continent contributed its share to the agitation in the shape of the familiar discussion of the rights of labor. Everywhere men were debating the nature and function of government. Revolutionary ferment was working. This stimulating intellectual argument stung into action the lumbering mind of Cooper.

Hitherto the novelist had preferred, almost by instinct, a Van Rensselaer to a busy, money-making John Jacob Astor. Certainly he had preferred a large landholder to a noisy leveling frontiersman. But imperceptibly the world had moved ahead of the Cooper way of thinking. The big argument was not between the large landowner and democrat, or between the landowner and the factory owner. It was between the laborers and small farmers on the one hand and the opposing party consisting of business men and manufacturers. In trying to find his bearings in this debate, Cooper lost himself completely. He was a man of stalwart loyalty without any party to which he could give allegiance. He became too European for America, and too American for Europe. He broke with every one, carried on innumerable quarrels and lawsuits, and died a disappointed man, disgusted with his generation. It was the European trip that began this misunderstood and unfortunate episode in the life of Cooper.

Throughout the eighteen years of acrimonious debate with his countrymen Cooper remained a stalwart American, proud of his nation's achievement, hopeful of her future, but savagely critical of the forces then controlling her fate. He was bitter over America's failure to become a nobler and more satisfying home for her citizens; he waxed furious over the real and fancied failures of democracy; but his whole contention was over the method by which the country might be bettered, although in the course of the quarrel he became embroiled in many curious and trivial side-issues.

During the last years of his stay in Europe Cooper wrote three books, *The Bravo*, *The Heidenmauer*, and *The Headsman*, with the rather bumptious intention of demonstrating the superiority of American life over European. Returning to this country he found that much of the vaunted superiority did not exist. *The Monikins*, one of our bitterest satires, was the result of his discovery. Of his critical books probably the most offensive to his contemporaries was *Home as Found*, a headlong attack on the principal of majority rule, a doctrine to which America was then hopelessly committed. To make his offense still more unpardonable he wrote his anti-rent trilogy in defense of the landowners of New York who were faced with the growing unrest of their tenants. Of these three novels, *Satanstoe,* *The Chainbearer,* and *The Redskins,* the latter was the most distasteful, for it again attacked the principle of American democracy. As intelligent critics have often pointed out, these critical books are a perfect mine of information to the social historian who wishes to know something more about our country than is told in political histories.

In these critical novels and discussions Cooper sustained the point of view of his ancestral Federalism. According to his own lights he was a good American democrat, but by a democracy he meant a government carried on by representatives of the people with the mass of the people meek and tractable under the control of their betters, the landowners. Government is a matter that should concern only gentlemen, and good citizens are those who are docile enough to defer to the judgment of the gentry in all governmental affairs. Accepting this definition Cooper was a good enough democrat, but a frontiersman would not have thought much of such a definition or of such a democrat.

Cooper and the Frontier.—Inevitably the question arises as to the relation of Cooper to the frontier. There is no argument as to his handling of frontier scenes and incidents; the question is whether or not he was in sympathy with frontier character. Was Leatherstocking a true frontiersman? Was Cooper himself a frontiersman?

To argue that Cooper was a frontiersman because he wrote of frontier characters and events is like arguing that Shakespeare was a Roman because he wrote plays about Roman history. Cooper's background has already been indicated, and that background appeared in all his works, even in the Leatherstocking series. Natty Bumppo shows almost none of the fundamental frontier traits. Rather he is an eighteenth century servant dressed in a buckskin hunting shirt. Many virtues has this character, but they are the virtues that Cooper valued in a retainer and not the virtues that flourished on the frontier. Natty Bumppo is quiet, restrained, efficient, scrupulously observant of established law, and consistently respectful to the things that Cooper thought deserved respect. The virtues of the frontiersman, such as the insistence upon the leveling of class distinctions, the perfect willingness to adapt law to his needs, and the sense of a right to participate in governmental decisions— these things Cooper could not have accounted virtues.

In short, Cooper's frontier hero was a frontiersman only in the superficial, unimportant aspects. Place him beside a swaggering fellow from the West like Crockett or some of Longstreet's characters, and the difference is at once apparent. Bumppo can unerringly follow a cold trail; his ability as a marksman is phenomenal; he can imitate the cry of beast and wild fowl; he can endure unmoved the ingenious tortures inflicted by his foes. But there his likeness to a real frontiersman ends. Fundamentally he bears a closer resemblance to John Adams than he does to Davy Crockett. The very fact that Cooper is transplanting eighteenth century virtues in frontier soil accounts for some of the stiffness and artificiality in the Leatherstocking tales that cannot be explained by the literary style of the books or by the stilted language in which the characters converse. Cooper was no frontiersman, and his sympathy was not with the aspirations of that type of man. He wrote frontier stories because he lived in a romantic age when even the least romantic novelists took at least the setting of romance for their background. There were three sources of material for the American romancer, the early colonial period, the Revolution, and the frontier. Cooper used the last two, especially exploiting the frontier.

Cooper in American Literature.—But discussions of Cooper as a master or a bungler of literary style, as a critic of American life, or as an eighteenth century aristocrat who wrote about the frontier simply because such novels were popular, all miss the abiding worth of the novelist. For a century the exploits of Leatherstocking have held old and young alike in the power of a born story teller whose great narrative ability is nowhere more strikingly proved than by the fact that it breaks through to the reader in spite of a host of literary blunders that could have been avoided by a lesser writer. But the lesser writer could not have gained the interest, the breathless suspense, that gives undying vitality to the novels. Readers in France, England, Austria, Germany, Russia, know the thrill of Leatherstocking's deeds, and the American reader who misses that thrill is missing one of the finest things in American literature.

JAMES KIRKE PAULDING

(1779-1860)

James Kirke Paulding, novelist and politician, had a much closer connection with American affairs than did either Cooper or Irving.

Paulding spent no time in searching for the picturesque or in mourning the passing of a landed aristocracy. He was acutely aware of the fact that he was living in nineteenth century America and that the problems of America were his problems. Nor did he blink western democracy, with its noise, swagger, and unrealized promise. In fact, better than most men in America Paulding realized the implications of the West in our national life. He understood to the full the meaning of the American party battle, a struggle that at times seemed to lose all meaning. It is the insight of Paulding into our problems of the time that gives the man considerable significance in our literature.

Paulding, the Eulogist of Democracy.—Paulding is another of our neglected early novelists. Every one has said—or tried to say—"Peter Piper picked a peck of pickled peppers," but very few know that the line is from Paulding's satire on the Whig party. Paulding is not the best of our early novelists, nor is he the worst, but he is a very significant writer. In his books one can chart the social and political current of the time very easily.

Paulding came of staunch revolutionary stock, his father having espoused the cause of liberty when such a course was highly dangerous in his neighborhood. The boy was reared to hate England and all her ways, and to the end of his life he believed that the European class system was responsible for all the ills of the Continent and that the free democracy of America was responsible for all our felicities. Few American authors have taken so little from European culture as did Paulding. The sole influence of foreign life and thought was only to drive him into a deeper admiration for America.

Paulding was a product of New York State, a country product. For the first twenty years of his life he knew the poverty and aspirations of the common people, the small landholders, and never did he forget the lessons of his youth. At the age of nineteen he went to New York City to live with his sister who had married Washington Irving's older brother. A friendship between young Irving and Paulding resulted in the *Salamagundi Papers,* humorous skits on New York life. Soon Paulding entered the employ of the navy department, in which he remained for a number of years, becoming secretary of the navy under Jackson's friend and successor, Martin Van Buren.

During Paulding's life one of the chief sports of English travelers was the writing of books that belittled American institutions and manners. Such productions always nettled Paulding, for they seemed to him only the slurring comments of an aristocracy-ridden nation upon the free and happy life in America. Paulding replied to the English critics, giving them shot for shot in a lively series of publications. But praising America was the chief literary task that the man set for himself. This he conceived to be the most effective answer to America's critics.

In all of his writing Paulding reveals himself as a thorough-going equalitarian, a Jeffersonian who would have neither an aristocracy nor a class of money-getters in this nation. None of our writers, save Jefferson alone, has ever been so wholly of the soil. Paulding was utterly opposed to the city and its business, holding with Jefferson that the middleman sought only the exploitation of the farmer. Imbued with physiocratic economics, he went so far in his praise of the countryside as to declare that he never "saw an industrious farmer forsaken or 'his seed begging bread.' "

In his praise of America Paulding used verse and prose, fiction and fact. The first of his productions was. *The Backwoodsman,* a long poem that celebrated the freedom that awaited him who fled from the city to the frontier. The author set forth, with probably more enthusiasm than poetry, the material blessings and the mental development that attended the backwoodsman. *Koningsmarke,* a lively satire of the Whig gospel of progress, has been pronounced by most critics the author's best book. It is more than a satire, for it is a burlesque of Scott's Waverley novels. Scott and Byron were Paulding's two pet aversions. Both of the English writers were aristocratic in tastes, Byron having inherited a title and Scott always carefully choosing his leading characters from the upper classes. Such flagrant offenses Paulding could not allow to go unpunished. *Westward Ho!* is a novel that takes up the theme of the backwoodsman but without marked success. *The Puritan and His Daughter* is a long work that tells of the power that America has to heal old wounds that are brought to this country from Europe. Cavalier and Puritan could fight to the death in the old world, but when they came to this continent, the new environment forced them to forget their old differences. Again it is the power of America to undo the wrongs perpetrated by the class distinctions of Europe. It is significant that Paulding dedicated this work to the "sovereign people of America."

Paulding as a novelist has probably passed into an oblivion so deep that it will never be penetrated by the average reader. This fact is to be deplored. America never produced a writer who was more thoroughly homespun, or one who more resolutely defended the influences that made him what he was. Furthermore *Koningsmarke* is a well-written book, easily surpassing in literary merit much of the prose and poetry of the time that we have so scrupulously preserved. In both manner and content Paulding little deserves the oblivion that has overtaken him.

WILLIAM CULLEN BRYANT

(1794-1878)

Bryant is an example of an American author who has been neglected only in one part of his work. For less than ten years Bryant divided his allegiance between poetry and law, producing a thin volume of the best poetry written in the United States before 1830. For the last fifty years of his life he rendered a distinguished service to his nation as the liberal editor of the influential *New York Evening Post*. Yet histories of literature devote pages to the man's poetry and dismiss his admirable work as a journalist with a sentence, saying merely that he wasted fifty years in a newspaper office. It is conceivable that Bryant himself would not like such an appraisal.

Bryant's Early Life.—Bryant was born in the Berkshire Hills in western Massachusetts where the principles of old-time Puritanism had not ceased to train the people in the ways of personal piety and stern ethical thinking. That the boy's family were not Jeffersonians is shown by the fact that the future poet first practiced his art in a rhymed lampoon of Jefferson and the Embargo Act. After a rather sketchy preparatory education, Bryant entered Williams College, where he remained only a few months. Lack of money preventing any further academic training, he began the study of law. For a number of years he practiced his profession at Great Barrington, Massachusetts, quitting both the profession and the town to accept a position on the staff of the *Evening Post*. He was connected with the paper for more than fifty years, forty-nine of which he spent as editor-in-chief.

Bryant the Poet.—After tasting more than local fame with his poem on the Embargo, Bryant continued to experiment, until at the age of seventeen or eighteen he produced "Thanatopsis," the poem upon which a large part of his popular fame has always rested. The poem was not first published in the form that we have it in to-day. The original lacked the first sixteen and the last sixteen lines. The complete poem consists of eighty-one lines, hence the first draft was only a little more than half of the whole poem in length, and the later additions contain the famous lines of the piece. The introduction and conclusion were written about ten years after the early part.

In almost every syllable "Thanatopsis" gives evidence of its Puritan ancestry. The Puritans spent much of their time in a contemplation of death, and "Thanatopsis" is one of the notable "graveyard" poems of the English language. Furthermore the conclusion, beginning with the words, "So live that when thy summons comes," is typical didactic poetry, written with the primary aim of imparting a lesson to the reader. Such traces of ancestry are not necessarily defects in the poem. Although to-day those characteristics seem old-fashioned, they were quite the mode in New England when Bryant wrote. One is reasonably safe in assigning to "Thanatopsis" the highest rank of all old-time Puritan poems written in this country.

The note that Bryant struck in his great success he repeated again and again in all his best poetry. He is always serious, deeply impressed with the ethical meaning of life, and grimly determined to leave the reader with an unmistakable moral lesson. Usually this lesson is stated at the end of the poem. Some of Bryant's typical conclusions are:

> Be it ours to meditate,
> In these calm shades, thy milder majesty,
> And to the beautiful order of thy works
> Learn to conform the order of our lives.
>
> (From "A Forest Hymn")

> I would that thus, when I shall see
> The hour of death draw near to me,
> Hope, blossoming within my heart,
> May look to heaven as I depart.
>
> (From "The Fringed Gentian")

> He who, from zone to zone,
> Guides through the boundless sky thy certain flight,
> In the long way that I must tread alone,
> Will lead my steps aright.
>
> (From "To a Waterfowl")

Although Bryant is usually regarded as our most successful Puritan poet, there are many of his poems in which he shows a decidedly non-Puritanical spirit. These are his nature poems. It is true that in some of his poems of outdoor life nature is used simply to convey a moral lesson to the reader, as in the excerpts cited above, but in certain poems like "The Evening Wind," "Robert of Lincoln," and the love song, "O Fairest of the Rural Maids," nature is celebrated for its own sake. In his conception of nature Bryant was essentially romantic. Rejecting the old Puritan belief that nature offered no approach to God, Bryant felt that the forests, streams, and flowers triumphantly exhibited the spirit of God in tangible form. The poet celebrated this aspect of nature in some of the most sensitive and colorful poems of our early literature.

Bryant's poetic style never varied throughout his long life. Although two-thirds of his poetry had been written when he moved to New York in 1825, he continued to write an occasional poem down to the very year of his death. During all these years his style never changed, and his poetic thoughts never showed the softening touch of the warm liberalism that he acquired in his later life. The reason for this is not hard to discover. After 1825 Bryant was primarily an editor and not a poet. He had already developed an effective poetic style that had won general approval, and it was only natural that he should write his occasional later poems in the style that he had early mastered. If he had written a large body of poetry after 1825 one may well suppose that he would have allowed new fashions and new ideas to enter his poetry as they entered his editorials. Poetry was not his primary concern after going to New York, and the constant writing of editorials is not conducive to the development of a poetic style.

Granting all the weakness that can be urged against Bryant as a poet, still much can be said in his favor. A genuine poetic talent such as he unmistakably had, joined with a sensitive appreciation of nature, will cause the reader to pardon many literary shortcomings. We forgive Bryant for his didactic conclusions because of the successes that he scored in the preceding lines. We forgive him for his limited range because within that range he was a true poet. Some of his poems will not soon pass out of American literature.

Bryant, the Liberal Editor.—By the time that Bryant left Massachusetts for New York his feet were already on the path of liberalism, and on that path he continued to travel to the end of his days.

Exactly what the forces were that first began to lead him away from the narrowing influences of his early Calvinism and Federalism, we can only surmise. It is pretty certain, though, that he was touched by some of the winds of romantic doctrine that were blowing through the whole nation during his young manhood. That the Bryant family felt a liberalizing influence is shown by the father's acceptance of Unitarianism, which was only the romantic version of the old Calvinism. Moreover Bryant set himself a course of reading in his last months in the law office that did much to change his way of thinking. Exactly what his reading was, we do not know, but probably it included a considerable amount of liberal thought. At all events when he appeared in New York, he had an open mind. He next fell under the spell of English liberalism with its firm insistence upon the duty of the state to make itself as inconspicuous as possible. This desire for a weak government led him into a position that was not far removed from Jeffersonianism.

This last was the position held by Bryant for the remainder of his life. He always thought in the terms of the farmer and laborer. Financial speculation of all kinds he despised, tariffs he rejected as a mode of exploiting the poorer classes, and any abuse of the laboring man he instantly challenged. With these views he naturally supported the program of Jackson and his party, he worked incessantly for the rights of the laboring class, and when the slavery controversy broke he was to be found on the side of Lincoln. His last years were spent fighting against the powers of corruption for common decency in governmental affairs. However much Bryant may have failed to develop as a poet, as a liberal editor and as a champion of human rights his development was logical and constant.

Certain touches of his Puritanism Bryant was never able to shake off. Enthusiasms were simply foreign to his nature. Not for him was the flaming passion of Garrison or the buoyant reform spirit of Horace Greeley. No agitator was he, but a rather slow-thinking man of intense but quiet convictions. His inability to grow enthusiastic kept him from becoming a popular leader of unpopular causes, but the same characteristic made him an excellent balance-wheel in the whirling social and political discussion from 1830 to 1860. His influence was great, and it was always on the side of human rights. Under his guidance the *New York Evening Post* became a great liberal paper, speaking for the moderate group of reformers and humanitarians just as the *Tribune* under Greeley spoke for the radicals.

It is to be regretted that the editorial work of Bryant is so little known. However, journalism is for the day and not for eternity. Nothing is so obsolete as yesterday's newspaper. The students of Bryant soon discover this fact when they find some of his slight poems assured of at least relative permanence, while his very valuable editorial work is entirely slighted. Judging the man by either phase of his activity he belongs in American literature, no less as an editor than as a poet.

HORACE GREELEY

(1811-1872)

One may look through anthologies of American authors and histories of American literature without number and find no mention of Horace Greeley. Seldom is he noticed in our elementary political histories save as the recipient of a crushing defeat when he aspired to the presidency in 1872. Yet no one need apologize for including Greeley in any account of the development of the American mind. Probably the most influential editor in all our journalism, for more than two decades he led the extreme liberals of America in their attempt to solve the problem of social well-being. Horace Greeley, far better than any other figure, represents the common man of America during the forties and fifties, remarkably endowed with intelligence, and expanded to huge proportions. A little grotesque was Greeley, a trifle too prone to accept proposed reforms without a close examination, but underneath the glowing enthusiasms lay a heart that was never animated save by a love for humanity. Nor was Greeley only a crack-brained fanatic. His enthusiasms never kept him from weighing his decisions in the balance of common sense. He was a practical politician, and such men cannot lose touch with reality. It is as an epitome of a period that Greeley is admitted to a discussion of the American mind.

Greeley combined in himself the three elements that were stirring up most of the political and intellectual tempests in America from 1840 to 1860. These were, first, the agrarian movement, the pulse of the frontier which kept constantly before the nation the question of the open land and our land policy. The second element was the laboring class of the cities, fast in the grip of the industrial revolution and trying desperately to better its condition. Last was the great intellectual awakening, the romantic movement, that culminated in the reforming wave of the forties. Greeley as a product of the New England backwoods never lost touch with his early environment, and his constant desire was to see "young men go West" and settle as small farmers on the public domain. As a mature man he worked in New York City where he was compelled to see the sickening conditions under which laborers were forced to live. The humanitarian reforms he grasped at because he was a keen intellectual, obsessed with the desire to help solve the ills of society. These influences made Greeley.

The New Task of Romanticism.—The earlier American romanticism, that of Jefferson, Paine, Barlow, and Freneau, was compelled to be destructive. Its task was the uprooting of old institutions, the abolition of over-seas tyranny, autocracy, aristocracy, and outmoded customs that hampered the free development of man. That work was accomplished. The generation that came of age between 1830 and 1840 found, to its surprise, that although the evils of a former day were no longer existing, society had not achieved the desired degree of social well-being. The new generation sensed that constructive measures were needed to accomplish the desired results. Horace Greeley was in a real way the epitome of all those optimistic Americans who began experimentation with constructive reforms.

By 1840 several appalling facts had forced themselves upon American romantics. The very essence of romanticism was freedom, personal and social, freedom from governmental interference and from the control of other individuals. This freedom implied a simple, inexpensive form of government and an economics founded upon agriculture and home manufacturing. The industrial revolution, which had set in not far from the beginning of the romantic movement, upset all these calculations. Industry was coming to be fearfully complicated. Factories were growing in size, more workers were congregating in the towns, living conditions were becoming progressively worse, and, worst of all, the newly invented machines were pouring out a constantly increasing stream of products, some of them extravagant luxuries, that had to be sold to people of hitherto simple tastes and desires. Men, women, and children worked furiously in factories to make various commodities. The desire to possess these very commodities forced the laborers to work harder and for longer hours to get more money; the harder work produced more and still more things that in turn whetted the acquisitive appetites of the people. Thus humanity was in the grip of an endless, evil chain, the industrial system. The growing complexity of the industrial system was forcing a corresponding growth in the complexity of the government. At a glance the new generation of romantics saw the danger. Jeffersonian simplicity was in danger of becoming an unrealizable dream. Something must be done.

It was to the doing of this something that Greeley and his generation applied themselves. Some, like Thoreau, thought that the solution lay in the resolute return to the bosom of nature, at one stroke freeing the mind from the desire to possess more goods and the body from bondage to the machine. Others like George Ripley began experimenting with social organizations that would allow people to live together in groups enjoying the benefits of association without paying the penalty in the shape of elaborate governments and burdensome factories. Still others like Emerson watched all experiments and discussed all proposed solutions in the light of romantic individualistic philosophy. It was with the second group, the experimenters, that Greeley was most nearly allied.

Greeley and Fourierism.—Charles Fourier (1772-1837), a French social philosopher, worked out a plan for the organization of society in such a way that the evils of industrialism and excessive governmental regulation might be avoided. Fourier thought that society should be divided into small groups, each of which should be housed in a large building or group of buildings. A community thus formed was known as a phalanx. Members of the phalanx should so distribute labor that no one should be compelled to work at an uncongenial task or to continue a work after it became irksome. Private property and the right of inheritance were to be allowed, but the products of labor within the phalanx were to be equitably distributed, five-twelfths to labor, four-twelfths to capital, and three-twelfths to talent. Ample leisure was to be allowed for the moral and spiritual improvement of the members.

Fourierism became very popular in the United States, where it was usually known as associationism. At least thirty-four phalanxes were formed in this country, an official newspaper, *The Harbinger*, was established for the spreading of the doctrine of associationism, and a society with the same aim was organized under the presidency of Horace Greeley. Greeley never belonged to any of the phalanxes, but he was a frequent visitor at several of them and he owned a body of Pennsylvania land upon which one was established. Although most of the phalanxes disbanded after a few years, Greeley's enthusiasm for Fourierism did not wane. He opened the columns of the *Tribune* to all exponents of the system, and by his constant agitation for that particular reform did much to make America socially minded.

Greeley and Labor Reform.—From Fourierism Greeley proceeded naturally and logically to the more specific question of the laborer. In answering this question Greeley showed his fundamental agrarianism by saying that the evils of industry were directly traceable to our public land policy. Land speculation and the practice of the government to sell the public domain only in large tracts kept many from the possession of farm homes and forced these same people to the cities where naturally they were the easy prey of a vicious industrialism. "The freedom of the public lands to actual settlers, and the limitation of future acquisitions of land to some reasonable amount, are also measures which seem to us vitally necessary to the ultimate emancipation of labor from thraldom and misery." This statement by Greeley in the *Tribune* became the working platform of many refomers and the basis of a considerable body of proposed legislation both state and national. Out of these proposals ultimately came the homestead act of 1862 which allowed each bona-fide settler a tract of 160 acres. Greeley himself introduced the first homestead bill in Congress in 1848. The devotion of Greeley to the cause of labor enabled him in 1854 and 1856 to carry most of the working men with him into the newly formed Republican party.

Greeley was never far from the spirit of the frontier. His hatred of land speculation, his aversion to large landholders, his enthusiasm for the freedom and independence of the small farmer all reflect his interest in the West. "Go West, young man, go West," was his most famous bit of advice, and the widespread acceptance of his words caused the line of settlement to surge westward at a great speed. The implications of the frontier bothered Greeley not at all, and its demands he regarded as only reasonable and just. It would not be hard to prove that Greeley was a Jeffersonian equalitarian who was the product of frontier thought, just as Jefferson himself was.

Greeley and Other Reforms.—Greeley was one of the foremost American opponents of slavery. Like Lincoln his opposition to the institution was twofold. His hatred for its unhumanitarian aspects was increased when he saw that the institution meant the extinction of his beloved small farmer in the districts where it was introduced. "Free homesteads, free soil, and free labor," was a slogan that received its finest elaboration and defense in the columns of the

Tribune, and the vast influence of that paper in western states like Ohio and Illinois did much to commit those regions to the anti-slavery cause.

But Greeley's list of reform measures is not easily exhausted. He was an early and ardent advocate of temperance at a time when drinking was almost universal. And Greeley practiced what he preached. He was opposed to the use of tobacco, caring almost as little for it as he did for alcohol. Dietary reform was one of his early enthusiasms, and he met his future wife at a Grahamite boarding-house where meat, white-bread, stimulants, and pickles were rigorously forbidden. He took up the cause of women's rights when that proposed reform was the laughingstock of all "practical" men and freely opened the columns of his paper to a discussion of the question. All his life he opposed capital punishment. Universal peace and international good-will gained his ready support, and his last great fight was a protest against bribery and corruption in government. In short Greeley was one of the most valuable converts ever made to the cause of reform. He was a thorough-going reformer, but, what is more important, he gave to the reformers a widespread publicity and an impressive personal influence.

Greeley's reputation as a writer lies buried in the files of the *New York Tribune.* When his editorials are exhumed by some student and made accessible to the modern reader, it will be found that his career very nearly epitomized one of the great epochs of American history, and not the least glory of that epoch is the fact that in those days things spiritual and intellectual were not regarded as inferior to things material.

SUGGESTED READINGS

Bigelow: *William Cullen Bryant.* Boston. 1890.
Bowers: *The Spanish Adventures of Washington Irving.* Boston. 1940.
    Not of extreme importance but fills a gap in our knowledge of Irving.
Boynton: *James Fenimore Cooper.* New York. 1931.
Brooks: *The World of Washington Irving.* New York. 1944.
    A typical Brooks work. All the details are there but little direction.
Canby: *Classic Americans.* New York. 1931.
    Contains chapters on Irving and Cooper.

Commons: "Horace Greeley and the Working Class Origins of the Republican Party." Political Science Quarterly, 24: 468-488.
> Every student of American political development should know this article.

Cooper: *Correspondence of James Fenimore Cooper*. New Haven. 1922.
> It is doubtful if we ever have a thoroughly satisfactory life of Cooper. These letters are not even a fair substitute.

Hellman: *Washington Irving*. New York. 1925.
> Not a well-rounded study, though it contains some material which was new in 1925. Superseded by Williams.

Herold: *James Kirke Paulding*. New York. 1926.
> Remains useful.

Irving: *Life of Washington Irving*. Out of print.
> The official life by a nephew.

Macy: *The Spirit of American Literature*. New York. 1912. Cooper, pp. 18-34; Irving, pp. 35-44.
> Despite its age, Macy's book is still a good introduction.

Nevins: *The Evening Post—A Century of Journalism*. New York. 1922.
> This history of a distinguished paper has a valuable account of Bryant's journalistic work.

Parrington: *The Romantic Revolution*. New York. 1927. pp. 193-237.
> Parrington's account of Irving is slight. In other respects a valuable work.

Pattee: "Cooper the Critic." Saturday Review of Literature, 5: 1107-1108.

Pattee: *Sidelights on American Literature*. New York. 1922. Bryant, pp. 293-326.

Rourke: *Trumpets of Jubilee*. New York. 1927. Greeley, pp. 239-365.
> Remains the best study of Greeley.

Seitz: *Horace Greeley*. Indianapolis. 1926.

Spiller: *Fenimore Cooper: Critic of His Times*. New York. 1931.

Van Doren: *The American Novel*. New York. 1921.
> Contains chapters on Cooper and Paulding.

Williams: *Life of Washington Irving*. New York. 1935.
> By far the best in the field.

CHAPTER XIII

THE NEW ENGLAND RENAISSANCE

CONFLICT OF ROMANTICISM AND INDUSTRIALISM IN NEW ENGLAND

In New England American romanticism reached its fullest development. Indeed no aspect of the romantic movement in this country, save the southern dream of a Greek democracy, is missing from the roll of New England activities between 1830 and 1850. The gospel of individualism was preached more eloquently by Emerson than ever it was by any other American. New England discovered the doctrine of nature, and Thoreau became its prophet. A large group of shrill-voiced reformers declaimed the coming of a new day in social relations. The Utopian socialism of Fourier here had some of its most ardent advocates, and the most famous of all the phalanxes was that at Brook Farm, Massachusetts. The past glories of New England were celebrated in more than one novel. The medieval world and picturesque beauties of modern Europe enthralled a whole generation of New England students and travelers, including such men as Longfellow. Above this swirling medley of social reform and intellectual awakening steadily sounded the clear note of ethical responsibility. So brilliant and manifold were the aspects of New England romanticism that some critics fail to see the movement in other portions of the country. Such a judgment is inaccurate, but certainly New England developed the flower of American romanticism.

For fifty years after the outbreak of the Revolution the intellectual sterility of New England was disheartening. During the revolutionary agitation Massachusetts had been the hatching place of many an idea, but independence once achieved, the merchants and seagoing men of New England settled down to the dull routine of making money. After 1800 Federalism, dead elsewhere in the United States, gave up the ghost in New England with many a gasp and death struggle. Iron-clad Calvinism, reeling under the double impact of frontier optimism and the new romantic philosophy, was still strongly entrenched in its native hills, and every Sunday its clergy thundered against such pernicious innovations as the ideas that were seeping in from across the Atlantic. The fact that some of the new thought was coming by way of Virginia made it only the more odious. Intellectual sterility was the order of the day.

But a new order was coming. Slowly, imperceptibly, romantic thought entered the forbidden ground, and at its transforming touch every New England institution blossomed into something new and fine. With the impact of romantic doctrine upon the Puritan mind, everything—the church, the state, the family, social relations, industry—was subjected to a close and sometimes exasperated examination. Few things were left in their original form. Most of all was the New England mind transformed. Little was preserved of the older Calvinism save the ethical interests, and these became social instead of individual. The diverse reactions of the New England mind to romanticism form one of the most interesting and fruitful chapters in the history of American thought.

New England and the Frontier.—The romantic revolution in New England showed less influence of the frontier than did the same movement in other portions of the country. This was perfectly natural. The frontier was far away from Boston and moreover there were certain western characteristics—roughness and lack of social polish, for instance—that did not appeal strongly to Bostonian culture. There was, however, one way in which New England felt the effect of the frontier. Whenever a Yankee villager or farmer heard the call of the West or experienced the lure of free land, he packed up and moved to the Mississippi Valley. In this way New England lost some of its most substantial citizens, and the new states of the Northwest gained a desirable element in their population. However, it is not correct to say that New England was not aware of the meaning of the frontier. Emerson, Thoreau, and Parker, to name no more, all watched the experiment of western democracy with a most friendly interest. Emerson's *Journals* contain many references to the Westerners and their leaders, including several to Andrew Jackson, who was one of the author's favorite public figures. The men who preached the gospel of nature had too much in common with western life to ignore the frontier completely.

New England and Old World Thought.—Romanticism was more of a cultural movement in New England than it was elsewhere in America, and as a natural result it drew very largely from the old seats of culture across the Atlantic. French philosophy, for long connected with the excesses of the French Revolution and stigmatized by the ugly epithet of atheistical, was forced to enter Boston surreptitiously, but enter it did, even though in disguise, and there found some of its warmest disciples. German romantic philosophy entered more slowly, but with less of a struggle. However, the bar to the entrance of German philosophy was the ignorance of the language, for until 1820 few New England students had been in German universities, and the German language was known to almost none. Emerson learned it rather late in life at the suggestion of Carlyle, but it remained for Theodore Parker to be the first New Englander thoroughly to understand German romantic philosophy and religious thought.

One of the chief sources of New England romanticism was the teaching of such English writers as Wordsworth, Coleridge, Shelley, and especially Carlyle. From Coleridge and Carlyle came much of the German thought, while from other English sources came variations and transformations of the earlier French philosophy. Certainly the Emersonian doctrine of nature owed much to the poetry of Wordsworth. In the beginning an inordinate proportion of New England romanticism came from or by way of England but later the Boston and Concord writers drew their ideas directly from the original sources.

Another foreign influence in New England romanticism was the warm humanitarianism that traces, however indirectly, from France. With its strong ethical bias and its willingness to accept social responsibility, the mind of romantic New England was vastly concerned with problems of right and wrong. Virginia could temper its romanticism by economics and politics, the West might base its objection to slavery on economic grounds, but these actions were not for New England. Here all questions were answered in terms of ethics warmed and ennobled by a deep humanitarianism.

The Question of Industrialism.—But romanticism was not destined to possess the New England mind without undergoing a sharp challenge from an opposing force. This force was industrialism. Indeed romanticism was not destined to possess permanently the mind of any portion of America, and even during the short time when it was in the ascendancy, industrialism was slowly winning the field. Romanticism first entered the land of the Puritans in various guises about the time of the Revolution. By 1800 it was making its influence distinctly felt, especially in religious thought. By 1820 it was noticeable everywhere. By 1830 it reached its height, a pitch that it maintained for twenty years only to decline during the fifties. After the Civil War the disgraceful welter of the Gilded Age made the early romanticism seem positively old-fashioned.

Industrialism came to New England some time after the dawn of the romantic movement, but it set itself the task of opposing doggedly every point in its rival's program with the irresistible argument of "common sense" and the irrefutable logic of facts. Romanticism looked upon nature as the revealed mind of God, the inspiriting tutor of man; industrialism saw in nature only the potential wealth of natural resources awaiting development for the profit of the developer. Romanticism exalted the individual man as "only a little lower than the angels"; industrialism could see in man only a unit of energy whose labor was necessary to the transformation of natural resources into salable articles. Romanticism preached the doctrine of the simple life close to nature with all material desires reduced to a minimum; industrialism impelled men into cities and there proceeded to sharpen their appetites for material goods. Romanticism offered man a life of freedom without wages; industrialism chained man to the machine but paid him for his servitude. Romanticism promised a life of spiritual satisfaction to all with pecuniary profit to none; industrialism promised material progress to society, wages to the many, and great wealth to the successful business enterpriser. Romanticism was a way of life; industrialism was a way of making a living. Thus the two great rivals came to a show-down in the narrow arena of New England, and, as it happened, the verdict there reached was to be accepted without question by the American people. With the decision in the hands of a population addicted to commercial gain and to the gospel of getting on in the world, the outcome of the struggle could not long remain in doubt. Industrialism was the choice of New England, and that choice was seconded vociferously by America at large. From the material standpoint the wisdom of the choice certainly cannot be questioned; from the standpoint of the spiritual and intellectual life it is doubtful if so much can be said.

Although victory rested with industrialism, few are acquainted with the leaders of that movement, and every schoolboy knows such romantics as Emerson, Thoreau, Garrison, and Hawthorne. In fact industrialism triumphed because of the unimpeachable "common-sense" of its appeal to a middle-class people like Americans whose intense desire has always been to acquire worldly goods. The romantic leaders left their monuments enshrined in the heart of American literature. The industrial leaders left their monuments in the shape of mile after mile of factory windows, surmounted by tall, smoking chimneys. The industrialization of a whole nation was the enduring memorial wrought by these men. Of the spokesmen for industrialism Daniel Webster is the one outstanding figure, and he, coming into public life too early to be caught in the full tide of industrialism, kept many friends among the romantics until almost the end of his life.

Daniel Webster (*1782-1852*).—Webster is very dear to the Yankees because he is a person of very commanding understanding with every talent for its adequate expression. His external advantages are very rare and admirable; his noble and majestic frame, his breadth and projection of brows, his coal-black hair, his great cinderous eyes, his perfect self-possession and the rich and well-modulated thunder of his voice . . . distinguish him above all other men.

The faults that shade his character are not such as to hurt his popularity. He is very expensive, and always in debt; but this rather commends him, as he is known to be generous. . . . All is forgiven to a man of such surpassing intellect, and such prodigious powers of exertion which have so long been exerted. . . . He has misused the opportunity of making himself the darling of the American world in all coming time by abstaining from putting himself at the head of the Anti-slavery interests. . . .

Thus Emerson in his journal characterized a man whom he both admired and criticized, whose doctrines he accepted in part and rejected in larger part. Two men could not be farther apart than were Emerson and Webster. The first was an explosive dreamer, contemptuous of economics, who would allow no institution or habit of the past to stand between him and the realization of his selfhood. On the other hand Webster kept a firm grasp on economic expediency and the great gospel of material progress. Steeped in law and absorbed in the active practice of politics, the great orator turned his back on romantic promise and became the realist of New England.

There are two periods in Webster's life that every one should keep distinct. The first culminated in the great reply to Senator Hayne in 1830 when Webster affirmed the perpetuity of the union in this sonorous peroration.

When my eyes shall be turned to behold for the last time the sun in
heaven, may I not see him shining on the broken and dishonored fragments of a once glorious union; on states dissevered, discordant, belligerent; on a land rent with civil feuds, or drenched, it may be, in fraternal
blood.   Let their last feeble and lingering glance rather behold the gorgeous ensign of the republic, now known and honored throughout the
earth, still full high advanced, its arms and trophies still streaming in
their original lustre, not a stripe erased or polluted, nor a single star obscured . . . but everywhere, spread all over in characters of living light,
blazing on all its ample folds, as they float over the seas and over the
land, and in every wind under the whole heavens, that other sentiment,
dear to every true American heart—Liberty and Union, now and forever,
one and inseparable.

This oration, a masterly piece of rhetoric, caught the fancy of the
North where it was widely circulated in pamphlet form.   For ten
years from the delivery of this speech Webster was the acknowledged
leader of New England, and, as Emerson said, virtual president of
the United States.   In 1830 the ground that he took was sufficiently
advanced for the time, and if the great orator had kept pace with
the intellectual and spiritual development of Massachusetts, he
might have gone down in history as the popularizer of the principles
of the New England Renaissance.   But Webster failed to keep pace
with his generation.

During the early forties the cross currents of slavery and abolition
began to chop up the hitherto fairly smooth waters of our politics.
The abolitionists were becoming insistent, and the slave power was
growing defiant.   Many Northerners who were not abolitionists deplored the haste and radicalism of the extreme agitators and yet took
a firm anti-slavery stand.   Many Southerners who were not "fire-
eaters" saw with increasing clarity that there was no middle ground
in the great controversy.   A line was being drawn between the two
portions of the country, and on both sides of that line public opinion
was rapidly unifying.   The successful national politician could offend
neither opinion.

During the forties Webster was consumed with an ambition to be
president in name.   This marks the later period of his career.   His
refusal to head the anti-slavery movement of the North, coupled
with his efforts to placate southern opinion, brought upon him the
censure of the Massachusetts romantics.   The growing ill-feeling
toward him culminated in a burst of rage when he delivered his
famous Seventh of March speech advocating the passage of a fugitive

slave act. The anger of the Massachusetts reformers knew no bounds. Whittier's poem, "Ichabod," "the glory departed," gives some hint of the depth of feeling against the old leader. Two years later at his death, resentment had so far abated that Emerson could write, "The sea, the rocks, the woods, gave no sign that America and the world had lost the completest man. Nature had not in our days, or not since Napoleon, cut out such a masterpiece. He brought the strength of the savage into the height of culture. . . . Cities had not hurt him." For so cultivated a romantic as Emerson to praise a man for having both natural strength and acquired culture was indeed high praise. But against those words Emerson could write, "Webster wants the power of the initiative, the affirmative talent, and remains, like the literary class, only a commentator." This last criticism was caused by the orator's failure to take a positive stand on questions raised by the New England Renaissance.

In his thinking Webster showed little influence of the frontier and little of foreign thought. Fundamentally every one of his economic and political doctrines coincided with those held by the industrialists of Massachusetts. For years the man's superb command of rhetorical statement prevented a break with the romantic thinkers, and later on when a choice had to be made between the reformers and the business men, he did not hesitate. A practical politician and a trained constitutional lawyer could scarcely have done otherwise than support the cause of material prosperity and progress over the cause of romantic dreaming. Frontier agrarian economics in his make-up or humanitarianism might have added another element to his intellectual and spiritual fiber and might conceivably have shifted his position in American history—and not for the worse.

ROMANTICISM AND THE NEW ENGLAND RELIGION

During the latter part of the eighteenth century and the early part of the nineteenth, the religious thinking of America underwent a striking change. This change was brought about largely by the frontier and the romantic revolution. By 1750 religion in this country had settled down to a cold and dispiriting repetition of dogma unwarmed by any emotional content. Edwards had stated the Calvinistic doctrines so well that there was little left to do save to repeat without change the formulas and arguments that he so ably elaborated. To an unbiased observer the churches of America were

suffering from inanition. At all events vitality of thought and action
was lacking, save for the short period preceding the Revolutionary
War. But under the impulse of new forces the churches took on a
life of revived energy and helpfulness.

Religion of the Frontier.—As previously pointed out, iron-clad
Calvinism was incompatible with frontier life. Social and political
equalitarianism, optimism, and faith in the innate goodness of human nature were the very breath of frontier existence. The elder
Calvinism denied every one of these beliefs and practices. Furthermore Calvinism was cold and unemotional; it rested on a basis of
revelation fortified by logic. Now frontier life itself was a cold,
disheartening, realistic experience, and the demand of the Westerner
was for a religion that would afford him an emotional release.
Warmth and enthusiasm he wanted from his church, not the logical
restatement of accepted creeds. These wants the frontier ministers
were compelled to supply.

The warmly emotional Methodists and Baptists flourished exceedingly in the West from early days. The Presbyterians on the
frontier for a time held fast to their Calvinistic doctrines, but about
1800 they began to reconstruct their official beliefs to accord with
the spirit of the time and place, and about 1810 the Cumberland
Presbyterians departed from the older group as a protest in part,
at least, against the belief in predestination held by the parent body.
About the same time Thomas and Alexander Campbell, Scotch Presbyterian ministers, led another withdrawal from their church that
resulted in the formation of the Disciples of Christ, frequently known
as the Christian church. This group became particularly strong
in the Ohio Valley. After 1800 the Congregational church ceased
emphasizing its Calvinism as stated by Edwards and became one
of the strongest frontier denominations, having most of its strength
in the northern Mississippi Valley.

With the coming of the new groups and the changing of their
doctrines by those that were already on the ground, the western
settlements underwent a great religious revival. Camp-meetings and
religious debates were the chief emotional outlets for the people,
surpassing even political campaigns, for politics waxed warm only
once in two or four years, while revival meetings for weeks on a
stretch were to be enjoyed every fall and winter. If religious enthusiasm at some of the camp-meetings reached a point that seemed
excessive to some of the staider denominations, it must be remem-

bered that a starved emotional life will always demand relief, and the only relief on the frontier, with its dearth of literature, art, music, and drama, was to be found in the church. Whatever the practices of these specific churches may have been or however much they may have differed, they were alike in holding no dogma that conflicted with the fundamental beliefs of the frontiersman: optimism, freedom, the possibility of progress, and the essential goodness of human nature.

The political consequences of the frontier religious revival were marked. Dr. J. Franklin Jameson has pointed out that the extension of political equality coincided quite closely with the growth of those denominations that rejected the Calvinistic doctrine of strict predestination and salvation by election. The equalitarianism of the frontier could not abide any belief or practice that was erected upon a caste system. A competent investigation of the frontier revival and its effects on American life still awaits the work of scholars.

Romantic Religion in New England.—In his amusing poem "The Deacon's Masterpiece," Oliver Wendell Holmes tells of the story of a "one-hoss shay" that was built with so great care out of specially selected materials that there was positively no weakest spot in its construction. Hence the vehicle lasted on and on for a hundred years, until one day, when it seemingly was in as good condition as ever, it suddenly fell to dust under its astonished occupant. Such was the downfall of orthodox Calvinism in New England. The doctrines as put together by so skillful a logician as Jonathan Edwards were so argument-proof that they lasted for a long time after their day was really past, and then disappeared with amazing rapidity. The destroying force was the warm breath of romantic philosophy.

For at least twenty years before the opening of the nineteenth century there had been certain stirrings of theological liberalism in the New England pulpits, and about 1800 one after another of the most eminent divines announced their allegiance to new doctrines. Quickly most of the churches of New England followed their ministers. When the old First Church of Boston, John Cotton's former charge, and the Second Church, the Mather stronghold, went over to the liberals, and especially when a liberal was elected professor of theology in Harvard College, then broke the new day in the religious life of New England. Liberalism was almost everywhere triumphant. By general consent this liberalism has been called Unitarianism, though this name but imperfectly expresses the significance of the movement.

Unitarianism is only romantic philosophy in strange garb. Romanticism in other places might have strong economic and political connotations, but in New England the chief manifestation had to be religious and intellectual, for the Puritans of that region were primarily religious and were gifted with great intellectual possibilities. Thus when the new liberal thought seeped into New England, it was forced to take a garb and speak a language that was familiar to its prospective followers. But if the student penetrates below the surface, he is sure to find in Unitarianism the familiar features of romanticism.

Unitarianism never formulated a body of official doctrine. Each minister preached the gospel to his parishioners according to his own intelligence and conscience. Naturally no two ministers agreed exactly in all details, but there was a broad common meeting-place that can be easily set forth. Starting from the basic assumption that human nature is essentially good and that man is created in the image of God, Unitarians agreed on the fatherhood of God and the fellowship of all men under the leadership of Jesus. They further held that salvation is dependent on individual character and that both man and society enjoy the possibility of unlimited progress. Man's will is free, and the exercise of that will to follow the teaching of Jesus and the dictates of one's own conscience is the chief duty of man. Such in essence is the unofficial statement of liberal religious thought in Boston about 1815.

The implications of such a belief are plain. Like its mother-force, romantic thought, Unitarianism placed immense emphasis upon the individual. Faith in the goodness of man and belief in the possibility of progress made the Unitarians consistently friendly to the cause of education, while those reformers who were working for the removal of social evils drew most of their recruits from the same ranks. Strongly individual as Unitarianism was, its principle of the fellowship of all men gave its adherents a sensitive social conscience that is reflected again and again in the literature of the New England Renaissance. Conscience and spiritual freedom came to be the points most often dwelt upon by Unitarian ministers, because spiritual freedom guided by a rational conscience was considered the gateway to man's illimitable spiritual development. Progress means growth, and under the new liberalism static society and static theological dogmas are alike impossible. In short Unitarianism was of necessity the first step in the romanticization of New England thought. Without it the Renaissance would never have dawned.

William Ellery Channing (*1780-1842*).—The life and teachings of William Ellery Channing represent the progress and principles of New England Unitarianism. His career proves that out of the bitter can come forth sweetness, for as a boy the man who was to become Boston's most lovable and revered expounder of the love of God sat under the preaching of Samuel Hopkins, the strictest of old-time Calvinists, who propounded as the final test of one's piety the question, "Are you willing to be damned for the glory of God?" Such a query must have violently repelled the young Channing, for in later years he repudiated the question in every syllable and in every implication, preaching always the boundless love of God which finds its earthly prototype in the love of man for his fellows.

After taking his degree at Harvard in 1798, Channing went to Virginia to serve as a tutor in the family of a wealthy planter. For twenty-one months he remained in the heart of the Jeffersonian domain, and there came in contact with a new intellectual stimulus. Concretely this stimulus was represented by the writings of Rousseau, by William Godwin's *Political Justice,* and by Mary Wollstonecraft's *Rights of Woman.* While he was reading these books, the sensitive young tutor saw exemplified all around him the social and political principles of Jefferson. Ever after he remembered the gentle courtesy and the pleasant demeanor of the Virginians. This Virginia experience, both the reading and the fellowship, gave Channing's mind the bent that it followed.

Returning to New England, Channing took his theological work at Harvard and, accepting a Boston pastorate, began preaching the doctrines that have since been connected with his name. He developed very slowly, and it was almost twenty years before he became the accepted leader of the liberals. The development of Channing was very much like that of William Cullen Bryant, cautiously progressive, never extreme, but always safely liberal. In his famous sermon preached in Baltimore at the ordination of Jared Sparks, Channing set forth the principles upon which Unitarianism was destined to develop. Liberal theology never received a clearer or a more finely tolerant exposition than the preacher gave it in this discourse. The sermon is an examination of the principles of old-time Calvinism in the light of the new day. The minister could have summarized his discourse in words that he had written a decade earlier. "A man of plain sense, whose spirit has not been broken to this creed [Calvinism] by education or terror, will think that it is not necessary for us to travel to heathen countries to learn how mournfully the human mind may misrepresent the Deity." The last nine words of this sentence, Barrett Wendell said, thoroughly express "the change which the Renaissance brought to the leading spirits of Boston."

In his relations with the abolition movement Channing showed his truly liberal temper as well as his limitations as a popular leader. Despite his insistence upon the universal brotherhood of man, Channing was at heart an intellectual aristocrat without the unsympathetic temperament that so often mars the patrician. Controversy, the spontaneous expression of violent feelings, the appeal to sentiment—all were highly distasteful to him. Hence the extreme abolitionists like Garrison and Phillips rather repelled his interest. However, the righteousness of the cause of freedom mightily appealed to him, and, firmly disregarding passion and the appeal to economics, he examined the case of slavery in the light of his views on the respect due to the worth and goodness inherent in every human soul. Starting from such a basis Channing could not remain cold to the pleas of the abolitionists; he enlisted in the cause of freedom and ever after gave the reformers an intelligent support that was dignified by the temperance of his utterances as much as by the character and courage of the minister. "No matter how ignorant the slave may be, the capacity of improvement allies him to the more instructed of the race," Channing declared. "Every human being has in him the germ of the greatest idea in the universe, the idea of God." It was sinful he concluded to keep in bondage any soul that held so sublime an idea.

In his examination of the anti-slavery cause, Channing was led to question the rights and powers of the state. Slavery was recognized by law in many of the states, and its legal existence was implied by the Constitution. These facts brought the question of political ethics into the range of his thought. In his conclusions on this subject he was close to the position of Jefferson. Power once delegated to rulers is so apt to be abused, and the powerful government is so liable to foolish extravagance and display that "no more authority should be confided to rulers than is absolutely necessary to repress crime and preserve public order. . . . There should exist, if possible, no office to madden ambition. . . . The less of power given to man over man the better." Jefferson would have agreed with every statement, for these are the fundamental political principles inherent in romantic thought with its belief in the excellence of human nature and in the ability of man to lead himself aright if unhampered by the restrictions of society.

In all his discussions and controversies—for despite his dislike for public arguments he was often forced to defend his views—Channing was always characterized by one crowning virtue, an insistence that a man's utterances should be governed by his conscience. Once Theodore Parker preached a sermon that was violently repugnant to the ideas of many Unitarians. Some of the preachers attacked Parker, but Channing would not join them. "As for Mr. Parker," he said, "I wish him to preach what he thoroughly believes and feels. . . . Let the full heart pour itself forth." The last sentence, one of the noblest in our intellectual life, summarizes the ruling desire of Channing and the keynote of New England religious liberalism.

But Channing more than summarizes the Unitarian movement. In his insistence on the divine right of the individual to live his own life according to the dictates of his own conscience, the preacher was the forerunner of such later romantics as Emerson, Thoreau, Parker, Garrison, and Margaret Fuller. Without the emphasis on individualism and the doctrine of the possibility of human perfectibility, the romantic movement in New England would have been a thing of appearance and not of substance.

TRANSCENDENTALISM

Transcendentalism is an obscure subject, and efforts to clarify it usually result only in augmenting the obscurity. The very name itself is unfortunate, for it carries a flavor of gaseous mysticism that succeeds at the start in convincing the student that the transcendental teaching is involved in doctrines so profoundly metaphysical that they are beyond the grasp of the ordinary person. If the group of writers known as transcendentalists could have gone down in American literature under a name not quite so polysyllabic, it is probable that their doctrines would have been read by the young student rather more hopefully and profitably. As a matter of fact, transcendentalism never was a classroom philosophy, reeking of the study lamp and super-subtle definitions; it was in its elements a simple and even popular guide to the best way of living. Certainly not a little of the obscurity attaching to the name has been caused by the efforts of the transcendentalists themselves to relate their thought to English and German thinking. Probably more of the obscurity has been caused by the wholly unsuccessful efforts of classroom philosophers to make a complete philosophical system out of a simple American suggestion for living the Good Life.

Transcendentalism was neither a religion nor a philosophy. The traditional emphasis of religion has been upon eternal salvation; daily life is considered as merely a means to an end, the end being life eternal. Transcendentalism concerned itself almost wholly with day by day living as an end in itself. When Thoreau, the most consistent of the transcendentalists, lay dying, a friend asked him if he was giving any thought to the future life. Straight the answer came back, "One life at a time; one life at a time." The true transcendentalist was eager to wring as much satisfaction as possible out of this life, believing full well that, if he lived in the wisest fashion, the future life would take care of itself. Furthermore in the modern world the term "religion" implies a more or less formal adherence to an organization that holds a body of doctrine. Adherence to a consistent body of doctrine or to any type of organization would have been the very negation of everything that transcendentalism stood for. Again we have the very direct evidence of most of the religious leaders of the early nineteenth century that transcendentalism was not a religion. Some of the Unitarians looked upon it with favor, but most of the ministers repudiated it for its emphasis upon the duty of self-reliance, for its rejection of ministerial guidance, and for its trust in conscience as the sole moral guide. Certainly transcendentalism was never recognized as a body of religious thought by those who lived during its brief period of life in New England.

Nor was transcendentalism a philosophy. To be a philosophy a body of thought must contain a rational and consistent explanation of the chief problems that have confronted the human race. Among these questions are the nature of God, the place of man in the universe, truth, goodness, and the problem of knowledge. It is true that transcendentalism touched all these points, but the various thinkers did not agree among themselves on any one, and indeed no individual thinker ever bothered himself to be consistent with his own previous utterances. "A foolish consistency is the hobgoblin of little minds, adored by little statesmen and philosophers and divines. With consistency a great soul has simply nothing to do," said Emerson, evidently thinking himself no more a philosopher and divine than a statesman. Once Walt Whitman, the great poet of transcendentalism said, "Do I contradict myself? Very well then, I contradict myself." Upon one point and one only did all the school agree, and that was the eternal validity of the command, "Trust thyself." This ringing imperative is a sufficient basis for the gospel of self-reliance, but it is a meager platform for the holding of a complete philosophical system.

Starting with the invigorating text, "Trust thyself," transcendentalism neither preached a sermon nor expounded a philosophy; it inculcated an attitude of mind. Strictly speaking this attitude at its most concrete form was an implicit faith in the "inalienable worth of man."

But this attitude had other implications that are correctly associated with transcendentalism. The inalienable worth of man, as enunciated by Emerson and lived by Thoreau and Parker, implied the most intense individualism known by the nineteenth century. Not even Nietzsche, the arch-individualist, surpassed these men, save in the vigor of his phraseology; in content the New Englanders anticipated some of the German's views. The romantic ideal, as expressed by liberal thought from Rousseau to Walt Whitman, never reached a higher or more ecstatic pitch than that achieved by Emerson and his circle in their doctrine of individualism. By 1830 the goodness of human nature was a commonplace of romantic thought that had recently been restated by the Unitarians, but the transcendentalists, moving ahead a step, declared the divinity of the human soul. Not satisfied to rest here they asserted that everything in the universe contains a divine core. "What is there of the divine in a load of bricks?" asked Emerson. "What is there of the divine in a barber's shop? . . . Much. All." This belief in the divine nature of man puts the capstone on individualism; the doctrine could go no further.

Transcendentalism, with its unflinching faith in the worth of the individual and its reliance on the goodness of his nature, brought a full close to the doubt and pessimism of early Puritanism. The high destiny of man and society could no longer be questioned when the guide was the unfettered conscience of man, for this conscience was the audible voice of God speaking through the divinity that ennobled each individual. The optimism thus reached was achieved by no use of reason but by a more potent influence, the feeling. The following lines clearly express the idea:

> I am immortal. I know it. I feel it.
> Hope floods my heart with delight.
> Running on air, mad with life, dizzy, reeling,
> Upward I mount,—faith is sight, life is feeling,
> Hope is the day-star of night.
> Chance cannot touch me. Time cannot hush me.
> Fear, hope, and longing at strife
> Sink as I rise, on, on, upward forever,
> Gathering strength, gaining breath—naught can sever
> Me from the Spirit of Life.

The pages of Emerson glow with just such expressions, while many readers profess to be wearied by the strident note of optimism that runs through the whole body of Whitman's verse. Thoreau, shrewd Yankee that he was, saw in the future only an unbroken serene. Cheerful hope sets the march for the whole body of transcendental thought.

Naturally the transcendentalist, with his belief in the divine right of the individual to do each day what was pleasing, was no worshiper of the past. Never would he suffer the cold hand of a dead past to restrain the living heart and conscience of the present. "This is the place," they said in effect, "the present is the time, the living are the people." This typically new world doctrine pretty effectively denied respect for European tradition and allowed little inclination to follow old world advice. The voice of the present in America is far more important than that of the past in either Europe or America, said Emerson, and one of his first popular appeals was for American scholars and literary men to break the hampering bonds of the past. "We must be expressed," he wrote once in his journal and by the "we" he meant himself and all men of his generation.

The Mystic Element in Transcendentalism.—The mystical element, easily discernible in all transcendentalists, was shown in many ways, but it was especially prominent in the doctrine of the relations of man, nature, and God. The transcendentalist conceived of man as the center and pinnacle of all created things. All around him as a part of his being stood nature that was the reflection of the mind of God, the embodiment of the divine love.   Similarly the mind of man contained and reflected the mind and goodness of God.   Hence man had an identity with both nature and God. He felt more than kinship with the beauties of the visible world; he felt an identity with them.   He felt more than kinship with other men; he and they were one, for they were all of the same divine essence.   Emerson's doctrine of individualism, Thoreau's concept of nature, and Whitman's identification of himself as the universal man all rest upon this mystical element.

Transcendentalism and European Thought.—Altogether too much has been made of European influence on New England transcendentalism.   Lowell dated the beginning of the movement by the publication of an essay by Carlyle, but it is very doubtful if one can be so definite as to date or influence.   It was not in the very nature of transcendentalism to accept much from alien sources, and one may well question whether the publication of an essay by an unknown Scotchman would result of itself in a widespread intellectual movement among the intensest individualists of the country.   A safer position is one that holds that transcendental tendencies were developing in the New England soil and that the work of Carlyle and Coleridge afforded a respectable sanction for what was a very radical movement.   At that, such men as Thoreau and Whitman never looked beyond their hat-brims to find any sanction for their ideas.   The close relation of European thought and the Emersonian group has been traced usually by those who are fond of discovering literary influences and lines of thought.   A more likely place to look for the origins of transcendentalism is in the soil of the new world watered by romantic idealism.

However, it is certain that the name "transcendentalism" came from the old world.   Rousseau contended that the intuitions of the natural mind are good.   With this as a starting point Immanuel Kant, a German philosopher, soon reached the view that knowledge does not always come by the physical senses.   He held that certain truths do not arise from external sources but transcend human experience.   In other words they are perceived intuitively by the human mind.   Among the ideas thus acquired are our conceptions of God, duty, immortality, and the like.   Although the existence of these things cannot be proved, they are as real as a stone or a hat or anything that we can see and grasp.   They are known to be true when we examine our own minds and find every fiber of our being crying out for them. "The blazing proof of immortality," said Emerson, "is our dissatisfaction with any other explanation." Carlyle and Coleridge read this German philosophy in the original and popularized it in England. Emerson and the earlier members of his group read the English authors, but Theodore Parker went directly to German sources for his reading. But in spite of this known connection between the English and New England transcendentalists, it still remains doubtful if the new world group derived from European philosophy much more than a name for their movement.

Transcendentalism and the West.—The pioneer was the last person in the world to bother about transcendental knowledge or attempt to sound the bottomless gulf of Immanuel Kant's philosophy, but, waiving the formal philosophy, the Westerner carried a full stock of transcendentalism as he faced the hard life that he led. The pioneer did not receive his optimism and whole-hearted individualism from any intellectual source. They were native to his life, and just as inevitable and necessary as the rifle or the plow. However, this does not argue that the New England romantics received their impulse from the pioneer. But there is a close relation between the West and Emerson's study at Concord.

Without the West it is doubtful if New England transcendentalism could have developed. The immense reservoir of free land that nature had provided in the Mississippi Valley, the successful rush of the pioneers to possess this domain, the buoyant optimism of the Westerner—all these things were keenly known and appreciated in New England. And then Emerson and Whitman were far enough away from the hardships of pioneer life to see only the glamor without sensing any of the disturbing realism. In short, the New England transcendentalist was vastly encouraged by his rough but highly successful cousin, the natural man of the West. Emerson has many words of praise for the spirit and nerve of the pioneer, though he may hardly suppress a smile at western bluster or lack of polish. If any one wishes to trace an influence from a non-literary source to its appearance in our literature, let him write a weighty volume on the effect of the West upon New England transcendentalism.

Transcendentalism and Literature.—Transcendentalism is expressed in our literature in the essays and journals of Emerson and Thoreau, in the sermons of Theodore Parker, and in the poetry of Walt Whitman. However, some of the most precious part of the doctrine was lost by the failure of certain members of the group to write books or articles. Bronson Alcott spent a life of ninety years in conversation, and thus we have missed the ideas of one who was declared by his listeners to be the most persuasive of the group. Margaret Fuller was another who expended most of her energies in talking and lecturing. Although the literature of the transcendental group is but a fragment of what we might have had, still it is the most valuable portion of our national product. Emerson, Thoreau, Parker, and Whitman would dignify the literary life of any country of the world, and in most nations they would have been better received than they were in their own. No group can be accounted slight in accomplishment that produces such things as Emerson's "Nature" and "Self-reliance" and Whitman's "Song of Myself."

To many people the most enjoyable pieces of transcendental litera-ture are the *Journals* of Emerson and Thoreau. In these voluminous works the reader gets the full flavor of the authors' spontaneity, originality, and native force. Because transcendentalism stressed the intuitive expression rather than the reasoned utterance, its best pas-sages were short and pungent epigrams—oracular, Mr. Parrington calls them—that frequently throw flashes of wisdom upon the deep questions of life. To speak the truth that was in them was the aim of both Emerson and Thoreau, and in the *Journals* this speaking was spontaneous and vivid.

RALPH WALDO EMERSON

(1803-1882)

No man in American literature has been more variously appraised than has Emerson. To some he is the too-enthusiastic preacher of a dead and gone romantic idealism; to others he is the ever-inspir-ing expounder of individualism; to others still the sensitive lover and philosopher of nature. He has been called democrat, aristocrat, transcendental pioneer, and Puritan, and those who dubbed him with these epithets have never lacked citations from the author's own works to fortify their arguments. Emerson in the hands of his critics reminds one of the descriptions of the elephant by the seven blind men of Hindustan. Each critic seizes upon a striking passage from one of the essays or the *Journal* and concludes that, since this para-graph is stated with great clarity and force, it must be the gist of

Emersonianism. Such procedure is highly dangerous, for it is liable to make Emerson shoulder the responsibility for doctrines that are completely opposed to his prevailing ideas.

Probably only one of his own doctrines is never contradicted by Emerson. This doctrine is a belief in the divine self-sufficiency of the individual. In his consistency to this belief the essayist fills his pages with contradictory sentences, for the aim of Emerson, the individual, was to say from day to day the truth that was uppermost in him. If this truth varied and forced the writer into inconsistency, so much the worse for consistency. "If you would be a man, speak what you think to-day in words as hard as cannon-balls, and to-morrow speak what to-morrow thinks in hard words again, though it contradict everything you said to-day." This rule Emerson never violated, for only by observing it could he be true to the ruling passion of his life and teaching—the right and duty of the individual to live his own life and to speak his own thoughts. Decent individualism can go no further.

Emerson's Life.—Emerson made his life the emphatic expression of his individualism. Never did he allow concern with the mere business of living to interfere for long with the more serious undertaking of his life, the development of his mind and soul.

Emerson was born in Boston in 1803. As the son and grandson of preachers notable for their pulpit eloquence he naturally went to Harvard and prepared himself for the ministry. Shortly after his graduation he became pastor of the Second Unitarian Church of his home town, the old Mather church. His work was absolutely satisfactory to his congregation, but he soon began to question the advisability of his continuing in the ministry. He felt that he could no longer administer the communion in the sense in which it was accepted by his parishioners, and he objected to the use of ritual or even a fixed order of service. Meditating seriously on the questions raised by his doubts, Emerson came to the conclusion that his only course was to resign. This he did partly to quiet his conscientious scruples and partly to drop his affiliation with an organization that might hamper his individual development. Once he wrote: "A sect or a party is an elegant incognito devised to save a man from the vexation of thinking." Emerson never shrank from such a vexation; he asked only that he might be allowed to think unimpeded by the hand of tradition or the necessity of conforming. This resignation was the most important step in Emerson's career.

Shortly thereafter he established his home in Concord where he lived the remainder of his life, devoting all his time to meditation and writing.

"Loafing and inviting his soul," Walt Whitman would have called Emerson's use of his time in Concord, and more descriptive words could not be found, for out of the leisure found in the little Massachusetts village came one of the finest souls that ever ornamented the life of a people. And in living his own life Emerson became the great American teacher of those who seek the good life through self-cultivation.

Emerson resigned his pastorate in October, 1832. After spending several months in Europe, where he met Coleridge, Carlyle, Wordsworth, and Landor, he returned to America, and in 1834 established his residence in Concord. His very simple wants were met in part by the income from a small amount of money that he had inherited from his first wife, who had died in 1831. The remainder of his income was derived from the sale of his books and the delivery of lectures. From 1830 to 1860 was the great age of the lyceum in this country, and Emerson was one of the most popular lecturers. He spoke all over the East and Northwest, sometimes receiving as much as fifty dollars an evening, a large fee in those days. At this rate a rather short season would supply him with a living for a year. Apart from his lecture tours he spent his time in his study or on walks through the fields and woods near Concord, sometimes talking with Thoreau or Alcott, but most often turning over in his mind eternal questions or current problems of our national life. Out of so tranquil a life came some of the abiding passages of our literature.

Convinced individualist that he was, Emerson was blessed with a sweet disposition and a tolerant temper. These characteristics are strikingly shown by the notable circle of friends that he soon gathered about him. Thoreau, Margaret Fuller, Bronson Alcott, Hawthorne, George Ripley, the younger Channing, Theodore Parker, and many another came to Emerson for friendship and guidance. These friends were more notable for their quality than for their number. Matthew Arnold once declared that Emerson was the "friend and aider of those who would live in the spirit," and the number of the New Englanders who would so live can be told by the number of Emerson's friends for the twenty-five years beginning with 1835.

The Basis of Emerson's Individualism.—Like the good romantic that Emerson was, he based his individualism on the premise that human nature is divinely good. In the very nature of the individual he found the root and spring of everything good, and the best of guides he declared to be the conscience and instincts of man. "I will trust my instincts," he wrote only a few months after resigning his pulpit, and again, "Trust to that prompting within you." These oracular statements would lose all force, would become the most despicable of ethical guides, if they were not based on the proposition that man's nature is good.

Emerson does not leave the reader groping for his ideas on the individual. "A man contains all that is needful to his government within himself," he wrote in his *Journal.* "He is made a law unto himself. All real good or evil that can befall him must be from himself. The purpose of life seems to be to acquaint a man with himself; the highest revelation is that God is in every man." Passages like this are the foundation upon which all the other passages rest, for the worth and sanctity of the individual are the basic facts of transcendental teaching.

However, some will object that such a doctrine will lead to a pronounced egotism. Emerson saw the danger, acknowledged it, but flatly refused to call it a danger. To him the great man was the egotist, and he would define egotism as the desire to develop to the fullest one's own nature and to act according to the promptings of that nature. Without egotism "Luther, Mirabeau, Napoleon, John Adams, Andrew Jackson, Greeley, Parker, Garrison would lose their vigor," he said in his *Journal,* and these were not the words of an ardent young man, but of a man sixty years old. As a part of egotism he included strength of will and determination. The old Calvinistic doctrine of bondage of the will received scant attention from him. "Luther and Napoleon are better treatises on the will than Edwards's," he remarked, revealing his low estimate of philosophical systems when confronted with the living fact of a human will shod with iron determination.

Emerson did not fear egotism—he courted it—but he had a complete aversion to conformity. "I like the sayers of No better than the sayers of Yes," he declared, and to him the yes-sayer was apt to be a weakling anxious to conform to the ideas of those about him. The no-sayer was the individualist, insistent upon living and speaking according to the light that was within him. "Who would be a man must be a non-conformist. . . . Nothing is at last sacred but the integrity of your own mind. . . . No law can be sacred to me but that of my nature. . . . A man is to carry himself in the presence of all opposition as if everything were titular and ephemeral but he. I am ashamed to think how easily we capitulate to badges and names, to large societies and dead institutions. What I must do is all that concerns me; not what the people think." In our own day of standardized clothing, standardized motor cars, standardized radio programs, and standardized thinking, the knowledge that America once harbored a man who was so defiantly and triumphantly non-conformist heartens many in their protest against our regimented living and thinking.

Moreover, Emerson was aware of the perils of non-conformity, which were only slightly less acute in the period of romanticism than they are to-day. "For non-conformity the world whips you with its displeasure," he warned his readers, but his whole conclusion is that one can stand the displeasure of one's neighbors better than the self-accusation of treason to one's own nature.

Emerson's Political Theory.—With a philosophy founded fundamentally on the divine worth of man, Emerson made his ideal state surrender most of its powers to the individual, holding with Jefferson that a government should have no more authority than that absolutely necessary for defense and the preservation of order. Jefferson as the executive head of a nation stopped at that point, but Emerson, the transcendental thinker, pushed on to the logical conclusion. If man is good and if his instincts are to be implicitly trusted, is not the use of force by government a deplorable mistake? To this question Emerson returned a ringing affirmative. Force he always hated, for it implied compulsion, and compulsion meant that the individual was forced to bend his will to suit the fancy of another. "I do not like to see a sword at a man's side. If it threatens man, it threatens me. A company of soldiers is an offensive spectacle." To Emerson the wise and just man was not greater than the state; he was the state. If political authorities passed laws that forced him to violate his conscience, it was man's duty to disobey those laws. He said frankly that good men must not obey the laws too well, and when the fugitive slave law was passed he wrote in his *Journal,* "This filthy enactment was made in the nineteenth century, by people who could read and write. I will not obey it, by God." He did not obey it, and his friends, Thoreau and Alcott, carried this doctrine to the extent that they refused to pay their taxes. Both went to jail rather than violate their consciences. As Mr. Parrington has pointed out, no distinction can be made between the political theory of Emerson and philosophical anarchism.

At the end of his essay on "Politics" Emerson gives a brief but definite exposition of his ideal state founded on a repudiation of force and an appeal to the moral feelings of mankind.

We live in a very low state of the world, and pay unwilling tribute to governments founded on force. There is not, among the most religious and instructed men of the most religious and instructed nations, a reliance on the moral sentiment, and a sufficient belief in the unity of things to persuade them that society can be maintained without artificial restraints, as well as the solar system; or that the private citizen might be reasonable, and a good neighbor, without the hint of a jail or a confiscation. What is strange too, there never was in any man sufficient faith in the power of rectitude, to inspire him with the broad design of renovating the state on the principle of right and love. . . . Not the less does nature continue to fill the heart of youth with suggestions of this enthusiasm, and there are now men . . . to whom no weight of adverse experience will for a moment make it appear impossible, that thousands of human beings might exercise toward each other the grandest and simplest sentiments, as well as a knot of friends, or a pair of lovers.

One cannot find a more explicit repudiation of the political state founded on force and the substitution for it of a state founded on the divine principles of peace, justice, and good-will.

A recent book lists Emerson among the eminent American opponents of democracy, including on that list John Adams, Hamilton, and H. L. Mencken. Such a judgment is egregiously in error. It is true that Emerson occasionally let himself break out in criticisms of democracy, but these strictures were caused not by any defect in the theory of democracy, but because the actual system was so far below the ideal. He based his theory of democracy upon the same principle that sustained his individualism, belief in the innate worth of human nature, declaring that the root and seed of democracy is the doctrine, "Judge for thyself, Reverence thyself." Again he said that democracy has its root in the sacred truth that every man has in him the divine reason and that all men are capable of living according to the dictates of reason. This, he concluded, is real equality. Evidently a man who holds such views cannot be set down as the enemy of democracy.

Emerson took his practical politics with a large measure of indifference, so long as the state did not interfere with him. Part of this indifference was caused by his inability to decide which party he should support. The Democrats he liked because of their principles and disliked because of their demagogic leadership. The Whigs he liked personally for their breeding and culture, but disliked because of their high regard for the rights of property. Talking about the rights of the individual appealed more to Emerson. In one of his statements which he does not seem ever to have repudiated he said, "The philosopher, or the poet, or the religious man will, of course, wish to cast his vote with the Democrats for free trade, for wide suffrage, for the abolition of legal cruelties in the penal code, and for facilitating in every manner the access of the young and the poor to the sources of wealth and power." In these words he placed himself squarely with Jefferson and the humanitarians, though his support of the Jeffersonian party was frequently impossible on account of the blatant leadership that it suffered from. Emerson, like Brackenridge, believed in democracy but deplored its shortcomings.

Emerson's exasperation with democracy and with human nature was always momentary and always caused by the failure of humanity to come up to the high ideal set for it. The Concord thinker lived on a plane whose altitude was surely too great for those with weak hearts. The ideal set was too high for struggling humanity, however much man might want to fulfill all hopes placed in him. When the inevitable lapse came, Emerson always spoke his disappointment straight from the depths of his heart. Some of these blasts are blighting, but in none of them did he permanently repudiate his faith in unspoiled human nature, and so long as he kept that faith he is not to be numbered with the opponents of democracy.

Emerson and the Reform Movement.—Emerson's connection with the New England reform movement, like most of his intellectual relations, was a trifle inconsistent. A pronounced individualist is very apt to begin and end his reforms within himself and to trust all others to do the same. If all should do this, the need for widespread social remedies would disappear. Emerson was so imbued with the spirit of individualism that instinctively he considered the problem of reform one for each person to settle for himself. Although he certainly was not unfriendly to the general principles of reform, yet he looked askance at any suggestion for social amelioration that involved the use of force or that considered society as a whole and not as a mass of individuals. Force he particularly mistrusted. "It is better to work on institutions by the sun than by the wind," he told the workingmen of Boston in his lecture on "Man the Reformer," meaning that moral suasion was preferable to legislation. Furthermore, the use of force allows for no individual differences in men and impels society in a body to adopt reforms that are not sincerely accepted by each individual. This method would result in Emerson's two chief aversions, enforced conformity of thought and the failure to bring about good deeds through appeal to the individual conscience. The danger of regimented thinking Emerson clearly saw inherent in the reform program, yet he retained a friendly interest in all proposals for social betterment.

Emerson's preference for individual reforms is shown by his attitude toward Brook Farm. This community was founded by a group of transcendentalists with the aim of giving its members a chance to live their lives according to their beliefs. Although he was on terms of intimacy with the founders of the community, and although he was in complete sympathy with their aim, yet he remained aloof from the experiment, for he saw that entrance into a communistic group would necessitate the surrendering of certain individual rights and prerogatives. Such a life as that proposed by the Brook Farmers meant a continual compromise, and Emerson's individualism chose never to compromise. His personal aim was to release himself from all outward compulsions and restrictions, a hard enough task in the life of solitude that he lived in Concord, and Brook Farm would but add to those evils that he feared. The day after the Ripleys, Alcott, and Margaret Fuller discussed at Emerson's home the plans for the new community, the great individualist confided these words to his *Journal:*

I do not wish to remove from my present prison to a prison a little larger. I wish to break all prisons. I have not yet conquered my own house. It irks and repents me. Shall I raise the siege of this hen-coop and march baffled away to a pretended siege of Babylon? It seems to me that so to do were to dodge the problem I am set to solve, and to hide my impotency in the thick of the crowd. I can see too, afar,—that I should not find myself more than now,—no, not so much in that select, but not by me selected, fraternity.

Thus Emerson refused to join Brook Farm, although he did not sneer at the project. He simply preferred his own life.

Alcott's experiment at Fruitlands drew the same interested attention and criticism. At first everything went well and Emerson wrote in his *Journal*, "The sun and the evening sky do not look calmer than Alcott and his family at Fruitlands. I will not prejudge them successful. They look well in July. We will see them in December." Later on, when the experiment was going to pieces, he wrote, "The fault of Alcott's community is that it has only room for one." This was Emerson's first reaction to Brook Farm, and the final failure of all the communistic experiments showed him that he was not far wrong. The individual is community enough within himself.

Although Emerson refused to become entangled in some of the reform programs, he characteristically contradicted himself and became a vigorous supporter of abolition. As early as 1837 he said, "Right-minded men have recently been called to decide for abolition." The decision once reached was never recanted, and he was a firm opponent of slavery until the institution was no more. The reason for his support of abolition when he had refused his aid to other reform measures can be explained without recourse to any metaphysical subtleties. The degradation of the individual by slavery was so violent a wrong that it outraged every one of Emerson's moral sentiments, and the desire to abolish that wrong was so great that it overcame whatever misgivings he might have had as to the desirability of mass reform movements. Whenever one of Emerson's minor beliefs clashed with his major doctrine of individualism, the minor belief had to give way. In one respect Emerson was the most consistent of men.

Emerson and Nature.—As a romantic Emerson was anti-scientific in his attitude to life. This disposition kept him from using nature as it is so often employed to-day, as an illustration of the fixed and immutable laws of science. To Emerson nature was not an illustration of a law but a demonstration of freedom, not an example of conformity but of unfettered development. This was the usual romantic view, and in Emerson's works it reached its completest statement in America.

The Emersonian doctrine holds that man is a part of nature and that nature in turn is a part of the deity. Thus the three manifestations of the same spirit are held together in the closest bonds of fellowship. According to early Calvinism nature was simply a veil that served only to hide God from the sight of men. Emerson held that nature is the connecting link between God and man. No separation can be possible so long as the two can meet on a common ground, the beautiful natural world. Man is a part of the world, every particle of which is animated by the divine spirit. Thus man receives his crowning glory of divinity. As a matter of course, this beautiful world of nature that reflects the mind of the deity proves the existence of a God whose every impulse is one of benevolence, justice, and truth. Nature is like a mirror; it reflects what lies before it. It is of surpassing benevolence, therefore the God whom it reflects must also be of surpassing benevolence. In turn man has in his heart a spark of this divine goodness.

In a world thus conceived of man, nature, and God intertwined and all bathed in divine goodness and peace, the existence of evil could hardly be admitted. Evil could arise only from the failure of man to discover himself and to live according to the dictates of his conscience, or it might come from the repressions of society. The avoidance of evil was a simple task. To live the good life man needed only to live close to nature and to God. Then all would be well. With so simple a remedy for the age-old problem of evil, it is no wonder that Emerson and his followers became devotees of optimism. To them man was already good, and, what was more important, he was inherently capable of complete perfection. In fact perfectibility meant only the development of the divinity that was within him. To Emerson nature was superlatively good; if man would approach perfectibility, let him only approach the ways of nature. Above all, the God who presided over man and nature, whose spirit animated the two, was of unalloyed goodness. In such a world optimism was the only possible workaday philosophy.

The Humanitarianism of Emerson.—Although Emerson is not usually looked upon as the great humanitarian of transcendentalism —that distinction is reserved for Walt Whitman—still that element is constantly recurring in the essays and the *Journal*. Emerson could not escape the touch of humanitarianism. To him every man was divine and worthy of divine honors. His towering egotism stopped short of imposing his will upon others. As an individual he demanded everything, but his whole message was to encourage every man to demand for himself the same privileges and rights that Waldo Emerson demanded for himself. Thus the egotism of Emerson, tempered by a fine humanitarian regard, left room in the world for as many other egotists as there were men.

In his conception of humanity Emerson frequently felt an identity of himself with every other person. This projection of one's personality into the personality of all mankind was carried to its fullest development by Whitman, but there are traces of it in the *Journals* of Emerson. In a passage referring to the use of force, previously quoted, Emerson says, "If it threaten man, it threatens me." This is an explicit avowal of the identity of the one with the many. Again he says, "I stand here for all humanity." With these for texts Whitman wove into the great fabric of his poems the goodness of humankind and the all-inclusive humanitarianism of his nature. In a very true sense Emerson was the spiritual father of *Leaves of Grass*.

The Puritanism of Emerson.—Although Emerson has been claimed by many critics as the supreme Puritan in our literary history, it is obvious that such a claim must be preceded by a careful definition of Puritanism. Certainly no man who held the romantic views of the relations of man, nature, and God could be a Puritan of the Mather school. Emerson's optimism, his belief in the power and freedom of the human will, and his fundamental doctrine of the divinity of man's nature, all separate him widely from the Puritans of the first generation who held closely to the stern dogmas of Calvin. In speaking of his Puritan forefathers Emerson said: "Great, grim, earnest men, I belong by natural affinity to other thoughts and schools than yours, but my affection hovers respectfully about your retiring footprints, your unpainted churches, strict platforms, and sad offices; the iron-gray deacon and the wearisome prayer rich with the diction of ages." Deep respect Emerson had for his ancestors, but by his own words he was not of their school of thought. He could never allow respect for the past to bind his own actions in the present.

If by Puritanism one simply means an ethical outlook on life, then Emerson must be admitted to be a Puritan. Any man who teaches a way of life is an ethical teacher, whether that man be Christ, Buddha, Spinoza, Kant, Nietzsche, or Emerson, yet one would have a great deal of difficulty in proving that any one of these men was a Puritan of the original American variety. An ethical teacher Emerson was, by far the most exhilarating yet produced by our people. His whole work was an effort to find the way to the good life, and if he did not find the way completely to his satisfaction, at least he approximated it and led countless others into a better life. He belonged to the second generation of Puritans, those men whose fully socialized consciences repudiated the harshness and unloveliness of the early Puritanism and lived in the cheerful glow of a good world warmed by the beneficent face of a loving deity. The ethical background alone came down from the older time.

Emerson's Literary Work.—From the age of seventeen to the age of seventy-five Emerson kept a journal. It was not a diary, such as countless people have kept, telling of the events of one's external life. An occasional reference to his daily life will creep in, but in general such remarks are quite abrupt, as "House burned," "I was married to Lydia Jackson," or "Waldo [his son] walks alone." Such passages are rare. Most of the space is given to a full record of the writer's spiritual life and development. The journals are the one and only primary source of information about Emerson and his ideas. They contain his estimates of public men, his reaction to public questions, and his constant speculation on the eternal problems of life. It is by far the most important literary bequest left us by the writer.

When Emerson wished to prepare a lecture or essay he would go to his spiritual diary and select passages bearing upon the topic that he wished to discuss. These he would weave together without much regard for smoothness of thought or logical arrangement. As a result some of the essays are quite hard to read in consecutive fashion. For instance, parts of the essay on "Self-reliance" sound like collections of texts for lectures or sermons. Each sentence has an unmistakable relation to the general subject but the transition between the individual thoughts is rough. Emerson referred to his *Journals* as his savings bank, and his characterization was strikingly apt. He saved his best thoughts in these pages and used them at need.

The *Journals* were published about twenty years ago in ten good-sized volumes. Recently (1927) Professor Bliss Perry published *The Heart of Emerson's Journals,* an abridged edition in one volume.

Emerson owes his chief reputation in American literature to his numerous essays on various subjects. These were drawn originally from the *Journals,* and many were delivered as lectures. In them the author gave his thoughts their most extended public presentation, for the *Journals* were not published until thirty years after the author's death. To-day the essays are invaluable, but the close student of Emerson will wish to determine the spiritual and intellectual background of these works by constant reference to the *Journals.* The most characteristic essays are those on "Self-reliance," "Nature" (the first essay, published in 1836), "Politics," "The American Scholar," "Man the Reformer," "Uses of Great Men" and "Compensation."

Aside from his essays Emerson wrote two or three books that are remembered. Chief among these are *English Traits*, and *Representative Men*. The latter work seems to suffer from comparison with Carlyle's *Heroes and Hero-Worship*. As a matter of fact both of these books are collections of essays, but each chapter is linked to the general subject, whereas in his early works the essays are unrelated.

Thus far nothing has been said about Emerson's poetry, but that omission was not caused by a feeling that the poems are slight in value. On the contrary they are of high worth. The great fault is that notable ones are difficult reading. Some one has remarked that Emerson skimmed the cream off his diaries to get his essays, then churned this cream and called the resulting pat of butter a poem. Certainly his best verse is highly concentrated. In it he makes even fewer concessions to the comfort of the reader than he does in his essays, and consequently he manages to pack a great deal of his doctrine in a few stanzas. The heavy content frequently makes the verse extremely rough and unmelodious, and often the thought of the writer is too swift for the slow reader. As a result the best known poems are those that are less characteristically Emersonian. Among these are "The Mountain and the Squirrel"— more correctly known as "The Fable"—"The Snow-Storm," "The Concord Hymn," and numerous others that have an immortality in our school readers. More typical poems are "Good-bye," "The Rhodora," "Each and All," "Brahma," "The Sphinx," "Threnody," "Ode to W. H. Channing," and "Waldeinsamkeit."

The subjects of the poems are the subjects of the essays; nature, the mystic relations of God and man and the natural world, duty, and the call to self-trust are the favorite topics. Emerson's success as a poet is to be attributed more to his ability to interpret transcendentalism in metrical lines than to his verbal melody or sensuous beauty. These last qualities he totally lacked. Although he was probably the best poet of the Concord group—and nearly all of Emerson's friends attempted poetry—he had not sufficient command of poetic technique to qualify as a great poet. To-day we usually read his more notable verse as an expression of his ethical teaching, but at his best he is far below the great philosophical poets like Lucretius, Dante, and Goethe.

American society has swung so far from the position that it occupied during the transcendental period that to-day Emerson sounds hopelessly old-fashioned, but the very distance that we have traveled from his ideal throws into higher relief the main elements of his doctrine and more sharply points the lesson that he sought to impart. The dangers that he saw have encompassed us. The rising tide of industrialism has submerged the individual. To-day the individual is no longer considered brother-in-the-spirit to God and to the wholly excellent natural world; he is only an economic unit, a necessary adjunct to our machines, and a potential purchaser of the products of those same machines. In our haste to accommodate ourselves to the demands of the machine age we have lost sight of the dignity and worth of the individual, and in our enjoyment of material goods we have lost many a cubit from our spiritual stature. We are tending to become "robots," soulless manikins. Against the evil tendencies of industrialism Emerson's voice is the clearest. He calls man back to his former relations with God and the world about him; he beseeches the individual to remember that he is a man and not merely a machine; he summons all to the high duties of life, the highest of which is the reverencing of our own selves and the placing of implicit faith in the self-sufficiency of the individual.

HENRY DAVID THOREAU

(1817-1862)

Emerson was the clearest preacher of transcendental individualism, but Thoreau lived that gospel. Emerson taught the duty of non-conformity; Thoreau put his lesson into practice by refusing to conform to any institution that he disliked. Emerson praised a life close to nature; Thoreau built himself a hut on the bank of Walden Pond and lived alone with nature as his only companion until he was satisfied that the theory of his friend was sound. In short, Emerson and the other Concord transcendentalists gave oracular directions for leading the good life; Thoreau with canny Yankee practicality tested these directions.

Of all the nay-sayers of Concord, Thoreau had, if not the loudest, certainly the most incisive voice. To so many things did he say

"No" that many have gravely wronged the man by putting him down as a chronic objector. Part of the fault must be attributed to Emerson, whose sincere attempt to praise his closest friend took the form of a catalog of negations: "He was bred to no profession; he never married; he lived alone; he never went to church; he never voted; he refused to pay a tax to the state; he ate no flesh; he drank no wine; he never knew the use of tobacco; and though a naturalist he used neither gun or rod." At various times in his life Thoreau would not have made some of these denials, others were permanent, but whether permanent or temporary each refusal had for its aim the practical testing of a certain precept. If the denial was satisfactory it was made permanent. To the chronic objector nay-saying is an end in itself, but to Thoreau it was only a means to an end, the desired end being a satisfactory life.

But there is more than nay-saying in the life and writings of Thoreau. In all his works there are thundering affirmatives, and not the least emphatic of these is the answer to the query: Is life worth living? Thoreau devoted every day of his existence to the wringing of the ultimate satisfaction out of life, and when he lay on his death-bed, dying with "pleasure and peace," so his marveling neighbors reported, there escaped from his lips not a single regret. He had made of life what he wished it to be, and he was satisfied. If the possession of the peace that passes understanding is the test of a happy life, Thoreau was successful in his quest for happiness. A few days before he died a well-meaning friend anxiously asked, "Have you made your peace with God?" The dying man responded without a quiver, "Sir, I am not aware that we ever quarreled." In answer to certain questions of superlative importance Thoreau's life was one long-drawn affirmative.

Thoreau and the Problem of Living.—Thoreau left to others the nebulous problems of philosophy that led some of the transcendentalists into the way of airy speculation and gossamer-like theories. He devoted himself to finding the answers to the ordinary questions of everyday life like: "What shall a man eat? What shall he wear? Where shall he live? What about the problem of making a living? Is wealth worth getting? What shall be the average man's attitude toward the political state?" With a practical man's mistrust of speculative answers born of the study he went to the open fields and the streams, to his simple home beside Walden, and to the streets of his native Concord for solutions of his problems.

The problem of making a living presented itself to Thoreau, as it does to every one. When he was graduated from Harvard he taught for a short time. This work was unsatisfactory, and he turned to his father's trade of pencil making. He soon became so expert in his work and made so good a pencil that Boston business men urged him to become superintendent of a factory that they were about to establish. Thoreau promptly rejected the offer. Thereafter he did some surveying for his neighbors, but gained most of his livelihood by working at any manual labor that he wished to undertake. By a careful calculation he had discovered that he could make enough by working a few weeks each year to support himself the remainder of the time. After he made this discovery, he cut his work to the very minimum.

In solving his problem of how to live a satisfying life Thoreau approached the question with only one preconception: he was determined to be the servant of no institution, custom, machine, or superfluous desire. It is said that once some one gave him a paper-weight. He carried his present home to his bare hut and for a time used it, but use entailed an occasional dusting. This was too much bother, and he cast the troublesome thing into the depths of Walden. The anecdote is highly illuminating, for it shows exactly how Thoreau solved the problem of money-making and wealth-getting. Living was the only thing that could be allowed to occupy much of his time; making a living was too trivial a question to bother with for long.

Thoreau soon saw that there were three ways in which he might solve the question of money-making. He could hire himself out to some one who would exploit his labor, as for instance, the Boston pencil makers wished to do. He could hire other men and exploit their work to his gain. Finally, he could reduce his wants almost to the vanishing point and get along without any kind of exploitation. This last was the only satisfactory plan, and he determined to follow it. Manual labor was the most pleasant form of work, therefore he discovered how little work was necessary when wants were brought to the irreducible minimum, and did no more than the required amount.

As it was with the question of making a living, so was it with his other problems. Thoreau refused to have anything to do with anything that made requirements upon his time and energy. These were treasured as divine gifts, to be used only in the grand experiment of living. As he said himself, he "drove life into a corner and reduced it to its lowest terms," for he knew that only by getting rid of all extraneous material could he enjoy the full flavor of living. Getting a living was not to be his trade but his sport; living was his trade. The church was about to make certain demands upon his time and energy, and he "signed off" in the following memorable fashion: "Know ye, all men, by these presents, that I, Henry Thoreau, do not wish to be regarded as a member of any incorporated society that I have not joined." And the chief point with Thoreau was that he joined nothing. The state into whose citizenship he was born, he repudiated.

Many have objected to the wholesale renunciation that Thoreau practiced, and still more have been repelled by the ascetic life that he led in the pursuit of his aim, but hostile critics must remember that the man was putting into practice the doctrine of individualism and that he made no claim that his solution was the only correct one or even that other people would be better for following it. Like Emerson's his egotism was supreme, but it stopped dead short of imposing views on others, however futile or foolish their lives might seem. Thoreau's renunciation and his ascetic life hurt no one. They were his own prescription for himself. Other people need not touch them.

Thoreau and the Reform Movement.—The reform movement in general left Thoreau profoundly unmoved. He was far too busy living his own life to be bothered with the multitudinous vexations that were throwing the New England reformers into spasms of white-hot indignation. Did Dr. Graham propose the amelioration of human ills by eating not a mouthful of meat or white flour? Well, Thoreau had already found out the most healthful and inexpensive diet for himself, and as proof of his discovery had published his menus in *Walden*. Did the long hours of labor outrage the sensibilities of Horace Greeley? Thoreau had discovered the sure cure for that evil. He had quit working. Universal peace was engrossing the attention of certain Boston intellectuals, but out at Concord Thoreau lived on terms of peace and good-will with God and man, and he was sensible enough to argue that if every one else did the same the abolition of war might be effected with precious little oratory and high-flown resolutions. Reform was a matter of individual effort, and not a thing to be effected by mass-meetings and the enactment of restrictive legislation.

Like Emerson, Thoreau was urged to join Brook Farm. He refused to try the experiment, writing in his journal that it was better to keep bachelor's hall in hell than to live in a boarding house in heaven. Walden Pond offered society enough, and the hut housed enough of a community to suit its occupant. Joining Brook Farm would have been the very negation of all that Thoreau lived for; it would have been an acknowledgment that his way of life had failed. Certainly he never was in the mood to make any such admission. Every reform proposal drew the same reply from Thoreau; he had come into the world not to "make it a good place to live in, but to live in it, be it good or bad." Brook Farm was only another attempt to make over the world.

Thoreau and the State.—Enough has already been said to indicate that Thoreau is our great social rebel, our foremost protester against the tyranny of institutions. Nor did his protest stop short of a flat repudiation of the political state.

In a very real sense Thoreau was the spiritual and intellectual heir of the great liberals of the preceding age, Rousseau, William Godwin, Paine, and Jefferson, writers whose belief in the fundamental goodness of man led them to advocate a state whose powers would be reduced to the minimum. Just what this minimum was these thinkers did not say. Emerson had implied that the minimum was complete abolition of government, but he had not stated his views in so many words, nor had he ever acted on the assumption that his views should be adopted. It remained for Thoreau to give a practical demonstration of transcendental political theory.

In only one reform was Thoreau interested. That was the abolition of slavery. Involuntary servitude was so heinous a fate, and those who held men in slavery were so drenched with guilt that Thoreau would have been willing to forgo any of his theories or his mode of living in order to abolish the hated institution, but up to 1847 his opposition to slavery had been theoretical just as his opposition to the state had never been definitely expressed. The Mexican War precipitated the crisis. Thoreau thought—quite correctly, it seems—that the slave power was the instigator of the war. Massachusetts as a member of the federal union was equally guilty with the slave states, for it had sent its own state troops to the battle field. Thereupon Thoreau refused to pay his poll tax. For his refusal he was placed in jail, much to the consternation of his neighbors who only advocated the doctrine that their practical friend was putting into practice. It is told, upon doubtful authority, that Emerson went to see his companion in the Concord jail. "Henry," began the older man solicitously, "why are you here?" "Waldo," came Thoreau's ready reply, "why are you not here?" If the story is true, we may be sure that Emerson was in some perplexity to find a suitable answer. After spending one night in jail, Thoreau was released. One of his friends paid the tax, greatly to the disgust of the prisoner.

Soon after this episode Thoreau wrote his famous essay "On Civil Disobedience" to set forth his views on the political state. This little work is the most explicit statement of philosophical anarchism ever penned by a well-known American. Accepting the theory of Jefferson that that state is best which governs least, Thoreau carries that proposition to its logical conclusion and declares that that state is best which governs not at all.

When men are prepared for it, that will be the kind of government which they will have. . . . How does it become a man to behave toward this American government to-day? I answer, that he cannot without disgrace be associated with it. I cannot for a minute recognize that political organization as my government which is the slave's also. . . . It is not a man's duty, as a matter of course, to devote himself to the eradication of any, even the most enormous wrong; he may still properly have other concerns to engage him; but it is his duty, at least, to wash his hands of it.

In this essay there is the rage of an Old Testament prophet thundering denunciations of the iniquities of his rulers, but with the Concord thinker the people themselves, as rulers of the land, are denounced as the authors of slavery, the greatest of iniquities. When we get the full flavor of the radicalism expressed in "Civil Disobedience," we do not greatly wonder that most of Thoreau's commentators have neglected entirely to mention the essay. However laudable the intention of the commentators may have been, the omission is inexcusable. That essay puts the cap-stone on Thoreau's work. It states explicitly the social philosophy toward which his earlier life and work were tending. Without it the author becomes too much of an echo of Emerson, far too much of a naturalist. Thoreau was neither; he was, as he said himself, "a poet, a mystic, and a transcendentalist." Above all he was a social philosopher who carried to its flinty, logical conclusion the pleasant liberalism of Jefferson, Paine, Godwin, and Rousseau.

Emerson and Thoreau.—Although the relations of Emerson and Thoreau were close and long continued, still it is a mistake to con-

sider the younger man only a weak echo of the older. Certainly there
was a reciprocal influence existing between them. Each influenced
the other, but Thoreau was possessed of too original a nature and
too acute a mind to become a mere copy of any one. He was strictly
a product of the good rich earth of Concord watered by transcendental doctrine. Nothing bookish was there about him, and he never
aspired to philosophical profundities. His everyday life as described in his books is the best possible argument in support of the
contention that transcendentalism was a native American product
and that it would have developed in this country without the slightest foreign influence. Without the influence of Emerson, Thoreau
would not have had his conscious connection with transcendentalism,
but he would have been the same poet, the same mystical lover of
nature, and the same implacable foe of society.

This reciprocal influence existing between the two men probably
can never be disentangled. It was the custom of the older historians
and critics of American literature to speak of Thoreau disparagingly,
as one of the "minor men of Concord," or as a rustic imitator of
Emerson. Such characterizations are no longer attempted. To-day
we realize that he was a major figure in our literature. His style
alone would compel such an appraisal, even if he had no other claims
to eminence, and other claims he has in plenty. But with the elevation of Thoreau's position the problem of his relations with Emerson become more difficult of solution, for so long as he was only a
minor figure it would suffice to admit that all his good qualities were
a reflection of his friend. To say that the problem is a tangled one
is stating only half the truth.

It has been proposed to settle the difficulty by acknowledging
Emerson to have been an original thinker and Thoreau an original
doer. This suggestion seriously raises the question if Emerson was
not as much stimulated by the life of Thoreau as Thoreau was by
the utterances of Emerson. When Emerson established his residence
in Concord in 1835, Thoreau was a boy of eighteen, far more mature
in mind than in years. At that time the older man had written virtually nothing, though his first essay on "Nature" appeared the next
year. Presumably his mind was maturing rather slowly, and certain
it is that his striking social and political doctrines were not yet elaborated. In 1838, when Thoreau was twenty-one, Emerson has the
following entry in his diary: "My good Henry Thoreau made this
else solitary afternoon sunny with his simplicity and clear perception.

How comic is simplicity in the double-dealing, quacking world. Everything that boy says makes merry with society, though nothing can be graver than his meaning." This entry seems to indicate that in his social thought Thoreau was already as advanced as Emerson was. Again Emerson wrote, "Thoreau gives me in flesh and blood . . . my own ethics." Certainly a man who consistently practices what another preaches must not be without influence on the preacher.

The Walden Episode.—Critics of Thoreau have talked about the life at Walden far too much. Some have considered it the turning point in Thoreau's life, while still more have considered it as his major concern. It was neither. Living at Walden for two years and two months was only an episode in Thoreau's life, an experiment. When the experiment was successfully completed, he went back to Concord, not because he did not like life in the woods, but because he had something that he wished to do in the village. In the beginning Thoreau borrowed Alcott's ax and built a little cabin beside Walden Pond on land belonging to Emerson. He says that he went to the woods "because he wished to live deliberately, to front only the essential facts of life, and see if he could not learn what it had to teach, and not, when he came to die, discover that he had not lived." In other words he went to Walden to see if a life of solitude would not help him in extracting the last bit of flavor from existence. His experiment convinced him that his theory was correct, as any one can discover by reading a chapter or two of *Walden*. When he was satisfied, he went back to Concord, for such an experiment too long protracted might become onerous, or might grow to be the very aim and reason for life itself. Thoreau wisely ended his stay in his cabin after twenty-six months.

Thoreau as a Naturalist.—Although Thoreau deserves his highest place in the development of our national mind as a social critic, or rather as a tester of social philosophies, yet the idea that he is primarily a naturalist obsesses the minds of many. It is fairly clear to any one who reads Thoreau's books and journals in chronological order that the author was first of all a critic of human institutions, and only incidentally a student of nature. A close student of nature he probably never was, for scientific naturalists have pointed out many instances of his careless observations or mistaken conclusions. He began life as a lover of nature, for it was only in the fields and woods and along the ponds and creeks that he could find an antidote to society. In his early books and journals there is more interest shown in social criticism than in nature. The natural world obviously affords a relief from the shortcomings of man. However, the longer he lived, the more engrossed he became in the contemplation of nature, and in the later journals volume after volume is filled with his observations. One is reasonably safe in saying that in his early years Thoreau courted nature like a lover, with more ardor than critical acumen, but in his later years he tended more and more toward the scientific attitude.

Works.—Like Emerson, Thoreau kept a voluminous journal, even more voluminous than that of his friend. He published only two books during his lifetime and both of these were drawn from the journals. These two books are *Walden* and *A Week on the Concord and Merrimack Rivers.* After his death in 1862, his friends and family published *Excursions, The Maine Woods, Cape Cod, The Yankee in Canada,* and the letters. These books appeared within a space of four years. Later various excerpts from the journals were published, but it was not until forty years had passed that we got the full text.

As a literary figure Thoreau occupies a high position because of his excellent prose style. A finer vehicle could not have been perfected for its intended use. It abounds in the most specific words imaginable, in wit, and in crystal clarity. No man can mistake the meaning of Thoreau's sentences. Simple Anglo-Saxon words flowing in melodious sequence make such works as *Walden* or *The Week* the easiest books to read in our whole literature. Thoreau avoids the disjointed oracular style of Emerson that seems to be a string of epigrams. If the epigram comes, he does not scorn it, but he fills up the space to the next pithy utterance with a prose so well-ordered that the reader unconsciously floats along with the stream of thought.

General Characteristics.—It is superfluous to point out that Thoreau was an individualist, a mystic, a believer in the fundamental goodness of the individual, and an optimist. These things are implied in the transcendental faith that he openly professed. It is more to the point to think of him as the tartest critic of society produced by the romantic movement, and one of the chief manifestations of this movement was the criticism of human institutions. If he did not like the state he would let his life be a "counter friction to stop the machine" and to those who remonstrate with him for not conforming at least outwardly he blandly replies, "If a man does not keep pace with his companions, perhaps it is because he hears a different drummer. Let him step to the music which he hears, however measured or far away." For who knows, thought Thoreau, but what the distant tune may be the proper march to follow.

It cannot be too strongly emphasized that Thoreau, supreme individualist that he was, never insisted upon imposing his views upon others. "If the shoe fits," he would say in homely phrase, "wear it." It was every man's duty to live not according to the light that others held for him but according to the light that was within him. "Let every one mind his own business and endeavor to be what he was made."

Some have dwelt too strongly on the point that a society composed of Thoreaus would be quite impossible. Surely the contention is correct, but let no one become alarmed over the prospect. In two hundred years our continent was able to bring forth only one Thoreau, and it is not likely that the feat will be soon duplicated. Really the danger is not in having too many Thoreaus but in having too few.

In many ways Thoreau was the most fortunate of men. He lived to the full, wrung every drop of juice out of life, and died reconciled to both life and death. His was the golden day of romantic individualism, and his own life marked the high noon of that day. Death saved him from the twilight and darkness of the human spirit. Fortunate was he in life, and fortunate in death.

AMOS BRONSON ALCOTT

(1799-1888)

Bronson Alcott belongs to what some critics have facetiously called the "lunatic fringe" of transcendentalism, but as a matter of fact neither Alcott nor the fringe are half so bad as they have been made to appear. The trouble with Alcott was that he carried to an extreme the transcendental inclination to speculate on the meaning and origin of the universe rather than trying to live in it on decent terms. Furthermore he was as rebellious as Thoreau toward all institutions, and his ability to earn a living could be measured only in minus quantities. Unlike Thoreau he accepted the responsibilities of a family, and his inability to provide for his dependents, as much as his nebulous speculation, made him the jest of his time. He is a truly amus-

ing figure most of the time, but he is also worthy of serious consideration because of his contribution to American education.

Alcott was the son of a Connecticut farmer whose lack of means
made impossible an education for his son. As a young man Alcott
was a peddler in Virginia and North Carolina for a number of years.
During his sojourn in the latter state he came into contact with
numerous Quaker families. The lives of these people so favorably
impressed him that he accepted their chief doctrine, a belief in the
validity of personal inspiration. Back in New England with a firm
mystical belief in the inner light, he naturally joined the transcendentalists.

His first work after returning to the North was the management
of a school in Boston. His ideal was the mental, moral, physical,
and esthetic development of his students. This work was to be accomplished in part by a plan of organized play, by the use of the
honor system, by the beautifying of the schoolroom, and by a great
deal less dependence upon corporal punishment than was then customary. Not an idea was tested that is not to-day a commonplace
in even our most backward communities, but at that time the theories
were far too advanced for Boston. The introduction into the curriculum of an elementary lesson in physiology caused the withdrawal of
about two-thirds of the students. Finally when Alcott admitted a
little Negro girl to the school, the remainder of the pupils departed.

Alcott's next scheme was the famous communistic experiment of
Fruitlands, concerning which Emerson remarked that the chief difficulty was that there was room in it for only one member. As a firm
supporter of all the reform movements of the day, Alcott founded his
community on a strictly vegetarian basis. He refused to allow the
use of eggs, milk, cheese, and butter, and limited the choice of vege-
tables to those "aspiring" plants like peas and beans that grew up-
ward. Base edibles like potatoes, carrots, radishes, which grew in the
ground, he strictly forbade. As a result menus at Fruitlands were
somewhat restricted in scope. Furthermore the labor of horses was
not allowed. This necessitated the use of manual labor exclusively,
and since the men of the community were fonder of attending reform
conventions than of working in the fields, the community soon came
to a dismal end.

After a long struggle with poverty, a struggle for which he was
totally unfitted, Alcott was appointed superintendent of schools in

Concord. In this post he gave eminent satisfaction to his patrons, not all of whom were transcendentalists. Among his additions to the curriculum were group singing and systematic lessons in physiology. About this time he began his famous "Conversations," which were nothing more than lectures by Alcott himself. These efforts brought him in a little money and gave him a chance to indulge in his favorite task, speculative talk, but it was not until his daughter, Louisa May, wrote *Little Women* that his financial worries were at an end.

The chief trouble with Alcott was his obsession by a grandiose desire to answer at once all possible questions as to the origin and meaning of the world, to give in one breath the answer to the riddle of the universe. In striving for such an answer he swept aside as irrelevant all details however pertinent. Generalities alone interested him; particulars were of no concern. The natural result was that the talker built a castle of clouds a mile high and then attempted to climb to the top. The results were ludicrous to practical-minded onlookers. It was as the dreamer of vast, misty dreams that Alcott delighted his sympathetic hearers, and when the audience was congenial his talk was said to have been of the most attractive variety. Emerson, who was not uniformly pleased with him, said of his talk: "His discourse soars to a wonderful height, so regular, so lucid, so playful, so new and disdainful of all boundaries of tradition and experience."

Certainly the boundaries of experience never for a moment confined the man's speculative flights, nor did repeated disillusionment ever cure him of his unconquerable optimism. Thoreau spoke of Alcott's unquestionable knowledge, "overlaid and concealed by a faith in the unseen and impracticable. . . . He will be the last man to be disappointed as the ages revolve. His attitude is that of greater faith and expectation than that of any man that I know." Moreover he was never bound by any view that he had previously avowed, however recent his avowal might have been. So great was his inconsistency that even Emerson, that apologist for inconsistency, was moved to protest. "He never remembers. . . . His topic yesterday is Alcott on the 17th of October; to-day, Alcott on the 18th of October; to-morrow, on the 19th. So will it be always."

As a speaker Alcott occasionally let ideas drift in through the haze of speculation, but as a writer he retained all his wordiness as a talker and entirely omitted all ideas. A hostile critic said of one of his publications that it was like a railroad train of fifteen cars and only one passenger. He has no place in our literature as a writer, save for some of his very effective sonnets. Just how a man, so verbose that he could not express an idea short of an entire day of talk, could compress his thought into the compass of a fourteen-line poem will always remain one of the literary mysteries of America. However, the fact is embalmed in type in many an anthology.

But despite his literary lapses, Alcott was a force among the undoubted men of letters of his day. He enjoyed close personal relations with such men as Emerson, Thoreau, Parker, Greeley, and Hawthorne, and all of these men found his talk wearying in its sum total but curiously stimulating. He had the faculty of suggesting many lines of thought that he took not the trouble to carry out. Other men profited from his suggestions. In his fundamental views, in so far as we have them, he much resembled Thoreau whom he preceded to jail by several years for his refusal to pay taxes to a government that condoned slavery. His philosophy was that of an extreme transcendentalist, and his humanitarian ideals were those of the most advanced reformers. Intellectually he was thoroughly of his age, save when he talked himself into cloudland. Probably his best characterization is by Emerson, who set him down as a "tedious archangel."

THEODORE PARKER

(1810-1860)

As a minister Theodore Parker had all the characteristics of a great molder of public opinion. He possessed what was probably the most impressive mind in America. His stock of exact information was surpassed by that of no contemporary. His marvelous industry held him at his desk from twelve to seventeen hours a day. He was said by one of his fellow ministers to have had the most sensitive social conscience since the days of Luther. His appearance in the pulpit was made memorable by an eloquence that was a compound of courage, child-like simplicity, and unquestionable sincerity. And not the least notable feature of the man was his theology which he gradually reduced until it carried only two points, the God of love and the love of God. This beneficent God manifested His love in every object of the visible universe and in the depth of every human heart whose greatest duty it was to love that divine spirit whose indwelling presence made all nature and all men one, "even as Thou and I are one." With this superb moral and intellectual equipment Theodore Parker shook America as it was never shaken by the preaching of one man.

Parker was the son of a Lexington farmer in whose veins there was good fighting blood—Theodore's grandfather was the Captain Parker who commanded the colonial troops at the Battle of Lexington—and the Boston Brahmins have not yet forgiven their greatest preacher either for his lowly birth or for his courage that did not stop short of calling to account the most dignified citizens of Massachusetts. After graduation from Harvard he accepted a pastorate at West Roxbury, going from there in 1846 to Boston, where he preached every Sunday to huge throngs, at first in the Melodeon, later in the Music Hall. America was in a great intellectual and spiritual ferment during his years in Boston, and no man did more to create this ferment than did Parker. Every minute of his waking hours was filled, and his sleep was cut to the minimum. The incessant study that was a fixed part of his régimé, letters to friends or total strangers, visitors who dropped in to talk over the political situation, addresses, sermons, conventions, and committee meetings all made his days a grueling task and so sapped his strength that he died at the early age of fifty, looking as if he were seventy. Emerson said, "Theodore Parker has filled up all his years and days and hours; a son of the energy of New England, restless, eager, manly, brave, early old, contumacious, clever. . . . He was willing to perish in the using. He sacrificed the future to the present, was willing to spend and be spent; felt himself to belong to the day he lived in, and had too much to do than that he should be careful for fame."

Parker was a grand combination of scholar and practical man. He once expressed the desire to live with men and think with philosophers, and if we can believe those who heard him preach, he fully realized his desire. It was said that his most scholarly addresses sounded like stump speeches. A transcendentalist of the extreme variety, he could express the subtleties of that philosophy in words of one syllable. A reformer with his hands in almost every ameliorative scheme, yet he remained a man of great practical sense, never losing sight of the weaknesses of the flesh or the human desire to take the path of least resistance. When he arose to speak to his people, it was with the spirit of a moral aristocrat and the words of a commoner.

One of Parker's great contributions to the life of his time was the translation of current social and political problems into terms of divine justice. Too often the romantics, absorbed in their contemplation of the ideal, lost all grip on reality. Their discussions of contemporary political issues always tended to run off into the hazy reaches of transcendental speculation with never a glance at the economic or social basis of the questions at issue. Such discussions may have been satisfying to the philosophers, but the average man, striving desperately for practical guidance in the everyday matter of casting his vote, demanded more information and less theorizing, more interpretation and less Utopian dreaming. To this man Parker's was the clear steady voice in the midst of a meaningless babel. No person of the time understood better than the great preacher the real causes of political action and the ultimate aims of our obscure national policy, but never for a moment did concern with the practical aspects of our politics distract his eyes from the fixed light of truth and justice beside which all earthly policies had to be tested. In the testing if it became necessary to mention eminent and respectable Bostonian names, Parker never hesitated, nor did he shrink from applying harsh epithets to those names if the holders were guilty of wrong-doing or of condoning wrong. Boston never forgot or forgave the famous address on the Nebraska Bill and the still more famous one on Webster in 1852. The last was the most merciless and realistic analysis that an American statesman was ever subjected to at the very close of his career. In this as in every public utterance Parker never lost his hold on either mundane facts or his romantic idealism.

Parker's Political Views.—In his political views Parker was the nearest to an agrarian democrat of all the New England romantics. He never forgot that he was the son of generations of Lexington farmers, whose democracy, like that of the frontiersman, was the practical equalitarianism of the small landholder. In the eyes of Parker all men stood on a footing of absolute equality of rights and privileges, just as they did on the frontier, just as they would before the bar of divine justice. The fugitive slave, the scholar, the farmer, the aristocrat could alike claim to be partakers of the divine spirit inherent in all men, each had in him possibilities of progress, and each could demand the right to live according to his conscience. Such views boldly expressed made Parker one of the most unpopular figures of the time. He and the Boston Brahmin probably never understood, certainly never admired, each other. To the Brahmin

Parker was guilty of excessive loyalty to his ideals and of bad taste, this last being the worst of offenses in the eyes of respectable Boston. To Parker the Brahmin was guilty of temporizing with truth and justice and of elevating the dollar to an equality with the man.

Fundamentally the difference between Parker and such men as Webster and the Boston notables was the difference between industrialism and humanitarianism. Webster once said that the function of government is the "protection of property at home and respect and renown abroad." Beside this materialistic definition Parker put his own contention that the duty of government is to "erect God's justice into human laws." The immense gulf separating romantic democracy and New England Whiggery can be measured by computing the distance between these two views.

That Parker was a great genuine democrat can never be doubted. In point of development he stood midway between the two American democrats whom he most resembled, Jefferson and Lincoln. Without question he was influenced by the earlier thinker, and he certainly influenced the development of Lincoln. His correspondence with Herndon, Lincoln's law partner, is one of the significant documents of American history. Parker's idea of a satisfactory democratic government is best expressed in his own words, afterwards immortalized by Lincoln with only a slight change in phraseology: ". . . a government of all the people, by all the people, for all the people."

Significance of Parker.—Parker's importance lies not in his literary work so much as in the awakening touch that he laid upon his generation. "The center of a thousand minds and the center of a thousand hearts," he has been called. He forced unpopular issues upon his community and state, he made men think of political questions in terms of divine justice, and he welded romantic idealism and social reality into a compact union. For years he and Horace Greeley were accounted the most powerful influences in America, and the two were one in aim and background. Both were romantic reformers and exponents of social justice, calling a time-serving generation to account for its deeds.

Parker was undoubtedly the last great American preacher of national importance. When he began preaching moral opposition to slavery, many ministers were apologizing for the institution, and condoning it on grounds of history, tradition, and economic necessity. Parker made such apologies deep moral offenses. With evil he admitted no compromise. Many men hated him because he would give them no peace of mind, but he would not be silenced. His task was to make popular the unpopular cause of social justice. Too many of his successors in the American ministry have devoted themselves to the championing of movements that were already popular.

MARGARET FULLER

(1810-1850)

At the opening of the nineteenth century woman was in possession of few things that might be called rights. From the cradle to the grave her course was controlled by men—father, brothers, or husband—and under their tutelage the only career open to her was that of housewife. However mentally brilliant a girl might be, she could look forward to no other epitaph than that she was "a loving wife and a devoted mother." Few educational advantages were provided for her in the elementary schools, and none at all in the colleges. Under the laws her husband could dispose of her earnings and could even mortgage or sell the property that she inherited. Woman suffrage was considered the very height of the ridiculous.

It was the reform movement that began the woman's rights agitation in this country. During the thirties when anti-slavery and temperance societies were being formed all over the United States, especially in New England, women were among the early and the most ardent advocates of the proposed reforms. Up to that time they had never been given the right to speak in public at any kind of meeting. Among the early abolitionists were the Grimké sisters, two Carolina Quakers who emancipated their slaves to forward the cause of freedom. With these women working beside their masculine associates, it was ludicrous to enforce the ban of silence on women. Garrison, Phillips, and other reformers allowed women to participate in their meetings, although the practice was frowned upon by the conservatives. In 1837 a church convention in Massachusetts passed resolutions declaring that the work of the Grimké sisters was unchristian and demoralizing. However, in spite of opposition women were gradually allowed to speak at and to preside over conventions and public meetings.

During the thirties Frances Wright, a gifted Scotch woman, aroused great interest and opposition in this country by her lectures on questions of the day. During this decade Harriet Martineau, an Englishwoman, also visited here, writing and speaking in favor of the rights of woman. These visitors acquainted Americans with the advanced thought of England on the question of the position of woman in society, an issue that was raised in 1792 with Mary Wollstonecraft's *Vindication of the Rights of Woman.* In 1833 Oberlin, a new college in Ohio, opened its doors to men and women alike. Owing to the efforts of the reformers, the foreign lecturers, and a few other forces, the cause of women's rights made steady progress from 1830 to 1840.

During the forties the tide of feminism ran high. The cause of women's rights became the subject of a separate reform movement that held its first convention in Seneca Falls, New York, in 1848. This meeting was followed by others in various parts of the country. The chief result of the Seneca Falls convention was the publication of a women's Declaration of Independence that demanded political, economic, and social equality. Among the native reformers identified with the cause of women's rights were Lucy Stone, who was the granddaughter of a captain in Shay's rebellion, Elizabeth Cady Stanton, Lucretia Mott, and Susan B. Anthony. By 1850 the cause had made so great progress that suffrage seemed to be within the easy grasp of women. Educational facilities had been expanded, divorce had been made easier, woman was gaining control of her property, and numerous other innovations were marking minor but significant victories for the reformers. Without question the Civil War and the resultant social confusion postponed the winning of national woman suffrage by many decades, and it was not until 1920 that the constitutional amendment giving women the right to vote was finally ratified.

In the two decades preceding the Civil War many of the advances made by the feminists were due to the large number of women who were demonstrating beyond question that the feminine mind is susceptible of a high degree of development. France produced George Sand; England the Brontë sisters, George Eliot, and Florence Nightingale; and America a large number, of whom none was more brilliant or influential than the famous Margaret Fuller.

Work of Margaret Fuller.—Margaret Fuller could not help being a non-conformist. She was the daughter and granddaughter of nonconformers, and accepted to the full the extreme doctrines of transcendental individualism; and, gifted with an exceptional mind, she was constantly brought into contact with the stupid inhibitions and restrictions that hedged about woman's activities in the America of 1840. Born in Cambridge, the daughter of a prominent lawyer and politician, she was brought up in an atmosphere of intellectual interests. Her father had broken with Massachusetts Federalism and espoused the cause of Jeffersonian democracy. As a girl Margaret carefully read the letters of Jefferson, and from the political romanticism here expressed she constructed the framework of her own romantic philosophy that later developed in many directions.

From Jefferson the young woman proceeded to a reading of Rousseau and the French romantics, Mary Wollstonecraft's defense of woman next interested her, and from the English romantics she went to German literature where she found the greatest inspirations of her life. Especially was she influenced by Goethe with his god-like grasp of the problems of life. However, she never escaped from the power of Rousseau, whose mark is to be found on almost every act of her career and in almost every line that she wrote. Rather late in her life, after visiting the library of the Chamber of Deputies in Paris where the manuscripts of Rousseau are preserved, she wrote:

Yellow and faded age has made them [the manuscripts], yet at their touch I seemed to feel the fire of youth, immortally glowing, more and more expansive, with which his soul has pervaded this century. He was the precursor of all we most prize . . . his spirit was intimate with the fundamental truths of human nature, and fraught with prophecy. There is no one who has given birth to more life for this age.

With such an intellectual background it was natural for Margaret Fuller to become one of the Concord group of transcendentalists. Here she was accepted without question as the equal of Parker, Emerson, Thoreau, Alcott, and the other notables. She became the first editor of *The Dial,* the magazine of the group. She refused, like Emerson and Thoreau, to join Brook Farm, but she often visited the community. Horace Greeley was so attracted by the intelligence and vivid personality of the young woman that he took her to New York to live in his family and write literary criticism for *The Tribune.* The work that she did here was fully as good as the best critical writing then being done in this country. Her adverse comments on Longfellow cost her friends among the Harvard group, but she was generally looked upon as an authority on contemporary European literature.

In 1846 she went to Europe where she served for a while as a foreign correspondent for the *Tribune*. She met many of the writers whose works she had read with so much pleasure, and at Rome met Mazzini and the other members of the Italian revolutionary party. She was in Rome during the uprising of 1848, and had charge of one of the hospitals during the siege. Here she married Count Ossoli. Upon her return voyage to America she was drowned together with her husband and small son.

Like Alcott Margaret Fuller was more of a personal influence than a literary figure. Her striking personality and her allegiance to so many causes and intellectual movements made her the most prominent woman of her time. Her early death removed the influence of her commanding presence but did not still the slanders and innuendoes of her enemies. As a result the reputation of the woman tends to vary from the fantastic to the disreputable. The real Margaret Fuller must be studied in connection with the ferment of her age. To the multitudinous activities of Emerson, Thoreau, Parker, and Greeley she added the task of demonstrating to a skeptical world the fitness of woman for equality with men. This task was accomplished by the persuasive charm of her personality and conversation no less than by the possession of characteristics that made her the equal of Parker as the epitome of American romanticism.

THE DIAL

From 1840 to 1844 the Concord group published *The Dial*, a quarterly magazine of transcendentalism. Margaret Fuller was the editor for about two years, and Emerson succeeded her for the remainder of the time. Every prominent transcendentalist wrote for the periodical, giving it a most distinguished list of contributors. It was considered radical, just as the Concord group was radical, and the Harvard group, Longfellow, Holmes and their followers, did not publish anything in its pages. For a first-hand statement of transcendental interests the historian of to-day can go to no better source than *The Dial*. The very number of contributors insures the expression of various points of view, a thing that is not certain in an essay or book written by one author.

Reform and the Reformers

The general significance and manifestations of the romantic reform movement have already been discussed. It remains only to mention briefly one of the curious products of reform and to speak of a few of the most notable reformers who made their influence felt in literature.

Perfectionism.—Calvinism has for two of its main doctrines a belief in the depravity of human nature and a firm disbelief in the possibility of progress. When the romantic revolution rejected both these dogmas and caused the liberal churches to substitute a belief in the goodness of human nature and in the possibility of progress, it was only a matter of time until some idealist would set up the doctrine of the possibility of moral perfection here on earth and the consequent abolition of sin from human society. This doctrine was announced by John Humphrey Noyes (1811-1886).

While Noyes was a student at Yale he became convinced of the possibility of moral perfection and declared to the horror of the orthodox that he was then living a sinless life. For his audacious heresy he was expelled from his seminary, barred from the pulpit, and dropped from the church roll. Determined in his way of thinking, he went to his old home at Putney, Vermont, where he preached his peculiar doctrines, at first quietly but, as his followers increased, with greater ardor. Soon he had around him a considerable number of disciples.

The implications of perfectionism are staggering. A person who is living a perfect life is incapable of sinning, according to Noyes, and his contention was that a state of perfection once reached could not be lost through any act. Therefore, any person who is perfect is absolutely freed from the domination of any law, command, custom, or institution. Such a person is a law unto himself. He is his own interpreter of moral law, for any admission that the views of others are binding upon him would be an admission that some one else was more perfect than he. The perfectionist disregards the law of the state, for such a law is founded upon force or at least upon majority will. Thus perfectionism implies a condition of complete social and political anarchy.

Nothing speaks more eloquently of the height reached by the reform movement and the open-mindedness of Americans during the thirties and the forties than the fact that these amazing doctrines were not laughed out of existence by "right-thinking" people. As a matter of fact Noyes made many converts, some of them in high places. Garrison became attached to the perfectionist theories, largely because Noyes stressed the abolition of churches along with all institutions that might ever attempt to guide the individual. In short perfectionism wiped the slate clean and began its reconstruction of society with no other aim than the removal of all possible restrictions on the perfect man.

Obviously such a doctrine could receive fair trial in this far-from-perfect world only in a community where those perfected in the faith could live undisturbed by the worldly. Noyes saw this and began a community near Putney where the members could live according to their beliefs. In this community private property was unknown, the private home did not exist, the presence of the political state was unacknowledged, and all laws, ethical considerations, and moral codes were declared null and void. In spite of the absence of many institutions that society has known for long, the followers of Noyes were declared to be quiet, very peaceable, industrious, and intensely religious.

Opposition to the perfectionists developed in the village of Putney, and Noyes led his followers to Oneida, New York, where he founded the famous Oneida community that had so long and so flourishing an existence. Noyes avoided the economic mistake that so many American communists made, for he relied slightly on agriculture as the economic basis of his community. He early introduced manufacturing and gradually evolved an industrial system that was admirably suited to such a group. After the Civil War, financial troubles never gave any further concern. Oneida was disbanded as a communism in 1879, but it still flourishes as a joint stock company.

Perfectionism merely carried to a logical conclusion many of the views and movements current in New England. Nearly all of the writers of the day came into contact with this strange, subversive doctrine, but few of them showed deep influence. The whole question of perfectionism is worthy of serious study, because the work of Noyes is a symptom of a widespread feeling that underlay much New England thinking.

WILLIAM LLOYD GARRISON

(1805-1879)

It should be borne in mind that the abolition of slavery was not the only reform proposed during the hectic years preceding the Civil War. It is true that abolition was probably the most important, certainly the most conspicuous, reform, but there were literally dozens of others, and very few of the reformers limited themselves to one cause. Those who were conspicuous in the ranks of the abolitionists could be found on occasion promulgating temperance, woman's rights, peace, or some other proposal, though each reformer usually had a main issue with a large number of sidelines.

Garrison and Abolition.—The most strident and insistent voice lifted against the institution of slavery in the United States was that of William Lloyd Garrison, one of our few really great propagandists and journalists. Born in Massachusetts of miserably poor parents, he educated himself before the type-case in a newspaper office. Nature gave him a social conscience that would not hold its peace before any moral wrong, and a courage that rendered him immune to threats and intimidation. He perfected himself in the art of writing vivid, denunciatory English until his pen was feared more than that of any other man. With these qualifications, but without money, friends, or influence, Garrison flung himself upon the oldest and the most strongly entrenched social wrong in America.

After serving an apprenticeship in a newspaper office and a term in the Baltimore jail for criticizing a Massachusetts slave dealer, he founded *The Liberator* in 1831 to preach the violently unpopular doctrine of abolition. Entirely repudiated by his own town and state, he kept doggedly at his work even though he was mobbed and almost killed in 1835 by a crowd of respectable Boston business and professional men. The southern states offered rewards for his delivery into the hands of their authorities, but still he kept indomitably at his self-chosen task. Slowly the sublime audacity of the man and his insistent calls to the humanitarianism of his readers won attention and converts to his cause. Other leaders came up, like Wendell Phillips, who shared the burden of leading the cause, and soon Garrison was at the head of determined and well-organized groups of men and women who preached the gospel of abolition without ceasing. By 1840 the movement had gained the semblance of respectability, and by 1850 its work was done when the social conscience of the North became pretty well aroused. From that time the moral issue was superseded by the economic, and the appeal to the conscience was abandoned for political action at the polls. From this time the influence of Garrison declined, but he published an issue of *The Liberator* every week until the close of the Civil War.

As a propagandist and journalist Garrison rivals the best ever produced in America. By his very insistence he made people listen to his plea, by his fierce invective and fiery appeals to the moral sense of his readers he made converts of people who disliked him, but as a steady leader of a great popular movement he was impossible. And it was his very finest characteristics that made him impossible, his idealism, his crusading spirit, and his habit of thinking of moral questions far in advance of the thought of his time. But for thirty-five years *The Liberator* called men to repent of the grievous sin of slavery, and at the end of its days the sin was no more. In his first number Garrison had said:

I am aware that many object to the severity of my language; but is there not cause for severity? I will be as harsh as truth, and as uncompromising as justice. On this subject, I do not wish to think, speak or write with moderation. . . . I am in earnest—I will not equivocate—I will not excuse—I will not retreat a single inch—and I will be heard.

General Characteristics.—As a political theorist Garrison was an extreme idealist. He based his whole politics on the Jeffersonian doctrine that all men are created equal and endowed with certain inalienable rights, and he thought that the proper place for the exercise of these rights was within a state whose powers were almost at the vanishing point. In fact after he met John Humphrey Noyes he accepted the perfectionist view that the state was an impertinent meddler in the affairs of an individual. Furthermore he was bitterly hostile to the political organizations existing in this country because all of them allowed or recognized slavery. Because of this fact, as well as because of his perfectionism, he spent much of his life in sharp opposition to all political organizations. At one time in the heat of the anti-slavery controversy he publicly denounced the Constitution as "a covenant of death and an agreement with Hell." His idealism blossomed in the philosophical anarchy of Thoreau and of perfectionism.

However, Garrison was no political theorist; he was a moralist

Political expediency meant less than nothing at all to the great abolitionist; economic arguments infuriated him. Nothing mattered to him save the moral question involved. Harsh, unyielding, intolerant, violent, he might be called, but he was fighting an evil that had all the unlovely traits attributed to him, and he was striving to awake a public conscience that much preferred to slumber. Against such odds it is no wonder that his voice reached a strident pitch or that his temper frequently escaped control. He set his face against evil, and he would not be deterred. For three decades he was an Old Testament prophet, striding gauntly through the pleasant New England scene armed with the lash of truth and justice, and when he struck, he cared not whom he punished.

But it is unfair to Garrison to present him solely as a lash of righteousness laid in anger upon the shoulders of the sinful. He was literally forced into his extreme and violent outbursts because of his deep love for humanity—a love that could not tolerate the thought of men suffering in human bondage. At the top of the first page of *The Liberator* he always carried a short motto borrowed from Thomas Paine, "Our country is the world—our countrymen all mankind." Underneath the harshness of the Hebraic prophet was a heart that beat with tenderness and pity for humanity, and not the least notable thing about Garrison is the fact that he could make the hearts of others beat in unison with his own.

JOHN GREENLEAF WHITTIER

(1807-1892)

The fame of Garrison must of necessity be largely historical, for he wrote almost exclusively for the cause of abolition, and when the Emancipation Proclamation freed the slaves, his writings lost their appeal. On the other hand, Whittier, the poet of abolition, wrote a large number of poems that reflect the life of rural New England, and upon these rests his permanent reputation in American literature. However important historically the anti-slavery poems may be, they are all occasional, and when the specific occasion passed for which they were written, much of their interest perished. To the contrary, such a poem as "Snow-Bound" can never lose its interest so long as our taste allows us to enjoy the quiet and restrained presentation of simple life.

Whittier the Abolitionist.—Whittier came of a long line of Quaker ancestors, who accepted literally the doctrine of the inner light as the only true guide to one's own action. This inner light was thought of as a bit of the divine spirit dwelling within man. Thus if all men are in constant communion with an immediate deity, all are equal in the most important sense. Furthermore the adherents of Quakerism are extreme individualists, fully tolerant of all other men and views, and wholly opposed to the use of force in any way. All these characteristics Whittier possessed as the heritage from his family. The abolition controversy often put a great strain on the doctrine of non-resistance, but throughout all the bitter struggle, the poet's personal attitude was one of gentle kindness.

As a boy he received little education, a misfortune that undoubtedly did much to restrict the scope of his interests and performance. Evidently one of the strongest educational influences was the reading of a volume of Burns. The warm humanitarianism and the deep love for simple rustic life in the pages of the Scotch poet left their mark on much of Whittier's work. The Quaker farm-boy began to write poetry early and had his first verses published in a paper edited by William Lloyd Garrison. In 1831 came his book, *Legends of New England,* the first volume of poetry published in the New England Renaissance. He became an editor and practical politician, and for a time contemplated a political career. This he resolutely put behind him in 1833 when he publicly avowed abolition sentiments. In that year he published a little volume of prose, *Justice and Expediency,* and signed the Anti-slavery Declaration. From this time on he was wholly allied with the abolitionists.

He broke early with Garrison and the more radical reformers on the question of political action. Garrison, as we have seen, was a perfectionist anarchist. Whittier, believing in the divine guidance of the inner light, naturally thought that elections could be made the voice of God, if only people would hearken to the spiritual voice within each one. Acting upon this belief he became one of the founders of the Liberty party that developed into the Free Soilers and later into the Republican party.

Whittier's abolition poetry comprises the greater part of all that he wrote, but few of the titles are read to-day. The stanzas to Garrison and "Massachusetts to Virginia" are assured of an immortality in our anthologies, but "Ichabod" deserves a higher place. This poem is a stinging rebuke to Webster when the Massachusetts senator temporized with the slave power and made his infamous Seventh of March speech in advocacy of the fugitive slave law. It is hard to think of a more searing poetic censure than Whittier compressed in nine short stanzas. The poem is all the more blasting for its Quaker-like quiet and restraint. Not a bad-tempered line or a word of vituperation mars the rebuke. It comes from the pure heart of a man moved to deep righteous indignation and heavily burdened with sorrow and disappointment. Of its kind our literature has nothing finer. Certainly nothing that Whittier wrote better shows the spirit of the Quaker-reformer.

Whittier as a Poet of New England.—All through the abolition controversy Whittier was writing poetry of New England, and when the Civil War closed he sat down to write his one undisputed masterpiece, "Snow-Bound." In the last lines of the poem the author gives his work its best characterization, "Flemish pictures of old days," for it is a quiet and homely presentation of a New England landscape and household during a snowstorm. The charming intimate descriptions of the people and of the life that they led have won the praise of successive generations of readers, and by none has it been more lauded than by those who best knew the life depicted. The idyllic rural note in our literature just about reaches its truest pitch in this poem.

The other New England pieces by Whittier are not uniformly good. "Skipper Ireson's Ride" has a note of crude authenticity about it that makes it very attractive to many people. "Cassandra Southwick" and "Amy Wentworth" have been much admired, but the famous "Maud Muller" is simply a poor poem with scarcely a redeeming feature. "The Barefoot Boy" has found its true level in our school readers, though it contains lines that indicate the poet's native democracy. "Telling the Bees" is a graceful account of an old New England custom, and "The Huskers" with its closing section known as "The Corn Song" is another interpretation of the farm life that the poet knew so well. Whittier was a self-trained man, but he totally neglected to train himself in the art of self-criticism. As a result his poetry, especially that dealing with his own life, displays a wide variety of excellence. However, at his best no one has approached him as the poet of rural New England.

Whittier's intensely religious spirit frequently found outlet in poetry. Some of this work is so good that it seems to occupy a permanent place in our hymnals. "Laus Deo" is an outburst of religious joy upon the ratification of the constitutional amendment abolishing slavery. It is probably the best of the religious poems.

"Margaret Smith's Journal."—Whittier's prose work that seems likely to live longest is a little book called *Leaves from Margaret Smith's Journal of the Province of Massachusetts Bay.* This is an understanding and illuminating account of the life in Massachusetts in 1678 written from the standpoint of the gentle Quakers who were subject to great hardships and punishments. Recent investigation into the social history of the colony shows that Whittier's understanding of conditions was extraordinarily acute and accurate. This book is worth reading for the expression of the Quaker spirit if not for the social history that it contains.

General Characteristics.—Although Whittier belongs squarely in the heart of the romantic movement by virtue of his mystical conception of human nature and of democracy, his reform activities, and his deep interest in the humble life, it is probable that at least part of his work is not so hopelessly outmoded as is that of some of his contemporaries. The present-day interest in the lives of our ancestors and our admiration for records of the humble life of the past will pretty surely give such poems as "Snow-Bound" a long if not a permanent place in our literature. Certainly there are parts of the New England idyll that ought not to be forgotten.

It is useless however to try to make out that Whittier is a great poet or even one of America's major figures. His place is among the minor writers who have presented with truth and feeling the limited experiences that were theirs. His note is true, but it is never the utterance of a great poet. His feeling is often deep and sincere, but it is not the feeling of a sensitive artist of the first rank.

MRS. HARRIET BEECHER STOWE

(1811-1896)

Mrs. Harriet Beecher Stowe shows as clearly as any of our writers do what happened when the original Puritan spirit of old New England once became convinced that a social institution was morally wrong. Mrs. Stowe was of the sternest Calvinistic stock. Her father was Lyman Beecher, a redoubtable defender of orthodoxy in Boston when the Unitarians were carrying all before them; her brother was Henry Ward Beecher, the most successful emotional preacher of the time, whose sensational methods never kept him from preserving at least the name of orthodoxy; her husband was Calvin Stowe, a more scholarly man than Lyman Beecher and even more firmly rooted in the Calvinism of the past. Old time Puritanism was in the very air that the woman breathed.

Lyman Beecher took his college training under the famous guardian of orthodoxy, Timothy Dwight, and began preaching in Connecticut, the most conservative of all the states. He so distinguished himself by his opposition to all religious and political liberalism that in 1826 he was invited to Boston to combat the Unitarians on their home ground. He left there in 1832, without having achieved notable success, to assume the presidency of Lane Theological Seminary in Cincinnati. Harriet went to the West along with the remainder of the family. Here she was married to Dr. Stowe in 1836, and in the following years became busied with the care of many children. During this time she had a good chance to observe slavery at close hand, for although Ohio was free territory, Kentucky with its thousands of slaves lay just across the river. Mrs. Stowe went with her husband in 1850 to Maine, where he had accepted a position in Bowdoin College.

"Uncle Tom's Cabin."—1850 was the date of the fugitive slave law, and it was this law that loosed Mrs. Stowe's wrath against slavery. During 1851 and part of 1852 she wrote *Uncle Tom's Cabin,* publishing it in the latter year. It was the most effective emotional protest ever made against slavery. This book visualized the evils of the system for northern readers who had been only momentarily stirred by Garrison, Phillips, Whittier, and the other agitators. Mrs. Stowe dramatized the sorrows of negroes and the inhumanity of the institution so vividly that she did more to arouse public sentiment than any other one agitator was able to accomplish. Without the passage of the fugitive slave law that set off the explosion of Puritanical morality in Mrs. Stowe, the North might have remained unmoved against slavery until economic and political pressure became unendurable.

The faults and excellencies of *Uncle Tom's Cabin* are easy to enumerate. A hurried reading, however superficial, will show one that the book is carelessly written and hopelessly sentimental. No one could be expected to produce a faultless book with six children clamoring for attention. Besides, it was a first novel, although the author had written a collection of sketches almost ten years previously. But the major flaw in the book is its excessive sentimentality. It literally wallows in tears. There is no subterfuge and no artistry about appealing to the simplest emotions of the reader, but a direct attempt to touch one's sympathy. Naturally the writer overstresses her case, exaggerates the conditions that she was attempting to depict, and creates her characters by so simple a method that they become mere outlines of human beings and not persons of flesh and blood.

Every one who has read the novel must have been struck by the fact that the characters are types and not individuals. Uncle Tom is not an individual negro but the typical faithful slave. Little Eva is not a personality but a type of innocence. Simon Legree is the typical villain. In drawing her characters thus Mrs. Stowe did a common thing among American novelists. Types are more easily handled than are individuals, and the reader grasps their significance without effort. It is especially desirable to use them when the writer is interested in imparting an idea rather than in creating character. Since the American novelist has been very much interested in promoting ideas, the type has not passed, for some authors use their characters to illustrate psychological cases or laws. Hence all individualizing traits are omitted.

However, some of the very faults of the book assisted in its successful appeal. The aim of the book was to create a moral revulsion, an emotional protest, against slavery. If the book had not been sentimental, it would not have appealed to the millions who read it only to become embittered against slavery. If the characters had been fully drawn, the average reader would have been so lost in a maze of psychological subtleties that he would have missed the aim of the writer. If there had been no exaggeration in the novel, its appeal would have been greatly curtailed, for the emotions of many are aroused only by a vigorous shaking. But above all these weaknesses that turned out to be strong points there is one characteristic that unquestionably made for success. That was the human element, the elusive quality that makes people interested in the actions and fate of characters. This quality *Uncle Tom's Cabin* had in abundance.

Uncle Tom's Cabin is our first well-known sociological novel. Its aim was the remedying of a social wrong, and its method was the method of socially minded writers of more recent days. It is interesting to compare this book with other sociological studies like *The Jungle* by Upton Sinclair or Ernest Poole's *The Harbor*, and note similarities and contrasts. Bearing in mind that Mrs. Stowe wrote more than fifty years earlier than the other two novelists, the modern reader has no trouble in awarding her a high rank for her emotional study of slavery.

Mrs. Stowe as a Novelist of New England.—Just as Whittier turned aside from the writing of abolition poetry to the description of New England life, so did Mrs. Stowe proceed from *Uncle Tom's Cabin* and its successor *Dred,* a more reasoned anti-slavery argument, to a series of novels that lovingly displayed the homely virtues of Puritan New England. Probably the best known of these is *Old Town Folks,* a sketchy composition with many effective chapters that was composed from the boyhood recollections of the writer's husband. Another is *Poganuc People,* a similar book made up of Mrs. Stowe's own recollections. Still another is *The Minister's Wooing,* a romance written about a personally likeable Puritan minister who preached the most amazingly terrifying theology and practiced the friendliest and most charming manners in his personal relations. In all these books Mrs. Stowe displays a fine sense of humor and a sensitive feeling in her search for the human qualities of the Puritans whose worst side was exhibited in their harsh and crabbed theology. It is doubtful if Mrs. Stowe would have attracted a large audience by these works, but her position as a competent American novelist would be just as high to-day if she had never written her anti-slavery stories.

To say that Mrs. Stowe is a competent novelist is dismissing her without excessive praise. Her emotional argument against slavery is crude, but the next novel, *Dred,* is much better done, and the New England stories are extremely well written. *Oldtown Folks* and *Poganuc People* have just the right to remain in American literature that "Snow-Bound" has. All are made from the same cloth, and that cloth was woven of the life of old New England.

THE GENTEEL TRADITION OF NEW ENGLAND

Custom, sanctioned by school histories of literature, dumps Emerson, Thoreau, Mrs. Stowe, Whittier, Longfellow, Lowell, and Holmes into one large category and names them "The New England Writers." The attributing of all these figures to New England cannot be very successfully impeached, but certainly geography is the only thing that they all have in common. The ideas of Emerson resembled those of Longfellow about as much as the democracy of Calhoun resembled that of Lincoln. Thoreau and Holmes were about as much alike as were Davy Crockett and Cooper. It is quite necessary to distinguish between the transcendentalists and reformers of New England and the members of the genteel school, Lowell, Longfellow, and Holmes, nor need the distinction be a fine one, for the differences are clear to any one who can read.

The Brahmins, as the New England aristocrats are called, have always held themselves aloof from the middle-class Yankees. Family connections, money, and culture have long been considered the hallmark of Brahmin respectability. Behind this triple protection the upper class of New England society developed its inviolable code of customs and prejudices beside which it tests all things to determine if they are "respectable." The touchstone of this respectability is the possession of good manners, a genuine but frigid culture, a scrupulous regard for appearances, and a genteel determination to admit the existence of nothing unpleasant. To the representatives of Brahminism, truth, to be acceptable, was required to stop short of the disconcerting or unpleasant fact, justice as a matter of social expediency ought not to violate any of the sacred taboos, and although it was theoretically desirable to see "God's justice erected into human law," it was not expected that any gentleman should demean himself by insisting too strongly that immediate steps be taken to effect the desirable end.

Naturally the transcendentalists and reformers were too far from conforming to the Brahmin code to be acceptable in the high places of Harvard society or in the frigidly correct drawing rooms of the best Boston society. In 1838 Emerson gave the graduating class of the Harvard Divinity School an exposition of his idea of transcendental religion. It was one of his epoch-making utterances, but the result was that for almost thirty years thereafter he was not invited to speak on the campus of his university, although during that time he was the tonic moral influence of all America and one of our most popular lecturers. Thoreau angrily accused Lowell, one of the chiefest of Brahmins, of trying to blue-pencil one of his essays, and Lowell retaliated, after the death of Thoreau, in a critical appraisal that is the very essence of priggish misunderstanding. Theodore Parker was never admitted to the inner circle of Boston respectability, and down to our own generation there are detractors who deplore the man's "bad manners" and "intemperate speech," criticisms that imply that Parker excoriated evil, all apologists for evil, and especially those who closed their eyes and declared that they saw no evil. Garrison was the most unpopular man in New England—though Alcott, Parker, and Emerson all claimed the same distinction; his manners were "bad." Wendell Phillips, the great orator of abolition, was the cause of much disappointment and sorrow among the Brahmins, for he deliberately deserted the upper class into which he was born and espoused the cause of noisy and "intemperate" reform movements. After the Civil War the survivors of New England romanticism met on a common footing, for Thoreau and Hawthorne were dead, Melville and Alcott were in abeyance, Garrison and the reform movement were extinct volcanoes, and Emerson's individualism had been dulled by the passage of years. Longfellow and Lowell could afford to treat the survivors of the war and the industrial triumph with condescending respect; the genteel tradition was well established in New England, and all America was taking its literary cue from Boston.

However, the Genteel Tradition in letters had not been immune to the romantic revolution. It exalted a European background, but it insisted that such a background consist more of romantic legends and picturesque landscapes than of the ebullient romanticisms of French revolutionary philosophy or the spiny individualism of Godwin and Shelley. Rousseau's appeal to Longfellow would have been negative, for the Frenchman warmly advocated the disavowal of the man-made culture that the Harvard professor found so comfortable and the substitution of a state of natural culture and equality, an idea abhorrent to the Brahmin. Europe was admitted to be the mother of our civilization, but European culture to be acceptable in Boston had to be carefully selected and thoroughly denaturized. The Genteel Tradition accepted the optimism of romanticism, but washed out the buoyant jauntiness of Emerson and Whitman to a pallid hope that all would be well in due season if no one offended the sacred taboos. The guardians of the genteel, however, did accept the romantic version of religion in the shape of conservative Unitarianism, for old-time Calvinism insisted on the very unpleasant fact that ninety per cent of men were to be everlastingly lost without regard to wealth or social status, and, as some wit has remarked, the Brahmins cheerfully insisted that they were too good to be damned. Unitarian the Brahmins were, for it was highly respectable to follow Channing and the other early romantics into the way of genteel religion, but Parker was wholly without the pale because of his insistence upon interpreting questions of everyday politics and economics in terms of religion. The genteel could not echo Channing's remark concerning Parker, "Let the full heart pour itself forth," for the possession of a full heart implies the presence of an ecstasy that may disregard the canons of "respectability." In short, the Genteel Tradition was romantic, but it demanded that its romanticism never disagreeably disturb the placid gentility of Brahminism by insisting upon a new way of life.

HENRY WADSWORTH LONGFELLOW

(1807-1882)

In Longfellow New England Brahminism probably gave us its best product. He was born in Portland, Maine, of a well-to-do and strongly Federalist family. During his undergraduate days at Bowdoin, he showed such aptitude for foreign language and literature that the college offered him a professorship of modern language. In preparation for his work he spent three years in Europe, where he joyously discovered the picturesque legends and literature of the Continental countries. Returning to America he taught for a time at Bowdoin, leaving his alma mater to accept a chair at Harvard. A second trip to Europe gave him a fuller knowledge of his beloved field and led him into a study of the minor German writers whose sentimentalism greatly appealed to him. Upon his return to America he established his residence in Cambridge near the Harvard campus, where he lived for the remainder of his life. A second marriage in 1843 brought him wealth, domestic happiness, and an assured entrance into the best circles of Boston.

There is no question about the popularity of Longfellow. He has even yet more readers than any other American poet can boast. During his lifetime his books sold as well in England as did those of Tennyson, and on the Continent he is read by school children from Paris to Constantinople, from Madrid to Leningrad. The reasons for this appeal to the general reader are not hard to find. Longfellow makes no demand upon the intellectual powers of his audience; every idea is as easily grasped as are those of the Grimm brothers and Hans Christian Andersen. Again, his poems are always of the types that attract ordinary people. One of his favorite forms is that of a simple narrative, the story of which trips easily and gracefully along with the pleasant rhyme; another form is the didactic poem that urges the reader to practice one of the simple obvious virtues. However naïve "The Psalm of Life" may be, it is pretty sure to retain its place in our anthologies and school readers so long as our people want their moralizing "done up in neat packages and tied with rhymes." The very weaknesses of Longfellow—his lack of ideas, his child-like simplicity, and his detachment from the deep and awesome problems of human life, all become elements of genuine strength in his appeal to the common men.

It is as the poet of childhood and of the unsophisticated reader that Longfellow must take his place in literature, and a high place it is. However, to praise the poet for having written virtually all his work within the grasp of the grade school student is not all praise. Such a poem as "Paul Revere's Ride" was aimed at the child reader, as were many others, but certain works like "Evangeline" that have since been taken over by children were written for mature readers. To write a poem expressly for a child is one thing, but to write a poem for mature readers and have it settle down to the level of the seventh-grade boy is quite another. But when all the adverse comments are over, it remains to be said that Longfellow is a part of the democratic culture of England and America, whatever that culture may be worth.

Longfellow did a great service to his own time in making Americans acquainted with certain phases of European literature. Especially successful was he in his adaptations and translations of popular ballads from almost all nations of the Continent. He was the Chautauqua of his time. He brought culture to the stay-at-homes, not a very impressive culture, to be sure, not intellectual or disturbing to the petty round of duty that makes up life, but pleasant and gently insistent upon the homely virtues. Recent critics of Longfellow, searching diligently for something pleasant to say about our best known poet, have settled upon the sonnets with something like a sigh of relief. Certainly these poems can be praised with little reservation, especially those prefaced to the translation of Dante's *The Divine Comedy*. However, a comparison of these sonnets with Miss Millay's "Euclid Alone Hath Looked on Beauty Bare" leaves the impression that Longfellow was hopelessly bookish. An attempt to compare him favorably with the great sonneteers of England may have a most laudable patriotic motive, but it certainly lacks convincing critical support.

It is probable that bookishness, as much as lack of deep spiritual interests, kept Longfellow from achieving a higher place in poetry. His references to nature are all taken from books and not from the sky and the fields and the moving water. His best poems reflect something that he has read and not something that he has felt. Professor Barrett Wendell expressed this criticism when, speaking of the academic note in Longfellow's anti-slavery poems, he said: "One may fairly doubt whether in all anti-slavery literature there is a more humorous example of the way in which philanthropic dreamers often constructed negroes by the simple process of daubing their own faces with burnt cork." The only criticism of the statement is that Longfellow did not daub his own face with black to create his poetic slave; that method would have put too much of the personal element into the poem to suit the gentle poet. He merely used a black man that he had been reading about. Almost the clinching argument in favor of Longfellow's overwhelming bookishness is to be found in his great number of translations that culminated in a new version of *The Divine Comedy*. Usually poets who can draw upon their own lives for material do not need to translate; they have in their souls more poetry than they can ever write in a lifetime. It seems that Longfellow must go down in American literature as a minor poet who generally used insignificant material for his verses. There are adventures of the human soul that never were Longfellow's. Not for him were the heights and depths of passion, righteous indignation, leaden-eyed despair, tumultuous ecstasy, or even the all-inclusive pity that blossoms as gentle humanitarianism. All his emotions were second hand, bookish. For that reason he is read to-day most by those whose experiences have been limited or whose capacity for reflective thought is slight.

OLIVER WENDELL HOLMES

(1809-1894)

As a town wit whose reputation has become national and as a creator of light poetry, *vers de société*, Oliver Wendell Holmes stands without a serious rival in our literature. He was the perfect columnist, who, if he were alive to-day, would revel in the conducting of a humorous column in a daily paper, like "The Conning Tower" of F. P. Adams. But Dr. Holmes lived before the days of personally conducted columns, and since he was too much given to jesting to attempt much literature on the grand scale and too serious-minded to sit down in his club and spend his life in delightful conversation, he never quite found his element. He wrote much light poetry, gave innumerable after-dinner speeches with most felicitous results, and in the Breakfast Table series put several hundred pages of conversation into print. The mutual admiration society that the Boston writers became after the Civil War extolled Holmes as a major figure, and it has remained for the present century to undertake the ungracious task of deflating his reputation. To-day we rank him very high in his chosen field of literature, but it is surely not unkind to remember that one does not discuss a town wit as if he were a Shakespeare or even an Emerson.

Like Longfellow, Holmes led a life too much sheltered from the intellectual breezes that were disturbing New England. He was born in Boston of a good family and received his degree from Harvard. After some indecision he studied medicine, rounding off his education with two and a half years in Paris. Upon his return to this country he taught for a time in Dartmouth, and beginning in 1847 he was for thirty-five years professor of anatomy and hygiene in the Harvard medical school. Holmes was happy in his work, in his domestic relations, and in his social contacts. To him Boston was in all seriousness the hub of the universe, and the Saturday Club, a social organization of distinguished men, was the very center of the hub. Never a ripple, save that of kindly laughter, marred the current of his life. Romantic idealism meant nothing more than the subject of a clever jest.

Holmes's reputation seems to-day to rest upon a few poems and *The Autocrat of the Breakfast Table*. Time and critics uninfluenced by the genial doctor's winning personality have not dealt kindly with the novels and the later volumes of the Breakfast Table series. The poems that are best known, save the favorite "Chambered Nautilus," are usually humorous or occasional. Holmes was in steady demand as a poet for class dinners and similar functions, and some of his happiest verse owes its inception to social obligations. Among the best known poems are "The Last Leaf," "The Boys," "The Height of the Ridiculous," "The Ballad of the Oysterman," and "The Deacon's Masterpiece." The last was published in the pages of *The Autocrat of the Breakfast Table*.

As a humorist Holmes has all the characteristics and all the tricks of the columnist. He likes witty epigrams, verse with a smile in it, clever retorts, nor is he above employing a pun. His humor is quite without a sting, just as one would expect a poem or story to be that was composed with the idea of amusing every person present in a crowd. If he had been a satirist intent on chastising some of the follies or vices of society, his humor would not have had its pleasant flavor. Humor rightly employed is one of the most effective social weapons. Dr. Holmes never so employed his wit. He was content to make his readers smile. Reform he left to other hands.

Holmes never carried his romanticism very far, save in the field of religion. The son of a minister, he was unalterably against the system of elder Calvinism, and for this outworn body of dogma he reserved the sharpest of his darts, and even they left slight stings as any one can see who reads "The Deacon's Masterpiece." As a physician he brought to a discussion of religion a certain flavor of rationalism that reminds one more of the eighteenth century than of the romantic period. Rationalism was not the only connection that Holmes had with the time of Pope and Queen Anne. He doted on the town wit style of the eighteenth century, on the pleasant but artificial society of the period that chatted its leisurely way through the years, and on the polished light verse of the time that frequently became clever. As a boy he read Pope's translation of Homer, and the finished charm of the verse and the urbanity of style gave him a lasting taste for the age that produced it.

JAMES RUSSELL LOWELL

(1819-1891)

James Russell Lowell had more variety in his life and works than either Longfellow or Holmes could claim. He was born in the most correct circles of Brahminism where the political theory of Webster, the poetry of Pope, and the easy theology of moderate Unitarianism were alike accepted as superlative achievements in their respective fields. But in the "roaring forties" he ventured out of his sheltered haven and for more than a decade took all the stormy winds of New England romanticism. By the time of the Civil War his romantic inclinations had effervesced, and his last thirty years were spent in a complacent contemplation of the Genteel Tradition and all its works.

The Lowells have long been prominent in the affairs of Boston and Massachusetts. Of James Russell Lowell's immediate family, the grandfather was a leading patriot in revolutionary days, the father occupied one of the important Unitarian pulpits of Boston, one uncle was an influential Federalist, and still another founded and gave his name to the factory city. A family of more dignity and honor it would have been hard to find in all Brahminism. After his graduation from Harvard in 1838, James Russell Lowell deserted the comfortable precincts where his name meant so much and cast his lot for a time with the reformers and romantic idealists who were filling New England with so great a clamor. In 1840 he met Maria White, poet, mild transcendentalist, and ardent abolitionist, who had by all accounts the better mind of the two, and under her tutelage he busied himself for more than a dozen years with the varied intellectual activities that were adding zest to Massachusetts life. He never became a transcendentalist, but abolition claimed a prompt and warm adherence. During these years he wrote the poems by which he is best known and a considerable amount of fiery prose that he later repudiated. Lowell and Maria White were married in 1844. The next six years were his most productive period. By 1850 he was beginning to weary of reform, and after Mrs. Lowell's death in 1853 he swiftly declined to the placid indifference of his distinguished caste to social wrongs and proposed remedies.

In 1855 Lowell succeeded Longfellow as professor of modern language in Harvard, a position that he held for twenty years. After quitting Harvard he was American minister to Spain and then to England, serving eight years in the diplomatic service. His last days were spent at Elmwood, his ancestral home in Cambridge, where he presided as the dean of American letters and issued his pontifical edicts on all questions of the day, civic as well as literary. When he died in 1891 the twilight of American romanticism was past. Knocking at the door stood a new generation whose literary taste was formed on French and Russian realism and whose social and economic philosophy drew from sources utterly repugnant to the genteel. The early romanticism had passed in the triumph of industrialism, and with the death of Lowell even the Genteel Tradition was rapidly to become submerged under the flood of new ideas that poured into this country from 1885 to 1917. The passing of Lowell meant the passing of an age.

Lowell as a Poet.—Lowell enjoyed his great poetic year in 1848 when he published "The Vision of Sir Launfal," "A Fable for

Critics," and the first series of "The Biglow Papers." These are the three poems by which he will probably keep his place in anthologies of American literature.

"The Vision of Sir Launfal" is a thoroughly romantic production. It is a bit of New England moralizing placed in the form of a medieval legend and framed in some really good descriptive poetry of nature. The two preludes still retain their cultivated admirers and it is probable that many more generations of school children will be required to memorize the famous lines celebrating the perfection of a June day. Like so much of the poetry of the New England Renaissance, "Sir Launfal" is rarely read for the first time by the mature person; its place is in the upper grades or the first years of high-school training. As a poem for that class of readers it is surely one of the most successful in our literature.

In "A Fable for Critics" Lowell pays his respects in two thousand lines of poetry to all the contemporary writers, not overlooking himself. Lines from this poem are quoted whenever early American criticism is discussed. These are a few of the best known passages:

> There is Bryant, as quiet, as cool, and as dignified
> As a smooth, silent iceberg, that never is ignified,
> Save when by reflection 'tis kindled o' nights
> With a semblance of flame by the chill Northern Lights.

> If I call him an iceberg, I don't mean to say
> There is nothing in that which is grand in its way;
> He is almost the one of your poets who knows
> How much grace, strength and dignity lie in Repose.

> There is Hawthorne, with genius so shrinking and rare
> That you hardly at first see the strength that is there;
> A frame so robust, with a nature so sweet,
> .   .   .   .
> Is worth a descent from Olympus to meet.

> There comes Poe, with his raven, like Barnaby Rudge,
> Three-fifths of him genius, the two-fifths sheer fudge.

> There is Whittier, whose swelling and vehement heart
> Strains the strait-breasted drab of the Quaker apart.

Sometimes the humor is not so gentle as when the author pays his respects to Margaret Fuller, for that rather waspish lady had vigorously criticized him for certain poetic shortcomings, and Lowell was anxious to repay in her own coin.

"A Fable for Critics" is a medley of sophomoric poetry, clever wit, and sound sense. Some of the lines are inexcusably crude and amateurish, and others are excellent tabloid criticism. A drastic revision would have helped the poem, but Lowell never had the desirable quality of self-criticism. He wrote hurriedly under the impulse of momentary nervous energy, and when the burst of energy disappeared, there remained not even the ability to read critically what he had previously written.

The first series of "The Biglow Papers" seems to-day to be the best thing that Lowell ever did. The Mexican War aroused all the fighting abolition spirit that the poet possessed, and his indignation welled over in these poems that give in native Yankee dialect and mother wit the homely and pointed objections to foreign conquest for the benefit of the slave power. The second series, written at the time of the Civil War, has its effective moments, but as a whole it is inferior to the earlier production.

Some of the shorter poems of Lowell are general favorites. "The Present Crisis," a piece of rousing rhetoric inspired by the anti-slavery struggle, is still read and quoted. "To the Dandelion," "The First Snow-fall" and "The Shepherd of King Admetus" still have their places in collections of poetry, while some of the sonnets and "Rhoecus" are worthy of serious attention. The poems written after 1860, mostly occasional and commemorative verse, reflect far too plainly the author's feeling that he is expected to do something dignified and profound. The best of these is the Harvard "Commemoration Ode" with its justly admired tribute to Lincoln, but even this poem seems to-day to lack the dignity and effectiveness that once were so much praised. Formerly "The Cathedral" had many admirers, but it is significant that the most recent collections of American poetry for college use omit this effort.

Lowell as a Critic.—After 1855 Lowell gave more and more of his attention to critical work. During his twenty years at Harvard the most important of his essays dealt with literary subjects, but in the last period of his life he divided his time between literature and public questions.

As a literary critic Lowell is the subject of a considerable amount of contemporary debate. His detractors allege that he said nothing new, that his approach to literature was that of the cultured dilettante and not that of the scholar, and that he showed timidity and a lack of interest in his own age by sticking to the classical figures in literature rather than attempting an appraisal of less known writers. The charges can be substantiated. Most of the literary essays were dashed off during his teaching days as visible proof that the writer had not succumbed to his indolence. They were largely the material given to his undergraduate classes in Harvard. Now there is one test and one only of the classroom critic. He must always be judged by the success that he achieves in making his students want to read the literature that he talks about. The men who were in Lowell's classes testify to the interest in reading that their teacher inspired, but a good classroom lecture does not always make a permanent contribution to the subject under discussion. Lowell probably should not have published some of his essays. As lectures they were successful, but as printed studies they are not so highly regarded.

As a critic of contemporary questions Lowell can fairly be accused of achieving even slighter success than in his pronouncements on classical literature. The essay on Thoreau is a masterpiece of misunderstanding and muddleheaded thinking, but for forty years it blasted the fame of its subject, and even to-day our histories of literature show the effect of this essay by a consistent belittling of Thoreau and by a complete misinterpretation of the man's work. The publication of that essay was one of the many tragedies of American literature. Furthermore, as a contemporary critic Lowell had great limitations. For instance, he disliked and disregarded the work of Taine, the great French historian and critic of literature, one of whose critical contributions was the theory that literature is a direct product of race, time, and environment. To-day Taine is regarded as the founder of one of the schools of criticism, but Lowell gave the Frenchman's theories only a condescending notice followed by a curt dismissal.

In his discussion of public affairs Lowell resolutely set his face against innovation, contending that, while matters were not proceeding very satisfactorily, further tampering with social and economic questions might lead to disaster. The last twenty years of his life were spent in the Gilded Age, an era of unparalleled corruption in American public life. The small farmers of the West were vehemently pointing out the causes and cure of the ills that beset the body politic, and the workingmen of the cities were even more noisily directing attention to their grievances by the very effective use of strikes and boycotts. Lowell shut tight the doors of his study against the entrance of either faction. The agrarian agitation he condemned as the brazen efforts of dishonest men to get what was not rightfully theirs. The demands of labor found him as hostile; no use had he for the eight-hour day, but only a contempt for the man who "pretends to believe that eight is equal to ten." Agitation in England to extend the suffrage drew from him the grave warning that such a step might be attended by immediate danger. It has been said that Lowell's essays on political subjects are "indispensable to an American." They are quite indispensable to any one who wishes to see how strangely the idea of modern democracy can be perverted by the Brahmin brain.

It is probable that the trouble with Lowell's later utterances is the fact that our nation traveled too rapidly from 1855 to 1870 for the pace of a sedate professor. The triumph of industrialism and the Civil War loosed a welter of get-rich-quick enterprises and corrupt politics. Under the brazen leadership of such unlovely characters as Daniel Drew and Jim Fisk, American business dropped its pretensions to decency and became a thing dedicated to exploitation by the financial pirate who scuttled corporations and cut individual purse-strings with neither fear nor compunction. Corruption spread from our local and state governments to the higher circles of national administration. Lowell saw all this and was troubled. He was a high-minded man who desired most of all common decency in the conduct of affairs, and common decency was then the scarcest commodity in all America. In his confused search for a remedy for the distressing condition Lowell naturally went to the ideals of his class; for Brahminism, although not productive of many new ideas or conducive to rapid social progress, at least was honest and scrupulous of appearances. His rather nonplused suggestions for the bettering of society were never heard in the mad scramble that followed the Civil War.

SUGGESTED READINGS

Anthony: *Margaret Fuller.* New York. 1920.
    Psychological study. Intelligent.
Bazalgette: *Henry Thoreau: Bachelor of Nature.* New York. 1924.
    Gurgles ecstatically.

Bell: *Margaret Fuller.* New York. 1930.
> Gives many sidelights on other romantics.

Brooks: *Emerson and Others.* New York. 1927.

Brooks: *Life of Emerson.* New York. 1932.
> Not very satisfactory. R. L. Rusk is preparing a biography of Emerson which will probably be the standard work for many years.

Brooks: *The Flowering of New England.* New York. 1936.

Cabot: *Memoirs of Ralph Waldo Emerson.* Boston. 1887.

Canby: *Classic Americans.* New York. 1931.
> Contains chapters on the chief New England writers.

Canby: *Thoreau.* Boston. 1939.
> Despite the scholarship and clean writing, Thoreau never quite emerges as a human being.

Christy: *The Orient in American Transcendentalism.* New York. 1932.
> This valuable work is to be used with caution.

Commager: *Theodore Parker.* Boston. 1936.
> An excellent study. Minimizes the controversial aspects of Parker.

Dwight: *Letters from Brook Farm.* Poughkeepsie. 1928.
> Gives an excellent picture of everyday life at Brook Farm.

Emerson, Channing, and Clark: *Margaret Fuller Ossoli.* Out of print.
> This first estimate of Margaret Fuller was written by three of her friends. It has a certain quality that no subsequent biography has been able to recapture.

Foerster: *American Criticism.* Boston. 1928. Emerson, pp. 52-110; Lowell, pp. 111-156.

Frothingham: *Transcendentalism.* Boston. 1876.
> Misty but valuable contribution.

Garrison and Garrison: *William Lloyd Garrison.* New York. 1885-1889.
> One of the really great biographies. It remains the best history that we have of the reform movement.

Gilbertson: *Harriet Beecher Stowe.* New York. 1937.

Goddard: *Studies in New England Transcendentalism.* Out of print.

Gohdes: *The Periodicals of American Transcendentalism.* Durham. 1931.

Gorman: *A Victorian American, Henry Wadsworth Longfellow.* New York. 1926.

Hibben: *Henry Ward Beecher.* New York. 1927.
> This highly controversial work contains some valuable pages on Harriet Beecher Stowe and the other Beechers.

Hilen: *Longfellow and Scandanavia.* New Haven. 1947.
> Good study of one aspect of Longfellow. The poet needs other studies of this type.

Howells: *Literary Friends and Acquaintance.* New York. 1902.
> As the genteel impressed an ambitious Westerner.

Macy: *The Spirit of American Literature.* New York. 1912.
> The chapter on Thoreau remains just about the best thing written on the subject.

Matthiessen: *American Renaissance*. New York. 1941.
    A notable book.
Michaud: *Emerson the Enraptured Yankee*. New York. 1930.
    A cool appraisal by a distinguished scholar. Valuable.
Michaud: *La Pensée Americaine: Autour d'Emerson*. Paris. 1924.
    Some of the essays in this volume are of great value.
Mumford: *The Golden Day*. New York. 1926. pp. 85-120.
Newton: *Lincoln and Herndon*. Cedar Rapids. 1910.
    Contains the Herndon-Parker correspondence.
Noyes: *The Religious Experience of John Humphrey Noyes*. New York.
    1923.
    Valuable for the background of Perfectionism. Most of the book
    is a reprint of the writings of Noyes.
Parrington: *The Romantic Revolution*. New York. 1927. pp. 271-472.
Robinson: *Jeffersonian Democracy in New England*. New Haven. 1916.
Rourke: *Trumpets of Jubilee*. New York. 1927.
    Gives glimpses of many participants in the Romantic Revolution.
Rush (ed.): *Letters of Ralph Waldo Emerson*. New York. 1939.
    Indispensable.
Sanborn: *Life of Henry David Thoreau*. New York. 1917.
Schlesinger: *Orestes Brownson*. Boston. 1939.
    Good biography of a strange figure.
Scudder: *James Russell Lowell*. Boston. 1901.
Sears: *Fruitlands*. Boston. 1915.
    Excellent account of the Alcott experiment.
Shepard: *Pedlar's Progress*. Boston. 1939.
    Superlatively fine life of Alcott.
Shepard (ed.): *Alcott's Journal*. Boston. 1938.
    This book and the preceding throw much new light on Alcott.
Sherman: *Americans*. New York. 1922.
    Contains an essay on Emerson.
Tyler: *Freedom's Ferment*. Minneapolis. 1944.
    A confused but valuable account of the reform movement.
Villard: *John Brown*. New York. 1943.
    Understanding treatment of a fanatical abolitionist.
Wade: *Margaret Fuller: Whetstone of Genius*. New York. 1940.
Weiss: *Life and Correspondence of Theodore Parker*. New York. 1864.
    Long out of print. Despite the work of Commager this book is
    still of high value to a student of Parker and his times.
Wilson: *Crusader in Crinoline*. New York. 1941.
    Good biography of Mrs. Stowe.

CHAPTER XIV

WALT WHITMAN
(1819-1892)

"Why should we grope among the dusty bones of the past?" asked Emerson as he was preparing to declare our intellectual independence. The culture of centuries gone is to be used reverently but judiciously, he continued, never is it to be allowed to cabin and confine the human spirit of the present. The chief disgrace is not to be ignorant of the thoughts of the past, but to allow the ideas of the past to force us into stereotyped thinking. Then Emerson proceeds to give the creed by which the American scholar and literary man should be guided. "We will walk on our own feet; we will work with our own hands; we will speak our own minds." These inspiring words, spoken in 1837 and dropped on the transcendental seed-bed of the New England mind, were certainly not without their effect, but it was not until 1855, when the first issue of Walt Whitman's *Leaves of Grass* came from the press, that an American writer took the declaration at its full value and proceeded to speak his own mind in native words. As Thoreau lived the life that Emerson advocated, so did Whitman write the poetry that the Concord prophet had predicted.

Whitman spoke his own mind in *Leaves of Grass*. It was original; nothing quite like it had previously appeared in the world of literature. To-day we are beginning to realize that the poet was reproducing in his individual fashion many things found in Emerson's essays, but the startling ideas of transcendentalism were so expressed in the new book that they seemed wholly original and far more startling than those of Emerson and Thoreau. The towering egotism of the poet overwhelmed people. Here was a man who spoke of himself by name in his own poetry, and the longest and most characteristic poem was called "Song of Walt Whitman," afterwards changed to "Song of Myself." This frank egotism was bad enough, but far worse, even unspeakable, was the nonchalant way in which the poet had celebrated the body as well as the soul, declaring that the body

348

and all its physical members were as sacred as the spirit of the individual. This declaration was only Rousseau's views on the sanctity of the natural man carried to their plain conclusion, but it was a new thing in poetry. And such poetry! It had neither rhyme nor meter, nor nicely constructed figures of speech, nor anything else that one ordinarily met in a book of verses. And such words! The nineteenth century poet was supposed to have a special vocabulary that no one else ever used. It abounded in "poetic" phrases and figures of speech and quite omitted the homely Anglo-Saxon monosyllables of everyday speech. That was only another tradition that Whitman fractured. His words were taken from the lips of bus drivers, street-car conductors, carpenters, politicians, tramps, loafers, and obscure Americans of every type. Truly the book had all the outward appearance of an original work.

Immediately the argument began. The Genteel Tradition gave its most genteel shudder and either answered the book with a stony silence or declared that it was utterly lacking in importance. Whittier cast his copy of the book into the fire; the natural man was too much for him. Before reading the poems Lowell declared offhand that this sort of thing "won't do," and if he ever afterwards altered his views he refrained from making a public recantation of his error. Some of the newspaper critics denounced the book as an atrocity, mucky with arrogant egotism and insufferable indecencies. One outraged gentleman recommended the whipping-post as the reward of the author. Other commentators timidly approved, though they were confused as to the author's meaning. In all the riot of noise and argument, a few clear voices were raised in defense of the poems. These were the voices of the transcendentalists who recognized in *Leaves of Grass* the fruition of their own strivings and the poetic statement of their own teachings. Emerson approved of the book. Thoreau and Alcott, even more enthusiastic, made a trip to Brooklyn to meet the author, and several members of the group sensed that Walt Whitman was really one of themselves.

The argument thus inaugurated continued for many years, but to-day the detractors of Whitman are only a few feeble and very academic critics. Every commentator of intelligence admits the power and significance of *Leaves of Grass,* and not many are disposed to question the influence of the book upon our literature. But when it comes to attributing a final position to the poet, critics fall into disagreement—or silence. Is Whitman worthy to take rank beside the supremely great poets of all time, beside Dante, Homer, and Shakespeare, or is he to find his place beside those men who have finely summarized their time as did Milton, Wordsworth, Spenser, Shelley; or is he merely a stimulating influence in a new field, a pioneer like Burns with all the crudities and good qualities of this type? These questions are fruitful subjects for speculation, but they are not to be answered. In the final appraisal of Whitman, this generation is not saying the last word; that task must be delegated to later ages.

The purpose of the present slight discussion is to consider Whitman as the last and the most fluent of the transcendentalists and as the epitome of the Golden Day of American romanticism with all the bombast, all the ennobling ideals, and all the chaotic strivings of its newly released human spirit. In the man who sets for himself the appalling task of speaking for a nation in a great hour, inconsistencies and contradictions must count as naught.

> Do I contradict myself?
> Very well then I contradict myself,
> (I am large, I contain multitudes)

In Whitman one finds the pioneer of the West and the teeming life of the city, the egotism of the assertive individualist and the quick pity of the humanitarian, the song of Walt Whitman and the chant of praise for democracy, the highest flights of poetry yet attained by an American and the repellent anatomical details of the autopsy. Yet when all the conflicting elements are set forth, it remains that the inconsistencies of *Leaves of Grass* are those of a transcendentalist and that the contradictions are those of romantic America. His book is not "chaos of death—it is form, union, plan—it is eternal life—it is happiness." But the form, the life, and the happiness are those of our Golden Day, foregathered in the capacious embrace of Walt Whitman.

If Whitman can be summarized in a few words, his message is that of Emerson made only a little more spacious. He held a contagious faith in the divine self-sufficiency and all-inclusive power of the individual. Like Emerson's this individualism was based on a mystic conception of human nature that made Walt Whitman the very center of the universe and wholly identified him in the spirit with every other individual who in turn was the center of a universe just as real and as meaningful as that of Whitman. Every human being was the poet in another guise. The reader must make a reconciliation of this individualism and this mystic brotherhood of man in order to understand *Leaves of Grass,* for the poems vacillate between praise of Whitman, the individual, and triumphal pæans to democracy. No one recognized this fact better than did the author, for with these clearly explanatory words he makes his bow to the world:

> One's-self I sing, a simple separate person,
> Yet utter the word Democratic, the word En-Masse.
>
> Of physiology from top to toe I sing,
> Not physiognomy alone nor brain alone is worthy for the Muse,
> I say the Form complete is worthier far,
> The Female equally with the Male I sing.
>
> Of Life immense in passion, pulse, and power,
> Cheerful, for freest action form'd under the laws divine,
> The Modern Man I sing.

Life of Whitman.—Walt Whitman was born on Long Island at the little village of West Hills. His parents were of the ordinary American type, distinctly middle class. The father was a farmer whose very moderate success in getting a livelihood out of the soil for his nine children was indicated by his removal to Brooklyn. In the city he worked as carpenter and contractor. The mother, who was a Quaker, seems to have had a great influence on her poet-son. The second boy, Walt, so called to distinguish him from his father who was named Walter, received a rather hasty and incomplete education, however not so incomplete that he could not later teach country school for a time. Although the family lived in the city, Walt took many opportunities to spend much time in rural Long Island. After his schooling was over, he was there frequently for months at a time, teaching school, editing a paper, or simply "loafing and inviting his soul." In his teaching he is said to have resembled Alcott in his refusal to use force and in his appeal to the better instincts of his pupils. After a few years of desultory life on Long Island, during which time he came into close contact with the common people whose aspirations and ideals he afterwards so triumphantly expressed, Whitman went to Brooklyn where he worked as a journalist for a number of years. This period of his life was rounded off by two years of service as editor of the *Brooklyn Eagle.* By this time, 1848, Whitman was fixed in his political and social views. As a democrat he was of the line of Jefferson and Lincoln, taking a firm stand against southern slave-holders in their efforts to open the western territories to their peculiar institution. However, his democracy differed a bit from that of his two great prototypes in that it sprang as much from association with the workingmen in the cities as from friendship for the small farmer. But both elements can be found in Whitman's political views. He was a member of the Democratic party and prominent in its councils, but when that organization swung to the support of slavery, he joined the radicals. For doing so he lost his editorial position. In his fundamental political philosophy he was very much like Jefferson, holding always that that government is best which governs least. He rested his hope for the future on the Westerners and city laborers. "Radical, true, far-scoped and thorough-going democracy may expect great things from the West," he once remarked. He admired the West so much that he declared that there is something refreshing even in the extremes of western character.

Whitman's career during the years 1848-1855 was long uncertain, and even yet not all the facts are determined, though we are now sure that these were among his most important years. Soon after quitting the *Brooklyn Eagle,* he accepted a place with a New Orleans paper. In his new home his chief experience was a love affair, one of the momentous events of his life, for he discovered through the experience of love a mystic kinship with all mankind. He further gained from his stay in the South an augmented opposition to slavery, because he saw more plainly than ever before that the western pioneer, capable and self-reliant as he was, could not compete with the slave power in the settlement of new regions. Slavery was economically ruinous to the free settler. After a few months in New Orleans Whitman went back to Brooklyn as a Free Soil editor. Again politics threw him out of work, and he took at least one more trip to the South. Then he worked in Brooklyn for a time as a carpenter and extended his acquaintance among the bus drivers, ferry-men, laborers, and floaters of the city. His fundamental equalitarianism, his constant association with the practical exponents of democracy, and his recent political and personal experiences all set him to thinking. Into the ferment of thought thus started entered the stimulating teaching of Emerson. About 1853 Whitman read Emerson's essays, and for two years thereafter he labored on a book of poetry that he had already contemplated for six years.

In July, 1855, *Leaves of Grass* was published with the results previously described. In 1856 and in 1860 new editions appeared. In the meantime Whitman had gone to the support of the new Republican party in its opposition to the slave power. When the war broke out the poet showed that his humanitarianism was not merely theoretical by volunteering as a hospital nurse and caring for wounded and sick soldiers with so great a devotion that he permanently injured his own health. There is nothing finer in the history of self-sacrificing idealism than the story of Whitman as the volunteer nurse, supplying the wounded with tobacco, dressing wounds, reading the Bible to dying Protestant boys, looking through the city to find a priest for expiring Catholic soldiers, buying freezers of ice cream to treat a whole ward, interceding with incompetent medical directors to make another—and successful—effort to save a leg that they had decided must be amputated, and doing the thousand things that an energetic and humanitarian nurse can find to do in an overcrowded hospital. Whitman asserted after the war that he had probably met 80,000 men in his work. Many of these remembered him with deepest affection.

After the war, the poet obtained a clerkship with the Interior Department as clerk in the Bureau of Indian Affairs. He was dismissed from this position because the secretary of the interior, his superior, objected to certain passages in *Leaves of Grass*. However, a place was found for him in the attorney general's office where he remained for eight years. His work here was ended by a stroke of paralysis. For the remainder of his life he lived in Camden, New Jersey, where he died in 1892.

Whitman, the Transcendentalist.—The influence of Emerson upon Whitman was deep and enduring, and Emerson was the chief of American transcendentalism. *Leaves of Grass* shows unmistakably transcendental paternity in its conception of human nature, its optimism, its idea of nature, its tolerant individualism that created democracy, and especially in the mystical background of its whole thought. Both Emerson and Whitman acknowledged the relationship of their ideas. In a record of Whitman's conversations covering only a little more than a year, Emerson is mentioned about two hundred times. Writing once of the Concord teacher the poet said: "He pierces the crusts that envelop the secrets of life. He joins on equal terms the few great sages and original seers. He represents the freeman, America, the individual." Again he said: "Emerson is great—oh! very great: he was a far reaching force; a star of the first, the very first magnitude, maybe; without a doubt that." In the 1856 edition of the *Leaves of Grass* he spoke of Emerson's work in awakening a new social conscience in America: "Those shores you found. I say you have led the States there—have led me there. I say that none has ever done or ever can do a greater deed for the States than your deed."

Writing to Whitman in July, 1855, the month of the publication of the first edition, Emerson said:

I am not blind to the worth of the wonderful gift of *Leaves of Grass*. I find it the most extraordinary piece of wit and wisdom that America has yet contributed. I am very happy in reading it, as great power makes us happy . . . I give you joy of your free and brave thought. . . . I find incomparable things said incomparably well, as they must be . . . I greet you at the beginning of a great career. . . . The solid sense of the book is a sober certainty. It has the best merits, namely of fortifying and encouraging.

In the height of his rapture over *Leaves of Grass*, Emerson exclaimed: "Americans who are abroad may now return: unto us a man is born." Emerson probably was never so enthusiastic about another book; well might he be enraptured, for he was applauding his own intellectual offspring. Such lines as the following are undiluted Emersonian doctrine:

I do not trouble my spirit to vindicate itself or be understood,
I see that the elementary laws never apologize,
(I reckon I behave no prouder than the level I plant my house by, after all)

Whimpering and truckling fold with powders for invalids, conformity goes to the fourth-remov'd,
I wear my hat as I please indoors or out.

It is perfectly true that Whitman might have reached his distinctive views without having read Emerson, for transcendentalism was rife in the very air of America during the forties, but the fact remains that he did not. He read Emerson and acknowledged his indebtedness to him in a public utterance, and Emerson acknowledged his approval of the doctrine in *Leaves of Grass* by a letter of warm appreciation.

In Thoreau, Whitman had even a more intense admirer than he found in Emerson. For this there was a reason. Thoreau was much more of a natural man than Emerson was, more like a wild animal, more in love with the ecstasy of living. He was enough of a child of nature not to be frightened by a catalog of anatomical names, and he was enough of a practicing transcendental individualist to recognize his kind when he saw it. Emerson once wrote in his journal: "Perhaps his [Thoreau's] fancy for Walt Whitman grew out of his taste for wild nature, for an otter, a woodchuck, or a loon." Whitman's poems are filled with lines that, but for their rhetorical peculiarities, might easily fit into *Walden* or the *Week*. Thoreau's disdain for money and the material things of life are echoed in: "And you or I pocketless of a dime may purchase the pick of the earth."

The intense individualism which found the whole universe in a Concord bean-field, even under one's very hat-brim, would be satisfied with this declaration of the importance of self:

I exist as I am, that is enough,
If no other in the world be aware I sit content,
And if each and all be aware I sit content.
One world is aware and by far the largest to me, and that is myself.

He who came into the world "to live in it, not to make it over" would find a congenial spirit in Whitman, who declared himself to be "the caresser of life wherever moving," and all transcendentalists in New England and elsewhere must have found epitomized in the following lines their mistrust of formal learning, their joy in simple life and occupations, and their abounding egotism:

And to glance with an eye or show a bean in its pod confounds the learning of all times,
And there is no trade or employment but the young man following it may become a hero,
And there is no object so soft but it makes a hub for the wheel'd universe,
And I say to any man or woman, Let your soul stand cool and composed before a million universes.

Whitman's Mysticism.—Like all the transcendentalists Whitman based his whole workaday philosophy on a profoundly mystical basis. From his mother, a good Quaker, he received the belief that "the unseen is proved by the seen," that the inner light, the intuition, is the safest guide to conduct, and that God dwells in all men and all men in Him.

Swiftly arose and spread around me the peace and knowledge that pass
    all arguments of the earth,
And I know that the hand of God is the promise of my own,
And I know that the spirit of God is the brother of my own,
And that all the men ever born are also my brothers, and the women my
    sisters and lovers,
And that a kelson of the creation is love. . . .

Again:

Why should I wish to see God better than this day?
I see something of God each hour of the twenty-four, and each moment
    then,
In the faces of men and women I see God, and in my own face in the
    glass,
I find letters from God dropt in the street, and every one is sign'd by
    God's name,
And I leave them where they are, for I know that wheresoe'er I go,
Others will punctually come forever and ever.

The mystical aspects of transcendentalism could not be more
clearly stated, for the lines acknowledge the constant and immediate
presence of God in every human being and the ability of each to
receive messages directly from the Deity at all times. To the person who holds such a view and allows it to others, as Whitman did,
equalitarian democracy is not a vague possibility or a desirable
though remote ideal but rather a necessity based upon the sacred
duty of allowing each man to follow and express the divinity that
is within him.

Twenty years after the first edition of *Leaves of Grass* Whitman
again uttered his belief in the divine origin of the inner light, the
still small voice of the conscience:

O I am sure they really came from Thee,
The urge, the ardor, the unconquerable will,
The potent, felt, interior command, stronger than words,
A message from the Heavens whispering to me even in sleep,
These sped me on. . . .
. . . Thou O God my life hast lighted,
With ray of light, steady, ineffable, vouchsafed of Thee. . . .

Such a mystical conception of the union of God and man can
hardly be treated as a practical consideration; it is an attitude of
mind which colors all facts that come into its influence. The mystical union is not regarded as the exclusive prerogative of any one

man or group of men. It is a universal possibility, and if man errs
it is simply because he does not follow the plain guidance of the
light within. By bringing the individual into direct communication
with God, it creates a tremendous individualism, but by allowing
to all men the same relations with God it makes a complete spiritual
equalitarianism, a firm and sure basis for equalitarian democracy,
both spiritual and political.

Whitman does not allow his estimate of human nature to be implied in a general statement of his mysticism. Again and again he
explicitly declares his faith in the indwelling presence of God, and
beseeches all men to remember that their bodies are temples of the
divine spirit.

> None has begun to think how divine he himself is.

Upon a battle field the body of his slain enemy moves him to pity.

> My enemy is dead, a man as divine as myself is dead.

Nowhere does the seen mirror the unseen more accurately than
in the relations of the soul and body.

Was somebody asking to see the soul?
Behold the body includes and is the meaning, the main concern, and in-
    cludes and is the soul;
Whoever you are, how superb and how divine is your body, or any part
    of it.

Again:

> I have said that the soul is not more than the body,
> And I have said that the body is not more than the soul,
> And nothing, not God, is greater to one than one's self is.

This close interlinking of the soul and the body and the rapture
over the divinity of man's physical structure led to the fleshliness
and primitiveness that have repelled so many from Whitman's poetry. In the closing section of the "Song of Myself" the poet says:

> I too am not a bit tamed, I too am untranslatable,
> I sound my barbaric yawp over the roofs of the world.

Many, many critics of Whitman seem to have read no other lines
of his poetry. The genteel, impressed by the wildness of his "barbaric yawp," have set him down as the defiant apologist of sheer

animalism, and with this estimate have condemned his verses to the limbo of unspeakable indecencies. In his self-characterization Whitman was guilty of poetic exaggeration, for he is perfectly translatable, and his most barbaric passages are merely glorifications of the physical body as the divine home of the soul. Whitman is no more indecent than a book on physiology is indecent. He only permitted to "speak at every hazard nature without check with original energy." Concerning this aspect of *Leaves of Grass* Thoreau makes the best criticism: "As for the sensuality of Whitman's *Leaves of Grass* I do not so much wish that it was unwritten, as that men and women were so pure that they could read it without harm."

In short, Whitman had the transcendental view of human nature. He considered it divine, and he went one step beyond the New Englanders in insisting that the body, the home of the soul, is equally divine with the spirit. The individual considered alone is divine, and no less divinity attends him in the democratic mass, the congregation of the common man. Furthermore, the best moral guide of man is the individual conscience, the voice of God, which always attends every man, whether he be a solitary figure or one of a huge society.

Whitman's View of Nature.—Just as Whitman and the transcendentalists were one in their conception of human nature, so did they agree upon a mystical interpretation of the relations of man and the natural world. "Letters from God dropt in the street" are merely manifestations of God in nature, and since the poet found these everywhere, he was at no more of a loss than Emerson was to find the Deity in the landscape itself and in every detail of that landscape. The most universal and insignificant thing, equally with the most conspicuous object, became the messenger of God.

A child said What is the grass? . . .
. . . I guess it is the handkerchief of the Lord,
A scented gift and remembrancer designedly dropt,
Bearing the owner's name someway in the corners. . . .

I believe a leaf of grass is no less than the journey-work of the stars,
And the pismire is equally perfect, and a grain of sand, and the egg of
    a wren,
And a tree-toad is a chef-d'œuvre for the highest,
And the running blackberry would adorn the parlors of heaven,
And the narrowest hinge in my hand puts to scorn all machinery,
And the cow crunching with depress'd head surpasses any statue,
And a mouse is a miracle enough to stagger sextillions of infidels.

Furthermore just as a mystic of the Whitman variety looks upon other men and sees in them resemblances to himself, becomes part of them and makes them part of him, so he becomes a part of the nature around him.

There was a child went forth every day,
And the first object that he look'd upon, that object he became,
And that object became part of him for the day or a certain part of the day,
Or for many years or stretching cycles of years.

One of the most characteristic minor aspects of transcendental literature is the frequently expressed rapturous delight in the external beauty of nature. Whitman frequently voices the same delight. "The earth never tires," he declared, rejoicing in the beauty of the physical scene, and in the quiet of the night he absorbed immortality and peace. With Emerson he testifies that "The air tastes good to my palate," and like his teacher in the transcendentalism of nature, he realized the fullness of his individuality only in the presence of the natural world.

We also ascend dazzling and tremendous as the sun,
We found our own, O my soul, in the calm and cool of the day-break.

The Optimism of Whitman.—The size and grandeur of Whitman's scope can be seen nowhere better than in his optimism.

> My foothold is tenon'd and mortis'd in granite,
> I laugh at what you call dissolution,
> And I know the amplitude of time.

A good deal of foolish chattering over Whitman's "jaunty, back-slapping optimism" would never have come into being if the critics had read those three lines which have the radiance and repose of eternity itself. Such lines can come only from a soul that is sustained by a quiet but unshakable faith that all will be well in God's own good time. No flamboyance is here, but only a steady belief in the final goodness of man and the beneficence of the universe in which we live. In the face of so much goodness and in the prospect of the final triumph of good, "the wonder is always and always how there can be a mean man or an infidel." Whitman's universe is good without reservation. In fact at times he is inclined to say that there is no evil. The poet who can sing: "All seems beautiful to me" should be pardoned for a bit of exuberant joy, because he is an antidote for the excessive pessimism that to-day is almost universal in American and European literature. But once Whitman's optimism did not seem excessive. To-day any cheerful note sounds "jaunty" by comparison with the prevailing mood.

It would be well if we could stop talking about Whitman's optimism for a time, and consider it as transcendental idealism grappling with the problem of death and evil. In such a light *Leaves of Grass* drops much of its "jauntiness" and becomes a grave and reverent defense of man's right to hope in his most critical hours. So divine a thing as human nature was not meant for annihilation, says the poet, and some of his most memorable passages bid humanity to take heart even when in the grip of the last enemy.

The smallest sprout shows there is really no death. . . .
All goes onward and outward, nothing collapses,
And to die is different from what anyone supposed, and luckier.

Again:

I know I am deathless,
I know this orbit of mine cannot be swept by a carpenter's compass,
I know I shall not pass like a child's carlacue cut with a burnt stick at
    night.

Nothing can shake so great a faith and so steady a confidence in the goodness of life and death. Sorrow and disaster become straws on the current that is slowly but irresistibly moving toward ultimate triumph.

And as to you death, and you bitter hug of mortality, it is idle to try to
    alarm me.

The peace that passes understanding has come upon the poet, and "no array of terms can say how much I am at peace about God and about death." Why should he not be at peace? God dwells in him and he in God, and death has vanished utterly before the calm face of high idealism.

Whitman's Cosmic Significance.—"Cosmic significance" has for long been a favorite phrase of the friendly critics of Whitman, and so ponderously have they labored the rather cryptic characterization that they have almost submerged their ideas under a deluge of polysyllables. Cosmic means universal, and the whole phrase attempts to give in tabloid form the reasons for the poet's claim to speak for each and all men. Whitman could speak for all men because of his "cosmic significance"—he was the universal man. "Walt Whitman" stood for more than the Brooklyn editor and carpenter; it stood for every separate unit of the human race just as did the term "man." It represented the free man and the slave, the black and the white, the Southerner and the Northerner, the city dweller of the East and the trapper of the West, the American and the European. It was in the completest sense a universal term.

Some of the difficulty with "cosmic significance" has been caused by the egotism of *Leaves of Grass*. Whitman was a rank egotist; he recognized that fact in many a passage, but his individualism stopped short of the cave-man variety that must kill, maim, or conquer every other individual in the world besides himself. Such lines as these are not calculated to impress any one with Walt Whitman's insignificance:

Having pried through the strata, analyzed to a hair, counsel'd with doctors and calculated close,
I find no sweeter fat than sticks to my own bones.

Or these:
          I am larger, better than I thought,
          I did not know I held so much goodness.

But one can never insist too strongly that any claim made by Whitman might also be made with his approval by any man anywhere. In fact he insists upon making it for his mute brethren:

          And what I assume you shall assume,
          And every atom belonging to me as good belongs to you.

Again:

In all people I see myself, none more and not one a barley-corn less,
And the good or bad I say of myself I say of them.

Or this:

My spirit has pass'd in compassion and determination around the whole earth,
I have look'd for equals and lovers and found them ready for me in all lands,
I think that some divine rapport has equalized them with me.

But Whitman does not allow his universality and his deep feeling for innate equality to be spent in mere political or social theorizing; he led them to a practical fulfillment in a rich humanitarianism that some have thought is Whitman's finest bequest to literature

> Behold, I do not give lectures or a little charity,
> When I give I give myself.

Or this:

> I know perfectly well my own egotism . . .
> And would fetch you whoever you are flush with myself. ·

Too often a laudable humanitarianism has been lavished upon those who are not particularly needing it or upon the respectable element in our society. Such was not the case with Whitman. The outcast, the despised, the law-breaker, the unfortunate he held in his vast embrace, never refusing his mercy to a one. "Not until the sun excludes you do I exclude you," he assured an outcast, and the deeper the agony the quicker and the more complete the response:

> Agonies are one of my changes of garments.

If there is any Puritanism to be found in Whitman it appears in the form of an insistence upon the duty of every man to cultivate a ready sympathy as one of the great unifying bonds in the brotherhood of universal man. "Whoever walks a furlong without sympathy walks to his own funeral dressed in his shroud," he once declared, and in speaking of an unfortunate he says, "I am the man, I suffer'd, I was there." One can take with a good grace many lectures from Whitman on humanitarianism and the beauty of sympathy, for the poet freely spent his health during the Civil War ministering to the sick and wounded in the crowded hospitals. His actions during those grim days were a heartening demonstration of the doctrine that he had just been preaching in *Leaves of Grass*.

Whitman and the Frontier.—In a very true sense Whitman's mystical equalitarianism, his sympathy, and his other romantic traits epitomize the spirit of the western frontier. Although the poet saw rather little of the West, he was wholly in sympathy with its social and political aspirations. He saw the economic reason for western opposition to slavery, and he became successively an anti-slavery Democrat, a Free Soiler, and a Republican under the leadership of Lincoln. The spirit of the West is plain in *Leaves of Grass* and in almost any of the prose, and the facts of Whitman's political career have been public property for a number of years. What is not even yet so well recognized is the fact that the poet found in the cities a new frontier, very much like that one which was receding into the West so rapidly.

Without a doubt the city frontier does resemble our historical line of settlement as much as a crowded tenement can resemble open land, as much as a factory can resemble a homestead. The spirits of the city laborer and the frontiersman are much alike. Much alike also are the aspirations of the two men. Each is greatly concerned with economics. The frontiersman demands social and political equality, by which he thinks to have a chance to possess the economic resources of the frontier on an even footing with his fellows; the city laborer also wants equality, political, at least, for by this means only can he gain economic security, the right to work for a fair wage in a reasonably permanent position. In choosing social and political leaders both men are alike in their contempt for the pretensions of birth and culture when unsupported by other qualifications. Both prefer the practical man of affairs who can do things to the theorist, however intellectual he may be, and both are very liable to succumb to the appeals of the demagogue.

For a hundred years the tone of American democracy was set by the West. Although the city man united with the frontier to elect Jackson and Lincoln, so predominant was the voice of the Westerner in our politics that insufficient credit was given to the laborer for his share in the victories. Since 1900 the voice of the city is becoming more and more noticeable in party councils, and with the rush of our people to the large centers of population it is safe to say that the American democracy of the future will be determined on our new frontier, the large city with its teeming laboring population.

Although Whitman did not sit down and reason out the likenesses of the city laborer and the pioneer, for he was not a reasoning man, he sensed these similarities and as the poet of American democracy put into his ample lines the songs of the commoners, wherever they might chance to live.

> O such themes—equalities! O divine average.

"Memories of President Lincoln."—Whitman gained two sections of *Leaves of Grass* from his Civil War experiences. The first of these, "Drum-Taps," gave his direct reactions to the great conflict

and the sights that he saw on the battle fields and in the hospitals. Among the most admired poems in this group are "Beat! Beat! Drums!" "Strange Vigil I Kept on the Field One Night," "The Wound-Dresser," "Give Me the Splendid Silent Sun," and "Ethiopia Saluting the Colors." But the two master works from the war are to be found in the section called "Memories of President Lincoln." The shorter poem, "O Captain! My Captain!" has been a favorite of all classes of Americans for many years. Its simplicity, direct-ness, and note of personal grief appeal to all readers. The longer poem, "When Lilacs Last in the Dooryard Bloomed," is one of the superlative literary productions of the nineteenth century. "A sono-rous nocturne," Swinburne called it, and this characterization ac-curately describes the tone-color and music of this great lyric ex-pression. Whitman probably never reached a higher level than he achieved in this poem with the chant beginning "Come lovely and soothing death." "Memories of President Lincoln" is a fitting tribute to a great American leader by the man who is generally considered as our greatest poet.

Whitman's Verse Form.—It is useless to speculate upon the poetic qualities of *Leaves of Grass*. Some have even questioned Whit-man's claim to recognition as a poet on the grounds that he dis-regarded all the external characteristics of poetry, even disdaining meter, that basic requisite of verse. The most casual reader of Whitman can see that the poet did not mean to have any fixed pattern for his lines. They are rhythmical, but the rhythm is that of good prose and not that of poetry. The nearest literary parallel to the lines of *Leaves of Grass* is to be found in Elizabethan prose, especially in that of the Bible. But there is a rhythm of nature that might easily have been the model for Whitman, and that is the rhythmical but irregular beat of the ocean waves. Whatever the model was, the poet captured a rhythm that is exceedingly effective and not easily imitated.

In attempting to voice in poetry the aspirations of a new people, Whitman broke with the past in form as in content. He could no more have caught the spiritual significance of America in conven-tional verse than Shakespeare could have written Hamlet's soliloquies in the form of villanelles. Every great poet has been something of an innovator, and Whitman was only a little more daring than most. His claim to poetic renown rests on a more secure basis than an adherence to or a defection from conventional rules. He is entitled to recognition because of the fundamental poetry in the amplitude of his imagination and in the sustained majesty of his utterances. He was not always great, it is true, but neither was Shakespeare, neither was Wordsworth. Only a shortsighted critic would make final judgment of Wordsworth on some of the flat lyrics that grieve all sensitive readers, and it would be only a perversely wrongheaded critic who would insist upon discussing Whitman in terms of some of his screechy, flamboyant lines.

"Leaves of Grass."—Beginning in 1855 Whitman published all his poetry in successive editions of *Leaves of Grass*. About twelve editions came out during the poet's lifetime, and many more have been published since 1892. The best edition for the beginning student of Whitman is that so admirably edited and abridged by Professor Emory Holloway. This collection of about 100 poems contains the full flavor of Whitman with judicious omissions of the debatable passages.

In addition to *Leaves of Grass* Whitman left a considerable amount of prose. Perhaps the most valuable single bit is the preface to the 1855 edition, which gives the poet's critical defense of his work. As such it is one of the significant prefaces in the history of literature. Another important piece is *Democratic Vistas,* a statement of his faith in democracy in those dark days following the Civil War, when it seemed that the worst features of American life were permanently in control of our national destiny. In some passages this little pamphlet is not effective, but in others it has an imaginative grasp and a grandeur of utterance equaled only by his best poetry.

Whitman's Influence.—Every great artist has a tendency to ruin his particular vehicle as a mode of expression for his immediate successors. The grand style of Michael Angelo, so triumphantly achieved, led his successors into the fatal mistake of confusing grandeur and mere size. As a result, the first few years after the death of the old master saw canvases acres in extent but totally lacking in merit. All dramas in blank verse since the Elizabethan period have been inevitably compared with Shakespeare's to the vast discomfiture of the later dramatists. Following the death of Beethoven all symphonies sounded like imitations of the master's until the rise of Brahms. To this day German opera is under the huge shadow of Wagner. So it is in American poetry. Many have imitated Whitman, but few have been successful.

However, this statement does not mean that Whitman has had

no influence in American literature. It is true that such poets as Carl Sandburg, Edgar Lee Masters, and many another have written in verse as free as anything in *Leaves of Grass,* but the younger men have used free forms that are their own individual possessions. There have been and still are many close imitators of Whitman, but they are not among our leading poets. They are destined to go down in literature as imitators. On the other hand those poets who are most successful have gone far along the path first traveled by Whitman. In the content of recent literature Whitman has been as influential as he has been in the form. The poet's study is no longer a thing of four walls and rows of books; it is the noisy whirl of American life, the city, the factory, the farm, and the small town. Bookishness is no longer the rule of our poetry. Furthermore the themes of our literature are to-day drawn from that vast field indicated by the wide gesture of Whitman. Our novelists and our dramatists have quit copying Dickens, Thackeray, Victor Hugo, and the pallid imitations of Shakespearean poetic dramas. Dreiser, Sinclair Lewis, Sherwood Anderson, Eugene O'Neill, and Willa Cather reflect various phases of their America just as Whitman hoped his successors would do.

Poets to come! orators, singers, musicians to come!
Not today is to justify me and answer what I am for,
But you, a new brood, athletic, continental, greater than before known,
Arouse! for you must justify me.

The old poet has had his wish. His aims and achievements are justified in every book that falls into the main stream of our literature, and it is almost certain that the fullness of his justification is not yet reached. Emerson, Whitman, and Mark Twain achieved our literary independence of Europe. Foreign literary fashions may give us many things in years to come; they may once more dictate the subject matter and the methods of our authors, but in the works of our three great writers American literature has achieved a splendid independence and a noble sonority of expression.

SUGGESTED READINGS

Arvin: *Whitman.* New York. 1938.
    Stimulating study by a liberal critic, but it should not be taken literally. Whitman's socialism needs more definition than Mr. Arvin gave it.

Bailey: *Walt Whitman*. New York. 1926.
> Excellent interpretation.

Bazalgette: *Walt Whitman, the Man and his Work*. New York. 1920.
> This study needs a new translation.

Bucke: *Walt Whitman*. 1883.
> An early biography which still has considerable value.

Burroughs: *Notes on Walt Whitman as Poet and Person*. 1867.
> Whitman himself seems to have had a considerable hand in the writing of this book. For this reason it has unique value. A later work by Burroughs, *Whitman: a Study* (1896) is a complete revision.

Canby: *Whitman*. Boston. 1943.

Carpenter: *Days with Walt Whitman*. London. 1906.
> Valuable sidelights on the poet.

Ellis: *The New Spirit*. Boston. 1926.
> There are many other editions of this work. Contains fine discussion of Whitman.

Fausset: *Walt Whitman: Poet of Democracy*. New Haven. 1942.
> Restrained but penetrating. Extremely valuable.

Foerster: *American Criticism*. Boston. 1928. pp. 157-222.

Holloway: *Whitman, an Interpretation in Narrative*. New York. 1926.
> Mr. Holloway is probably the outstanding authority on Walt Whitman, but he did not succeed in writing a definitive study.

Keller: *Walt Whitman in Mickle Street*. New York. 1921.
> Personal reminiscences.

Masters: *Whitman*. New York. 1937.
> As usual, Masters is arbitrary in his judgments and autocratic in tone. The book, however, is not to be overlooked.

Matthiessen: *American Renaissance*. New York. 1941. pp. 517-625.

Mumford: *The Golden Day*. New York. 1926. pp. 121-137.

Perry: *Walt Whitman, his Life and Work*. Boston. 1906.
> After more than forty years this book remains of more than a little value.

Santayana: *Interpretations of Poetry and Religion*. New York. 1900.

Symonds: *Walt Whitman: a Study*. London. 1893.
> Of more value than many of the later works on Whitman.

Traubel: *With Walt Whitman in Camden*. New York. 1906-08-14.
> Traubel's intimate acquaintance with the poet gives this book a high position. Indispensable.

CHAPTER XV

THE DEVELOPMENT OF THE AMERICAN NOVEL TO 1860

Of all the common literary forms the novel was the latest to develop. Centuries after many varieties of poetry were well known in England and almost two centuries after the drama reached its full development, Samuel Richardson wrote *Pamela* (1744), generally known as the first English novel. The author followed his great success with *Clarissa Harlowe* and later with *Sir Charles Grandison*. Americans read and liked all these books, for Richardson was very anxious to leave a moral lesson with his readers. Indeed *Pamela* has for its sub-title, "Virtue Rewarded." *Sir Charles Grandison* was especially popular in this country. Even so strict a moralist as Jonathan Edwards read it and approved so heartily of its style that he resolved to pay more attention to his own writing. One of the earliest of the great American religious revivalists, Charles G. Finney, was named by his mother for the morally perfect hero of Richardson's last novel.

However, Richardson's great contemporaries, Henry Fielding, Tobias Smollett, and Laurence Sterne, were not so immediately popular in America. Certainly they were not widely accepted in New England, for almost every character and idea set forth by any of the three would have been anathema to the Puritans. These three novelists were realists, that is, they were concerned with setting down the various aspects of human nature, good, bad, and indifferent, with no regard whatever for the lesson imparted or the lack of one. These men were interested in action and in the external manifestations of character, while Richardson was interested in character analysis and in the presentation of the moral. Humor was a chief consideration with the three realists, while the moralist dealt largely in sentiment.

The first American novel was *The Power of Sympathy* by Mrs. Sarah Wentworth Morton of Boston. It is a poor thing, written in the form of letters, as were the novels of Richardson, and simply drowned in sentimental tears. To-day it lives only as a historical relic of a taste and form that have alike vanished. Another sentimental novel was *The Coquette* in which Mrs. Hannah Foster told a touching story of the sad fate that befell a young woman who jilted a minister. This book was very popular, but it was far exceeded in general favor by Mrs. Susannah Rowson's *Charlotte,* one of the greatest sellers in the history of American fiction. Indeed in length of days the popularity of this book surpasses that of any other native novel. There have been more than 100 editions published and of that huge number at least three are for sale by present-day publishers. *Charlotte* is also a tearful story of the misfortunes of a beautiful but injudicious young woman.

While the sentimentalists were reaping popular favor and the other rewards that usually accompany that prize, the realists were beginning their work. The first of these was the genial satirist, Hugh Henry Brackenridge, whose *Modern Chivalry* is a perfect mine of information about the early frontier democrats. Fielding was one of Brackenridge's acknowledged masters. Certain critics have seen in our earliest satire enough of a likeness to the machinery of Cervantes to call *Modern Chivalry* the "Don Quixote of the frontier." For many years the book retained its popularity, and nowhere was it more read than in the West. To-day it is to be had in a recent edition. Another realistic story was *The Algerine Captive* by Royall Tyler. This book follows the method of Defoe's *Robinson Crusoe* in relating the story of a man who fell into the hands of pirates. Fact and fiction are cleverly woven together by Tyler as they were by his great master.

Just at the close of the eighteenth century Charles Brockden Brown introduced to American fiction the whole romantic ferment with its discussion of the rights of woman, French revolutionary philosophy, and the philosophical anarchism of Godwin. Joining these alien influences to native materials Brown became the first American novelist to win lasting critical approval coupled with a considerable amount of popularity.

Within two or three decades after the death of Brown, American romance had developed its three topics—the settlement, the Revolution, and the frontier. At once the whole romantic school, Cooper, Kennedy, Bird, Simms, Paulding, Caruthers, and many a less renowned writer, flung themselves on the wealth of material at hand in a hasty attempt to satisfy the voracious appetite of American readers for sensational melodrama. The romantics started out well enough, but slowly the level of their performance dropped to meet the lower levels of public taste, and soon romance was in the hands of the bloodthirsty but futile hack-writers who turned out "Wild West" stories by the thousand. One man alone is said to have the credit—or discredit—for 600 titles. Obviously romance had committed suicide in pandering to a depraved taste. By the close of the Civil War it was apparent that the novel must receive a fresh impetus from another school of writers.

Meanwhile sentiment was in as bad a way. In the days before the war the "weepful" school was dominated by the egregious Mrs. E. D. E. N. Southworth, Mrs. Mary J. Holmes, and Augusta Evans. The masterpiece of this group without doubt was *St. Elmo*, a perfect revel of saccharine delight written around a Byronic hero whose air of mystery and handsome appearance were the source of never-ending feminine sighs. But sentiment was no monopoly of women readers or writers. Donald Grant Mitchell with his *Reveries of a Bachelor* and George William Curtis with the weakly sentimental *Prue and I* showed that men could fall into the way of writing appeals to the tender emotions. By the time the war came on, sentiment had about reached the lowest level.

Uncle Tom's Cabin was too great a success not to have imitators. In fact Mrs. Stowe wrote one of these imitations in *Dred*, but it was reserved for T. S. Arthur to do the most popular reform novel of the century next to the great anti-slavery appeal. This book was *Ten Nights in a Bar Room*, a melancholy record of the evils of drink. The author's appeal to tears and maudlin sentiment was probably never surpassed in unconcealed effrontery, but despite the literary sins of the book it was long popular both as a novel and as a drama. In this last form it successfully competed for popular favor against a field that included such stand-bys as *Uncle Tom's Cabin* and *East Lynne*.

The fifties seems to have been our most sentimental decade. When the romantic appeal to imagination was made by any other than a master, it was very apt to be to weak sentimentality. Tears were the obsession of our sentimental romancers, and under the constant urge of such novelists American readers were losing their taste for homely literature that reflected the humor and the color of life. Literary realism was the cure for the disease, but the path of the realists was to be a hard and slow one to travel. Notwithstanding the shortcomings of the fifties, those years saw the major activities of two of our greatest novelists, Hawthorne and Melville. It might be remarked in passing that the greater of the two, Melville, was almost totally rejected by his time.

NATHANIEL HAWTHORNE

(1804-1864)

For long Hawthorne was considered the leading American novelist, but to-day the claims of other men are being urged with so great insistency that he is no longer permitted to occupy alone the highest pedestal of our fiction. The partisans of Mark Twain, Henry James, and Theodore Dreiser are urging that their favorites be considered at least the equal of Hawthorne, and there are very few critics of the younger generation who do not acclaim *Moby Dick* as the supreme achievement in American fiction.

No one wishes to remove any laurels from Hawthorne's brow. He would be considered a competent novelist in any country, and until our writers have made some immense advances he will continue to occupy a leading place in our literary history. However, it is not ungracious to point out a few of his shortcomings that are serious enough to keep him from treading a measure with Fielding, Thackeray, Hardy, and Conrad—to name no more of the chief novelists of the English tongue. So serious and obvious are these defects that many cannot consider him the equal of Mark Twain and Melville in his own land. The chief of these defects is a lack of human interest in the affairs of life, and especially in people. Hawthorne so often wrote in the allegorical strain that one always suspects him of using his characters as mere symbols of ideas. Of course symbolism is a recognized literary device, but its use by a novelist is very apt to lead the writer into a greater interest in the abstract idea than in the character. Certainly the creation of character is one of the main concerns of fiction, and the writers who stand highest are always those whose characters are the best conceived and presented.

Moreover, despite the interest of Hawthorne in ideas, his intellectual range was neither wide nor deep. He was a taster of many a concoction, but never a one did he drain to the dregs. In fact he tasted of so many conflicting ideas that ultimately the last became the antidote for its predecessor in the series. No intellectual interest ever grew into a transforming force in his life. He became a transcendentalist only to drop that engaging way of life when it yielded no immediate results. A moderate romantic individualist, he could still accept favors from an administration put into office by the slave power. So it was with all his ideas. They were superficial.

The last count against the man is his lack of human warmth. This is implied in his inability to create character, but the defect becomes unconcealable when he starts his men and women on their round of experiences. The various episodes of his novels become as impersonal as scientific lectures. In the hands of a novelist like Dostoievsky or Tolstoy or even—to drop to a lower level—Dickens, *The Scarlet Letter* would have been one of the most poignant works in literature, as unforgettable as the sufferings of Lear. But in the hands of Hawthorne the persons in his novel become only figures of subdued pastel shades against a somber background. Warm, creative imagination, that soul-shaking force in literature, is simply not present. We close the book politely deploring the tragedy, but our emotions are not deeply stirred.

Estimates of Hawthorne.—A peculiar thing about the fame of Hawthorne is the curious inability of critics to agree on anything about the man except his competence as a novelist. Dr. Carl Van Doren calls him the "prime source" of information concerning the romantic era and says that his self-appointed task was to "sum up and body forth the inner vision of his age." This estimate would imply that the novelist was a close observer and describer of the material and intellectual interests of contemporary life. On the other hand Mr. John Macy points out that Hawthorne was a born romancer in his distaste for his neighbor and his neighbor's interests. The author of *The Scarlet Letter* alone, of all the literary men of his time, was not deeply stirred by black slavery or any of the burning issues of the age. He was as far removed as Poe, declares Mr. Macy, from any sort of ethical tradition about or before him. Mr. John Erskine says that Hawthorne's genius was formed in transcendentalism. Dr. and Mrs. C. A. Beard, in an appraisal of the novelist that contains some impressive statements from his own writings, classify Hawthorne as a truly democratic spirit in his acceptance of the people and in his mistrust of aristocracy, pointing out, however, that his disinclination to go the full distance in romantic idealism was shown by his early withdrawal from transcendentalism. The historians finally conclude that the man was temperamentally a skeptic. Mr. Parrington, starting at this point, goes further than the other critics in bringing out the inconsistencies of Hawthorne's temper by showing that, although he was a member of Brook Farm and nominally a romantic idealist, he had no belief in human perfectibility, that he mistrusted man's instincts, and that he was barred from participation in transcendentalism by his lack of mysticism. Certain recent biographers seem never to have heard of the tumultuous intellectual life of the thirties and forties which must be considered as the background of every American romantic writer.

From these contradictory estimates one may justly conclude that it is high time for a new critical appraisal of Hawthorne. When such an estimate is made, it will probably be not far from the ground occupied jointly by the Beard and Parrington estimates, for these are not violently contradictory and they come nearer than any others to explaining the novelist's point of view.

One of the chief implications of the romantic movement was an attempt to abolish sin and evil. To such men as John Humphrey Noyes and Walt Whitman the attempt was an accomplished fact, and to virtually all the other romantics, especially those of New England, the immediate future held out the most rosy promise of success. Hawthorne was temperamentally incapable of accepting this promise. He was too intelligent not to be curious about the problem of evil, but his mental equipment was not sufficient to make him a deep student of the eternal problem. The whole urge of his age was to acquiesce in the romantic promises of glowing idealism, but his common sense acted as a constant brake on his romanticism. He sampled all theories and filled himself with none. As a result, his whole life was a constant testing of ideas in his clear but thin, cold intelligence. To none of these could he give his full allegiance or his whole-hearted opposition. The temperamental skeptic is capable of nothing but skepticism.

There is probably a great deal of Hawthorne himself in "The Great Stone Face," for the chief figure is a cautious skeptic to whom at last comes the reward that the unthinking had so often tried to bestow upon others. Incidentally it might be said that Daniel Webster was the original of old Stony Phiz. A statement that clearly shows the self-contradictory element in Hawthorne is the one that he made on commerce and trade: "Traffic seems to be an evil, but who knows but high moral results may flow from the most unattractive stream of human action?" During the Civil War the novelist complained that a "man's opinions can take no catholic or philosophic range nowadays but they call out some shrewish accusation of disloyalty." The ability to throw himself wholly into any cause or idea was denied Hawthorne.

Life of Hawthorne.—Solitude was in the very blood of Nathaniel Hawthorne. When the boy's father, a Salem sea captain, died while on a voyage to the tropics, the mother became a recluse, and the care of the four-year-old child was largely intrusted to the mother's brothers, well-to-do men who did not stint their nephew's educational opportunities. Hawthorne as a lad spent a considerable period of time in a quiet country home in Maine owned by one of his uncles. Here he read widely and gave himself over to his inclination for brooding meditation. In 1825 he was graduated from Bowdoin College in the class with Longfellow and Franklin Pierce. Pierce and Hawthorne remained lifelong friends. Upon his graduation, Hawthorne returned to his mother's home in Salem, where for more than ten years he lived in almost unbroken solitude. He wished to make writing his life work, and during these years he was practicing his chosen art and trying to perfect his style. In 1839 he obtained a post in the Boston Custom House which he kept for a short time. In 1841-1842 he spent about a year at the transcendental communistic experiment, Brook Farm. This experience was rather distasteful, and ever after he looked with more than usual skepticism upon soaring theories of social betterment. In July, 1842, Hawthorne was married to Sophia Peabody, and the young couple settled at the Old Manse, the old home of Dr. Ezra Ripley, orthodox minister of Concord. From 1846 to 1849 he held another governmental post in the Salem Custom House. Franklin Pierce became president in 1853 and appointed his old friend consul at Liverpool, one of the most lucrative positions at the disposal of the government. He held this position for four years and afterward traveled on the Continent. After 1860 he lived in Concord, where he was on terms of friendship with all the literary circle and intimate with none. He died suddenly while on a trip to New Hampshire with Pierce and was buried in Sleepy Hollow, the Concord cemetery.

Hawthorne's Early Work.—When he was only twenty-four Hawthorne published an immature novel called *Fanshawe,* which completely failed to attract popular or critical attention. It did one thing, however, in that it opened the way for some contributions to *The Token,* a Boston annual publication. The next book from his pen was a collection of short stories, *Twice-Told Tales.* This book was so successful that a second series appeared in 1842, five years after the first publication. As the collection stands to-day it contains some of the best and most characteristic work of the author. Some of the favorite stories included are "The Minister's Black Veil," "The Gray Champion," "The Gentle Boy," "The May-Pole of Merry Mount," and "The Ambitious Guest." The next important book was *Mosses from an Old Manse,* another collection of short stories. Among the pieces in this book are "Young Goodman Brown," "Rappaccini's Daughter," "The Celestial Railroad," and "Feathertop."

"The Scarlet Letter."—*The Scarlet Letter* (1850) is almost unanimously rated to-day as the best work of its author and one of the indubitable masterpieces of American literature. The novel owes its rating not to the fact that it employs a historical background, as some have said, for strictly speaking the book is not historical. Hawthorne uses all the freedom of an accomplished artist in the handling of the Puritan background, carefully suppressing everything except the deep shadows from which the grim tragedy naturally proceeds. In its presentation of the facts of Puritan life *The Scarlet Letter* is not to be compared with Whittier's little book, *Margaret Smith's Journal.* Hawthorne was interested only in creating a harmonious setting for his story. In his effort he succeeded and thus gave the book a firmer grip on fame than he could have done by the most carefully presented historical background. Almost any one with a bit of time and access to a good library can discover and write down the elementary facts of history. It takes an artist to paint the dark and foreboding shadows of *The Scarlet Letter.*

In its lowest terms *The Scarlet Letter* is a poetic treatment of sin and its consequences. Without doing violence to the author's intent, one can say that the thesis of the book is "The wages of sin is death." But the novel set out to prove nothing. As little argumentative as a Chopin nocturne, it as completely captures a mood, or rather a harmonious collection of moods, for each character is less a person than a disembodied human emotion. The moods created are those of remorse, sorrow, and despair. So completely are these feelings woven into the story that characters, action, and background blend into a delicate but enduring work of art. One of the most commendable characteristics of the book is its economy of effort. The story is reduced to its simplest elements, and those elements are presented in a series of tableaux that move along with deliberate haste to the appointed end. The narrative is not exactly consecutive, for each tableau corresponds roughly to an act of a drama, but the unquestioned tone-unity of the book is accomplished by the author's skill in the selection of his material and in the composition of each scene. The unity of impression is as marked as it is in "The Fall of the House of Usher."

The Scarlet Letter ought not to be compared with a great novel which grasps as its material an immense segment of life. It should not be likened to *Les Miserables, Vanity Fair, The Return of the Native, Tess of the D'Urbervilles,* or *Lord Jim.* Rather it should be classed with those books that set out to capture a mood, tragic or otherwise, and in a relatively short space create the atmosphere and set the figures that completely embody the desired effect. It belongs with such undoubted masterworks as its own author's short stories, the tales of Poe, Melville's *Benito Cereno,* Hardy's *Under the Greenwood Tree,* Conrad's *Youth,* Mrs. Wharton's *Ethan Frome,* and Miss Cather's *Lost Lady.* Never should the brevity of these stories lead one to underrate them, for size has relatively little to do with the merit of a work of art. Chopin's short piano pieces are just as remarkable as are his sonatas. The class that *The Scarlet Letter* belongs to is a high one, and in that class the book is entitled to an eminent position.

Hawthorne's Later Work.—The later work of Hawthorne is excellent, but it never once quite reaches the level of *The Scarlet Letter.* Probably the best of the later books is *The House of Seven Gables,* another novel invested with an artistically true and delicate background that affords a perfectly harmonious back-drop for the joyless drama that is enacted before it. It too is a poetic treatment of life in the shadows of an old house. It uses more major characters and more detail than *The Scarlet Letter,* but the story never quite attains the starkly classical perfection that the earlier novel reaches.

Blithedale Romance is the most interesting of Hawthorne's works to a reader who is concerned with the author's point of view, for this book uses Brook Farm as the scene of the action. In no other place is the author's lack of sympathy with romantic idealism more clearly marked. In Zenobia the novelist has given a spiteful picture of Margaret Fuller, and in other characters he has rather belittled the aims and intelligence of the reformers. The book does not give a very good picture of Brook Farm, but it gives an excellent portrayal of Hawthorne's mind. Henry James and William Dean Howells have given *Blithedale Romance* the highest praise. It is natural that these two critics would do so, for they were completely wedded to the realistic method, and this is the only novel by Hawthorne that is at all realistic.

The Marble Faun is another exploitation of the question of evil, this time in an Italian setting. For some quite inexplicable reason numbers of teachers have preferred that their classes make the acquaintance of Hawthorne in this story. Certainly the novel is a good piece of work, especially in the treatment of the Italian background. Every critic remarks that it is a "handy guide to Rome," but the book lacks the poetic glow that makes memorable *The Scarlet Letter* and *The House of Seven Gables*.

When Hawthorne is appraised from the standpoint of his romantic environment, he must be called a skeptic, a constantly doubting observer of current idealisms. Because he went back to the problem of evil in his best novels he has been called a Puritan, as if Puritans were the only people ever to have an interest in sin and its consequences. Puritan he was not; few of our writers have been less touched by the spirit of old New England. To Hawthorne the problem of evil was merely evocative of a mood. Once in hand, this problem was treated as a poetic theme and not as a text for moralizing. The novelist stood aside from Puritanism just as he stood aside from his own age. When all is said Hawthorne was preëminently an artist, interested more in presentation than in argumentation, more concerned with tone-color than with intellectual interests. It is as an artist and not as a thinker that he must be considered, and as such he stands almost unique in his generation. Nor has the passage of years dimmed the artistry of *The Scarlet Letter*. Fragile though it is, that book stands secure in its place in American literature.

HERMAN MELVILLE

(1819-1891)

The reputation of Herman Melville has had the most curious vicissitudes. His first book achieved a considerable degree of popularity, but each succeeding work met with less and less favor until the writer was forced to abandon a literary career for the monotonous duties of an inspector of customs. Although Melville lived for forty years after the period of his relative popularity, he meant so little to the readers of the seventies and eighties that when he died in

1891 few people seemed to recognize the significance of his work. A history of American literature published in 1901 gives him one sentence. Another of about ten years later fails to mention him in the body of the work but allots him three lines in the appendix and gives the names of five of his works. The four-volume Cambridge History of American Literature (1918) gives him three pages and a careful bibliography. The centenary of his birth awakened a considerable interest in the man, and in 1921 came the first biography, an admirable work by Raymond Weaver. Since that time Melville has been the subject of innumerable articles and of at least two excellent biographical and critical studies. Furthermore we know that more books on the man are in the making. The last published work, *Herman Melville*, by Lewis Mumford, says that the novelist "shares with Walt Whitman the distinction of being the greatest imaginative writer that America has produced: his epic, *Moby Dick*, is one of the supreme monuments of the English language; and in depth of expression and religious insight there is scarcely any one in the nineteenth century, with the exception of Dostoievsky, who can be placed beside him." Thus in the short space of thirty years the reputation of Melville has risen from complete obscurity to an equality with that of the greatest writers of all time. In another evaluation Mr. Mumford places *Moby Dick* beside *The Divine Comedy, Hamlet, The Brothers Karamazov,* and *War and Peace.*

Although it certainly is not easy to determine why Melville lost all his popularity there are discoverable reasons for the disfavor of the vast majority of American readers. In the first place the novelist so often and so bluntly stated his contempt for society and civilization that his offended public set him down as a misanthrope, a hater of mankind, and in this country no curse is so blastingly condemnatory as the accusation that a man is not willing to hob-nob with the crowd and to slap backs with the most vulgar. A similar charge caused our historians for fifty years to regard Thoreau as merely "the queer man of a New England village." In book after book Melville overlooked no chance to repudiate society and to excoriate the fruits of its most revered institutions. In his copy of Schopenhauer, the philosopher of pessimism, this sentence is underlined: "When two or three are gathered together, the devil is among them." Such was the feeling of Melville, and from the touch of man he shrank aghast. In one of many impersonations he appeared in *Moby Dick* as Ishmael, the outcast, the wanderer, and when men flee from society, they are very apt to create for themselves a dream-land from which all the plagues of earthly life will be banished. Thus did Jean Jacques Rousseau, Edgar Allan Poe, and James Branch Cabell, to name no more. Melville, too, had his own Utopia, his land of forgetfulness, but, unlike Mr. Cabell, he made the fatal mistake of visiting this land in person. The South Seas were Melville's Utopia, but a stay of four months in the tropic vale of Typee created in the visitor only an insuperable desire to escape. Thereafter all Utopias were subjected to Melville's skeptical criticism. Society simply would not do, and there was no escaping the company of man.

In the next place Melville, like Hawthorne, was burdened with the problem of evil, its origin, its meaning, and its final destiny. Especially prominent was this question in the greatest of his books, *Moby Dick*. Unlike Hawthorne, who set his discussions of evil in the dim shadows of the past, Melville insisted upon talking about the question in terms of contemporary civilization, and more than a few times his hot satire seared some object of unquestioned respectability. Such a novelist is bound to be uncomfortable, and if there is anything that the American of the fifties wanted to find in his literature it was comfort. Sentimental readers can snivel agreeably over the misfortunes of a wayward youth or maiden, but such people can get no pleasure out of a realistic analysis of comforting hypocrisies. Hawthorne's romanticism kept him from offending most readers; Melville's realism repelled many.

Finally, Melville was declared to be obscure. It is true that such a charge cannot be successfully denied in the case of *Mardi* and *Pierre*, and the full meaning of *Moby Dick* is not exactly crystal-clear, but the meaning of *Typee, Omoo, Redburn,* and *White Jacket* is not debatable. Four more lucid and straightforward works are not to be found. But the charge of obscurity was effective. *Pierre* was declared to be a hodge-podge of German philosophy. The charge was damaging, for Kant and Hegel were not so attractive to the general reader in 1855 as they were to Emerson and Parker in the first flush of discovery many years earlier. While the reasons here given might not have been potent enough to account for all of Melville's lack of popularity, they would account for at least some of it.

Life of Melville.—Herman Melville was born in New York City. Both his mother and his father belonged to old and rather distinguished families. His mother was a Gansevoort, one of the Dutch families long prominent in the life of the city. In 1832 the father died, leaving the mother burdened by the care of a large family of small children. Herman received no college training whatever, and the cold, hampered environment in which he grew up was hardly a desirable training school for a genius. A good deal of his early life can be glimpsed in the first chapters of *Redburn*. This book, the third of the author's, gives a most interesting account of Melville's first voyage, a round-trip from New York to Liverpool in 1837. So far as one can ascertain to-day there is a very slight fictitious element in this account, though one does have difficulty in telling whether all the bitterness in the heart of Wellingborough Redburn was really in the heart of the young Melville, or whether it was placed there by the author of 1849 who had then suffered many embittering experiences and disappointments.

After returning from his first voyage Melville engaged in a variety of occupations until early in 1841, when he shipped as a sailor from New Bedford, Massachusetts, on the whaler "Acushnet," immortalized as the "Pequod" of *Moby Dick*. In about four years the whaler returned with her holds filled with oil, but Melville was not in the crew. After serving on the ship for about eighteen months he and a young companion, Toby Greene, deserted at the Marquesas Islands, an archipelago in the south Pacific. Five days of hardship and thrilling adventure followed the desertion, and then the boys came into the beautiful valley of Typee. The whole story is given in *Typee* and there is hardly a reader who will not thank the one who sends him to that delightful source for his information. The inhabitants were savages—cannibals, Melville feared—but their manners were kind, and they inhabited a veritable paradise. Toby soon escaped, and after Melville had been held for four months "in an indulgent captivity" he too managed to get away.

An Australian whaler rescued Melville, but service on this ship was too distasteful to be endured, and he left the vessel at Tahiti. In company with a ship's doctor, Long Ghost, he had some interesting adventures on this island, adventures which are vividly related in *Omoo*, another book that seems destined for immortality. After knocking about the Pacific for some time, Melville finally started for home on board a United States war vessel, arriving in Boston in October, 1844. The story of this trip is told in *White Jacket*.

Upon reaching home Melville wrote all his books in quick succession. He began in 1846 with *Typee; Omoo* followed a year later. In 1849 came two books, *Redburn* and *Mardi,* with *White Jacket* appearing the following year. By this time Melville was married, and the question of a steady income was becoming increasingly important. All these books had had a certain sale, but none had reached enough popularity that the author could call himself a success. In 1850 he bought a farm in the Berkshire Hills of western Massachusetts, and here he settled down to the task of writing *Moby Dick.* In the Berkshires the novelist had Hawthorne for a near neighbor, and between the two men there developed a close friendship, one of the most intimate that either ever enjoyed. It is a question whether the writers influenced each other. Certainly they had relatively little in common save a deep pessimism, much more pronounced in Melville, and a desire to probe the question of evil. In the congenial neighborhood of another writer, *Moby Dick* was completed and published in 1851 with a dedication to Hawthorne. The great epic of the sea did not sell very well. In 1852 came *Pierre,* a work that some critics have called a "desperate book." Certainly it was most confusing, and its unpopularity was assured from the start. Thereafter Melville wrote less, and with the exception of *Israel Potter* and *The Piazza Tales,* a collection of short stories, his books could not be expected to appeal to a general audience.

The necessity of making a living led Melville in 1867 to take a position in the New York Custom House. In 1886, when Mrs. Melville inherited enough money to give the two a competence in their old age, the novelist resigned his position and essayed a little writing. *Billy Budd,* the one interesting result of this period, was not published until many years after the author's death. The long-forgotten novelist and traveler of the South Seas died in 1891.

"Typee" and "Omoo."—Melville discovered the South Seas for literature. The discoverer has been followed to those delectable isles by Robert Louis Stevenson, Pierre Loti, Somerset Maugham, and Rupert Brooke—a goodly company—to say nothing of the dozens of less distinguished writers who have given us more or less truthful narratives of life in the southern Pacific, but of all the books produced about the South Seas, it is gravely to be doubted if any exceed the first two in literary merit. Of these two *Typee* is probably more widely admired than is *Omoo.* The earlier book has a freshness of presentation and a sparkle of genius about it that the latter does not always possess, though the portrait of Dr. Long Ghost in *Omoo* is one

of Melville's triumphs. But *Typee* has many triumphs. It spread before the ravished gaze of the culture-sick European the sun-drenched greenery of an Eden uncursed by culture and its penalties, unmarred by the blight of civilization. Fayaway is an imperishable figure; in her the primitive beauty of a long-vanished past and the transient youth of all mankind are made eternal. "She was neither a mystery nor a sin," but a goddess of classical antiquity, imagined by the clear-headed Greeks, who rejoiced in the objective beauty and color of the world and left brooding sorrows and vain misgivings as the melancholy birthright of a less joyous time. Then, too, the episodes of *Typee* are related with a vividness and dramatic skill that give each one as sharp an outline as if it were the personal experience of each reader.

The curious thing about the two books is the fact that they represent the recollections of a young man of twenty-six, and yet they have in them the acrid reflections that usually follow a spent youth and the disillusions of middle or old age. Nor do these books reflect the indefinite and indefinable green-sickness of youth. Each contains numerous and specific indictments of civilization, and every indictment is fortified by concrete evidence of objective evils that are traced to the influence of society. The point of view is that of a scientific but hostile critic, not that engendered of a romantic melancholy, vaguely objecting to things present and known. The prospect of life in the valley of Typee was so attractive that it raised Melville's estimate of the human race, an estimate that went down precipitously when the writer again reached so-called civilized men. Whence came this bitterness, this black rage against civilization? Did Melville carry it into Typee, or did the unspoiled life in the tropical valley first make him realize the festering sores of civilization? In the answer to that question lies one of the keys to the riddle of Herman Melville.

There is one more question that perplexes: why did Melville leave his island paradise? It is true that over him constantly hovered the dread of being eaten by his hosts, who, he suspected, were cannibals. Did this fear drive him from the island? The answer is highly uncertain. Melville's fear could have been removed completely and permanently by his submitting to the process of tattooing, an act that would have made him a blood-brother of the tribe. But tattooing was the thing that he constantly refused, and in his refusal he rejected the happiness of Typee. After all, perhaps happiness was not for Melville. He had tasted of the bitter waters of civilization, and not all the sweet springs of Typee could bring forgetfulness. All his life he was tortured by his recollections, hopes, and aspirations; never could he find peace. Hawthorne once said that Melville would gain no rest until he could get hold of some definite belief. "He can neither believe nor be comfortable in his unbelief, and he is too honest and courageous not to try to be one or the other." This is one of the best criticisms of Melville ever uttered, and liberally interpreted it explains many things in the man's life. It can be made to explain his departure from Typee and his subsequent idealization of life among the savages.

"Redburn" and "White Jacket."—*Redburn* and *White Jacket* are among the best sea stories in our language. They are too factual to be compared with Conrad's poetic interpretations of the sea, and far too good to be likened to the ordinary travel books. They belong in the class with such works as Dana's *Two Years Before the Mast*. Mr. John Masefield, himself a sailor and writer of the sea, declares that he likes *Redburn* best of all the books by Melville. Certainly the description of the ship and her motley crew, the events of the voyage, the unforgettable misery that Melville saw in the slums of Liverpool, and the sinister figure of Jackson, one of the ship's company, are all set forth with a literary skill that makes the reader a participant in the experiences described. In *White Jacket* the outstanding achievement of the writer is the creation of Jack Chase, one of the most admirable figures that has ever entered any book of the sea. Incidentally *White Jacket* presents so vivid an indictment of the evils of flogging in the navy that copies of the book were given to every member of Congress when the abolition of that evil was under consideration.

"Mardi" and "Pierre."—*Mardi* and *Pierre* are alike in that they are both fantastic extravaganzas that many critics have pronounced hopelessly incomprehensible. To-day one has difficulty going the full length with these critics, but certainly the books are far from clear.

Mardi starts out like an ordinary romance of the South Seas. There is an escape from a whaler, the meeting with an apparently deserted brigantine, and a shipwreck, but in the second half of the book the atmosphere of reality changes to one of complete fancy. From then on the story becomes a chaotic allegory of life with the pursuit of the maiden Yillah by the hero of the book representing the fruitless quest of man for beauty. All the kingdoms of the world and all the still more extensive kingdoms of philosophy become parts of Melville's satirical allegory. (The machinery of the book is simply the search for happiness by mankind, eternally disillusioned, eternally hopeful.) *Mardi* is not totally incomprehensible, but understanding the book is no child's play.

Pierre is probably the wildest, bitterest book ever produced on this continent. It was the last of the author's great works in point of composition and to it he brought his full powers, but when he sat down to write, he was laboring under the inescapable fact that he had just poured his very life blood into *Moby Dick* to no purpose. Into *Pierre* went all the pent-up anger of an outraged soul. It is Melville's "spiritual autobiography," worthy of comparison with the confessions of Rousseau or St. Augustine. When the author looked at life, especially when he considered how his own days had been spent, his heart was black within him, and out of this blackness came *Pierre*. Naturally his own generation would have none of it, and for seventy years (until 1929) it was very hard to find a copy of this novel.

"Moby Dick."—On the surface *Moby Dick* is a book of the whale. Everything that is known of the leviathan is here written down, his anatomy, his habits, his different varieties, his economic importance, and especially his capture and transformation into whale oil. 1851 was a good time to tell the story of the whale. Nantucket and New Bedford ships were nosing into every corner of the seven seas in search of their quarry, and the fame of the harpooners and boatmen was a magnet to attract thousands of New England boys away from the safe but monotonous hill farms. And wealth waited the successful whaler, for did not Nantucket have a Pacific Bank, whose capital stock came out of the western ocean? Whaling was the romantic occupation that gold-mining was shortly, that railroad building and air-plane flying later became.

The plain story of *Moby Dick* is simple. The narrator, Ishmael, leaves Nantucket on the whaler "Pequod." The vessel is commanded by Captain Ahab, who has lost a leg in a combat with a huge white whale. The whale escaped, and the brooding over his misfortune and the deep thirst for revenge made Ahab a monomaniac. His one overpowering desire is to kill the white whale, and the story is that of an eager, relentless search for Moby Dick by a crazed captain at the head of a wild crew. Thus far the book is simplicity itself, for despite its length, the meaning of the informative passages and the thread of the narrative need no explanation.

But the plain facts and the simple narrative are not all of *Moby Dick,* though one may read the book with much pleasure and profit and see nothing else there. The acute reader does not go far before he begins to sense that there is more to the story than the mere words indicate. Symbolism makes an unmistakable appearance; certain episodes seem to be allegorical. The beginning reader need not be worried by such things. Any one will be reasonably safe in considering that Moby Dick stands for evil, the ocean for life, and Captain Ahab for the unconquerable soul of man. The long search for Moby Dick, the combat, and the ultimate catastrophe are the allegorical representation of the spirit of man grappling with the vast problem of evil. Melville says: "That unsounded ocean you gasp in is Life." Once more: "The White Whale swam before him as the monomaniac incarnation of all those malicious agencies which some deep men feel eating at them."

An exact analysis of the symbolical meaning of *Moby Dick* is impossible, for Melville wrote the book, according to his own statement, with no clear grasp of the allegory. Some have interpreted the whale as the universe; some have seen in Ahab the very image of Melville. With these interpreters there is no quarrel; their reading of the story does not differ materially enough from the one given to allow a very clearly distinguished difference of opinion. It is probable that the chief figures may have meant one thing to Melville to-day and quite another to-morrow, for he said: "What the White Whale was to them, or how to their unconscious understandings, also, in some dim, unsuspected way, he might have seemed the gliding great demon of the seas of life—all this to explain would be to dive deeper than Ishmael can go." The meaning of *Moby Dick* is no clearer than is the ultimate meaning of *Hamlet.*

Moby Dick is a book of many inconsistencies and contradictions. Certain passages are very clear, others are not; sometimes the action is swift and dramatic, sometimes it is wholly suspended for pages and pages of exact but irrelevant information. Notwithstanding the lapses of the narrative, *Moby Dick* has more compelling power than any other book has in the whole field of American literature, and one must go to the heights of English drama and Russian fiction to find its equal. Few sensitive readers can scramble to the deck of the "Pequod" and there meet the monomaniac captain without becoming a passenger on that strange voyage that does not end until ship, captain, and crew are buried in the "great shroud of the sea."

Whatever *Moby Dick* may mean to various people, a sea voyage, a treatise on whales, or a study of abnormal psychology, it will have its wisest reading as a symphony or huge epic of the sea. The book must be read for one to see how effectively the author captured the mood of the ocean and with what power he transferred that mood to paper. For sheer artistry there are unsurpassed chapters in *Moby Dick*. The style of the prose is admirably fitted to the material and the mood. Indeed it is not prose; it is poetry. Pages and pages of the story have the majesty and power of great verse, and at times the characters talk in a language that has never been equaled for force and rhythmical beauty since the days of Shakespeare. *Moby Dick* is more than a book—it is an experience, just about the greatest experience that recent literature can offer. Talking about it is futile; it must be read to be appreciated.

The Minor Works.—This inadequate discussion leaves untouched a number of Melville's minor works. The chief of these are *Benito Cereno* and *Israel Potter*. *Benito Cereno* is a story of an adventure encountered by an American sea captain off the coast of South America. The framework of the narrative was taken almost verbatim from official records, but Melville touched the cold, lifeless facts of a captain's reports with the genius of a born story-teller, and the result is a perfect evocation of atmosphere. Over every word of the narrative hangs a nameless dread, a feeling of horror and disaster. The story creates a mood as well as does "The Fall of the House of Usher," but Poe could never get the reality into his lines that Melville achieved so deftly. *Israel Potter* is a good historical novel with John Paul Jones and Franklin among the characters. It deserves more readers than it has ever had.

The story of the romantic revolution is at an end. At the close of the Civil War the Golden Day was ready to plunge into the gray and undistinguished twilight. Walt Whitman alone of the romantic writers was still producing, and he was but amplifying a chant that he had first raised ten years earlier. Industrialism had triumphed; war had only emphasized the completeness of the victory of expediency and material interests over romantic idealism. A vague romanticism lingered on through the twilight in the shape of the feeble enthusiasm of the Genteel Tradition. Poetry was in the hands of the imitators of Lowell and Longfellow. Fiction was in the hands of the local colorists.

Even though the romantic revolution was lost in the murky smoke from factory and battle field, it accomplished a great work in America. An intellectual movement that gave birth to every first-rate novel, poem, and story written in America from 1820 to 1860 cannot be dismissed as a futile, Quixotic charge against the whirling mills of materialism. Even if romanticism had produced nothing more than the *Journals* of Emerson, *Walden, Leaves of Grass,* and *Moby Dick,* the revolution would have been considered a notable fact in any modern literature.

SUGGESTED READINGS

Melville in the last twenty years has come to be a favorite subject with critics, scholars, and aspiring candidates for the doctorate. The list given below is highly selective.

Anderson: *Melville in the South Seas.* New York. 1939.
> If this work is not the last word on the subject, it is very nearly the last. Strictly factual.

Arvin: *Hawthorne.* Boston. 1929.

Arvin (ed.): *The Heart of Hawthorne's Journals.* Boston. 1929.

Cantwell: *Nathaniel Hawthorne, the American Years.* New York. 1948.

Freeman: *Herman Melville.* New York. 1926.
> Good brief discussion.

Hawthorne: *Nathaniel Hawthorne and His Wife.* Boston. 1884.
> Written by Julian Hawthorne, son of the novelist. Valuable, but it has the faults of most biographies written by members of the subject's family.

Lawrence: *Studies in Classic American Literature.* New York. 1923.
> A most peculiar work but stimulating.

Macy: *Spirit of American Literature.* New York. 1912.
> Contains good chapter on Hawthorne, but when this work was written Melville was not rediscovered.

Matthiessen: *American Renaissance.* New York. 1941. Hawthorne, pp. 179-368; Melville, pp. 371-514.
> Despite frequent lapses into incoherence, this work is one of the most important in the whole American field.

Morris: *The Rebellious Puritan.* New York. 1927.
> The value of this psychological study of Hawthorne is disputed.

Mumford: *Herman Melville*. New York. 1929.

> An interesting and valuable critical study, but the tone throughout is one of uncritical laudation. The book is marred by many errors of fact.

Reed: "Self-Portraiture in the Works of Nathaniel Hawthorne." *Studies in Philology*, 23: 40-54.

Sedgwick: *Herman Melville*.. Cambridge. 1944.

> Recent critical study of some little value.

Stewart (ed.): *American Notebooks of Nathaniel Hawthorne*. New Haven. 1932.

> The editor is an authority on Hawthorne.

Stewart: *Nathaniel Hawthorne, a Biography*. New Haven. 1948.

Thorpe: *Melville*. New York. 1938.

> This book of selections has a good introduction.

Van Doren: *The American Novel*. New York. 1921. Hawthorne, pp. 77-108; Melville, pp. 68-76.

Weaver: *Herman Melville, Mariner and Mystic*. New York. 1921.

> This first biography of Melville is still most valuable, but much research since 1921 has uncovered a large amount of new material.

BOOK IV

THE TRIUMPH OF REALISM

I. THE GILDED AGE (1865-1890)

CHAPTER XVI

THE INDUSTRIALIZATION OF THE UNITED STATES

INDUSTRY DURING THE GILDED AGE

The term "Gilded Age" is coming to be applied to the quarter of a century between the close of the Civil War and 1890. The epoch is so called because it was a time when everything in our social and business life was colored by gold, when money was sole criterion by which everything was judged, and when our whole nation was engaged in a mad, vulgar scramble for the possession of dollars. Americans have never been loath to accept wealth, and usually they have been quite willing to work hard to get it, for our people have always been dominated by middle-class ideas, not the least of which is the urge to "get on in the world." In the beginning this continent was settled by men who were seeking to better their economic status. In the eighteenth century Benjamin Franklin spent a great deal of his time in pointing out the way of success to his eager disciples, and the westward rolling line of settlement was forwarded by land hunger, more than by any other motive. The factory system was started in this country by those who wished to produce revenue from large-scale industry, and one of the chief concerns of Alexander Hamilton and Daniel Webster—to name no more—was to protect our manufacturing interests. Certainly we have never been despisers of wealth, but money-getting activities never reached so great proportions or degenerated into so frenzied a scramble as they achieved in the twenty-five years following the Civil War.

From 1800 to 1865 industry was beset by two vigorous rivals. In the first place business enterprise was confined very largely to the northeastern seaboard. It was highly sectional. As such it was opposed by the small farmers of the Middle West and fought furiously and determinedly by the planters of the South. In the hands of the last class was vast political power, and every ounce of that power was hurled against the manufacturing interests of the northeast. This would have made the way of industry hard enough, but in addition the implications of commercialism were opposed by the romantic spirit that was reaching so vigorous an expression in New England. The southern planters fought industry in the political arena, while romanticism used every effort to discredit it by an appeal to the individual longings and spiritual desires that were very apt to be swallowed up by rapacious commercial and manufacturing interests, if these interests were much extended. But despite these handicaps industrialism won. "Things are in the saddle," was the melancholy observation of Emerson that seemed to prophesy evil to romanticism. Prophecy or observation or both, it was amply confirmed. Industrialism could not be checked; it was destined to control the country, despite the efforts of agriculture and the moral opposition of romanticism. In the struggle romanticism was killed, and there are those who say that agriculture was wounded unto death.

Romanticism was ended by science, technology, invention, in short, by the industrial revolution and the subsequent development of manufacturing and its allied interests, commerce and finance. Industry stood for monetary profit, material progress, and the rule of common sense and expediency; romanticism stood for high idealism and the life of the spirit. Since 1860 the business man has been without a serious rival as the dominant figure in American life.

Conditions After the Civil War.—The Civil War marked the achievement of a double revolution in American life and thought. It signalized the triumph of the philosophy of industrialism over the philosophy of romanticism, and it gave unmistakable notice to the world that the political power of the southern planters was at an end. As a matter of fact both aspects of the revolution had been consummated before the first gun was fired at Fort Sumter. While no one can be very definite in dealing with so intangible a thing as the spiritual and intellectual life of a people, one is fairly safe in asserting that the romantic movement was showing signs of a sharp decline by 1860. The thirties and forties were the heyday of romanticism, but by the middle of the next decade most of the familiar aspects of the great movement were noticeably waning. Certainly by 1865 the chief tenets of romanticism were as old-fashioned as the laws of Hammurabi, and it is very doubtful if so complete a downfall could have been accomplished in so short a time as the duration of the war if the romantic movement had not been on the decline before 1861.

The other aspect of the revolution, the overthrow of the planting aristocracy, was also virtually effected before 1860. At least the South had lost the war long before the outbreak of hostilities. It had lost it to the wealth, industry, and population of the North, although it required the force of arms and four years of time to demonstrate to the Southerners that an agricultural society cannot dominate more than twice its population sustained by vastly superior wealth and industry. The Civil War was won in the factories and money markets of the North, and those institutions had been developing rapidly for more than half a century. From the southern point of view the outcome of the war was as calamitous as possible. Southern agriculture was prostrate, the land was fallow, the horses and mules were among the casualties of the battle field, the buildings were burned or in dilapidation, and the field workers, worth from three to five billion dollars before the war, were freed from any obligation to till the crops. Furthermore the business life of the South had simply disappeared. Confederate paper money was worthless, hard money was not to be had, and the state governments were forced to repudiate their bonds. Worst of all from the southern standpoint, national political leadership had passed from the hands of the landed aristocrats to the hands of the "mudsills of society," the mechanics of the North.

In only one respect was the southern estimate mistaken; political power had passed from the South, but into the hands of the industrialists and farmers of the North and West. In the strange political partnership thus created the real power was wielded by the manufacturing and commercial interests, though a western president usually was in the White House. One of the largest concessions made to the western farmer by the partnership was the passage of the Homestead Act in 1862, a law that the southern planters and the commercial interests had formerly opposed with equal vigor. But the war had taken the Southerners out of political life, and the industrialists were so situated that it was necessary to placate their political partners. Out of the legislation passed during the progress of the war, industry seized the opportunity to achieve its long-desired aims. These aims were embodied in laws that provided for a high tariff, for a system of national banks, and for generous grants for the construction of a transcontinental railroad. The first two of these measures had been vigorously opposed by the western farmers and by the southern planters, while the Southerners had looked dubiously upon a proposal to finance a railroad to the Pacific until the suggestion was made that Memphis or New Orleans be made the eastern terminus. While the war was in progress, the passage of all these acts was easy. The western farmers, elated over the Homestead Act, were in a mood to acquiesce in the suggestions of their benefactors.

The Nationalizing Effect of Industry.—The effect of the three measures passed by the industrialists was to nationalize and consolidate the country more firmly than ever before. In the days before the war all the forces that opposed the spread of industrialism made for diversity and disunity; they tended to develop local and sectional characteristics rather than the growth of national feeling. The southern planters were notoriously in favor of state and local government, and the western farmers were as thoroughly committed to the principles of personal independence and self-direction through their own local governmental agencies. The whole implication of romanticism was individual development and government without the intervention of a strongly centralized state. These were formidable forces of opposition, and they effectively checked for many decades the growth of a strong nationalism. But under cover of the war cloud the industrialists passed the measures that helped insure the steady and permanent nationalization of the country.

The process of nationalization in the abstract was probably the last thing that the industrialists thought of; they were interested in gaining and consolidating a rich market for their wares. The tariff law built a wall of protection around the nation that effectively prevented the entry to our home markets of competitive foreign goods. This law simply meant that the American manufacturer would be allowed to treat this nation as his own private domain, and whatever market he could find or create here would be his without interference. The national bank law stabilized the money and banking system of the country and thus greatly facilitated the transaction of business. This act made a large and very important group of banks independent of state control and placed them under national supervision. Hitherto each state had passed its own banking laws, and while the national bank act did not supersede all these laws, it allowed the formation of banking houses all over the country under one jurisdiction. The building of a transcontinental railroad bound the country more closely together physically, and guaranteed the manufacturers a swift and inexpensive way of distributing their goods to markets that had hitherto been almost inaccessible. It is often said that the nationalization of our country was effected by the Civil War. Such a statement needs a bit of qualification; the most powerful nationalizing forces loosed in this country as the result of the war were three acts that were passed without direct reference to the struggle that was being decided on the field of battle.

Industry looked with no favor upon the Homestead Act, but when the manufacturers found that immigrants would replace the workers drawn west by the attraction of free land, they consented to the passage of the bill. Accordingly for fifty years after the passage of the act and for twenty-five years after the virtual disappearance of the free land, our lenient immigration laws were a constant invitation to foreigners. During that time millions of aliens came to our shores, many of whom found employment in the shops and mills of American industry.

The greatest favor that industry gained from the Civil War was the passage of the fourteenth amendment to the Constitution that in one provision forbids a state to deprive any person of property without "due process of law." Since an incorporated business is legally a person, the importance of this amendment is immense. It is probably safe to say that more important cases originate under "due process of law" clause than under any other two or three sections of the Constitution.

The Reign of Business.—The imagination is staggered by a recital of the cold facts that show with what energy and avidity the business interests of the United States availed themselves of their self-made opportunities to pile up huge profits. Within twenty-five years the value of the manufactured products in this country increased from less than two billion dollars to more than nine billion, and with the improved methods of manufacturing there is no very good reason for not thinking that the increase in profit was greater than the increase in production. Figures showing the amount of governmental aid given the Union Pacific Railroad will give some idea of the official attitude toward all private business enterprise. It has been estimated that the corporation that built the line from Omaha to Ogden, Utah, received from the government 12,800 acres of land for every mile of road completed and a cash subsidy that varied from $16,000 to $48,000 for each mile. With so great a sum of money being thrown about recklessly it is no wonder that soon every one was frantic with the acquisitive fever.

The building of railroads was not the only way by which men

made quick and easy money from 1865 to 1890, though the construction of almost every other important line during that period saw a repetition of the methods used by the builders of the Union Pacific, except that money grants were not so lavishly bestowed. The western railroads opened up the richest body of timber in the world for exploitation by lumbermen. Untold riches in oil, coal, and other minerals lay in the earth waiting for the driller or miner, and other fortunes were ready for the men who would prepare for the market the droves of livestock that soon were to replace the slaughtered buffalo on the western plains. Soon every industry had its millionaires, and there were few that did not boast their plutocrats, men whose wealth ran into fabulous figures. The Gilded Age saw the rise of such men as Gould, Harriman, Hill, Rockefeller, Morgan, W. A. Clark, Philip Armour, and a thousand others who varied from their prototypes only in the possession of a lesser amount of money.

From 1865 to 1890 the first steps were taken toward the complete industrialization of the United States. The making of great fortunes became the primary aim of our people, and there was no very effective social philosophy to counteract the results of unbridled commercialization. Romanticism was gone, and it was to have no immediate successor. Manufacturing, transportation, and financial enterprises were being conducted on large scales, and profits accrued that were worthy of the scale of the undertakings. The social, intellectual, and spiritual results of this widespread industrialization were enormous. Modern America is the product of the Gilded Age, not the product of the earlier romantic period. The heritage of the Gilded Age can be seen in the problems of our huge cities, in our labor questions, in the dilemma of the farmers, and especially in the workaday psychology and philosophy of the American people.

The Problem of Labor.—Industry cannot flourish in a rural population, and a rural population cannot thrive where industry is dominant. Manufacturing and commerce are irresistible magnets drawing people to large centers, and one of the first results of the industrial wave was the beginning of the shift from the rural districts to the cities. The growth of the cities meant the outbreak of acute social questions. Housing, public health, police and fire protection, and municipal government all became pressing problems during the Gilded Age, but the question that created the greatest amount of ominous comment and conjecture was that of labor. Such a problem could not have arisen in a rural society like that envisioned by the southern planters or by the romantics of New England. It took industrial America to bring it to life.

In the old days of home manufacturing labor questions were impossible. Every man was his own employer. He set his own hours of labor, bought his own raw materials, and sold his product in the best possible market. But the advent of factories changed all this. The factory system meant the aggregation of capital in quantities far beyond reach of the average individual. It meant the hiring of laborers in large numbers who worked at highly specialized tasks with the aid of machinery. Whereas it was once hard to learn a trade like shoemaking, it became easy to work in a shoe factory, for a man or woman could quickly become reasonably proficient in the use of a machine. Gone was all the old-time independence of the laborer. He was no longer his own master. Frequently he no longer lived in his own house, but occupied one that was exactly like rows of others, all belonging to the company. The worker was no longer a self-controlled individual; he was a unit of industry. The object of the employer was to work his men the longest possible time for the smallest possible wage. Similarly the object of the laborer was to demand shorter hours with no appreciable loss of pay. Capital and labor were squaring away for a mighty struggle.

Organization of Labor.—Although labor unions have existed in the United States since 1825, the labor question did not become acute until after the Civil War. Before the great struggle and the beginning of the vast industrial boom, the unions had been weak and rather purposeless organizations, but after the war there was a rapid accumulation of dissatisfaction and a swift effort to unite all workers in one union. The result was the National Labor Union, founded in 1866, that tried to be all things to all workers. In general it suffered from a lack of concrete aims, and though it took a stand for the eight-hour day, for the establishment of a national bureau of labor, and for the exclusion of Chinese, it could never decide whether it wished to accept the privately owned system of industry or whether it was in favor of factories owned by the state or the workers. After a chaotic existence this organization came to an end in 1872.

The National Labor Union was succeeded by the Knights of Labor, an organization that admitted to membership any one except professional gamblers, saloon keepers, lawyers, and bankers. This group had rather more definite aims than did its predecessor, but it too suffered from grandiose schemes for the reorganization of society, and it had quite a bit of the economic radicalism of the romantic period. It played with all kinds of ideas from almost every source. Western agrarianism, socialism, and various other theories found their way into meetings of the Knights of Labor. All this aroused opposition, but the chief weakness of the organization was the attempt to place all laborers, skilled and unskilled, in one group. For more than a decade this was the only labor organization in this country, but in 1883 a group of practical men formed the American Federation of Labor.

This new group made no attempt to become one big union of all laborers, but started with the idea of federating trade unions in one inclusive organization. Thus a man did not belong to the American Federation directly but held his membership there through his affiliation with a trade union. Such a plan of organization eliminated some of the weaknesses of the earlier attempts. The hangers-on and well-wishers of labor found no place in the new group. The membership was solidly from the laboring class, and an overwhelming percentage was from the skilled trades. These facts gave a unity of ideas and aims to the Federation that the earlier "one big unions" had not possessed.

From the beginning the Federation was rather conservative. It naturally supported such demands of labor as the eight-hour day, high wages, and general good working conditions, but it refused to have anything to do with the socialistic movement that was beginning to assume some little importance, and moreover it declined to form a new political party with the laboring class as its basis. Samuel Gompers and the other men who formed the Federation accepted the present capitalistic system of industry, that is, private ownership by the capitalist-employers. This acceptance of capitalism somewhat reassured the moneyed class, which had looked with great alarm upon the radical tendencies of the National Labor Union and the Knights of Labor.

However conservative the American Federation may have been in its acceptance of the capitalistic system and in its refusal to form a new political party, the organization exerted a great influence for liberalism in our state and national politics. Among other things it stood for a graduated income tax, generously supported education for all children, direct election of United States senators, control of legislation by the voters through the initiative, referendum, and the recall, and various other proposals that were advanced from time to time. Many of these proposals were made into law after being incorporated in the platforms of both major political parties, for the Federation held steadily to the policy of rewarding its friends and punishing its enemies irrespective of party.

The Great Strikes of the Gilded Age.—The oft-repeated prophecy of the southern planters that the North would ultimately see a civil war between capital and labor seemed to be promised a speedy fulfillment during the Gilded Age. Before the smoke of battle cleared, industrial trouble broke out in various parts of the North, the most serious being bitter and expensive strikes by the shoemakers in a number of industrial centers. But it was not until after 1873 that strikes became a serious national question.

The panic of 1873 was responsible for a widespread financial distress and a consequent lack of employment by laborers. Millions of people were in the grip of grinding poverty, and thousands of unemployed walked the streets of our cities seeking desperately for work. At the height of the industrial depression came two strikes of national importance, one among the textile workers of New England, the other among the anthracite miners of Pennsylvania. Both were serious affairs, and both ended in defeat for the strikers, but these affairs were only skirmishes in the great struggle that was brewing.

In 1877 some of the eastern railroads announced wage cuts of ten per cent. At once virtually all the railroads east of the Mississippi and north of the Ohio were paralyzed by the walkout of their workers. Attempts to run the roads with the aid of strike-breakers met with determined opposition. In several cities the militia, reënforced by troops of the regular army, were summoned to preserve order. The results were numerous bloody clashes between the soldiers and the strikers; property to the value of millions of dollars was burned; dozens of lives were lost; and hundreds were wounded in the pitched battles fought in the streets of various cities. Over large portions of the country it seemed that law and order were at an end. The most serious situations arose in Baltimore, Pittsburgh, and Buffalo, but rioting occurred in Chicago and St. Louis and as far away as San Francisco. After many days of tumult and street fighting the railroads began to run their trains under the protection of the military. The tragic affair ended in total defeat for the workers, but the immediate results of tragedy, property loss, and social disaster were far exceeded by the lamentable after-effects. The strike brought an atmosphere of suspicion and hate into our industrial life that was not lost for at least a generation. The whole affair came very near breaking out into class war, the dread event long foretold by Southerners, and peace, when it finally came, was not peace, but a suspension of hostilities. The fire of class antagonism smoldered on, ready to break into flames at a moment's notice. Never did the whole social structure of the country seem so near to disaster as it did in the seventies, and the most ominous threat came from the relations of capital and labor.

Industrialism had already proved one thing: it had demonstrated that the shift of our population from an agricultural basis to an industrial and financial basis means the loss of a certain independence of thought and action, and the substitution of collective thought and action. The whole tendency of events after the Civil War was to organize our society into classes. Labor unions and federations, strikes, the great combinations of capital, and the very processes of industry all assisted in the growth of class consciousness. Gone was the old independence, the feeling of self-sufficiency, the buoyant faith that all would end well. The employer became a unit in a complex organization, and the laborer became a unit of energy in the factory. Both faced certain facts that could not be romanticized into something pleasant. The unpleasantness of inescapable facts and the substitution of collective thought and action for individualism were sure to have great effects in our national literature.

CHANGES IN AGRICULTURE DURING THE GILDED AGE

While the American industrial system and the status of the laborer were undergoing great changes from 1865 to 1890, agriculture was experiencing a revolution no less momentous. The final results of this revolution are not yet apparent, but the main effect has been to lay the standardizing hand of industrialization on the farmer almost as sharply as it has been laid on the laborer and the employer.

Agriculture in the South.—For the purpose of this study agriculture in the South is of relatively slight importance, though the great changes that the basic occupation underwent in the Kingdom of Cotton were paralleled by just as great changes in other portions of the country. Before the war three-fourths of southern agricultural products were produced by slave labor in fields that belonged to large landholders. The remainder of the products came from lands held by the despised middle class who were often struggling with dire poverty. After the war the tendency was for the large plantations to pass into the hands of the former slaves or the middle class. Not all the large estates were broken up, for tenant farming has been common in the South ever since 1865, and with the passage of the years its importance has increased. In the last decade or two there is said to be an increasing tendency toward the system of large holdings worked by tenants or hired laborers. The war changed the labor system and abolished the aristocracy, but other features of the old order have been retained.

Along with the growth of large plantations on the plan of those before the war has gone the industrialization of agriculture. To-day machinery is much more prevalent and far more complicated than ever before. Fewer hands are required in the fields, and if it were not for the necessity of picking the cotton by hand, the same methods would be used in the fields of Alabama and Mississippi that prevail in the wheat fields of Kansas, Minnesota, and Washington. As it is, the southern farmer has lost much of his old-time independence and his mistrust of industrialism. In fact, he is in a fair way to be industrialized.

The Exhaustion of Free Land.—From the earliest days of settlement one of the dominant influences in American development, material, intellectual, and spiritual, was the presence on the western frontier of a vast amount of open land. The existence of that land determined the character of much of our politics, our economics, our thought, and our conception of the problems of human existence. Without the great reservoir of western land as one of the chief impelling forces in American life, much that is most significant in our history would never have occurred.

Before the Civil War government land had been sold in varying amounts to speculators as well as to bona fide settlers, but none of it was given away as a home to the man who was willing to live on it. In 1862 the system was changed. Land was still sold, but any one could get a title to a homestead of 160 acres by living on it for a specified number of years. Under this impetus there was an unprecedented rush for public land, and within thirty years from the passage of the Homestead Act, the government officially announced the disappearance of the frontier and the virtual disappearance of our open land.

It is absolutely true to say that these facts actually shocked all our society, and the shock was not confined to this country. Gone was the time when any man dissatisfied with his lot could pack up his goods and find a new home in the West where he would at least be his own master. Gone was the time when the farmer who had impoverished his land by careless methods could find virgin soil of great richness out on the frontier. Gone was the time when the laborers of the cities and the oppressed peasants of Europe could dream of finding a new and comfortable home on the open lands of western America. But most important of all, gone was the source of all that spiritual force and energy that Americans drew from the presence of free land, a knowledge that blossomed in our life in the shape of our optimism, our feeling of self-sufficiency, and our sustaining faith that every man is the captain of his own fate. After 1890, when the American farmer and laborer found conditions unpleasant, there was no possibility of obliterating them by romantic dreams of better days to come in the West. Facts had to be faced realistically; romantic optimism was no longer in vogue.

The passing of the free land caused a cry of distress from the American farmer and laborer. They realized acutely what such an event meant to them. Mingled with the distress was an unmistakable note of anger, for millions of acres of the public domain had not gone into the hands of actual settlers but had become the property of land speculators and the railroad companies. Many Americans looked upon the directors of railroads as mere speculators, as indeed they were, for they were holding for a high market price the great areas that had been given them by an indulgent government. Every American social thinker during the Gilded Age considered land speculation one of the major crimes. The inability of farmers to get cheap land in the West forced them to pay an excessive price or a very high rent for lands in the older settled portions of the country. Laborers objected to land speculation on the same grounds, for they realized that so long as the price of land was kept high they would have a slender chance of becoming landowners. Henry George was the first man to state the fears of the American farmers and workers in a coherent social theory, and Hamlin Garland's stories gave the same fears their first literary expression.

The Industrialization of Agriculture.—The farmer of the earlier day had been almost completely self-supporting. He lived a simple life and had few material wants that could not be satisfied from the products of the farm. The land was tilled with the simplest and most inexpensive implements. The plow was altered scarcely at all from the design of Jefferson, and the other implements were not infrequently made on the farm. The horse was the source of all power used in the tilling of land and in the threshing of grain. Farm life was hard but very simple, and it offered a type of satisfaction that can come only from the individual's ability to satisfy his own wants.

This idyllic system was shattered by the industrialization of the nation. One of the chief faults of our modern industrial and selling methods is that they create desire to possess economic goods. When a wealthy person purchases a luxury or even a convenience, his example is followed by his well-to-do neighbor and so on down through the whole economic scale. The rural districts are infected and soon every one possesses an article that only the rich should purchase. The luxurious and extravagant display of our newly made millionaires during the Gilded Age was aped by all classes of people, rural as well as urban, and one of the first results of the pernicious habit was to throw the farmer into the way of spending more and more.

Furthermore, the very processes of farming became more and more complicated. The old wooden walking plow gave way to a steel one, the steel one was followed by a riding plow, and this in turn by a more elaborate piece of machinery that in our generation has developed into eight or nine plows drawn by a tractor. The old-fashioned scythe was followed by a mowing machine. This was superseded by a reaper that was soon made obsolete by a self-binder, and this last has been replaced on western wheat farms by a combined harvester that cuts, threshes, and sacks the grain in one operation. To-day most of those combines are driven by gasoline motors and are drawn through the fields by tractors. The farmer was forced to industrialize his farm. His old way of raising grain was too expensive to allow of great profits, and the farmer was thinking of profits just as were the manufacturers and other business men. He had to raise grain to buy machinery to raise more grain to pay for more machinery, and so on in an endless sequence. His standard of living was raised, and while he handled much more money than he once did, he soon discovered to his dismay that he was not keeping much more of it than he had been. Hard times were chronic in the West from 1865 to the opening of the twentieth century, and even then, except for short periods, economic distress continued almost unrelieved.

The result of all these changes in agriculture was to destroy much of the farmer's traditional independence, to bring him into the industrial movement, to run him into debt for land and machinery and thus bring him closer into touch with the world of finance, and to place him in a situation that he often thought a very bad one and then give him no way out. If the supply of free land had kept up indefinitely, the farmer might have maintained his feeling of independence, but the supply was exhausted. The farmer could only face the stubborn facts and try to work out his happiness in spite of untoward conditions. Like the laborer and the employer, he was industrialized. Romantic dreams could no longer bring him surcease of his desires. Realistic desires demand realistic satisfaction.

PUBLIC MORALITY AND PRIVATE TASTE

Political corruption and bad taste in architecture and literature were by no means introduced to American life for the first time during the Gilded Age, but that period certainly saw the most extensive and brazen bribery and graft that was ever perpetrated in the history of our nation, just as it saw erected many a monument to the atrocious artistic taste of our people. The reasons for both the political corruption and the deplorable private taste go back to the same ultimate source. The riotous and ostentatious extravagance that accompanied the industrialization of all American life with its deification of money led some men to sell their votes and influence and led others to erect marvels of bad taste in the effort to show that they were the happy possessors of great wealth.

State and Local Political Corruption.—There is probably no getting at the specific origin of the political corruption that disgraced the seventies, the Dreadful Decade as those years have been aptly called. Before the war certain state legislatures had been accused of selling bank charters and other concessions, but the dishonorable proceedings of the earlier period were swept into insignificance by the flood of political debauchery that followed in the wake of the war. (However, let it be said that the war cannot be blamed for all the unlovely aspects of the Gilded Age.) Rather it was the mushroom growth of huge fortunes that corrupted our political life by substituting for the earlier American ideal of deliberate earning and saving a frenzied desire to grasp great wealth in a day by luck, by speculation, by any means that promised to capture the dollars. In an atmosphere reeking with demoralizing influences and saturated with constant talk of quick wealth, it is very difficult to maintain untarnished political rectitude. Railroads and other private corporations insisted upon special privileges that usually meant immense illegitimate returns from the public, and they were willing and anxious to pay huge sums to public officials who would assist in the getting of such privileges.

The war was scarcely over when *The Nation,* a weekly paper that kept up a consistent fight for common decency and honesty in the conduct of public affairs, charged that there was hardly a legislature in the country that was not suspected of corruption. Within five years enough scandals had been uncovered to show that the suspicion was not entirely imaginary. In the South the carpet-bag legislatures were indulging in an orgy of corruption that was a disgrace to civilization, and conditions in the North were not noticeably better. Open scandals occurred in a dozen northern and western states, and of these scandals that connected with the Erie Railroad in New York was typical, though the New York legislature was probably no worse than many another. The scandal arose over a struggle for the control of the Erie Railroad. "Commodore" Vanderbilt attempted to dispossess Daniel Drew, Jay Gould, and Jim Fisk from their control of the road. None of the three attacked was noted for scrupulous honesty or for high ideals of public service. Drew managed to combine a hypocritical piety with the business morality of a pirate, and Gould was never known to sacrifice a penny to save friend or principle, but of the three Fisk was by far the most spectacular and audacious. He was the bloated figure of vulgar and ostentatious extravagance, possessing not the slightest vestige of public or private morality. Vanderbilt never withheld his hand from any business transactions because of conscientious scruples, but when he struck for the control of the Erie, he had probably not calculated exactly the corrupt resourcefulness of his three opponents. The struggle progressed from the stock market to pitched battles between gangs of hired thugs, then to corrupt courts, and finally culminated in the wholesale bribery of the state legislature. It was probably one of the most disgraceful performances ever perpetrated in this nation, but the level of public opinion can be gauged very accurately by the fact that the voters of certain New York legislative districts were outraged, not because their representatives had sold out, but because the improvident men had sold out for less than the market price. It was seriously contended that the conduct of such legislators was derogatory to the dignity of their constitutents. Such was the conception of public morality during the Dreadful Decade. Again, it must be said that affairs in New York were more brazen but probably no worse than they were in a dozen other states.

In virtually all states where there were legislative scandals there were corresponding municipal disgraces, and of the city political rings formed for the purpose of bribery and corruption none was so odoriferous as the Tweed ring of New York City. William Marcy Tweed, the son of immigrants, started his career as a chair maker, but membership in a volunteer fire company threw him into the current of city politics, and within fifteen years he was the dictator of the largest city on the continent and the possessor of millions of dollars, every one of which had been illicitly acquired. He and his ring steadily rose in power until they gained control of the city government, and then with his henchmen in a majority in the municipal council and in complete possession of the financial and accounting offices of the city, Tweed began a career of unparalleled audacity and corruption. The opening of new streets, paving contracts, public construction and the like all brought in a stream of money to the coffers of the ring. Public contractors were forced to pay Tweed as much as eighty-five per cent of the contract price of work. The New York court house was designed to cost two hundred and fifty thousand dollars, but when the ring was overthrown the building had already cost more than eight million and was still incomplete. Just how much Tweed and his associates stole from the public will never be known. A moderate estimate places it at seventy-five million dollars, though there is reason for thinking that the figure may have been more than twice that sum. The success of the Tweed ring in New York led to the rise of imitators in other cities who fell short of Tweed's success only in the smaller amount of money that they were able to lay hands on.

National Scandals.—It would be pleasant to be able to say that political corruption during the Dreadful Decade was confined to state and city governments, but the melancholy record indicates that the legislative halls of the national capitol were polluted by the presence of undenied bribery.

The first of the great scandals to rock the nation was that connected with the building of the Union Pacific Railroad. The actual building of the railroad was handed over to a company known as the Crédit Mobilier which took the contract for construction at figures that would allow exorbitant profits. Most of the stockholders of the Crédit Mobilier were also owners of stock in the Union Pacific. These men manipulated the business of the railroad in such a way that shares of the Union Pacific, authorized by acts of Congress to sell only at par, were given over to the Crédit Mobilier at about one-third of their face value. When the profits from these were added to the already huge profits made from the construction of the road, the total earnings of the Crédit Mobilier were enormous. When the construction company in 1868 returned $3500 in dividends for every thousand dollars originally invested, the secret could no longer be kept. A congressional investigation disclosed a most amazing state of affairs. Many members of Congress had purchased Crédit Mobilier stock at half its recognized value, apparently with no thought of any impropriety. One representative boasted that he had accepted seventy-five shares in his wife's name and loudly lamented that he had not been able to get more. The disclosure of the scandal shook national confidence in our representatives, a few of whom were permanently disgraced, though many who had bought stock in the Crédit Mobilier were afterwards elevated to still higher positions.

The odor of the Crédit Mobilier frauds had not died down when the country was called to gaze upon the disclosure of scandalous laxity in the collection of internal revenue from certain whisky distilleries. The "Whisky Ring" as this fraud was known, was composed of a number of prominent politicians who were enriching themselves at the expense of the government. The facts of the case as finally disclosed resulted in the trial of the president's private secretary for participation in the profits. Although the accused was acquitted, public sentiment forced him to resign his position. He was afterwards indicted for conspiring to dynamite a safe in order to lay his hands on certain incriminating documents. Soon after the "Whisky Ring" came the Belknap case in which the secretary of war was forced by public opinion to resign his office under charges of collecting for his own use huge sums of money from federal office-holders. Later the "Star Route" cases disclosed that carriers of mail over certain lines were drawing more money than their contracts called for. Again politicians were the beneficiaries of this fraud. So ran the story with melancholy repetition during the entire Dreadful Decade. The acquisitive passion, once aroused in industry and in agriculture and given possession of the country, could not be kept out of our governmental affairs.

Business Morality.—The sordid record of the time cannot be closed without reference to the fast and loose methods played by promoters of business enterprises that were alleged to be legitimate. Numerous railroads were started that "began nowhere and ended nowhere," and thousands of investors lost all their savings in the inevitable crash. During the seventies more than twenty-five insurance companies failed, and the losses came in every instance from the pockets of men who had paid for the policies in good faith. Dozens of banks failed, carring down to ruin thousands and thousands of depositors whose accounts represented the savings of years. Many business men engaged in honest and high-principled enterprises cried out at the shameful dishonesty which was besmirching the name of American business, but there was no legal redress, for the various states had been remiss in the passage of regulatory laws and criminally lax in the enforcement of such feeble laws as were in existence.

The depths of depravity to which business of the seventies could sink unless controlled by men of high personal honor is best illustrated by the exploits of three previously mentioned pirates, Gould, Drew, and Fisk. Following the "Battle of the Erie," which was won by this trio, they started out to recoup themselves for the trouble and expenses incurred in getting possession of the railroad. In short, they planned the plunder of the road. This was neatly done by the process known as "watering the stock," a phrase that was coined by Daniel Drew himself. To water stock those in control of a corporation simply issue more stock than is justified by the physical valuation of the company. For instance, in the case of the Erie the three conspirators printed stock certificates that increased the capital of the road from thirty-five million dollars to more than fifty-seven million. This act was committed without adding a cent to the value of the physical property of the road or without increasing its earning capacity by a penny. The shares thus issued brought into the hands of the three men about ten million dollars and beat down the price of stock to a very low point. Still the conspirators were not satisfied. They wished to buy back at still lower prices the shares that they had just sold. This stroke they effected by precipitating a money panic in the New York market. Their scheme was successful. Suddenly money became very difficult to obtain, and holders of stock sold their property at ludicrously low prices in order to get cash. Drew, Gould, and Fisk had precipitated the panic by withdrawing all their deposits from the banks. With the money that they held in hand they bought vast quantities of stock, triumphantly regaining control of the Erie holdings that they had just sold at so enormous a profit. Examples of similar high-handed robberies could be indefinitely extended.

Henry Adams, who lived through this period, wrote in his autobiography this estimate of the Dreadful Decade: "The worst scandals of the eighteenth century were relatively harmless by the side of this, which smirched executive, judiciary, banks, corporate systems, professions, and people, all the great active forces of society in one dirty cesspool of vulgar corruption." When we look upon only a few of the moral lapses of the Gilded Age, we are very apt to decide that Henry Adams was a lenient critic of an unbelievably corrupt period.

The Collapse of Taste.—One of the chief characteristics of the Gilded Age was its atrocious taste in architecture, interior decoration, personal adornment, literature, and art. Space is lacking to discuss all these, but the art which reveals most clearly the soul of a nation is architecture, and architecture was the most obvious artistic atrocity of the Gilded Age.

Early American architecture had not been uniformly good, but a great deal of it had been most satisfying. To realize that this statement is true, one has only to call to mind the dignified and comfortable homes of colonial New England, the attractive Dutch houses of the Hudson Valley, Jefferson's Monticello, Washington's Mount Vernon, Westover on the James River, the White House, and dozens of southern plantation homes. These houses were commodious, as comfortable as the architects of the day could make them, and quietly in good taste. The Gilded Age brought a new note to the architectural development of the country. For a house to be acceptable to the newly rich of the period, it had to be a screaming testimony to the wealth of the owner, and no qualities save size and abundance of decoration could give such testimony. As a result many of the houses were very large, and the architects, unwilling to gain impressiveness through simple decoration of large masses, stuck on bay windows and "gingerbread" woodwork until the building was covered with garish and useless decorations. To gain especial "impressiveness" ingenious architects would combine incongruous elements of diverse schools of architecture to make the resulting building a hodge-podge of every known style. They have been known to place on the same building the pointed arch of medieval Gothic, columns from the classical style, a turret from the French château, colonial Georgian windows, and cover the whole with an assortment of fantastic "gingerbread," and then call the result an Italian villa. Almost every town in the country has a few specimens of domestic architecture dating from the Gilded Age, and almost every such specimen is easily distinguished from the earlier and later houses by its ostentatious decoration. America was being filled with newly rich, most of whom had been farm boys, butchers, clerks, and small business men. When these people wished to build a residence, their lack of culture too often betrayed itself in the bad taste of the house and its decoration. (Industrialization brought money, but it was rather slow about bestowing good taste.)

The interior decoration of the houses was as bad as that of the exterior. Every ornament had to be gaudy, and if it were not costly it had to imitate something that was extravagantly expensive. Pictures, hangings, rugs all had to shriek and writhe in loud colors and tortured designs. Huge red roses of the largest and reddest variety were found on everything from rugs to chinaware, from tapestries to candy boxes, and if the rose had a rival for public favor it was to be found in the white lily, emblem of a purity that was so distressingly scarce in our political and business life.

In literature the over-wrought taste of the time preferred the spectacular and the sentimental in about equal proportions. One of the approved novelists was E. P. Roe, who catered to popular taste with such books as *Barriers Burned Away, He Fell in Love with His Wife,* and *Opening a Chestnut Burr.* These romances, dripping with sentiment, warmly exhort readers to eschew evil and do good. The inability of literary art to do great good or great harm to the reading public was never more strikingly illustrated than by the failure of these very popular moral novels to elevate the level of political and business morality. General Lew Wallace, who was probably the best liked novelist of the time, lived a very colorful life. After participating in both the Mexican and Civil wars and serving on the court that tried the Lincoln conspirators, he became governor of the territory of New Mexico just at the time when the noted bandit, Billy the Kid, was leading his short but devastating career in the Southwest. Living in the old palace of the Spanish governors in Santa Fé, General Wallace turned his back upon his own adventurous and exciting life and wrote *Ben-Hur*, a highly colored, spectacular historical novel of two thousand years ago. Although the book purports to be religious, the main theme is revenge—a revenge that is pursued for almost five hundred pages with a most unchristian relentlessness. However, the readers of the Gilded Age did not notice this little incongruity; they were satisfied with the historical glitter of the book and its superficial interest in religious themes. Other favorite books were General Wallace's *Fair God* and *A Prince of India*.

It will perhaps be objected that taste is a minor thing, and that the political corruption of the seventies was confined to a relatively small class. It is true that few Americans were implicated in bribery, but far too many of the officeholders were, and the significant thing is that there was no general protest and no country-wide attempt to correct the abuses. The prevalent moral apathy was the most discouraging feature of the age. Furthermore, taste is not a minor thing. In art and literature a people finds its national expression. The art of the Gilded Age was tawdry, and its favorite literature was mawkish or sentimental. The best-sellers failed to grasp the problems of the time, and in that respect they were quite typical of the readers who were equally indifferent to corruption and appallingly bad taste. National taste is never a minor consideration in the study of a civilization.

But one of the worst features of the taste of the Gilded Age was its tendency to become standardized. Factories were turning out thousands of uniform rugs, tea-cups, horse-hair sofas, and gilded picture frames. Modern methods of distribution and selling were scattering them all over the country. The old local fashions in furniture, rugs, architecture—and thought—were tending to disappear under a wave of standardization. The first steps were taken during the Gilded Age toward a goal that we have not yet reached, though we are pressing toward it with increasing speed. That goal is the complete standardization of American life, and it is the result of the industrialization of America.

THE MIND OF INDUSTRIALIZED AMERICA

Enough has already been said to show the tendency of American thought during the Gilded Age. It will suffice to recapitulate briefly.

It may be a fact that the romantic thinker of the thirties and forties was a muddleheaded idealist. It may further be a fact that his ideals were quite incapable of realization. But these facts, if they are facts, are of little importance to the historian. The romantic assumed that he was right, and he acted on that assumption. It then becomes the duty of the historian to record the romantic's faith and opinions and to chronicle the resultant actions. Let the philosopher ponder on the ultimate truth or falsity of those opinions.

Romanticism succeeded an opposing philosophy of life that is usually referred to as Puritanism. According to the Puritan, human nature is evil, man's will is in complete bondage to a predetermined course of events, social progress is impossible, and the prevailing tone of thought is a gray pessimism. Under the pressure of a free economics engendered by the frontier and under the additional weight of foreign thought this hopeless philosophy gave way to the romantic temper. Romanticism denied every major allegation of Puritanism. It asserted that man's will is free and that the individual is the master of his fate; it held an implicit faith in the possibility of unlimited social and individual progress; it based its main contention on the innate goodness of original human nature and waxed fervent in the denunciation of the corrupting influences of custom and tradition. First and last it colored all its speculations with the rosy tint of its unconquerable optimism. Placed side by side Puritanism and romanticism collide at every point. Romanticism set the prevailing tone of thought from 1800 to 1860, but it was destined to succumb to the thought fostered by industrialism.

Broadly speaking industrialism is the product of science. Science makes possible inventions and improved methods of technology or manufacturing, and these two forces create modern industry with all its myriad ramifications. The genuine romantic always had a tendency to despise science. To him a fact was never an inescapable thing. His buoyant optimism enabled him to disregard any fact by calling into play his faith in the possibility of progress. If man is capable of unlimited progress there is no reason for supposing that he cannot nullify or evade the most stubborn and disagreeable facts. Man is the architect of his destiny; the superlative fact is the importance of catching the vision of a sufficiently exalted destiny. Once the vision is caught, realization will be an easy and natural consequence. Certainly to-day science is not without its visions and its exalted ideals, but the first result of the scientific movement was

the overthrow of romanticism by the thought inculcated by industrialism. This thought was founded upon the unimpeachable validity
of the fact.

Growth of Social Complexity.—The Gilded Age saw the passing
of a comparatively simple social structure and the coming of a complex order. It saw human society tend to become crystallized in certain strata that might ultimately become almost as fixed as a caste
system. It saw the stratification of society emphasized by such
things as strikes of one class against another, the threatening talk of
class war, and the established principle of collective bargaining by
means of which thousands of people spoke as a unit. In such ways
did the Gilded Age see the passing of old-time American individualism, and with the individualism went most of romantic thought. No
man, employer or laborer, who was moved around in an industrial
struggle like a pawn in a chess game, like a private soldier in a huge
war, could believe longer in the inspiring doctrine that his will was
subject to his individual control and that he was the captain of his
fate. No farmer caught in the strangle hold of industrialized agriculture could cleave steadfastly to a romantic faith that all would
be well in the near future. When the average American citizen saw
the unrebuked corruption, extravagance, and avarice that seemed
to control America, he could no longer have a deep confidence in
either the innate goodness of human nature or in the possibility c.
unlimited social and individual progress. How did the honest business man caught in a panic or the depositor ruined by the failure
of a bank feel about the forces that were controlling their lives?
Naturally they felt that they were in the grip of tremendous and
inscrutable powers over which they had but slight control. The
romantic impulse had lost its ability to control the thinking of men.

Passing of Individualism.—During the Gilded Age the American
began to realize for the first time since the eighteenth century that
he was not master of the situation in which he found himself. He
began to suspect that his career was determined by certain inescapable facts, and when this suspicion dawned on him, he tended
to revert to the eighteenth century way of thought. The feeling
of individualism was swallowed up in a feeling of class solidarity.
The desire to control one's social destiny became an iridescent
dream totally impossible of realization. Romantic optimism died
a much harder death, but it showed an unmistakable tendency to
become more and more a thing to be lauded in public and repudiated

in one's private meditations. Certainly there remained much optimism in the country, but it was an optimism born of the certainty of science and not produced by the mere hope to see everything end well. The gray melancholy that colors so much European literature first began to appear in our national life in the later years of the Gilded Age. Our pessimism, unoppressive as it was at first, had its roots in the same feeling that gave rise to so much of the great literature of the older nations, the feeling of the helplessness of man in the face of impersonal forces that he cannot exorcise as his primitive ancestors rid themselves of the powers of evil and that he could not dream out of existence as his immediate romantic ancestors did their unpleasant experiences. There was only one way to begin to cope with these immense forces, and that was to discover the fact that lay behind them. The beginning of the search for this fact tended to make the American a realist, for a realist is a man who is willing to face a fact, however unpleasant.

Literary realism had a long road to travel before it was accepted in America. Our readers were wedded to their idols of sensationalism and sentiment, and they relaxed their taste for adventure and tears only with the deepest reluctance. Before realism could make much headway it was necessary to produce some national critics who were willing to attempt a diagnosis of America's ills. In literature the Gilded Age was a period of a wide wandering of the creative spirit. Many of the writers were hopelessly lost. Even a colossal figure like Mark Twain had his moments of indecision, doubt, and muddled intentions. Henry Adams, one of the acutest minds of the period, acknowledged that he lost his way and spent years of meditation in a fruitless effort to find it again. Howells and Hamlin Garland knew what they were trying to do, but it was not until the very end of the Gilded Age that Howells found himself, and Garland published his first book at the beginning of the nineties. Mark Twain finally thought himself clear of the material comforts and the financial profits of industrialized America, but most of the books in which his later thoughts are embodied appeared near the end of his life or after his death. Rumor has it that there are certain of his manuscripts that have not yet been published.

The first notable critics of the Gilded Age, aside from Mark Twain in his *The Gilded Age*, were three in number: Edwin Lawrence Godkin, journalist and advocate of civic reform in the interests of common decency and good government; Henry George, who based his reform notions on the evils of land speculation and the disappearance of the free land; and Edward Bellamy, who first brought into America an enthusiasm for Marxian socialism.

SUGGESTED READINGS

Adams and Adams: *Chapters of Erie and Other Essays.* Boston. 1891.
Two members of a distinguished family give a depressing picture of finance during the Gilded Age. Out of print.

Beard: *Contemporary American History.* New York. 1914.
Gives attention to the agrarian movement.

Beard and Beard: *The Rise of American Civilization.* New York. 1927.
Vol. II, pp. 122-479.
The best discussion of the age.

Bowers: *The Tragic Era.* Boston. 1930.
The Reconstruction Period, 1865-1877.

Brooks: *Agrarian Revolution in Georgia, 1865-1912.* Madison. 1914.
Gives a good account of agrarianism in one state. Valuable.

Buck: *The Agrarian Crusade.* New Haven. 1920.
The best short account.

Commons: *History of Labor in the United States.* New York. 1918.
Very full and valuable.

Fuller: *Jubilee Jim.* New York. 1928.
The life of Col. James Fisk, Jr.

Haynes: *Social Politics in the United States.* Boston. 1924.
Excellent.

Hillquit: *History of Socialism in the United States.* New York. 1910.
Out of print.

Lynch: *"Boss" Tweed.* New York. 1927.
Good account of municipal corruption.

McVey: *The Populist Movement.* Amer. Econ. Asso. 1896.

Mumford: *The Golden Day.* New York. 1926. pp. 157-195.

Myers: *History of Tammany Hall.* Out of print.
Sometimes called a muckraking history, but it seems to be reliable

Norton: *Letters of C. E. Norton.* Boston. 1913.
The reaction of a scholarly gentleman to the Gilded Age.

Seitz: *The Dreadful Decade.* Indianapolis. 1926.
Unsavory episodes from the 1870's.

Tarbell: *History of the Standard Oil Company.* New York. 1904.
Big business during the Gilded Age.

Werner: *Tammany Hall.* New York. 1928.

CHAPTER XVII

THREE CRITICS OF THE GILDED AGE

The theory of socialism has long been known in America, though it has not always been called by its right name. In the first months of the Plymouth colony the Pilgrims held all things in common, dropping the system of communism only when its disadvantages became apparent. In the nineteenth century there were dozens of communistic experiments attempted in all parts of the country. The most famous of these, Brook Farm, the other Fourieristic groups, the Owen experiment in Indiana, and the Oneida community are familiar to all students. The distinguishing feature about most of these groups is the dislike that their members bore to industrialism and the consequent rejection of the industrial basis of modern society in favor of the agricultural ideal. This rejection of one of the prime facts of nineteenth century life was ultimately a weakness. Another weakness was the naïve assumption that man's shortcomings such as his vast acquisitive appetite and his zest for competition are fruits of a faulty society. Naturally these nineteenth century communities were very Utopian in their extreme romanticism.

Marxian Socialism.—In the middle of the century Karl Marx (1818-1883), a German economist, revolutionized the whole body of socialistic thought and founded modern socialism. To-day there are many types of socialism, but most of them, certainly the more important ones, are derived more or less directly from the teaching contained in Marx's huge work, *Capital,* often referred to as the "Bible of Socialism." Probably no two of Marx's followers will agree on the exact doctrines of their master, but there are certain theories found in *Capital* that are at once fairly clear and fairly typical of Marxianism.

Marx founded his system squarely upon the discoverable facts of history and of human nature; he was thoroughly realistic in his approach inasmuch as he depended for his material upon the facts of science and history rather than upon any idealistic conception of society or of human nature. The result of his studies was to give

Marx his first important theory, that of the economic interpretation of history. According to this theory economic factors are the determining force in human affairs and in the development of history. This view was opposed to that of the Utopians, but it was in the elaboration of his second theory that Marx broke most sharply with Utopian socialism. This second theory was that of class struggle. The Utopians were so obsessed with the idea of the brotherhood of man that they overlooked or disregarded the division of society into the rich and the poor. They hoped to establish the ideal state simply by holding up before the eyes of men the example of a community in which there would be neither rich nor poor, nor class struggle, nor hard labor, nor any of the objectionable features of prevailing industrialism. Marx was realistic enough to accept the facts of the evolution of modern industry and to build his theory on these facts. He saw that capital was tending to accumulate in the hands of a few, that the working class was tending to increase its numbers at an inordinate rate, and that the old middle class was about to be ground to death between the rich and the poor, the capitalists and the proletariat. This process was to result in a struggle between the competing classes, and Marx held that it would not cease until the workers took over the ownership of the instruments of production and managed them for their own benefit. Upon these main points Marx rested his system.

Marx spent less time in describing the ideal socialistic state than he did in telling his readers how to take the political steps that would enable them to realize their aims. It was this translation of economic ideals into terms of present-day politics and his realistic discussion of the class struggle that gained for Marx, a mild-mannered gentleman with the tastes and habits of a scholar, the reputation of being a noisy revolutionist much inclined to violence. The earlier socialists had spent all their time in giving glowing pictures of the ideal state when all their dreams should be realized, but they were distressingly vague as to the means by which their aims might be effected.

The Marxian program was announced in Germany in the late forties and brought almost at once to the United States. The doctrine did not flourish here at first because of the backwardness of industry and the large amount of open land that offered an immediate way of escaping any evil that might be felt by dissatisfied laborers. At that time Utopian socialism was so popular that the more realistic Marxian type was not regarded with pleasure even by the advanced reformers, but after the Civil War, the rapid increase of labor troubles and social unrest caused Marx's views to receive closer attention. Socialists of the newer variety were numerous in the National Labor Union (1866-1872), and many were found in the Knights of Labor. During the seventies and eighties the progress of socialistic thought was so inextricably entangled with anarchism and the general labor movement that a short statement of the situation is impossible. Many socialists were to be found in the ranks of the strikers during the time, and some of them bore parts in the violence that attended the great industrial struggle. The violence of the Gilded Age had a typical outburst in the Haymarket Riot in Chicago when a policeman was killed and several wounded by the explosion of a bomb. For this affair four men were hanged and three sentenced to life terms in the penitentiary. It is quite characteristic of the muddle-mindedness of the period that the identity of the man who threw the bomb was never established. The Haymarket Riot is the theme of Frank Harris's striking novel *The Bomb*. Despite violence and misunderstanding, Marxian socialism made slow but steady gains through the Gilded Age and in the nineties became one of the recognized political parties of the country.

EDWARD BELLAMY

(1850-1898)

The ideal socialistic state received a great deal of attention just at the close of the Gilded Age because of the publication of Edward Bellamy's famous book, *Looking Backward*. In giving his version of the perfect state, the author made a curious combination of Marxian ideas and Utopian idealism.

Bellamy was a novelist whose heart seems to have been principally in social reform. A discussion of the writer is difficult, because no adequate biography has yet been written. He was born in Massachusetts in 1850, just at the close of the romantic outburst, and in his boyhood he seems to have been familiar with the ideals of the early reform movement. He was educated partly in this country and partly in Germany. In the latter country he must have come into contact with the Marxian theories then to be found in many of the universities. At all events the social conditions of Europe aroused in him a desire to remedy bad social conditions everywhere. Upon his return to America he entered journalism, serving for a time with the *New York Evening Post*.

In 1879 Bellamy began his first novel, *The Duke of Stockbridge*, a story founded on Shay's Rebellion, the agrarian revolutionary movement in western Massachusetts immediately after the Revolutionary War. The study of this episode in his first book betrays Bellamy's strong reform tendencies. This work was not published in full until after the author's death. After his first attempt at social criticism in fiction Bellamy turned to the facile and rather pointless fiction that was preferred at the time. In this field he achieved marked success. In 1888 he published the book upon which his reputation rests to-day, *Looking Backward*. For the next ten years the author was engaged in various reform movements, all of which grew out of the conditions pictured by the book. His only notable literary product of the nineties was *Equality*, a sequel of his earlier success. Bellamy died in 1898.

"Looking Backward."—The framework of *Looking Backward* is very simple. A young man of Boston awoke in the year 2000 after a sleep that had lasted since May, 1887. During this long nap the whole social and political structure of the United States had been drastically changed, and most of the book is taken up with explanations of the new order. There is enough romance to allow the work to be called a novel, though certainly the interest of the author was not in the love story.

In constructing his ideal state Bellamy accepted the industrial revolution and the large advances that science had already made toward creating a more convenient mode of life. Furthermore he called prophecy into play and forecast many of the inventions that we have since seen perfected. For instance, in one passage he closely predicted the radio and the central broadcasting station, though he spoke of his receiving set as a telephone. In his whole-hearted acceptance of science Bellamy gave us the first scientific Utopia, a type of work since produced by H. G. Wells.

In the year 2000 the United States knew no labor problem, for there was neither a laboring class nor an employing class. Every industry had been nationalized, and the land and factories were under the control of the workers from whose ranks alone were the rulers chosen. The president of the United States had to be a man who had come up from the ranks of labor. He was assisted by ten men, each of whom was head of one of the great industrial groups of the nation. Under these men the workers were organized like an army in which every man and woman had a place. From twenty-one to forty-five every person was a working member of this army. After forty-five no work was required. In the distribution of labor every effort was made to equalize the burdens. Those who held easy positions worked longer hours than did those who held harder. Only volunteers were used on dangerous tasks. Every worker was paid the same, not on the ground that all did equal amounts, but on the argument that all put forth the same effort. A moron or a cripple would try as hard as would a skilled and accomplished mechanic. Therefore he should receive the same wage.

Every worker was given an annual allowance equal to four thousand dollars. Since there was no money in circulation this allowance was in the shape of a credit at one of the nationally owned banks. Purchases were made in stores where only samples were displayed. The buyer would select the articles that he wanted, pay for them in tickets or orders against his bank, and the goods would be delivered at his home much more rapidly than they would have been from the old-fashioned store. The people had very little private property, most of it being only personal belongings.

In accounting for the change in the United States from privately owned industries to socialism, Bellamy said that the concentration of capital in the hands of a few during the last years of the nineteenth century and the tendency of many separate corporations to unite under one control, trusts, the resultant companies were called, enabled the change to be effected with the least amount of trouble. Only a relatively few corporation owners had to be dispossessed by the public. The primary cause of the change to socialism was the intense and constantly increasing class struggle. This class struggle that preceded the economic revolution and the revolution itself were not closely described, but they both are plainly enough mentioned in *Looking Backward*.

Bellamy is usually classified as a Utopian socialist who was entirely untouched by the teaching of Marx. It is not so certain that this is a correct estimate. Willingness to accept industrial and commercial evolution as that development causes a greater and greater concentration of capital is certainly a characteristic of Marxian socialism, and almost every one knows that the doctrine of class struggle had its first statement at the hands of Marx. In the light of these facts it is dangerous to announce that Bellamy was wholly non-Marxian. It seems probable that the man cleverly combined the salient features of Marxian socialism with the naïve idealism of the Utopian variety so that the repellent and disquieting aspects of Marx's teaching would be obscured. So successful was Bellamy in hiding the rough side of Marxianism that many refuse to see in *Looking Backward* anything more than a scientific Utopia.

Effect of "Looking Backward."—Bellamy's book had a sensational success in this country and abroad. In two years the United States bought more than 350,000 copies and the work has remained a good seller down to the present. Even to-day it can be found in many circulating libraries that cater chiefly to the demand for recent fiction. But the success of the book cannot be judged by sales alone. Nationalism was the name given by Bellamy to the type of socialism that he had described, and within a few months Nationalism was one of the accepted reform movements of the time. Thousands of people joined the clubs and for a time there was an attempt to form a national organization. In practical affairs the results of Nationalism were to forward discussion of municipal ownership.

Although the agrarians disliked the importance that Bellamy assigned to industry, the platform of the People's party in 1892 embodied many of the ideas of Nationalism. The appearance of *Looking Backward* in 1888 was a significant fact. It came in the Gilded Age, a time of vast industrial development and consolidation. It grew out of the conditions in America and a theory of social betterment derived from the old world. Furthermore it was almost the only suggestion for social reform that accepted the great advances of science and invention and called eagerly for more.

HENRY GEORGE

(1839-1897)

If Bellamy was a critic of the Gilded Age who foresaw the ideal state that might arise from concentration of capital and the nationalization of industry, Henry George was a critic of the same period who based his whole critical and constructive work on the problem of land ownership. By 1875 the scarcity of land had begun to make itself felt by our shifting agricultural population. There was still much open land in the country, but it was not in the unlimited quantities that the preceding generation had known, and the amount available was not of first quality. Speculators, the vast railroad grants, and the rush of homesteaders to the West had pretty well depleted the choice. Henry George was the first man to attribute the ills of the Gilded Age to the problem of land, and his importance in the development of the American mind lies in the fact that he devised a thoroughly domestic remedy for a domestic problem. Seemingly he was little influenced by any foreign thought; all his influence came from the frontier.

Career of Henry George.—Henry George was born in Philadelphia, but as a boy he went to sea and, after a variety of adventures, reached California in 1858. Here he worked as a printer, supplementing his meager education by wide reading and study. In 1868 he published an article in *The Overland Monthly,* then edited by Bret Harte, and three years later he published a pamphlet called "Our Land and Land Policy." This work was the result of the observations that George had made of social and economic conditions that were then prevailing in his state. The chief problem that he faced was that of land speculation and the huge profits that frequently accrued from the monopolistic control of land.

From 1871 to 1875 George participated in the active political life of California and formulated his theories about landholding and taxation. At this time one of the chief problems of the state was the presence of huge tracts owned by a few men. The landlords naturally held up the price of their land and prevented migration from the cities of thousands of underpaid laborers. In 1878 George organized the "Land Reform League of California" to spread his views. The following year he published his best known work, *Progress and Poverty,* which contains his social theories in their final form. In 1880 he went to New York City where he resided for the remainder of his life, carrying on a constant campaign of speaking and writing in defense of his views. He became recognized as the champion of the worker and twice was candidate for mayor of the city and ran once for governor of the state. George was not a politician, but he was a great propagandist and used his political campaigns as a means of getting his theories before the public. He died in 1897 in the middle of his last mayoralty campaign.

Henry George was more than an effective propagandist; he was one of the best and clearest writers on social and economic conditions yet produced by America. His style is clear, precise, and interesting, and his whole body of thought is animated by a fine humanitarianism. Proof that his books reached the heart of America is found in the fact that by 1905 more than five million copies of his books had been sold, most of them in America, though Great Britain bought many.

"Progress and Poverty."—In his best known and most representative work, *Progress and Poverty,* George attempted the solution of such problems as unemployment, inadequate wages, the excessive price of land, and various other phases of social injustice. His final conclusion is that most of the objectionable features of our social life are caused primarily by a wrong land policy. By "land" George meant the land proper and the natural resources of the earth like minerals and timber. In short, his proposal was to remove all taxation from personal property, buildings, and all types of improvements and to levy a tax solely on the land proper. This is the well-known theory of the single tax. To the support of his theory George brought effectively a large array of arguments.

In the first place the right of man to life and liberty implies the right of equal opportunity to possess the natural resources of the land. The mere limitation of the amount of land held by each person will be of no avail, for land differs so widely in fertility that one hundred acres of rich soil will make its owner wealthy while the same amount of the poorer will not be sufficient to make a living for its owner. In view of this fact George argued that a real equality of opportunity will be assured by taxing all land the full amount of its economic rent. This economic rent is the difference in return between the poorest land and the piece under consideration. Thus an acre of the poorest land under cultivation will barely pay expenses of operation, while an acre of good land will return five dollars above all expenses. This five dollars represents economic rent. George held that by virtue of the right to equality of opportunity this rent belongs to the entire community and should be collected in the shape of taxes.

George further held that as population increases, poorer and poorer lands are brought under cultivation, thus constantly increasing the economic rent on a given piece of land. The farmers who are living on the poorest land are hard driven to make a livelihood, and their standard of living tends to decrease. This decrease is reflected in the wage scale of industry, for the laborer is paid only as much as will keep him from migrating to the poorest land, for only the most undesirable will be open to the man without means. Interest will also go down, for George held that capital is only another form of labor. Inventions, industrial combinations, the increase in population, all tend to create a sharper demand for the products of land and thus increase the amount of rent by forcing men to go to poorer and poorer tracts to make their homes. In brief George thinks that "progress" is synonymous with poverty. From this view comes the title of his book.

As a final argument for his theory George set forth the allegation that a single tax would make capital wealth much more productive by removing from it all forms of taxation. Furthermore, a single tax would make impossible the holding of land for speculative purposes. One of the problems of Henry George's time was that of men who would buy up a tract of land either in the city or the country and allow improvements made by other men on neighboring tracts to increase the value of the original purchase. This increase in value, known as the unearned increment, would simply be taxed out of existence under George's plan. Thus there could be no incentive to land speculation.

George was directly opposed to socialism and the nationalization of the land. He thought that the state had the right to tax real estate to the extent of its economic rent, but at that point he stopped short. He defended the right to possess private property, and that right he wished to respect in every way, drawing a line only at land speculation.

Influence of Henry George.—In 1880 America was still largely enough agrarian that such a proposal as that made by Henry George was sure to be warmly received. The urge was still to possess cheap land, and to many people it seemed that the single tax offered the quickest way of realizing their desires. Consequently George's followers were numbered by the thousands, and since much of his concern was with the problem of wages, he had as many followers in the cities as in the rural districts. Many prominent Americans accepted the proposals of George, and his influence is clearly to be seen in some of our literature. The most notable literary figure influenced by the new reform movement was Hamlin Garland, a son of the middle border, whose attention was directed by his environment to the question of land speculation. Garland's interest in single tax and in Henry George can easily be seen in such books as *A Son of the Middle Border* and *Main Traveled Roads*.

EDWIN LAWRENCE GODKIN

(1831-1902)

E. L. Godkin brought to his criticism of the Gilded Age a mind and a spirit that were richly endowed with almost every trait that the age so greatly needed. He was first of all a gentleman whose gentility was founded on the seasoned culture of the Old World and on a high ideal of public morality and civic responsibility that was almost repellently austere in its inflexibility. He stood for culture, for the spirit of honesty and common decency, and for an intelligent and seemly conduct of our political and economic life. To these inestimably valuable qualities he joined a fighting temper that could not be intimidated and a mordant wit that could pierce the thickest skin.

To many people Godkin's criticism of the Gilded Age seems superficial. His brilliancy no one denies, but his plan for reform was not so sweeping as were those of some of his contemporaries. Unlike Bellamy he did not begin with a demand for a wholesale reordering of society upon a socialistic basis, nor did he agree with Henry George in thinking that the salvation of the age lay in cataclysmic changes in our systems of taxation and landholding. He was not displeased with a civilization founded on business enterprise; he was not averse to private property or to our existing political organization. His first demand was for an end of public corruption; all other reforms were secondary. To him a public office was a public trust, and there was no deeper treachery possible than the betrayal of this trust. Once corruption was removed, Godkin had many ideas about the political and economic management of a state, but none of his ideas involved drastic changes. In the same issue of *The Nation* in which he excoriated some corrupt municipal ring, he would read a pungent lesson in economics to the western farmers who were shrieking for more paper money, or he would lecture severely the laborers who had the effrontery to say that wages might properly be the subject of legislation.

Godkin called the culture of his time a "chromo civilization," a characterization that describes the Gilded Age better than any other epithet or descriptive title ever coined. In those words are epitomized the vulgarity, tawdry ostentation, and hypocritical sham of the generation. In the castigation of this "chromo civilization"

Godkin developed the most brilliant editorial ability of his time, and it is gravely to be doubted if many journalists of England or America have surpassed him. It took America of the Gilded Age to bring out most of his salient qualities. In a country that lacked our "chromo civilization" he might have been only a capable but undistinguished editor.

Life of Godkin.—Edwin Lawrence Godkin was born in County Wicklow, Ireland, of a family of English descent. His father was a Presbyterian minister who was forced from his pulpit because of his activity in the "Young Ireland" society, a revolutionary group that favored the use of violent methods in the securing of Home Rule for Ireland. Godkin was educated at Queen's College, Belfast. After spending some time in the study of law, he became a correspondent in the Crimean War. In 1856 he came to America and traveled through the South, making some very shrewd and penetrating observations on the real status of that section under the slave régime. During the Civil War he was a correspondent for a London paper and at the same time an editorial writer for the *New York Times.*

In 1865 he founded *The Nation,* a weekly paper that soon achieved a great influence among thoughtful and educated people. Although Godkin became editor of the *New York Evening Post* in 1883, his name is chiefly associated with that of *The Nation.* The paper was brilliantly written, caustic in manner, and completely non-emotional in temper. Godkin's exacting nature and his tart criticism of all shortcomings led one critic to call *The Nation* a "weekly judgment day." By his enemies Godkin was reviled as a snob, and even his friends felt that his criticism was occasionally too haughty, yet with all his faults he made *The Nation* a sensible and high-minded advocate of reform in a period of almost unbelievable political and industrial corruption.

Godkin's Influence.—Certainly Godkin was not patient with frauds, hypocrisy, or sentimentality, but he was far more than a chronic fault finder. He advocated currency reform, a tariff for revenue only, and the abolition of the "spoils" system. Under this last method the civil service of the nation had been degraded to the level of a payment for political work. His contribution to civil service reform constitutes Godkin's chief public performance. In his economic belief he was a member of the English laissez-faire school, the group that believed in right of business to proceed without hindrance from the government. As a laissez-faire economist he mistrusted socialism, agrarian reform, and all schemes looking toward a larger governmental control of business.

But valuable as E. L. Godkin's political contributions were, he did a finer service for American culture. He injected into his paper a tone of gentility that had been distressingly rare in earlier American journalism. Too often the editorial writers of the older day had relied for their effects upon coarse personal invective or vituperation. Godkin wrote with an air of good breeding flavored with wit, and every one of his editorials was based upon an exact knowledge of the facts involved. He convinced his readers by his presentation of his facts rather than by his appeal to prejudice or passion. Many testimonials have been given by the most cultivated and best informed men and women of America as to the influence that *The Nation* had on their thinking during the days of Godkin's editorship.

In immediate results achieved, Godkin was probably the most effective of all the critics of the Gilded Age, for a large and influential group of voters followed his advice, and he had the satisfaction of seeing many of his proposals enacted into law. He was not superficial in his diagnosis of what was wrong with America; he was only a clear-minded, practical journalist who refused to be misled by proposals for civic and economic betterment that had no possible chance of being adopted. His suggested reforms were sadly needed, and they always had the virtue of being expedient. Indeed if one started out to find the most useful citizen of America during the Gilded Age, the choice might easily fall upon E. L. Godkin of *The Nation*.

SUGGESTED READINGS

George: *Life of Henry George*. New York. 1904.

Haynes: *Social Politics in the United States*. Boston. 1924. **Henry** George, pp. 117-136; Bellamy, 138-151.
> Best brief discussion of George and Bellamy.

Hertzler: *History of Utopian Thought*. New York. 1923. Bellamy, pp. 225-236.
> Excellent.

Mumford: *The Story of Utopias*. New York. 1922. Bellamy, pp. 159-169.

Nevins: *The Evening Post, a Century of Journalism*. New York. 1922.
> Has many references to Godkin.

Ogden: *Life and Letters of Edwin Lawrence Godkin*. New York. 1907.
    Thin background.
Pollak: *Fifty Years of American Idealism*. New York. 1915.
    The story of *The Nation*. Good account of Godkin's work.
Villard: *Some Newspapers and Newspaper-men*. New York. 1926.
    Godkin, pp. 282-301.
    Fine discussion by a distinguished newspaper-man.

CHAPTER XVIII

THE TWILIGHT OF ROMANTICISM

Even if the industrialization of America and the vulgar material-ism of the Gilded Age were erected upon the ruins of the great romantic movement, it is not to be thought that all writers who considered themselves romantics turned to social criticism or to the realistic presentation of their material immediately upon the col-lapse of the spiritual inspiration upon which romanticism was founded. Indeed their failure to realize the worst and accept it was one of the major faults of these later romantics. The fact was that the romantic movement of Emerson, Thoreau, Melville, and Whit-man was gone. It was no longer a living force. The soul had departed from it leaving only the shell, and this shell was often nothing more than the traditional subject matter of the older writers. For a full generation after they should have ceased, the lesser roman-tics kept harping on the old strings. The poets wrote pallid imi-tations of Byron and Shelley that were so far removed from the spirit of the originals that they sound like imitations of imitations. The novelists turned gladly from their unlovely surroundings and wrote historical romances, mystery stories, and character sketches that were carefully modeled on Poe, Thackeray, Dickens, or Haw-thorne. Of fresh, original inspiration there was none. Romanti-cism was dead; the flash and color of the older generation had de-generated into cheap and gaudy "gilt and tinsel."

The lesser romantics are not wholly to be despised. Notwith-standing their utter lack of vitality they possessed great technical mastery, and many men who had absolutely nothing to say wrote so skillfully that they deceived their own generation into thinking that they were literary stars of considerable magnitude. Many of these men were quite influential in their day, for they came into control of the best magazines to which they would naturally admit nothing that was not unmistakably their kind of literature. With such men as J. G. Holland and Thomas Bailey Aldrich in editorial positions, realism and social criticism had to be carefully disguised

in order to see print, and even after they were disguised they had
to be presented with deft literary technique. This insistence upon
smooth and adroit style was probably the only contribution of value
made by the lesser romantics.

Sidney Lanier (*1842-1881*).—Sidney Lanier was the one poetic
artist of the Gilded Age and one of the very few true poets of
America. With the exception of Poe, he gave us the most melodious
lines of any of our older men, and it is doubtful if Poe himself was
so deep a student of the laws of English verse. Lanier was a melodious worshiper of beauty, born into an age of crass materialism.
That he could write at all during the years after the war is proof
of the sincerity of his poetic impulse.

Lanier was born in Georgia where he received an education that
he afterwards spoke of with scant respect. He served in the Confederate army during the war and emerged from the struggle broken
in health. An overpowering desire to live in an atmosphere of
culture led him in 1873 to go to Baltimore where he soon obtained
a position as flutist in the great Peabody orchestra of that city.
He read omnivorously and during the last two years of his life
his study was rewarded by his appointment as lecturer in English
literature at Johns Hopkins University. He died at the early age
of thirty-nine from consumption contracted during his service in the
army.

Lanier dedicated his whole life to the arts of music and poetry,
and to him the two were but slightly different manifestations of the
great art of melodious utterance. Hence the first aim of the poet
was to create beautiful lines. Although the content of his verse
was of slight moment, any one can trace a firm idealism in his
dislike of the ugliness that was so conspicuous during the Gilded
Age. The rationalism of science repelled him, for he instinctively
mistrusted reason and relied upon feeling.

> Vainly might Plato's brain revolve it,
> Plainly the heart of a child might solve it.

Alcott, Thoreau, Emerson, and Whitman would have understood
and approved of those words.

In the opening lines of his first celebrated poem "The Symphony"
Lanier exclaims:

> O Trade! O Trade! would thou wert dead!
> The time needs heart—'tis tired of head.

And again:

> Shall Trade aye solve his conscience-aches
> With jibes at chivalry's old mistakes—

Lanier was a true romantic born into an age that was violently unromantic. His poetry is inclined to lack the note of authenticity, that oracular tone that the earlier romantics fell into so easily, but the fault is not to be found in any personal shortcoming of the poet. No poet can chant his verses with ringing assurance who does not feel behind him the moral support of his age, or at least of a living and articulate element of that age. Lanier was born with his romantic temper; he could not help writing romantic verse. The unfortunate thing was that romantic verse in the Gilded Age was an isolated phenomenon, and the feeling of isolation gave to Lanier much of his unsureness. If he had ever felt the quickening touch of the early and genuine romanticism, as Whitman did, he might have written differently, but a man born in Georgia in 1840 had little chance of being affected by Emerson and Whitman. The lack of any living sympathy around him drove Lanier to the library for much of his inspiration. This gives some of his lines a distinctly bookish tone, as when he says:

> David to thy distillage went,
> Keats and Gotama excellent,
> Omar Khayyám, and Chaucer bright,
> And Shakespeare for a king delight.

In another poem he says:

> Now in the sea's red vintage melts the sun,
> As Egypt's pearl dissolved in rosy wine,
> And Cleopatra night drinks all.

But in the very next stanza Lanier nobly atones for his bookish figures of speech by these lines of pure music:

> Come forth, sweet stars, and comfort heaven's heart,
> Glimmer, ye waves, round else unlighted sands.
> Oh, night! divorce our sun and sky apart,
> Never our lips, our hands.

Even when due allowance is made for Lanier's most obvious weaknesses—his lack of universality, his thinness, his excessively refined technique, and his failure to achieve buoyant authenticity—such poems as "The Symphony" and "The Marshes of Glynn" stand as the best poetic work of the seventies with the sole exception of Whitman's output. The faults, or at least many of them, must be attributed to the age and not to the man. The excellencies, and there are many of these, were the personal work of Sidney Lanier himself, who wrought alone and unencouraged in an age whose very spirit warred with his own.

Lesser Poets of the Gilded Age.—Bayard Taylor (1825-1878) is a good representative of the lesser romantics after the Civil War. He was a talented man of undeniably romantic temper who satisfied his romanticism by traveling in the Orient and developing a passion for spices, perfumes, coffee, and warm colors. As a capstone to his exotic romanticism he wrote a volume called *Poems of the Orient* which contained the famous "Bedouin Song."

> From the desert I come to thee
>   On a stallion shod with fire
> And the winds are left behind
>   In the speed of my desire.
> Under thy window I stand,
>   And the midnight hears my cry;
> I love thee! I love but thee!
>   With a love that shall not die
> Till the sun grows cold,
>   And the stars are old,
> And the Leaves of the Judgment Book unfold.

So maudlin a romanticism needs nothing so much as the lash of satire wielded by a Mark Twain to bring the moon-struck poet to his senses. It is typical of Taylor and his fellows that such events as the Civil War, the completion of the Pacific railroad, the slaughter of the buffaloes, and the whole romantic vista of western life moved them to no poetic fervor. They preferred to visualize a fictitious Arab from a dream desert, standing before a hypothetical window and singing an imitation of Shelley. Such poetry is on a parity with the martial valor of the redoubtable Jim Fisk, who liked to load himself with a sword and gold lace and parade at the head of his regiment, though his ardor did not lead him to participate in the Civil War. In the seventies Taylor was the crown-prince of the Genteel Tradition under the benign despotism of the First Triumvirate, Lowell, Longfellow, and Holmes. As such he has received from many school texts a space out of all proportion to his real importance.

Another poet of exotic oriental splendor was Richard Henry Stoddard (1825-1903), who voiced his yearning romanticism in this plaintive ditty:

> We parted in the streets of Ispahan.
> I stopped my camel at the city gate;
> Why did I stop? I left my heart behind.
>
> I heard the sighing of thy garden palms,
> I saw the roses burning up with love,
> I saw thee not: thou wert no longer there.
>
> I send thee gifts by every caravan,
> I send thee flasks of attar, spices, pearls,
> I write thee loving songs on golden scrolls.
>
> I meet the caravans when they return.
> "What news?" I ask. The drivers shake their heads.
> We parted in the streets of Ispahan.

Truly the romanticism of the Gilded Age was a shabby thing.

One reads this unbelievable poem and asks in amazement what madness had fallen upon the author who was born "of sailor ancestory" in Hingham, Massachusetts, and worked his way to authorship through blacksmithing, iron molding, and journalism. The sixth line is a brilliant example of a futile attempt to achieve beauty by stark simplicity. The attempt failed and the author for all his pains had only childishness.

Other romantic poets of the Lesser Generation were Edmund Clarence Stedman (1833-1908), Thomas Bailey Aldrich (1836-1907), and Richard Watson Gilder (1844-1909). The last two were of more than a little importance, for Aldrich edited the *Atlantic Monthly* for almost a decade, while Gilder directed the *Century* for twenty-eight years.

LOCAL COLOR IN THE GILDED AGE

Although most Americans were never bound to the soil as were the countrymen of the Old World, the years following the Civil War saw an immense increase in the amount of travel in the nation. The war itself took millions of men out of their old homes and threw them into strange environments, and after the close of the conflict the improved means of transportation made easy the journey from one part of the country to another. Thousands from the East and the Mississippi Valley went south or west looking for new homes. Other thousands moved from the rural districts to the cities where they joined the ranks of laborers or professional men. The Gilded Age saw a nation in motion.

This increase in travel and permanent migration caused our people to become conscious of their sectional differences. Before the war America was strongly sectional. New England had its dialect, its typical Yankees, its distinctive architecture, and its peculiar customs, just as surely as it had its typical landscapes. The South had its strongly defined sectional characteristics, and so had Kentucky, Indiana, the western frontier, and California. Travelers on the overland stage frequently remarked upon the changes that they saw in the inhabitants and their customs, as the lumbering vehicle rolled along day after day into a new world. Once on the frontier travelers or immigrants carried with them for a time the unmistakable marks of their native localities. There was no more danger of confusing the man from Pike County with the man from New England than there was of confusing a Chinese with a Caucasian. In the city, everywhere the newcomer went, he carried with him traces of his origin. Other people noticed these traces and became curious. Reading of the customs and manners of another part of the country was the next best thing to a visit, and there was no better place to read of these things than in the pleasant fiction that made a specialty of exploiting "local color."

Moreover the emigrants from one part of the country to another took with them something more enduring than dialect, dress, or customs. They carried fond memories of their old homes, and nothing could be more agreeable to them than idealized descriptions of life in the regions that they had just quit. Distance and incorrigible sentimentality blurred all the unpleasant facts and left only a recollection of the good times and pleasant experiences in the old home. Stories of plantation life in the South "focused out" of the picture the dire financial straits that a slave economy frequently brought on a region. Omitted too were the unhappy aspects of domestic slavery. Such things were not for the local colorist, but he did not fail to emphasize the gay parties and the tender romances that occurred in the "big house" with the great white columns. In the New England stories the narrowing provincialism and the life of grinding toil were omitted in favor of the corn-huskings and the festivals in the maple sugar camp.

In short, local color as it was practiced in the Gilded Age was a pleasant and often sentimental presentation of typical life in a certain definite locality that had characteristics of manners and customs peculiar to itself. The pleasant portrayal of manners in the chosen locality is the primary aim of the local colorist. When he becomes concerned with character or with the impact of overpowering influences upon the individual he is no longer representative of his school. Hamlin Garland is no local colorist; he is a realist of locale. Willa Cather writes of life in Nebraska, but she is so much concerned with character and with the effect of the environment upon human life that she is far from being a local colorist. If local color were her primary aim, she would stop with a pleasant description of life in a Nebraska homestead. The new school of writers engaged in depicting the life of the southern Negro is far removed from that of the earlier period which wished to catch only the outward aspects of Negro life through dialect and broad humor. The new school is attempting to plumb the soul of the black man, and there is as much difference between a book like *Porgy* and a local color story as there is between a jangling Negro musical comedy and a spiritual that springs from the deep heart of a race. Local color has little to do with character presentation and nothing at all with the unpleasant. Manners and turns of speech that the emigrant cannot think of without a twinge of homesickness are the aims of the local colorist.

How Local Color Is Achieved.—Local color is easily achieved by a writer who knows his chosen background. First of all, to be successful he must use dialect; that is the prime requirement. An absolutely accurate ear for local peculiarities of speech is not essential, but the main liberties with good English must be presented, preferably in a horribly garbled spelling. Actually the rage for dialectical spelling so possessed some authors that in their attempts to achieve local color they occasionally spelled correctly in phonetic fashion, and if these words are pronounced as spelled they will be spoken according to accepted English usage. Dialect must be achieved. If one's supply runs a bit low, good English can be dressed up to resemble provincial pronunciation.

The second obvious necessity of the local colorist is the use of typical characters. In the creation of such personages great attention must be given to costume and manners, while flesh and blood and spirit are of slight importance. A southern colonel must wear a broad-brimmed hat and a bow tie, and a cowboy without a trunkful of accouterments can easily be proved to be no cowboy but a plain case of misrepresentation. Given a knowledge of dress and manners, a writer has little trouble in fabricating typical characters by the dozen. The preference of our novelists for types is a crying national weakness, and nowhere is the choice so often displayed as in the volumes so repetitiously compiled by the local colorists.

Still another injunction laid upon those who exploit their native localities is the necessity of using typical scenery. The backgrounds used by the local colorists of a certain region are as monotonously alike as are the backdrops in a cheap vaudeville theater. Visitors to strange parts of the country who have already formed their impressions of those localities from the reading of local color stories frequently have to look rather earnestly over the landscape before they can find the objects that they naturally supposed to be universal.

Bret Harte (*1839-1902*).—Bret Harte was the founder of the local color school and probably the most popular author of this group. It was he who determined the major characteristics of the local color story, and in the execution of his plans he achieved a deftness that few of his followers could match. This remark is not equivalent to claiming for Harte the eminence of greatness. Great he was not, though he was an accomplished story-teller, and he produced a few very good stories. But the very deftness of the man and the enthusiasm with which his California stories were received were his final ruination. For years he was content to repeat his formula that had been so effective in the sixties and seventies, and when one tries to make an estimate of the man's contribution to American literature, most of the considerable bulk of his writing fades out, and one is faced with a consideration of three or four of his stories and not more than that number of poems. The California of the fifties afforded one of the most striking sights that America has seen. It held the concentrated essence of frontier life fiercely agitated by sensational discoveries of gold on almost every hand. Harte made no attempt to portray this scene in its entirety. He deliberately circumscribed his effort by setting out to treat only the dramatic incident that was participated in by picturesque characters, each of whom was typical of a group. So narrow a field is soon worked. If Harte in later years attempted to leave his familiar material he was always driven back, either by the importunities of editors or by the personal desire for popularity. Early success and facility were the undoing of the man.

Bret Harte was not a Westerner. Indeed it is gravely to be doubted if he liked the West that he did so much to immortalize. He was taken to California as a boy of fifteen, and he left there at the age of thirty-two and never went back. Harte was born in Albany, New York, of a cultured family that possessed an excellent library. It is somewhat ironical that the discoverer of Pike County in literature and the romanticizer of western frontier life should have been the product of great cities, but Harte spent his youth in Providence, Boston, Philadelphia, Brooklyn, and New York. The boy began to read early, and at the age of seven he had a fair acquaintance with the works of Dickens. This was a matter of great importance to the development of the future writer, for Dickens always remained his literary master.

In 1854 Harte removed to San Francisco with his family, going by way of Nicaragua. When he arrived in California he did not fit easily into the society that he found there. Perhaps this is just as well, for if he had slipped agreeably into the way of life around the Golden Gate and in the mining districts, he might not have been able to see and appreciate the manners of his environment so keenly. In his new home Harte continued the studious habits that he had formed earlier, and much of his time was spent in reading and attempting to write. Within a short time he became an express messenger in the northern part of the state, and like so many of our literary men, worked at the printer's trade. All the time he was experimenting with his own writing. In 1864 he became secretary of the San Francisco mint, a position that gave him much time for his literary work. Soon he began to contribute to *The Golden Era*, a local magazine, and when *The Overland Monthly* was established in 1868 he became its first editor.

By this time Harte had written a considerable amount of material. Very early in his career he indicated the bent of his talent, for his first sketches that have been preserved have a strong flavor of romance laid in the distinctive atmosphere of Spanish California. In 1867 he wrote "M'liss," a story that is unmistakably of the local color school, and in the second number of the new magazine he published the work upon which rested his sudden popularity, "The Luck of Roaring Camp." Two years later came his equally famous poem, "Plain Language by Truthful James," and America had a new literary idol and a new type of literature, that of local color. Instantly Harte became the most popular writer in the country. In 1871 he went East and seven years later took a consulship abroad. He never returned to his native land.

It is no exaggeration to say that every pen-stroke by Bret Harte has for its literary inspiration the methods of Charles Dickens. If the typical works of the great English novelist be examined they will be found to be achieved by an unvarying formula. Dickens used typical characters that were almost grotesques, so intent was he upon having each figure in the story personify a type of person or an aspect of human temper. With as economical number of strokes as possible the author created his characters, sometimes only outlining them as human figures are drawn in cartoons. The characters thus created were then allowed to enter into various situations in the unfolding of a plot, each episode being designed to evoke the feeling of humor or pathos. Bret Harte worked in almost exactly the same fashion. His characters are types, and so close did he stay to the Dickensian formula that he frequently gave his personages grotesque descriptive names. Instances of such nomenclature are the names of Culpepper Starbottle and Calhoun Bungstarter. Again, Harte uses his characters only to give the reader a blend of his favorite emotional reactions, humor and pathos. "The Outcasts of Poker Flat" and "Tennessee's Partner" are prime examples of his emotional range. It is such a range as Dickens preferred.

This comparison of the two men does not mean that Harte was as great a writer as Dickens. The Englishman was one of the supreme literary cartoonists of all time, and Harte was only an imitation of his master. Dickens had moral fervor and a depth of sincerity that Harte never reached and that he approximated in only one or two stories. Dickens is a master of a peculiar type of literature; Harte is only a second-rate writer even when he is compared with Americans. In the vast scope of world literature Dickens is still a fair-sized figure; Harte is lost in the mass of greater men.

Harte further showed the influence of his master in selecting only the dramatic and picturesque for his stories, and in his most facile narrative the action becomes melodramatic and theatrical. The critical reader feels that the situations in the story are as obviously the result of theatrical manipulation as they are in artificially constructed dramatic "thrillers." Just as Dickens exercised artistic selection in extracting laughter and tears out of English life, so did Harte deliberately turn his back on the dominant but unsensational element in California society and create a frontier life that never existed anywhere except in sporadic eruptions that were promptly quelled by quiet and unpicturesque men who had no desire to have their ordinary existences enlivened by thrilling adventures.

Harte left two influences on our literature. He created the local color school or at least popularized it, and he gave new form and intent to the short story. Under his hands the story no longer sought so much for dominant tone and mood as for action. Poe's favorite appeal to sadness or fear soon appeared old-fashioned. Harte speeded up the narrative and gave compactness to the situations. Dramatic tenseness punctuated by sentiment or laughter became the aim of writers. This innovation was in many ways a dangerous contribution, for it tended to exalt facility over truth, humor and pathos over sincerity. In the hands of O. Henry and many another of Harte's followers the short story became a marvel of facility and artificiality.

John Hay and the Discovery of Pike County.—By the discovery of Pike County is meant the first use of the distinctive and ungrammatical dialect used by the natives of the Mississippi Valley before that dialect was subjected to the refining influences of schools and colleges. A fair example of this dialect is that spoken by the whites in *Tom Sawyer*. Whatever may be said of the bad grammar and garbled pronunciation used by the Middle Westerners, it must be admitted that their dialect was picturesque and swiftly expressive. Pike County is generally supposed to have been discovered by Bret Harte, but it is quite possible that the honor belongs to John Hay (1838-1905).

Concerning the "pike" Bayard Taylor says:

A pike in the California dialect is a native of Missouri, Arkansas, Northern Texas, or Southern Illinois. The first emigrants that came over the plains were from Pike county, Missouri; but as the phrase, "Pike County Man" was altogether too long for this short life of ours, it was soon abbreviated into "a Pike." He is the Anglo-Saxon relapsed into semi-barbarism. He is long, lathy, and sallow; he expectorates vehemently; he takes naturally to whisky; he has "the shakes" his life long at home, though he generally manages to get rid of them in California; he has little respect for the rights of others; he distrusts men in "store clothes," but venerates the memory of Andrew Jackson.

Such was the subject of the Pike County literature.

Harte was so popular as a result of the publication of his poem "Plain Language from Truthful James" that he followed the success of this venture with a volume called *East and West Poems*. Seven pieces in this volume are in the Pike County dialect. Almost at the same time John Hay published a collection of his poems bearing the significant title *Pike County Ballads*. The question of priority has never been settled, though certain competent critics have pointed out that Hay's poems had appeared in obscure country newspapers several months before they were incorporated in a volume. It is quite probable that the solution of the question has been effected by the suggestion that Hay first put the Pike County dialect into poetry but that poetry of this type was popularized by Harte.

A variety of the Pike county dialect appeared in American letters as early as the thirties when Longstreet's *Georgia Scenes* were seeing the light in southern papers. Later certain of the western humorists made use of the dialect in their writings, but it required the enormous popularity of Harte and the poetic skill of both him and Hay to introduce the "Pike" to a large audience. After Harte and Hay, the exploitation of Pike County was continued by a large number of western writers, many of whom never rose above the dignity of anonymous contributors to small weekly newspapers. Probably the most effective use of the dialect to be found in our literature is in the books of Mark Twain, whose native language was the vernacular of Pike County.

John Hay was born in Indiana of a cultivated and well-to-do family. At the age of fifteen he was sent to a private school in Pike County, Illinois (just across the Mississippi from Pike County, Missouri). From this school he went to Brown University where he had a distinguished career. Upon graduation he returned to Illinois where in the little river town of Warsaw he wrote verse imitative of the poetry of cultured circles. Going to Springfield he studied law, but before he could begin to practice Abraham Lincoln took him to Washington in 1861 as assistant secretary to the president. After the Civil War he entered the diplomatic service and later collaborated in the writing of a huge biography of Lincoln.

He was American ambassador to England and closed his career as Secretary of State in the cabinets of Presidents McKinley and Roosevelt.

Hay wrote very little that was in the Pike County vein. Usually his poetry is melodious and technically correct, but it is not very stimulating. Too much of it resembles the poetry of the Gilded Age that was sponsored by the Genteel Tradition, the verses of Taylor, Gilder, Aldrich, and Holland. Hay deserves a place in our literature because of his assistance in introducing the realistic poetry of the West to literature, for the discovery of Pike County was nothing more than the dropping of insincerity and the use of reality in presenting the record of western life in verse.

George Washington Cable (1844-1925).—George W. Cable, the local colorist of New Orleans, had the most romantic material of any of the writers of his school. New Orleans, with its colorful background of French and Spanish culture and with its mixed population of whites, blacks, and creoles, offered a background of unsurpassed possibilities. It had an old world atmosphere that no other American city could claim, a romantic past that was little known to ordinary readers, and a seasoned culture that few other communities on the continent could equal. The city was for many decades the chief center of French influence in America, and as such it enjoyed grand opera, concerts, and ballet dancing when many parts of the country were finding their chief cultural influences in the spelling bee, the singing school, the revival meeting, and the political campaign.

Cable was born in New Orleans and there received his scant education. He was forced to stop his schooling at the age of fourteen and take a minor position in the custom house. He enlisted in the Confederate army when he was seventeen and served all through the war. From 1865 to 1873 he was employed as clerk, journalist, or surveyor. In the latter year his first story was published in *Scribner's Magazine*. This effort was followed by a number of others, and in 1879 he published his first book, *Old Creole Days,* one of the great successes of the time. Later he produced *Madame Delphine* and *The Grandissimes*. These books all used the background of Louisiana, and all attracted large numbers of readers. Cable's later work is rather unimportant.

Cable was a true artist. His exotic background, his characters alien to American ways, and the dramatic incident required by the taste of the time, all were combined in the very effective stories that lacked little of possessing great power. There is nothing in our literature quite like *Old Creole Days*. The barbaric splendor and mystery of the background has a reality that Poe could never touch. The action is direct, swift, and not so obviously manufactured as it is with many of the local colorists, while the effect of brooding melancholy attained by some of the stories is hardly surpassed by that of the "Fall of The House of Usher." It is regrettable that the great popularity of Cable's early books was followed by a period of indifference that has come down to the present, for *Old Creole Days* and *Madame Delphine* are worthy of more readers than they have.

Irwin Russell (*1853-1879*).—Irwin Russell of Mississippi is usually credited with being the first man to discover the literary possibilities of the Negro character and Negro dialect. In *Uncle Tom's Cabin* Mrs. Stowe had attempted to utilize Negroes and their peculiar speech, but to any one who knows the black man her knowledge of Negro character is as lamentable as is her presentation of Negro dialect. Men who have made the widest and most effective use of the Negro in literature have agreed that Russell's poem "Christmas Night in the Quarters" opened a new field for writers.

In Irwin Russell the South possessed another true poet. He was immeasurably beyond most of the rhymesters of his time in his insistence that poetry must have its roots in the affairs of everyday life. Scoffing at the artificial orientalism of such men as Taylor and Stedman he set out to make poetry of the commonest and most despised thing in the South, the life and speech of the newly liberated slave. Competent observers of Negro life have testified to the success that attended Russell's effort, and any reader who has an ear for the music of English verse will be caught by the flowing melody of his lines. "Christmas Night in the Quarters" is one of the distinctive triumphs of American poetry. In its striking presentation of humble life it has been compared to "Cotter's Saturday Night," but it is a question if the bubbling humor and buoyant spirit of Russell's poem do not find a closer counterpart in "Tam O'Shanter."

The early death of Russell was a great loss to our national literature, for if he had lived he would have lent able assistance to those who were trying to rid our poetry of sham orientalism and the banalities of both the lesser local colorists and the so-called romantics. Russell was striving for reality in his verse, and to get this reality he was going to the life of common people, just as all men have done who have helped bring in a poetic renaissance.

Joel Chandler Harris (*1848-1908*).—Working the field opened up by Russell, Joel Chandler Harris produced Uncle Remus and his immortal tales. Immortal is a strong word, and few American literary productions can claim it with any show of conviction, but it is probably safe to say that, so long as there are children in the world or adults with the easy imagination of childhood, Uncle Remus will be assured of appreciative readers. That ought to be immortality enough to satisfy any one.

Erudite men have laboriously traced Harris's connection with the plantation tradition, and others have commented ponderously on his peculiar dialect, but such work is the product of unimaginative minds. Harris belongs in literature with the Grimm brothers and the dozens of others, frequently anonymous, who have kept from oblivion the folklore of a people. The stories of Uncle Remus are the familiar legends of animals and men that are in circulation during the childhood of a people. Æsop, Grimm, and the medieval animal stories like those of Reynard the Fox spring from the same source. Harris wrote to give delight to those who cared to read, just as true literary artists always write.

Harris was born in Georgia and spent all his life in his native state. The stories of Uncle Remus were first published in the *Atlanta Constitution*, a newspaper with which the author was long connected. The chief qualities of the legends put in the mouth of Uncle Remus are a whimsical humor and a simple and direct appeal to the reader's primitive imagination. Sophisticated readers who get their pleasure only from the super-refined literature of the élite see little in Harris's work, and some people have been known to make foolish objections to the bad grammar of the plantation Negro, but to those who rejoice in the discovery of simple literature coming straight from the heart of a people, Uncle Remus is a perpetual delight. Children, the most exacting of all critics, care nothing about the primitive qualities of the stories, they are interested in the humor and in the dramatic action. That they are satisfied is sufficient proof that both qualities are present.

Thomas Nelson Page (*1853-1922*).—The plantation tradition that was brought down to the Civil War by such men as Kennedy and Cooke was picked up by Thomas Nelson Page and given all the habiliments of the local color story. Page used the Virginia of the large plantations and the spacious hospitality of the stately mansion houses; he saw a chance for tearful sentiment in a land broken by battle beyond recovery; and in the tender relations of kind master and faithful slave he glimpsed possibilities of unlimited pathos; finally he found the requisite dialect in the soft language spoken by the blacks. That he never sharply individualized his characters but always tended to make them more typical than individual was in keeping with the practice of the school. From almost every test Page is a thorough-going local colorist.

Page was born in Virginia on a plantation in the old Tidewater region. He was educated at Washington and Lee and at the University of Virginia. From 1875 to 1893 he practiced law in Richmond. In 1884 his first story appeared in *Scribner's*. It was "Marse Chan," and although it was wholly in dialect it was at once acclaimed as a great work. "Meh Lady" was another success. These two and several others were published in 1889 under the title, *In Ole Virginia*. This is perhaps Page's best work, in spite of its excessive tendency to pathos. Probably the best of the author's novels is *Red Rock*, a story of reconstruction in Virginia. It has all the characteristics of the short stories.

"Charles Egbert Craddock" (*1850-1922*).—Mary Noailles Murfree, writing under the name "Charles Egbert Craddock," first attempted the literary presentation of the poor whites living in the mountains of Tennessee. In recent years much has been written about these people. Travelers have told us of their pure Anglo-Saxon blood, their customs and curious superstitions, and their dialect that contains words current in the days of Shakespeare but long since obsolete among the users of "correct" English. But not all the inquiry of the curious and the industrious has nullified the work of Miss Murfree or cast doubt upon the authenticity of her stories. The field she opened is yet only partly explored, but it is probable that before the work can be reasonably completed, an interpreter of the mountain whites must come from the ranks of those people. There are many indications that such an interpreter may appear within a short time.

Writers of New England.—Mrs. Stowe's contributions to the wave of local color novels and stories have already been mentioned. In her *Oldtown Folks* and *Poganuc People* the author did what is probably her most finished work. Certainly they are the books that the reader can turn to most often with a feeling of pleasure. In them she has sketched a life that every New Englander dwells upon with fond recollections and that few readers, however far they may have been born from the soil of New England, would wish to see disappear from our literature. In these books Mrs. Stowe followed the methods that were being fixed by the local color school, and her success in handling them made her the leader of the large group that exploited the literary resources of New England.

Sarah Orne Jewett (1849-1909) and Mary Wilkins Freeman, (1862-1930) are called local colorists of the decline of New England, though their methods differed from those of their school. There was none of Bret Harte's preference for the sensational and the picturesque in the stories of these two women, and in the pages of Miss Jewett there was a very sparing use of dialect. Both writers took for their tasks the portrayal of the narrow, repressed, and barren lives led by the men and women—especially the women— on the deserted farms and in the quiet villages of New England. Both were realists who rejected utterly the pleasant and facile writing of Harte, and both emphasized the minor occurrences of everyday living. They differed in the depth of their tragic conception of life. Mrs. Freeman was a genuine pessimist who blocked out of most of her stories anything that might be called romantic. In many ways her work reminds one of the novels of Hardy without the comic relief, though of course she was never the artist that the great Englishman was. Miss Jewett is more restrained and less grim. She approached her task with a mind open to all the suggestions that might come from her environment. Mrs. Freeman approached her work with a mind already saturated with a gray melancholy, a sense of utter futility. Miss Jewett reminds one of the Dutch painters who presented the joy and sorrow of the common people in quiet colors. Mrs. Freeman's pessimism is like that seen in the hopelessly tragic stories in Garland's *Main Traveled Roads;* Miss Jewett's influence is to be found in the stories and early novels of Willa Cather. In fact it strains the language to call either of these writers local colorists. Their importance is to be found in their realistic presentation of New England life, for in this respect they are worthy forerunners of American realism.

It is only because they confined their efforts to the New England scene that they are ranked with the local color school.

James Whitcomb Riley (1849-1916).—Americans of the seventies and eighties were never too busy in the pursuit of money or political prestige to refuse to drop a tear over the sentimental recollections of their childhoods spent on the old farm. Will Carleton proved this fact by selling more than half a million copies of his sentimental *Farm Ballads,* and James Whitcomb Riley so profited by Carleton's example that by 1890 he was the acknowledged poet laureate of the United States. Riley was not a great poet, for his amazing popularity could not have belonged to any one who had the message or power of Whitman, but he knew how to combine fond recollection, pathos, humor, and the Indiana dialect in such a way as to appeal to an enormous following.

Riley was born in Indiana and after a roving youth that took him into close contact with the heart and mind of the average American he began newspaper work. His first poems were published in the *Indianapolis Journal,* and in 1883 he issued his first book, *The Old Swimmin' Hole and 'Leven Other Poems.* These verses immediately established his standing as the poet of "the people" as distinguished from the literary class. Everything that Riley wrote is easily understood by any student halfway to high-school standing, and many of them are among our best known nursery rhymes. Such poems as "The Old Swimmin' Hole," "When the Frost Is on the Punkin," and "The Old Man and Jim" have been recited at grange meetings, church socials, chautauquas, and school programs for more than forty years, and they have never been without appreciative audiences. Truly Riley is the "people's laureate."

As a poet Riley had serious limitations. He consciously excluded from his pages all serious thought, for it could never be grasped by his chosen audiences, and he hopelessly idealized American farm life, but the man's besetting sin is a perfect mania for trying to make his audience weep. His attempts were never made by way of high passion or moving tragedies of the spirit, but always by an appeal to shallow pathos. But whatever Riley's shortcomings may have been, his audience liked his poetry, and that reward seemed to him a sufficient recompense for his work. Probably his readers would not have liked him so much if he had not possessed the very faults that he had.

Joaquin Miller (*1841-1913*).—Most of the local colorists narrowly limited their fields. Harte wrote of the gold mines of California, Cable of New Orleans, Miss Murfree of the Tennessee mountaineers, and Riley of the Indiana farm home. Joaquin Miller, as true a local colorist as we have ever had save in his preference for Byronic rhetoric over dialect, was less modest in the limitation of his territory. With a sweeping gesture he took the whole West as the subject of his poetry. Naturally with so great a subject he felt called upon to treat it in the grand manner, and that style was simply too great for him to handle. As a result, his descriptions are overdone, and many of his attempted flights of verse are only rhetorical ranting that is woefully lacking in sincerity.

Miller was a true son of the West. He was born in either Ohio or Indiana, the exact site is uncertain, when those states were decidedly western. In 1852 stories of the promising regions of the Pacific coast led his family to migrate to Oregon. Here the boy grew up, obtained the rudiments of an education, ran a newspaper, practiced law, mined for gold, campaigned against the Indians, rode pony express, and in general participated in the colorful life of the northwestern frontier. The statement that Miller led an adventurous and even thrilling life in the Oregon country is not to be doubted, though his vivid accounts of certain dramatic experiences are decidedly open to question.

In 1868 Miller published a volume of his poetry that was not enthusiastically received. The next year he produced another volume called *Joaquin et al.* that met with little more favor. Disgusted at the indifference of his countrymen, he went to London where he failed even to find a publisher. At his own expense he printed *Pacific Poems,* and to the surprise of every one the success was tremendous, sensational enough to satisfy the author. This volume was immediately republished as *Songs of the Sierras.* With English recognition firmly in his grasp he turned to his native land where his poetic claims could no longer be denied, especially by the numerous critics who took all their opinions ready-made from London. However, many Americans never took Miller at his own very extravagant appraisal. His faults were too numerous and too glaring not to attract considerable critical comment.

The chief fault of Miller is an inveterate tendency in almost every poem to leave off writing poetry and begin waving his hat and shouting at the top of his voice. At his best he was a true poet, but he could never draw the line between poetry and noisy rhetoric. The West of the Gilded Age was a crude, colorful place of flamboyant manners, and Miller allowed the characteristics of his chosen region to interfere seriously with artistic qualities of his poetry. If inspiration failed at a critical moment he would attempt to gain his effect simply by raising his voice. Frequently the result is lamentable. Miller undoubtedly modeled much of his poetry on that of Byron, but too often in his hands the inimitably easy lines and apt descriptions of "Childe Harold" become only bombastic and splotchy word-paintings. He lacked the restraint and quiet power that can be achieved by the true writer without the use of superlatives.

The very best of Miller is to be found in a few scattering poems like his well known "Columbus" and in his most successful descriptions of western scenery and life. Occasionally he has the ability to make one see and feel the West and the spirit of the pioneer. Even in the poems that are least successful he has left us valuable social documents, because he was completely of the West—too completely for his artistic good, for he was never able to make effective selection when dealing with his vast material.

There are many more local colorists who helped fill the magazines from 1870 to the middle nineties, but the ones enumerated are fairly representative of the various parts of the country.

The local color school was not of vast importance in the development of our literature. Bret Harte gave new life to the short story, Russell and Harris discovered that the Negro race has possibilities for literature other than that of illustrating social injustice, and Hay and Harte made a step toward western realism in the use of realistic dialect. But to-day few of these contributions seem to be important. The short story of the present, save that in the inferior magazines, shows no influence of Harte. The methods of Russell and Harris were so debased by the efforts of their followers to get tears and laughter out of using the black race that contemporary novelists and dramatists of Negro life have had to start their work from a new approach. The writers of western dialect who followed Hay and Harte descended to appalling inanities, and to-day we think that the best presentations of western life are being done by such novelists as Miss Cather, Mr. Rolvaag, and Mr. Sherwood Anderson, whose interpretations depend little upon dialect.

A few of the so-called local colorists like Miss Jewett and Mrs. Freeman gave considerable impetus to the development of realism, but it is gravely to be doubted if such writers are genuine members of the school of local color.

SUGGESTED READINGS

The material for this chapter exists in enormous quantity. The student is referred to a few of the more useful items.

Bikle: *George W. Cable; His Life and Letters.* New York. 1928.
Blair: *Native American Humor.* New York. 1937.
    Treats Harte and the local color school.
Boynton: *Bret Harte.* New York. 1903.
Harris: *Life of Joel Chandler Harris.* Boston. 1918.
Harrison: *Bret Harte.* New York. 1941.
    Excellent introduction.
Howells: *Literary Friends and Acquaintance.* New York. 1911.
    Contains a short passage on Harte.
Matthiessen: *Sarah Orne Jewett.* Boston. 1929.
    A model biography of a minor figure. Willa Cather has some illuminating things to say about Miss Jewett. See *Not Under Forty* and the preface to a volume of stories by Miss Jewett.
Merwin: *The Life of Bret Harte with Some Account of the California Pioneers.* Boston. 1911.
Mims: *Sidney Lanier.* Boston. 1912.
    For Lanier see the prefaces to the collected edition.
Pattee: *The Development of the American Short Story.* New York. 1923.
Pattee: *A History of American Literature Since 1870.* New York. 1915.
    pp. 3-24; 63-135.
Rourke: *American Humor.* New York. 1931.
Stewart: *Bret Harte, Argonaut and Exile.* Boston. 1931.
Walker: *San Francisco's Literary Frontier.* New York. 1939.

CHAPTER XIX

WESTERN HUMOR

Critics of our literature have indulged in a vast amount of loose
talk about western humor. Some have traced the laughter of the
West back to one man, but those who did the tracing have not
agreed on the same man, for "John Phoenix" and "Artemus Ward"
have both been acclaimed the founder of western humor; some have
said that it came directly from a certain class or profession, like
the early river men of the Ohio and Mississippi; still others have
intimated that it was a gift miraculously bestowed upon the pioneers
and that any attempted examination of its origin is destined to be
a fruitless task. All such contentions proceed upon the assumption
that western humor is so different from all preceding types of humor
that it is in effect a unique variety. Certainly it is different from
the usual humor of literature, and there are elements in it that surely
come from the presence of the frontier, but it is to be questioned
if western humor is not simply the universal humor of the lower
and uneducated classes placed in literary garb. Humor is the most
personal thing in the world, and that of the West reflects the conditions of frontier life, but the elements of that humor are not
peculiar to western literature.

It is probable that every generation in every nation has had its
humor, its broad witticisms, and its practical jokes that were current among the lower and uncultured classes and were seldom admitted to the dignity of literature. Literary men have usually been
educated, or at least they have been subjected to educational processes. As educated men their taste in humor has been refined and
made intellectual. In their writing they prefer wit to slap-stick
comedy, and they are quick to draw the veil over most of the humor
that springs from the everyday lives of the commoners. Despite
the reticence of literary men there is plenty of evidence to show
that Chaucer, Shakespeare, Fielding, and Hardy—to name no more
—knew the broad humor of the tavern, the countryside, and the
crowded city streets. In America the very class whose humor was

450

largely excluded from literature poured into the Ohio and Mississippi valleys and formed a homogeneous society that roared with laughter at whatever amused it. When western journalists began their trade, they naturally filled their columns with the material that their readers wished to see. Often this material was humor, broad, unpolished, free and easy, but frequently very funny.

Causes of Western Laughter.—Of course the West and the presence of the frontier influenced the traditional humor of the people. Many of the inhibitions and repressions of the old world were removed. Respect for rank, a sense of social inferiority, the fear of economic disaster caused by the employer's whim were all removed by frontier equalitarian forces. Western laughter was democratic; it gloried in its irreverence for caste and in its jaunty impertinence. Why should the laugher fear economic reprisals from him laughed at? The frontier held too grand a promise of free land and too great a threat over the head of the aspiring aristocrat for any one to forgo laughter because of fear. There certainly was nothing obsequious in the humor of the West. Operating just like western democracy, it played on all alike and brought all to the same level.

Another incentive for frontier humor is to be found in the emotional sterility of western life. The pioneer knew very few emotional outlets such as music, art, the theater, and literature. He was reduced for his relaxations to revivals and political campaigns, and these outlets came at infrequent and irregular intervals. Hence the telling of countless stories and the "swapping of yarns" became recognized as major amusements in the West, comparable to the operas, the dramas, and the art galleries of older portions of the country. Laughter is always the easiest response obtainable by the unskillful story-teller, and the stories that provoked laughter became amazingly popular. Davy Crockett, Abraham Lincoln, and many another backwoods leader first became known through the ability to tell stories. The art was practiced in country stores, at political meetings, at public auction sales, on court days, everywhere and every time people came together.

Another motive that powerfully though unconsciously influenced the Westerners to tell humorous stories was the very hard life of the frontier. Conditions were hard enough to break the spirits of the strongest, and humor was used as a moral tonic, a freshening and invigorating influence. The frontier promised much, but sometimes its promises were long deferred, and in the seasons of disappointment and disaster humor may have eased many a rough place for the struggling pioneers. They could laugh because the unchangeable conditions of western life made optimism inevitable, and humor became a passing aid to the disappointed. Still another reason for the laughter of the frontier can be found in its use as a means of social criticism. The frontier insisted upon bringing every one to the same level in virtually every important respect. It suffered few variations from the norm. Aristocracy was the pet aversion of the pioneer, and even if economics and social life had not made aristocracy impossible in the West, it would have been laughed out of existence. Humor and satire are by far the most effective instruments of social criticism, and these means were widely employed upon the frontier. Moreover, in the West they were not veiled as they might have been in Europe or in other portions of this country. In the hands of the pioneer they were forthright and exceedingly sharp.

Characteristics of Western Humor.—One of the most noticeable characteristics of western humor is the habit of gross exaggeration. Any of Mark Twain's books will give sufficient examples of this method of getting a laugh. The author was a mild-mannered man, yet he is constantly longing to criticize some person with a revolver, and he never wearies of slaughtering offenders and adding greatly to the population of the cemeteries. Some have thought that the habit of exaggerating was caused by the incorrigible western optimism. That is a pretty theory, but it probably is too far-fetched to be even approximately correct. Exaggeration is a familiar device of the humorist. If a listener is expecting a certain moderate statement and receives instead one that is ludicrously extravagant, he laughs. Now the exciting of laughter is the aim of much humor, and when a story-teller finds an easy way to achieve his aim, he is apt to use it often.

Another characteristic of western humor is its sharp common sense piquantly and sometimes extravagantly stated. When "Josh Billings" says, "Honesty iz the best polisy. But dont take my wurd for it; tri it," he is compressing a sensible sermon into a few words. "Flattery is like kolone water, tew be smelt of, but not swallowed," is a homely saying that contains a great amount of common sense stated in a way that will get a laugh. This last example contains another prime characteristic of western humor, its incongruities and unexpected comparisons. Every one of the humorists uses this device repeatedly, and it is usually effective. Mark Twain is especially adept at it, and in such a book as *Roughing It* some of the most humorous passages are those in which the comparisons are the most illogical and absurd. Some writers have said that this method was fostered by the incongruities of the frontier. This, too, is probably only another pretty theory. An illogical comparison gets a laugh, just as exaggeration does, by its unexpectedness.

Early Western Humorists.—It is impossible to call any man "the first western humorist." Benjamin Franklin had many of the characteristics of the frontiersman, and he was something of a humorist. Washington Irving made an attempt to absorb some of the frontier spirit, and he too was a humorist; in fact, his first book, *Knickerbocker's History of New York*, is a genuinely humorous work, probably the first ever written in this country. Augustus Longstreet was certainly both a Westerner and a humorist, as were certain other obscure writers in the first half of the nineteenth century.

George Horatio Derby (1823-1861) writing under the name of "John Phoenix," has been called the father of the new school of humorists. He was a native of Massachusetts and a graduate of West Point. During the middle fifties he was in the Far West with army engineers, and at this time he wrote most of the sketches that made him famous. He died at the early age of thirty-eight. Derby used most of the tricks that were later in the repertoire of all western humorists. Solemn but gross exaggeration, illogical comparisons and conclusions, irreverence, and homely philosophy seasoned with wit all are to be found in his pages. Moreover Derby saw and described the "pike" and used a considerable amount of Pike County dialect in his humorous sketches. One of Derby's best efforts is a mock review of a piece of descriptive music, a most amusing burlesque in which the "pike" appears dressed in his familiar garb and using his familiar dialect. Evidently Derby had considerable vitality, for his writings afford fair entertainment to-day. This remark cannot be made of every western humorist.

"Josh Billings," whose real name was Henry Wheeler Shaw (1818-1885), carried the art of expressing homely philosophy in epigrammatic form to the highest pitch reached by any of his school. This form of humor has always been popular with Americans, and with very good reason, for it is the natural expression of a practical, sensible, and hurried people. Benjamin Franklin immortalized Poor Richard, Emerson was constantly uttering shrewd epigrams, Lincoln frequently clinched his argument with a penetrating sentence, and Mark Twain never did anything better than the sayings of Pudd'n-head Wilson. But "Josh Billings" excelled them all in the number and whimsical drollery of his epigrams. He is truly American in his desire to leave a moral lesson and to inculcate the teachings of common sense. During his lifetime he was best known through his "Farmers' Allmanax" that surpassed Poor Richard's annual offerings in popularity and circulation. While all of the western humorists took liberties with spelling and grammar, "Josh Billings" had a positive genius for misspelling.

"Artemus Ward."—"Artemus Ward" was the name under which Charles Farrar Browne (1834-1867) wrote his satires and burlesques of American life. Browne was a native of Maine, and when only a young boy he began work in a newspaper office. While working in Boston he began to experiment with humorous writing, but it took a trip west to reveal to him the possibilities of the field. As a writer for the *Cleveland Plain-Dealer* he began to describe the experiences of a traveling showman whom he named Artemus Ward. In 1861 he became editor of a New York comic magazine, the old *Vanity Fair,* and in 1863 and 1864 he lectured on the Pacific coast. In Virginia City, Nevada, he spent three weeks with Mark Twain, and it is probable that Twain's future was determined by his association with the more experienced writer. In 1866 he became editor of the London *Punch* and one of the most popular lecturers of England. He died in the following year.

Humor has a tendency to change fashions along with the changing years, and jokes that our fathers laughed at need solemn explanation before we can see the point. Such is not the case with the humor of Artemus Ward. Naturally there are passing allusions that must be explained, but the main aim of the writer was to expose the soul of a people, not to raise a laugh at a passing weakness, and the soul of a people evidently changes but slowly if at all. Ward was a keen satirist of society, and as such he has passed from the position of a popular favorite to that of a writer for the "civilized minority." He has taken this place because his criticisms of America during the Civil War are shrewd, penetrating, and good-humored. No ill temper soils his pages, and there is not a sign of personal irritation or petulance. This absence of personal temper

gives Ward a decided advantage over many of our present-day
social critics. His penetration joined to his humor seems to insure
him appreciative readers for generations to come. So long as men
enjoy the blessing of being able to laugh good-naturedly at the
foibles of their fellows, just so long will Artemus Ward have gratefully appreciative readers.

Of all men who are writing to-day Will Rogers most resembles
Artemus Ward, and inasmuch as he is both a typical western humorist and a social critic, he is one of the most significant figures of
the time. When Rogers says, for example, that six thousand people
of Los Angeles watched a golf champion play a round and then
drily remarks that ten years ago you could not get six thousand
California people to lie to you about anything except real estate,
he strikes in true Artemus Ward fashion at both our unholy zest
for money and at our national habit of taking our sports in mass
formation. Rogers delights in exposing such of our national weaknesses as class jealousies, ignorance, intolerance, our groveling worship of money, and our mob thinking. Such was the work of Artemus Ward during the Civil War when thinking was about suspended in favor of passion and prejudice. Both men, it might be
remarked, have pungently commented on the intellectual sterility
of the Genteel Tradition in our literature and in our society.

One can read a volume of Ward's selected works and see the same
weaknesses during the Civil War that flowered so obnoxiously during the Gilded Age and that still afford targets for the satirical
thrusts of Will Rogers. Ward caricatured with no animus but
with penetrating satire our extravagantly boastful patriotism that
finds its release in inflated orations rather than in laudable actions.
He shows us the "home guard" of the sixties who, like his latter-
day prototype, suffered acutely for waffles and fruit cake while the
soldiers were undergoing genuine privations at the front. Especially
does he comment on the reformer who thoughtlessly failed to begin
reforms at home. The man who viciously denounced the weaknesses
in others that he himself secretly possessed receives a neat and
humorous rebuke at the hands of Ward, as does the selfish office-
seeker who thinks more of getting position for himself than of public
service. According to Ward the Battle of Bull Run was lost because news came to the northern army that there were three vacancies in the New York Custom House, and every officer and man
turned about and started for a "job." Times have probably not

changed so much as either the pessimists or the optimists like to think.

During the fifties and sixties the American reading public had a vast appetite for sentiment, and the more sugary the better it was relished. Ward, like Mark Twain and Will Rogers, hated insincerity, and sentimentality is always the epitome of insincerity. The sentimental songs, novels, poetry, and pictures of the time he lampooned with exquisite skill and huge gusto.

Ward is one of the important minor figures of our literature. He has suffered at the hands of the genteel who have been repelled by his roughness and his crudities and he has further suffered at the hands of those teachers who see nothing in a writer whom they cannot discuss profoundly in sonorous polysyllables. Ward certainly had all the characteristics of a western humorist at the very time when the guardians of the genteel were lamenting the overthrow of culture by hordes of "western Goths," and he and Mark Twain were numbered among the Goths. Certainly he is hard to discuss in ponderous phraseology; he is to be read and enjoyed by persons of thoroughly civilized tastes. He will never be highly esteemed by those whose adamantine allegiance to a cause makes them lose that sweetening sense of humor that is so invaluable a part of every well-balanced nature. He will never be gladly read by the stupid or the stodgy, but to a small number he will remain as one of the most significant and enjoyable figures in our literature.

SUGGESTED READINGS

Blair: *Horsesense in American Humor*. New York. 1942.

Blair: *Native American Humor*. New York. 1937.

Blair and Meine: *Mike Fink, King of the Mississippi Keelboatmen*. New York. 1933.

Chittick (ed.): *Ring-Tailed Roarers*. Caldwell. 1943.

Nock: Introduction to *Selected Works of Artemus Ward*. New York. 1924.

Rourke: *American Humor*. New York. 1931.

Stewart: *John Phoenix, Esq*. New York. 1937.

CHAPTER XX

LOST IN THE GILDED AGE

The sins of the Gilded Age are numerous and grave, but in the whole list none is quite so unforgivable as the disasters that it wreaked upon Mark Twain and Henry Adams. Utterly unlike in personal and cultural backgrounds, these two men fell into the grip of the Gilded Age, and hopelessly embittered, both left the world feeling that life had cheated and made a fool of them by rejecting their best gifts and gratefully accepting unworthy offerings. Mark Twain was formed on the frontier into a social satirist of rare abilities for whom there was an urgent need in the seventies and eighties, but the age did not enjoy criticism so well as it liked humor, and under the urging of family and friends he became the popular and highly paid humorist of the day. The colossal social injustices of the Gilded Age, combined with a reading in science and an observation of life among the ancient peoples of Asia and Europe, curdled the frontier optimism that was his birthright and turned it into a black pessimism. He was almost the first American writer to come to the melancholy conclusion that man is powerless in the grip of circumstances over which he can have no possible control. Holding so pessimistic a philosophy Mark Twain felt the success of his early humor turn to dust and ashes in his mouth. He left the world glad to be gone from a life that gives so great a capacity for suffering and then heaps up personal and social sorrow until it is almost unendurable. If Twain had been allowed to follow his natural bent and become a satirist of society, it is probable that he might not have looked back upon his life as a record of utter futility. The Gilded Age had worked its will upon him.

Henry Adams felt the weight of displeasure fall upon him, and he too without reluctance left a world that despised his best gifts. Public service was a tradition in the Adams family. Henry's great-grandfather, John Adams, and his grandfather, John Quincy Adams, were both presidents of the United States, and his father, Charles Francis, was our very successful minister to England during the critical days of the Civil War. Adams was his father's secretary in London, and returned to this country in 1868 after years of valuable training in London, fully determined to offer his talents to his nation. He was surprised and sharply hurt by his discovery that he was not wanted in public service. The Dreadful Decade was just beginning its foul course, and to those in charge of our government an Adams meant no more than the obscurest one of the innumerable Smiths. To his chagrin Henry Adams found that his country had nothing more to offer him than the editorship of a magazine and the position of professor of history in one of our colleges. The man whose immediate family had contributed so much to America wanted to help make history, not to write it. Shortly after he was forty he quit his uncongenial tasks and spent the remainder of his long life contemplating with philosophic detachment the spectacle of American life, and speculating on the meaning of existence. When he died he left in unpublished form *The Education of Henry Adams,* an autobiography, that closes on a note of bitter despair. He too was a lost soul, lost in the Gilded Age.

Saying that Mark Twain and Henry Adams were lost does not mean to imply that they left works of no value. Quite to the contrary. Their books are of extreme significance, but no little of this significance lies in the fact that their works are the records of two men who were deflected from their natural bents by the Gilded Age and forced into ways of thought that brought them no happiness. Adams bridges that measureless chasm that separates the New England of the older Adamses from the age of Jim Fisk and Jay Gould; Mark Twain bridges a similar chasm between the frontier of Lincoln and industrialized America. Both men are very significant, but neither felt that he had been quite true to his possibilities.

MARK TWAIN

(1835-1910)

For fifty years critical controversy has raged about the figure of Mark Twain. When he first broke uproariously into the somnolent placidity of our national letters, college professors and other keepers of the Genteel Tradition gave him a frigid appraisal and unanimously dismissed him as a shaggy barbarian quite insensitive to the refined appeal of Great Art. But a few critics like William Dean Howells, assisted by the author's irresistible personality, secured for him a fair and competent critical appraisal that directed attention to the man's unquestionable greatness of scope and power. Thus encouraged, the historians of our literature began to give Mark Twain a place in their discussions, at first very gingerly in a few noncommittal remarks but finally loosing page after page of uncritical laudation. To-day the voice of the detractor is again heard grumbling about the "final place of Twain in literature" and hinting solemnly at his deficiencies. Surely he had deficiencies, but to make too much of certain of his shortcomings is like regretting Shakespeare's inability to play the saxophone or Dante's ignorance of the Russian ballet. With these arguments and barren regrets the historian of literature ought to have but little to do. His main duty is to record the facts, melancholy though they may be, and attempt to comment on their significance.

There are certain admitted facts about Mark Twain and his literary work. Almost every one concedes that he began his career as a western humorist and developed almost at once a capacity for social satire. Under certain influences he turned from satire back to humor and achieved his most enduring work in a humorous treatment of his past that was far enough away to have gathered the romantic glow of fond recollection mingled with imagination. As he grew older even this romantic treatment of the past failed to satisfy. He was a close observer of his time, he traveled abroad for many years, and he read widely, especially in history, biography, and science. His observation and reading led him into a new way of thinking, and he died hating the cruelty of the human race and holding grimly to the despairing feeling that man is an automaton moved about by combinations of incomprehensible forces. Under the shadow of this belief in the late nineties he wrote a number of deeply pessimistic works, and in the autobiography, written about this time, though not published until 1925 and then perhaps only in part, he gave further evidence of what some have called the dual nature of the man, his pessimism and his humor. These seem to be facts upon which almost every one is agreed.

The following brief and inadequate discussion of Mark Twain will be built upon the foregoing facts. Furthermore, an attempt will be made to comment upon the significance of these facts in the light of his frontier training, his environment during the Gilded Age, and his living through the nineties and the first decade of the twentieth century. In many ways Mark Twain is an excellent recorder of the intellectual changes of his time. With deep sorrow he watched America turn its back upon the easy ways of frontier life, and with still deeper sorrow he found himself so entangled in the new scheme of things that he could not extricate himself. The satirist was almost lost in the humorist; the humorist winced under the knowledge that jokes were the last thing that the Gilded Age ought to have. All in all, his life was a great compromise, and compromises are usually unsatisfactory. Like Melville, Mark Twain wrote so much of his life into his books that it is necessary to understand certain biographical details before discussing his literary work.

Life of Mark Twain.—Mark Twain was born in 1835 in the diminutive frontier village of Florida, Missouri. His father and many of his relatives were dreamers who were always expecting to become fabulously wealthy overnight through the development of mines, or waterways, or some other gift of nature that needed only a bit of enterprise to be turned into immense wealth. The father in particular placed implicit faith in the potentialities of a tract of wild land in Tennessee. He died extremely poor, but with his last breath he besought his family to keep the land.

The Clemens family, for Twain's real name was Samuel Langhorne Clemens, moved from Florida to Hannibal when the boy was only five or six years old. He received the whole of his education before he was twelve, for his father died in 1847 and the boy was then taken from school and apprenticed to a printer of Hannibal. Prior to that time his life had been as happy and carefree as that of Tom Sawyer. Hannibal was a sleepy village that had its only connection with the outside world by means of the great river. Along the Mississippi came the steamboats that spelled romance to young Sam Clemens, and upon the banks of the stream he and the other boys of the hamlet fished, hunted, loafed, and "played hookey." The river got into the boy's blood, and in later years when the whole world delighted to do him honor he could never think of the happy romantic days of his life on the Mississippi without a sigh of genuine regret.

Like many another American writer Clemens got most of his education in a printer's office. After staying in Hannibal long enough to learn his trade, he started on the traditional vagabond life of a printer, visiting New York, Philadelphia, and other towns before returning home. He happened to read about the land of promise that awaited men in Brazil, and like his father, stung by a desire to have a share in the discovery of great wealth, he resolved to go to South America. He went to New Orleans looking for a ship sailing to the south but despaired when he heard that it might be years before one would set out. Then he turned to the river, his first love, determined to be a pilot. He learned the work under one of the best men on the river and for a short time enjoyed such pleasure as he never knew before or after. These glorious years were brought to an end by the Civil War.

The Clemens family was southern, and in a characteristically impetuous moment the young pilot enlisted in a Confederate cavalry troop. There is little to be said for him as a soldier. He disliked the work, and an attack of boils and a sprained ankle so disgusted him with war that he made a precipitous withdrawal from military life. His brother had been appointed secretary of the territory of Nevada, and Clemens decided to accompany him to the new country. The prospects sounded entrancing, for silver had been discovered in the territory. Here began his third and last period of high romance. The first had been his boyhood in Hannibal, the second was his life as a Mississippi River pilot, and the third was the time he spent on the far western frontier. In Nevada he devoted himself principally to the task of having a good time, but here he discovered his talent for humor and satire. Artemus Ward came along on one of his lecture tours and taught Clemens how to tell a story, and shortly after Bret Harte initiated him into literary work. To these two men he owed his start. A quarrel with a rival editor in Nevada led to a bloodless duel, and he was forced to go to California. Here he did a little mining and a little more newspaper work and settled down at the age of thirty as a good-natured failure. In sheer weariness he went to Hawaii, came back and delivered a lecture and discovered that he could make people laugh. In 1867 he published a droll sketch called "The Jumping Frog of Calaveras County," and this story together with his fame as a humorous lecturer made the East clamor to hear him. After his first appearance in New York he was for the remainder of his life the undisputed king of the American lecture platform.

In 1867 he visited Europe and Palestine with a group of tourists. The resulting book was *Innocents Abroad*, one of his great successes. Encouraged, he then published his *Roughing It*, a much better book than its predecessor. This work told of his experiences in the Far

West. In 1870 he married Olivia Langdon, the daughter of a very respectable and wealthy business man of Elmira, New York. Three years later in collaboration with Charles Dudley Warner he wrote *The Gilded Age,* a satire on the orgy of speculation and money-madness that had possessed the American people. Clearly the genius of Twain was in the direction of social satire, but under the urging of his wife and friends he retold the story of his boyhood in *Tom Sawyer,* one of the undisputed glories of our literature. *Life on the Mississippi* described those satisfying days when he was pilot on the river, and later he returned to the material of *Tom Sawyer* and wrote its sequel, *Huckleberry Finn,* the book that most critics call his masterpiece.

Meanwhile Mark Twain was making a large amount of money each year but not enough to satisfy him. He undertook the business of publishing books and started with the hugely successful *Memoirs of General Grant.* But before long the firm failed for a large sum and Mark Twain was left at the beginning of old age burdened with immense debts. He resolutely set himself to the task of paying every dollar and succeeded in doing so within a few years through the royalties on his books and the proceeds from a lecture tour around the world. After the middle nineties the romantic recollections of his youth and his boisterous humor became things of the past. A brooding melancholy settled like an ache in his bosom, and the things that he wrote were either short but terrific blasts of temper aroused by some imbecility or glaring injustice, or they were sketches so bitter and pessimistic that some waited for years before publication. It is currently reported that some of this material has not yet been seen in printed form. Two short works coming from this period are *What Is Man?* and *The Mysterious Stranger,* both written in 1898. The first was published in 1908 and the second in 1916. *The Man That Corrupted Hadleyburg* (1899) is a melancholy record of the effect of greed on the ordinary amenities of life. Coming when it did, it is a very significant story. Mark Twain's character was not polluted by the Gilded Age, but his mind and heart were profoundly touched by the evil genius of the period.

During the years of his deepening depression, honor after honor was heaped upon the head of Mark Twain. Several American universities gave him honorary degrees, and in 1907 Oxford, the oldest and most renowned of the English universities, made him a Doctor of Literature. Three years later he died. His life had extended over a changing and colorful period of our history. Born in the golden day of the pioneer and reveling in that life, he lived through the industrialization of America and well into the Machine Age. Upon his sensitive soul all the changing forces of our life etched their marks, and out of his varied experience came the strange bundle of affirmations and denials and inconsistencies that puzzle us every time we look over the collected works of Mark Twain.

Conflicting Elements in Mark Twain: The Frontier.—Mark Twain was a true product of the frontier. William Dean Howells, himself a son of the Middle West, once remarked that Twain was the Lincoln of our literature, and a juster estimate of the man was never uttered. Furthermore, he was a product of the old frontier, the same one that produced Lincoln. He was well past his most impressionable years before the industrialization of America and the pinch of unsatisfied land hunger began the transformation of our freely shifting race into an unhappy static order. Mark Twain was born into a frontier society that abominated class distinction and practiced a genuine equalitarian democracy. Along with a regard for the equality of men, he absorbed the other social ideas of the frontier. He loathed the cruelty and injustice that are so often visited upon the weak by the powerful or better situated. To him social justice was a real thing to be obtained in the swiftest and most direct method with no regard for technicalities; certainly it was never a thing to be explained away by appealing to psychology or to metaphysical subtleties. Other frontier principles that gained his full support were the implicit faith in the possibility of progress and the belief in the right of every man to share in that progress and in the material things of life. But most of all he seemed to prize the sense of personal freedom that the old frontier inculcated, that flutter of romantic expectancy that anything agreeable is "rather more than apt to happen," that blessed feeling that man is the master of his fate and the captain of his soul. The immediate conditions of pioneer life may have been hard, but the constant promise of the old frontier to bestow imminent wealth made many of the hardships but passing annoyances. Optimism was the natural heritage of the pioneer, and Mark Twain surrendered his heritage only after a struggle.

Mark Twain was formed on two frontiers. His earliest pioneering was done as a boy and youth in the easy ways of ante-bellum Missouri, the most westerly point reached by true Jeffersonian democracy. Life in Missouri before 1850 bore many resemblances to that in frontier Virginia during the formative years of Jefferson's life. Slavery was known but its effects were completely submerged under the flood of frontier influences. From Missouri Mark Twain went to Nevada and California where a more congenial climate, especially in the latter state, a more romantic background, and the discovery of vast mineral wealth exaggerated the ordinary cheerful optimism of the pioneer into what was almost a caricature of frontier spirit, so emphasized were some of the sensational and romantic features. In the Far West the romantic dreams of such men as Mark Twain's father were coming true every day. Mark Twain himself carried through life the ineradicable imprint of Jeffersonian equalitarianism, and for many years he had the grandiose air of the Far Westerner who is about to discover the boundless wealth of El Dorado.

The Frontier in Mark Twain's Books.—Traces of the frontier spirit can be seen in all of Mark Twain's books, even in those of the most somber mood, but naturally that spirit is more pronounced in the earlier productions. However, Jeffersonian equalitarianism is most noticeable in *A Connecticut Yankee at King Arthur's Court,* which appeared when the author was fifty-four years old. Western humor, introduced only for the sake of the laugh, disappears early from his books, though there are still readers who insist upon splitting their sides over *A Connecticut Yankee,* and *Following the Equator.* The person who can laugh over the descriptions of the queen's dungeons in the former book can laugh heartily over the madness of Lear or the sufferings of the tortured in Dante's *Inferno.* It is a mistake to look for humor in all of Twain's works, even though the author is a true Westerner, and humor is one of the western characteristics. There are other marks of the Westerner that Twain soon substitutes for humor. Among these are sharp social satire and a cold hatred of tyranny, injustice, and inhumanity. As these elements find their way into his books, Twain becomes less uproarious but no less western.

However, Mark Twain made his bow to the East as a humorist of the Pacific coast, and it was hard, almost impossible, for him to live down his early reputation. His first published story, "The Jumping Frog," is simply an episodic western anecdote that owes what little humor it contains to very obvious tricks, every one of which was designed to get a laugh. The story has little of the significance that Artemus Ward would have given one of his sketches, or that Twain would have conveyed a few years later. But it was successful in its appeal to the public, so successful that shortly after its publication, the posters announcing Twain's first appearance in New York showed the lecturer mounted upon a frog. Despite its lack of literary significance, "The Jumping Frog" is wholly of the frontier.

The first book, *Innocents Abroad*, is one of the author's most significant works. There is humor in it and a strong tang of western breeziness, but the chief element is a running commentary of sharp satire. In 1870 America was being deluged by sentimental travel books that sniveled or waxed rhapsodic over every romantic or historical scene of the old world. American tourists, taking their cues from these books, rhapsodized and wept all along the tourist routes of Europe, northern Africa, and western Asia. Mark Twain went abroad every inch an American. He had seen all the marvels of his America; in fact, as a frontiersman he was one of them, and he stalked unabashed into regions sanctified by the victories or the glorious defeats of the human spirit, disdaining to grovel or to thrill with exaltation before most of the sights of Europe. His finest satire is reserved for those who exclaim or sigh according to dictates of the guide books. Everywhere he went Mark Twain held up his head and remarked audibly on the excellencies of America. Here is true western independence. But the story is not finished. If Twain failed to understand or appreciate anything, he jeered at it. Through the art galleries, libraries, and museums of Europe clumped this western frontiersman venting the same grotesque buffooneries upon the finest creations of European culture that he used upon mendacious guides and cheating landlords. "If you don't understand it, laugh at it," seemed to be his motto. *Innocents Abroad* is a glad, sad book. One reads it gladly to see contempt heaped upon the hypocritical sentiment and sham romantic raptures of the American tourist, but one also sadly reads in it the cultural limitations of Mark Twain. And his limitations were those of western America. The frontier is too self-sufficient. It too confidently faces the present and too heartily despises the past. It has no regard for any culture, save that which is to be created on some future day in Cactus Center, Jonesville, or Grizzly Gulch. Thus it is with *Innocents Abroad*. But whatever else that book may be, it is frontier to the core.

Roughing It is the saga of the Far West. Infinitely more truthful and realistic than the frontier stories of Bret Harte, it was conceived and written in the spirit of high romance. To Mark Twain the trip across the plains was the Great Adventure, and Nevada was the Promised Land where the old dreams and desires of the frontier might find fulfillment. It was in this spirit that he visited the West, and more than ten years after his arrival in Virginia City, ten years filled with romantic recollections and pleasant memories, he sat down to write his book of the Golden West. The book is uneven and much too long—almost all the latter half should have been omitted— but its best pages glow and sparkle with color and vivacity. The reader is not to be envied who has not enjoyed this re-creation of old times in the West.

The Gilded Age is a different type of book from any of its pred-ecessors, more restrained than *Innocents Abroad* and far more prom-ising, and less humorous and more satirical than *Roughing It*. Many people have spoken loosely of the "tragedy of Mark Twain," but the real tragedy of his life was his failure to fulfill the promise of *The Gilded Age*. The book was the result of a collaboration with Charles Dudley Warner, who wrote certain chapters. The part done by Warner may be passed without consideration, for it contains a pointless love story that is out of harmony with the remainder of the work. The portion of the book done by Twain includes the chapters dealing with Colonel Sellers and the conditions in the na-tional capital. This part of the book is a gorgeous piece of social satire. Taking the frontier optimist who was always about to "strike it rich," Twain injected him into the wild speculative temper of the seventies and surrounded him with gaudy rascals and contempt-ible ignoramuses that characterized the business and politics of the age. The satire ranges in temper from the broadly good-natured to the acridly tart that could easily slide over into bitterness. In *The Gilded Age* Mark Twain stood on tiptoe ready to take off on his literary flight. He promised to become the great American satirist, but in the deft touch with which he handled the scenes of his boyhood there was another promise—a promise to turn his back on the satire of *The Gilded Age* and to become the chronicler of a time and a place that had departed with his youth. This last was the promise that he fulfilled, and while his fulfillment gave us three of the glories of our literature, the sensitive reader must feel, as the author himself felt, that *Tom Sawyer, Life on the Mississippi,* and *Huckleberry Finn* gave us only a part of the full potentialities of

Mark Twain. The man never fully realized himself, never followed up relentlessly the powers exhibited in *The Gilded Age.*

From satire Twain went to a romantic treatment of his boyhood and youth. *The Gilded Age* showed his ability to satirize the weaknesses of the frontier as well as those of the politics and business of the seventies, but in *Tom Sawyer, Life on the Mississippi,* and *Huckleberry Finn* the fond contemplation of the far away and long ago submerges the satire, save for occasional irruptions. In these three books the poetry and romance of the Mississippi flood every page with the glow of kindly recollection tempered by fine literary art. For Mark Twain was an artist. Certain passages in *Tom Sawyer,* the first twenty chapters of *Life on the Mississippi,* and the whole of *Huckleberry Finn* bear the mark of genius. These books hold in solution the golden memories of a day that is past. The author avoids the unpleasant or laughs it off while dawdling fondly over the pleasant. The result is a placid, unhurried story whose words are formed in affection. A discussion of the relative merits of the books is useless. They are all very good, so very good that no literary man of the nineteenth century would have sensibly disdained to be the author of any one. *Tom Sawyer* is probably a bit more artificial than the others, but in some of its episodes, as in the celebrated "showing-off" of Tom at Sunday School, it has a bubbling spontaneity that is fairly hypnotic in its power. *Huckleberry Finn* is an unquestioned masterpiece. If to the inner circles of great fiction only two American books can penetrate, it is pretty certain that the bulk of critical opinion would award the honor to *Huckleberry Finn* and *Moby Dick.*

Twain's three great books are representative of a certain phase of frontier life, but no one asserts that they give the whole picture. One would have very great difficulty in reconstructing the life of Lincoln upon the frontier background described by *Tom Sawyer* and *Huckleberry Finn,* and Lincoln developed in the environment set forth in the books. Mark Twain always had a strain of incorrigible romance in him that came to a beautiful flowering when he wrote of the Mississippi River. Just as the great waterway had once brought romantic dreams to young Sam Clemens of Hannibal, Missouri, so did the recollection of days and nights on the Mississippi bring a greatly desired release to the mature Mark Twain. Romantic memories of boyhood served as an excellent excuse for not satirizing the follies of the Gilded Age. With a feeling of genuine relief Twain wrote the pages that allowed him to forget the unpalatable present in the pleasant memories of days long past. If the material had held out and if the ideas of the author had not changed, he might have added many volumes to his Mississippi romances, but the books are autobiographical, and as such their material was soon exhausted. Besides, the spirit of the author was restlessly surging on to other fields. Romantic pioneering is a delightful business, but it could not hold Mark Twain indefinitely.

A Connecticut Yankee gives Twain's fullest expression of his innate frontier spirit. The book simply sweeps away thirteen hundred years and dumps an enterprising American into the atmosphere of chivalry and aristocracy. The Yankee finds everything wrong at Camelot. Aristocratic ideals cramp and hamper the development of natural ability, injustice and sheer cruelty flourish everywhere, the groveling of the lower classes before the clerics and nobles is disgusting, chivalric ideals outrage every suggestion of common sense, and not the least of the worries is the primitive method of working at all tasks. Twain spilled page after page of mordant criticism upon the social order of Arthur's realm, and beside every glaring wrong he conspicuously displays the ideals of frontier America. Western individualism and initiative replace class-mindedness, justice and humanitarianism alleviate social wrongs, and liberty and personal freedom are exalted far above the chivalric ideals of group loyalty. Thus Twain would substitute for a static, stratified society, one that was closely modeled upon that of the West. Furthermore into the archaic industry of Camelot the Yankee introduced modern American inventions and enterprises. In all these criticisms and innovations Mark Twain was voicing the ideas of the pioneer.

In many ways the ideal society hinted at in *A Connecticut Yankee* is comparable to that in Bellamy's *Looking Backward*. Twain did not go so far as Bellamy did in the creation of a Utopia, but both wished to keep the benefits of science and invention without suffering the ill effects of the widespread industrialization of society. Twain founded his ideal state upon the principles inculcated by frontier life; Bellamy hastened the process inaugurated by scientific invention and rushed to a perfect society founded upon machinery and functioning in the interests of justice and happiness. The fundamental aims of the two men bear considerable resemblance to each other, but the methods used to reach those aims are different. Many have wondered why Twain took the trouble to direct so elaborate a criticism at a civilization that was ended five hundred years ago. Indeed the wonder is legitimate, but the chief question is whether he was criticizing the civilization of Camelot or the gross faults of America during the Gilded Age, for many of the wrongs and stupidities attributed to medieval Camelot flourished in the America of the seventies and eighties. It is quite conceivable that Twain, feeling himself unable to criticize his age directly as did Godkin, Bellamy, and Henry George, did his work by indirection. Whatever his ultimate aim may have been, we know that he greatly admired Bellamy and that *Looking Backward* delighted him. It is a bit significant that Bellamy's work appeared the year before *A Connecticut Yankee*.

The frontier molded and shaped the ideas of Mark Twain. Had he remained permanently in the easy life of California or had he been born at the opening of the nineteenth century, he might have escaped a sharp challenge of his ideas. But he was born in 1835, he went east from California, married an eastern woman, and took over many of the prepossessions of the Gilded Age. Mixing the Gilded Age and the spirit of the old frontier is like mixing oil and water. The later Mark Twain is composed of two or more incompatible elements very imperfectly blended.

Conflicting Elements in Mark Twain: The Gilded Age.—The frontier made Mark Twain; the Gilded Age ruined him. When he went east in 1868 in the confident flush of young manhood, he naturally wanted to be acclaimed a success. He soon found that success was measured in two ways, by popular favor and by monetary return. The latter was the surest sign; it left no room for doubt. His marriage into the family of a prosperous and ultra-respectable business man of Elmira accented his desire to gain popular favor and a good income. With new associations many things changed. Some of his old ideals became blurred by the noise and prosperity of the Gilded Age. He became intimate with business men and political figures that he should have been the first to rebuke, but they belonged to his circle. He had taken on some of their aspirations and ideals. Shortly his old pioneer desire to get on in the world was caricatured into its grotesque, unlovely counterpart of wanting to get rich quickly. And Twain was naturally unable to attack anything fiercely with which he had identified himself. He was the sponsor and publisher of Grant's *Memoirs,* and as such felt a sense of loyalty to the book and its author. He was a scathing critic of poor writing, as any one will testify who has read his opinions of Cooper's literary sins, and yet when Matthew Arnold sneered at Grant's style, Twain rushed to the defense and talked as if he actually considered the *Memoirs* the literary equal of Gibbon's *Decline and Fall of the Roman Empire*. In just such fashion did the Gilded Age silence Mark Twain's caustic criticism.

Furthermore the desire to be thought quite respectable took some of the primitive force away from Twain. He lived in New England where the Genteel Tradition held literature in its keeping. Writers that it approved had to be quiet, inoffensive, and very innocuous. Certainly buoyant western humor and satire could not hope for critical recognition by the genteel. Hence Twain allowed himself to be led away from the satirical presentation of life. Minor journalistic critics, who were hardly capable of reading the proofs of his books, gravely revised his manuscripts and suggested sweeping emendations that were humbly accepted. A few years ago Van Wyck Brooks, a very capable critic, wrote *The Ordeal of Mark Twain*, in which he attempted to show by means of psychological analysis that Twain was the victim of an ultra-respectable wife who yearned to have her husband write "nice" literature. In spite of a harrowing lack of humor, Mr. Brooks made an impressive case for his contention. But he made one very great mistake in laying all the sins of the Gilded Age upon the head of Mrs. Clemens. In a very true sense Mrs. Clemens was a symbol of the age, but alone she could have done little toward deflecting the genius of her husband. The whole Gilded Age aided and abetted her.

The Gilded Age put Mark Twain in a position where he could not criticize it, but it could not keep him from seeing both its faults and his own weakness in failing to rebuke them. He realized the monstrous injustices of the time in economics and politics, he understood the bitter cry of the oppressed, and though he raged in private, he never unsheathed his pen. The knowledge of these facts would not tend to make the man a bubbling fountain of humor and good nature. Furthermore he saw the disappearance of a free self-determining people that the frontier had fostered and the substitution of a stratified society that came in the wake of industrialization. He saw disappear the very real basis of American optimism—our free economic life—and the coming of the first shadows of a national pessimism. He saw all these things, and as a result he was one of the first Americans to fall into a pessimistic way of thinking.

There were other reasons for Twain's pessimism besides those pushed upon him by the Gilded Age. He read largely in many fields, never touching poetry or fiction but assimilating much history and science. The human race has been so wasteful of life and happiness that history can hardly be called a highly optimistic study, and the first implications of science are downright pessimistic. Besides reading, Twain traveled a great deal, and his observation of life in the older parts of the world confirmed him in his suspicion that the free and brave life of the frontier required a spacious background that would be impossible in a few generations. His gloomy conclusions about the future of the world were shared by such men as Hardy and Anatole France. The suffering and distress of humanity offered a problem that these three men could never resolve to a cheerful conclusion.

Sharp jets of satire directed at the Gilded Age can be found in even the early books of Twain. In *The Gilded Age* the satire becomes sharper and more unconcealed. It goes into "asides" and interpolated remarks in the books dealing with the Mississippi, and it appears by indirection in *A Connecticut Yankee*. Thereafter its place is taken by a black despair, a brooding sense of futility, that sees in life a melancholy dream that has its ending only in the last long sleep. It was certainly a curious conclusion for any one to reach who had come out of the West intoxicated with the buoyant ideals of the frontier. But the satirist had been thwarted. He was forced to live and write in ways foreign to his original nature. The Gilded Age had worked its will.

The midnight of Mark Twain's spirit is best found in two short works, *What Is Man?* and *The Mysterious Stranger*. The first of these is a philosophic dialogue that expounds the opinion that man is an automaton entirely at the mercy of powerful influences that he does not yet understand and cannot even begin to control. The second is one of the supreme expressions of pessimism in literature. It ends on the note that life is a dream, a bad dream, and the last word is an exhortation to dream "other dreams, and better."

HENRY ADAMS

(1838-1918)

Although Henry Adams owes his reputation chiefly to two books that bear publication dates of 1913 and 1918, and despite the fact that he has been called a contemporary American, he can well be discussed with Mark Twain, for the Gilded Age put him in a way of thinking that thirty years later developed into the dark skepticisms of *The Education*. The conclusions reached by Adams are not unlike those of Mark Twain in philosophical temper, though in coming to their final views the two men started from entirely different points and traveled different roads, but both routes lay through the muck of the Gilded Age.

Life of Henry Adams.—Henry Adams suffered many misfortunes but none was greater than to be born into the Adams family and then be forced to live through the Gilded Age. The Adamses revered their high ideals of public service; they were slaves to duty; and they considered culture of supreme importance, second only to conscience. To be sure, they were not noted for their popularity, for they never dropped the air of moral and intellectual superiority that was their birthright, and it was confidently asserted of them that they could always do the right thing more disagreeably than any other family in America. Henry Adams inherited all the family characteristics, and with every one of these eighteenth century virtues weighing him down, he plunged into an appallingly demoralized America that was unimpressed by the ideals of public service, duty, and culture. He was a man of ability—competent critics have called him one of the ablest members of the family—but he found in 1870 that the talents of the Adamses were as archaic as their virtues. Henry Adams was surprised, but not out of his family traits. Clutching his feeling of "spiritual superiority," he withdrew in silence to his house, designed by the best architect of the country, and seating himself at the window leisurely watched the passing show of late nineteenth century America. His sense of aloofness never left him, nor did his cynical humor and his biting irony, and he found nothing more amusing than the fact that four generations of training fitted him only to become a contemplative onlooker of the pageant that his great-grandfather and grandfather had started.

The big task of Henry Adams was to educate himself. It was not that he lacked money or the chance to attend college classes; his trouble was his inability to find any one who could teach him anything. The education started inauspiciously, for he always declared that his experience at Harvard and at a German university was no slight misfortune. He learned nothing at either place, but in Germany he acquired the language, and he grudgingly admitted that this was a step toward his education. The education proper was really started in London where he went as secretary to his father, the American minister to England, and where, as Adams whimsically remarked, he was under the most expensive tutors in the world, Lord Palmerston and W. E. Gladstone among Englishmen, and W. H. Seward and Charles Francis Adams among Americans. In other words, Adams was beginning his education by watching the game of politics played by masters. Politics is a manifestation of social force, and from watching the political scene Adams was moved to wonder about the nature of such a force and about what gives it direction and intention, provided that it has intention. This is the problem that ever after engaged his educational efforts, but the education was never finished, for he could never answer the question that he asked.

The remaining facts of Adams's life are few. He returned to this country in 1868 and became assistant professor of history in Harvard and editor of the *North American Review*. Within ten years he dropped these uncongenial tasks, and for another decade he devoted his time and energy to the study and writing of American history. Among the works produced during these years were biographies of John Randolph and Albert Gallatin and a long and masterly history of the Jefferson and Madison administrations. During the years of his research and writing his "education" was not neglected, but after 1892 it occupied the whole of his time.

The Problem Faced by Adams.—Henry Adams deliberately set to work on one of the profoundest questions that can engage the intellect of man. He wanted to discover no less than the origin and nature of the force that gives direction to the current of human affairs. The answer to this question will be a key to the philosophy of history. Many forces are at work in the world, but to the ordinary observer not one can be called the parent-force. Adams attempted to reduce all these forces to their lowest terms in order to study the unity instead of the multiplicity of influences. The discovery and examination of the great parent-force was his problem. It was not enough to see and describe mere motion of human affairs; the influence setting the direction and goal of the motion had to be understood. When he first met Darwin's theory of evolution by natural selection, it seemed to Adams that he saw the answer to his problem, but a swift glance at the United States in the years after the Civil War convinced him that Darwin did not hold the answer. A survey, however fleeting, of American life from Washington, Franklin, and Jefferson to the politicians of the Dreadful Decade does not indicate a very satisfactory amount of evolution or even an intelligently ordered change. It indicates change; that is all. Evidently Darwinism could not give him the answer that he wished. Puzzled, he sought other explanations and still others, and never was he satisfied. He closed his "education" dubiously shaking his head at all suggestions and ominously regarding the future of the human race.

Seemingly Adams started on his education hopefully enough, but he finished his search for the riddle of existence, baffled and pessimistic. His pessimism reminds one of that of the eighteenth century before the dawn of romanticism suffused thought with rosy promise. Although he decided that he could not fathom the secret of force, he concluded that American life had only four prospects, all of them quite unattractive. He asserted that our political thinking would take on the pessimism of the dying civilization of Europe, or that we should be compelled to submit to a tyranny of either labor or capital, or that we should fall back into religious mysticism and clerical domination, or that the age-old social processes would be ceaselessly and senselessly repeated. It was depressing enough to admit that Force defies unification and definition, but it was far more so to predict that an incomprehensible power is carrying us irresistibly to a melancholy fate. One ends by questioning the very word progress.

"The Education" and "Mont-Saint-Michel."—To determine whether there is such a thing in human history as progress it is necessary to have a point from which the movement and direction of human drift can be measured. The most satisfactory point, Adams decided, would be that time when man held the "highest opinion of himself as a unit in a unified universe." Considerable investigation convinced the historian that this time was the century from 1150 to 1250. The measurement of progress over seven centuries entailed the close study of the early period and a correspondingly close appraisal of contemporary times. From these studies came two books that have been justly called "among the best American books that have yet been written." The study of the medieval century is *Mont-Saint-Michel and Chartres: a Study of Thirteenth-Century Unity,* and the examination of contemporary society grew

into *The Education of Henry Adams: a Study of Twentieth-Century Multiplicity,* an autobiography that can be neglected by no student of American life. *Mont-Saint-Michel* was gratefully received by the whole reading public that had sufficient background to read the work. It was lavishly praised by architects, students of church history, lovers of medieval life, and literary critics, all of whom united in calling it a satisfactory interpretation of medieval life and thought. The reception of *The Education* was not so gratifying. Discerning readers at once saw the significance of the book, but drawing-room apologists for American faults, professional optimists, and superficial thinkers belittled the autobiography as the record of a sour and disappointed failure. Some particularly obtuse readers, misled by the sustained tone of ironical humor, have foolishly insisted that the writer was not in earnest. No criticism could be more pointless; Henry Adams was so deeply in earnest that he constantly hid the depths of his feeling, like the aristocratic gentleman that he was, by a show of raillery. But the book is establishing itself in American literature, though, like *Mont-Saint-Michel,* it is too closely written and too subtly suggestive to be easy reading for any one.

Adams ended his life with none of his questions answered and with the extent and direction of human progress not fully determined. "Dispute was idle, discussion was futile, and silence, next to good temper, was the mark of sense." His silence is not that of a man pleased to think that there is nothing more to say; it is the grim silence that settles upon the self-conscious victims of futility. What different conclusion Henry Adams might have drawn had he lived in the eighteenth or twenty-first centuries it is impossible to say certainly, and speculation is fruitless. It is sufficient to know that when he turned his contemplative gaze from the rational order and leisurely happiness of the thirteenth century to the meaningless chaos of the Gilded Age, he had reason to be disquieted.

SUGGESTED READINGS

Adams and Mark Twain are both best studied in their own writings.

Adams: *The Adams Family.* Boston. 1930. Henry Adams, pp. 305-352.
Beach: *The Outlook for American Prose.* Chicago. 1926. Adams, pp. 202-214.

Benson: *Mark Twain's Western Years*. Stanford University. 1938.

Brashear: *Mark Twain, Son of Missouri*. Chapel Hill. 1934.
> Sound and useful piece of work.

Brooks: *The Ordeal of Mark Twain*. New York. 1920.
> Not to be trusted in its major points. This work was later revised but not improved.

Cater (ed.): *Henry Adams and his Friends*. Boston. 1947.
> This collection of letters has a long introduction which is probably the best piece of writing yet done on the subject of Henry Adams.

Clemens: *My Father Mark Twain*. New York. 1931.

De Voto: *Mark Twain's America*. New York. 1940.
> De Voto, an authority on Western life, has written a book of extreme value for an understanding of Mark Twain's background. Mr. De Voto does not care for the theories of Mr. Brooks.

De Voto: *Mark Twain at Work*. Cambridge. 1942.
> Three essays. That on *The Mysterious Stranger* is the most enlightening comment on that book.

De Voto (ed.): *Mark Twain in Eruption*. New York. 1940.
> Hitherto unpublished portions of Mark Twain's autobiography. Of prime importance.

Ferguson: *Mark Twain: Man and Legend*. Indianapolis. 1943.
> An admirable one-volume biography. Characterized by accuracy, restraint, and good literary judgments. Demolishes Van Wyck Brooks without ever mentioning the gentleman's name.

Hemminghaus: *Mark Twain in Germany*. New York. 1929.

Howells: *My Mark Twain*. New York. 1910.

Lawton: *A Lifetime with Mark Twain*. New York. 1925.
> Glimpses of an author from an unusual point of view.

Mack: *Mark Twain in Nevada*. New York. 1947.

Macy: *The Spirit of American Literature*. New York. 1912. Mark Twain, pp. 248-277.

Mumford: *The Golden Day*. New York. 1926. Mark Twain, pp. 199-230.

Paine: *Mark Twain*. New York. 1912.
> The authorized biography in four volumes. This work has many flaws, though it has not been superseded.

Shafer: *Science and Progress*. New Haven. 1922.
> This book contains a chapter on Adams.

Thayer: *Life and Letters of John Hay*. Boston. 1915.
> Contains many references to Adams and his circle.

Wagenknecht: *Mark Twain: the Man and his Work*. New Haven. 1935.

Walker: *San Francisco's Literary Frontier*. New York. 1939.

Webster: *Mark Twain, Business Man*. Boston. 1946.
> This work covers more ground than the title indicates. Many of the letters here published for the first time are of prime importance. The book has not received the attention that it deserves.

Whipple: *Spokesmen*. New York. 1928. Adams, pp. 23-44.

CHAPTER XXI

THE RISE OF REALISM

After the Civil War a change came rather rapidly over the spirit of American fiction. Before 1860 our novels had been predominantly romantic in tone because American life was romantic. Poe, Cooper, Simms, Kennedy, Paulding, all were romantic. After the war our fiction became realistic because the industrialization of the country and the disappearance of the frontier were removing the romantic element from our national life. By 1890, the close of the Gilded Age, our attractive free land was exhausted, "big business" held control of our industry, organized labor was extremely self-conscious, and our traditional feeling of freedom was fast disappearing. Naturally literature came to reflect this new life. However, the artificial romanticism of the seventies and eighties, all "gilt and tinsel," stubbornly disputed the field with its new rival. Nor was it ever completely routed, for the pseudo-romanticism of Lew Wallace and E. P. Roe can hardly be counted extinct so long as Zane Grey, Harold Bell Wright, James Oliver Curwood, and Peter B. Kyne number their readers by the hundred thousand for each of their books. The public whose taste was formed on the shallow and artificial romance of the Gilded Age opposed the new method in fiction as uninteresting, grim, sordid, and even as immoral. This new method was called realism. It was fostered by a variety of influences and first given a place of dignity in American literature by the fiction and criticism of William Dean Howells and Hamlin Garland.

What Is Realism?—"Realism is nothing more and nothing less than the truthful presentation of material." This definition by William Dean Howells can be accepted as a fair statement of the aims of the realistic novelist. It indicates a complete break with the methods of our early romanticists, all of whom assumed in their fiction the same grandiose attitude that characterized our national life during the first half of the nineteenth century. The romanticist did not pretend to tell the truth about life. He used the unpleasant only as an obstacle over which his hero would vault to final victory.

Melville found that the idea of inevitable defeat was not attractive to the early American reader. Now if the average man of the romantic period imagines himself to be the master of his personal and social fate, and if he thought of the world only as a theater for the display of his talents, how natural it was for the novelist to assume that he could fashion the play world of his imagination according to his own ideas. He never thought that he was taking liberties with the truth; he considered that he was only doing with his dreams what any man could do with the world of reality. Hence unusual characters, interesting action, and thrilling climaxes were the aims of romantic novelists. Furthermore, these writers always showed their characters under the spell of a consuming passion like deep love or relentless hate. The realist quietly set to work with a new method. He sought out those quiet, unobtrusive aspects of life that occupy the average man almost exclusively. This step eliminated a great many of the stock characters and situations from the novel, for the realist contended, quite correctly, that man is not naturally the colorful, melodramatic figure visualized by the romantics, and that life was more placid and commonplace than climactic, and that heroes were distressingly scarce. The realist had only one great aim; to reproduce the material of everyday life as truthfully as possible. This aim created an entirely new type of fiction that contained no interpretation of values.

Influences Behind Literary Realism.—Disregarding the general tendency of American life during the Gilded Age there were at least three specific influences making for literary realism between 1870 and 1890. These were the influence of science, of democracy, and of foreign writers who adopted the realistic method before Americans used it extensively.

Science is one of the immediate ancestors of realism in that it gave a method of procedure to the new school of novelists. The method of science is to observe closely, to record scrupulously everything observed, and to attribute quite as much importance to the ordinary quiet and normal ways of nature as to the unusual and spectacular. The unusual always has an interest to the curious, but no scientist allows one spectacular happening to blot out the significance of ninety-nine ordinary occurrences. One of the chief requisites of a scientist is the ability and patience to carry out sustained observation and experimentation. Darwin announced his epochal theory only after twenty-five years of observation. A bac-

teriologist will devote years to the study of microscopic life in order
to isolate and describe a single germ. Agronomists, "hunger-fight-
ers," they have been called, will spend half a lifetime in the development of a new variety of wheat. It was from the procedure of such
men that the realist derived his new method of writing fiction. Just
like the scientist, the writer has a wide field from which to choose
his material, but once the choice is made the realist allows himself
as few deviations from the truth as the scientist takes. Jane Austen,
Turgenev, Flaubert, Henry James, Howells, and Hamlin Garland
chose widely differing material for their novels, but in the handling
of that material each novelist stayed as close to truth as he was
temperamentally capable of staying. Each tried to keep his work
true to "the motives, the impulses, the principles that shape the
actual life of men and women."

Realism took its method from science, but its material came from
democracy. The old novel had been aristocratic. It was filled with
people of rank and title or at all events with very unusual heroes,
for these characters seem, as Howells said, to be essential to the
happiness of readers with "weak and childish imaginations." But
democracy had made all men of the same rank, and the aristocratic
hero and lord were as much out of place in the literature of a democracy as they were in its social and political systems. The new
fiction concerned itself with the merchants, professional men, laborers, farmers, and the other components of everyday America. "I
do not ask for the great, the remote; I sit at the feet of the familiar
and low," said the realists quoting Emerson, and thereupon they
proceeded to the writing of an ever-increasing stream of novels that
presented the ordinary aspects of our national life. To-day no
material, no class of people, can be called "non-literary" subjects.
Everything is literary, and every human being can be made the
subject of interesting and important fiction. This idea is the great
bequest of democracy to the novel.

The third influence behind the rise of American realism was purely
literary. This force was the example of foreign novelists. In the
mid-nineteenth century all over Europe creative artists were striving
for truth and sincerity. Under the influence of the new mood
sculptors quit modeling careful imitations of Greek goddesses and
struck boldly out toward the truthful presentation of men and women
of contemporary life. Following the lead of the French artists,
painters began to seek sincerity in the interpretation of common

life, and idealized heroes began to be replaced by such figures as those of Millet's peasants. (This tendency toward the truthful representation of material and the accompanying tendency to seek subjects in the common and ordinary were shared by fiction.) In France such writers as Balzac and Flaubert did more than any others to set the method for the new generation of writers; Turgenev, Tolstoy, and Dostoievsky wrote a memorable group of Russian novels; George Eliot and Thomas Hardy gave realism a vast impetus by their truthful but poetic interpretations of English country life; and roving at large over Europe was the American-born Henry James, more at home in Paris and London than in Boston, the first international novelist, whose aim was the realistic analysis of the finest shade of emotion. Those writers all had their effects upon our fiction.

During the seventies and eighties Americans had their first contact with this foreign realism. The more cultivated and widely read picked up the new books in Europe or imported them, while translations were speedily prepared for those whose command of language was limited to English. From the number of realistic novels reviewed during the Gilded Age in the more intellectual papers like *The Nation*, it can be judged that there was a good-sized group of advanced readers in this country. Certainly thoughtful Americans like Henry Adams would not be satisfied with either the historical sentimentalities of Lew Wallace or the sugary romances of E. P. Roe. Such readers turned with a feeling of sympathy to Flaubert, Turgenev, Tolstoy, Henrik Ibsen, and even to Émile Zola, the naturalist. When our native realism began to produce its works, it found waiting for it a small but intelligent and appreciative audience.

Changes in the Technique of the Novel.—Enough has already been said to indicate that realism made great changes in the technique of the novel. The new school of writers tried to avoid all plot manipulation, holding, quite correctly, that life has so few climaxes that they may be discounted in a novel which attempts to tell the truth. The new novelists contended that life is ordinarily without glaring high lights and deep shadows and that the forcing of events into a plot with climaxes and suspenses is wholly artificial and untruthful. The romantic novel moves toward a carefully planned happy ending, usually a wedding in the very last chapter that gives every one highest hopes for future bliss. The realist sometimes came to the wedding in the early or middle chapters of his novels and spent the remainder of his time in studying the effect of the marriage upon the characters involved. The whole point of the new technique was to avoid the unnatural and the spectacular both in action and in character and to stress the ordinary and usual. This method had the effect of subduing both the comedy and tragedy, but with the quieter results came an added sincerity.

The Early Realists of America.—Since realism is a relative term, it is impossible to tell who is the earliest of American realists. As early as the sixties Rebecca Harding Davis, mother of the romancer and adventurer, Richard Harding Davis, wrote a realistic story of life in the steel mills of Pennsylvania. Others may possibly have been thinking and writing in the same strain, but to Edward Eggleston (1837-1902) must go the credit for being a pioneer realist who was consciously trying to present truthfully various aspects of life in his native region.

Eggleston was an Indiana clergyman whose professional duties brought him into close contact with the intimate lives of the people. The reading of Taine's defense of quiet, homely realism in his book, *Art in the Netherlands,* led Eggleston to attempt the same type of realism in a literary medium that the Dutch painters had so successfully practiced. He set out to write quiet but truthful novels of life in the Ohio Valley. His aim was to remain as impersonal as the Dutch painters had been and by so doing to give a truthful picture of home life in Indiana uncolored by his own personal views. This theory, carried to any extent whatever, will result in limiting the novelist to an expression of fact without comment as to its desirability or undesirability. The first result of Eggleston's effort was *The Hoosier Schoolmaster* (1871), which is entitled to rank as an excellent and faithful presentation of western life about the middle of the nineteenth century. For more than fifty years this book has held its own with readers, and to-day it is generally recognized as one of the minor classics of American literature. The second of the author's books, *The Circuit Rider* (1874), is another general favorite that handles the same material that is so successfully used in the earlier novel. In addition to these two, Eggleston wrote *The Graysons,* a book that introduces the young Lincoln very effectively without resorting to any of the heroics that seem to plague most novelists when they try to introduce into the pages of a novel a great historical figure like Washington, Lincoln, Queen Elizabeth, or Napoleon. In all his novels Eggleston revealed a close knowledge of his material and a consistent desire to present that knowledge in a truthful fashion.

Eggleston's main interest in writing novels is pretty well revealed by his attempt to write a *History of Life in the United States*. This work, left unfinished at the author's death, is a most laudable attempt at a social history that gives careful attention to the everyday life of the people and little to the sensational political and military events that are usually emphasized by historians. In his history Eggleston used the same material that he utilized for his novels, and he presented it in much the same fashion.

As a novelist Eggleston is a typical early realist. His stories excel in characterization, the plot is always slight, and close attention to detail marks the descriptions of scenery, interior settings, and manners. His three books are worthy of places in the long and distinguished line of realistic studies of American life.

Joseph Kirkland (1830-1894) was another pioneer realist who chose the Mississippi Valley as his field. He was the son of Caroline Matilda Kirkland, one of the earliest of western writers. He was born in Geneva, New York, and when only a small child was taken by his parents to their new home in Michigan, then a genuine frontier state. From 1842 to 1856 he lived in New York City, and after serving in the war, made his home in Illinois. His one important book is *Zury; the Meanest Man in Spring County* (1887). This book is a stern and convincing novel of western farm life that is important partly for its own sake and partly for the impetus that it gave to Hamlin Garland, who was just beginning to attempt his first stories when the book appeared. *Zury* has many crudities, and to-day it is little read, but it deserves to be kept alive by intelligent readers who are interested in the historical development of American realism.

Ed Howe (1853-), the very original and capable editor of the Atchison, Kansas, *Globe,* wrote one work that trembles on the brink of a greatness comparable to that of *Huckleberry Finn* and *Moby Dick*. This book, *The Story of a Country Town,* a grim and terrible novel, relentlessly lays bare the savage aspects of western life that too often have been untruthfully concealed by the purveyors of sweetness and optimism. As a writer of fiction Howe has his faults, the most glaring of which is an inability to write easy and natural dialogue, but the man's honesty of purpose and his grim power are so great that they sweep all faults before them in achieving a memorable picture drawn in dull shades of life on the middle border. Howe has an eye for human personality, a strong feeling for the individual flavor in each of his characters, and it is this that makes his book notable. The action of the book develops naturally out of the personality of the characters, a method that has always been used by the best realists.

The Story of a Country Town is a brilliant example of a book that appeared too early to be appreciated. If the novel had appeared in 1913 instead of thirty years earlier it would have shaken contemporary literature as Masters' *Spoon River Anthology* did in 1915. It is not exactly accurate to speak of the book as a milestone in American letters: its chief service was that of a beacon, far in advance of the body of writers, toward which our novelists slowly labored for more than a third of a century. To-day many writers have caught the spirit of *The Story of a Country Town,* but relatively few have ever achieved its power and truthfulness. The reading public has paid a distinct tribute to Mr. Howe's novel by giving it a steady circulation for more than forty-five years, while thousands of other far more sensational books have run their little course and disappeared into permanent oblivion.

WILLIAM DEAN HOWELLS

(1837-1920)

Out of the unlovely turmoil, the perplexed indecision, and the conflicting tendencies of the Gilded Age there emerged one definite and purposeful literary movement that steadily progressed, despite many vicissitudes, until it had all American writers either clearly in its train or just as clearly in opposition. This literary movement was realism, and William Dean Howells was its major prophet and chief practicer. Kirkland, Eggleston, and Howe were pioneer realists of the West, and as such, were relatively uninfluential among eastern writers. Howells was also of the West, but his manner and personality were so ingratiating that the old school of New England writers cordially adopted the man and shortly made him editor of *The Atlantic Monthly.* As such he had great influence in eastern literary circles. It is only correct to say that Howells was the leader of the realists in the long and hard literary battle that ended in the triumph of realistic standards in American literature.

So confused was the Gilded Age that Howells was not allowed by circumstances to give a clear statement of his aims and a correspondingly clear exemplification of his theories. He was deflected but not entirely baffled by the Gilded Age. But even to-day his work is often misunderstood. To some he appears to be merely the novelist of the decline of New England, the last recorder of the Genteel Tradition. To others he is the forerunner of modern sociological fiction, and to another group he is the shrinking realist who wished to tell the truth about his material but always carefully limited that material to the trivial, the obvious, and the pleasant. Each of these estimates has something to commend it. The diversity of estimates was caused in part by a change in the subject matter treated by Howells. Long after he became a major figure in our literature, a consideration of the social problems of the Gilded Age and a wide reading in Tolstoy led him into the way of sociological thinking. This change in tone and material, however, did not extend to his method, for he remained a realist, as he had always been, but his realism was less frank, less sweeping in its acceptance of life than is the realism of Turgenev, Flaubert, or George Moore.

Howells was not a great novelist. He lacked the color, the sense of dramatic values, and the quickly responsive sympathy with human aspirations that most great novelists have possessed. Many critics curtly dismiss him as uninteresting, and certainly the charge is not easily disproved. A typical Howells novel contains far too much irrelevant talk, and too little significant action and character revelation. There is very little of the close analysis of character that we find in the novels of Henry James and the later psychological novelists, but there is the everlasting dawdling over the tea-cups until frivolous and temperamental women talk themselves down. As a result of his weaknesses, more apparent in his earlier works than in his later, Howells cannot fairly claim a place among the great novelists, but none will question his deep significance, and certainly none will fail to give him high honors as a literary critic. Howells is of significance in the development of our literature because he popularized European realism among American readers and successfully introduced the methods of that fiction to our writers who were trying to interpret the native scene. Howells was admirably fitted by nature and his literary art to become the successful introducer of foreign realism. He was of a most pleasant and genial disposition, and this characteristic combined with his good standing with the older writers of New England allowed him to speak with authority and persuasiveness in behalf of his literary theories. He was moreover so clear and graceful a writer that many read him for his discriminating use of words who in the beginning vigorously disapproved of his realism. The natural thing happened. From the pleasant and suave pages of Howells, readers were led insensibly into the grimmer and more forthright studies of those men who penetrate into the depths of human nature. Without the work of Howells, the deeper and more truthful realists might never have had an appreciative audience in this country.

Life of Howells.—The significant facts of Howells's life are few, and those few are generally limited to some literary interest or activity. His external life was almost devoid of events or influences that tended to determine his career. Almost the only ones were his residence in Venice where he came into contact with European literature and the years spent in Boston, the literary capital of America.

Howells was born at Martin's Ferry, Ohio. His family was exceptional among its frontier neighbors in that it enjoyed good books and had a small but well-chosen library. The boy received but little formal education. Most of his early book-learning he acquired while standing before the type-cases in his father's printing shop, but so rapidly did he improve upon the start thus made that, by the time he was twenty-one, he had a fair working knowledge of five or six languages. In addition to his linguistic accomplishments he had acquired an adequate grasp of our national political and economic development. At an early age he began writing, and when he was twenty-three, he collaborated with a friend in the writing of a book of poems. In the same year, 1860, Lincoln was a candidate for the presidency, and Howells wrote a campaign document in the form of a life of the nominee. In return for the preparation of the biography Lincoln appointed the author United States consul at Venice.

Howells remained at his post for four years, and most fruitful years they were for a young consul with literary tastes and ambitions. He himself later said that his residence in Venice changed the whole course of his literary life. His early days had been spent in a frontier environment, and naturally his earliest writing had been shaped by this environment and by the romantic way of thought that was then so potent in America. In Italy he came rapidly under totally different literary influences. From the study of Dante he progressed to the reading of modern Italians like Goldoni, Manzoni and D'Azeglio, who attempted a truthful and unbiased presentation of life. Under such influences Howells's own writing soon changed its aims. The new direction of his literary interests can be gauged by the fact that he had gone to Venice to write romantic poetry but his first published works were two well-written books of travel, *Venetian Life* and *Italian Journeys*. His years in Venice had divorced him from the romantic interpretation of life and had made of him a student of manners. And a student of manners he remained to the end of his days.

Upon his return to America he became first a member of the staff of *The Nation* (1865-1866) and then assistant editor and editor of *The Atlantic Monthly* (1866-1881). During these years he read widely in European literature and made the acquaintance of such men as Björnson, Turgenev, Zola, Hardy, and Tolstoy, realists all, and all were influential in the formation of Howells, the realist of American life. During his residence in Boston, Howells did his first novel, *Their Wedding Journey*, a quiet study of ordinary life, utterly devoid of the sensational action and heroic figures that are the framework of romantic fiction. This novel indicated the literary method that Howells was to follow in his later career as a realist. The method is that of a close observer of manners who is interested solely in recording the life that he sees about him. Other admired books of this period are *The Lady of the Aristook, A Modern Instance,* and *The Rise of Silas Lapham.* The second of these is generally looked upon as the novel that marked the author's arrival at his full power as a writer, and the last is often called his most finished production. The usual material used in these books is composed of commonplace happenings of contemporary New England society.

Next to his Italian residence the greatest single influence that ever touched Howells was the work of Tolstoy, the great Russian humanitarian novelist. So strong an artistic and ethical force was Tolstoy, that Howells wrote scarcely a book after 1886 that does not in some way exhibit this influence. Tolstoy brought to Howells an intimate knowledge of the depths of human nature and a contemplation of life's problems that is tempered by an intense feeling of moral earnestness and responsibility. The first visible fruits of the Tolstoy influence was *A Hazard of New Fortunes* (1889), a book that forsakes the commonplace happenings of genteel life for the sociological consideration of certain new problems that were coming into Howells's horizon. These problems were those of wealth, poverty, and the social responsibility of the individual, and Howells treated them with a moral earnestness that derives from Tolstoy.

A Hazard of New Fortunes marks the beginning of a new period in the development of Howells. The writer never lost his humanitarian principles that he probably first had from Tolstoy, and as further evidence of his interest in sociological questions he became an ardent socialist of the Marxian variety. This belief, too, he never abandoned. About the same time that he became interested in social conditions the novelist left Boston and established his residence in New York. In his new home he was brought into close contact with cosmopolitan thought, with a brutal and ruthless economics, and with distressing social conditions. In grappling with the questions raised by these conditions and with the issues created by the rapidly shifting current of thought during the nineties, the social theories and example of Tolstoy were a fixed influence with Howells just as the artistic methods of the Russian were a constant guide in the writing of novels. Other books written under the influence of Tolstoy and sociological thought are *A Traveler from Altruria* and *Through the Eye of the Needle*. The first of these is a Utopian study that sets forth the joys of a society where there is no class distinction and where labor is honorable. Howells did not confine his examination of current social problems to the pages of his fiction. He raised his voice in behalf of the Chicago anarchists, condemned to death for participation in the Haymarket Riot, and he manfully advocated independence for the Filipinos. It has been truly said of him that "no good cause lacked the support of his voice." He was one of America's most valuable citizens in our spiritual and intellectual life, and no little portion of his value was caused by his acceptance of the eminently Christian teachings of Leo Tolstoy.

Howells the Realist.—In considering the realism of Howells a sharp distinction must be made between his theories of fiction and his practice. He advocated a type of realism that he did not practice and, in fact, that Americans were not ready for. As a critic he was notable for his advanced views and for the audacity with which he advocated them, but in his novels he was the rather timid realist who carefully confined his labors to a certain narrow field in our society. This criticism is especially true of the early books. As a result of this lack of consistency between his theory and practice, it is not improbable that later generations may value Howells more highly as a critic than as a creative artist.

The most valuable work that Howells did in the development of American fiction was to advocate and introduce a new technique in the writing of the novel. He insisted from the first to last upon verisimilitude, the truthful presentation of facts. In order to be truthful he discarded all forms of plot manipulation, insisting that life is largely a commonplace thing that never reaches the thrilling climaxes of fiction. Furthermore he refused to distort facts to gain plot interest or to encompass the happy ending. "The novel ends well that ends faithfully," was one of his remarks. Just as life sacrifices romance to truth, so should the novelist part company with romance when it refuses to follow him into the ways of truthful presentation of material. In harmony with his rejection of plot manipulation, Howells also rejected the hero of romance. He felt that the hero was an out-moded survival of aristocratic culture and that the superman in fiction should be replaced by the ordinary men and women of our democratic society. He also insisted that fiction treating of the strange and remote should accompany the hero and the dramatic climax into the limbo of past and gone things. He urged the writers to pitch their fiction in a lower key and to find tragedy and comedy, not in the grotesque and unusual, but in the ordinary and common. In short, Howells tried to democratize the material and methods of the American novel.

Thus far Howells advocated a type of fiction that was not far different from that supported by Turgenev, De Maupassant, Flaubert, or Zola, but he hastily added to his first specifications certain amendments that would keep the tender-minded American reading public from taking fright at the threatening grimness of our newly arrived realism. As the first of his amendments Howells laid down the rule that the American novelist must reflect the cheerful and pleasant temper of our national mind, holding that the more smiling aspects of life are the more American. This view was naturally more tenable in 1890 than it is to-day, but even then it was a highly questionable opinion. Last of all, he thought that fiction should always teach a moral lesson. Only a superficial reading of Howells shows that the weaknesses of the novels arise in part from the rigid application of the first of the two amendments, the one enjoining cheery optimism. His critical theories were sound, but it was when he began to adapt the criteria of European realists to the American public that he got into difficulties.

The method used by Howells in his novels is usually called "reticent realism," a term coined by the author himself, and it is quite the customary thing to attribute all the weaknesses of the earlier novels to the writer's reticence. It is doubtful if Howells can be successfully impeached in so easy a fashion. Indeed it is quite difficult to state in concise form the chief flaw in his novels. Probably the weakness lies in the very tone and atmosphere of the work rather than in any specific fault. Certainly the verbal composition of the books is not lacking in strength, for Howells was a finished and vigorous writer. The lack of vitality and significance may probably be attributed to certain shortcomings in the material selected for treatment. If material that lacks vitality and prime significance is used by a novelist of the commonplace who writes under the dictation of Howells's two amendments to the criteria of realism, the result is very apt to be a colorless novel totally devoid of virile interest or even passing significance.

Despite his knowledge of European literature and his advocacy of realistic methods, Howells selected the material for his early novels under the eyes of the Boston Brahmins of the Genteel Tradition. Rather uncritically he accepted the society about him with all its petty interests and timorous misgivings as the proper field for the exercise of his talents. This society in which and of which he wrote was one of considerable wealth, great social prestige, and excessive refinement. And yet it was completely devoid of vitality. New interests and new horizons of thought were inconceivable. That human culture did not come to a complete halt at some time during the earlier years of the living generation was an idea that never encountered a doubt, and quite as unanimously accepted was the placid conviction that Boston was the best of all possible worlds and that those upon whom it smiled were the most favored of mortals. Genealogy and social proprieties were subjects of intense interest, while the intellectual leaders in even their most exalted moments confined their cultural activities to a chaste and quiet admiration of ancient glories. Under such conditions a vital, dynamic culture takes flight to be succeeded in the interests and affections of people by a meticulous refinement. In such an intellectual atmosphere Howells lived and wrote his earlier novels, all of which reflect the refinement, the lack of vitality, and the intellectual sterility of the time and place.

The New England of the Gilded Age had settled back into a smug quiescence after the exuberant days of romanticism. The West was attracting many of the more ambitious and energetic young men, and many of the women stayed at home to become the New England spinsters of tradition whose days were spent in endless introspective probings of conscience and in equally endless small talk. Both exercises were conducted with the utmost refinement, and both were utterly barren of results. These old maids, who had nothing more important to occupy their time than their trivial small talk and milk-and-water discussions of conscientious scruples, naturally developed cases of "nerves." They became neurotics in whose disordered gaze insignificant trifles were magnified to the size of portentous events. And the obsessions of these neurotic women became, with only slight modification, the major interests of their entire social group. Abnormally sensitive consciences, neurotic dispositions, and the inability to see events and actions in their proper perspective are all penalties visited upon a stubbornly provincial society that has enough money to support it in genteel idleness, that has sacrificed culture to an over-refinement of speech and manner, and that has a vital interest only in the contemplation of the trivial. Such was the society that New England had during the Gilded Age, and such was the material that Howells used until he fell under the influence of Tolstoy.

The early Howells closely reflects the society of his time and place. Most of his women are abnormally serious, and many are undoubtedly neurotics. The pages of his novels are cluttered with these characters, their interminable small talk, and their doubts and apprehensions that flow from disordered, super-sensitive consciences. Little happens in the early novels, and the less action, the more talk. A dinner party is good for two hundred pages. First, there is the minute discussion of plans and invitations, then comes the party occupying pages of table-talk, and finally the event drags to a slow close through the post-prandial discussion by the family after the departure of the guests. Howells does all this very skillfully, but at the end the reader carries away a feeling of great technical ability wasted upon trivial material.

It has been aptly remarked that Howells took a vow to tell the truth and nothing but the truth, but that he was quite careful not to commit himself to tell the whole truth. Much as he admired the spirit and method of the Europeans, he never attempted to practice rigorously their literary axioms. There are depths of human nature that he never wished to plumb; there are aspects of life that he never wanted to see. What he told about his characters was the truth, but he made no effort to tell the whole truth.

Significance of Howells.—But adverse criticism of Howells should not blind the student to the man's great significance in the development of the recent American novel. Too reticent he may have been, and his material may have been essentially thin, but it should not be forgotten that in the long and bitter fight during the eighties and nineties between moribund, tawdry romanticism and the newly arrived realism, Howells was the suave and competent leader of the realists. His best critical work was in defense of his chosen literary method, and his novels were a sufficient refutation of those romantics who declared that realism meant only the exploitation of the sordid and repellent. Timid he may have been in practice, and his novels may not have squared consistently with his theories, but if he had been as audacious in his fiction as in his critical support of European realism, it is probable that his boldness would have done great harm in the long run to the welfare of the realistic movement. Timorous readers had to be led gently into the enjoyment of realism, for many Americans in the eighties, capable of praising Turgenev and Flaubert, strenuously objected to the application of those authors' methods to the treatment of our native characters and background. Such readers had to be dealt with easily, and a less diplomatic course than that followed by Howells might have postponed popular acceptance of the new literary school for many years.

From 1875 to 1900 the chief literary event in America was the long battle between realism and romanticism, and Howells was at once the most conspicuous and important figure in the combat. Under his leadership the realists slowly won critical and popular acceptance, until at the time of his death in 1920 there was not an important literary man in this country who did not admit, either expressly or by implication, that the major claims of the realists were substantially sound. In short, these claims are that life is a succession of commonplace happenings, that man is usually far from the heroic, and that fiction writers are not warranted in torturing the plain facts of life into dramatic climaxes or in thrusting prosaic man into heroic attitudes. To-day the old flamboyant romanticism is to be found in the pages of such writers as Harold Bell Wright and in the "pulp" magazines, those inexpensive periodicals that are designed largely for news stands. Realism, with its numerous ramifications and variations, stands triumphant in American letters. No one man is more responsible for this triumph than is Howells. Without his pioneer work in both critical and creative writing it is doubtful if our literature could have claimed such later figures as Hamlin Garland, Stephen Crane, Frank Norris, Robert Herrick, Upton Sinclair, Theodore Dreiser, Edgar Lee Masters, and Sinclair Lewis, to name no more. Many of these men have repudiated Howells's leadership because of his "reticent realism," and all have gone beyond him in an attempt to express the truth, but without his early efforts to accustom and reconcile the American public to realistic methods, the popular acceptance of these men would have been slower and more grudging than it was.

Furthermore the implication of Howells's work is interesting. It can be pretty well established that one fundamental reason for the realistic treatment of life is an underlying antipathy to the materials that are set forth. This may not have been the case with Howells but it certainly was with many of his successors. However that may be, it is only a step from the truthful presentation of material to the truthful presentation of conditions that the novelist wishes remedied. Thus out of realism came the whole school of social critics in our recent literature from Howells himself to Sinclair Lewis. Another movement that came directly out of realism was that of naturalism or pessimistic realism. The chief practicers of this method are Crane, Norris, Dreiser, and Anderson. Even the latest development in our letters, the so-called "new romanticism," would never have come into existence without realism, for the new romantics all agree with the realists that life is a quiet affair, far removed from the heroic and dramatic. These romantics disagree with the realists only in the definition of the aims of fiction, for they hold that the function of literature is not to present life as it is but as we should like to have it. It is quite true that the work of James Branch Cabell and Robert Nathan, leaders of the new romanticism, is a reaction from realism, but that very fact establishes realism as one of their determining factors, a factor that, by forcing them into opposition, gave rise in no slight degree to the latest form of romanticism. All these movements spring directly or indirectly from the methods advocated by Howells.

HAMLIN GARLAND
(1860-1940)

One of the most significant followers of Howells is Hamlin Garland, a son of the middle border, who became the first important realist in America to deal with farm life. Garland is frequently referred to as a local colorist, but such a classification is misleading. In the first place he does not have the romantic outlook that seems to be essential to the local colorist, and furthermore the creation of local color was not his p. imary aim. His first object was to present farm life as the working farmer actually endured it. The creation of character did not concern him so much as did the representation of the harsh realities of life, and plot was of no moment whatever. To his self-imposed task Garland brought an intimate and thorough knowledge of his material, a grim determination to tell the truth regardless of its unpleasantness, and a gray philosophy that had been imposed upon him by his harsh struggle as a farmer against relentless economic difficulties and the adverse forces of nature.

Early Work of Garland.—Hamlin Garland was born on a Wisconsin farm in 1860. His father, a typical farmer of the middle border, served in the Civil War and later moved to Iowa and then to Dakota. In both new states he and his family slaved at their tasks of making homes on the virgin prairie. Here the young boy watched the drudgery of pioneer farming dash out the sparks of life and ambition in the people around him, and he vowed that he would escape the numbing toil. It is rather noteworthy that in Garland's early stories the characters are very often obsessed by the desire to escape. Garland received a slight education, but it took no effort to awaken in him a love of reading and a determination to know and enjoy great music and art. After completing a course at an Iowa academy, he taught school for a year and then went to Boston where he met Howells and began his career as a writer. His first important book was *Main-Travelled Roads,* a group of realistic short stories of life in a western farm.

Garland's early life and struggles and his first literary triumphs are told at length in his *Son of the Middle Border* (1917), an autobiography that demands a high rating even when compared with the acknowledged masterpieces in its field. It gives a memorable picture of farm life in the Middle West in the first two decades after the Civil War, and this social order produced millions and millions of Americans of our own generation. It is probably not too much to say that this autobiography occupies a place in western literature corresponding to that held in eighteenth century American literature by Franklin's account of his early struggles and triumph.

With the publication of *Main-Travelled Roads* western farm life received its first competent, realistic treatment. Early pictures of the farmer and his work had been pretty little descriptions of make-believe country life. The milking was always done by dairy maids whose playful antics and studied poses make one think of Marie Antoinette and her ladies-in-waiting playing at dairying. The cows were sleek, contented creatures that placidly chewed their cuds or browsed peacefully on immaculate greensward. Hay-making was always a romp between buxom Maud Mullers and handsome country swains, while the scent of the new mown hay perfumed the air for miles around. In short, farm life was treated in the rhapsodic manner of country idylls. With the advent of Garland as a writer the truth was told. He had existed for twenty years in the unspeakable discomforts of pioneer farm life; he knew that nature is sullen and that her extravagantly praised bounties must be snatched from her; he knew what cow barns looked like and smelled like; he knew that farming on the middle border was one of the most grinding, ill-requited, and deadening forms of labor; and he knew that beside the life of a country woman of that region the life of a field slave in the old South was one of comparative ease. Garland told all these things, and his telling lacked nothing in the way of concrete illustrations.

In his early stories Garland had none of the optimistic philosophy that impressed Howells as being so profoundly American. The new western writer was grim, pessimistic, almost despairing, when he contemplated the fate of man in the struggle against great odds. One of his characters says: "A man like me is helpless; just like a fly in a pan of molasses. There is no escape for him; the more he tears around the more liable he is to rip his legs off." The speaker concludes that man can do nothing. The author agrees, remarking that "the farmers must live and die practically as he saw them to-night." To a far greater extent than Howells, Garland embodied the first American appearance of an old world pessimistic realism that was to be of great importance in the development of our literature.

Garland the Reformer.—Successful as Garland was in *Main Traveled Roads,* he ultimately allowed his pity for the western farmer and his deep aversion to country conditions to wreck him as a writer of realistic fiction. He had presented his unlovely pictures with the idea of directing attention to the dark shadows of life on the middle border, and from such a purpose it is only a step to the espousal of reform measures designed to abolish by law the objectionable evils. Such a course Garland followed.

The first reformer to attract Garland was Henry George, who attributed all the woes of the western farmer to speculation in land. Such a doctrine was bound to command attention from any thinking man who had watched the gradual disappearance of the public domain and the subsequent enrichment of land speculators at the expense of actual farmers. Garland was ready to believe the worst about land speculation, and soon after hearing the impressive mass of evidence gathered by George and listening to the promises made by the reformer, the young man was exhorting single-tax meetings. The association of the beginning writer with George was very important in the mental development of Garland, for it marked his first deflection from the narrow path of the artist toward the alluring field of propaganda and reform. Unfortunately it was not the last of such deflections.

Soon after meeting with George, Garland came under the influence of Benjamin Orange Flower, editor of *The Arena,* an egregious fellow ready and willing to swallow any proposed reform without the slightest preliminary examination. Flower welcomed to the pages of his magazine some of Garland's early stories, including some that were later published in *Main Traveled Roads,* and he evidently converted the young contributor to some of his most cherished reform movements. After Garland joined the ranks of the single-taxers, he needed but little encouragement to continue the work of a practicing reformer. This encouragement Flower supplied.

While Flower was initiating his young neophyte into the ways of reform, one of the most spectacular political insurrections was brewing in the Middle West. This particular insurrection was populism. The populist movement of the eighties was the culmination of a long line of agricultural troubles that began right after the Civil War. In 1890 the grievances of the farmers were of the usual variety, but they were stated with unusual vehemence. The disappearance of the free land had ended the farmer's traditional independence. A man burdened with a mortgaged farm could no longer abandon his land to his creditors and establish a new, unencumbered home on the government domain. Moving might only intensify his economic distress. Furthermore, the money in circulation had dropped from $31.18 per capita in 1865 to about half that amount twenty years later. Thus, farmers who borrowed money in the late sixties when money was plentiful and the prices of their products correspondingly high were forced to pay their loans in a time of scarce money and low prices. As a result, economic distress was prevalent on the middle border. The farmers sought relief by an agonized appeal for governmental assistance. Such assistance could be gained only through vigorous political agitation. It was this agitation that attracted the attention of Flower and Garland.

Naturally Flower approved offhand of the principles of populism. He asked Garland to write a story illustrating the revolt of the farmer, and to give the fiction proper local color he sent the writer on a trip through the disaffected portion of the Middle West. This trip just about finished Garland as a creative artist. He was thrown in with a group of fervent reformers whose extravagant proposals knew no bounds, and he accepted these proposals with the glowing enthusiasm of a convert. Previously Garland had looked upon the distressed condition of the western farmer with the eye of an artist who seeks a sympathetic knowledge of human woe and then tries to express this knowledge in such form that the representation will move others to fear and pity. His crusade with the roaring devotees of populism took Garland outside the pale of artistic endeavor. Thereafter the strivings of men called not for literary delineation but for governmental relief; the helplessness of a mortgage-burdened farmer was matter for a political speech, not material for a grim study of human life. Romantic political dreaming had blinded Garland to the worth of the realities of life as matter for artistic treatment. Flower and the populistic wave completed the debacle of a very promising young realist.

Garland the reformer could no longer bear to go over the old unreformed material that he had earlier used with so great success. After his fling with populism he usually sought his material in the gaudy and superficially romantic atmosphere of the "Wild West." In his later novels and stories he never admitted that anything could be wrong with his material, and it would be a bold critic who would assert that any sorrow could conceivably enter this world, for it is fashioned of the dreams and make-believe fancies of every boy attracted by the fictitious glamor of the Indian and the cowboy. The later stories and novels of Garland were competently written, but they had no significance, no connection with life. Their counterpart on a lower level can be found in the "Buffalo Bill" stories. To call them fitted to juvenile taste is more complimentary to the stories than to the taste of youth.

Significance of Garland.—Despite his downfall as a realistic novelist, Garland is one of the significant figures in recent American literature. Eggleston and Kirkland had both done earlier books of western realism, but the performance of Garland was infinitely superior in literary merit to that of the other men. He had surpassed in technical finish the very striking work of Ed Howe. Furthermore Garland had concentrated upon a certain phase of western life that had not previously received literary attention. He is truly the pioneer realist of country life in middle America. And his work is enduring, as all works are that are competently blended of sincerity and truthfulness. To-day his early stories seem as fresh and vivid as if they were done yesterday, and it seems quite probable that age will not wither or changing fashion discard the stark sketches in *Main Traveled Roads*. The intelligent reader of to-day can fitly deplore with Howells the withdrawal of Garland from the field of realism, for the decision of so competent a writer to confine his literary work to tawdry romanticism was one of the calamitous events of recent American literature. One who feels the compelling power of *Main Traveled Roads* is moved to wonder what Garland could have done if he, like Hardy or Conrad, had industriously worked for years the material that he used so effectively before he reached the age of thirty.

In only one other place has Garland reached the mastery attained in his early stories, and this place is his admirable autobiography, *A Son of the Middle Border*. This book richly deserves all the praise that it has had.

INFLUENCE OF HENRY JAMES

Henry James (*1843-1916*).—Although Henry James is a most engrossing subject to the sociological critic of literature, a discussion of his work seems not exactly apropos to a discussion of American literature as an expression of the national mind. James was hardly American except by birth. He was an international novelist and critic, one of the first of a race that is certain to become numerous and influential. It is conceivable that James, when compared with an international novelist of 1975, will seem provincial, but compared with men of his own generation like Mark Twain, Howells, and Garland, he is positively un-American, despite his frequent use of American characters. Indeed, it is to be questioned if he knew American life or if he was interested in more than one aspect of our people. This one aspect is the psychological effect wrought upon the crude American when he first becomes aware of the authenticity and binding force of European tradition that has been established and maintained by every social sanction at the disposal of a genuine aristocracy.

If James gives little sign of his American blood in the content of his novels, he gives even less in his form and technique. The foreign writers who have most influenced American fiction are Fielding, Dickens, Thackeray, and Hardy, and to none does James bear fewer resemblances than to these novelists. He belongs in the line of Richardson, Stendhal, and Proust. In fact, the last named may have been influenced considerably by the expatriated American, for in general James has been far better known by and more influential with foreign writers like Ford Madox Ford and the recent psychological novelists of England than he has been among American writers. In the beginning of his work he was influenced by Hawthorne, but after he went to Europe he developed his literary technique under the tutelage of men like Flaubert and Turgenev. In American fiction the story has usually been accounted important, but to James it may be said to have been almost non-existent. His close psychological studies were dissections of situation and character, rather than elaborations of conventional plots. The little masterpiece, *Daisy Miller*, is much less Jamesian than are most of the books, and it is also much closer to the traditional structure of the American novel, but even this work is built around a situation that most of our writers would have deemed a bit unexciting.

Henry James was born in New York City of a wealthy family that had an easy familiarity with things European. The father, Henry James, Sr., was a well-known exponent of the Swedenborgian philosophy, and eminent European visitors to America were frequently entertained in his home. The younger Henry was educated partly abroad and partly in America. After taking some work in Harvard Law School, he turned his attention to literature, publishing his first writings in the *Atlantic*. From 1869 to 1875 James spent much of his time abroad, and after the latter date he maintained his home in Europe, living for a short time in Paris and later in England.

We are in no doubt as to why James left America, for he has detailed his reasons with great care. First of all, he could not bear the thinness of American life. He felt that a writer should be able to feel beneath him a deep cultural soil, the layers of which have been built up by successive ages, each rich in history and tradition. Furthermore, he felt that civilization—at least the agreeable portion—was represented by concentric rings of varying thickness. England, the inner circle, is by far the thickest; America evidently lies on the periphery where the culture is only shellac-thick. London is even better than Paris, though exactly why James seems never to have said. It may be that Paris was a bit light-hearted in the presence of certain conventions that Anglo-Saxons are taught to respect religiously. At all events, the English society in which James moved was austerely dignified, very respectful to tradition, and completely equipped with all those things that America so deplorably lacked, a sovereign, a court circle, personal loyalty, an aristocracy, an established church, a clergy, a diplomatic service rich in memories and tradition, country gentlemen, cathedrals, and literature—to take James's own enumeration. Naturally, an acceptable literature reflected all the preceding appurtenances of English society. Moreover, the literary legends and associations of England were almost overpowering to a man in flight from the raw crudity of American life. London was full of ghostly echoes, each gently titillating the seeker for authentic culture. To see how far one particular seeker strayed from America, one has only to compare James with Mark Twain, or, to be more extreme, with Jack London or Jim Tully.

Works of James.—Against the background of old-world society which he found so satisfying, James projected the characters of his psychological novels, frequently exploiting his compatriots, few of whom resembled the novelist in his easy acceptance of European conventions. Rather they were crude specimens of western democracy who usually collided disastrously with adamantine usage or prejudices. The young girl, Daisy Miller, is typical of a whole host of James's characters.

But however much James may have been interested in dissecting the last fine reaction of a character to a given stimulus, he is not at all oblivious to the moral significance of the situations that he sets up. Quite distinctly he has a lesson to impart, and if the lesson is not a moral one, it comes very close to being such. James's point of view is given its most brutally forthright statement in the thesis, attributed to the author himself, that no one has a moral right to be ignorant of or to hold lightly those social usages and appendages that are so highly esteemed by Henry James. Indeed a desire to leave a lesson may have led James into taking liberties with the reality of some of his characters, for if his Americans had been so crude and unsophisticated as they were represented, it is highly improbable that they would have been sensitive enough to feel just the reactions that James attributed to them. But this objection may be pure cavil. At all events, one must admire the precision and consummate artistry that enabled James to pick his deliberate way through a leisurely psychological study, making no end of digressions or random voyages on the stream of consciousness, and at the end leave a feeling of intensity and a sense of inevitability in the foredoomed clash of crudity against the authentic conventions of an old social structure.

In describing this clash James is superficially cold and lacking in emotion, but he is not unaware of the power and meaning of passion. When he writes, the fires are drawn from his characters, but he knows that once they were there, and he exhibits the cold marks of the flames, realizing their deep significance. The flames may break out again, he hints; but they never do. James is too reticent and too leisurely to be much attracted by a driving, dynamic passion. Repose, not action, is the characteristic quality of most of his subjects, and white-hot passion is not conducive to repose.

It is true that James is not the easiest of novelists to read, though his complexity has been grossly exaggerated. However, one of the later novels like *The Golden Bowl* is rather apt to repel the reader who has no knowledge of modern psychological fiction or of some of James's earlier works. Once when James was asked to name the order in which his typical books should be read, he indicated for "beginning" readers the following sequence: *Roderick Hudson, Portrait of a Lady, Princess Casamassima, The Wings of a Dove,* and *The Golden Bowl.* For more "advanced" readers he preferred this order: *The American, The Tragic Muse, The Wings of a Dove, The Ambassadors,* and *The Golden Bowl.* It is very likely that most readers will find the way to *The Golden Bowl* somewhat smoothed if they include early in the course *Daisy Miller, A Passionate Pilgrim,* and *The Europeans.*

The themes of the early books are nearly always some aspect of Europe *vs.* America. *A Passionate Pilgrim* (1871), James's earliest notable work, is of considerable interest to students of the author, for the central figure is that of an American who made a passionate pilgrimage to England in search of culture. Six years later *Roderick Hudson* had the same general theme, except that this time the pilgrim was an American sculptor who sought artistic inspiration in Rome. This is the earliest of the books to win the author's later approval. *The American* (1877), another piece of work that had James's lasting favor, is the study of the love of an American for a woman of an aristocratic French house. The theme was admirably suited to a writer gifted with James's literary method and social predilections. *The Europeans* (1878) was a rather formal contrast of New England and Europe. This work was followed by *Daisy Miller* (1879) which tells the story of a rashly impulsive American girl, who disregarded the conventions of Europe only to suffer tragically. *The Bostonians* (1886) is notable for its chilly attitude toward the New England romantics. Evidently Swedenborgian philosophy was one thing, and romantic reforming zeal quite another.

After 1890 James wrote no novels for about ten years. During this time he produced a number of short stories, but the drama was his chief interest. Although the natural and acquired qualities of his mind and art fitted him not at all for dramatic composition, yet he produced a number of plays. All were unsuccessful. From 1902 to 1904 he wrote the three books that mark the culmination of his peculiar powers as a novelist. These three are *The Wings of a Dove, The Ambassadors,* and *The Golden Bowl.* The second of the group the author liked best of all his works.

The most obvious characteristic of James is his inordinate deliberation in dissecting character and his thrice inordinate deliberation in presenting his findings. He writes in a curiously oblique, zigzag style, thickly interlarded with parenthetical explanations and deprecatory qualifications, as if propriety had ordained that truth must not be abruptly disclosed to the common gaze. In all probability the style is no affectation, though long practice gave James the ability to handle it with so confusing a facility that it seems the height of artificiality. It is the natural expression of a sensitive mind that uses every subterfuge to ward off the impact of jagged reality. In the earlier books the style, though never forthright, is clear, but a growing interest in the minute analysis of the last fine shade of feeling and a corresponding desire to describe the analysis in language as exact and painstaking as the method make the later books masterpieces of evasiveness.

His later stylistic peculiarities notwithstanding, James is undoubtedly one of the great figures of recent literature. He helped point the novel toward psychological analysis and thus became the artistic progenitor of a whole troop of descendants, few of whom have been able to reach the mark set by the old master. But when all is said, James hardly belongs to American literature; he is international in every respect. Incidentally, it is hardly reassuring to our wonted complacency to know that the greatest figure that America has contributed to world literature since 1855, Mark Twain alone excepted, is the least American of all our writers.

MRS. EDITH WHARTON

(1863-1937)

It is quite safe to say that Henry James suffered one of his greatest misfortunes in the shape of his American disciples. Most of his followers in this country succeeded in acquiring only his mincing gait, his habit of qualifying a plain assertion until it loses all force and meaning, and his dainty air of unimpeachable refinement. These superficial characteristics of James are the very ones to appeal to third-rate copyists who are hopelessly incapable of even understanding his immense powers as an analyst of character. It remained for Mrs. Edith Wharton to become both a disciple of James and a first-rate novelist in her own right. Beginning her career as a follower of James, she took from her master what she needed in the way of technique and then combined this element with material of her own choosing to produce novels that are little, if at all, inferior to those of James and that are much more in the main current of American thought and ways.

Very often Mrs. Wharton has used the favorite theme of James, the conflict of the individual with social convention, but in her typical works she has used the American background peopled by native characters. However, in many of her novels one of her chief characters or a group of characters will be chosen from an environment that is not that of the main action of the story. Frequently she has depicted the assault of raw American stock upon the closed circles of the old aristocracy of New York City, gently satirizing both the slavish conformists and the inept newcomers. The similarity of Mrs. Wharton and Sinclair Lewis has not been sufficiently stressed. Both are social satirists of American life, and both are highly critical of many institutions brought under consideration. Mrs. Wharton finds her subjects in those who belong to a restricted upper caste, while Lewis finds his in the crude bourgeoisie of the midland villages and cities. Lewis's charmed circle of those who belong is very much more spacious in its embrace than is Mrs. Wharton's and infinitely easier in its social code, but defection from convention is punished in Gopher Prairie and Zenith no less surely than on Fifth Avenue. Lewis seems to be aware of a kinship with Mrs. Wharton, for *Babbitt* is dedicated to her, and when the critical clamor arose over his receiving of the Nobel prize, Lewis declared that he was paying no attention to his detractors but that he would be concerned if Mrs. Wharton criticized the award. If Mrs. Wharton openly disapproved of the honor paid to Lewis, her words were not very widely reported.

In her indictment of men and institutions Mrs. Wharton reveals herself as an aristocratic intellectual, critical of the loose standards held by most Americans. In society she particularly dislikes the accepted standard of pecuniary success by which all things are to be judged, and in the realm of the intellect she contemns gross stupidity no less than the affectation which is so often summoned up to gloss over unintelligence and lack of culture. Like a true aristocrat Mrs. Wharton has no aversion to arrogance, either in social or intellectual life, but democratic virtues do not leave her so completely unmoved. Although she has never pointedly attacked any specific institution, as so many of our critics have done, she unmistakably belongs in American literature as a high-bred realist and satirist of an undistinguished society which seems to her to be growing steadily more and more undistinguished. It is the cultural atmosphere of our society which gives her concern. Intellectually, morally, and spiritually our whole social organization fails to pass her scrutiny, and it is probable that she feels that this failure is caused in part, at least, by the chaotic state of American life, a condition that in turn seems to be inherent in a society unregulated by an aristocracy and untempered by the presence of stabilizing traditions and institutions. Even the family is tending to lose its former status, and as for family rights or a deep pride in one's blood connections, such things simply are non-existent. Mrs. Wharton discovers that American character is formed by external stimuli rather than by spiritual interests, and not the least disturbing of her discoveries is that Americans are liable to be drugged by luxuries and great wealth into an unprotesting acceptance of a life that is wholly formless and aimless in its lack of spiritual and social sanctions. In such a society as Mrs. Wharton depicts, woman is certain to be the chief sufferer, for her swift intuitions tell her that the time is out of joint, while her relatively minor rôle in a world of predatory wealth prevents her from altering conditions that are placidly accepted by the more pragmatic male. Secure in her superior intelligence and taste Mrs. Wharton makes a cool diagnosis of our maladies, disdaining utterly to offer any suggestions for the remedying of the offensive conditions. She remains an aristocrat to the end; never does she fall into the ways of the propagandist or sociologist. Even if she has ideas about the better ordering of our society, her habitual tone of satire and irony would prevent her from expressing them directly. Her ordinary attitude toward persons or institutions is well indicated by these short characterizations from *The Old Maid:*

The Ralstons were of middle-class English stock. They had not come to the colonies to die for a creed but to live for a bank-account. The result had been beyond their hopes, and their religion was tinged by their success. An edulcorated Church of England, which, under the conciliatory name of the "Episcopal Church of America," left out the coarser allusions in the Marriage Service, slid over the comminatory passages in the Athanasian Creed, and thought it more respectful to say "Our Father *who*" than "which" in the Lord's Prayer, was exactly suited to the spirit of compromise whereon the Ralstons had built themselves up. There was in all the tribe the same instinctive recoil from new religions as from unaccounted-for people. Institutional to the core they represented the conservative element that holds new societies together as seaplants bind the seashore. . . .

Frederick John listened, obeyed, married a Halsey, and passively followed in his father's steps. He belonged to the cautious generation of New York gentlemen who revered Hamilton and served Jefferson, who longed to lay out New York like Washington, and who laid it out instead like a gridiron, lest they should be thought undemocratic by people they secretly looked down upon. Shopkeepers to the marrow, they put in their windows the wares there was most demand for, keeping their private opinions in the back-shop, where through lack of use, they gradually lost substance and colour.

Mrs. Wharton's Novels.—When Mrs. Wharton began her literary career, she was so largely under the domination of Henry James that in some of her earlier novels and stories she used the European background. In an extremely interesting letter written in 1902 James shows a very friendly interest in the younger novelist and issues a warning to her in these provocative words:

Only they've made me again . . . want to get hold of the little lady [Mrs. Wharton] and pump the pure essence of my wisdom and experience into her. She *must* be tethered in native pastures, even if it reduces her to a back-yard in New York.

Such a critical admonition makes one wonder if James wished that he had stayed closer to native pastures.

However that may be, Mrs. Wharton had a mind essentially different from that of the scrupulously careful and analytical James, and even if she had not ultimately selected different materials for her novels, her art would have eventually come to a different flowering. As it was, she achieved her first marked success with *The House of Mirth* (1905) a treatment of an American subject, that demonstrated her peculiar ability to depict certain aspects of our national culture.

The general theme that has concerned Mrs. Wharton is not James's desire to expose social ignorance and ineptitude in the face of authentic culture and social grace. It has been rather the clash of an individual or a group with convention. Mrs. Wharton gives no very definite indication that she particularly approves or disapproves of either the convention or its antagonist; James nearly always leaves the impression that he approves of European ways. So equally does Mrs. Wharton satirize both the conformist and the rebel that she has made confused readers ask anxiously if she approves of any type of person or society. In her satire it is pretty clear that it is the authentic aristocrat who is speaking. Mrs. Wharton was born into the charmed circle of New York society in the days when Manhattan Island had the nearest approach in America to a true aristocracy. One of her most successful themes is the attempt of an outsider to break into the inner social life of Fifth Avenue. In the handling of this subject in *The Custom of the Country* she holds that convention is not to be broken without incurring penalty. Society has a sense of oneness, a solidarity, that inflicts punishment for the non-observance of its conventions, however pointless or unsanctioned these conventions may be.

Of Mrs. Wharton's distinctly social studies the best are probably *The House of Mirth, The Custom of the Country, The Age of Innocence,* and the four novelettes published under the inclusive title, *Old New York*.

In *The House of Mirth* Lily Bart, a member of an exclusive social circle, is guilty of a breach of convention. For her error she is summarily expelled from her group, and she finds that re-admission is a task of exceeding difficulty. In *The Custom of the Country* Undine Spragg, a spoiled child of a wealthy but socially deficient family, enters upon marriage and divorce easily and indifferently. At the end she is married to a man who has vast wealth and a certain social standing, but she finds that, as a result of her earlier indiscretions, she cannot climb to the social pinnacle to which her wealth seems to invite her. Undine Spragg is one of Mrs. Wharton's best characters in vividness of presentation, but her creator pretty surely does not approve of her lack of personal standards and respect for tradition. *The Age of Innocence* shows that those who belong to a circle and implicitly obey its behests must pay a penalty no less drastic than those who fracture convention at will. Judging from the studies of Lily Bart and Undine Spragg, one might suppose that Mrs. Wharton approves of social convention, but *The Age of Innocence* leaves one in a fine state of indecision, for in this book she is at pains to show that conformity sometimes exacts the price of personal happiness. *Old New York* consists of four novelettes, *False Dawn, The Old Maid, The Spark,* and *New Year's Day,* each of which gives a glimpse of New York society during successive decades of the nineteenth century, beginning with the forties. These short works are among the most deft and accomplished of the author's books.

By general acclamation *Ethan Frome* (1911) has been declared Mrs. Wharton's masterpiece and one of the finest triumphs of all American literature. This little novelette tells in a relatively short space a tragedy of rural New England that is caused by a country-man's challenge of convention. Just as in the upper circles of New York society, the challenge is answered by punishment, a punishment in this case so appalling in its grim terror that beside it death would be a positive relief. The art of Mrs. Wharton is seen at its very finest in this story. Reducing the materials of the tragedy to the minimum and telling the story with a clipped spareness of phrase, the author achieves a powerful intensity that is excessively rare in our literature. In spite of the great economy of the story, Mrs. Wharton has managed to invest *Ethan Frome* with the authentic atmosphere of New England and to bestow upon the characters a convincing reality. Volumes of explanation could not adequately describe the high pitch of the story, the passion which animates it, and the grim, lingering punishment of the end. *Ethan Frome* is to be read, not discussed.

Summer is another novel that approaches *Ethan Frome* in both materials and power.

As a craftsman Mrs. Wharton is one of the finest novelists now writing in English. In all her fiction there is hardly to be found an episode or even a line that is unworthy of the author's fine intelligence and great artistic powers. She never cheapens her novels to gain a bit of popularity, nor does she ever descend from objective presentation to support a popular cause or to attack an unpopular one. If there is any criticism to be made of her work it is that her reticent objectivity sometimes leads her into a chilliness of temper, but this fault is so rare among American writers that it may almost be said to give the reader a refreshing change.

SUGGESTED READINGS

Beach: *The Method of Henry James*. New Haven. 1918.
  An early but most useful study.
Beach: *The Twentieth Century Novel:* Studies in Technique. New York. 1932.
Blackmur (ed.): *The Art of the Novel: Critical Prefaces by Henry James*. New York, 1934.
  The editor brought together all the critical prefaces written by

James for the collected edition of his own works. No student of
James or of fiction can afford to neglect these prefaces.

Bosanquet: *Henry James at Work*. London. 1924.

Interesting and important. The author was James' secretary.

Brooks: *The Pilgrimage of Henry James*. New York. 1925.

The thesis of this book is that James failed, in the last analysis,
because he did not firmly root himself in any country. See also
New England: Indian Summer, Chapters XI and XIII. Many students of James reject the Brooks thesis.

Conrad: *Notes on Life and Letters*. New York. 1924.

The short essay on James is interesting because it is the tribute
of one master technician to another.

Dupee: *The Question of Henry James*. New York. 1947.

A symposium which maintains a remarkably high degree of excellence. Among the writers are Howells, Max Beerbohm, Conrad,
Lubbock, Beach, Beer, Eliot, Brooks, Parrington, Wilson, Matthiessen, Spender, Gide, and Barzun.

Edgar: *Henry James: Man and Author*. New York. 1927.

Distinctly unsatisfactory.

Firkins: *William Dean Howells*. Cambridge. 1924.

Grattan: *The Three Jameses*. New York. 1932.

Howells: *Life in Letters of William Dean Howells*. Garden City. 1928.

Of prime importance.

Matthiessen: *Henry James: The Major Phase*. New York. 1944.

Matthiessen: *The James Family*. New York. 1947.

A first-rate family history told largely in excerpts from the writings of the Jameses.

Matthiessen and Murdock (eds.): *The Notebooks of Henry James*. New
York. 1947.

The publication of the notebooks was one of the most important
contributions ever made to the study of Henry James. The editorial
work is emphatically good.

Perry: *The Thought and Character of William James*. Boston. 1935.

Many sidelights on Henry James. A great biography.

Pound: *Instigations*. New York. 1920. pp. 106-67.

Quinn: *American Fiction*. New York. 1936.

Warren: *The Elder Henry James*. New York. 1934.

Satisfactory study of a man who was, in Bernard Shaw's estima-
tion, more interesting than his son.

West: *Henry James*. New York. 1916.

A brief but skillful study.

Wharton: *A Backward Glance*. New York. 1934.

Henry James appears in this autobiography.

Wilson: *The Triple Thinkers*. New York. 1938. pp. 122-64.

THE TRIUMPH OF REALISM

II. The Machine Age (Since 1890)

CHAPTER XXII

NATURALISM

Naturalism may be defined as a literary method which uses the material ordinarily utilized by realism, the common and ordinary along with the more elevated, and at the same time attempts to appraise the value of this material in terms of a pessimistic philosophy. It has been called pessimistic realism, but this definition cannot stand, because the essence of realism is an objective presentation of facts with absolutely no personal or philosophical interpretation. Toward his characters and the incidents of his novels, the naturalist is quite detached but in his interpretations, either implied or stated, he drops his objectivity and becomes a philosophical pessimist. One of the primary criteria of naturalism is the rejection of the principle of free will, and no man can reject this romantic doctrine and not immediately become more or less pessimistic in his philosophy. The naturalist usually conceives of man as an impotent figure in a world that is not even remotely controlled by an intelligent force. That there is force in the world all naturalists admit, but they are unwilling to ascribe to this power any such anthropomorphic qualities as benevolence, foresight, or intelligence. They frankly say that the struggle of man with this force is very apt to be in vain and that whatever success may be achieved is caused by a chance combination of circumstances over which human will has no control. Success thus attained is liable to become a tragic jest at the next turn of the inscrutable force. With such a philosophical basis naturalism is of necessity a product of a sophisticated and disillusioned people. It could not have existed in America before the days of the Gilded Age.

To say that naturalism is an old-world product is not to say that hints of it were not found in this country prior to the beginning of the naturalistic movement. It is true that *Moby Dick* is a romantic book, yet there is a clear strain of pessimism underlying the narrative, and the very end of the story might have been done by an admitted naturalist. Mark Twain in his later years was decidedly naturalistic in his temper, and Hamlin Garland started his career evidently thoroughly imbued with the spirit of naturalism. But it was only during the nineties that the naturalistic movement became a recognized literary force.

Naturalism had its beginning in France, though it flourished in Russia, England, Germany, and the Scandinavian countries. The movement in French literature can be traced back to the writings of Stendhal, a novelist who wrote in the early part of the nineteenth century. Balzac (1799-1850), one of the supreme novelists of all literature, showed a tendency to naturalism. But the great names in the development of the movement and the real founders of naturalism are Flaubert, De Maupassant, and Zola. The theory was worked out by Zola in two books of criticism, *The Naturalistic Novelists* and *The Experimental Novel*. Naturalism was the product of literary realism combined with two things emphasized by nineteenth century science: analysis and causation. During a great part of the last century, thinkers were probing and dissecting institutions and organisms largely to discover the causes of such things, the determining factors in biological and social life. From the efforts to find the law of causation there developed two schools of thought, the biological determinists who followed the leadership of Darwin, and the economic determinists who followed Karl Marx. Zola's theory and practice of fiction developed from his knowledge of these two schools of scientific and economic thought. Although Zola certainly did not minimize the importance of economic questions, he attempted to explain the behavior of man, the animal, through an appeal to biology. "We take men solely from the hands of the physiologists," he declared, "to solve scientifically the question of how men behave in society." This attempt to make a scientific study in fiction of man's actions from the biological viewpoint originated with and reached its highest development among the French novelists of the second half of the nineteenth century.

Main Tendencies of Naturalism.—Not all naturalists write from the same point of view, and not all novels written by the same author are conceived in the same fashion, but in general naturalism exhibits two well-defined tendencies. The first tendency is to study in great detail a social background that contains a large number of characters, not one of whom is allowed to usurp the central interest of the story. Such a novel usually tends to become sociological; its chief aim is to examine the background and through this examination to set forth the conditions that govern man's actions in a given environment. Such a method is extremely valuable for the study of the individual in great impersonal social movements like a war, an economic struggle, or a mass migration. Typical novels of this description are Zola's *La Débâcle* (*The Downfall*), an account of the Franco-Prussian War in which huge masses of men are handled as the older novelist handled individual characters; Frank Norris's *The Octopus,* a close study of man's reaction to his physical and economic environment; Zola's *Germinal,* an account of life in the French coal mines. Other novels that show a tendency to emphasize the environment rather than to dissect character are Freeman's *Joseph and His Brethren,* Arnold Zweig's *The Case of Sergeant Grischa,* Stephen Crane's *The Red Badge of Courage,* Remarque's *All Quiet on the Western Front,* and Hardy's *The Return of the Native.* The last five novels named are not so typical of their class as are the first three, but all are examples of the naturalistic tendency that stresses the importance of environment.

The second tendency of naturalism is to dissect character and to give relatively slight attention to environment. Typical examples of this tendency are Flaubert's *Madame Bovary,* a merciless vivisection of an ordinary woman; Zola's *Nana,* a novel written about a character whose touch brought death and disaster; Hardy's *Tess of the D'Urbervilles,* a story of a woman at once weak and strong; Dreiser's *The Financier* and *The Titan,* two studies of a powerful American business man; and Frank Norris's *McTeague.*

Although all the illustrations thus far have been taken from prose fiction, it should not be assumed that the novel alone of literary forms has felt this new influence. Naturalism started in prose fiction, and there it has received its highest and most typical development, but it is also felt in drama and in poetry. It is to be found in varying degrees in such dramas as O'Neill's *Beyond the Horizon* and *Strange Interlude,* Murray's *Autumn Fires,* Arthur Richmann's *Ambush,* Gorki's *In the Depths,* Chekhov's *Cherry Orchard,* Ibsen's *Hedda Gabler.* In poetry it can be found unmistakably in the work of such Americans as E. A. Robinson, Edgar Lee Masters, and Robinson Jeffers.

The Aims of Naturalism.—As indicated in the preceding discussion of naturalism, the naturalistic writer has two fundamental aims: objective presentation of facts and philosophical interpretation.

To gain objectivity the naturalist attempts to be impersonal and scientific. He allows his personal tastes, prejudices, and desires to interfere with his presentation of facts just as little as the scientist allows his to interfere with the performance of a biological or chemical experiment. In the presentation of his facts he refuses to pass moral judgment or to reject material because it does not conform to accepted ethical standards. For him there is neither right nor wrong, pure nor impure; he is concerned only with the mechanism of the animal called man, the conditions under which it operates, and its modification by heredity and environment. In describing the mechanism of man, the naturalist uses the utmost frankness of speech. And since this frankness, like the whole naturalistic method, is directed toward the divesting of man and his emotions of romantic glamor, it is particularly distasteful to the lovers of romance. The naturalist takes the romantic thrill out of life; to him every emotion is susceptible of being explained in terms of biology, physics, or chemistry, and the love element of the old-time romancers is no exception to the rule. It has been said that in naturalism physiology takes the place of romance, a statement that certain of the naturalists would accept as high praise, so intent are they upon being impersonal and scientific.

Although the naturalist exerts himself to be impersonal and scientific, he consistently maintains one philosophic point of view. He is always pessimistic. This pessimism is found in the belief that the dominant forces controlling the world are either evil and hostile to man or so casual and indifferent as to give man a feeling of hostility. Often this pessimism is implied in the acceptance of determinism; rather seldom is it given direct statement. The naturalist further holds that man's actions are determined for him by forces quite beyond any one's control. He accepts the principle of determinism quite as thoroughly as did the old-time Calvinist, only the modern writer does not think that the determining forces are of divine origin. To the naturalist, free will, so dear to romantics, is a mere spark of fantastic imagination; to him man appears as anything but a free agent possessed of a purposive free will. The naturalists themselves are not agreed upon the exact nature of the force that impels men, but usually they accept one of three suggestions—that it is biological, mechanistic, or fatalistic. Those naturalists who hold to the idea of biological determinism think that man's actions are determined by the forces of heredity and environment. Zola is typical of this class. Those who think that the universe and all physical and intellectual life are the results of mechanical forces attempt to explain everything in terms of physics and chemistry, just as a dynamo or a chemical precipitant can be explained. Dreiser represents this class of naturalists. The fatalists think that the universe is a matter of pure chance, a chance directed by neither intelligence nor benevolence. To such thinkers the determining force has only one quality, strength. Further than that it has nothing; it is only a vast imbecility given enormous power. Some of the novels and many of the poems of Hardy illustrate this type of naturalism.

With so depressing a view of free-will and of man's inability to captain his soul, it is not strange that most naturalists write their studies in minor keys. The characters may be strong and noble, but in the end disaster, failure, or futility awaits as the final reward of human endeavor. This is the feeling that is always in the background of naturalistic writing. Naturalists are often reproached for not seeing life whole (as if any one ever did) and for holding too closely to the tragic strain. Although there are excellent comic passages in many naturalistic novels, a writer who is committed to the philosophy and literary methods of De Maupassant, Hardy, and Zola can hardly do anything light and cheerful as a whole. Such a work would be an utter contradiction to all that naturalism represents. A naturalistic comedy is not an impossibility, but in writing one an author will have to take certain liberties with the traditional definition of comedy. There are probably some such comedies in existence, but they are not generally recognized.

Temptations of the Naturalists.—Admittedly there are few successful and consistent naturalistic writers, for the novelists of that school are beset by a variety of temptations that relatively few have been strong enough to withstand. Literary history contains the names of many who began as naturalists and finished in other schools.

The most insistent temptation of the naturalist is to desert his austere standards of scientific detachment when he contemplates the influence of a bad environment on his characters and to assume a warm personal interest in the betterment of social conditions. From the scientific study of the effect of drink it is only a step to active opposition to intemperance. However laudable the moralist may find such a progression, the literary naturalist cannot take it without becoming a sociologist instead of a naturalistic novelist.

The study of a cruel, oppressive environment has led many writers into espousing a reform intended to better the undesirable conditions. This has been the fate of many a naturalist. Some of Zola's works show this tendency. Robert Herrick began writing as a potential naturalist but soon became a sociologist. Frank Norris in *The Pit* was as much concerned with social conditions and ethical problems as with scientific naturalism.

The desire to exhibit proof of his deterministic theories leads the naturalist into his second temptation, a tendency to choose exceptional characters, sometimes almost inhuman, in whom the deterministic forces can be seen operating in plain view. To show these forces most clearly the naturalist does not endow his characters with the full complement of human emotions and impulses; he denudes his figures of all save the desired qualities. Such procedure creates characters that look more like carefully supervised scientific experiments than like human beings. Sometimes these exceptional characters are of subnormal mentality and strong animal instincts and impulses, for such characters readily exhibit the operation of primitive tastes and desires. (McTeague in Frank Norris's novel of the same name is an example of a subnormal, almost moronic character who is driven by animal instinct.) Sometimes to illustrate his theory of human actions the naturalist will use a character of excitable, neurotic temperament. Emma Bovary in Flaubert's *Madame Bovary*, Sue in Hardy's *Jude the Obscure*, and Nina in O'Neill's *Strange Interlude* are all examples of this type of character. Again the naturalist may show figures of strong commanding personalities, some of whom may control affairs, at least temporarily, to the weal or woe of many other people. Joanna in Sheila Kaye-Smith's *Joanna Godden* and George Hurstwood in Dreiser's *Sister Carrie* are examples of strong figures who suffer defeat. Frank Cowperwood, the massive figure in Dreiser's *The Financier* and *The Titan* is an excellent example of a strong Nietzschean character who forces compliance with his will only to fail in the end. In the creation of most of these figures the naturalist has dropped his impersonal, scientific examination of human nature to present a laboratory-made illustration of a theory. Insomuch as a writer yields to this temptation he falls short of following the strict canons of naturalism.

In recent years and especially in American literature there has been a strong tendency among the naturalists to use "grotesques"

grotesque Character

instead of characters. A grotesque is not a well-rounded human figure. It is, in terms of drawing, only an outline or tracing of a figure distorted for the sake of emphasis. Such characters are created with the greatest economy of words, and only those points or characteristics are mentioned that are essential to the author's need. This method inevitably results in distortion. A grotesque in a book is only an imperfectly embodied emotion, repression or desire. It is an outline of a character that possesses only one trait, such as mother-love, smug hypocrisy, or a futile yearning for companionship. Sherwood Anderson uses grotesques very frequently and often very effectively. The sub-title of his book, *Winesburg, Ohio,* is "A Book of Grotesques." Edgar Lee Masters in *Spoon River Anthology* and Eugene O'Neill in a few of his dramas have both used this kind of character.

Naturalistic Tragedy.—Naturalism has succeeded in making obsolete the old conceptions of tragedy. Definitions of tragedy are very numerous, but in general critics have held that tragic art should represent the overthrow of evil and the subsequent triumph of good, despite suffering and temporary failure, or they have insisted that tragedy results when a noble character, usually called the hero, transgresses an immutable moral law and suffers the penalty exacted by eternal justice. This last conception, which seems to have the authority of Aristotle, is erected on the belief in the absolute justice of the world-plan. Now an examination of recent tragedies in the light of these definitions is sufficient to show either that such books as *Madame Bovary, An American Tragedy, McTeague, Nana,* and *L'Assomoir (The Dram Shop)* are either not tragic or the traditional definitions of tragedy are inadequate. Obviously the books just named are tragedies. Hence a new definition of tragedy is needed, though presumably no one has yet attempted it.

The older definitions fail at a number of points. In the first place, many modern tragedies end in the triumph of personal or impersonal forces that no metaphysical subtlety can transform into manifestations of good, and in some tragedies the triumphant forces are frankly evil. In the next place, many of the naturalistic characters whom we follow with interest and even with compassion cannot be called noble. To-day any character is looked upon as a fit protagonist of a moving tragedy. Furthermore, the second of the two definitions assumes the presence of a fixed moral law and a purposive power behind the universe capable of punishing transgressors of that law. The naturalist questions the validity of both these assumptions. He admits the existence of a power, but beyond this admission he will not go. To impute intelligence and purposive will to this power seems to him totally unwarranted.

It seems that when the new definition of tragedy is achieved, it will be forced to recognize that futility of effort may constitute a true tragedy, even if the one who strives has violated no moral law and even if the end outrages our feeling of poetic justice. It furthermore appears that degeneration of body, mind, or character can create tragedy, as can the strokes of blind, undirected fate.

The Reception of Naturalism in America.—Naturalism ran counter to too many cherished ideas to be received gladly by the guardians of traditional Americanism. Although many sensible critics, including Howells, commented intelligently on the naturalists and their aims, the publications of almost every novel from this school was greeted by critical clamor and by pretty general popular disapproval. Despite the uproar, the naturalists and their publishers persevered, and finally won a unanimity of sensible critical opinion and a satisfying popular following. Milestones in the progress of naturalism in America are the publication of Zola's novels during the seventies and eighties, the success of Crane's *The Red Badge of Courage* in the nineties, the appearance of Hardy's *Jude the Obscure* (under the title *Hearts Insurgent*) in *Harper's Magazine* in the same decade, the appearance of Dreiser's *Sister Carrie* in 1900, and of the same author's *The Financier* twelve years later, the enormous success of Masters' *Spoon River Anthology* in 1915, and the general acclaim that greeted Dreiser's *An American Tragedy* in 1925. The progress of naturalism has extended over half a century, and during most of that time the new school of literature was engaged in a bitter, uphill fight against unintelligent, even dishonest criticism and an instinctive hostility on the part of the American public.

This hostility was caused largely by the conflict of naturalism with two definite elements in American thinking. These elements were Puritanism and the frontier spirit. Puritanism stressed above all things the supremacy of the moral law and the existence of an eternal purposive will that governs the universe to the minutest details. The existence of both these things naturalism denied. Hence the Puritan moralists fell upon the new school of literature with righteous disapproval in an attempt to discredit it as irreligious and subversive of morality. On the other hand optimism was the pioneer's great bequest to American thought. The gray pessimism of naturalism was just as displeasing to our professional optimists as its amoral attitude was to the few surviving Puritans. Defenders of optimism tried to read naturalism out of good society by decrying the new books as "grim," "sordid," and "depressing." Cosmopolitan thought has seldom been welcomed by Puritanism and the frontier spirit, but never was an old-world idea so relentlessly mauled as was naturalism.

Despite this mauling, naturalism kept on so steadily winning writers and readers to its cause that some began to suspect the entrance of certain new conditions into our national life that were more hospitable to the naturalistic philosophy than were the conditions of early America. Such, indeed, was the case. Naturalistic determinism would have been impossible in America before the Civil War. Frontier economics, the huge area of free land, and the consequent temper of our thinking encouraged every man to consider himself the master of his fate. Under those conditions no type of determinism was possible. But those conditions were changing. The machine age was giving America a new mind, and the new way of thinking was not positively averse to the ideas of naturalism.

Beginning about 1860 the mind of America tended with increasing vehemence to be dominated by the machine. Social life became increasingly complex, and the old-time feeling of individual independence was giving way to a feeling of helplessness. The new feeling was fostered, first of all by the very organization and methods of industry. Formerly industry had been carried on by the independent craftsman who was his own master in his own workshop. The industrial revolution changed all this, and after the Civil War, American factories rapidly became larger and larger to house more and more intricate machinery. To tend these machines men, women, and children were used who had only a rudimentary knowledge of the complete processes of industry. The individual workman was no longer master of his trade or of himself. If he showed too restless or independent a spirit, he could be discharged and replaced at a minute's notice. Naturally he began to lose his cheery optimism and his confidence in himself as he realized with increasing conviction that he was the slave of the machine.

Another process that tended to denude Americans of their last shreds of independent thought was the rapid congregation of the population in the cities. In the spacious days of the pioneer a man might be cramped in his point of view, or he might be lacking in a broad tolerance, but at least he had elbow room on his farm or in the country village. Certainly the oppressive nearness of neighbors did not tend to make him feel like a powerless and useless unit, identical with millions of others, all crowded together in a great mass that dominated its parts. The city tended to create a mass psychology, for when a man can never rid himself of the presence of his fellows, he begins to think of himself in terms of the crowd rather than in terms of John Smith, the independent American.

Along with the loss of independence inculcated by the factory system and the growth of the cities, the individual lost his feeling of economic democracy, that sustaining faith that he enjoyed the same economic opportunity possessed by his fellows. The accumulation of wealth in the hands of a few gave the poorer classes a strong feeling that they were living in a society rigidly divided into economic castes. Looking at a wealth and power of a billionaire the ordinary man realized his lack of present power, opportunity and future. The employer of thousands of men holds a position and wields an influence far beyond the wildest dreams and aspirations of his underlings. To laborers economic regimentation and the loss of individualism are no grisly specters of the future; they are already existent.

All these social and economic facts united during the machine age to rob the American of his feeling of optimism, and everywhere that he looked for comfort he found only added confirmation of his doubts and black forebodings. And of all the aids and abettors of the gay philosophy of naturalism, none was more potent than science, the mother of the machine age. The first results of nineteenth century science were not quite reassuring to the optimist, for among the laws discovered was that of heredity, a force which man might well despair of controlling. Moreover, twentieth century psychology conceives of man as a mechanism that is certain to return a given response to a given stimulus. It emphasizes the fact that the human machine is driven by ducts and glands, deeply hidden impulses, and complex physio-chemical actions and reactions far beyond the individual's control or even present understanding. Just as theology dominated the thought of the seventeenth century and rationalistic philosophy the eighteenth, so does science dominate the machine age. Certainly no influence is more powerful to-day in the preparation of American thinking for the favorable reception of the naturalistic philosophy than is the school of modern psychology.

It is not the purpose of this discussion to examine the principles of naturalism and to render judgment on their philosophical validity. The sole aim is to tell what naturalism is and why it is gaining a foothold in this country. It gained its footing for the reasons just indicated, and there is apparently no very confident promise that it will soon give way to another school of literary interpretation. For forty years naturalism has been the strongest influence in American letters. It has produced some notable writers, and, what is quite as important, it has been the incentive to many other literary movements that are not usually thought of in connection with it. The sociological school was a direct development of naturalism, and the revival of romance in the late nineties was only a reaction to the same influence. The village controversy in our literature was precipitated by a naturalistic study of the small town in *Spoon River Anthology,* and the new romance accepts the basic contention of naturalism as the excuse for its romantic treatment of life. These are the important literary movements since 1890, and each one has a direct kinship with the naturalistic movement.

STEPHEN CRANE

(1871-1900)

According to the testimony of most competent critics, Stephen Crane was the genius of his generation. He seems to have been that rarest of beings, a born writer. His first book, *Maggie: A Girl of the Streets,* written when he was twenty years old, is a strikingly effective and finished piece of work that indicates a number of departures from the usual course of American novels. Some of these departures are seen in the absence of mawkish sentiment in handling a tragedy of the poorer classes, in the complete failure to pass moral judgment on any character or situation in the story, and in the note of irony that runs through the book and upon which the story ends. Both the writing and the conception of the book are amazing pieces of work for a twenty-year-old boy. *The Red Badge of Courage,* finished when the author was only twenty-three, is to-day seemingly assured of a permanent place in American literature. It is worthy of a place beside such novels of war as Tolstoy's *Sevastopol*, Zola's *La Débâcle*, Barbusse's *Under Fire*, and Remarque's *All Quiet on the Western Front*. [Crane's effectiveness lies largely in the power and skill with which he transmits impressions of light, color, sound and physical feeling.] His ability to describe swiftly and accurately seems never to have been learned from book or teacher.

Crane was the fourteenth child of a minister of Newark, New Jersey. The boy was a good student in those subjects that he liked but his chief delights were baseball and experimentation in the use of new and expressive words. He liked books, and before he was twenty he had read, among many other authors, Flaubert, Hamlin Garland, and Tolstoy. Tolstoy he considered the greatest of all novelists. He particularly admired that writer's *Sevastopol* and some of the early stories of Hamlin Garland. Crane attended Lafayette College and Syracuse University, though he completed the course in neither institution. For a time he was a reporter for a New York paper. According to his own statement he was "fired" from this position, but one cannot say if his discharge was caused by his over-use of impressionistic description to the slighting of news interest in his stories.

"Maggie: A Girl of the Streets."—While he was living a desultory life in New York, Crane became interested in slum life on the Bowery and out of this interest developed his first book, *Maggie: A Girl of the Streets*. As previously mentioned, this story was different from anything ever before attempted in American fiction. The author made no concession to the devotees of the Genteel Tradition; he threw no sop to the lovers of gilt and tinsel romanticism, and he gave nothing to those who dote on finished plots. The story "begins casually and ends casually," yet it leaves a feeling of utter reality that is seldom achieved in the pages of fiction. The language is that of the slums, the action is only what might be expected from the given characters, and the atmosphere is that of unrelieved realism. The book is a bit of slum life presented with utmost objectivity.

When Crane finished his story, he took it to Richard Watson Gilder, editor of *The Century Magazine*. Gilder is said to have had a "bad evening" with the manuscript. Theoretically he was not averse to realism, and he insisted upon good writing in the pages of his magazine. Here was a book that was both realistic and well written, yet it deeply disturbed him. It went too far. The reticent realist was supposed to do nothing more than hint at the unpleasant, but here was a young man who insisted upon describing unpleasant scenes in Bowery dialect interspersed with short descriptive sentences that were flaming jets of iridescent words. He failed to relieve the tension with a single sugar-coated sentiment or with a pleasant ending that showed all the coarse characters resolving to lead better and more refined lives. The story was a tragedy, and it closed on a note of grim irony. Plainly it would never do. Mr. Gilder sorrowfully admitted that the book was too good, too truthful, for his purposes. He could not publish it. Soon Crane discovered that no one else could. Finally *Maggie* made a surreptitious appearance, at the expense of the author, in paper covers. A copy that found its way to the hands of Hamlin Garland attracted the attention of that writer. He sent for Crane and helped him to sell some of his short stories, he lent the young fellow money, and, most important of all, he sent a copy of *Maggie* to William Dean Howells. The leader of the realists was enchanted, declaring that "here is a writer who sprang into life fully armed." But all his enthusiasm could not get a publisher for *Maggie*. However, he gave a dinner in honor of the author and read to his guest some of the poems of Emily Dickinson. Both incidents were of importance to Crane.

Maggie was a complete market failure. It enjoyed the sincere praise of our best novelists and critics, but it did not sell. Indeed it was not until 1896, three years later, that it appeared under the imprint of an established publishing house. Still the little tragedy was worth the money and effort that the young author had expended on it. Through this novel Crane met Garland and Howells, he sold some short stories, he became a figure in the literary world, and he read the poems of Emily Dickinson.

"The Red Badge of Courage."—One day Crane read Zola's great war novel, *La Débâcle*. He did not much care for the book, and a sarcastic challenge from one of its admirers may have stung him into writing *The Red Badge of Courage*. From his boyhood Crane had heard talk about the Civil War. Every street corner, every country grocery store had its group of veterans who exchanged countless stories of their experiences in the struggle between the states. A few, a very few war novels had been published, and most of these deserted the simple and moving truth to wallow in a mixture of melodrama and thin sentimentality. The early war book had specialized in plot, thrilling action, and heroic figures. Crane

had a good enough native taste to avoid the literary sins to which the other writers had succumbed. He went straight to the heart of his problem by leaving out every vestige of the heroic and by recording truthfully only the sensations that come to an obscure young soldier. So far from the heroic is the youth, the leading character in the book, that he is not distinguished by a name, and never does he rise above the level of the ordinary fellow. Crane attempted in this way to make the reader share the soldier's feeling of submergence in the mass. In this attempt he was successful. [The sympathetic reader feels the conflict between the war machine and the inner impulses of the soldier.] One senses the casual nature of life and death, defeat and victory. One sees that victories are largely accidental, and that war, even life itself, is a clash of blind, miserably directed forces. But the book contains no philosophizing and no moralizing. It is as coolly objective as if it were a report of a scientific experiment. The dialogue is done in a most life-like manner, as it was in *Maggie,* and the descriptive passages are notable for their brevity and intensity. Here is the closing sentence of a chapter: "The sun was a red wafer pasted in the sky."

The Red Badge of Courage was a great success. It contained little of the repellent that had been so disastrous to the success of *Maggie,* while in sheer literary deftness and effectiveness it marked an advance over its predecessor. It had an enthusiastic critical reception and a great popular success. The other work of Crane is so little known that it is not too much to say that the author's position as the founder of the contemporary school of fiction and as one of the great novelists of our literature rests upon his work in *The Red Badge of Courage.* In this book American naturalism had its first triumph.

There has been some doubt expressed as to the thoroughness of Crane's naturalism, but doubt is unwarranted. Crane was a real naturalist, though his impressionistic method kept him from laboring over detail in the manner of many of his fellows. Testing his work by the canons of naturalism, one discovers a scientific impersonality in the treatment of material, and a resolute purpose to record facts and impressions without passing moral judgment upon anything. Furthermore the principle of determinism appears in both novels by Crane. Maggie was the victim of a slum environment that she could neither conquer nor escape, and the youth in *The Red Badge of Courage* was the victim of various forces, not one of which was controlled by his free will. He was the victim of society when he entered the army, and once in the regiment he was the plaything of crowd psychology, conflicting impulses, and mere chance. In the first pages of this book Crane wrote: "It occurred to him that he had never wished to come to war. He had not enlisted of his own free-will. He had been dragged by a merciless government." Crane says these words in spite of the fact that the boy had not been compelled to enlist by any visible force. In fact he had done so against his mother's wishes. Tested from almost any angle Crane shows strong naturalistic conceptions.

Impressionism, a term borrowed from painting, is the name given to Crane's descriptive method, a method that to-day is in wide use. In literature it simply means the discarding of detailed description and narration for a "snapshot" that is as notable for its effectiveness as for its economy of words. The author sees things at a rapid glance and with equal rapidity transfers his impressions to his readers. The following sentences illustrating this method are taken from the opening page of *Maggie:* "His small body was writhing in the delivery of great, crimson oaths. . . . From the window of an apartment house that upreared its form from amid squat, ignorant stables, there leaned a curious woman. . . . Over on the island, a worm of yellow convicts came from the shadow of a gray ominous building and crawled slowly along the river's brink." From *The Red Badge of Courage:* "Tents sprang up like strange plants. Camp fires, like red, peculiar blossoms, dotted the night. . . . From this little distance the many fires, with the black forms of men passing to and fro before the crimson rays made weird and satanic effects." From "The Open Boat," a short story: "These waves were of the hue of slate, save for the tops, which were of foaming white. . . . The horizon narrowed and widened, and dipped and rose, and at all times its edge was jagged with waves that seemed thrust up in points like rocks. . . . These waves were most wrongfully and barbarously abrupt and tall, and each froth top was a problem in small-boat navigation." From "An Experiment in Misery": "It was late at night, and a fine rain was swirling softly down, causing the pavements to glisten with hue of steel and blue and yellow in the rays of the innumerable lights."

Crane as a Poet.—Crane's poetry is of considerable intrinsic merit and of more than a little historical interest in that it is the lineal predecessor of certain phases of the New Poetry, a literary move-

ment that came into being twelve or fifteen years after Crane's death.
In his poetry Crane did not achieve the emphatic intensity that was
his in almost every sentence of his prose, and much of his verse is
lacking in the fundamental impersonality that is so attractive an
element in his fiction. It does not have the studied detachment and
swift power that we find in the pages of *Maggie* or *The Red Badge
of Courage*. Crane, the poet, seems constantly striving to say something very good, very important. Occasionally he succeeds with his
poetry, but the success is never heightened by the self-conscious air
of oracular wisdom found in too many of his lines.

At his best Crane has a fine command of verbal imagery in his
poetry and the ability to say much in a few words. He is a true
predecessor of the Imagists in his attempt to create concrete images,
and many later poets copied his short, nervous lines of free verse,
so different from the melodious chanting of Whitman's lines. He
never quite reached the poetic deftness that was Emily Dickinson's
glory, but that statement is no very adverse comment on Crane's
poetry, for Miss Dickinson was one of the true poets of all our literature. The two poets together, the recluse spinster of New England
and the shy young man who loafed along the Bowery, bridge the gap
between Walt Whitman and the beginning of the New Poetry. Crane
published two volumes of poetry, *Black Riders* and *War Is Kind*.
The first book was dedicated to Hamlin Garland.

Such a poem as the following shows the author's naturalism:

> God fashioned the ship of the world carefully
> With the skill of an all-master,
> Made the hull and sails,
> Held he the rudder
> Ready for adjustment.
> Erect stood he, scanning his work proudly.
> Then—at fateful time—wrong called,
> And God turned, heeding.
> Lo, the ship at this opportunity slipped slyly,
> Making cunning noiseless travel down the ways,
> So that, forever rudderless, it went upon the seas,
> Going ridiculous voyages
> Making quaint progress,
> Turning as with serious purpose
> Before stupid winds.
> And there were many in the sky
> Who laughed at this thing.

The same feeling is shown in these few lines:

> A man said to the universe:
> "Sir, I exist."
> "However," replied the universe,
> "The fact has not created in me
> A sense of obligation!"

Crane's best poem is the one called "War Is Kind." In these lines the author uses the simple imagery and irony that he utilized so skillfully in his prose.

Other Work of Crane.—In his short life of thirty years Crane published several other books besides *Maggie, The Red Badge of Courage* and the two volumes of poetry. *George's Mother* is a short novel that deals with the material used in *Maggie*. This work is virtually unknown. It is probable that next to the two successful novels Crane's best work is a short story "The Open Boat." H. G. Wells declares that this effort is the author's finest performance.

In 1900 Crane died in Germany where he had gone for the benefit of his health. His early death was clearly one of the great disasters to contemporary American literature. In his short life he had by the force of sheer genius founded the contemporary school of fiction, and he, with Emily Dickinson, became the forerunner of New Poetry. No American writer ever did as much in so short a time.

FRANK NORRIS

(1870-1902)

Although Frank Norris was probably a romantic at heart, his early and intimate contact with the works of Zola and other Continental novelists influenced him to write three naturalistic novels. These three are *McTeague, Vandover and the Brute,* and *The Octopus.* His once-famous novel of Chicago business life, *The Pit,* falls midway between realism and romanticism. His other books are all romantic. In all his novels Norris reveals his innate romanticism by an extreme fondness for the unusual, the bizarre, and the spectacular, but in the three naturalistic works this fondness is made to serve the tenets of naturalism. Another non-naturalistic tendency is his inclination to pass moral judgment upon characters and actions. This concern with ethical values is most pronounced in *The Pit,* which is concerned with speculation in wheat.

Norris was born in Chicago, but while he was a young boy the family moved to San Francisco. A marked talent for drawing led him to prepare for a career as a painter. He spent a number of years in Paris where he studied art and read widely in the works of the contemporary French novelists. Zola, the most defiant of all the naturalists, became the favorite master of the young American. When Norris returned to America he completed his academic training at the University of California and at Harvard. Literature soon supplanted art as his major interest, and at this time he was never seen "without a yellow, paper-covered novel by Zola in his hand." While he was still a student he began two of his naturalistic novels, *McTeague* and *Vandover and the Brute*. The first was completed and published in 1899; the second was never finished. After passing through the San Francisco fire, the manuscript of *Vandover* was discovered and published in 1914, twelve years after the author's death. Upon leaving Harvard in 1895, Norris became a newspaper correspondent in South Africa. While at his work he was stricken by African fever. For a time he was near death, and he never fully recovered from the attack. Six years later the effect of the fever was a contributing cause of his death. The passing of Norris at the early age of thirty-two, a year after the untimely death of Crane, left American naturalism with only one avowed practicer. This writer was the slowly maturing Theodore Dreiser, who published his first novel in 1900.

Norris, the Naturalist.—In the writing of his early works, Norris was completely under the domination of Zola. The Frenchman had in him a strong dash of the sensational, and he never hesitated to employ even melodramatic effects to make the pages of his novels more vivid and memorable. This element of sensationalism appealed strongly to Norris, who deliberately planned his novels with the intention of using the most striking effects that he could command. He sought unusual subjects, many of which required for their proper elaboration the use of huge canvases crowded with a multitude of figures. He began a prose epic in three volumes that would tell the story of wheat from the field where it is produced to its consumption in Europe. Only two books of this trilogy were ever written, *The Octopus* and *The Pit*. Norris planned another trilogy that would give a huge cyclorama of the Battle of Gettysburg. One volume was to be devoted to each day of the gigantic struggle. Not a line was ever written of this grand conception. Even in his single-volume novels Norris was greatly influenced by Zola, for *McTeague* owes much to *L'Assomoir*. Both are naturalistic studies of character degeneration; both stress the influence of environment upon the individual, and both illustrate essentially the same literary method.

Despite his marked use of the sensational and his striving for immensity of effect, Norris held rather closely in the novels under discussion to the canons of naturalism. He contended that fiction must tell the bare truth, however unpleasant such procedure might be. Truth might be punctuated by salvos of artillery or shaken by the death struggle of a nation but it remained his chief aim in his more significant books. Adherence to fact made the writer a realist, and in the course of the novels determinism always entered in some guise to bring the characters to an inevitable though unwished end.

McTeague is Norris's most powerful and impressive book, though there are parts of *Vandover and the Brute* that equal its best passages. Indeed the latter book has flashes that are the equal of anything in American fiction. *McTeague* is a careful study of the slow degeneration of character under relentless pressure. In the world of this book there are various determining influences. Sometimes the influence is economic demands; sometimes it is mere chance. And often chance is malignant, wrecking lives and characters without rational cause. In all these elements the book is naturalistic, and these are the important features of the novel. There are romantic elements in the symbolic use of gold, the presence in the book of certain romantic characters, and the use of the revenge motive—one of the most hackneyed of romantic devices. But these elements are superficial embroidery upon a background that is essentially naturalistic. As a work of art *McTeague* has its flaws. The main objection to the book is that it suffers from the insertion midway through the story of another narrative that detracts from the main thread of interest. But *McTeague* is too strong, too virile to be gravely injured by any such treatment. The central figure of a San Francisco dentist, sub-normal in mentality and almost pathologically avaricious in disposition, has a life-like reality and a compelling interest that mere technical flaws could never obscure. The book is an amazing performance for a first novel. Norris never excelled it, and he equaled it only in detached bits of his other writing.

Vandover and the Brute is a study in human degeneracy through the warring elements in man's dual nature. In the slow break-up of

Vandover's character, evil consistently worsts good, until the man succumbs to forces beyond his control. The closing scene of the book has been called pure naturalism. *Vandover and the Brute* was too strong a bit of writing for the late nineties, and the reluctance of publishers to issue it caused Norris to drop the manuscript before it was fully completed, but in 1914 it was published to the pleasure of a large group of readers, for naturalism had gained a great deal of ground since 1900. In *Vandover* and *McTeague* Norris achieved two lasting pieces of work, and not the least significant thing about the two novels is the promise that they gave of future development. If the author had lived for twenty-five years after 1902, and if he had developed the talent for naturalistic fiction that he displayed in the two novels, both begun when he was twenty-four, he might easily have developed into the Great American Novelist about whose imminent arrival critics chattered for many years.

But it is to be doubted if Norris would have developed along the lines marked out by *McTeague* and *Vandover,* for his later books show a rapidly increasing interest in sociology. A great interest in sociology leads a writer into considerations of ethics and social justice, and when a novelist becomes interested in these he ceases to be a calm, impersonal observer of the struggles and triumphs of mankind. He leaves off the work of the artist and assumes the rôle of an advocate; he quits writing novels and turns his attention to sociological tracts and arguments. Sociology and artistic fiction are not compatible, and the chief weakness of naturalism is the tendency of naturalists to become too much interested in sociology. At the time of his death Norris was plainly exhibiting this tendency.

The Octopus (1901), the first novel of the trilogy of wheat, was written while Norris was still under the domination of Zola, but the dominant influence is that of Zola, the sociological-naturalist, and not that of Zola, the pure naturalist. The novel tells the story of the struggle of an entire state against the irresistible, impersonal power of a railroad. The very situation around which the book is built tends to stress social questions, and Norris seems willing enough to be led into a discussion of sociology. In the descriptive passages it is probably more deftly and expertly written than were *McTeague* and *Vandover,* but as a novel it is clearly inferior in conception. It reveals a changing point of view. *McTeague* is the story of a man, told by an artist who is intent only upon making the reader see and hear and feel the inevitable descent of a victim into the abyss. In the face of the overwhelming powers of the universe, the author feels that he is as impotent as are the powerless characters that he depicts. The whole mood is that born of resignation tempered by pity. In *The Octopus* Norris's heart swells with indignation. The evils that he pictures are social. Nay, more; they are remediable. And Norris longs to apply the remedy. From *The Octopus* to the soap-box and the indignant, perfervid eloquence of Upton Sinclair is only a step. Norris never took the step, but he came dangerously near doing so.

The Other Works of Norris.—Although *The Pit* is not the most successful work of the author, it is a very significant novel both in the development of Norris and in the history of American fiction. In this book Norris indulges his tendency to discuss questions of social justice, and the resulting strong sociological emphasis was the portent of a long line of novels that helped to block or deflect the activities of potential naturalists. *The Pit,* as the second member of the trilogy of wheat, used as its primary material speculation in grain on the Chicago Board of Trade. The book has many excellencies. Its narrative is rapid and coherent, and many of the descriptive passages are good enough to have been embalmed in books of selections for the guidance of young writers. But as a novel of Chicago business it is not a great success. Norris never quite caught the characteristic tone of Chicago. To feel the extent of Norris's failure, one has only to read the novels of Herrick and Dreiser dealing with the same subject. The characters of *The Pit* never quite take form. Norris sees them with neither the sharp, incisive glance of Stephen Crane nor the brooding observation of Theodore Dreiser. He is probably too much concerned with the social results that may flow from the actions of his characters to spend much time in the delineation of the figures themselves. Another and more objectionable fault is to be found in the absence of a coördinated dynamic drive, such as is found in *McTeague,* that gives force and meaning to every line of the novel. In short, *The Pit* must stand as an example of what a naturalist can produce when he becomes too much interested in sociology. It is not an unsuccessful novel, but when it is measured by Norris's earlier works, it is discovered to contain too much sociology and too little impersonal observation and too little artistic presentation of the strivings of men.

In addition to the novels already discussed Norris wrote a large number of sketches and short stories. Few of these are well known to-day. Indeed, most of them are inferior productions, though some are much better than most of the short stories that are so respectfully preserved in anthologies. *Blix* and *Moran of the Lady Letty* are two well-written but frankly romantic novels. During Norris's life they were very popular, and even to-day they find readers, but they cannot be considered on the same artistic level with his other books.

THEODORE DREISER

(1871-1945)

Theodore Dreiser is the most consistent and uncompromising exponent of naturalism who has thus far appeared in American letters. Both temperamentally and philosophically he is a naturalist, for his spontaneous reactions to the spectacle called life have always been those of a naturalist, and as he has matured, the philosophy that he has consciously accepted is that of extreme physical naturalism. Nothing has been able to deter or deflect him from his self-appointed task as the naturalistic novelist of contemporary America, the America of the big cities and big business. Neither the glitter of romance with its fat royalties for its favorites nor the attractive field of sociological fiction, neither moral censure nor the open contempt of academic critics has been able to turn Dreiser one hair's breadth from his chosen course. That he began his literary work as a well-developed naturalist is proved by *Sister Carrie,* his first book, which is fundamentally a sound piece of naturalism. And his latest novel, *An American Tragedy,* shows nothing new except a maturer literary talent and a more intense devotion to his avowed philosophy.

Two things have made Dreiser the interpreter of American life that he is to-day. These two things are his natural temperament and his long service as a journalist in our large cities. The chief characteristics of Dreiser are the brooding care and sense of pity with which he watches the struggle of "this animal called man," his conviction that existence is entirely without meaning or reason, his belief that the determining forces of life are physio-chemical actions and reactions, and his conclusion that the business of living divides mankind into the strong and the weak, not into the good and the bad, as would be the case if life had a moral purpose. Thus

Dreiser is a purely mechanical naturalist, probably the only one in our literary history, though Mark Twain toyed with this conception. Some of these characteristics may have been acquired from Dreiser's slow-moving, thoughtful German ancestors, but all of them could have come to a man of his temper who watched life in our modern cities.

Dreiser was born in Terre Haute, Indiana, of German parents. He was educated in the public schools and in the University of Indiana. After leaving the university without a degree, he became a newspaper reporter. This profession he followed with considerable success in several of the large cities of the East and the Middle West. The work done during this period left an indelible imprint upon Dreiser's method and style, for to this day he is essentially a reporter whose aim is to observe events closely and to record the facts with absolute impersonality. *An American Tragedy* is simply a mammoth example of the reporter's art, for its author has recorded, as if for publication in a newspaper for deliberate readers, all the pertinent facts in the life of a young man. Even in his composition Dreiser has never shaken off all the faults of hurried and slovenly writing that he acquired as a reporter pounding out copy at top speed. He is still prone to use the easy or trite phrase in preference to the more expressive but more elusive word. Verbal magic and striking originality of diction are as far from Dreiser as they usually are from the reporter who is intent only upon telling the story.

In the late nineties Dreiser became acquainted with another young reporter who was writing some fiction for popular magazines. Under the urging of his new friend he wrote and sold three or four short stories. Then the friend suggested that he begin a novel. Dreiser demurred, for he had no plot in mind, and he supposed that a novel could not be written without an intricate plot. However, to still the importunities of his friend one day he casually wrote the words "Sister Carrie" at the top of a sheet of paper. Dreiser soon was struggling along with a novel that bore this name, and *Sister Carrie* became his first and, some insist, his best book.

After the publication of his first novel Dreiser continued in journalistic work. For a time he was editor of a women's magazine. Then he served as editorial adviser to a firm that specialized in Wild West stories and dime novels. About 1910 he discontinued his journalistic work and devoted his full time to literature.

Dreiser's Novels.—Although only six of his nineteen books are novels, Dreiser devotes his greatest activity to novel writing, and it is as a novelist that he will be remembered in American literature.

Sister Carrie (1900) was Dreiser's first book. Although it is naturalistic in its prevailing tone, it does not have the studied naturalism that colors grayly the later books. In a sense it marked no sharp break with other American novels of the time. In that it begins rather casually, proceeds without a closely woven plot, and ends on no preconceived climax, it bears a slight resemblance to *Maggie,* another story of a young girl, but in actual composition the slow, labored movement of *Sister Carrie* is far removed from the rapid and brilliant impressionism of Crane's little masterpiece. With infinite pains Dreiser watches the progress of Carrie Meebler along a path that was not of her own choosing. The woman is moved from place to place, from situation to situation, through no willing of her own. She is a pawn in the hands of mighty and mysterious forces.

But it should not be imagined that Carrie is a mere automaton, a puppet of wires and strings. She is a well-realized human being whose feeble power only increases the pity that we naturally feel for the victims of fate. Carrie Meebler takes form in the novel that bears her name, but the great creation of the book is the character of George Hurstwood, a finely imagined and executed figure that is impressive enough almost to deserve the epithet, Nietzschean. The very finest passage in the novel and one of the best in all of Dreiser's work is the account of the slow disintegration of Hurstwood. Under the strokes of adverse fate, the masterful man slowly and painfully sinks. Force, ambition, pride, the very desire for life, one by one drop away until the shell of the once strong figure gratefully finds death.

Jennie Gerhardt (1911), the author's second novel, appeared after an interval of eleven years. Although Dreiser had presumably written nothing during those years except facile and unimportant journalism, the second book marked a distinct technical advance over the first. It is more smoothly written and more deftly put together than *Sister Carrie,* though it contains nothing that for poignant intensity and power approaches the story of Hurstwood. *Jennie Gerhardt* is another story of a woman who is compelled to be the passive victim of malignant chance. The chief character goes through life unaware of the meaning of it all, unaware even that there is a question about its meaning, and at the very end when she 'stands, broken, defeated, and denied, her actions are those of a person dazed by a blow from an unknown source. This book contains a number of characters, but the one that has attracted the attention of most readers is that of old Gerhardt, Jennie's father.

In his third and fourth novels, *The Financier* (1912) and *The Titan* (1914), Dreiser undertook the study of an American business man magnified to huge proportions. Frank Cowperwood, the business man, is a truly Nietzschean figure. From his boyhood he is possessed by the desire for great wealth and its attendant power. Nothing is allowed to stand in the way of the realization of his ambition. An experience that he had as a boy convinced him that mankind must "eat or be eaten," must conquer or be conquered. He determined to conquer. Upon the fragments of private honor and public trust he reared the malodorous reputation of a super-financier who was hampered by no such handicaps as conscience and word of honor. He had wealth and power and every accompaniment of these things that the unscrupulous could wish. At last his luck turned, and he went to the penitentiary for the embezzlement of public funds. Shortly after his release the Chicago fire precipitated a panic in which he made a fortune almost overnight. At this point *The Financier* comes to an end. *The Titan* picks up Cowperwood's career in Chicago whither he had gone from Philadelphia, his first home. The second book is built around the struggle of Cowperwood and his associates for permanent and lucrative control of the street railways. Just as he is on the verge of his greatest success, he fails again. It was the original plan of Dreiser to show Cowperwood in London working on new financial schemes, but the last member of the projected trilogy has not yet been written.

It is quite probable that future generations will think more of Dreiser's epic of American business than of any other portion of his work. Cowperwood is a huge but human and thoroughly convincing figure. The books deserve to remain in our literature for the sake of the chief character, if for no other reason. But there is another reason. Probably no other work of fiction or non-fiction in the whole range of our literature gives a more realistic account of American business during the Gilded Age. If the novels were social histories, extracted painstakingly from .legal documents and the files of newspapers, they could not be more scrupulously regardful of fact and the social background. Many have denied that

Cowperwood is a typical business man, but few have questioned the accuracy of the background, and as it becomes possible to take an unprejudiced view of the business man of the Gilded Age, it becomes more and more apparent that Cowperwood is fairly representative of his time and class.

Dreiser's next book, *The Genius* (1915), is a huge, sprawling, muddy biographical novel that uses New York City as the background. It suffers from two faults, indirection and inordinate length. Brevity is certainly never a characteristic of Dreiser's works, but the extreme length of his novels becomes objectionable only when the author allows his story to wander aimlessly. *The Genius* gives the reader a strong feeling that the writing of the book entailed the expenditure of great but undirected energy. When it is compared with such works as the story of Hurstwood in *Sister Carrie* or *The Financier*, or *An American Tragedy*, the sprawling aimlessness of the book becomes far too apparent. Furthermore in *The Genius* Dreiser allows his belief in the power of chance to reduce his story almost to a burlesque. The leading character, Eugene Witla, is catapulted so rapidly from obscurity to fame that the book sounds like a novel by Horatio Alger written in style of Jonathan Edwards's sermons. *The Genius* is said to be Mr. Dreiser's favorite of all his books. If such is the case, the fact merely adds point to the suggestion that no novelist should ever be allowed to pass critical judgment upon his own works.

For the first twenty years of his career as a novelist, Dreiser was the victim of chronic, unintelligent criticism that frequently descended to the level of personal abuse. Virtually all academic critics and most of the reading public were violently hostile to the man and all his works, and if it had not been for the insistent defense by H. L. Mencken, assisted by Randolph Bourne and a few other young critics, Dreiser would have been utterly without an advocate at the court of American letters. The charges against him ranged all the way from criticisms of his sentence structure to indictments of his personal morality, but they all sprang from one fundamental objection. That objection was lodged against Dreiser's naturalism. He was unsentimental, pessimistic, skeptical of accepted institutions and valuations, and he never passed a moral judgment upon any character or action. Hence he became the recipient of all the adverse criticism that could be conjured up by the imaginative minds of optimists, Puritans, and sentimentalists. This abuse continued until three or four years after the close of the World War.

But by 1925 the temper of American critics and readers had changed. Natural science, psychology, economics, and sociology had all accustomed thinking people to facts and theories that were sharply at variance with the older ideals of sentiment and optimism. The World War and the Treaty of Versailles had but deepened the pessimism in American thinking that hitherto had been apparent only to the very sensitive or the very observant. Moreover, Dreiser was then not the only naturalist in our literature. Other men of his temper were giving their interpretations of the American scene, and most of these frankly attributed to Dreiser the preëminence of leadership and authority. The attitude of the public toward him was softening. Then came *An American Tragedy* (1925), a long study in two volumes of a weakling whose weakness and passive acceptance of suffering and death made him a truly tragic figure. As usual with Dreiser, he had trouble getting started, and the first volume is a closely studied background, but the entire second volume that tells of the slow closing in by fate upon its unfortunate victim is a profoundly moving piece of naturalistic writing. *An American Tragedy* was a great popular and critical success. Even those academic critics who had derided and belittled Dreiser's earlier works spoke with respect of the massive bulk and impressive power of the new novel. The work was successfully dramatized, and with a flourish of trumpets a company paid a large price for the motion picture rights to the story. However, the tragedy has not yet appeared on the screen. With the publication of this novel Dreiser finally came into his own. And his own was domination of the field of American fiction.

An American Tragedy may be the best constructed of the author's books, but it is certainly not the most naturalistic. It is only the mature and carefully deliberated statement of a theme that had appealed to Dreiser's temperament twenty-five years earlier in the story of George Hurstwood, the tragic figure of *Sister Carrie*. In the quarter-century that elapsed between the two books Dreiser had only matured; he had not changed. It was American taste that had changed, and the great success of *An American Tragedy* was convincing proof of that change.

The student who is appalled at the great length of Dreiser's novels need not despair of finding a relatively short example of the author's style and method. Some of the short stories in the volume called *Free* are just as Dreiserian as are the novels, and the same can be said of some of the sketches in *Twelve Men*. No one who is interested in Dreiser should overlook *A Traveler at Forty* and *A Hoosier Holiday*. In the second of these books Dreiser has done some of his best work as a writer of English prose. *Hey-Rub-A-Dub-Dub* gives a very clear but somewhat self-conscious statement of the author's philosophy of life. It is decidedly worth reading. However, to the student of Dreiser one of the most valuable books is the autobiography, *The Story of Myself*. A reading of this book will convince one that many of the episodes in the various novels are drawn straight from personal observations.

Dreiser's Philosophy.—The prevailing note in the philosophy of Dreiser is a temperamental skepticism. He is certain of nothing, nor can he ever be certain, for he is constitutionally unable to make up his mind conclusively about anything. He has observed life closely—no man has watched it more intently—and he has set down his observations by thousands of pages. And yet he cannot be certain. He is not always certain that he is uncertain. Much of Dreiser's skepticism is expended upon the attempts of other men to guess the riddle of existence and upon the current valuations attached to actions, codes of social usage, and revered institutions. He has sought insistently for certainty, comfort, and that sense of satisfaction that comes from surety, but he has never found the object of his search. The most that he will permit himself to say is that life is constantly in motion. Change rules all, but he has never been able to discover an intelligent cause of the change. It just happens in response to mechanical or chemical forces. He admits that there is a world-mechanism, but thus far he has been unable to convince himself that this mechanism is under the control of an intelligent, purposive engineer.

Upon the shifting foundations of philosophical uncertainty Dreiser has reared a coördinated and consistent system of naturalistic thought. His literary method is that of a scientist, and his skepticism renders him deeply pessimistic. These two traits alone would make him a naturalistic writer. But he bears many other likenesses to the men of the naturalistic school. Dreiser's naturalism takes the familiar form of the conception of life in terms of Nietzschean struggle and will to power in a universe governed by physio-chemical forces. Dreiser holds that the events that set in motion these forces often proceed from pure chance. Man's happiness and woe are the result of casting dice with fate. His observation tells him that men are divided into two groups, the masterful and the weak, the conquering and the conquered. The weak meet their doom at once, and the tragedy of their existence is their passive acceptance of the strokes of fate. The strong may escape for a time, but finally chance fails them, and the tragedy of their downfall is the sense of pity and terror that the beholder gains from the sudden humiliation of the proud or from the slow disintegration of the strong. Human personality may be appealing in its weakness or imposing in its strength, but in the end it is of no avail against chance and the impersonal physio-chemical forces.

Dreiser's philosophy is one that could have been taken almost in its entirety from watching the shifting pageant of our large cities. But we do not know how much of it came from this source and how much came by inheritance from generations of brooding European ancestors. Probably both influences have left their marks in Dreiser's view of life, but certainly his philosophy could not have been what it is to-day if the author had not spent years observing the impersonal cruelty, relentless force, and blind chance of American city life.

Dreiser's Literary Method.—Besides his tendency to brood endlessly over the problem of existence, Dreiser has at least one other likeness to the peasant. This is his undying curiosity that makes him stand open-mouthed before a happening, mentally fumbling for some explanation of the mystery. Curiosity hangs over every book by Dreiser. With unhurried care he watches the progress of events and the part that men play in the ever-changing spectacle. To him no event is unimportant. Everything helps to satisfy his curiosity, and nothing that he sees is kept out of his pages. As a result of his lack of selective power, the novels are very long and unbelievably detailed.

In the process of changing his observations into literature, Dreiser is again slow and heavy-handed. His writing is wholly devoid of grace and subtlety. At times he is positively a poor writer, and at no time does he rise to stylistic elegance. And yet he is not a bad writer in the sense that he allows his style to diminish the effect of his narrative or in the sense that it is not suited to his material. One is forced to grieve over some of the rhetorical inelegancies, but

Dreiser's style in general is a good one for Dreiser, though one might hesitate about urging its general adoption. The slowly moving machinery of a Dreiserian novel would have a most unfortunate presentation if it were written in the nervous, monosyllabic sentences of Ernest Hemingway or in the studied archaisms of Mr. Cabell. Filled as it is with crudities so obvious that a school boy can detect them, still Dreiser's style is admirably fitted for the task at hand. One of the prime elements of a good style—an element frequently unmentioned by the dreary handbooks of writing—is the harmony of diction and sentence structure with the subject-matter. Whatever stylistic faults Dreiser may possess, certainly he has achieved this harmony. A gay, graceful writer he is not, and yet he is a much more effective writer than are some of his finicky critics, and his books are very much better written than they would have been had he taken the advice of all the teachers of English composition. Carping critics will always find fault with Dreiser's diction and sentence structure, but it is quite probable that judicious readers will go ahead for many years reading and re-reading his books.

Significance of Dreiser.—Dreiser is by far the most significant writer now working in the American field. He is certainly not the cleverest, or the most electric, or the most cheering, but he is the most powerful, and from the standpoint of literary development he is the most significant.

It is Theodore Dreiser, almost unaided, who has brought current American fiction into harmony with the tone of contemporary American life by making the novel a becoming and worthy medium for the presentation of the world about us. Our national life to-day so admirably lends itself to naturalistic treatment that it can be said almost to demand such presentation. The little flurry of naturalistic writing in the nineties would have come to an untimely end with the passing of Crane and Norris, had it not been for the stubborn persistence of Dreiser. Upon his head was cast all the contumely that could be hurled by outraged optimism and sentimentality, and still the man persisted in the honest presentation of life as he saw it. He sensed that naturalism was the one literary method adapted to the treatment of his material, and his forthright honesty forbade him to compromise. For almost forty years he has watched American society and its dominant figures, and what he has seen he has written down with perfect candor and with immense indifference to the prejudices and preconceptions of men.

Dreiser has had something of a reward for his persistence. To-day the major writers of the country recognize the naturalistic philosophy either by acceptance or by implication. E. A. Robinson, Edgar Lee Masters, Sherwood Anderson, Eugene O'Neill, Ernest Hemingway, Robinson Jeffers, Laurence Stallings, and many another accept the philosophy in some degree. James Branch Cabell, Robert Nathan, and many of the poets admit the validity of the naturalistic creed, yet they prefer to make their literature from their dreams and not from gray and cheerless facts. And the man who first recognized the congeniality of the naturalistic temper and the American scene, and who made naturalism the dominant literary mode in America is Theodore Dreiser.

SUGGESTED READINGS

Beach: *Outlook for American Prose*. Chicago. 1926. Dreiser, pp. 178-96.

Beach: *The Twentieth Century Novel*. New York. 1932.

Beer: *Stephen Crane*. New York. 1923.
> Brilliant biography. A new study of Crane is needed.

Bourne: *History of a Literary Radical*. New York. 1920. Dreiser, pp. 195-204.
> One of the earliest sensible estimates of Dreiser.

Cargill: *Intellectual America*. New York. 1941.
> Satisfactory treatment of naturalism.

Cowley: *After the Genteel Tradition*. New York. 1937.
> This symposium contains an essay on Dreiser.

Dondore: *Forgotten Frontiers: Dreiser and the Land of the Free*. New York. 1932.
> A very strange book. It may have some little value.

Garland: "Stephen Crane as I Knew Him." Yale Review. April, 1914.

Geismar: *Writers in Crisis*. New York. 1942.
> The views of a left-winger in criticism.

Hatcher: *The Foreground of American Fiction*. New York. 1935.

Kazin: *On Native Grounds*. New York. 1942.

Marchand: *Frank Norris: A Study*. Stanford University. 1942.

Mencken: *Prefaces*. New York. 1922. Dreiser, pp. 1-148.

Michaud: *The American Novel Today*. Boston. 1928. Dreiser, pp. 71-127.

Quinn: *American Fiction*. New York. 1936.
> The author is exceedingly conservative, but his work has value.

Rascoe: *Theodore Dreiser*. New York. 1925.
> Remains a good treatment of the subject.

Sherman: *On Contemporary Literature.* New York. 1917.

>One of the essays contains a vigorous attack on Dreiser's naturalism. Later Sherman changed his views radically. It is instructive and amusing to read the essay in this book and then turn to Sherman's review of *An American Tragedy.* Only some eight years separated the two utterances.

Van Doren: *Contemporary American Novelists.* New York. 1923.

>Good estimate written before *An American Tragedy.*

Van Doren: *The American Novel.* New York. 1921. Crane, pp. 258-60; Norris, pp. 260-4.

>The author hardly gave Crane too much space.

Wells: "Stephen Crane," *North American Review,* 171: 232-42.

Whipple: *Spokesmen.* New York. 1928. Dreiser, pp. 70-93.

CHAPTER XXIII

ROMANCE AND SOCIOLOGY

ROMANCE

Naturalism was not destined to possess the field of American fiction without encountering the opposition of other literary schools. Its opponents seemed to be divided roughly into two classes, the ones who objected because the new method was "sordid, cheerless and unsentimental," and the ones who wished to remedy the unlovely conditions set forth in naturalistic novels. The first found the desired sweet sentimentality, optimism, and false glitter in romances, especially in historical novels. The second found their desire in the hitherto unexploited possibilities of the sociological novel.

The Romance of the Nineties.—Confirmed sentimentalists will never be denied their tears, thrills, and happy endings. Ever since the beginnings of fiction there have been writers ready and willing to accept popular favor by supplying romances soaked in sentimentality and dipped in sugar, and at present there is no sign that uncompromising realism is about to capture the reading public of America. The historical novelists of the nineties still find a considerable number of belated readers, Harold Bell Wright and Zane Grey are among our most popular writers, and the crowded motion-picture theaters of every city and village are eloquent testimony to the existence of the "motion-picture mind," which finds its most satisfying relaxation in pleasant but extravagantly untrue pictures of life. To a greater or less degree we all possess this mind, and it is entirely possible that we shall become more and more susceptible to the attraction of unreal literature if social pressure continues to hold us hard against the harsh and unpleasant facts which we long to escape. Of all the literature of escape no variety has a wider appeal than has the romance, and of all types of romance historical novels have long been eminent for the number and fervor of their followers. This was the variety of romance that enjoyed

543

unusual favor during the nineties among those displeased with the grimness of the prevailing naturalism.

In the hands of Sir Walter Scott the historical novel first revealed its elements of appeal and its weakness. Its great appeal is in the ease with which it may be read, for it places the minimum of strain upon the mental capacity of the reader. Long before one begins the reading one has already visualized the chief characters, and the others are usually only foils and henchmen. The use of quasi-historical incidents, strange and beautiful costumes, exotic manners, and archaic trappings all pleasantly divert the reader from the consideration of things unwished in either life or fiction. The weakness of the historical novel lies in an excessive dependence upon the devices just mentioned and in a lamentable disregard for the accurate presentation of character. But Scott's readers, entranced by the facile art of their author, lose their critical powers, if ever they had any, in the contemplation of the variegated pageant that streams through such novels as *Ivanhoe* and *Quentin Durward*. Scott charted the sure route to popular favor.

The popularity found by the great Scotsman attracted a host of eager imitators among American writers. Cooper, Kennedy, Caruthers, Cooke, Simms, and Melville all wrote historical romances, and under their direction the province of this type of fiction soon embraced two of the three fields of the American novel of their period. These two fields were the colonial epoch and the Revolution. Relatively few frontier novels were historical. Before the Civil War much of the popular fiction was historical, but after 1865 the rise of realism tended to turn writers and readers from the traditional themes and periods. Still the lover of gaudy unreality could find diversion in pseudo-historical romances like *Ben-Hur* and *The Fair God*.

The nineties saw the flowering of our second great age of romantic fiction. By the beginnings of the eighties some of the English writers were in conscious rebellion against the rising schools of realism and naturalism. This revolt was led by Robert Louis Stevenson, whose romantic life and winning personality, coupled with a charming literary style, very deftly concealed the excessive thinness of his work. In America the call for colorful romance was joyously answered by many writers from 1890 to 1905. On the trail of Stevenson's *Treasure Island* and *Kidnapped* and Stanley Weyman's *The Red Cockade* came a huge flood of American romances, many of them distinctly of the historical variety. Among these may be mentioned S. Weir Mitchell's *Hugh Wynne,* Paul Leicester Ford's *Janice Meredith,* Maurice Thompson's *Alice of Old Vincennes,* Gertrude Atherton's *The Conqueror,* and Ellen Glasgow's *The Battleground.* To-day the sadly tarnished glitter of these books is a melancholy mark of the passage of time and the shift in public taste, though all of the titles are in considerable demand at public libraries, and almost any reader can find in the list one book that will assist in the lightening of a dull afternoon when the sluggish imagination refuses high flights and when the weather and the disposition alike refuse to welcome the unstimulating verity of realism.

Along with the relatively successful historical romances of the period went a group of indisputable failures, and one of the disheartening aspects of our taste for sugared history is the fact that the artistic failures sold as well as the more successful books. George Barr McCutcheon's *Graustark,* and Robert W. Chambers's *Cardigan* seemed to be caricatures of the historical romance, but the nadir of inanity was reached in Charles Major's *When Knighthood Was in Flower* and *Dorothy Vernon of Haddon Hall.* The silliest motion picture of to-day is no worse than these confections.

Historical novels were immensely popular in this country from 1890 to 1905, but unaided they could not satisfy our appetite for romance. Many authors forsook the standardized pattern of the historical romancers and wrote dozens of popular novels that owed their great successes to the sentimental treatment of some stock theme that could hardly be called historical. Many of these novels were only local color stories of the preceding decade refurbished to suit the demands of the nineties and expanded to book form. Thomas Nelson Page's *Red Rock* retold with tearful sympathy the sad story of life in Virginia just after the Civil War, but it should be noted that this story ends happily with the marriage of the southern hero and the northern heroine. F. Hopkinson Smith in *Colonel Carter of Cartersville* idealized the southern gentleman. Owen Wister wrote *The Virginian,* a story of Wyoming life, that became the respectable ancestor of a whole flock of tawdry and meretricious descendants done by innumerable hack-writers. Edward Noyes Westcott's *David Harum,* the best-seller of the day, was a book-length portrait of the canny Yankee trader and "crackerbox" philosopher. John Fox, Jr., did unspeakable violence to the poor whites of the Cumberlands in order to produce the drooling sentiment of *The Little Shepherd of Kingdom Come* and *The Trail of the Lonesome Pine*. And just as Charles Major succeeded in taking the historical romance into hitherto unexplored depths of imbecility, so did Gene Stratton-Porter outdo her rivals in the sentimental treatment of nature and human character. *Freckles* (1903) was Mrs. Porter's first contribution to the orgy of debased romance. Unfortunately it was neither her worst nor her last. Upon the sure foundations laid by the preceding writers, Harold Bell Wright has continued to rear his sugar castles, each containing a moral that is indisputably unchallengeable and equally hackneyed.

The Romance of Business.—During the years of our great national prosperity following the election of McKinley in 1896, another distinct type of romance was devised for the glorification and delight of the hard-working, successful American business man. This type has been variously denominated. Mr. Parrington refers to it as "Rotarian romance," while others have called it "the romance of business" or the "S.E.P. School," after the *Saturday Evening Post*, the jealous guardian of the school's traditions as well as the Mæcenas of those writers fortunate enough to capture its favor. It was fitting that George Horace Lorimer, the editor of the *Post*, should himself set the pitch for his writers. This act he performed in *Letters from a Self-made Merchant to His Son* (1902). These letters preach the gospel of thrift and industry in no strikingly original fashion and at the same time gently satirize the college bred who is forced to unlearn everything for which he has just spent his time and money, before he can be a fit and capable unit in our undistinguished middle-class society.

Most of the products of this school had but little distinction, and few of them ever saw book form. In its flower, probably *Calumet K* by Samuel Merwin and Henry K. Webster, the Rotarian romance is a pæan to the American business man's hustle and his ability to surmount such hurdles as can be raised by labor organizers, unscrupulous rivals, or adverse business conditions. Efficiency sets the tone for the whole story. A love affair can be tucked in between the dictation of momentous letters and an important business conference just as dexterously as the hero can take care of two jobs in the time allotted to one. Naturally the interest of the characters and their creator is in business success, and this interest pretty effectually eliminates all consideration of ethics. George Randolph Chester wrote some delicious satires, consciously or otherwise, of this school in his stories that centered about "Get-Rich-Quick" Wallingford.

Francis Marion Crawford (*1854-1909*).—There are three romancers of the period who deserve slightly more than casual notice. These three are Francis Marion Crawford, Mary Johnston, and Winston Churchill.

Crawford was born in Italy, he lived in that country most of his life, and his most successful novels were placed in the society of modern Rome, but he is always considered an American writer, and with very good reason, for he kept in close touch with the tastes and desires of a portion of the intelligent American reading public, and he typifies the best aspects of our last period of romance.

Crawford consciously set himself to oppose Howells and the realists by insisting that the novel should be concerned primarily with the story. Writing books that accorded with his theory of literature, he stressed vivid color, action, adventure, artificial plot, and unusual characters. He declared open opposition to the problem novel, evidently because that type made certain intellectual demands upon the reader, for he tried to write novels that would concentrate the whole attention upon plot development, just as the well-made play attempted to keep an audience interested in a cleverly arranged sequence of artificial situations. But on the other hand he refused to let the local colorists beguile him into their extravagances. To Crawford the novel had to be a "pocket-drama" with quick action. He thought that the scene should be laid far enough away from present problems that no reader could be teased into doing any serious thinking as the result of perusing a novel, and he insisted that the writer must not make too close a study of the manners of any one generation, for it was the business of a novelist to tell a story and not to write a social history. So clearly did Crawford state his creed, and so intelligently did he construct his novels according to that creed, that he became the most capable champion of the American romantics, just as Howells was the acknowledged leader of the realists.

Crawford wrote a large number of novels in a rather short life, but in all his books he is entertaining, and in some he reaches a high degree of narrative skill. His first book was *Mr. Isaacs* (1882), the story of a Persian jewel merchant. The great success of this novel determined the course of his future career. *A Roman Singer* (1884) is built about the love of an Italian singer of low birth for a Prussian noblewoman. *Via Crucis* (1898) is a story of the Crusades. *In the Palace of the King* (1900) compresses into the action of a few hours much of the traditional romance that has gathered about Don Juan of Austria. Nearly all recent critics have agreed that Crawford's best work is to be found in his four novels of modern Rome that tell of the fortunes of the Saracinesca family. These books are *Saracinesca* (1887), *Sant' Ilario* (1889), *Don Orsino* (1892) and *Corleone* (1896). The series is highly unified in that all the books have about the same characters, but the first two novels in the group seem to have more vitality than the other two. It is something of a commentary on the taste of the present age that the Saracinesca series should be the most popular of Crawford's works, for these novels are the ones in which the author came nearest to realistic methods. Crawford knew Roman society, and in these books he did not exclude all his knowledge of this interesting subject in order to speed up the action.

As a novelist Crawford excels only in plot movement. He tells a story well, so very well that the reader overlooks the flagrant use of time-honored melodramatic devices, the inability to create convincing characters, and the many artificial props used to sustain the suspense.

Mary Johnston (*1870-1936*).—Mary Johnston is one historical romancer who has refused to allow the calls of realism, sociology, satire, or local color to divert her permanently from her original interest. For more than thirty years she has ranged the field of American history to choose with an accurate judgment the periods and episodes that lend themselves most agreeably to the needs of the romancer. Her first novel, *Prisoners of Hope* (1898), is an excellent though very romantic treatment of life in early colonial Virginia. She followed this book with such titles as *To Have and To Hold, The Long Roll, Cease Firing, Croaton, The Slave Ship* and *1492*. Despite the essential monotony of these books, all of them are good reading. Certainly they give the author a high position in the ranks of our historical novelists.

Like most of her school, Miss Johnston uses many ancient but efficacious devices of narration and characterization. She has almost an obsession for imperious heroines and for heroes who are ambidextrous in the use of deadly weapons, either rapier, pistol, or rifle. Nor is she a stranger to the venerable trick of disguising the highborn gentleman as a serving-man. In short Miss Johnston seldom startles the reader with an original turn, though occasionally the ordinary appeal to sentiment is whetted by the use of a tragic ending. The highest possible praise for the author is to be found in her continued popularity in an age that considers historical romances old-fashioned.

Winston Churchill (1871-1947).—The Spanish-American War startled the nation out of the spiritual sloth of the Gilded Age. The ostensible idealism of the crusade to free Cuba from the tyranny of alien rule and the surging patriotism that followed our triumph of arms almost made our people explode with pride over the greatness and the altruistic motives of the United States. In those hectic days Mr. Roosevelt came to the Presidency and under his strenuous leadership the naïve, moral fervor of the nation had no chance to grow sluggish. Tirelessly the President flogged our civic conscience into activity, appealing always to the heroic strain in us with strident exhortations to achieve high ideals through the exercise of simple virtues. As a result of the Spanish war and the moral earnestness of Mr. Roosevelt, we Americans thrilled to the discovery that we lived in a great and noble nation. Just at this moment Winston Churchill appointed himself to the task of demonstrating that our past was altogether worthy of our glorious present.

Churchill was well qualified for his chosen work. He was born in St. Louis, a city that was sharply divided in allegiance during the Civil War, and in the novelist's boyhood the passions of the struggle slowly cooled to a sympathetic understanding of both antagonists. He was educated at the United States Naval Academy, where, it is not unlikely to suppose, he absorbed some regard for the history and destiny of his nation. He had sufficient intelligence and learning to invest the backgrounds of his novels with a satisfying air of veracity. Furthermore Churchill's temper was as idealistic as even Mr. Roosevelt could have wished in either a historian or a romancer.

Thus admirably equipped, both intellectually and temperamentally, to provide the desired fiction for his contemporaries, Churchill naturally became one of the favored novelists of all time in our literature. His reputation as a historical romancer rests on three books, *Richard Carvel*, *The Crisis*, and *The Crossing*. The subject matter of each of these novels was chosen with a fine discernment of what the American public wanted to read. First came *Richard Carvel* (1898), a story of the Revolution with a good patriot for a

hero and a Loyalist for the villain and with John Paul Jones contributing to both the historical atmosphere and the heroic strain. Of
course there was a satisfying love element, and the end showed the
conclusive triumph of patriotism, moral goodness, and youthful love.
The nineties would have had to be far more critical of literary performances than they actually were, if they had rejected this agreeable dénouement. In *The Crisis* Churchill chose another climactic
moment in our history, the days of the Civil War when St. Louis
was torn between two hostile factions. For purposes of dramatic
interest he typified the cavalier spirit of the South in a proud,
vivacious heroine, while he embodied the phlegmatic Puritanism of
the North in a quiet, determined hero. Again the novel moved on
through a variety of thrills and complications to a most satisfactory
ending. With *The Crossing* Churchill seized upon what seems to be
the most dramatic and the most neglected aspect of our history,
the migration to the West from the Atlantic seaboard. The action
of the book starts in the days of the Revolution with the bombardment of Charleston and proceeds westward into Kentucky with a
goodly number of Indian fights on the way. Then comes the sensational expedition of George Rogers Clark against the English posts
of the Northwest Territory. The latter half of the book declines
sharply in spite of the introduction of young Andrew Jackson, but
the first half glows with genuine romantic ardor. *The Crossing* was
a worthy end to Mr. Churchill's romanticization of our past.

By 1905 the historical romance was clearly becoming out-moded.
We had been most satisfactorily reassured as to the worthiness and
nobility of our history. Then the horrid thought intruded that
perhaps our present was not all that it might be, notwithstanding
the labors and the certitude of President Roosevelt. The idealistic
Mr. Churchill never hesitated. He plunged into a series of competent social studies that completely removed him from the province
of the historical romance and transferred him to the ranks of sociological novelists. Better than any other one writer he typifies
the progress of our national hopes and fears from 1898 to the
outbreak of the World War.

SOCIOLOGY

The Sociological Novel.—The second opponent of naturalism was
the sociological novel, a literary type so congenial to the spirit of

the American people from 1903 to 1917 that it swept the historical romance out of existence and kept the naturalistic novelists in an inconspicuous position for more than a decade. So popular was the new variety of fiction that potential naturalists like Robert Herrick and Jack London were drawn into the new field, and many of the historical romancers permanently deserted their earlier tasks to write sociological novels.

From the opening of the century to 1917 we suffered our first acute attack of self-criticism. The work of the naturalists, both native and foreign, had directed the attention of many readers to deplorable conditions in modern social life, and from the presentation of undesirable facts to the discussion of ways and means for bettering them is only a step. Social problems in our cities and in the rural districts were demanding thoughtful consideration. A new critical spirit was abroad that spared no aspect of our national life, however ancient or respected. Furthermore the moral lash wielded by the President could not forever drive us into a crusading zeal that might be appeased by incursions against error in alien lands. The natural result of these influences was a righteous fervor against indigenous wrongs, and during the Roosevelt régime our nation developed a sensitive social conscience that was reflected in the work of our muck-raking journalists, in the multifarious activities of our political and literary insurgents, and in the huge output of deadly serious sociological novels.

The Problem Novel.—The problem novel was the product of the Gilded Age. This type of fiction consciously subordinates plot and characterization to the study of a definite question, usually social Such a novel does not suggest remedies for conditions discussed; it rests its case upon the statement of fact that is presented with absolutely no coloration or philosophical bias. This type of fiction is, therefore, rather simple, almost naïve in its method. It is the kind of novel that a man or a group first writes under the impact of the discovery that all is not gladsome in social life. The crass materialism of the Gilded Age forced intelligent citizens to give heed to the questions of social import, and out of the fact-finding and the thinking of many writers came our problem novel.

This novel as it was written from 1870 to 1900 covers a wide expanse, though it generally treats some aspect of our political or economic life. However, some of the most valuable are studies of our national culture, using the term in a rather narrow sense. Probably the first problem novel in our literature after the Civil War is *The Gilded Age* by Mark Twain and Charles Dudley Warner. This book is about the only one of its class that can be read to-day with pleasure, and its owes its longevity to the satirical power of Mark Twain. Albion W. Tourgée presented some of the problems of reconstruction in *Figs and Thistles, A Fool's Errand* and *Bricks Without Straw,* novels that are not so well known as they should be. In 1880 Henry Adams anonymously published *Democracy,* a work quite typical of its class both in the indifferent telling of the story and in its trenchant observations on national politics. Three years later Adams's friend, John Hay, wrote *The Bread-Winners,* a study of capital and labor that was notable for its chilly attitude toward the worker. Francis Marion Crawford attempted a problem novel in *An American Politician* with no marked success. Bellamy's *Looking Backward* is generally regarded as a problem novel. Among the many other writers who did fiction of this type the most successful were H. H. Boyesen, Henry B. Fuller, and Harold Frederic. These last dwelt on the tawdry vulgarity of the age and the brazen audacity of the social climber who had no qualification save well-financed ambition. The efforts of the established order, the old respectables, to repel the assaults of the newly enriched "Goths" later afforded Edith Wharton with an agreeable theme.

The Muck-rakers.—The study of American life from 1870 to 1900 convinced many that the one original evil in our national life was a rabid economics that controlled our politics, our newspapers, and even our educational system. The sole cause of our political corruption was declared to be the willingness of the beneficiaries of special privileges to pay huge bribes for the legal right to plunder the people through excessive charges for various services. Those who devoted themselves to the odoriferous task of digging up proof of this contention were called muck-rakers. The energetic labors of these writers exhumed an appalling number of ancient scandals and many a one that was not so antique. Admittedly the muck-rakers were guilty of excesses, but the facts that they uncovered certainly tended to support their charges that an alliance existed between rapacious business concerns and corrupt politicians. The alleged facts did not convince every one, indeed, some declared that few facts had been established, but the good result of the muck-raking movement was the turning of many people, believers and skeptics alike, into socially minded critics or defenders of our economic and political establishments.

Contrary to the opinions of many, the muck-raking movement was not launched against the mere possession of wealth. Government by a rapacious autocracy was the object of the attack. The din of the attack fell pleasantly on the ears of critical Americans, for by 1905 many people were convinced that the time was out of joint and that vociferous advice to achieve social well-being through the individual living of simple, virtuous, and heroic lives might not be based on a correct diagnosis of our ills and might not contain the proper prescription for the social malady. Popular magazines gladly joined the crusade against Mammon and its auxiliaries, and scarcely a month passed that some newly discovered scandal was not given a public hearing. The possession of wealth did not of itself lay a man open to attack, but many a captain of industry found to his surprise that his money did not make him immune to criticism in the magazines and newspapers.

The names of the chief muck-rakers became household words, and many are remembered to this day. Among the most conspicuous were Gustavus Myers, Ray Stannard Baker, Ida Tarbell, Lincoln Steffens, Charles Edward Russell, and Upton Sinclair. To-day the old crusading spirit seems to have departed from all except the last. Mr. Sinclair still has the divine gift of righteous indignation, but most of the others have sunk into respectable desuetude. Probably the best and most scientific work produced by the school was *The Shame of the Cities* by Lincoln Steffens. This book bares the machinery of our extra-legal city governments and shows how corruption comes through the willingness of greedy corporations and individuals to give bribes and the corresponding alacrity of avaricious politicians to grant inordinate privileges in return. Mr. Steffens pointed out that the monstrous conditions were caused by a surreptitious but widespread system that was really the governing body in virtually all our largest cities.

Upton Sinclair (1878-   ).—The career of Upton Sinclair shows what has happened to American artists times without number. Sinclair is at heart a fine creative artist. He sees vividly, he has a warm human sympathy, he has intelligence, and above all he has an enviable facility in the apt and forceful use of words. He began his work as a novelist of more than a little promise, but social studies gradually led him into the ways of the propagandist, and to-day he is more interested in politics than in art, more concerned with economics than with the wizardry of words, more anxious to pillory capitalism and all its minions than to experiment with the nuances of style.

Sinclair completed his formal education with some years as a post-graduate student in Columbia University. He gained a bit of fame as a poet and novelist, and before he was twenty-seven he had written *Manassas,* a novel of the Civil War that was cast almost in epic mold. The turn came in 1906 when he assisted in a governmental investigation of the Chicago stock-yards. Out of that experience came *The Jungle,* an exposure of the nauseating conditions prevailing in the great meat-packing plants. This book was one of the most startling and effective ever to impinge upon American consciousness. It aroused a roar of indignation against the packers. The President ordered an investigation of the plants, and while public opinion still seethed, Congress passed our first national pure food legislation. After this episode Sinclair became a pamphleteer and propagandist, but that he can still write a moving novel he proved in the recent publication of *Boston.* However, this long and effective work grew out of the author's reactions to the famous Sacco-Vanzetti case.

In his later novels, Sinclair frequently allows argument to submerge art, but in some his narrative skill keeps the story from degenerating into a tract. *The Jungle* has tremendous power. The accounts of conditions in the packing plants are vivid enough in all conscience, but the finest thing in the book is the sympathetic treatment of the ignorant and helpless workers, exploited and debauched by brutal superiors, who in turn are fast in the grip of a callous industrial system. There are descriptions of physical sensations in this book that in effectiveness compare favorably with similar passages in any recent literature. One sees, and smells, and feels at the behest of the writer, and there is no stricter test of effective writing. *King Coal,* a story of the strikes in the Colorado coal fields, has been called Sinclair's most skillful book. Certainly it holds together better than most of the others. *Jimmie Higgins* and *100%* grew out of the hysterical fervor of our society during the World War. *They Call Me Carpenter* is a study of religion that has all the aspects of a tract. *Boston* was a deserved success. In this book Sinclair's deep and quietly expressed sympathy for the defeated and helpless gives the novel an impressive dignity and power.

In recent years Sinclair's critical studies of American society have received considerable attention. This series began in 1918 with *The Profits of Religion,* a vitriolic assault on organized religion in this country. With his deep suspicions of capitalism and his lack of sympathy with organized religion, Sinclair was quick to allege a corrupt coalition of the two. This study was followed by *The Brass Check,* a cogent attempt to prove the influence of big business upon the newspapers from which we are supposed to form our public opinion. Certainly the book is too strident, and many of the conclusions may be forced, but without doubt it caused Americans to do some serious thinking about the accuracy of the news that they had been accepting as unquestionable. *The Goose Step* is a study of the alleged influence of capitalism in our colleges and universities. *Mammonart* and *Money Writes,* the latest additions to the series, attempt to show the nefarious influence of wealth in our artistic and literary activities. The argument in the last two books becomes extremely tenuous.

This series of propagandist tracts shows Sinclair at his strongest and weakest. His strength is a passion for social justice and the ability to translate that passion into moving words. His weaknesses are a morbid distrust of capitalism and an insuperable desire to play the martyr. Wherever Mr. Sinclair can come across an audience he mounts his portable soap-box, lifts his hair shirt, and displays the marks of the knout. And so pathologically suspicious is he that he magnifies the most trivial affronts or mere coincidences into positive evidence of dark capitalistic conspiracies against society and especially against Upton Sinclair. But despite these debilitating weaknesses, he is an important figure in the history of American social protest. Certain critics have placed him with the "ragged philosophers" along with Tom Paine. The classification is apt. Both men loved the common man and hated oppression; both ardently desired freedom for all from every form of tyranny; both felt the lash of social disapproval; both, probably, would be satisfied with an appraisal that placed them together.

Insurgency in Politics.—However clamorous the muck-rakers became, and however salutary may have been some of the results that they achieved, their revelations had no effect whatever upon the steady progress of the centralization of our economics. Since the

Civil War corporations have been growing larger, and more and more essential products and services of industry have become the exclusive prerogatives of a few "trusts," as the huge monopolies were called. The critical papers of the late nineties and the early nineteen hundreds were filled with cartoons that showed the consumer helpless in the hands of some trust. Old-time competition was tending to disappear in the field of production and distribution. It was alleged that the great oil, coal, steel, meat, and machinery companies either had monopolies in their respective fields or had an agreement with their ostensible rivals which effectually abolished competitive selling and consequent lower prices to the consumer. Such conditions were immensely lucrative to the large companies, and almost all of the producing or service corporations in the country were trying to effect monopolistic control or an amicable agreement with their competitors. Defenders of the new system said that large corporations could pay higher dividends to the stockholders and allow lower prices to the consumer than could a system of cutthroat competition, for the formation of one company from a dozen small ones would bring many economies in buying, selling, and management. The money thus saved would mean larger dividends and lower prices at the same time. Despite these reassuring words, many took fright at control by the trusts, and the thoughtful discerned a serious problem in the situation.

The problem was political. The business interests of the nation have never been without influence in our national and state governments, but as the large corporations increased in size and number, they exerted a correspondingly increased pressure upon the government. Students of American life declared that they discerned a threat to political democracy through the breakdown of genuinely representative government, for the voice of big business seemed to be more potent in our legislative halls than was the collective will of the people. Many senators and representatives were publicly denounced as mouthpieces or flunkies of special privilege, and the state legislators were even more fiercely assailed. The whole problem, said the critics of business, was that of guaranteeing popular control of legislation in a highly undemocratic economic life.

Under the stimulus of popular unrest our state and national legislatures passed a quantity of new laws that were designed to curb the evils that were increasingly apparent. This legislation was in two fields, the purely economic and the political. In the latter field were waged most of the sensational battles from 1890 to 1917. The first attack made in the name of democracy was an attempt to wrest control of the political parties from the beneficiaries of special privilege and their henchmen and to make those organizations reasonably responsive to the will of the majority. The first blow in this battle was the reform of the civil service. Beginning in the early eighties and extending to the present, a series of laws, national, state, and municipal, resulted in the establishment of at least the principle of appointive officeholding on the basis of merit only. This legislation helped to banish the old system whereby party workers were rewarded by positions on the public payroll. The next step in the ridding of the parties from domination by professional politicians in league with privileged corporations was the adoption of the secret ballot. This reform greatly discouraged the practice of buying votes at the polls, for no purchaser could be sure of receiving what he paid for. These two innovations, civil service reform and the Australian ballot, as secret voting was called, were most needed and salutary reforms, but far more radical proposals were in the offing.

The most effective instrument for the restoring of popular control over representative government was the adoption of the initiative, referendum, and recall by numerous states. These expedients carried to its logical conclusion the major premise of American democracy by giving to the voters the right to initiate and pass laws, to annul laws previously passed by the legislature, and to remove from office those officials whose conduct was displeasing to their constituents. In some states the recall was extended to include judges. The battle over these proposals raged for more than twenty years, apparently coming to an end about 1920 with one or more of the reforms effective in about half the states.

Another sweeping reform was the abolition of the old-time nominating convention with its retinue of professional politicians, manipulators working for special interests, and nondescript hangers-on. Under pressure from political progressives, candidates for state offices generally came to be nominated by direct vote of the people, and in many states delegates to the national conventions that name candidates for the Presidency were placed under definite instructions to vote for a specific man. But the most spectacular and significant battle in this campaign was that joined over the direct election of United States senators. According to the federal constitution, senators were named by state legislatures without reference to the wishes of the electorate. Under this system the Senate had come to be the most exclusive club in the world. Usually those senators who were not themselves captains of industry and recipients of special privilege were the legal representatives of corporate enterprise, and the reformers insistently declared that popular rights and desires were about the last consideration of the august assemblage. Attempts to pass legislation that would make the Senate more responsive to popular will were checked in the very body that was under criticism. Finally certain states allowed the voters to express their preference of the candidates running for the Senate with the understanding that this preference would be ratified by the legislature. Then after the lapse of several years, a constitutional amendment was adopted that provided for the direct election of United States senators.

The reforms just enumerated are typical of the changes wrought by our political progressives. Virtually all of these innovations were first proposed by the agrarians of the West from 1866 to 1890, and most of them were elaborately discussed and advocated by the Populists of the eighties and nineties. Many were also to be found in the platforms and resolutions of the American Federation of Labor. The net result of the reforms was to establish more firmly the principles and practice of popular government. The new expedients carried on the tradition of Jefferson and Lincoln; they kept alive the faith of the romantics in the dignity and worth of the individual; at all events they tided traditional American individualism over a time of perplexity and enabled that valuable quality to stay alive until we recover our poise and set a new course in a totally changed social order. Certainly the old-time individualism is outgrown, and one of the chief tasks of our thinkers and seers is to define a new type. That task was begun in 1910, and in 1930 it is barely started. In the meantime the progressive reforms saved the people many a dollar that was doled out to privilege in the earlier day, but the innovations were more important in that they saved some shreds of popular self-respect.

Economic Insurgency.—The continued growth of great fortunes and the centralization of our economic life in a relatively small number of enterprises with immense power in the hands of a few men seemed to many people an ominous threat. If competition was at an end, to depend upon the old economic theory of laissez-faire was futile and even dangerous. The work of the muck-rakers and their kind had demonstrated to the satisfaction of many that political and social abuses generally rest upon an economic foundation. The firm conclusion was that something must be done to meet the threat to our institutions, to curb the power of predatory wealth, and to establish a measure of the democracy in economics that our new reforms had just set up in our political life.

There were three main proposals for proceeding. The ultra-conservatives, strongly supported by business enterprise, wished a continuance of the principle of laissez-faire. Another group urged a definite return to the competitive system with large numbers of competitors in every field. The aims of this group were best expressed in *The New Freedom* by Woodrow Wilson, but even this skillful advocate and acute thinker could hardly tell exactly how the desired consummation was to be brought to pass. Still another faction approved of the centralization of our economics and insisted that the process be allowed to continue under strict governmental supervision. People who held this view varied all the way in political complexion from liberal Democrats and mild Progressives to the most radical Socialists. From the viewpoint of 1930 it seems that the ideas of this group have been adopted in practice, but opinions are yet widely at variance over both the desirability and the efficacy of our governmental supervision. At all events the three-cornered debate generated enough heat that popular insistence forced the adoption of certain laws that were of some little immediate importance and of more than a little significance. The passage of this legislation extended over a period of thirty years.

Among the laws to regulate business, none was more important than were the various acts that established the Interstate Commerce Commission and gave that body its great powers over all matters pertaining to railroads. While the Commission was developing its powers to the lugubrious plaints of the reactionaries because of governmental interference with private business, a large body of anti-trust legislation was placed on the books. To-day most of the regulations seem to be as obsolete as the Salic Law, but in their time they helped to allay the fears of timid persons, and their sanction by the courts established permanently the right of government to regulate business corporations. Another step in the interference with private business was the establishment of a tax on incomes, both personal and corporate. In the early nineties a law levying such a tax was declared unconstitutional. Thereafter the question was intermittently under discussion until the Taft administration, when a constitutional amendment was adopted that permitted the collection of the tax. While the government was making these inroads upon the sanctity of wealth and the policy of laissez-faire, the individual states were passing similar laws. The most significant laws passed by the commonwealths were those protecting labor. Legislatures generally adopted the eight-hour day for industry, a minimum wage for women, industrial insurance, and employers' liability. Heated arguments and numerous judicial decisions marked the progress of these reforms, but in the end governmental control over private business seemed to be unreservedly sanctioned.

The net result of this legislation was unmistakable progress toward social democracy. The World War put an end to this period of ebullient reform, but whether the stoppage was only temporary or whether it was for all time, only the future can tell. The era of militant democracy, both political and economic, left its traces deep in our literature. Among the poets the new social conscience is shown by Masters, Lindsay, Sandburg, James Oppenheim, Arturo Giovannitti, and a whole flock of minor radicals.

Literary Insurgency.—The critical spirit loosed between 1900 and 1912 could not be confined to political campaigns and legislative halls. It overflowed into our literature, showing up in every place from newspaper editorials and political tracts to novels and poetry. To-day much of it is ancient history. A book like William Allen White's *The Old Order Changeth* sounds medieval, for it was written with the ecstatic fervor of a liberal who saw all around him the signs of a new day. Even the penetrating studies of the economic determinists are a bit aged, and people have ceased to be stirred to anger or enthusiasm by any of the political and economic critics. However, there was a small group of young and clamorous writers whose works done before 1918 still move the complacent conservatives to righteous anger.

These young social and literary critics made an impudent and vigorous assault upon all the fetishes of American cultural life. Some of the writers were of European blood, others had been educated abroad, while all had a well-filled arsenal of recent cosmopolitan thought from which they could draw ammunition to use in the bombardment of our native culture. The chief aversions of the youngsters were our venerable but rather antiquated Puritanism, our middle-class ideals, our oft-repeated optimism, our sentimentality, and the heavy stupidity of our national culture. Puritanism was a conspicuous target in the battle that was shortly joined, for truly it had lost much of its vitality and had become only the dead hand of a repressive tradition laid upon the present. The defenders of Puritanism were few in number and feeble in spirit, but around the standards of middle-class America rallied an army to give battle worthily for the ideals of their group. The most revered of these ideals was that of genteel respectability. It was the ideal of Longfellow and Lowell positively denuded of intellectual implications and wholly standardized to meet the cultural needs of a people to whom culture meant nothing more vital than vaguely polite references to literature that was far enough away from the tumultuous present to have no significance. Whatever may be the merits of that controversy which still rumbles on with diminished fury, the middleclass defenders fought fiercely, and in the young critics they found fit opponents who fairly reveled in breaking heads and sustaining savage blows. In the general combat sentimentality and optimism were discovered to have many devotees but few defenders.

The names of the young critics are well-known. H. L. Mencken and George Jean Nathan, at first editors of *The Smart Set* and later founders of *The American Mercury*, were probably the most conspicuous of the group. Both men are able writers and sensible critics, and no record of our recent critical activities can fail to take the two into account. As a controversial writer and as a dangerous opponent Mr. Mencken has no superior in this country and few equals. Randolph Bourne was another of the group. Still others were Walter Lippmann, Francis Hackett, Van Wyck Brooks, and Ludwig Lewisohn. The founding of *The New Republic* gave positions to certain of these critics on the editorial staff, while others were contributors. This paper was recognized from the start as an exceptionally well-written journal of independent opinion. Among intellectuals its influence has been large. After wandering for years in a very sterile wilderness, *The Nation* emerged during the war as the most outspoken of the liberal papers. Under the editorship of its owner, Oswald Garrison Villard, grandson of William Lloyd Garrison, this weekly is distinguished at once for its liberal views and its high journalistic standards. Such were the literary insurgents and some of their journals.

Although the representatives of the genteel still loftily refuse recognition to the younger critics and contemptuously refer to Mr. Mencken as a vulgarian, the importance of the new school cannot be overlooked and should not be minimized. A large amount of American literature since 1912 has come directly or indirectly as a result of some form of this literary insurgency. Among the infected writers who may be named are Sinclair Lewis, Sherwood Anderson, James Branch Cabell, Edgar Lee Masters, Carl Sandburg, Zona Gale and Ellen Glasgow. The so-called "Battle of the Village" in our letters was the direct result of the new social criticism, and the defense of the village by William Allen White, Booth Tarkington, and Dorothy Canfield Fisher was made necessary by these attacks.

The foreign thought previously referred to that supplied the young critics with some of their material embraced everything from musical criticism to psychology, from philosophy to communistic propaganda. Much of this cosmopolitan thought and great numbers of European writers were introduced to American readers through the work of James Huneker (1860-1921) whose critical writings on the drama, fiction, painting, and music of contemporary Europe mark a new era in our appreciation of the arts that he discussed and still more emphatically mark a new era in American criticism. Mr. Huneker first made readers in this country aware of the existence of such men as Degas, Monet, Manet, Cézanne, Huysmans, Barrès, Synge, Remy de Gourmont, Stravinsky, Schoenberg, Ibsen, and Nietzsche. The last two may not have been introduced to America by Huneker, but he first gave them intelligent critical treatment. In fact, he ranged over the whole of European thought, neglecting only economics and social philosophy, and then translated his findings for his American readers. His work may not be of eternal importance, but it was a most potent and liberalizing influence in the education of adult America from 1900 to 1921. During the years of Huneker's great activity, Mr. Mencken was spreading the essentials of the Nietzschean philosophy in this country. Linked with the current psychology Nietzsche's theory of biological aristocracy is one of the most popular ideas now abroad in the reputed cradle of democracy. Almost all of the other young critics popularized or introduced some phase of European thought on this side of the Atlantic.

Winston Churchill.—Mr. Churchill is notable for the acuteness with which he sensed the tastes of the American people and the closeness with which he followed those tastes in his novels. Accordingly in the early years of the century we expect to find him producing books that reflect the progressive political thought of the time. Nor are we disappointed. *Coniston* (1906) might have been done by one of the more temperate and competent muck-rakers as a political biography. The book sets forth the familiar thesis that the "interests" controlling legislatures are seekers after special privileges and that the chief worker for these privileged corporations is a corrupt "boss." *Coniston* is an occasional novel, almost a case-book in political manipulation, but it is done on a large enough scale and with a close enough knowledge of facts to make it an impressive document. The "interests" in *Coniston* are the railroads, and a few years after the publication of the novel, Mr. Churchill ran for governor of New Hampshire on a platform of opposition to the political power of the railroads. He was defeated. *Mr. Crewe's Career* (1908) tells of the control of legislation and other governmental activities of a state by the legal representative of the capitalist who lives in New York. It is an attack on absentee political landlordism with sharp insistence on the need for the development of a social conscience.

From politics Mr. Churchill proceeded naturally to economic themes, just as the thinking of the Americans proceeded. His first attempt in this field was *The Inside of the Cup* (1913), a discussion of the problems of the Christian church and especially of the socially minded minister in a capitalistic world. As a novel the work is not a great success, for argument so overwhelms art that some of the chapters read like sociological discussions. The underlying argument is that the church should discard the worn-out dogmas and revert to the teaching of a social Christianity. In his insistence that business usually controls the church because of the liberality of its contributions, Mr. Churchill joins hands with Upton Sinclair. *A Far Country* (1915) shows that personal satisfaction does not always follow great success in business. *The Dwelling Place of Light* (1917) is an attack on industrialism for what it has done to the native American stock that has not managed to climb into the employers' class. Churchill is greatly disturbed because industrialization is forcing a potentially valuable group in our society to lose its independence and its satisfaction in the accomplishment of individual, creative work.

Churchill's sociological novels are not widely read to-day, though all of them find occasional readers, but they deserve to keep a place in literary history because they so well represent our interests from

1900 to 1917 and because they are probably the clearest expression in our literature of the intellectual, crusading progressive who intelligently examined American life and found it lacking. Churchill is more intellectual than is William Allen White, and far more cosmopolitan in his background. However, his cosmopolitanism stops short of socialistic implications. He is committed to traditional American individualism, and he supports this commitment with the liberal philosophy of a Jeffersonian democrat.

Robert Herrick (*1868-1938*).—The novels of Robert Herrick show what happens when the fine old Puritan conscience, completely socialized to meet the present situation, is brought into contact with the modern industrialized city and its horde of attendant problems. Herrick was born in Cambridge, Massachusetts, and educated at Harvard. In 1893 at the age of twenty-five he joined the English department of the University of Chicago where he remained for thirty years. The Chicago of the nineties was a "boom-town" of the frontier on a huge scale, charged with dynamic energy and guided by men whose fortunes were in keeping with the spirit and size of the city. Just after the World's Fair in 1893, Chicago business was paralyzed by a panic and in the middle of the depression the grim Pullman strike in the car shops spread to the railroads and ultimately threatened civil war. The strike imperatively directed attention to the situation in Chicago. A few powerful magnates in finance, transportation, meat-packing, and manufacturing stood at the head of as conglomerate a society as the world ever saw. Below these magnates, far below them, the small business men, skilled workmen, and common laborers were ranged in economic importance. The upper class was complacently satisfied with the best of all possible arrangements. The middle class was nonplused or vaguely dissatisfied, while the lower class in swarming numbers sullenly labored, remembering such old sores as the Haymarket Riot and accumulating new causes for dissatisfaction. The panic of 1893 and the Pullman strike brought the problems of Chicago into high relief and loudly challenged the mind and conscience of the young English teacher at the new university.

Herrick brought to a consideration of these problems an admirable moral and intellectual equipment. He had a socialized Puritan conscience, a mind that carried a full complement of philosophical and sociological thought, and a disposition to inquire into the causes and results of Chicago life. One problem that particularly interested him was the question of the effect of capitalistic economics upon his own class of professional men. Again and again this question appears in Herrick's novels. Sometimes the protagonist is an architect, sometimes a lawyer, sometimes a doctor, but the underlying question is always the effect of unbridled acquisitiveness upon the group that traditionally supplies the finely idealistic leaders of society. Other problems enter the novels, such as the effect of business upon the business men's ideals, or the changing status of women and the home in a social order dominated by industry. These questions deeply disturbed the morally sensitive, intellectual observer that Herrick proved himself to be.

With such problems before him, Herrick consciously subordinated character and story to background and ideas, though his men and women are always human figures and not automatons. To Herrick the background creates the problems, hence it naturally assumes major importance in the study of those questions. In his study of the Chicago scene he has done many significant works, but three seem to be representative of the whole list. These three are *The Common Lot* (1904), *The Memoirs of an American Citizen* (1905), and *Waste* (1924). The first of these sets forth the clash of artistic ideals with the commercial spirit. The story is that of a young architect who is just beginning his professional career. He forms the acquaintance of a successful contractor for whom he designs buildings. The temptations created by sharp competition lead him into allowing his friend to erect buildings that do not conform to the specifications. Finally in return for an exceptionally bad concession he is promised some stock in a shoddily built hotel. Before the deal can be consummated, the hotel burns with the loss of eight lives, and the ensuing investigation brought the young architect's career down in ruins. The ideas of this novel are utilized also in *The Web of Life* and *A Life for a Life*.

The Memoirs of an American Citizen is one of the best studies in existence of an American businessman. Indeed many say that it is exceeded only by Dreiser's *The Financier,* but in restraint and narrative skill Herrick probably surpasses his fellow novelist. The story is that of a Nietzschean figure who climbs to the top of the meat-packing business over the remains of his less fortunate or less ruthless competitors and then goes to the United States Senate frankly as the representative of his class. This book has a thinness, not noticeable in *The Common Lot,* that probably arises from Herrick's lack of sympathy for his meat-packer. The architect and his problems in *The Common Lot* are more sympathetically presented. However, the story of Van Harrington's rise in Packingtown assuredly deserves better treatment than it has had from readers and critics.

Waste is reported to be the author's favorite book, and one has no difficulty in seeing the reason, for none of the novels contains so much of Robert Herrick. It is a long study with a host of characters that vividly dramatize the development of our social order in the generation marked by the World War. The book is the product of sharp observation and of unhurried reflection. Undoubtedly it is one of the most intelligent of recent novels. The most obvious flaw is indignation that at times almost chokes the author, though to many readers the chief defect is the lack of clarity and individualization in character creation. Like other books by Herrick, *Waste* can hardly be allowed to pass from our literature. Whatever judgment the esthetic critic may pass, the social historian will find it a quarry of pertinent facts and accurate observation. *Homely Lilla* (1923) seems to be a by-product of the huge labor that went into the making of *Waste*. Both of these novels show a tendency to make the woman an idealistic character in a world devoted to materialism.

The faults of Herrick as a novelist have been too often stressed by adverse critics. His style has been impeached for its lack of force and beauty, and his temper criticized because of his habit of rushing into indignation instead of checking himself at the more moving quality of pity. But his excellencies are too great to be overlooked, despite his failure to live up to canons set by men who have not a tithe of his honesty, intelligence, and social conscience and who have never engaged the problems that he set for himself. Not one of his novels lacks a definite idea behind it, and not one fails to give an intelligent discussion of that idea. Herrick hates the money-madness of our commercialism and the inanity of our cultural and spiritual life, and he has blazoned those hatreds on every page of his work. Such an accomplishment alone would give his work great significance to any student of our most critical epoch.

Jack London (*1876-1916*).—Herrick and Jack London were both potential naturalists. Herrick was deflected from his destined course by moral earnestness and intellectual interests, but Jack London was the bar-room socialist whose sympathies were enlisted in the cause of revolution through the feeling of kinship that he has with the lower classes. Herrick is the intellectual aristocrat, the austere Puritan with a chilly exterior and a flaming social conscience; London is a proletarian of vigorous, untrained intellect, who is ablaze with personal sympathy for the worker. The two are totally unlike in personality and background, yet they occupy neighboring niches in our library of social criticism and protest.

London grew up on San Francisco Bay. His formal education was rather sketchily accomplished, except for some work in the University of California, but his education in the ways and hopes of ordinary humanity was enviably complete. He went to sea as a common sailor, hunted seals in the north Pacific, joined in the rush to the Klondike, and tramped thousands of miles over this country and Canada; and these experiences, interpreted in the light of his enthusiastic reading in Darwin, Spencer, Nietzsche, and Marxian socialism, bore fruit in his best work.

London's first success, *The Call of the Wild* (1903), is a fine bit of writing, abounding in poetic descriptions of the primitive background, that tells of the relapse of a dog into the ways of his wild cousins, the northern wolves. It is altogether probable that in this book the author gave an allegorical treatment of certain unlovely and usually hidden aspects of human character, for the atavistic impulses of men never fail to interest London. *White Fang* is a kindred story. *The Sea Wolf* (1904) is a frank personification of Nietzscheanism. Wolf Larsen, the brutal sea-captain, stands as the ultimate of malignant will-to-power, housed in a body strong enough to force compliance with its demands. The book is amazingly effective, and if London had not slipped toward the end in the melodramatic introduction of a useless woman character, the novel would have been a masterpiece of dynamic strength.

London shows his true interests in such sociological works as *The War of the Classes* (1905), *The Iron Heel* (1908) and *The Revolution* (1910). These are socialistic predictions and descriptions of the impending class war and the resultant revolution in society. The socialism that London espouses is not founded upon intellectual premises or humanitarian argument but wholly upon his sympathy for the clean-cut will-to-power of the proletariat. As statements of such a social creed, the books are profoundly significant.

Jack London never realized a fraction of his power. He could have gone the path indicated by *The Sea Wolf* and have become a thorough naturalist, for the requisite temper and philosophy are present in this book. Or he could have gone further in the way of *The Revolution* and have become the prime spokesman for the proletariat. He did neither. Rather he succumbed to the temptation of large checks and often wrote to please the bourgeoisie that he affected to despise so heartily. Despite his truncated performance, London put deep meaning into a few of his works. In them one finds a fiery indictment of society, a close understanding of the "mucker," and enough poetry to supply a more voluminous writer. He, too, must have a place in any consideration of the development of our national mind.

Ernest Poole (*1880-   *).—London wrote his novels of economic revolution from sympathy rather than from exact knowledge, but Ernest Poole carefully studied our economic evolution and thoughtfully forecast the future from his understanding of the past and present. In his first book, *The Harbor* (1915), he gave us the most detailed sketch that we possess of the ideal proletarian state. This novel is an epitome of the past and the immediate future in America as interpreted and visioned by the radical socialist. The book sketches the development of business through the system of fierce competition among small independent firms. This era is succeeded by the period of consolidation. Then Poole describes the America of the future when the solidly organized workers will be in complete control of the government and all instruments of production and distribution. Such a Utopia has long been the syndicalist ideal. The book very skillfully and effectively uses the great harbor as the symbol of the changing world of business.

Poole was born in Chicago. Upon his graduation from Princeton in 1902 he made a first-hand study of social conditions in New York City, and in 1906 he assisted Upton Sinclair in the gathering of the material used in *The Jungle*. He served as war correspondent in Europe in 1914-1915, and after the revolution he lived in Russia for some time sympathetically watching the social and economic experiment that was being attempted in the country. Although *His Family* (1917) was awarded the Pulitzer prize, it does not have either the skill or meaning of *The Harbor*. The later novels are negligible.

SUGGESTED READINGS

Beard and Beard: *The Rise of American Civilization*. New York. 1927.
Vol. II: 480-800.
  The authors consider all aspects of the rising tide of liberalism.
The latter portion of the book discusses post-war society.

Beard: *The Economic Basis of Politics*. New York. 1922.
  Very unpleasant to some people.

Beer: *The Mauve Decade*. New York. 1926.
  The 1890's in a midnight revue.

Crawford: *The Novel—What It Is*. New York. 1893.
  The argument of the romantics by one of them.

Croly: *The Promise of American Life*. New York. 1909.
  Political and social liberalism presented by the man who later
founded *The New Republic*. Croly insists that democracy must have
a social program founded upon popular will.

De Witt: *The Progressive Movement*. New York. 1915.
  A study of the practical workings of the progressive movement.
The field covered is much larger than that of the Progressive party.

Hansen: *Midwest Portraits*. New York. 1925.
  Short discussion of Herrick.

Huneker: *Steeplejack*. New York. 1920.
  The autobiography of the chief cosmopolitan critic in America
during the early years of the century.

Huneker: *Selected Essays* (edited by Mencken). New York. 1930.
  Good examples of Huneker's criticism.

La Follette: *Autobiography*. Madison. 1913.
  The life story of the leading progressive. A very valuable social
document.

Lippmann: *Drift and Mastery*. New York. 1914.
  An analysis of the new democratic spirit in American life.

Lippmann: *Preface to Politics*. New York. 1913.
  The faith of a political liberal. Lippmann protests against abso-
lutism, formalism, and legalism.

Mencken: *Prejudices*. New York. 1919-1927. (Six volumes sold separately.)
  Best examples of the New Criticism.

Mencken: *Selected Prejudices*. New York. 1927.
  Selected from the six volumes.

Pattee: *A History of American Literature Since 1870*. New York. 1915.

Stearns (ed.): *Civilization in the United States*. New York. 1922. A
symposium.
  This book shows the post-war tendency to emphasize cultural questions rather than political or economic.

Sullivan: *Our Times*.
  The Turn of the Century. New York. 1926.
  America Finding Herself. New York. 1928.

Sullivan: *Pre-War America*. New York. 1930.

A review of the things that interested the average American from 1895 to 1912.

Underwood: *Literature and Insurgency*. New York. 1914. Out of print.

Has discussions of Twain, Howells, Norris, Churchill, and others.

Van Doren: *Contemporary American Novelists*. New York. 1923. Upton Sinclair, pp. 65-74.

Veblen: *The Theory of the Leisure Class*. New York. 1899.

Veblen: *The Theory of Business Enterprise*. New York. 1904.

Veblen: *The Instinct of Workmanship*. New York. 1914.

Veblen's works give the whole capitalistic domination of modern society the most caustic review that it has yet received. The author's peculiarly indirect style, his unfamiliar vocabulary, and his irony make these books very hard to read.

Weyl: *The New Democracy*. New York. 1912.

Conflict of plutocracy and democracy.

CHAPTER XXIV

THE NEW POETRY

The rise of New Poetry is a literary phenomenon of the twentieth century. By the middle nineties the older poets of America were all dead, and the younger generation, such men as Aldrich, Stedman, and Gilder, had not been able to say anything important in their polished imitations of Shelley, Keats, and Tennyson. The art of poetry was stagnant, and public interest in the art was correspondingly torpid. Although the New Poetry movement may be said to have begun in 1890 with the publication of Emily Dickinson's poems, the general reading public was unaware for more than twenty years that a poetic renaissance had been started. The development of the new verse was carried on by Stephen Crane, Richard Hovey, and William Vaughn Moody, but an engrossed attention in public questions and the treatment of those questions in the novel kept the reading public interested in fiction to the exclusion of poetry. Even Moody's poems on current problems did not gain for him a very large following. However, his work and that of his contemporaries performed an important task in the gathering of a small group of readers who had an intelligent interest in poets and their art. As late as 1910 most people would have been willing to aver that interest in things poetic was at a very low level, for the work of Miss Dickinson, Crane, and Moody had made little impression, and the publication of three really distinguished books by E. A. Robinson in 1897, 1902, and 1910 had utterly failed to penetrate public apathy. But within two years indifference was to be succeeded by an intense interest.

The presence of the adjective in the name "New Poetry" calls for some sort of discrimination between that type of verse and the older variety. Certainly chronology gives only a slight clew to the difference, for much of the verse published since 1912 is not new, and the work of Miss Dickinson and Crane undoubtedly is. A hard and fast division according to time fails at the first test.

In general the differences between New Poetry and the conventional variety may be seen in subject matter and in the form of expression. In expression the New Poetry does not bar any form of verse because of its antiquity, its newness, or its failure to adhere to rules. It privileges the poet to use any form that he thinks best fitted for the expression of what he has to say. It allows the use of the heroic couplet, the sonnet, blank verse, regular meter, rhyme, or any of the traditional forms and devices. On the other hand it uses free verse, polyphonic prose, or any other experiment that seems good to the poet. Carl Sandburg uses neither regular meter nor rhyme, and he is one of the distinguished New Poets. On the other hand, Robert Frost usually writes in a meter that is as regular as that of Keats, and often employs conventional rhyme, and he is no less a distinguished member of the new school. The effect of the New Poetry movement upon poetic form has been simply to enlarge greatly the range of the poet's choice when he begins to select his mode of expression.

In like manner the New Poetry has vastly enlarged the poet's vocabulary. The older writers tended to develop a specialized diction that was never used save in verse. They seemed to think that "vale" was more poetic than "valley," "azure" more elegant than "blue," and "ere" preferable to "before." Furthermore they had a positive mania for so-called poetic contractions like "o'er" and " 'neath." New Poetry is not so catholic in its acceptance of words as in its willingness to take any verse form, for the examples just given and dozens like them are not to be found in the writers of the new school. To-day poetic diction tends to be that of ordinary conversation, just as the rhythm of many of the New Poets is conversational rather than song-like. No word is unpoetic, and no special vocabulary is poetic. However, many words and expressions are banned for their triteness. Again, the New Poetry differs from the old in its figures. It has a sharp mistrust of rhetoric and of all rhetorical devices like carefully stage-managed figures of speech. Its own figures, when they occur, are more natural, or at least less standardized than are those of the lesser Victorians. All these changes in form, diction, and figurative language have tended to make the New Poetry a fit vehicle for the expression of contemporary life.

However, form is not all-important. Rather it is the content, the mental mood, that most accurately classifies poetry as old or new. The Genteel Tradition showed a tendency to restrict poetry to a definite range of subjects, and in no way did the poets after the

Civil War display their gentility more unmistakably than in their disinclination to write about contemporary life in their own country. Taylor and Stedman tried to write about the camel drivers and Bedouins of the desert, but they would have been aghast at the idea of making a poem about an Italian onion-seller or a Jewish fish-dealer. They adored picturesqueness—in Ispahan or Bagdad, not in Chicago or Pittsburgh. They doted on colors, but the colors that they preferred were those of some imaginary oriental city and not those of New York or San Francisco. New Poetry broke with all such nonsense. It reveals the quality of its newness by its insistent contemporaneousness. It expresses the ideas of present-day people. It describes what they see and how they act, and it especially tells how they feel. Even when the theme is as old as that of Tristram or the flight of Helen, it is interpreted from the viewpoint of the present generation.

Furthermore, the New Poetry excludes no subject-matter, however inherently ugly or beautiful it may be. It admits the spectacular and the awe-inspiring along with the trivial and the commonplace. A burst of sunlight on a country landscape, the railroad yards of a city, the Battle of Gettysburg, and a placard in a street-car have all proved to be susceptible of poetic treatment. This enlargement of the field of poetry is a reflection of the shift of life from a rural to an industrial basis. The new life, unspeakably ugly to one trained in the idyllic school of rural beauty, has forced us to find esthetic satisfaction in things hitherto considered ugly or trivial. New Poetry has accepted these findings, as have the recent painters and sculptors, and it gains much of its effectiveness from the use of material hitherto forbidden.

In the interpretation of the subject-matter New Poetry is thoroughly modern. It reflects the psychology and philosophy of the machine age. The naturalism, satire, realism, and new romance of recent fiction are all to be found in our poetry, and to-day verse is put to the tasks of social criticism and propaganda, just as it always has been in the great ages of poetry. "The Battle of the Village" was precipitated by the publication of Edgar Lee Masters' *Spoon River Anthology,* one of the really great products of the New Poetry movement. Vachel Lindsay and Carl Sandburg have written many a poem of social criticism, and the radicals have produced a whole literature of protest in verse form. Masters and Robinson are both touched by naturalism, though neither is so confirmed in the philosophy as Dreiser, for they are poets first, and only incidentally naturalists. In short, a good picture of America can be made out of our poetry, and such a picture would include the thinking of the country as well as its objective aspects. The interest of the early nineteen hundreds in social questions was very fortunate for the New Poetry, because the very contemporaneousness of the verse suited the mood of people who had just been reading either the state papers of our political liberals or the products of our socially minded novelists.

Although New Poetry frequently carries a passionate protest or states a highly individualized point of view, it is preëminently objective. It is concentrated upon externals rather than upon subjective communings. Personality is certainly not excluded, for the authors' dynamic personalities are not to be kept out of their verse, but no New Poet so loses himself in the mazes of personality that he fails to achieve sharpness of outline or detachment of utterance. In theory the New Poetry stands for clarity, even though it does not always realize its aim. It seeks individuality while laboring to gain a universal significance.

Furthermore, recent poets have prayed—not without success in some instances—to be delivered from the curse of fuzzy imagery, abstract utterance, and muddled thinking. Some of the very recent poets, despising the injunctions of their elders, have indulged in all of the vices just named, and a few have fallen into the tortured rhetoric and fantastic figures of the English metaphysical poets. But these men of the youngest generation are not of the New Poetry movement. They evidently belong to a new and as yet undefined school.

Influences Behind the New Poetry.—New Poetry is an outgrowth of Whitman's posthumous influence. When the old romantic died in 1892 he had a devoted group of personal friends but apparently no poetic heir-at-law. Fortunately his influence did not pass with his life, for in the twenty years between 1892 and 1912 he came slowly into a measure of his rightful fame and influence. He was widely read by intellectuals, and a few sensible critics and teachers labored to elucidate his poetry and to ascertain the more important facts of his life. People gradually quit calling *Leaves of Grass* an absurdity and its author a monstrosity. The machine age accented the need for that rich humanitarian spirit that underlay his work, and the slowly rising social conscience found comfort in his broad sympathies. Almost certainly without Whitman's influence the burst of poetic energy in 1912 would have been much different, and there are some who insist that without this impetus the renaissance of verse would never have started.

Another force behind the New Poetry was the influence of a group of French poets who drew from Whitman some of their inspiration and many of their ideas of form. One of the influential critical studies near the beginning of the poetic revival was Amy Lowell's *Six French Poets,* published in 1915. The poets discussed were Émile Verhaeren, Albert Samain, Henri Regnier, Remy de Gourmont, Francis Jammes, and Paul Fort. All of these poets were writing during the nineties and the first decade of the twentieth century, and the study of these men by Miss Lowell and other American critics, notably Ezra Pound, had a quickening and enriching effect upon the New Poetry. Many American writers of the small towns and villages, where De Gourmont and Regnier were totally unknown, were influenced by Miss Lowell who was in turn influenced by the Frenchmen.

Every new school of literature must have a way of reaching its potential audience. Before 1912 many of the magazines, traditional buyers of short poems, were in the hands of editors hostile to the new movement. Hence the reading public got imitations of Longfellow, Keats, and Tennyson, but it saw no experiments in the French fashion. However, in 1912 Harriet Monroe, herself a poet and sensitive critic, founded *Poetry,* a magazine devoted exclusively to the publication and criticism of verse. So successful has Miss Monroe been in her aim to encourage unknown poets that a satisfactory history of the New Poetry movement since 1912 could be done from the files of her magazine. Few periodicals so emphatically deserve the high place in our literary history that *Poetry* has for its encouragement of poets and for the cultivation of an audience that likes good verse but that is sympathetic to all experiments. The list of poets that Miss Monroe discovered or introduced to a wide group of readers sounds like the roster of the New Poets in America, and *Poetry* has always kept an intelligent eye upon the literary activity of other lands. The success of this magazine encouraged other periodicals that are largely or exclusively devoted to the publication of verse. Among these may be mentioned *Palms, The Fugitive,* and *Contemporary Verse.*

In the literary lineage of New Poetry there are more names than those of Whitman and the French writers. Stephen Crane wrote some poetry that is almost as striking as his prose, though it has never had so many readers. This verse has already been discussed. At the time it was written this poetry had little influence, but in about ten or fifteen years the experimenters of the new school were considering *Black Riders* and *Wounds in the Rain* as examples of unconventional but very effective poetry. However, the influence of Crane can hardly be compared with that of Emily Dickinson, the recluse of Amherst, Massachusetts. This New England woman seems to have supplied the inspiration for Crane's first attempts at verse, just as she supplied the literary impetus to many another writer.

EMILY DICKINSON
(1830-1886)

Although Emily Dickinson died twenty-six years before 1912, she belongs to the school of contemporary poets in both spirit and technique. The factual record of Miss Dickinson's life contains but little of importance. She was born in Amherst, Massachusetts, in 1830. Her father was a prominent lawyer of the town, and for more than forty years he was a trustee of Amherst College. The girl received the polite education that daughters of good families received in the thirties and forties. In 1854 Mr. Dickinson was elected to Congress where he served two terms. Emily lived for a while with the family in the national capital. About this time she seems to have had a very unhappy love affair, all the details of which are matters of argument. From the shock of this experience Emily Dickinson's sensitive nature so recoiled that she spent the remainder of her life in almost total seclusion, seldom leaving her yard and during the last eight or ten years never leaving the house. She died in 1886.

It was not until after her death that Miss Dickinson's poetry became known. She wrote voluminously, but during her lifetime only three or four of the poems were published, and before her death she instructed her family to destroy all her writings. Many of the letters were burned, but fortunately the relatives decided that the poetry belonged to the world. In 1890 the first collection of her verse was printed. Several other volumes have followed, and it is probable that a good many of Miss Dickinson's poems are still in manuscript.

Emily Dickinson took the stuff of her poetry from her personal experiences. Although she was born in the full flood of the romantic revolution, only thirteen years later than Thoreau and eleven later than Whitman, she seems to have absolutely nothing in common with the writers of her time. She is wholly original—a primitive, some have called her. Her ideas cannot be linked up with those of other poets and her verse form is just as truly her own. It is not correct to say that she turned her back on current literature and philosophy, for she seems never to have been aware of their existence. Moreover, one hastens to say that she built no ivory tower from which she presents exquisite poetic offerings utterly detached from the vulgar world. Emily Dickinson went to the one source open to such a solitary as she was; she dipped into her heart for her poetry, writing her verse simply as an easement to surcharged feelings. In so economical a fashion and with so personal and poignant a phraseology does she express her emotion that the experiences of the secluded New England spinster take on the air of the universal.

Emily Dickinson allowed nothing to stand between her and the expression of that burst of flame that was her emotion. So tremendous are her imaginative flights and so overpowering is her wish to make articulate her vision that grammar, rhetoric, and metrical rules are wrenched asunder by the amazing violence of the shy little woman. Almost any one can point out more than one flaw in these lines:

> The show is not the show,
> But they that go.
> Menagerie to me
> My neighbor be.
> Fair play—
> Both went to see.

Or in these:

> To fight aloud is very brave
> But gallanter, I know,
> Who charge within the bosom,
> The cavalry of woe.

Dozens of such poems are to be found in her pages, distinguished at once for essential poetry and audacity of conception and for complete contempt of rules. But as T. W. Higginson so aptly said in the first printed criticism of her poetry, "After all when a thought takes one's breath away, a lesson on grammar seems an impertinence." Emily Dickinson wrote with the effervescent naïveté of a child and the imagination of a great poet. With the most unaffected artlessness she wrote dozens of short poems that are dazzling imaginative feats.

> The overtakelessness of those
> Who have accomplished death,
> Majestic is to me beyond
> The majesties of earth.

In no way does she better display her lack of bookishness than in the very effective use of figures drawn from her own restricted life in an old New England mansion.

> You cannot fold a flood
>   And put it in a drawer,—
> Because the winds would find it out,
>   And tell your cedar floor.

She thus expresses one of the joys of eternity:

> Snug in seraphic cupboards
> To nibble all the day,
> While unsuspecting cycles
> Wheel pompously away.

The subjects of her poetry are those of solitaries everywhere, God, love, and eternity. But over these old themes she threw a shimmering ecstasy that was the trembling joy and fear of a deeply original soul. Her soul was too sensitive an instrument to respond to the rough, uncertain touch of the world; to transmit the ecstasy and fear of a solitary woman was task enough for it. "The wounded deer leaps highest," she once declared, and many a page of her poetry proves the truth of this assertion. In one of her triumphant successes she tells of her desire to be united with her lover.

> If certain when the life was out,
> That yours and mine should be,
> I'd toss it yonder like a rind,
> And taste eternity.
>
> But now, all ignorant of the length
> Of time's uncertain wing,
> It goads me, like the goblin bee,
> That will not state its sting.

It is her reduction of life to its lowest terms and the statement of those terms in short jets of unmistakable poetry that has made her an American classic. Her poetic technique or the lack of it is not material to her accomplishment or influence. The important thing is her way of phrasing in an impromptu fashion, almost carelessly, audacious imaginative flights that have at their core the love, desire, and fear that have been felt by all men. She is forever contemporary. Her banishment of the trivial and the transitory in favor of things elemental will make her contemporary with countless unborn generations.

> This is my letter to the world
> That never wrote to me—
> The simple news that nature told
> With tender majesty.

RICHARD HOVEY

(1864-1900)

Richard Hovey occupies a place somewhat analogous to that held by William Ernest Henley in English poetry. Despising both the musty bookishness of the Genteel and the pallid estheticism of Oscar Wilde's imitators and followers, Hovey sang lustily of the joys of life and the blessedness of fellowship with Brother Man. He was not an important poet, but he was an important figure, for he helped to make poetry popular both by making it readable for the common man and by making it expressive of present hopes and ambitions.

Hovey was an Illinois boy who, after a wide variety of experiences, settled down to the teaching and writing of poetry. In his life as a theological student, actor, vagabond, journalist, and teacher he tasted of many experiences and seemed to find them all good. The lines from his *Songs from Vagabondia,* written in collaboration with Bliss Carman, career and shout with the joy of living:

> For we know the world is glorious,
> And the goal a golden thing,
> And that God is not censorious,
> When his children have their fling. . . .

The gusts of patriotic ardor that shook the country in the late nineties did not leave Hovey untouched. In his "Unmanifest Destiny" he gives a reverent expression of an emotion that too many sentimentalized into a mawkish caricature. Addressing his country he said:

> I do not know beneath what sky
> Nor on what seas shall be thy fate;
> I only know it shall be high,
> I only know it shall be great.

WILLIAM VAUGHN MOODY

(1869-1910)

William Vaughn Moody and Robert Herrick are much alike. Each was trained in Harvard, each joined the English department of the University of Chicago, each had a mind of a scholar and the sensitive conscience of a socially minded gentleman, and each gave his reactions to contemporary affairs in the shape of literature.

Moody was born in Indiana of a rugged, capable, pioneer family. After his graduation from Harvard he taught there for a short time and then went to the University of Chicago where he remained until 1903. The last seven years of his life he devoted exclusively to writing. During his teaching years his time was occupied by classroom drudgery and with such activities as the publication of texts and articles and the editing of Milton's poems, but he managed to snatch a little time for writing each year. It was his numerous distractions undoubtedly that kept Moody from developing earlier, for it was only in his last few years that he began to realize his powers.

Moody's first popular success was his drama *The Great Divide*, a play that has been aptly described as a melodrama written by a scholarly Puritan. It held its place in the theater for a rather long time. Later he wrote another drama, *The Faith Healer*, which was not successful. His most ambitious project was the planning of a poetic trilogy in dramatic form that would tell the story of man's return to God through the redeeming power of woman who first caused man to fall. The influence of Milton upon the design of the project is very obvious. The trilogy was left uncompleted at Moody's early death. The first two sections, *The Fire-Bringer* and *The Masque of Judgment*, were finished, but only one act of the last section, *The Death of Eve*, was completed. The problems raised in the work were to have resolved in the last section, hence it is unfair to pass too adverse a criticism upon the unfinished work. However, as far as the plan is revealed its execution fails utterly to equal the sublimity of the theme.

It is not by his dramas and poetic trilogy that Moody will live. His fame to-day seems to be based rather securely upon the short poems that express either his general philosophy or his specific reactions to a particular social problem. "Gloucester Moors" is decidedly naturalistic in its conception of the world as a slave ship lurching on without intelligent direction. The hold is crammed with suffering humanity whose agonies move not at all the indifferent crew. "Menagerie" is a half-humorous treatment of the theory of evolution in which a little man, "slightly jagged," realizes that he, "the last product of the toiling ages," is hardly a fit stopping place for the vast evolutionary process. The poem goes on to speak of the Perfect Man, "radiant and loving, yet to be." The poem called "The Brute" is one of the finest treatments that we have of man and the machine. After indicating the most obvious of the evils of machinery, the poet visualizes the new day, when man will be the master and the whirling machine will be the docile slave that makes for happiness.

In his discussions of specific questions Moody is very much like his colleague, Herrick, except that his vision of both problem and solution is more national and less restricted to Chicago or a city civilization. At the opening of the twentieth century two national questions engrossed Moody. One was the proposed partition of China by the so-called civilized powers and the other was the problem of America in the Philippines. In "The Quarry" the poet praises America for its high-minded idealism in protesting against the division of the ancient Chinese Empire. This poem represents a very effective use of symbolism. China is represented by the elephant, the European powers by the beasts of prey, and the United States by the eagle. Moody thought the work of John Hay in preventing the spoliation of Chinese territory worthy of the finest American traditions. Not so worthy was our decision to keep the Philippines. The short poem "On a Soldier Fallen in the Philippines" is a dirge for the fallen soldier and a moving injunction not to whisper to the dead that "the blood on his sword was his country's own heart blood."

Let him never dream that his bullet's scream went wide of its mark,
Home to the heart of his darling land where she stumbled and sinned in the dark.

Another utterance on this same subject is "An Ode in Time of Hesitation," probably the finest of Moody's poems. To the poet the slightest hesitation about setting the islands free was a lamentable betrayal of our national idealism, and it was especially reprehensible in that it occurred so soon after our allegedly disinterested efforts to free Cuba.

> . . . The wars we wage
> Are noble, and our battles still are won
> By justice for us ere we lift the gage.

The poem moves to a solemn warning:

> O ye who lead,
> Take heed.
> Blunders we may forgive, but baseness we will smite.

Moody was one of our most sensitive and intelligent critics during a confused and disordered period. We were emerging as a world power in international politics, and in our domestic life we were in the middle of the great social and economic upheaval wrought by the machine age. Moody did not welcome either change except as it offered the prospect of improved moral and social well-being to us and to all whom we touched. He was far more concerned in keeping our soul than in consolidating our military and economic conquests. His thinking is characterized by a personal and social idealism that coming events were about to render as archaic as transcendentalism, for the World War and the subsequent change in our national temper seem to have made Moody's misgivings and hopes dreadfully old-fashioned. But there are certain archaic spiritual qualities that might be wholesome forces in our nation to-day if ever they were allowed to function. Moody died eight years before the crash of American guns at St. Mihiel gave proof that our period of doubt and hesitation was over and that we were in pursuit of our manifest material destiny. Whether or not that pursuit was worth the price only the future can tell.

Moody is not always successful in his verse. At times he is plainly laboring, and often the diction seems very erudite or very forced. Then, too, many of his lines are so overweighted with meaning that reading them becomes a trying task. However, when all the adverse criticisms are accounted for, Moody still deserves a high place

n the history of New Poetry. His verse is personal, direct, and
colored always by the problems or philosophy of the present.

EDWIN ARLINGTON ROBINSON

(1869-1935)

Edwin Arlington Robinson has appropriately been called "The
Dean of the New Poetry." Before some of the pioneers of the new
school were born, he was writing a firm, clear, and close-clipped
ine that definitely stamps his verse as of the new variety. Super-
icially his poetry is quite conventional, for he has never experi-
nented in the use of extravagantly free verse. In fact, most of his
poems are written in traditional English forms, but the poet's adherence to conventional verse forms is no sign that his poetry is
conventional. Even when he uses so artificial a form as the vil-
anelle, he manages to put into it some of his own personality and
enough of the modern spirit to make the poem qualify as an example
of New Poetry. He always makes content and his individual style
dominate any form that he may choose to employ, and both are unmistakably modern.

Robinson grew up in Gardiner, Maine, the town that he has since
made famous as Tilbury. After two years at Harvard, he was compelled to abandon his college course; but already he had determined
to be a writer, and as he worked on the New York subway and at
other distasteful jobs, he was writing verse. In 1896 he published
privately a volume called *The Torrent and the Night Before*. The
next year *Children of the Night* appeared, to be followed five years
ater by *Captain Craig*. At this time interest in poetry was at a
ow ebb, and Robinson had a hard time winning an audience. He
night have had a much harder one had he not attracted the atten-
ion of President Roosevelt, who wrote a favorable review of *Cap-
ain Craig*. The President also gave Robinson a position in the
New York Custom House, after the poet had refused the offer of a
Mexican consulate. Since 1910 he has devoted his full time to
poetry. In recent years he has spent his summers in the MacDowell
Colony at Peterboro, New Hampshire.

Robinson's Debt to Older Literature.—At first glance it would
seem that a wide and sympathetic acquaintance with books has

molded all of Robinson's verse. Hardy and Crabbe are his acknowledged masters, and he has a warm admiration for Zola. The influence of the last seems to be discernible in Robinson's tendency
toward the naturalistic philosophy, while the influence of the two
English poets appears in his direct, almost abbreviated lines and in
the gray autumnal tone of the verse. However, his economy of
words comes partly from a mind that is naturally direct and incisive. He never pours out a gush of rhetoric in an effort to express
a fine shade of feeling. Sometimes he crowds thought into his lines
until they become turgid with meaning but never with rhetoric. He
has followed too closely the patterns of his masters ever to make
such a mistake.

Another way in which Robinson seems to owe an indebtedness
to literature is through his use of old themes that have been sanctified by the poets of other ages. For instance, he levies upon the
Arthurian legends for the stories of Merlin and Lancelot, and in one
of his very finest efforts he gives a new version of the old story of
Tristram and Isolt. But the use of legendary material often used
by other poets is no sign of Robinson's bookishness, for he has so
infused the medieval stories with his own personality and with the
spirit of the modern world that the age-old legends become finely
interpretative of contemporary life.

Robinson and People.—Robinson's knowledge of books has never
obscured his view of life and never dimmed his interest in people.
Studying the individual man is his self-imposed task. Only to run
through the table of contents of his collected poems will give one
some idea of his interest in people, for a large number of the titles
are the names of men, while others indicate the treatment of dramatic
episodes in the lives of people. Typical titles and poems are to be
found in "Flammonde," "John Gorham," "Ben Jonson Entertains
a Man from Stratford," "Bewick Finzer," "Bokardo," "John Ever-
eldown," "Richard Cory," "Captain Craig," "Isaac and Archibald,"
and "The Master."

Twenty years before Edgar Lee Masters achieved his sensational
success with *Spoon River Anthology*, Robinson was doing sparingly etched portraits—character sketches—frequently in sonnet
form. The aim of the two poets is essentially the same in individual
poems, for each wishes to present a personality in as few strokes
as possible. The difference between the two poets comes in Rob-

nson's willingness to consider each personality as an isolated phenomenon.   He makes no effort to frame his portraits together in
uch a way as to interpret a particular time or place.   On the other
hand, Masters gives us his pictures in a large frame so that the
group taken as a whole interprets a middle-western village.   Robinson is not so particularized; his portraits are more universal, even
though each one is distinctly a product of a New England mind.
But his mind has none of the stultifying provincialism that has so
often cramped and distorted New England literature.   Rather it is
a free mind, gifted with uncanny penetration and immense sophis-
ication.   Furthermore, Robinson is more sympathetic than Masters
is, though both are prone to glorify defeat and renunciation, and both
are apt to find ideal victory in failure.   It is in his unadorned portrait etchings that Robinson is at his very best.

Robinson's Philosophical Temper.—In temper Robinson is altogether modern.   The traditional verse form might mislead the careless reader into an erroneous judgment of the poet's modernity, but
here is no mistaking the tone color for one of an earlier day.   Robinson has the philosophy of Dreiser, only in the case of the poet
it is not a relentlessly maintained philosophy but rather a ques-
ioning mood that implies a background of thought.   He is not
primarily a thinker; he is a poet, but as such his is not an exposed
emotion.   His is a thoughtful poetry that interprets a mood, a char-
cter, or an episode without attempting to build up a consistent
philosophy.   Although Robinson has too broad a point of view to
be a thorough naturalist, he bears many resemblances to one.   He
celebrates success equally with failure, he sees in futile strivings an
occasional triumph of the spirit, but under all his poetry sounds the
steady, droning organ-point of philosophic naturalism.   Again and
again it voices a question, sometimes to be answered by a ringing
refutation, sometimes to be left unanswered, but always it returns
with a steady insistence that cannot be ignored.   Only one thing
seems to stand between Robinson and complete naturalism, and
that one thing is his belief in justification by faith.   He seems to
think that absolute despair is unwarranted so long as faith in one's
endeavor enables one to snatch a modicum of respect from the wreckage piled up by failure and the undirected forces of life.

Here is the conclusion of "The Man Against the Sky," a poem

that gives the title to Robinson's most typical and effective book
of verse:

> If after all that we have lived and thought,
> All comes to Nought,—
> If there be nothing after Now
> And we be nothing anyhow,
> And we know that,—why live?
> 'Twere sure but weaklings' vain distress
> To suffer dungeons where so many doors
> Will open on the cold eternal shores
> That look sheer down
> To the dark tideless floods of Nothingness
> Where all who know may drown.

The question here is like that of Hamlet in his musings, but Rob
inson shrinks from a direct reply, contenting himself with an im
plied answer that must be pieced together from the reading of other
poems.

Probably the finest poem that Robinson has done is "Ben Jonson
Entertains a Man from Stratford," a monologue placed in the
mouth of the rugged, honest, dogmatic Jonson that reveals the most
human and appealing Shakespeare ever set forth by scholar or
imaginative writer, and at the same time gives us almost as good
a picture of the speaker himself. Robinson's Shakespeare is the
Shakespeare of Stratford, the ambitious, successful, disillusioned
man, who wrote the sonnets and *Hamlet* and *Lear* out of his soul's
midnight. It is not the Shakespeare who flattered courtiers who
in turn flattered the queen. It is not the Shakespeare of *Henry V*
and the rolling patriotic fervor of the chronicle-histories. It is the
man who knew blackness and futility and unsatisfied longings and
who yearned somewhat incomprehensively for a life of rustic em
inence in a quiet English village. Robinson would be something
more than a minor figure in contemporary letters if he had never
written anything besides this poem and the eighty-two sonnets in
the 1928 edition.

And here are the seemly words that Robinson gave to Shakespeare
to express a philosophy that may not be Elizabethan—and may be—
but that is certainly modern:

> "No, Ben!" he mused; "it's Nothing. It's all Nothing.
> We come, we go; and when we're done, we're done . . .
> Spiders and flies—we're mostly one or t'other—

Your fly will serve as well as anybody,
And what's his hour? He flies, and flies, and flies,
And in his fly's mind has a brave appearance;
And then your spider gets him in her net,
And eats him out, and hangs him up to dry.
That's Nature, the kind mother of us all.
And then your slattern housemaid swings her broom,
And where's your spider? And that's Nature, also.
It's Nature, and it's Nothing. It's all Nothing.
It's a world where bugs and emperors
Go singularly back to the same dust,
Each in his own time; and the old, ordered stars
That sang together, Ben, will sing the same
Old stave tomorrow."

Robinson is a bleak, spare writer of gray moods. Hopes and aspirations are tumbled about by transcendent forces that, if they are not actually malignant, are senseless and blind. Assuredly if there is benevolently ordered power in the universe, it carefully conceals both the benevolence and the order and reveals only strength. Still life is presumably worth living. Robinson is too much of a Maine Yankee not to have courage and fortitude and an instinctive admiration for these virtues. He is aware of the undesirability of the real world, but before he comes to the final renunciation, some glimmer of New England faith or idealism holds him from the final gesture. In *Merlin* and *Lancelot* it is the vaguely defined Light or Gleam that keeps the philosophy from turning unbearably bitter, while in the more plebeian characters the saving grace is old-fashioned fortitude.

Robinson has wrongly been called a difficult poet to read. Highly individual he is, but not difficult save in rare passages. His passion for exactness and his desire to be brief and direct give his poetry a peculiar quality. He can say much in little space. The rare passages that are obscure are caused by the writer's effort to avoid unpoetic directness of nomenclature. The most quoted of these passages is the place in "How Annandale Went Out" in which Robinson calls a hypodermic syringe a "slight sort of engine." Incidentally, this sonnet is an excellent example of his style and of his ability to compress a drama into a few lines.

Although Robinson is not to be called a poet of locale, he is distinctly of New England. He shows his ancestry in the gaunt, craggy lines, disjunct by burden of meaning but made poetic by imagery,

swift allusiveness, and intuitive insight. He shows it in the almos
niggard economy of his words, and he especially shows it in the
choice of "queer" characters who are indigenous to the soil of his
native region. The very background of his thought and materia
is to be sought in the characteristic colors and moods of rural New
England.

ROBERT FROST

(1875-   )

In the history of American literature it has usually been accountec
something to transmute into literary form the peculiar flavor, the
atmosphere, and speech of a particular locality. For more than a
century men have labored to describe the chill of New England winters, the pine woods under a deep snow, the beauty of the springs
and summers, the riot of autumn colors, and, above all, the taciturn
inhabitants, rooted to the soil, and distinguished from all other Americans by their canny ways and clipped speech. Local colorists would
have thought themselves successful if they had been able to depict
only these things. But it remained for Robert Frost to describe
lovingly and accurately the particularizing qualities of the New England land and people, and then to achieve a unique distinction in
our letters by penetrating far enough below local peculiarities to
reveal universal aspects of life and human nature.

Frost is certainly not the last person in the world to sense that
he is more than a poet of New England, for in his *New Hampshire*
he mildly objects to a local classification. The objection is rather
noteworthy, for he is generally the most reticent of men about his
own work.

> And when I asked to know what ailed the people,
> She said, Go read your own books and find out.
> I may as well confess myself the author
> Of several books against the world in general.
> To take them as against a special state
> Or even the nation's to restrict my meaning.
>
>   .   .   .   .   .
>
> Because I wrote my novels in New Hampshire
> Is no proof that I aimed them at New Hampshire.

Frost's statement that he "wrote the books against the world"
does not mean that he indulged in any type of social criticism. In
the last line of the excerpt he defines his meaning of locality. In

other words, he wrote his lines with the idea of giving them more than local significance.

Frost and the New England Character.—It is only half a truth to say that Frost is a great interpreter of the New Englander. He is wholly New England in his backgrounds and his characters, and he especially reveals his locality in the clipped phrases with which he gives his findings. But when we look intently at one of his poems that is at first seemingly only a factual record of some incident that happened in Vermont or New Hampshire, we realize suddenly that the facts may be local but that their significance is universal. "Mending Wall" is an excellent example of a poem that outwardly carries only the atmosphere of New England, but the poem has overtones that make it applicable to any age or any land.

His taciturnity makes Frost say only enough to make his meaning clear, and rather than raise his voice or elaborate his facts to get effects, he often takes recourse in understatement. His economical use of words frequently shows itself in his insistent habit of making the plain statement on the page do double duty. The words always mean precisely what they say, but above their denotation they carry an overtone of poetic or spiritual significance. This habit makes Frost a hard writer to skim over but an easy one to come back to again and again. With his quiet, homely facts, his habitual understatement and unhurried speech, and his elusive but satisfying spiritual overtones, Frost is one of the poets that readers may approach, knowing full well that he will not prod the jaded nerves already tired by the jangle of modern life. His poems have all the restful qualities of an utterly placid landscape.

> I'm going out to clean the pasture spring;
> I'll only stop to rake the leaves away
> (And wait to watch the water clear, I may):
> I sha'n't be gone long.—You come too.
>
> I'm going out to fetch the little calf
> That's standing by the mother. It's so young,
> It totters when she licks it with her tongue.
> I sha'n't be gone long.—You come too.

But for all his feeling that he is doing something more than a local color sketch, Frost is the last man to insist that his poems carry implications that are the breath of omniscience. He is too much of a modern not to be certain of his facts and rather skeptical

of his conclusions and speculations. He sometimes feels that there
is something beyond the facts, but he is too reticent to announce
confidently any discoveries in the realm of the unexplored.

> Others taunt me with having knelt at well-curbs
> Always wrong to the light, so never seeing
> Deeper down in the well than where the water
> Gives me back in a shining surface picture
> Me myself in the summer heaven godlike
> Looking out of a wreath of fern and cloud puffs.
> Once, when trying with chin against a well-curb,
> I discerned, as I thought, beyond the picture,
> Through the picture, a something white, uncertain,
> Something more of the depths—and then I lost it.
> Water came to rebuke the too clear water.
> One drop fell from a fern, and lo, a ripple
> Shook whatever it was lay there at bottom,
> Blurred it, blotted it out. What was that whiteness?
> Truth? A pebble of quartz? For once, then, something.

Frost as a Realist.—By a numerical computation of his lines, it
is probable that Frost will be found to be nine-tenths pure realist.
Line after line of his poetry will give us only facts, as if they were
his sole aim. "The fact is the sweetest dream that labor knows,"
he declares, but occasionally he lets fall, quite casually, a phrase
that will throw over the bare facts the radiant light of poetry. After
his *obiter dictum* Frost returns to the facts at hand with the steady
determination of a realist to tell only the truth. His habit of resting his poetic interpretations upon a realistic basis is one of his most
agreeable and characteristic traits. By it he makes the reader co-
discoverer and co-author of the poetry, and there are few readers
who do not feel the flush of creative accomplishment when they read
into "Mending Wall" and find beneath the briefly told story of a
commonplace "chore" on a New England farm the eternal conflict
between the old and the new.

To say that Frost is a realist is not to warn the reader against
the "unpleasant" in his lines. The poet is reported to have said
that there are two kinds of realists, the one who gives you the potato
with much dirt clinging to it to prove that it is a potato, and the
one who gives you the potato washed clean. Emphatically Frost
belongs to the latter class of realists. But he is a true realist in
that he gives the facts, uncolored by any preconceived philosophical
interpretation and unbiased by any prejudice of taste or temper

that would make him keep out of his picture either the high lights or the shadows. Both he gives with deep respect for truth and for good taste.

One of the satisfying things about Frost and his realism is the assurance that he "knows his subject." He knows the life of a New England farmer just as Hamlin Garland knows the life of a Dakota farmer—because he has lived it. The easy familiarity with which he handles his rustic material can never quite be gained by the summer boarder. Frost never sentimentalizes the fact and never laments its presence. That it exists is enough. In a matter-of-fact fashion, with not the slightest outward show of affection or aversion, he tells of the commonplace happenings of country life. He talks interestedly about mending wall, cleaning out the pasture spring, apple picking, wood chopping, and all the daily tasks of the New England farm, and in every reference and every syllable he gives evidence that he knows intimately what he is talking about. He has done all these tasks in the prosaic way of making a living, and when he comes to write poetry about them, he sees no reason why they should be sentimentalized or falsely colored. If the poet's bare account conveys to the reader something of the universal, Frost will probably not complain; but the reader ought not to complain if he misses the universal, for he still has before him the undoubted fact, and a fact related by Robert Frost is not to be despised.

Frost and Society.—Frost is difficult to discuss in the phrases that we apply to other poets. He has no philosophy, for his deep insight into the significance of a fact or episode can hardly be called philosophical. Furthermore it would strain the meaning of the word immensely to term him a humanitarian. Of course, it is not to be supposed that Mr. Frost is quite without humane sentiments, but he has never used his poetry to preach the gospel of social well-being or to lash the deplorable injustices that afflict men. When he writes, political questions might as well not exist, and economic problems are beneath contempt.

> The having anything to sell is what
> Is the disgrace in man or state or nation.

Although Frost has never tried to qualify as a humanitarian poet, he has the fine rural quality of neighborliness remarkably developed. He is a friendly spirit, a sociable man, as the rustics phrase it, sincerely interested in the small affairs that make up his neighbors' lives and always ready to stop in the road or drop his work to chat with a passer-by. In short, he is so fond of man in the specific that he has never felt it incumbent upon him to gather in a capacious embrace man in the abstract.

> When a friend calls to me from the road
> And slows his horse to a meaning walk,
> I don't stand still and look around
> On all the hills I haven't hoed,
> And shout from where I am, What is it?
> No, not as there is time to talk.
> I thrust my hoe in the mellow ground,
> Blade-end up and five feet tall,
> And plod: I go up to the stone wall
> For a friendly visit.

One of the many recurrent overtones in Frost's work is a note of distress at the thought of separation from other men. The poet cannot entertain the idea of isolation without a slight feeling of dismay.

> "Men work together," I told him from the heart,
> "Whether they work together or apart."

Again Frost says rather anxiously:

> Before I build a wall I'd like to know
> What I was walling in or walling out,
> And to whom I was like to give offense.

The deep personal interest that Frost has in people is extended to things. Although he has never taken all nature into his sympathy or confidence, as Whitman did, he evidently finds in the world of nature something besides an objective fact, something more responsive than a mirror. A revealing little poem is "Two Look at Two," beautiful in its facts and doubly beautiful in its overtones. It ends on these lines:

> Still they stood
> A great wave from it going over them,
> As if earth in one unlooked-for favor
> Had made them certain earth returned their love.

Frost's Career.—Notwithstanding his long line of New England ancestors and his own absorption in the land of his fathers, Frost spent his first ten years in San Francisco. He did not complete a college course, though he was registered in Dartmouth for a few months, and he spent two years at Harvard. After leaving college he made his living by farming, newspaper work, teaching, and working in a factory. From an early age he wrote poetry, but it was invariably refused by editors.

In 1912 he and his family went to England. Here he made numerous congenial and helpful friends, and here he published his first two books of verse. The first volume, *A Boy's Will*, appeared in 1913 and *North of Boston* the following year. The success of these volumes in England directed the critical attention of Americans to their new writer, and since 1915 Frost has held an undisputed position as one of the leading poets of the English-speaking race. Since returning to America, Frost has lived in New England except for a time that he spent at the University of Michigan as "poet in residence." He now lives in South Salisbury, Vermont.

Although some critics are now suggesting that Frost is the undoubted classicist among American men of letters, his position as one of the consistent exponents of the New Poetry is never to be questioned. He is modern in every essential. The unwary may be trapped into thinking that the very conventional appearance of his poetry, with its regular lines and its frequent use of rhyme, signifies a conventional verse. Such is far from the case. However conventional the poetry may look, it sounds very unconventional when it is read. Frost writes singing lyrics, character sketches, meditative verse, descriptive poems, and dialogues—one of his favorite and most successful forms—but whatever the form, the rhythm will be conversational like that of New England speech, and the flavor will be as pungent as the fruit that grows in some old Vermont orchard.

The tag with which critics may ultimately label Frost is of no immediate concern. An important position in the development of American literature is pretty sure to be his, and he has reached this position over difficulties that are not easily surmounted. Since the days of Samuel Sewall and Cotton Mather, the New England countryman has had a tendency to be satisfied with a provincial outlook, and, except for the generation or two when the romantic revolution was at its height, the qualities that make for provincialism have been most highly esteemed by all New Englanders. Against the tendency of these qualities Frost has raised no passionate protest. With the touch of a creative artist and the swift insight of a born poet, he has transmuted rustic provincialism into something of universal truth and spiritual significance. It is highly doubtful if any future caprice of taste or literary fashion will render Frost's achievement of little account.

VACHEL LINDSAY

(1879-1931)

If Robinson and Frost represent a late stage in the intellectual and spiritual development of New England, Vachel Lindsay is the epitome of the Middle West. Let it be said at once, however, that he does not give us the Middle West, as Masters does, with more of failure than of realization, more of frustration than of success. Only incidentally does he describe any of the aspects of Mississippi Valley life. The future historian of culture will draw infinitely more facts from *Spoon River Anthology* and *Main Street* than he will extract from Lindsay's poems, but Lindsay will give the authentic mood of the pioneer projected into the twentieth century and tempered by a sense of beauty that was almost starved among those of the earlier generations. Lindsay is the romantic evangelist of beauty preaching the felicities of an idealized Middle West. The acrid, salty savor of reality is not to be found in "The Congo" or "The Santa Fé Trail." Lindsay suggests rather than describes the energy, the ethical drive, and the spiritual temper of the Mississippi Valley.

The genius of the Middle West is strong. Men that it bears and fashions find that the obliteration of its marks is an almost impossible task. Mark Twain never lost the touch of frontier Missouri. Hamlin Garland rightly glories in his position as the acknowledged spokesman of the Middle Border. Sinclair Lewis has fought with extravagant bursts of energy against his early environment, but there is abundant reason for thinking that he has never vanquished it. Lindsay is more like Hamlin Garland. He is buoyantly, defiantly middle western. The good black earth of Springfield, Illinois, seeped into his bones, and all the prejudices and idealisms of the "valley of democracy" went into the formation of his mind and philosophic temper. William Jennings Bryan was the product of the same locality, and he and Lindsay had striking points of similarity. Both were ardent democrats and champions of the commoners. Both burned with fervent idealism, both earnestly desired that all men be happy and virtuous, both had unbounded faith in the efficacy of political and moral evangelism, and both interpreted politics, economics, and diplomacy in terms of middle-western morality. Neither man could have been formed in New York, New England, or San Francisco.

Conflicting Elements in Lindsay.—Into the formation of Vachel Lindsay has gone all the potent spirit of the Middle West, plus an alien and seemingly inharmonious element. This alien strain is the reverent love of beauty. In some people these two dissimilar impulses would have warred to the death, but Lindsay has managed to effect a compromise. He has become the itinerant evangelist of beauty, singing its praises in colloquial verse set to the infectious, booming rhythm of ragtime, both religious and secular. He is the minstrel of Springfield, the singer of idealisms once voiced by older democrats of the West. He is the orthodox Campbellite preaching the gospel of beauty, the Y.M.C.A. lecturer mingling religion and rhyme, the Anti-Saloon Leaguer intoxicated with the vision of a new day that will be stainless in purity and dazzling in spontaneous beauty. Heredity is partly responsible for this strange combination in Lindsay. We are told that his father was a religious evangelist and that his mother was an artist. Certainly both left powerful influences on the son, and nothing shows more clearly the sincerity and strength of Lindsay than the indisputable fact that he has combined both strains and has been a traitor to neither.

After spending his boyhood in Springfield, Lindsay attended Hiram College for two or three years. Here he met numbers of students who were enthusiastically training themselves for oratory, and he began to write verse in the swinging rhythm of the spoken line. He has never dropped this habit, for all of his poetry is meant to be read aloud, and some of it is printed with marginal directions for the guidance of the reader. Moreover much of his verse is written in the hortatory strain, the rather "preachy" style that exhorts the hearers to live better and nobler lives. This strain is inherent in the Middle West, and association with the youthful orators of Hiram College gave added emphasis to something that was already in Lindsay's nature. The next step in his education took Lindsay sharply away from the ideals of the Middle West, for he went to Chicago to study painting at the Art Institute. After three years in that city, he went to New York where he studied under the great teacher and artist, Robert Henri. An education in Hiram College and in an art school strengthened both sides of Lindsay's dual nature. By the fortification of this strange duality, the future poet was guaranteed the permanent possession of his characteristic trait, the spirit of the Middle West linked with a sincere love of beauty.

From the New York School of Art Lindsay went into Y.M.C.A. service, becoming one of the Association's lecturers for about four years. From this work he went to the kindred task of lecturing for the Anti-Saloon League in the state of Illinois. This work held him only a year, for the other side of his nature was demanding utterance. It is said, moreover, that the Anti-Saloon League objected to his combining the gospel of prohibition with the gospel of esthetic beauty. Then came the tramping years when the poet wandered over the Mississippi Valley and the Southwest actually trading rhymes for bread and lecturing to the farmers and townspeople on civic beauty and village betterment. One of the most revealing things that Lindsay has ever done was the making of a "Village Improvement Parade," a series of pictorial preachments interspersed with hortatory placards that read, "Bad taste is mob law; good taste is democracy," "Ugliness is a kind of misgovernment," "Fair streets are better than silver; green parks are better than gold." The improvement parade mixes esthetics and evangelism with a vengeance.

Lindsay's Poetry.—One of the early issues of *Poetry* carried a short piece by an unknown author, "General Booth Enters into Heaven." The poem began in the rhythm of "Are You Washed in the Blood of the Lamb?" and proceeded to a homely description of General Booth's entrance into heaven. The lines were full of figures taken from the Salvation Army and from life in the Middle West. Marginal notations indicated the accompaniment and told the reader how to chant the lines. This was the reading public's first introduction to Vachel Lindsay, and the poem was characteristic of the best that he was to do in later years. In 1913 he published his first volume. A year later came *The Congo,* a volume whose title piece is one of the great successes of recent literature. This poem is a free fantasia on Negro themes. It moves easily back and forth from the United States to Africa and includes overtones of cannibal dances on the Congo, race-riots, the burning of a Negro by a mob, a minstrel show, Conrad's "Heart of Darkness," and songs of Stephen Foster. The barbaric color and the pounding rhythm of the lines assist in making the poem enormously effective as an interpretation of the Negro soul. "The Santa Fé Trail" is another fantasy on a purely American subject. This poem appeared in the volume containing "The Congo." In 1917 Lindsay published his

Chinese Nightingale volume. The title poem of this book is said to be the author's favorite, but despite that preference it is flat and lacking in significance beside the poems just mentioned. However, one is forced to admit that the author's reading of the piece reveals a beauty and a coherence that are not immediately apparent to the reader dependent upon the printed page. In 1923 Lindsay issued his *Collected Poems*. Since that time he has done little that is original or that is even a good imitation of his earlier work, but very recently there have been indications that he is working through to a new form of expression, a new style, that will be very effective if and when it is achieved.

Better than any of the major poets of the country Lindsay has been able to give us an interpretation of the Negro. In addition to his splendidly successful "Congo" he has written his version of a Negro sermon in "How Samson Bore Away the Gates of Gaza." Others of his Negro poems are "John Brown," "Simon Legree," and "Daniel Jazz." The Negro camp-meeting and sermon supplied the incentive of most of these pieces. Lindsay's attitude in his treatment of Negro subjects is admirable. He has neither condescension nor the chattering enthusiasm of the person who has just discovered the black man. By an intuitive understanding of the color and imagery of the Negro mind and by a sympathy with the strong communal feeling of the African people, Lindsay has created his very effective poetry dealing with that race, always treating the Negro as a colorful spectacle and not as a problem.

Lindsay is far too much of a Middle Westerner to allow his artist-nature exclusive control of his poetry. In many of his works there is a strong humanitarian tone that at times reaches almost the fervor of religious piety. Lindsay grew up in the Lincoln country. Everywhere in Springfield there are memories of the Emancipator, and we may be very sure that a sensitive boy like Lindsay would not have been indifferent to the stories of the town's great hero. Many of the humanitarian poems invoke the spirit of Lincoln, and some of the finest refer to him by name. "Abraham Lincoln Walks at Midnight" is a quiet but deadly effective protest against war in the name of the workers, the "sober folk." In this poem there are strong overtones of bitterness at the exploitation of the peasants and commoners by the great war-lords.

"Factory Windows Are Always Broken" brings the social protest home to America. "The Leaden-Eyed" is very typical of Lindsay—

despite its quiet language—in that it protests against the failure of men to live lives of idealisms and high deeds. The poem to Altgeld is a noble tribute to the governor of Illinois who pardoned the Haymarket anarchists in the face of personal abuse and bitter political opposition. Lindsay is far too much concerned with moral questions and ethical values not to be affected by the literature of social dissection and protest. The ethical note is never completely submerged in his poetry. Even when he is writing his noisiest ragtime, he is ready to break out in impassioned denunciations of wrong or in exhortations to nobler ideas.

The *Collected Poems* of Lindsay contain many selections that are delightful children's pieces. He is about the only one of our major poets who has cultivated this very difficult type. Some of the pieces like "The Potatoes' Dance," that serious critics have deplored, are general favorites among children.

In making poetry popular Lindsay has done a real service to New Poetry and incidentally to all poetry, past and to come. In the early days of the new movement there was a genuine danger that the verse, although written for the most part in the diction of ordinary conversation and descriptive of contemporary life, would be known and appreciated only by the intellectual minority. Lindsay revived an old folk-art, communal reading. All of his poetry is meant to be read aloud, and much of it is very effective for group reading, with interlocutory passages for the leader and the ensemble. Lindsay aptly calls this type of entertainment "the higher vaudeville," although it is actually more like a poetized version of an old-time minstrel show. No one who has heard Lindsay lead a thousand people in the reading of his lines or who has heard the poet give "The Kallyope Yell" can doubt that the higher vaudeville has been successful in reaching the interests and feelings of a popular audience. The elements of Lindsay's verse that make it so effective when read aloud, either solo or ensemble, are its pounding rhythm and its obvious imagery.

Americanism of Lindsay.—Lindsay is probably the most American of all our poets. He is the articulate voice of the Middle West finding utterance in ecstatic minstrelsy, and the Middle West is about the most numerous and most unified group of the nation. Nowhere does Lindsay reveal his locale more plainly than in his very weaknesses. Hundreds of critics and observers from Mrs. Trollope to Sinclair Lewis have agreed that middle-western life is so far from being overstimulating that it tends to be intellectually somnolent. Lindsay has endeavored to break the monotony, characteristically enough by circus parades and camp meetings. The poet of "The Kallyope Yell" would make every day a circus-day. Every day should see the trappings of romance envelop the drab and ordinary things of existence. Every day should hear an appeal to men's better natures. Lindsay would rouse his hearers to activity as primitive people are roused to action by the rhythmical boom of a gong. The device is atavistic but it springs from a desire to create a diversion from the stultifying effects of too intense a preoccupation with the trivial and the ordinary.

However, Lindsay's chief heritage from the Middle West is his strong ethical drive. "I would rouse the Abraham Lincoln in you all" is the avowed intent of more than one poem. The aim is the inculcation of high moral idealism through a fierce crusading zeal. The poet is apparently not intolerant, but that there can be another type of goodness, aside from the middle-western variety, appears never to have entered his mind. Although his province is geographically broad, it makes for provincialism no less surely than the most secluded village. Narrow ethical interests are fundamental in Lindsay. Louis Untermeyer says that Lindsay is a Puritan by intention and an artist by intuition. A curious slip of the pen. Lindsay is instinctively ethical in all his thinking, feeling, and writing. His early environment is much stronger than the influence of the artist-mother. He knew Springfield before he met Robert Henri, and at the end of his student-life in Chicago and New York he returned of his own volition to his native town, where he washed the taste of forbidden things out of his mouth with draughts of Anti-Saloon League evangelism. His artistry is the self-conscious element.

The dualism of Lindsay is his greatest weakness—and his characteristic strength. The artist-soul bids his fancy soar; the crusading spirit makes it alight in the nearest pulpit. The artist in him presents a golden lyre; he trades it for a tambourine. Better than any writer of the present, Lindsay can say to his own soul, "Thou hast counseled a better course than thou hast permitted."

One can have but small patience with those supersensitive critics who deplore the *Collected Poems* and wish that Lindsay might live only by the selections in anthologies—chosen by themselves. Like Frost, Lindsay is the voice of a people's soul. He is broadly expressive of the Middle West, and if his contributions to poetry should be limited to pieces favored by the anthologists, his Middle West would be a distorted grotesque. He is the avowed poet of the "New Localism," and his locality includes much that is good and much that is not so admirable. It is represented by barren exhortations as much as by high idealisms. As a poet of such a locality, Lindsay is as significant in his poor poems as in his undoubted triumphs. In all his poems he preaches democratic politics and religion and hints at a democratic economics. His great American heroes are the great heroes of the Middle West, William J. Bryan, John P. Altgeld, and Roosevelt, although his enthusiasms range from village evangelists to Darwin, from civic improvement clubs to Nietzsche, from the rhythmic oom-pah of the jazz-band tuba to the moral idealism of Confucius. The artist in Lindsay, the inquisitive lover of beauty, may stray thousands of years or miles afield, but the instinctive interests of the midlander bring him back again to the beliefs and prejudices that were his boyhood daily bread. He is accurately called a cross-section of the Middle West. Sometimes the cross-section is presented by an artist, sometimes by an evangelist. But caviling aside, Lindsay is a great poet and a great figure in contemporary literature. There is a greatness even in his failures.

EDGAR LEE MASTERS

(1869-   )

Edgar Lee Masters stands midway between a cool scientific dissector of character like E. A. Robinson and a furious social evangelizer like Vachel Lindsay. He has both a responsive social conscience and a strong sense of curiosity about his neighbors. He would have people live better lives, but in order that they might know what evils they have to overcome before reaching the good life, he insists upon probing their souls to discover what devils possess them. Living in Chicago has had the same effect upon Masters that it had upon Herrick, Moody, and Sandburg. He became acquainted with the face of injustice and hated it, and when he came to write his most distinguished book, he held up injustice to the sight of all by laying the scene of the book in a village cemetery where the dead speak without reticence and where there are no distractions which are allowed to conceal or blur the sharp lines of the indictment. Judged by *Spoon River Anthology* Masters is dominated by a social conscience and the mind of a lawyer that is intent only upon finding out the truth about individual people.

Background of Masters.—Masters was born in Kansas, but at a very early age he was taken by his family back to Illinois where his father and grandfather had previously lived. Petersburg, Illinois, where he spent his boyhood is said to be an ordinary small town of the Middle West like thousands of others in its class. It is only about two miles from the site of New Salem, the now deserted village where Lincoln lived as a young man, and some of the finest sketches in "Spoon River" were inspired by memories of Lincoln. In Petersburg Masters gained his indisputable intimacy with small-town life.

Masters did not receive a college degree, although he was a student at Knox College for some time. After quitting college, he studied law in his father's office. In 1891 he began practice in Chicago and ultimately became a member of the firm with which Clarence Darrow was associated. Many of his cases grew out of labor troubles and industrial accidents, and in the handling of such suits Masters soon gained a reputation for legal ability and for political and economic liberalism. A token of his liberalism may be found in rather recent prose sketches of John P. Altgeld and William J. Bryan.

From his youth Masters has written poetry, and in 1898 he published his first volume, *A Book of Verses*. These poems, imitative of such men as Keats, Poe, Shelley, Swinburne, and Browning, gave rather slight promise of the author's future mastery of unconventional verse. Masters followed this first book with several others filled with dreams of Italy, odes to autumn, invocations to spring, and all the other diversions of the young poet of the nineties. As late as 1912 or 1913 he was still doing this type of work. About this time his good friend and frank critic, William Marion Reedy of the *St. Louis Mirror*, besought him quite pointedly, it is said, to desist from imitations of formal and classical poetry. It is also told that Reedy sent him a copy of the *Greek Anthology*. Acting upon the injunction and the hint given by his friend, Masters wrote *Spoon River Anthology*. It was published in Reedy's paper from May, 1914, to January, 1915, under the signature of Webster Ford. The most personal of all the poems in *Spoon River* is that spoken by Webster Ford. Immediately the work appeared in book form, and American literature received the greatest shock since the publication of *Leaves of Grass* in 1855.

"*Spoon River Anthology.*"—The anthology is a series of soliloquies, more than two hundred in number, spoken from the graves of a village cemetery. Each soliloquy is very brief, but every one is significant, and some are devastating commentaries upon life in the village. The first effect of these poems delivered as monologues is that of almost absolute objectivity. Masters seems not to obtrude in the slightest either by injecting personal opinion or by supplying a philosophical basis for the entire group. It is only by taking a view of the poems as a whole that one begins to get an understanding of the author's ideas and aversions.

Economy of means is the most obvious characteristic of the collection. The anthology is written in free verse with short lines, and curt, colloquial language. No poetic device is allowed to obscure facts. Despite his marked conciseness, Masters very often achieves a beautiful cadence, and sometimes his recital of bare facts rises to the level of majestic speech.

The poems of *Spoon River Anthology*, like the people whom they depict, cannot be divided into rigid classifications, but most of them fall into one of three groups: the purely factual with no explanations and no contrasts, the ironic sketches that gain their mordant tang from the contrast of smug appearance with crass reality, and the idealizations that show people breaking through obstacles to gain lives of satisfaction or that present a triumph of the ideal even in temporal defeat.

Critical Reception of "Spoon River Anthology."—The impact of *Spoon River Anthology* was enormous. Every literate American seemed to read the book either to attack it violently or to praise it vigorously. Critics whose tastes had been formed on conventional poetry had an especially hard time with the new book. Few doubted its power, but many of the more academically minded gravely disputed its claim to poetic worth. One critic called it "A miracle of veracious characterization; fiction of an unexampled kind; a new thing under the sun. But why drag in poetry?" One outraged critic—not a college professor, either—in a marvelously facile discussion of five or six pages examined the anthology from the standpoints of realism, lyricism, documentary value, illustrative worth, philosophy, psychology, diction, and atmosphere, only to find from every standpoint save the last that the poems were worthless, and he argued that the possession of atmosphere is itself a paltry thing. Therefore, he concluded that the poems were worthless. It is seldom that a book is submitted to a test that is so poisonously stupid and so superficially administered.

Other adverse critics ran the scale of accusation. Masters was accused of everything from naturalistic tendencies to the assassination of American character. The greatest cry of distress came from the sentimentalists. A large number of the soliloquies are ironic, and irony has always been about the most unpopular and consequently the scarcest article in American literature. Masters' reiterated note of irony was extremely displeasing to many, and the displeasure was immensely heightened by the frontal attack that *Spoon River Anthology* seemed to make on the small towns of the Middle West, for tearful sentimentalists have lavished quite as much romantic approbation upon the village as they have upon farm life. Unendurable these people called it to have a man quietly transcribe testimony out of the mouths of many witnesses that impeached the small town and its honored citizens of every sin and vice. The loyal defenders of the village seemed to read only the factual indictments and the ironic exposures; they totally missed the fine idealism of "Aaron Hatfield" and "Anne Rutledge." This clash was the first and probably the hottest fight in the long campaign that has been called the "Battle of the Village."

Any one can see to-day that Masters drew no blanket indictment against the American small town. Like Frost he was interested in getting beneath the surface of a life that had previously been insufficiently explored, and in his exploration it became necessary to knock off some of the sheen that false romance had spread around the village. Furthermore Masters is like Frost in that he has given us a picture of the general by carefully depicting the specific. By showing us the frustrations and spiritual triumphs, the deceits and the sincerities of Spoon River, Masters has given us a picture of humanity everywhere. The poet had spent his youth in a small village. Later he practiced law in Chicago where he saw social problems in the large. Then, when he started to write his book, he was able to cite universal faults and virtues in the villages of central Illinois. Louis Untermeyer has said that Spoon River is all America in microcosm, and a truer estimate was never uttered. But the anger of the sentimentalists at the exposure of vices in a small town quite swallowed up their potential pride in the revelation of village idealisms.

Masters makes absolutely no criticism of the rusticity of Spoon River. Lucinda Matlock sings a triumphal hymn of joy, and every note that she utters displays some rustic quality. Fiddler Jones is only a country fiddler, and Doc Hill is a country doctor, and Masters has not a word of criticism of them. However, he does hate the smug, meaningless conformity to convention that so often passes for acceptable morality, and he loathes intolerant provincialism, cruelty, hypocrisy, and stupidity. Of course, these qualities are by no means confined to the small town or the country. They are generally the products of environment. This fact makes Masters far more concerned with the immediate surroundings of his characters than with heredity or with philosophical discussions of free will. If he feels that a rural environment creates the qualities that he abhors, he would criticize the rustic community, but he finds no fault with country life as such. His insight could have found microcosmic America in Chicago.

The Later Work of Masters.—With ten books of poems to his credit since *Spoon River Anthology*, Masters is one of our most voluminous poets. Not all of his great number of pages rise to the level of the anthology, but it is totally unfair to the author to say that his later work is negligible. There are individual poems in his later books that are as good as anything that he has written, but the highly effective pages generally do not dominate the books, as they do *Spoon River Anthology*. Moreover in his later books Masters has returned to his old habit of writing imitative and derivative verse. The influence of Browning is especially noticeable in *Toward the Gulf* and *Domesday Book*, though both these volumes have many pages of beauty and significance. "Silence" from the volume called *Songs and Satires* is certainly one of the finest of our recent poems.

By far the most distinctive of Masters's later poetry is the work called *New Spoon River*. The entire plan and execution of this book are much like those of the early anthology, only the new volume has lost much of the factual presentation and the ironic contrasts that made the earlier one notable. *New Spoon River* contains too much abstract speculation and too little documentary evidence, though many of the poems are very effective, and the volume as a whole is a very significant work.

As the author of six volumes of prose fiction between 1920 and 1927, Masters demands some little consideration as a novelist. It is not a damning criticism to say that none of his novels attains the scope and power of either anthology. In his most effective prose like *Mitch Miller* and *Skeeters Kirby* he uses the familiar background of Spoon River. *Mirage* is the story of Skeeters Kirby grown up. *Nuptial Flight* is a long story of three generations of Illinois people. His longest and most closely documented novel, *Children of the Market Place*, is the story of Stephen A. Douglas. It is not very successful. His latest book is a critical biography of Abraham Lincoln.

The things that we value in Masters to-day are not the things that were so apparent to the critics of 1915 who were reeling under the impact of *Spoon River Anthology* and who were blinded by the blaze of controversy. They could see only the public dissection of personal and community character, the exposure of corrupt politics, venal journalism, and conforming hypocrisy. To-day we think no less of Masters's social conscience, but we see that he did more than show us plague spots to be eradicated. He has given us more than a glimpse of those who live happily and profitably in the spirit and win the ideal even at the cost of apparent defeat. His picture of life appears better balanced than it once did. To-day Spoon River seems to be all America, divested of irrelevant qualities and concentrated in a village cemetery. *Spoon River Anthology* is thought by many to be the most important single volume of poetry published in America since 1855.

CARL SANDBURG

(1878-   )

Chicago is the far-flung, ebullient spirit of the Middle West, drawn to a head and personified by a motley throng of foreign laborers, native merchant princes, and financial magnates, shop-girls, clerks, gangsters, bullying foremen, hoodlums, and ordinary folk from the surrounding prairies. But there is also much of the rural in the metropolis. Illinois, Indiana, and Wisconsin farmers tend their cornfields within sight of the tawny smoke-blanket that arises from the factories and stock-yards of the big city. And it is this environment that Carl Sandburg has adopted. Its speech is his speech, and its feelings are his feelings. It covers a big territory, not especially big in area but extraordinarily confusing in its variety of people and aspects. Thoreau found his universe in a Concord bean-field; Frost discovered his world under the crust of New England provincialism; Masters reconstructed his out of the dust and memories of a country graveyard; Carl Sandburg came upon his in the variegated pageant of Chicago and the contiguous country. He knows Chicago, "the city of Big Shoulders," but he reminds us that "I was born on the prairie and the milk of its wheat, the red of its clover, the eyes of its women, gave me a song and a slogan." Sandburg fuses city streets and corn-fields into a mass that is at once as unified and as multifarious as America itself.

Carl Sandburg was born in Galesburg, Illinois, where he lived for his first fifteen years. He is the son of Swedish immigrants who were satisfied with a few years of grade school education for the boy. He stopped school at thirteen and found work on a milk wagon. For the next six or seven years he did all the odd jobs that a strong, uneducated laborer usually finds in the towns and grain fields of the Mississippi Valley. He was bootblack in a barber shop, a common laborer in brickyards and harvest fields, scene shifter in a theater, and a hotel dishwasher. In 1898 he enlisted in the army to have a hand in the Spanish-American War, and upon his return to Illinois decided to get an education. He was admitted to Lombard College where he spent four years as the big "activity man" on the campus. Here, too, he met a discerning teacher who encouraged him to write. After his graduation he worked as a newspaper man in Milwaukee, served as secretary to the mayor of the city, acted as organizer for the Socialist Party, and held a place on the staff of an industrial publication in Chicago. Since 1917 he has been steadily on the staff of the *Chicago Daily News,* with the exception of a year that he spent as the Stockholm correspondent for a news association. While he was living in Milwaukee, he married Lillian Steichen, sister of Edward Steichen, the photographer.

His first success was *Chicago Poems,* published in April, 1916. This was followed by *Cornhuskers* (1918), *Smoke and Steel* (1920), *Slabs of the Sunburnt West* (1922), and *Good Morning, America* (1928). In addition to these volumes of poetry he has written two books of Rootabaga stories for children, and he has produced in his *Abraham Lincoln: The Prairie Years,* one of the finest biographies ever done by an American. Sandburg has a deep interest in the collection and preservation of the folk songs of America, often giving recitals of the material that he has gathered. His *American Songbag* is the best collection that we have of the folk balladry of all classes of American society.

Sandburg's Poetry.—In one of her sympathetic reviews of Sandburg's poetry, Harriet Monroe once quoted Debussy's saying, "Rules are made by works of art, not for works of art." The quotation is apt. In some future time critics and prosodists—or what will then pass as prosodists—may possibly cite the work of Sandburg as the beginning of a new and individual poetic form. At least no sensible critic of to-day will ever seek to measure the living beat and surge of the *Chicago Poems* by the dead standard of petrified rules.

It is perversely wrong to say that Sandburg's lines are only jumbles of words broken capriciously into meaningless line lengths. The poet does not always disdain regularity of stress, and he labors over his lines to gain the exact cadences that he is seeking. Such a poem as "Monotone" is usually not dashed off by a man who is contemptuous of stress and cadence.

> The monotone of the rain is beautiful
> And the sudden rise and slow relapse
> Of the long multitudinous rain.
>
> The sun on the hills is beautiful,
> Or a captured sunset sea-flung,
> Bannered with fire and gold.
>
> A face I know is beautiful—
> With fire and gold of sky and sea,
> And the peace of long warm rain.

But it is not to be denied that in general Sandburg is a very unconventional poet. His verse is unusual, his figures of speech are startlingly unconventional, and his diction is the most amazing thing about his poetry.

Sandburg does not strip his lines of all rhetorical adornment, but he assuredly does not borrow any clichés from older poets. One of these older writers, acting for the nonce as literary critic, solemnly protested Sandburg's figure in the line, "The past is a bucket of ashes." Notwithstanding its unconventionality, the line says forcefully and accurately what the poet wished to say, and it is probable that most of the older figures of speech arose in much the same way that this one did and over the same kind of objections. In his "Nocturne in a Deserted Brickyard" Sandburg sees reflected colors "make a wide dreaming pansy of an old pool in the night." In his "Killers" he says:

> I am singing to you
> Soft as a man with a dead child speaks;
> Hard as a man in handcuffs,
> Held where he cannot move.

In another sketch he writes:

I know a Jew fish crier down on Maxwell Street with a voice like a north wind blowing over corn stubble in January.

But not all of Sandburg's figures are startling either by their crude force or authenticity. Sometimes his most unconventional figures are as soft and tender as any ever written.

> The fog comes
> On little cat feet.
>
> It sits looking
> Over harbor and city
> On silent haunches
> And then moves on.

His "Blue Island Intersection" has a few lines that are not easily surpassed for imagination and for sheer beauty.

> In the false dawn when the chickens blink
> And the east shakes a lazy baby toe at tomorrow,
> And the east fixes a pink half-eye this way. . . .

The New Diction of Sandburg.—To the readers and the writers of the older type of poetry the most surprising thing about Sandburg is his diction. The saying of Synge that poetry ought to have its roots in the clay and worms Sandburg applied with a vengeance. He thrust the roots of his verse down into the sub-soil of Chicago speech and extracted poetic beauty from the strange place. His is not the smart, denaturized slang of an O. Henry. It is the lingo that passes current in the streets and dingy restaurants and speak-easies of Chicago, and he tosses it about with an easy familiarity that is born only of intimacy. English readers and distressingly cultured Americans, appalled at the unfamiliar monosyllables, vainly thumb their dictionaries of slang to interpret the crackling lines.

In "Cahoots" we find the following words that may be more or less unfamiliar to readers: "cahoots," "harness bulls," "dicks," "frontoffice men," "fifty-fifty," "dips," "stick-up," "gazump." In the vituperative outburst, "To a Contemporary Bunkshooter" we find lines like the following:

You come along . . . tearing your shirt . . . yelling about Jesus.
     Where do you get that stuff?
     What do you know about Jesus?
Jesus had a way of talking soft and outside of a few bankers and higher-
     ups among the con-men of Jerusalem everybody liked to have this
     Jesus around because he never made any fake passes and every-
     thing he said went and he helped the sick and gave people hope.

Go ahead and bust all the chairs you want to. Smash a whole wagon
     load of furniture at every performance. Turn sixty summersaults
     and stand on your nutty head. If it wasn't for the way you scare
     the women and kids I'd feel sorry for you and pass the hat.

In addition to his very vivid slang Sandburg writes occasionally in an easy, colloquial style that the older poets find almost as obnoxious and unpoetic as the use of such words as "bug-house," "wop," "four-flusher," or "nutty." For instance, his "Cool Tombs" is utterly American in its diction, and yet there are few who think that it is unpoetic.

But to make Sandburg live only as a harsh and violent poet of slang and colloquialisms is to skip over more than half of his poems. He is a poet of brooding beauty, a lover of fog and sunset colors, a tender worshiper of childhood.

> Desolate and lone
> All night long on the lake
> Where the fog trails and mist creeps,
> The whistle of a boat
> Calls and cries unendingly,
> Like some lost child
> In tears and trouble
> Hunting the harbor's breast
> And the harbor's eyes.

Sandburg's Chicago.—The Chicago of Sandburg is not exactly the same city described by Herrick and Dreiser. To get his impressions Sandburg has been only a pair of ears and a pair of wide-open eyes. He sees and hears, and then sets down his impressions in crisp, fresh words that transcribe the very jangle and color of the

great city. No writer has been so successful in giving us his physical
impressions of a city in the machine age. But he gives us only
emotional reactions. He never stops to philosophize, never pauses
to formulate a theory of social well-being. He is an exposed emotion in one of the most sensational cities in the world.

The whole of Chicago flickers and crashes through Sandburg's
poems with all the verisimilitude of a "sound" picture. The city
is a strange, noisy place, full of shocking cruelties and flashes of
dazzling beauty. Above everything it possesses energy.

Come and show me another city with lifted head singing so proud to be
    alive and coarse and strong and cunning.
Flinging magnetic curses amid the toil of piling job on job, here is a tall
    bold slugger set vivid against the little soft cities.

Of all the things in Chicago the dominant interest to Sandburg
is the people, and the people of his poems are simply the western
pioneers of Longstreet, Twain, and Garland, drawn from eastern
and central Europe and crowded together, some in wealth and some
in poverty, in a magnificent but monstrous city. And Sandburg is
the fit poet of such a people. Unthinkingly he accepts their aspirations as his, and over all his poetry hangs a western pioneer's dislike of inequality and oppression. If it is the sight of economic inequality that is always outraging him, it should be remembered that
the city of the machine age creates just such sights. The poet ex-
coriates the wealthy who overwork and underpay their helpers. He
hates the mill doors, symbols of a machine age, for they also symbolize the force that sucks the life blood and the joy of living out
of workers' veins.

                    You never come back.
        I say good-by when I see you going in the doors,
        The hopeless open doors that call and wait
        And take you then for—how many cents a day?
        How many cents for the sleepy eyes and fingers?
        I say good-by because I know they tap your wrists,
        In the dark, in the silence, day by day,
        And all the blood of you drop by drop,
        And you are old before you are young.
                    You never come back.

Like the sensible man that Sandburg is, he realizes that there is
no such thing as rejecting the machine age. It is an accomplished

fact. He does not even hate it or rebel against it except when it is guilty of twisting and hampering the lives and hearts of men.

Humanitarianism of Sandburg.—Fundamentally Sandburg is a mystic. He is not self-conscious like Whitman, but, as one would expect in a machine age, a very quiet, shy, elusive mystic who makes his concealed mysticism the foundation of all his work. In most of the poems the mystic identification of self and the other-self is revealed by hints and pervasive overtones. Occasionally, however, there is something more than a hint, as in this "Portrait."

> To write one book in five years
> or five books in one year,
> to be the painter and the thing painted,
> . . . where are we, bo?
>
> . . . .
>
> Can a man sit at a desk in a skyscraper in Chicago
> and be a harnessmaker in a corn town in Iowa
> and feel the tall grass coming up in June
> and the ache of the cottonwood trees
> singing with the prairie wind?

This poem is inscribed to "S. A.," initials that may perhaps stand for Sherwood Anderson, himself another mystical interpreter of American life.

Sandburg is a true mystic of the machine age. Other men may feel an identification with divine love or with nature or with all humanity, but Sandburg prays:

Lay me on an anvil, O God,
Beat me and hammer me into a steel spike,
Drive me into the girders that hold the skyscraper together.
Take red-hot rivets and fasten me into the central girders.
Let me be the great nail holding a skyscraper together through blue nights
    into white stars.

Occasionally Sandburg has an echo of the mystic humanitarianism of Whitman:

I cross the sheets of fire in No Man's Land for you, my brother—I slip a
    steel tooth into your throat, you my brother—I die for you and I
    kill you. . . .

It is undoubtedly this humanitarianism, this mystic sense of the brotherhood of man, that has made Sandburg so sensitive to the environment of his brothers. He is not a sociologist, for no sustained study of society and its problems has ever appeared in his poetry. He is not a propagandist, for he has no specific cause to advocate. He is only a mystic who resents the wrongs done to others by the environment as a wrong done to himself. He is a counterpart of John Woolman, Thoreau, and Whitman placed in most unusual surroundings.

Like most humanitarians Sandburg is opposed to war. He makes no argument based upon the futility of fighting; he simply gives the emotional reaction to wholesale slaughter of a tender poet who can never get far enough away from the battle to make the killing of a man an impersonal thing. "A. E. F." is one of the strongest indictments ever drawn against war, but the little poem never mentions bloodshed; it is simply an episode illustrative of universal truth. "And So Today" is the most enduring bit of literature that came out of the burial of the Unknown Soldier at Arlington.

The violence of Sandburg, that so many people find objectionable, comes from his humanitarianism. He is a tender man, a lover of humanity, whose natural speech is as shy and tender as the man himself, but the revolting cruelties and injustices of a mechanized world drive him into a frenzy. Then he raises his voice and speaks in the tongue that the world can understand. But inherently the brawling tones are not his own; they are taken over from the environment that is both noisy and cruel.

Other Work of Sandburg.—In his *Rootabaga Stories* Sandburg has achieved success in one of the most difficult of fields, that of fantasy written for children. The masterly biography, *Abraham Lincoln: The Prairie Years*, has already been mentioned. It is a closely documented history written by a poet who brings to his work infinite sympathy with the subject and an intimate knowledge of the surroundings of Lincoln's early life. The book is an illuminating study, and many portions are done in an exquisite prose style. It seems to be as sure of a long life as anything that Sandburg has written.

. . . .

Admirers of each of the contemporary poets never lack for arguments to show why their particular writer would be the best possible ambassador from the contemporary generation to generations yet unborn. Without expressing any opinion in the fruitless controversy, one can say rather assuredly that it will be a disaster to the future reputation of our time if the poetry of Sandburg is forgotten. The Chicago poet stands in poetry where Dreiser stands in fiction. He is the interpreter of a reckless, violent age that perforce submits to the ruthless domination of mechanical and scientific laws, and holds in utter defiance all spiritual obligations. But Sandburg does more than describe his time and place. He proves that the machine age, even in the city environment, cannot quench that mystic spark that has long guided the way to individual decency and high social ideals. He proves that with the coming of the mechanized life we have not allowed the divine gift of righteous indignation to be displaced by a mental gesture of passive acquiescence. He proves that men can look through the smoke of factories and still glimpse beauty untarnished by the smudge and that some few still dream of a better day that may be achieved through the exercise in an alien world of a few old-fashioned virtues.

ARTURO GIOVANNITTI

(1884-   )

The I.W.W. Movement.—To-day the early syndicalist movement in the United States seems to be as dead as the Whiskey Rebellion or the abolition controversy. It is only with difficulty that even those who remember well the period from 1900 to 1917 can reconstruct those turbulent days in our economic life when one labor disturbance succeeded another with portentous regularity. To-day we have forgotten the immediate issues of those savage contests, and the proletarian economic theories that lay behind the struggles have long since ceased to be of any concern save to the historian. Whether the eclipse of the radical economic thought is temporary or permanent, only time can assuredly say, but just now there seems to be a growing tendency on the part of all classes to accept the present economic system both in theory and in practice. This acceptance takes the form of acquiescence, granted without any discussion whatever.

The rise of such radical organizations as the Industrial Workers of the World during the period from 1900 to 1917 was no spasmodic outburst. It was the logical result of a long train of circumstances. Grave disturbances had marked the relations of capital and labor since the Civil War. By 1900 the capitalists were deeply exasperated over the recurring strikes, and the laborers becoming more bitter with each defeat and, as they became acquainted with radical economic doctrine, more forward in their demands for sweeping changes in the existing order. Many workers, especially migratory or seasonal laborers, utterly rejecting the official attitude of the large labor organizations, accepted the gospel of violence as the one practicable suggestion that might lead to a favorable result. Sometimes this recommended violence was to be active, as it was in the better known strikes, but quite as often—and probably far more often—it was of the passive variety. That is, laborers were to "strike on the job" by impeding the profitable processes of industry in every way while allowing those processes to continue without visible opposition.

The I.W.W. became the champions of active violence. From its origin in the Far West, where unionizing such groups as the loggers was difficult and where the migratory and seasonal workers were very numerous, this loosely organized syndicalist group spread to other parts of the country. Wherever an important strike was in progress, there hastened the apostles of violence to dash oil upon the smoldering embers of class hatred. Such work was never fruitless. In dozens of strike areas violence was met with violence until miniature civil wars resulted. The outcome of many of these strikes was inconclusive, save in the inculcation of hatred and social disturbances, but the I.W.W. were denounced by every constituted authority as enemies of society and fomenters of discord. During the World War the government proceeded vigorously against the organization, and by 1920 the order had been hounded out of existence. To-day only an odious memory remains of the once-feared organization devoted to violence. Yet before it disappeared, the order contributed one name to American literature. That name is Arturo Giovannitti.

Giovannitti's Life.—Giovannitti was born in Campobasso, a small city of the Abruzzi, in south-central Italy. His father was a physician and a chemist, and his two brothers were professional men, one a physician, the other a lawyer. Giovannitti had a fair education in his native province. About 1902 he left Italy and went first to Canada where he worked as a coal miner. Here he met the realities of class struggle in a new country, and the raw newness of the social environment, with the superior class not yet in possession of the non-economic sanctions that it gains in an older culture, simply brought the issue of the struggle into sharp relief.

In some way Giovannitti was attracted to a Presbyterian mission in Montreal, and when the director died, the Italian immigrant was placed in charge. From the Montreal mission, Giovannitti went to another in Brooklyn, where he served as teacher and preacher among the newly arrived immigrants. Next he enrolled in the Union Theological Seminary and took work in Columbia, but some of the academic work was distasteful to him, and he went to Pittsburgh to head another mission. Here in one of the great industrial cities of America he first became acquainted with socialism. Already his religious work had made him socially minded, and he was doubtless very receptive to proletarian economics. His interest in the new theories led him away from his early work, and he became a hostile critic of the church. While in Pittsburgh he worked in an Italian socialistic newspaper, *Il Proletario*. When the great textile strike broke out in the mills of Lawrence, Massachusetts, Giovannitti and Joseph Ettor went to the scene of the trouble. The two became leaders and advisers of the strikers. Giovannitti always denied having urged or countenanced violence, yet when a woman was killed in a street riot, both Ettor and Giovannitti were arraigned on capital charges of inciting to riot. The statute under which they were arrested had not been invoked since the anti-draft riots of the Civil War. For almost ten months the prisoners were kept in jail, though they were ultimately freed after a long trial.

"Arrows in the Gale."—During his months in jail Giovannitti first read the classics, both literary and philosophical. He was particularly attracted by the poetry of Byron and Shelley. Without doubt the unorthodox doctrines of these poets appealed to him, no less than did their literary merits. From reading verse, Giovannitti was moved to express himself in poetic form. The results of these efforts were afterwards printed in *Arrows in the Gale* (1914). This little book, now rather difficult to purchase, contains the essence of radical humanitarianism that swings with moving power from the white heat of passion to the tenderness of proletarian mysticism. The book makes no apology. Its "Proem" declares that the lines are

> . . . the blows of my own sledge
> Against the walls of my own jail.

Nor is there any effort to palliate the radicalism of the author.

> All that you worship, fear, and trust
> I kick into the sewer's maw,
> And fling my shaft and my disgust
> Against your gospel and your law.

The most striking individual poems in the group are "The Cage" and "The Walker," both written in long rhythmical lines of free verse. Some of the pieces are orthodox poetry. "The Thinker," a poem inspired by Rodin's statue, is a rousing lyric addressed to the common man.

> Aye, think while breaks in you the dawn,
>   Crouched at your feet the world lies still—
> It has no power but your brawn,
>   It knows no wisdom but your will.
>
> Beyond your flesh and mind and blood
>   Nothing there is to live or do.
> There is no man, there is no God,
>   There is not anything but you.

"The Sermon on the Common" is not so successful as some of its fellows, but it contains one sentence that might serve as the text of Giovannitti's message: "Blessed are the strong in freedom's spirit; for theirs is the kingdom of the earth." And the message that is built on this text is one of love, peace, fellowship, and social justice to all.

"The Cage" is an appraisal of that authority that seeks to "settle twentieth century troubles with sixteenth century justice."

In the middle of the great greenish room stood the green iron cage.

All was old and cold and mournful, ancient with the double antiquity of heart and brain in the great greenish room.

Old and hoary was the man who sat upon the faldstool, upon the fireless and godless altar.

Old were the tomes that mouldered behind him on the dusty shelves.

Old was the painting of an old man that hung above him.

Old the man upon his left, who awoke with his cracked voice the dead echoes of dead centuries; old the man upon his right who wielded a wand; and old all those who spoke to him and listened to him before and around the green iron cage.

Old were the words they spoke, and their faces were drawn and white and lifeless, without expression or solemnity; like the ikons of old cathedrals.

    .   .   .   .

Senility, dullness and dissolution were all around the green iron cage, and nothing was new or young and alive in the great room, except the three men who were in the cage.

    .   .   .   .

Love, then I heard for the first time the creak of the moth that was eat-

ing the old painting and the old books, and the worm that was
gnawing the old bench, and it was then that I saw that all the old
men around the great greenish room were dead.

They were dead like the old man in the old painting, save that they still
read the old books that he could read no more, and still spoke and
heard the old words he could speak and hear no more, and still
passed the judgment of the dead, which he no more could pass,
upon the mighty life of the world outside that throbbed and thundered and clamored and roared the wonderful anthem of Labor to the
fatherly justice of the Sun.

"The Walker" is the most remarkable poem by Giovannitti and
one of the great achievements of American verse. It is a magnificent
expression of proletarian mysticism, an impassioned chant that flames
with protest against conditions in a society where "all things natural
are things impossible so long as there are jails in the world—bread,
work, happiness, peace, and love."

I hear footsteps over my head all night.

They come and they go. Again they come and they go all night.

They come one eternity in four paces and they go one eternity in four
paces, and between the coming and the going there is Silence and the
Night and the Infinite.

For infinite are the nine feet of a prison cell, and endless is the march
of him who walks between the yellow brick wall and the red iron
gate, thinking things that cannot be changed and cannot be locked,
but that wander far away in the sun-lit world, each in a wild pilgrimage after a destined goal.

.   .   .   .   .

Wonderful is the supreme wisdom of the jail that makes all think the
same thought. . . . The democracy of reason has leveled all the two
hundred minds to the common surface of the same thought.

I, who have never killed, think like the murderer;

I, who have never stolen, reason like the thief;

.   .   .   .   .

My brother, do not walk any more.

It is wrong to walk on a grave. It is a sacrilege to walk four steps from
the headstone to the foot and four steps from the foot to the headstone.

If you stop walking, my brother, this will be no longer a grave; for you
will give me back my mind that is chained to your feet and the
right to think my own thoughts.

I implore you, my brother, for I am weary of the long vigil, weary of
counting your steps and heavy with sleep.

Stop, rest, sleep, my brother, for the dawn is well nigh, and it is not the
key alone that can throw open the door.

AMY LOWELL AND THE IMAGISTS

> Despite her traducers, there's always a heart
> Hid away in her poems for the seeking; impassioned
> Beneath silver surfaces cunningly fashioned
> To baffle coarse prying, it waits for the touch
> Of a man who takes his surfaces only as such.

Thus Amy Lowell truly characterizes herself in her "Critical Fable." If there is any objection to be raised against the self-portrait it is that sometimes she was too busy with the polishing to make sure that the heart was there.

Amy Lowell (*1874-1925*).—The lack of personal emotion in Miss Lowell's verse is due in part to two elements in her nature, her aristocratic ancestry and her great intellectual power. Her inherent pride keeps her from opening her heart too wide in public, and emotion is always somewhat alien to people of marked intellectuality. Emotion Miss Lowell had in plenty, but it was the emotion of the critic and controversialist, not the emotion of the creative artist. Her brilliant mind and her wide reading gave her an immense amount of material for her poetry, so much that it would have tended to crowd out personal experience, if she had been inclined to use it, and her fine critical powers made her labor on the surface of her poetry until it shone like burnished metal.

Miss Lowell was born in Brookline, Massachusetts, of a very distinguished ancestry. Her family had previously produced writers, statesmen, diplomats, men of affairs, and educators, and her two brothers were Percival Lowell, the astronomer, and A. Lawrence Lowell, president of Harvard. Her permanent home during the whole of her life was her estate, Sevenels, where she was born.

It was not until Miss Lowell was twenty-eight years old that she decided to devote herself to writing. Then for eight years she studied, read, and wrote to perfect herself in her art. She read widely in many fields, paying particular attention to contemporary French poets. In 1910 she published her first poem, and two years later her first book appeared. The title, *A Dome of Many Colored Glass*, taken from Shelley, admirably foreshadowed the contents of the volume. Most of the lines were carefully built on classical models, and many of them were obviously derivative. As a whole the book was not impressive either for its performance or for its promise, though it contained hints of an interest in exotic pictorial art that was later to develop richly.

In 1913 Miss Lowell visited England where she met the dynamic Ezra Pound, as keen of intellect and as vivid of personality as she herself was. She became interested in the work of the Imagists, a small group of poetic experimenters consisting of Pound, Richard Aldington, F. S. Flint, Hilda Doolittle, John Gould Fletcher, and D. H. Lawrence. Her brilliant mind and her fighting nature made her an admirable leader of the group. As was to be expected, she and Pound developed what has been called a "pleasant enmity." Imagism did not hold her for long, but her affiliation with the poets of that school marked an important step in her poetic development.

In 1914 came the second book, *Sword Blades and Poppy Seeds*. This volume represented an enormous advance along the path of the New Poetry. It was daringly experimental. Gone were the borrowed accents and the derivative lines, and in their place appeared *vers libre* and a new thing in English, polyphonic prose. This type of prose, many-voiced, the term means, is so called because it borrows all the poetic voices or devices such as meter, free verse, assonance, alliteration, rhyme, and refrain. It had been developed by Paul Fort, one of the modern French poets whom Miss Lowell had studied. "Red Slippers" is a good example of this literary form.

With the publication of this second volume Miss Lowell became the acknowledged champion of free verse in this country. It probably was in this work that she did her finest service to American poetry. She was an extraordinarily gifted and pugnacious propagandist, and most of our struggling young poets owe more than a little to her assistance. Her best, but probably not her most typical, critical studies are to be found in *Six French Poets*, discussions of contemporary French poetry with many translations, and *Tendencies in Modern American Poetry*, one of the very best treatments of the subject that we have. The last piece of criticism that she did was the two-volume biography of Keats, an excellent work.

Of Miss Lowell's poetic work those portions that seem to be of the most value are her pictorial sketches and her narrative poems. Her pictorial work translates every sensation into terms of sight and color, until the lines glisten and flash like a jewel.

> The throats of the little red trumpet-flowers are wide open,
> And the clangor of brass beats against the hot sunlight.

They bray and blare at the burning sky.
Red! Red! Coarse notes of red,
Trumpeted at the blue sky.
In long streaks of sound, molten metal,
The vine declares itself.
Clang!—from its red and yellow trumpets.
Clang!—from its long nasal trumpets,
Splitting the sunlight into ribbons, tattered and shot with noise.

Her narrative poetry is excellent. Usually choosing a subject that lends itself to a colorful treatment, she works in the color bit by bit until the story is like a painting with rich pigments and masterly shading. *Legends* (1921) probably contains the best of her narrative work. Her *Fir-Flower Tablets* are little poems that resemble exquisite paintings in miniature.

Miss Lowell had an excellent feeling for artistic form. Her judgment seldom led her into using a vehicle that was unsuitable for her material at hand, and some of her poems are models of good form. The best known is "Patterns," a *tour de force* of poetic composition, in which pattern dominates the content as well as the outward form of the poem.

Harriett Monroe says in effect that Miss Lowell's poetry is significant largely because it is an element in a great career. Amy Lowell had a great personality, and she did great work for contemporary American poets, but she herself was hardly a great writer. She had everything that a successful poet needs except the ability or the will to put herself into her lines. Somehow her verse usually lacked the heart that we have always looked for in our poets. But she consistently knew what she was doing. In the preface to an early volume, she said, "I wish to state my firm belief that poetry should not try to teach, that it should exist simply because it is created beauty, even if sometimes the beauty of a Gothic grotesque." This statement evidently means that it was the poet's intention to create pictorial beauty in her lines rather than to write poetry that is a cry from the heart. If this was her intention, she succeeded admirably.

The white mares of the moon rush along the sky
Beating their golden hoofs upon the glass heavens;
The white mares of the moon are all standing on their hind legs
Pawing at the green porcelain doors of the remote heavens.
Fly, mares.
Strain your utmost,

> Scatter the milky dust of stars,
> Or the tiger sun will leap upon you and destroy you
> With one lick of his vermilion tongue.

Miss Lowell made an immense contribution to our recent poetic development. She wrote an impressive amount of material, much of it frankly experimental, that ranged from sonnets in imitation of Keats to exotic legends in free verse and translations of Chinese poetry. Her dominating personality made her a good leader of new causes, and many poets followed her gladly. Nor was she one to take a position and then leave her followers to the fire of conservative critics. Indeed the smoke and clamor raised by Miss Lowell somewhat obscure even yet the genuine value of her own creative work. Thus far she has received no adequate critical appraisal. She who rescued so many reputations from premature oblivion deserves a discriminating biographical and critical study.

The Imagists.—About 1913 Ezra Pound, who has always had a positive talent for disturbing the placid dogmatism of critics, managed to bring together a group of young writers who were experimenting with New Poetry. The group called themselves Imagists. In 1914 Pound brought his protégés into public notice by supervising the publication of a small volume, called *Des Imagistes*, which contained poems by a number of hands. The new group, somewhat self-conscious, shortly made a formal statement of aims in a pronouncement characterized rather more by narrowness than by catholicity.

The Imagists declared that they were seeking to write poetry that would employ the exact word but that they would also use only the language of common speech; that they wished the new moods of the modern age to find expression in new rhythms; that they refused to be limited in any way in their choice of subjects; that they wished to create images and not vague generalities; that they wanted their lines to be hard and clear—not blurred; and that they sought concentration rather than diffuseness. These aims simply meant that grandiloquent rhetoric, muddled thinking and writing, indefinite reflective moods, and metaphysical speculation were to be barred from Imagistic poetry. As many were quick to assert, the aims were not exactly new, for they had recently been exemplified, in part, at least, by the Symbolists of France. Furthermore all schools of English poetry for the last two hundred years had agreed with most of the Imagistic creed in theory, though rather seldom in practice. Others saw in Imagism only a restatement of the aims of Wordsworth and Whitman, two men who had striven for the exact, ordinary word and for the creation of sharp images. However, the new school was quick to repudiate the attempted identification, specifically rejecting many of the lines of the two older poets because of their vague generalities. For instance, such a line as Whitman's

And the cow crunching with depressed head, surpasses any statue

would probably have been criticized by the Imagists. The first part of the line is a clear image, but "depressed" may not be the exact word, and the last portion creates only a vague generality.

For the bearers of a creed that had been sanctified by previous critical pronouncements and poetic practice, the Imagists were subjected to exceedingly rough treatment. The attitude of the new school was not exactly conciliatory, and the remarks of the conservative critics were quite irritating in their obtuse misunderstanding. Even some of the New Poets joined lustily with the older critics to pummel the upstarts. Such imbroglios were the breath of life to Amy Lowell, Ezra Pound, and one or two others of the group, and the literary journals from 1914 to 1916 resounded with the noise of combat. The debate probably generated more heat than light. To the non-combatant it seems that both sides ended by withdrawing from their high positions. Most of the Imagists went on perfecting their art on somewhat broader lines than indicated by their creed, and the conservative critics finished by grudgingly admitting the new school to the realm of poetry.

Imagism had obvious weaknesses, though it contributed much to the New Poetry movement. Its inherent limitations are indicated by its very name. Verse written in accordance with the celebrated creed must of necessity appeal almost exclusively to the visual sense. It tends to become word-painting, though Ezra Pound defined an image as "that which presents an intellectual and emotional complex in an instant of time," and his poetry was always broader in its appeal than was that of some of the others. However, all the Imagists have progressed beyond their original creed. The best things about the new school were its insistence upon directness, clarity, simplicity, and vivid imagery. These qualities were genuinely needed by the New Poetry that was in danger of succumbing to the facile and the eloquent. Imagism as a school is dead, but its influence is far from gone.

Ezra Pound, Experimenter (1885-   ).—Ezra Pound is a curious combination of contradictions. Born in the Far West in Hailey, Idaho, he has been a seeker after the exotic for the last twenty years, living in Italy, England, and France. At present his home is in Paris where he is one of the three famous English-speaking men of letters who live in that city. The other two are James Joyce and Ford Madox Ford. Furthermore, Pound is an erudite scholar of medieval literature and the most daring of experimenters in the New Poetry. He can write an imitation of an impersonal medieval ballad like "The Ballad of the Goodly Fere," or he can turn off a polished piece of personal criticism or vitriolic satire. He is a genuine intellectual Imagist and a poet of elemental feeling. Like Alfred Kreymborg and Amy Lowell, he can claim the distinction of helping start many a literary innovation, most of which he abandoned shortly for other experiments. One of his chief diversions has been the lending of a hand at the launching of many new magazines. *Poetry, Blast, Broom,* and *The Transatlantic Review* are among the journals that he has assisted.

Pound's early books, *Exultations* (1909), *Personæ* (1910), and *Lustra* (1916) contain rich combinations of exact imagery, poetic form, and hauntingly beautiful rhythms.

> Dark-eyed,
> O woman of my dreams,
> Ivory-sandaled,
> There is none like thee among the dancers,
> None with swift feet.
>
> I have not found thee in the tents,
> In the broken darkness.
> I have not found thee at the well-head
> Among the women with pitchers.

In his later work Pound has tended to concentrate upon poetic form and the most delicate nuances of rhythm rather than upon the imagery and personal feeling, as he did in his earlier poems. Probably as a result of his obsession with form he has largely forgone original composition for translation. He has borrowed from languages as diverse as Chinese, Provençal, Latin, and modern French and Italian, and, while he has often succeeded admirably, we are told, in conveying the atmosphere of the original work, his own creative writing has suffered because of his translations.

Pound is the most pronounced cosmopolitan in current American letters. He has ransacked all literature for material to turn into cunning rhythms and colorful imagery, and the exotic stuff that he has discovered has been of value in helping more than one American break the bonds of provincialism. But future literary critics may find that the greatest work of Pound has been in experimentation with new forms and rhythms.

Of the other Imagists only H. D. (Hilda Doolittle), now Mrs. Richard Aldington, has stayed fairly close to the articles of the original creed. She is one of the most accomplished workmen among recent poets, writing little, but giving that little the high distinction of fine art. John Gould Fletcher has gone beyond the position that he took in 1914, but he still writes a vivid colorful verse that is peculiarly fitted for some of the descriptive poetry that he has recently attempted with so great success.

EDNA ST. VINCENT MILLAY

(1892-   )

The indubitably fine lyric poetry of Edna St. Vincent Millay does not lend itself very readily to critical discussion, for any consideration of it against the background of the New Poetry is apt to run into negatives. Miss Millay seldom uses free verse or experimental forms; she has no conscious philosophy upon which she erects her beautiful lyric outbursts; she makes no argument for or against anything. So negative a characterization is very misleading, for of all modern poets none is more emphatically positive than she. But except in a few instances her poetry touches upon things more elemental than literary fashions, critical squabblings, and social questions. The disturbing actuality of realism, the dark broodings of the naturalists, and the problems raised by the clash of social forces all leave Miss Millay entirely untouched. The clear-eyed and high-hearted qualities of her poetry carry the echoes of other times, earlier days of the race, when to be alive was divine ecstasy. Satisfied with the bit of life placed in her hands, or at all events determined to make the best of it, never has she sought protection in the colorful exoticism that has attracted many of her fellows, nor has she guarded herself against disappointments by a philosophy of despair. Her themes are those of the joy of living, the bitter-sweet of love and its transiency, and the poignant note of child-like grief in the presence of death. Her grief is keen, but not enduring; at her blackest moments she is only a "little lonely child, lost in hell," and her darkest lines are things of fragile beauty. In the surging emotion of her poetry it is idle to look for philosophical implications or sociological relationships. Miss Millay is the vivid singer of the passing moment, and her naïveté, directness, and spontaneity place her songs of transient moods in the category of timeless literature.

Edna St. Vincent Millay was born in Rockland, Maine. She spent her childhood there and at near-by Camden. From an early age she wrote poetry, and when she was only a girl many of her verses appeared in *St. Nicholas Magazine*. It is an old story that she entered a poetic competition in 1912 with her "Renascence" and won only honorable mention. However, upon the publication of the competitive poems in book form, public interest was at once attracted to Miss Millay's composition. The publication of "God's World," the little poem beginning "O world, I cannot hold thee close enough," directed further attention to the youthful poet.

In 1913 Miss Millay entered Vassar where she kept up her writing, participated in dramatics, and carried regular college work. She was graduated in 1917, and the same year she published her first book, *Renascence*, a volume which took its name from the poem written five years earlier. After graduation the poet became a Greenwich Villager in those feverish days when the Village was probably more sincere and certainly less advertised than it is to-day. While living in the Village Miss Millay became a member of the Provincetown Players for whom she wrote some of her very effective short plays. In 1920 came the very slender volume, *A Few Figs from Thistles*, a work much deplored by the serious-minded but which admirably expresses the gay insouciance of Greenwich Village in the early twenties. The following year appeared *Second April*, a collection of lyrics which contained the six poems constituting the "Memorial to D. C." These poems are the most beautiful and memorable work that Miss Millay has done with the exception of a very few of her sonnets. "D. C." is said to have been Dorothy Coleman of Milwaukee, Wisconsin, a college friend of the poet who died shortly after her graduation in 1918. The "Prayer to Persephone" is a marvel of condensation and wistful beauty.

The Harp Weaver and Other Poems (1923) contains thirty-nine sonnets that definitely place the author at the head of all those American poets who have attempted the difficult sonnet form. The remainder of the book is made up of lyrics that show a steadier, surer technique and a quieter emotional control. Not all of the lyrics will bear comparison with such earlier performances as "Renascence" and the "Memorial to D. C.," but the superlative excellence of the sonnets, especially the twenty-two in Part Four, brings the whole volume up to a high average level.

In 1927 Miss Millay wrote *The King's Henchman* as the libretto for an opera composed by Deems Taylor and produced at the Metropolitan Opera House. While the work was a distinct disappointment to many of the poet's admirers and while many of the lines are not easy to sing, it is safe to say that Miss Millay succeeded in an almost impossible task. The libretto is poetic, and very few works of its kind possess that quality.

Miss Millay's last book, *The Buck in the Snow*, shows a decline from the high level of its predecessors. It is good poetry—many of the lines are excellent, but it is the kind of book that any good lyricist could have written, and none but a master could have accomplished "Second April" or the sonnets from "The Harp Weaver." *The Buck in the Snow* displays a consummate metrical technique, but the youthful zest of the author has somewhat declined without being succeeded by the placid depths of middle-aged emotion.

In some of her recently published poems Miss Millay reveals a growing concern with problems of social justice. The Sacco-Vanzetti case roused her to indignant protests, some of which appeared in verse form. "Justice Denied in Massachusetts" was published in *The Buck in the Snow*. This poem and the article, "Fear," which appeared in 1927, may be portents of an approaching change in Miss Millay's interests. Certainly there is a graver tone in some of her recent protests than she was wont to use.

> Down, down, down into the darkness of the grave
> Gently they go, the beautiful, the tender, the kind;
> Quietly they go, the intelligent, the witty, the brave.
> I know. But I do not approve. And I am not resigned.

Even a hasty reading of Miss Millay shows that she has every characteristic required of the lyric poet. She has passion, intuitive insight, verbal witchery, metrical skill, and a fine feeling for form. In addition she has an arch wit that gives piquancy to many a poem. Above all her other traits she possesses the quality of femininity. She is the modern woman speaking with unfettered frankness and power. To her, love is not a thing to be fled or accepted coyly. It is a beautiful thing to be sought openly, and, when past, to be mourned without shame. But when love palls on her she is not one to bear her cross with exemplary Victorian meekness.

However, it is probable that the widest appeal in Miss Millay's poetry is not to be found in her wit, her femininity, or her technical excellence. The poet always has something of the child's attitude of vivid expectancy, tip-toe on the brink of new adventures, and in the adventure of life fresh experiences and new places sting her into singing the joy of living.

> Long have I known a glory in it all,
>   But never knew I this;
>   Here such a passion is
> As stretcheth me apart. Lord, I do fear
> Thou'st made the world too beautiful this year;
> My soul is all but out of me,—let fall
> No burning leaf; prithee, let no bird call.

ROBINSON JEFFERS

(1887-   )

Robinson Jeffers has been called the greatest poet developed in America since the rise of Whitman. He was born in Pittsburgh. As a boy he traveled widely in Europe. The family moved to California, and he entered Occidental College at Los Angeles from which he was graduated in 1905. Later he studied at the universities of Zurich, Southern California, and Washington. In 1914 he married and established his home at Carmel, California, where he has since lived.

In 1912 he published *Flagons and Apples,* following this youthful volume four years later with *Californians.* These two books had little more than promise. After a silence of eight years, during which time Jeffers labored to perfect himself in the art of the poet, he published *Tamar* in 1924. The praise that greeted this book increased upon the appearance of *Roan Stallion* in the following year. In overwhelming force, vivid description, and magnificent symbolism, "Roan Stallion" is a contemporary masterpiece and one of the most powerful poems in American literature. *The Women at Point Sur,* a long narrative poem with many fine passages, appeared in 1927. The next year appeared *Cawdor* and *Dear Judas.* The latter volume contained "The Loving Shepherdess," a work that seems to be something of a departure for Jeffers and to give the lie to many of the adverse comments on his work. However, before the poet can be appraised on the ground of his work in "The Loving Shepherdess," he must follow that poem with some others in the same strain. But it is really no hardship to ask any poet of our generation to submit to critical estimate upon the strength of his performance in *Tamar, Roan Stallion,* and *The Women at Point Sur.* It is probably true that the unbroken tragedies of these three poems need the relief of humor, a glimmer of hope, and a touch of human sympathy, for they are vast, austere works, totally unrelieved by comic interludes or Hardian passages of grotesque irrelevancies, but the intense concentration of the three poems just named is far beyond the reach of most contemporary poets and utterly beyond the conception of those poetasters who have arisen since the war.

Jeffers is so largely concerned with primitive passions and with people unspoiled by society, that he may be said to be universal, but in his devotion to one particular place he is highly localized. This one place is the California coast immediately south of Carmel. Here the poet places the action of most of his poems, and the vividness with which he describes the peculiar characteristics of that region would alone make him a notable writer. The ocean, the tawny landscape, and the blue sky of this locality have become inseparable from his poetry.

The Poetry of Jeffers.—In the judgment of many Robinson Jeffers will develop into the most powerful poet in American literature. So sweeping a verdict may be premature, for the poet is young, and his first distinctive volume was published only a few years ago. However, it is indisputable that the primitive drive, the immense concentration, and the breath-taking vocabulary of Jeffers make him a poet of amazing performance. To pass from a man like Sandburg, with all his strength, to *Roan Stallion* is like going from the staccato noise and emotionalism of a modern city to the grim quiet of the troglodytic age.

Jeffers is a primitive. No poet of our time has drawn so little of his material from the outward facts of contemporary life. His active dislike of people makes him flee from society to the solitude of the natural world. He hates the volatile passions of the crowd, and he evidently has but little respect for the most elaborate monuments raised by the hysterical energy of man. People and their

changing moods are displeasing to him; he seeks the unchanging
aspects of rocks, mountain ledges, and the open sea.

I drew solitude over me on the lone shore,
By the hawk-perch stones; the hawks and the gulls are never breakers of
    solitude.
When the animals Christ is rumored to have died for drew in,
The land thickening, drew in about me, I planted trees eastward, and the
    ocean
Secured the West with the quietness of thunder—I was quiet. . . .
. . . . Humanity is needless.
I said, "Humanity is the start of the race
. . . The old rock under the house, the hills with their hard roots and the
    ocean hearted
With sacred quietness from here to Asia
Make me ashamed to speak of the active little bodies, the coupling
    bodies, the misty brainfuls
Of perplexed passion. Humanity is needless."
I said, "Humanity is the start of the race, the gate to break away from,
    the coal to kindle,
The blind mask crying to be slit with eye-holes."
Well, now it is done, the mask slit, the rag burnt, the starting post left
    behind: but not in a fable.
Culture's outlived, art's root-cut, discovery's
The way to walk in. Only remains to invent the language to tell it.
    Match ends of burnt experience
Human enough to be understood,
Scraps and metaphors will serve. The wine was a little strong for the
    new wine-skins. . . .

The characters with whom Jeffers peoples his poems are primi-
tives, victims of atavistic urges and aboriginal passions. They are
usually people who have never known compulsory conformity to
crowd-culture or who have fled from it in disgust. Such characters he places in a sun-tanned landscape, girt by mountain shoulders
and the ocean, a landscape that Jeffers has made peculiarly his own,
and here he watches with brooding care the workings of instinct and
primitive passion.

And yet in spite of his concern with the primitive, Jeffers is modern. His materials are not of to-day, but his mood is wholly contemporary. He has been called "western" by many unthinking admirers, and even his more intelligent critics have declared that he
is Greek in thought and expression. There may possibly be some
grounds for considering him akin to the Greeks in the majesty of
his impressive lines, packed with titanic import, but there is none

whatever for thinking that he is like the Greeks in mood. No writer is less objective than Jeffers. Every object in his reach, every abstract thought is colored by his personal temperament, and almost every poem that he writes projects the gray mood that is Robinson Jeffers. It is a mood formed in the pessimism of naturalistic determinism. Its tragedies are those of a naturalist and not those of the Greek who saw in the avengers an intelligently directed force. Even the supernatural elements in Jeffers are not like those in the Athenian or Elizabethan dramas. They are the creations of a modern mind that uses such elements to link the riddle of present humanity to the unknown and probably unknowable force that gives direction to the drift of affairs. Tested from every angle Jeffers is contemporary.

Jeffers has been called a mystic, though such a classification is very hard to justify upon historical grounds. In his so-called mystic concepts Jeffers stands midway between Thoreau and Henry Adams, and only the first of these was a mystic in any sense. Jeffers seems to have chosen for his task the reduction of the whole universe to a common denominator and the measurement of the unknown, unifying force in terms of the knowable. Like Adams he wishes to discover the nature of the force that makes the universe a unity. Jeffers is convinced that the force has power; of its dynamic drive and its universality he has no doubt. But at that point assurance deserts him. If he has any mysticism, his is only the tentative, wistful type, like that of Sherwood Anderson, who wishes for, rather than realizes, a mystic identification.

In his search for the irreducible, unifying dynamics of the universe, Jeffers has caught life and nature in their most primitive aspects, when they are least wrought upon by the distracting impulses that arise from a complex society. His search for this unchanging element, this prime force, has led the poet to despise shifting humanity and to seek an identity with such relatively changeless things as the ocean, the sea-rocks, the yellow shoulders of craggy mountains, and the great forest trees. Even in these he sees the marks of great struggles long past, but compared with effervescent humanity they are everlasting. Their mood gives him a hint of the eternal peace and rest that would come from a perfectly understanding mind, joined through knowledge to visible and invisible forces.

In his search for the eternal Jeffers waives as immaterial all consideration of ethical problems. He is the grim fatalist who sees in the workings of nature and in the actions of man only slightly different aspects of the same great force. His concern with force makes him almost obsessed with the idea of strength, either dynamic or static, though he never idealizes this power enough to endow it with prescience or even with consciousness. Strength is its sole human quality, and this strength is so displayed as to be inhuman. Humanity is blind. It constantly strives "to slit eyes in the mask," but it is no blinder than the parent force that moves it. It is cruel, but no more so than the senseless power that animates the human arm. Life is mechanistic, but it seems to borrow this characteristic from the earth-mover.

So intent is Jeffers upon the identity of the prime force, and so completely does his mysticism bring all things, both animate and inanimate, to the same level that the poet is lacking in warm human sympathy. In scope and power Jeffers has reminded many of Hardy, but no one can find in *Tamar* or *Roan Stallion* a hint of Hardy's compassion for suffering people. Jeffers is as cold as a scientist even in dealing with his major characters, and toward the ruck he is contemptuous.

BIRTH-DUES

Joy is a trick in the air; pleasure is merely contemptible, the dangled
Carrot that leads to market or precipice;
But limitary pain—the rock under the tower and the hewn coping
That takes thunder at the head of the turret—
Terrible and real. Therefore a mindless dervish carving himself
With knives will seem to have conquered the world.
The world's God is treacherous and full of unreason; a torturer, but also
The only foundation and the only fountain.
Who fights him eats his own flesh and perishes of hunger; who hides in
   the grave
To escape him is dead; who enters the Indian
Recession to escape him is dead; who falls in love with the God is washed
   clean
Of death desired and death dreaded.
He has joy, but joy is a trick in the air; and pleasure, but pleasure is
   contemptible;
And peace; and is based on solider than pain.
He has broken boundaries a little and that will estrange him; he is
   monstrous, but not
To the measure of the God. . . . But I having told you—
However I suppose that few in the world have energy to hear effectively—
Have paid my birth-dues; am quits with the people.

Because of his choice of subjects, rather more than because of his craggy lines, his gray philosophy, or his lack of human sympathy, Jeffers will probably never be a "popular" poet. His subjects are those of incest, unnatural love, and diabolic perversions of accepted values. All of these themes have been used by such writers as Sophocles, Shakespeare, and Shelley, but readers to-day are often prone to allow the past a greater freedom in the choice of literary subjects than they willingly permit to contemporary writers.

However much we may deplore Jeffers's choice of subjects, and however vehemently we may repudiate his philosophy, expressed and implied, his poems undoubtedly are typical of much American thinking from 1920 to 1930. The post-war disillusion that almost smothered our youngest generation, the black pessimism that was the first reaction to the realization that science and machinery, undirected, were leading us into a blind alley, and the sharp revulsion from the performances of democracy—all these attitudes find congenial echoes in the poems of Jeffers, even though the poet directly expresses more interest in personal experiences than in social problems or philosophy. Although he may shun people and look upon the crowd with the contempt of the disillusioned, Jeffers rooted his poetry in the deep heart of American life and thought during the years of his writing. It may be that the post-war mood is only transitory, or it may be that it is an ominous portent of our national mind in years to come, but whether it be followed by a similar mood or by a distinct reaction, the period from 1920 to 1930 is sure to be accounted an important and significant era in American thought and literature. It is the decade that saw the acceptance of Cabell, the rise of Sinclair Lewis, the friendly though nonplused attitude toward the philosophy of Oswald Spengler, and the momentary triumph of a noisy nihilism. And the poetry of Robinson Jeffers is more completely of its decade than is the work of any other writer.

STEPHEN VINCENT BENÉT

(1898-1943)

Stephen Vincent Benét represents a marked drift away from the naturalistic temper toward the uninterpreted verities of realism and the pleasant selectiveness of romanticism. *John Brown's Body,* his most distinguished work, ranges between authentic realism and the romantic lyricism that was once a commonplace of poetry. The poem was carefully built out of documentary material, but often the heavy-footed realistic lines give way to singing lyrics that are as frankly romantic as a local color sketch of the 1890's.

Before writing *John Brown's Body*, Benét experimented with several kinds of literary work. He had succeeded in many forms of the lyric; he had written narrative poems and novels, but his most congenial material seems to have been that taken from the lives of the uncultured classes, the mountaineers and frontiersmen, and given lyrical treatment. One of his most successful poems is "The Ballad of William Sycamore" in which he relates the story of an old pioneer. "King David" is a retelling of the biblical narrative in the style of a Negro sermon with overtones of Vachel Lindsay. This was a prize poem in 1923. Another very popular piece is "The Mountain Whip-Poor-Will," a performance of amazing metrical and rhythmical dexterity. This poem has a primitive gusto and a musical lilt that are extremely attractive.

Benét began writing when he was only a boy, and at the age of seventeen he published *Five Men and Pompey*, a group of dramatic monologues that has been called an astounding performance for a high-school boy. He followed this book with *Young Adventure* (1918), *Heavens and Earth* (1920), *The Ballad of William Sycamore* (1923), *King David* (1923), and *Tiger Joy* (1925). The best poems of these books are sparkling lyrics that show great compositional ingenuity. Some of the lines have a tendency to use the loud rather than the emphatic word, or to substitute technical virtuosity for poetry, but often Benét gains the striking pictorial effects of an impressionist who sees truly and rapidly and who puts his impressions into cunning rhythmical patterns.

Benét has written several novels. *The Beginning of Wisdom* (1921) and *Spanish Bayonet* (1926) are the best known.

"*John Brown's Body*."—In 1928 Benét published *John Brown's Body*, a long narrative poem of the Civil War, that became one of the most discussed books of the year. In fact, the poem is one of the most impressive efforts to make the Civil War the basis of a piece of belletristic literature. The poem moves rather deliberately through an invocation, a prelude, and eight long books of narrative, in all about 13,000 lines. It employs a huge number of incidents and a host of characters, and the literary devices used by the author are almost as varied as the incidents and people, for he utilized regular blank verse, rhyme, *vers libre*, swinging lyrics, and prose passages to tell his story. Despite the length of the work and its kaleidoscopic effect, the poem is not hard to read.

But it is far too much to say that *John Brown's Body* is an unqualified success. Strictly speaking it lacks unity. The only unifying elements are the war itself and the adventures of one or two characters who appear frequently in the course of the action. There is no sustained interpretative element, as there is in Hardy's *Dynasts,* to give the disjunct episodes a unity of effect. Nor is there an emphasis upon one man or a group of men as there is in epic compositions. So episodic is *John Brown's Body* that the reader is apt to get the feeling of looking at a long motion picture with the "continuity" left out. Even when a familiar character reënters the story, the plot mechanism often creaks dreadfully.

Furthermore, the poem contains some surprising crudities, not of poetic technique but of narrative. Some critics have hastened to explain that Benét meant to put in the crudities as a part of his plan, but it hardly improves a poor work of art to say, however truthfully, that the artist meant to make it just as it is. The most objectionable flaws in *John Brown's Body* arise from awkwardness in the telling of the story, from verbosity that was not excised in revision, and from little starts of self-consciousness. The last evidently accounts for those painful places where the author helps to change the scene by impromptu explanations to the reader.

Despite its defects, the poem has great merit. Many of the portrait sketches have extreme vividness, and many of the 'episodes are very realistic.

> Ewell goes by,
> The little woodpecker, bald and quaint of speech,
> With his wooden leg stuck stiffly out from the saddle,
> He is muttering, "Sir, I'm a nervous Major-General,
> And whenever an aide rides up from General Jackson
> I fully expect an order to storm the North Pole."
>
> .   .   .   .
>
> Then the staff—then little Sorrel—and the plain
> Presbyterian figure in the flat cap,
> Throwing his left hand out in the awkward gesture
> That caught the bullet out of the air at Bull Run,
> Awkward, ragged, and dour, the belated Ironside
> With the curious, brilliant streak of the cavalier
> That made him quote Mercutio in staff instructions, . . .
>
> .   .   .   .
>
> Stonewall Jackson wrapped in his beard and his silence.

Reading aloud is one of the hardest tests of a narrative poem, and parts of *John Brown's Body* read well to an audience, if the reader first gives his selections vigorous revision to get rid of the irrelevancies.

On the whole Benét may have given us one of the significant poems of our immediate time, comparable in a way to *Leaves of Grass* and *Spoon River Anthology*. He is no muck-raker, no philosopher of gloom, no cynical sophisticate intent upon exposing the clownish behavior of Americans. He is frankly looking for the soul of a people which he obviously considers more important than iconoclastic histories or the intimate scandals about our great men, and he thinks that he will find this soul in the accurate but reverent examination of our past. It is not hard to think that the poems of Robinson Jeffers have closed an epoch in our literary development and that *John Brown's Body* opens a new one. Benét is not the poet that Jeffers is; he lacks the power and overwhelming concentration. But he may indicate a coming change in our attitude toward our people and our past.

T. S. ELIOT
(1888-   )

The intellectual progress of Thomas Stearns Eliot is typical of a considerable body of thought since the World War. In 1917 Eliot published his *Prufrock and Other Observations*, a volume of poetry written in what we have come to know as the characteristic hard glitter of the poet's style. The pieces in this book, many of them mordant irony, were the detached brilliancies of a mind that felt keenly the futility and frustration of modern life. Eliot's expression of his mood was guided by a nature that was more metaphysical than lyrical, more intellectual than warmly emotional. In thinking his way through the welter of the contemporary, Eliot produced his *Poems* (1919) under a London imprint. A year later a volume bearing the same name appeared in America. This second book of *Poems* contained all the earlier pieces and a number of new ones, all in the same vein of futility and frustration. In 1922 came *The Waste Land*, a masterpiece of chaotic strivings and baffled desires.

In the meantime Eliot had been developing his philosophical and critical ideas that arose from the contemplation of the goalless activity of contemporary life. Starting with the assumption that the modern needs a steadying and directing influence, Eliot became convinced of the necessity of a standard. Such a standard, he felt, to be efficacious must be objective, or at least it must have the sanction of some external force, for without objectivity it would leave all men under the domination of their personal standards, innumerable in variety and widely differing in efficacy and desirability. Subjective standards plainly would not do. By 1930 Eliot had reached the point where he was ready to announce his allegiance to the principles of classicism in literature, Anglo-Catholicism in religion, and royalism in politics. Whatever one may think of Eliot's desire for standards and of his accepted sanctions for those standards, no one can question the logic of his final position or of his progress to that position, granting the validity of his premises. Eliot has expressed his critical and intellectual creed in *The Sacred Wood* (1920), *Homage to John Dryden* (1924), and *For Lancelot Andrewes* (1928).

Eliot's opposition to science and democracy and his insistence upon standards have caused the New Humanists to regard the poet-critic as one of their number. However, Eliot differs from his fellow humanists both in his impeccable logic and in the courage with which he accepts his inevitable conclusions. Many of the humanists are stimulating critics of modern life, and all seems to sense the need for standards, but few have taken the trouble to make definite suggestions for the setting up of any rule of life that is not based entirely upon an individual and subjective basis. Eliot seems to have done well in insisting that humanism without religion i. futile, but relatively few American humanists are willing to follow him in this conclusion.

Eliot is not classed to-day as an American, although he was born in St. Louis, and he is distantly related to the Eliots of Harvard. He was educated at Harvard, the Sorbonne, and Oxford. In 1913 he established his residence in London where he has since lived. In 1927 he became a British subject.

Eliot's Literary Style.—Eliot is a metaphysical poet, carrying on, in both literary methods and personal tastes, the tradition of the seventeenth century metaphysicians, especially that of John Donne, whose influence is to be seen in Eliot's verse. The characteristics of Eliot's metaphysical poetry are a marked intellectuality, a quick allusiveness, and a vivid though far-fetched imagery. Intelligence is Eliot's prime trait, and all his verse emphasizes this quality almost to the exclusion of feeling. It is not quite true to say, as many have, that Eliot is without feeling, but it is true that his feeling is negative. That is, his emotion is usually one of active aversion, rather than that of warm admiration which we usually associate with lyric poetry. Even when he attempts to indicate a favorable attitude, as in "La Figlia Che Piange," he is still coolly intellectual.

> Sometimes these cogitations still amaze
> The troubled midnight and the noon's repose.

Eliot's habit of quoting without credit, parodying, or alluding to other writers fills his poetry with literary echoes and makes many readers wish that all his poems were equipped with annotations by the author, as was *The Waste Land*. In this poem there are more or less distinct traces of about thirty writers, and yet the whole work contains only about 450 lines. Furthermore Eliot's practice of mentioning abruptly some recondite fact or theory demands a certain culture and alertness on the part of the reader. When these qualities are enlisted in the task of expressing the chaos of modern life through depicting a series of meaningless episodes, the resulting poetry becomes difficult of assimilation.

Eliot's vivid and unusual imagery is employed even more strikingly in his early poetry than in *The Waste Land*.

> Let us go then, you and I,
> When the evening is spread out against the sky
> Like a patient etherized upon a table.
>
> .   .   .   .
>
> The yellow fog that rubs its back upon the window panes,
> The yellow smoke that rubs its muzzle on the window panes,
> Licked its tongue into the corners of the evening.

In another place he says:

> I am aware of the damp souls of housemaids
> Sprouting despondingly at area gates.

"The Waste Land."—Upon its appearance *The Waste Land* had a large and discordant greeting. Some declared it to be a deliberate hoax. Others saw in it the ludicrous rhapsody of a mind unintelligible even to itself, while one critic called the "poem—in spite of its lack of structural unity—simply one triumph after another." Structural unity the work certainly did not have, nor was it meant

to have it. As a matter of fact the poem is a series of disjointed pictures, each of which is too short and too staccato-like to leave a deliberate impression, and each of which is in itself entirely without meaning. Just there is probably the key to the inner meaning of the poem, for the work as a whole does possess meaning and effectiveness.

The Waste Land is the epitome of chaos. The first effect is one of utter unintelligibility, but the final effect upon a serious reader is that the poem is the product of a brilliant mind completely disillusioned and fully aware of both the complexity and the meaninglessness of the contemporary scene. Episodes that begin nowhere and end nowhere are thrown together with scraps of memories, doggerel, and quotations from writers who lived when existence was less complex and when life, on the surface, at least, was directed toward a spiritual goal. In many ways *The Waste Land* is the negative aspect of earlier poetry. Its beauty lies in deliberate ugliness, its aim is the presentation of the lack of aim.

Wordsworth defined poetry as emotion recollected in tranquillity. Eliot's poetry might be defined as tranquil nothings, the disjointed futilities of commonplace episodes, jumbled together in paroxysmal recollections. Again and again an episode will begin to unfold only to disappear before a quotation flashed out of nowhere or to give way to a perplexed silence broken only by the meaningless whistle or hum of a man distraught.

> But at my back from time to time I hear
> The sound of horns and motors which shall bring
> Sweeney to Mrs. Porter in the spring.
> O the moon shone bright on Mrs. Porter
> And on her daughter
> They wash their feet in soda water.

> Et O ces voix d'enfants chantant dans la coupole.
> Twit twit twit
> Jug jug jug jug jug
> So rudely forc'd.
> Tereu.

In these few lines there are a quotation from an anonymous piece of doggerel, a line from Verlaine, and a group of meaningless monosyllables at the end.

The Waste Land is an impressive performance. To many it is very much more impressive than any philosophical or literary criticism that the author has ever written, but its impressiveness lies in the totality of its effect and not in its structural unity or its episodic details. It has tonal unity, a unity achieved by disjunction and not through cohesion. The final impression is one of a world in which there is neither order, nor beauty, nor meaning, a world of energy and dynamic life undirected toward any goal. The poem itself, like the life it represents, moves to no predestined end, just as contemporary life has neither predestination nor recognizable end.

Of course, Eliot is no apologist for such conditions. Beneath all the chaos, unguided struggles, and sordid ugliness of *The Waste Land* there lies the personality of the author who hates ugliness and earnestly desires that life may have unity and meaning. Eliot is typical of the generation that suffered most during the war, and that is the generation of young men who went bravely through a period of personal grief and disaster hoping to find at the end a recompense for their sacrifices. But when the resounding rhetoric of war-time promises was succeeded only by the disheartening realities of the post-war period, then the faith of these young men gave way to a bitter futility. The despair of some turned them into nihilists, skeptical of everything; some became anarchs against every institution; others sought to analyze the material and spiritual chaos around them in the hope of finding a way out. In this last category belongs Eliot. His love of beauty has led him to explore the ugly and the meaningless, but he has done so in the spirit of the realist who is determined to expose the worst of evil in order to bring its enormities home to his readers. Eliot would very likely repudiate any suggestion that his writing has an ameliorative aim, but notwithstanding the disavowal, his critical and philosophical writings show that he has revealed the chaos of modern life, not because he likes it but because he hates it.

NEGRO POETRY

For many years the Negro in American literature was satisfied with his assignment to the task of providing slap-stick comedy and sentimental tears. Until 1890 it seems seldom to have entered the minds of either whites or blacks that the Negro had a past that differed immensely from that of the white man or that he had a racial temperament far removed from that of other races. When the Negro attempted literature it was almost always as the purveyor of the expected emotions or as the close imitator of white writers. As late as 1900 Paul Laurence Dunbar was known wholly as the author of sentimental poems in a broken English. His non-dialectal pieces like the "Ode to Ethiopia" and his excellent sonnets were quite disregarded. There is a bit of justification for this disregard, for Dunbar's poems in good English were imitative of the older English poets, just as the lines of Phillis Wheatley (1753-1784), the first Negro poet in America, distantly echoed the finished couplets of Pope. There was, however, one great difference between Dunbar and Phillis Wheatley. Dunbar had a certain amount of race-consciousness, while the earlier poet gave no hint that she had anything in common with her people. Even when race consciousness was found among the earlier Negro writers, it generally received a mawkish treatment in an approximately correct dialect that aroused only the shallowest feelings of readers. The climax of this early Negro literature seems to have been reached in the stories transcribed by Joel Chandler Harris.

To-day all this is changed. The New Negro has gently dismissed Harris as the "kindly amanuensis of the illiterate Negro peasant" and he is no less critical of the imitative poetry of blacks who have lost touch with their race than of Dunbar's sentimental lyrics like "When Malindy Sings." The old humorous and sentimental aspects of Negro literature have disappeared before the critical approach of those men who seek the soul of their race far beneath external characteristics that always suspiciously resemble stage make-ups. The New Negro has attempted a piece of work in literature that is very much like that undertaken by the writers of the Irish Renaissance whose aim was the presentation of real Irish life divested of those pleasant but artificial accretions that came from years of service as the stereotyped comic figure in an alien literature. To-day the Negro in our poetry, drama, and fiction is neither a stage figure nor the unsophisticated representative of a servile people. He is a Negro, fully conscious of his race and not unaware of his true relation to our national culture.

The work of the New Negro in American literature is attended by at least one danger. It is evident that the black writer is very apt to forgo art for the sake of propaganda. Of course, the propaganda aims to forward the cause of the Negro in American life, and in pursuance of its aim it has taken two courses. One group of writers have constituted themselves the official apologists of the

Negro, explaining and interpreting with scientific thoroughness the black man and his relation to his American environment, while other writers seek to gain for the Negro an ungrudged share in our cultural and social life. That there is a need for both kinds of propaganda no one denies, but every one hopes that the exceptionally promising young Negro writers will not surrender their art to the transient needs of their race, grave as those needs may be. There are others better qualified than the artists to serve the cause of propaganda.

In general the New Negro writers are divided into two groups, the realists and the symbolists, as they have been called. The realists do not belie their name. They are interested in objective descriptions of Negro life, with all the details of costume, dialect, superstitions, and traditional customs. The symbolists, who might better be called spiritual realists, are concerned with the deep racial traits of the Negro, with his temperament and innate moods that might pass for a philosophy in a more sophisticated race, and with his distinctive idioms turned into good English. These writers seem to have a marked aversion to dialect. It is well that they have. The extravagant distortions of dialect in the hands of earlier writers just about discredited that particular literary device, and furthermore it is well known that a skillful writer can give the effect of a foreign language better by translating the foreign idioms literally into good English than by using an uncouth jargon. By translating the Negro's idioms into standard English, the symbolists have often raised crude folklore to the level of literature and have brought readers appreciably closer to the heart of the black race. Excellent examples of dialect turned into pure English may be found in James Weldon Johnson's *God's Trombones,* a collection of Negro sermons in verse form.

Weep not, weep not,
She is not dead;
She's resting in the bosom of Jesus.
Heart-broken husband—weep no more,
Grief-stricken son—weep no more,
Left-lonesome daughter—weep no more,
She's only just gone home.

And God sat back on his throne,
And he commanded that tall, bright angel standing at his right hand,

Call me Death!
And that tall, bright angel cried in a voice

That broke like a clap of thunder,
Call Death! Call Death!
And the echo sounded down the streets of heaven
Till it reached way back to that shadowy place
Where Death waits with his pale, white horses.

Other examples may be found in the "blues" poems by Langston
Hughes, though this writer frequently uses a small amount of dialect.

> If I was a mule I'd
> Git me a wagon to haul.
> If I was a mule I'd
> Git me a wagon to haul.
> I'm so low down I
> Ain't even got a stall.

Here is a stanza from "Po' Boy Blues":

> Weary, weary,
> Weary early in de morn.
> Weary, weary,
> Early, early in de morn.
> I's so weary
> I wish I'd never been born.

The attitude of the New Negro toward race prejudice is different
from that of the obsequious "darky" who shuffled through the stories
of the local colorists. The present mood is to be felt in these lines:

> Although she feeds me bread of bitterness,
> And sinks into my throat her tiger's tooth,
> Stealing my breath of life, I will confess
> I love this cultured hell which tests my youth.
> Her vigor flows like tides into my blood,
> Giving me strength against her hate,
> Her bigness sweeps my being like a flood.

Not all the Negro writers always reflect their racial heritage, for
there is still a tendency to drop into the easily imitated lines of
other poets. For instance, Jessie Fauset begins one of her poems
in this fashion:

> On summer afternoons I sit
> Quiescent by you in the park,
> And idly watch the sunbeams gild
> And tint the ash-trees' bark.

> Or else I watch the squirrels frisk
> And chatter in the grassy lane;
> And all the while I mark your voice
> Breaking with love and pain.

The author calls this poem "La Vie c'est la Vie." The lines might have been written by the least of the minor poets of the "yellow nineties" or by a moon-struck sophomore who yearned to be an expatriate on the left bank of the Seine.

James Weldon Johnson (1871-1938).—James Weldon Johnson, one of the true poets of the Negro race, was born in Jacksonville, Florida. After his graduation from Atlanta University, he became a teacher. Later he studied law and practiced his profession in his native state. He served for a time in the American consular service. For many years he has been secretary of the Association for the Advancement of Colored People.

Johnson's first publication was *The Autobiography of an Ex-colored Man* (1912). This work is a vivid and moving account of a Negro's experience in both the North and the South. It is a worthy addition to that list of distinguished autobiographies written by Americans. In 1917 Johnson wrote *Fifty Years,* a review in verse of the black man's achievement in fifty years of freedom. The large amount of propaganda and factual assertion in this poem leaves but little room for art. He has also edited a book of American Negro poetry and collaborated in the editing of two volumes of Negro spirituals. This last work was one of the most important ever undertaken in the name of the Negro, for it showed conclusively that the black man had developed a folk art of surpassing beauty.

Johnson's best original work is *God's Trombones* (1927), the collection of Negro sermons in verse already mentioned. Such pieces as "Go Down, Death" and "The Creation" remind one of the work of John Millington Synge in interpreting the temperament, imagery, and idiom of a people. Considered as artistic expressions of the race, these poems are the finest product of Negro writers in America. In sincerity and truthfulness they are immeasurably beyond the sentimentality of Dunbar, the chiseled correctness of Claude McKay, or the sophisticated cleverness of Countee Cullen. If he never produces another line, Johnson deserves to live in our literature as the author of *God's Trombones.*

Claude McKay (1889-   ).—Claude McKay was born in Jamaica. After serving in the constabulary of the island, he came to America in 1912 and spent two years in the Kansas Agricultural College. Upon leaving college he made his living in various ways, finally going to New York where he became a waiter in a club. He contributed some poetry to the brilliant but short-lived *Seven Arts* that attracted considerable attention. In 1920 he joined the staff of *The Liberator*, a radical journal of New York. Later he lived abroad for some time.

Before he left Jamaica, McKay published a volume of poems, but his first representative work was in *Springs in New Hampshire* (1920). His third book, *Harlem Shadows* (1922), contains some of his earlier published work along with many new poems. In 1925 he wrote *Home to Harlem*, a presentation of Negro life in the form of fiction.

McKay is defiantly a Negro. His mood is bellicose rather than apologetic, and the dynamic power of his defiant imprecations and the fearless candor of his words give his poems a bold power.

> If we must die—let it not be like hogs
> Hunted and penned in an inglorious spot,
> While round us bark the mad and hungry dogs,
> Making their mock at our accursed lot.
>
> .   .   .   .   .
>
> Oh, Kinsmen! We must meet the common foe;
> Though far outnumbered, let us still be brave,
> And for their thousand blows deal one death-blow!
> What though before us lies the open grave?
> Like men we'll face the murderous, cowardly pack,
> Pressed to the wall, dying, but—fighting back!

McKay is a master of the sonnet form—indeed, the lines just quoted are from a sonnet—though all his verse is distinguished by metrical exactness and melodious utterance. His fine sonnet, "The Harlem Dancer," has a crisp pictorial quality mingled with overtones of melancholy. McKay brings to his lines a sympathetic feeling for the temper and misfortunes of his race, but he lived too long in a place where black blood is not an irremovable stigma to suffer racial discriminations with meek resignation.

Countee Cullen (*1903-*   ).—The clearest lyric note among the Negro poets is that of Countee Cullen, one of the youngest members of the group. Cullen was born in 1903 in New York City where his father was a minister. He was educated at New York University and at Harvard, taking his M.A. at the latter institution in 1926. At the age of twenty-two he became famous as the author of *Color*, one of the fine lyrical outbursts of recent years. In 1927 *Copper Sun* and "The Ballad of the Brown Girl" both appeared, and the same year he edited a group of Negro poems that he called *Caroling Dusk*. His first volume had been a great success because of its lyrical and epigrammatic qualities, but *Copper Sun*, retaining the good points of the earlier book, possessed a depth of feeling and a sturdiness of thought that gave distinct notice that a new poet had arrived in American literature. During 1929 Cullen studied in France, and the same year saw the publication of his *Black Christ*, a lyric, half-mystical treatment of a lynching. Cullen is on the staff of *Opportunity*, a magazine of Negro life.

Countee Cullen is a born lyric poet with a gift for terse, epigrammatic expression. His poetry is a full-throated lyricism that is equaled only by the best singers in our literature. One of its most striking characteristics is an impromptu air which gives the impression of careless ease, but despite this quality, Cullen's lines have a technical perfection seldom seen in contemporary verse. In his poetry there are no muddy passages caused by the conflict of thought and form, no crude uncertainties of style. Every period rings with the finish of brilliant execution that never fails of its effect. Cullen's poetic style is shown by such lines as these:

> Africa? A book one thumbs
> Listlessly, till slumber comes.
> Unremembered are her bats
> Circling through the night, her cats
> Crouching in the river reeds,
> Stalking gentle flesh that feeds
> By the river brink; no more
> Does the bugle-throated roar
> Cry that monarch claws have leapt
> From the scabbards where they slept.
> Silver snakes that once a year
> Doff the lovely coats you wear,
> Seek no covert in your fear
> Lest a mortal eye should see;
> What's your nakedness to me?

But Cullen does not allow his great technical virtuosity, his lyrical gifts, or his talent for epigram to lead him away from his racial affiliations. In fact his chief claim to distinction is that he has used his endowment to interpret the Negro. His finest poem is

"Heritage," a lyric rhapsody on an African theme, part of which has already been quoted. Despite its vague resemblances to Ralph Hodgson's "Eve" and "The Bull," this poem is one of the great artistic triumphs of the Negro. Here are the opening and closing lines:

> What is Africa to me:
> Copper sun or scarlet sea,
> Jungle star or jungle track,
> Strong bronzed men, or regal black
> Women from whose loins I sprang
> When the birds of Eden sang?
> One three centuries removed
> From the scenes his fathers loved,
> Spicy grove, cinnamon tree,
> What is Africa to me?
>
> . . . . .
>
> All day long and all night through,
> One thing only must I do:
> Quench my pride and cool my blood,
> Lest I perish in the flood.
> Lest a hidden ember set
> Timber that I thought was wet
> Burning like the dryest flax,
> Melting like the merest wax,
> Lest the grave restore its dead.
> Not yet has my heart or head
> In the least way realized
> They and I are civilized.

Langston Hughes (*1902-*   ).—Langston Hughes owes his considerable prominence in current letters to the success with which he interprets Negro "blues" in poetry. He is a jazz singer crooning in modern parlance the old, old woes of the black man. Much of his poetry sticks in one's memory just as a haunting jazz phrase flashes again and again into the mind. The striking things about Hughes's poetry are the shifting rhythm, frequent repetitions, and syncopated accent.

> Once I was in Memphis,
> I mean Tennessee.
> Once I was in Memphis,
> Said Tennessee.
> But I had to leave 'cause
> Nobody there was good to me.

Hughes was born in Joplin, Missouri, in 1902. After graduating from a high school in Cleveland, he attended Columbia University for one year. He then became a sailor, making several voyages to Europe and Africa. Later he was a student at Lincoln University, an institution for Negro men near Philadelphia. He has published two volumes of verse, *Weary Blues* and *Fine Clothes to the Jew*. In 1930 his novel appeared, *Not Without Laughter,* a study of Negro life in a small town of the Middle West.

No one can tell how far Hughes will go with his poetic work. The field that he has chosen for his own is, thus far, a rather narrow one, but it is not hard to show that poets are more apt to be remembered by the intensity of their cultivation than by the immensity of their chosen fields.

> Droning a drowsy syncopated tune,
> Rocking back and forth to a mellow croon,
> I heard a negro play.
> Down on Lenox Avenue the other night
> By the pale dull pallor of an old gas light
> He did a lazy sway . . .
> He did a lazy sway . . .
> To the tune o' those weary blues.
> With his ebony hands on each ivory key
> He made that poor piano moan with melody.
> O Blues!
> Swinging to and fro on his rickety stool
> He played that sad and raggy tune like a musical fool.
> Sweet blues!
> Coming from a black man's soul.
> O Blues!

SUGGESTED READINGS

Aiken: *Scepticisms.* New York. 1919.
    Essays on a number of poets done by a competent critic.
Atkins: *Edna St. Vincent Millay and her Times.* Chicago. 1936.
Bianchi: *Life and Letters of Emily Dickinson.* Boston. 1924.
    The reliability of this book has been sharply questioned.
Brenner: *Poets of Our Time.* New York. 1941.
Cestre: *The Poetry of Amy Lowell.* Out of print.
Coffin: *The New Poetry of New England.* Baltimore. 1938.
Daiches: *Poetry and the Modern World.* Chicago. 1940.
    Contains criticism of T. S. Eliot.
Damon: *Amy Lowell, a Chronicle.* Boston. 1935.
Detzer: *Carl Sandburg, a Study in Personality and Background.* New York. 1941.
Deutsch: *This Modern Poetry.* New York. 1935.

Gregory and Zaturenska: *A History of Modern American Poetry, 1900-1940.* New York. 1947.

Hansen: *Midwest Portraits.* New York. 1923.

Hughes: *Imagism and the Imagists.* Stanford University. 1931.

Kaplan: *Philosophy in the Poetry of Edwin Arlington Robinson.* New York. 1940.

Kreymborg: *Troubadour.* New York. 1925.

    A charmingly written autobiography of a minor figure. It gives us one of the best intimate pictures of the New Poetry movement.

Lowell: *Tendencies in Modern American Poetry.* Boston. 1917.

    Amy Lowell is always interesting.

Masters: *Vachel Lindsay: a Poet in America.* New York. 1935.

    Excellent piece of work. Done without the usual asperity of Masters.

Matthiessen: *The Achievement of T. S. Eliot.* Boston. 1947.

    A new edition of a study which first appeared in 1935.

Monroe: *Poets and Their Art.* New York. 1926.

Monroe: *A Poet's Life.* New York. 1938.

    Harriet Monroe was so much a part of the New Poetry movement that anything which she wrote was of significance.

Neff: *Edwin Arlington Robinson.* New York. 1948.

Powell: *Robinson Jeffers, the Man and His Work.* Los Angeles. 1934.

Sanders and Nelson: *Chief Modern Poets of America.* New York. 1943.

    The poets themselves form the best introduction to the New Poetry. Sanders and Nelson edited a most useful anthology. The selections are admirable.

Taggard: *The Life and Mind of Emily Dickinson.* New York. 1930.

Thompson: *Fire and Ice.* New York. 1942.

    An excellent study of Frost.

Thornton (editor): *Recognition of Robert Frost.* New York. 1937.

    A symposium. Frost from many points of view.

Untermeyer: *American Poetry since 1900.* New York. 1923.

Whicher: *This Was a Poet.* New York. 1938.

    The best biography of Emily Dickinson.

CHAPTER XXV

THE BATTLE OF THE VILLAGE

After the World War the temper of American fiction made a sudden and complete change. Before 1918 naturalism and social criticism had been the dominant notes in our more distinctive novels. After that date social criticism was almost stilled, and naturalism took on new aspects. Criticism there was in the new fiction, but it was neither economic nor political. The surging liberalism that gave rise to the early critics had disappeared under impact of the war. The old faith of English and American liberals had been devised in and for a world relatively peaceful, and the compromises into which it was forced, added to its betrayal by its leaders, simply killed it. Furthermore, the war so much bettered economic life for many people that the old distinction between capital and labor became somewhat blurred. With the resultant better relations between capital and labor, social criticism became outmoded. The laboring man deserted his old affiliations that made for radical thinking and accepted the new order in a spirit of complete amity. Even agrarian discontent was stilled, though this condition was only temporary. The whole temper of American economic life and popular thinking had changed—probably more than conditions warranted—and our fiction reflected the change. Of the old agitators only Upton Sinclair kept up a drum-fire on the minions of capitalism, but aside from his work the old-time critical spirit in fiction disappeared, and the problem novel ceased to be written. Ernest Poole's *The Harbor* and William Allen White's *In the Heart of a Fool* were about the last of their varieties of fiction. Moreover, war-time psychology had helped put an end to social criticism. During the great struggle conformity to mass thinking had been imposed as the first price of concerted effort. No one took the trouble to draw a distinction between criticism and disloyalty, and any suspicion of disloyalty was punished severely.

Naturally literature early reflected the change. The older naturalism was based upon the physical facts of life, hence it is aptly called physical naturalism. Often it was concerned with politics or economics, and similar interests. The new naturalism dropped its externality and became psychological. The difference between the two types can be seen by comparing Theodore Dreiser and Sherwood Anderson. In philosophy the two writers are much alike, but in their choice of materials they are miles apart. Naturalism did not vanish. In 1930 its influence is still strong, but it has a new form.

But criticism is so native to our people that it could not be quenched by official repression or the social ostracism of the critics. After 1918 the fault-finders left economics alone and turned their attention to fundamental elements in our cultural life. Cosmopolitanism had a revival. Our younger critics, many of them fresh from Europe and all of them imbued with foreign ideas, fell afoul of our traditional Puritanism in all its ramifications. Its smug respectability was declared to be more concerned with superficial propriety than with fundamental virtue, and its traditional hostility to innovation was denounced as an obscurantist movement. The other great element in our middle-class life, the pioneer spirit, had no more considerate treatment. Its intellectual conformity, its gospel of thrift and industry, its democracy, and especially its optimism were subjected to every kind of attack from ridicule to a reasoned examination of premises.

The villages scattered over the Middle West had developed as living monuments to Puritanism and the pioneer spirit. In these small towns, rural communities in every sense except in the nearness of the houses to each other, the remains of our pioneer heritage had effected an amalgamation with the vestigial Puritanism of the late nineteenth century. As the home of such elements the village drew the first fire of the critics. The defenders of the small town had not waited for the attack of the hostile party, for Booth Tarkington and William Allen White had been defending the village with unctuous words for more than twenty years.

THE DEFENSE

The middle-western village, as visualized by Meredith Nicholson, White, or Tarkington, is a place of idyllic felicities. According to its friends its material happiness is matched only by its depth of spiritual satisfaction. It knows neither avaricious millionaire nor the lean and dispossessed proletariat. All its worthy citizens live in comfort; none in want, none in luxurious idleness. Labor is accounted a happiness, thrift is a pleasurable duty. By some magical feat unsatisfied desire has been exorcised from the hearts of these people, and all live together, happy in the performance of the daily round of homely tasks. In the village religion is a matter of simple faith, unspoiled by doubt and exemplified by good works, and in their social and political life the villages respect the tenets and practices of primitive American democracy. Such is the picture that the apologists have constructed of our small towns.

WILLIAM ALLEN WHITE

(1868-1944)

A more loyal or more typical son of the Middle West than William Allen White never lived. For many years he has been one of the famous editors of America, a politician of sincerely liberal principles, a novelist, and a publicist, and in all his activities he has never revealed a trait that is not native to the Middle West. White began his active life as a newspaper reporter in Kansas City, and when he was a young man, he became editor of the Emporia, Kansas, *Gazette*. He still lives in Emporia and directs his paper which has come to be one of the few famous small-town dailies in the whole country. Like his activities, White's major interests have been bounded by a relatively small portion of middle America. He is thoroughly local, and, unlike Robert Frost, he has never succeeded in raising the provincial to the rank of the universal. In recent years the Emporia editor has become a national figure, but he has made no contribution to our cultural or political life that is not indigenous to his home state.

White's first book was *At the Court of Boyville,* another story of boy life that used a romantic version of the small town as a background of the action. No reader can miss White's meaning in the descriptions of juvenile democracy in the village—as the boys are, so are their fathers. And if the young form the habit of rewarding the worthy and of following the capable, it is reasonable to suppose that those traits are not dropped with the donning of long trousers.

Future students will undoubtedly place a high value on White's study of moderate liberalism, *The Old Order Changeth*. This little book sets forth the political and social creed of those moderates who formed the center of the Progressive party in 1912. As a political guide for to-day, it is as archaic as a platform of the Know-Nothing party, but it gives the student an excellent idea of principles that were widely accepted during the first twelve or fifteen years of the present century.

A Certain Rich Man (1909), undoubtedly White's best novel, is the story of a small-town boy who forsook the virtuous simplicity of village economics and became a grasping monopolist. Of course, in the end, John Barclay, the monopolist, made an atoning renunciation and dies convinced of the wisdom of village ways. In the book Barclay stands for the centralized economics of the city, while the score of minor characters represent the freely competitive, simple life of early America. The novel is a genuinely moving statement of a belief in the rightness of village life and ideals, but its idyllic rhapsodies on the felicity of the small town would be more convincing if the author had left out the white lilacs, the songs of birds in the springtime, and the various other appurtenances of the tearful, lesser romantics. The characters are sharply observed and well presented. *In the Heart of a Fool* (1918) White has given the same major theme a slightly different treatment.

White is not usually granted the place in contemporary letters that is rightfully his. Ordinarily critics speak of him as a notable figure in American life, but as novelist they talk as if he were a minor Tarkington or a lesser Dorothy Canfield Fisher. He is not so clever as Tarkington nor so workmanlike a novelist as Mrs. Fisher, but he has a solid grasp of his thesis, an accurate eye, and a lucid, convincing style that will make his works very valuable to future students. White is the perfect embodiment of village ideals, endowed with fine sense and a gift for expression. If he had been able to shake off one of the village weaknesses, sentimentality, he would have been fortunate indeed.

BOOTH TARKINGTON

(1869-1946)

For more than thirty years Booth Tarkington has delighted a huge circle of readers with recurrent exegeses of the obvious, and in all that time he has taken good care never to offend even the most sensitive by an interest in any ideas other than those incontrovertibly fixed in the minds of his readers. Never has he nettled by his hypercritical temper, never has he wounded by excessive plainness of speech. In novel after novel he has pursued his one object of extolling middle-class virtues as they are admiringly exhibited in the course of pleasant courtships that move to a happy conclusion with only an agreeable amount' of make-believe obstruction. Most of his novels have been only *Monsieur Beaucaire* in a village setting. Instead of a sword or a dandy's cane, Tarkington's modern hero is equipped with a fountain pen or a cash register. Instead of a wig and cocked hat he wears an honest fedora, sold for five dollars by the "gents' furnishings store" diagonally across from the First National Bank. Despite the recurrent thesis that honest worth will shine through any disguise to win tangible rewards, Tarkington has been able to give variety to his novels through the extreme facility of his writing, his humor, and his skill at character creation. He lacks only one thing, and that is the ability to tell the commonplace truth about his people.

In *Beyond Life* James Branch Cabell has written a very true and discriminating criticism of Tarkington:

For if, as Stevenson declared, the fairies were tipsy at Mr. Kipling's christening, at Mr. Tarkington's they must have been in the last stages of maudlin generosity. Poetic insight they gave him; and the knack of story building; and all their own authentic elfin liveliness of fancy; and actually perceptive eyes, by virtue of which his more truly Tarkingtonian pages are enriched with countless happy little miracles of observation; and the dramatic gift of contriving and causing to move convincingly a wide variety of puppets in nothing resembling the puppet-master; and the not uncommon desire to "write," with just enough deficiency in common sense to make him willing to put up with the laboriousness of writing fairly well. In fine, there is hardly one natural endowment requisite to grace in a creative author that was omitted by these inebriated fairies. . . .

For the rest, his plots are the sort of thing that makes criticism seem cruel. . . . The world to us is not very strikingly suggestive of a cosmic gumdrop variegated by oceans of molasses: we dispute if Omnipotence was ever, at any time, a confectioner's apprentice: and to us whatever workmen may have been employed in laying out that "noble and joyous city" appear undoubtedly to have gone on a strike.

Tarkington's first novel was *The Gentleman from Indiana* (1899), a huge popular success, that discovered the now familiar formula by which the rewards of love and material success are placed admiringly in the hands of the worthy young fellow, college bred, who returns to his native village to become one of the folksy townsmen. This particular hero became the idol of his fellows by joining hands with them in putting down rowdiness and other influences disturbing to the village peace of mind. For his camaraderie he was rewarded by a seat in Congress. The book ends on a note often repeated in Tarkington's writings: " 'Aren't they the good dear people?' 'The beautiful people,' he answered." Other typical examples of the Tarkington canon are *The Conquest of Canaan, His Own People, The Turmoil, The Magnificent Ambersons, The Midlander,* and *The Plutocrat.* On a slightly higher level are *Alice Adams* and *Gentle Julia.* It is often declared that *Penrod* and *Seventeen* demand comparison with *Tom Sawyer* and *Huckleberry Finn,* but they are liable to profit very slightly by such an appraisal.

In spite of his superficial glitter and smirking optimism Tarkington is one of our most depressing novelists. One's spirit can hardly be permanently elevated by continuous exhortations to seek comfort at the ultimate cost of spiritual exaltation, nor is one always sublimely inspired by recurring assurances that success in village undertakings is preferable to failure in glorious impossibilities.

DOROTHY CANFIELD FISHER

(1879-   )

Mrs. Dorothy Canfield Fisher has perfectly good grounds for denying any interest in the battle of the village as such, but it is undeniable that some of her books have been very comforting to those people who charge Sinclair Lewis and Sherwood Anderson with perversely bad sight. Mrs. Fisher has never attempted a conscious defense of the village, nor has she implied a defense by attacking the city. Her chief interest is in culture rather narrowly interpreted, and all her books contribute something to a discussion of this subject. She is drawn into the village controversy through her insistent refusal to find anything in the small town that is innately hostile to culture. Specifically she is usually concerned with the problem of education and with the price that a shallow social life exacts of cultured people.

Mrs. Fisher is one of our most competent novelists. She writes a very clear, neat, and accurate prose; her characterization is firm; and her use of incident is well directed. From the standpoint of technique she is undoubtedly one of our distinguished writers. It is in the choice of her theses that Mrs. Canfield weakens her novels. Too intellectual to write a novel for the sake of character and incident, she always must have a substructure for her writing, and this foundation is usually a bit shaky or so universally conceded that a thesis novel on the subject is unnecessary. For instance, the thesis of *The Brimming Cup* is the contention that it is a commendable thing for a woman to prefer her husband and children to a thorough rascal. Yet despite the obviousness of the thesis, Mrs. Fisher has written around it a novel really notable for its study of family relationships and for its friendly observation of village life. Admiration for the art of the writer tends to make one condone the weakness of the thesis. *Rough-Hewn* is the story of an artistically inclined woman who travels widely and then settles down contentedly in a Vermont village. This book caresses tenderly the familiar enthusiasms of Booth Tarkington.

THE ATTACK

As far back as 1883 Ed Howe's *The Story of a Country Town* had indicated that the idyllic pictures of life in the small town were slightly inaccurate, but Howe's work was too early to stir up either a defense or further attacks on the village. By 1915, however, the muck-rakers, younger critics like Mencken, and the work of the political and economic radicals had attuned the American mind to critical pitch. In that year *Spoon River Anthology* appeared. This book was a startling assault on the venerable village tradition, and when it appeared readers at once caught the meaning of the poems. At once the battle of the village was on. Masters' exposure of the dullness, hypocrisy, and venality of the village caused a great uproar, but before the indiscriminate mêlée could take the form of orderly combat, the war put a temporary stop to the struggle. After 1918 critics went back to *Spoon River Anthology* to document their indictments against the small town.

If the indictments had been drawn in the spirit of the critical years from 1900 to 1917, they would have emphasized the venality, political corruption, and economic injustice of the village. But the war had made the earlier liberalism quite obsolete, and critics who came into prominence after 1918 were cosmopolitans interested in culture and the life of the spirit far more than in economics and politics. As a result, the assault on the village was centered on the spiritual aspects of the small town, and the qualities that drew the hottest fire were the long-sanctified virtues of middle-western America inherited from our pioneer ancestors. Thrift and industry, the most widely practiced of the village virtues, were denounced as respectable covers for avarice and sharp business practices and as the begetters of stinginess in both purse and spirit. The critics pointed out, probably with more than a little justification, that the typical American business man worked so hard and spent so frugally trying to accumulate money upon which to live that he died without ever having really lived. Village friendliness—the famed folksiness of Tarkington and White—was assailed as the mere "noseyness" of inquisitive neighbors. Furthermore, the critics contended that the once valuable pioneer asset of optimism had quite lost its reason for existence and had come to be only a noisy back-slapping that was useful as a defense mechanism.

But the chief criticism was leveled at dullness, "the village virus." The pioneer had assiduously uprooted from his society every vestige of aristocracy, but no upper-class trait was more relentlessly exterminated than was that of independence of thought. Lacking the secure sanction of name and family tradition for his thinking, the pioneer instinctively sought sanction in the solidarity of his group. Few ideas and speculations were tolerated that could not gain the understanding approval of the mass. This fact caused the intellectual life of the village to settle on a rather low level. The ambitious and the intellectually restless left the small town for the city. The cultural centers of the East were all well acquainted with the "back trailers of the middle border," and the left bank of the Seine knew a few of the most adventurous. But the home villages slumbered on generation after generation with little sign of change.

The chief critics were H. L. Mencken, George Jean Nathan, Ludwig Lewisohn, Randolph Bourne, and Van Wyck Brooks, and the leading critical magazines and journals were *The Smart Set* from 1914 to 1923, *The Dial, The American Mercury, The Nation, The New Republic,* and *The Freeman.* Sinclair Lewis and Sherwood Anderson were two novelists enlisted on the side of the assailants, and the works of these two men were the center of especially hot conflicts, for they were widely read in the villages where the hostile critical writings were only slightly known.

SINCLAIR LEWIS
(1885-   )

Sinclair Lewis is fundamentally a socially minded idealist who states his idealisms obliquely by means of realism and satire. His method is not always the same. Sometimes he is the impersonal reporter of what he sees and hears, occasionally he selects and deftly accents the comic element in his characters to barb the satire, and sometimes, in his earlier books, he selects his material and gives it a romantic interpretation. In general, he shows his idealism in his conception of the story as a whole, and his realism in the handling of detail. Such a novel as *Arrowsmith* is plainly idealistic in its broad aspects, but once in the novel Lewis presents details with the utmost reality. On the other hand *The Man Who Knew Coolidge,* literally a stenographer's transcript of a long monologue, is as impersonal in every respect as the dictionary.

Lewis has been compared with many writers of the past and present from Voltaire to Upton Sinclair, but he is most like Vachel Lindsay. Both men are products of the Middle West, both dislike the ugly and sordid features of the small town, both would have the village a better and more attractive place. Of course, Lindsay has a vast number of enthusiasms and collateral ideas that Lewis would pointedly refuse to touch, but that fact hardly vitiates a comparison of the two men. However, Lindsay promulgates his idealisms through glowingly romantic descriptions of the desired end, while Lewis states his by making ridiculous the folly and unloveliness that must be removed before the desired wisdom and beauty can be attained. Never does Lewis allow himself romantic rhapsodies; his reportorial instinct always saves him from such excesses.

Career of Lewis.—Sinclair Lewis was born in Sauk Center, a Minnesota village of about two or three thousand people. In his native town he seems to have been distinguished from the boys around him only by a zest for reading and study. After graduation from the Sauk Center high school, Lewis went to Yale where he is still remembered for his rebellious attitude. Professor W. L. Phelps, who had him as a student, says that he showed a deep interest in all kinds of reforms. It seems that he was particularly irritated by some of the outmoded but traditional ways of college life. There are at present no facts extant to show us when the reforming zeal set in, but by Lewis's third year at Yale it had become irresistible, for at the end of his junior year he joined Helicon Hall, the short-lived community of Utopian socialists founded by Upton Sinclair. Again we do not have enough facts about his life in the community to determine whether he had any experiences that would tend to give him a mistrust of facile Utopianism. At all events, Lewis, like many reformers, saw that a certain amount of destructive criticism is a prerequisite of social millenniums. After firing the furnace at Helicon Hall for some time, Lewis left the community and made his first attempts at writing. His first accepted works were children's poetry and jokes. In 1906 he returned to Yale and received his degree the following spring.

Lewis's Early Writings.—After finishing college, Lewis set to work seriously to learn how to write. He did journalism in Connecticut, Iowa, and California, tried free-lance writing, edited the *Volta Review*, a magazine for the deaf, became assistant editor of *Adventure*, and finally served as editor and advertising manager for a publishing house. In the meantime he had been writing a large amount of apprentice material. None of this seems to have been published, except for a few pieces just after his graduation from college. In 1914 appeared *Our Mr. Wrenn*, Lewis's first novel under his own name.

Those critics who regard *Main Street* and *Babbitt* as providential accidents perpetrated without warning have evidently never read *Our Mr. Wrenn*. It is quite true that the first novel is crude. It attempts many things that do not quite "come off," and the author is too prone to spoil an effect by "dropping character" to step forward and point out how clever he is and how close are his observations. But in general *Our Mr. Wrenn* sets the pattern for *Main Street* and *Babbitt*. The novel tells of a spiritless little clerk who spent his leisure reading advertising folders sent out by steamship companies. The dullness and stupidity of his life goad him into a mild revolt, and he goes adventuring to Europe on a cattle boat. Here he has a very romantic love affair with an artist. Shortly he returns to New York and his job, again the meek little clerk, who finds happiness reading newspapers aloud to a bovine woman whom he marries. At the end of the book Mr. Wrenn is carrying home to his wife seven cents' worth of potato salad. Several types in this book are familiar to readers of Lewis's later novels. The stupid and uninteresting man who finds release in gaudily romantic day-dreams, the heavy, unimaginative woman, and the girl who typifies romance are all to be found in later books. Furthermore, the revolt that ends in abject surrender appears plainly in *Main Street* and *Babbitt*, where the colorless endings give piquant meanings to the novels.

But there is more of Lewis in *Our Mr. Wrenn* than these elements. In this first work one finds that absolutely accurate transcription of the American idiom that may easily be considered Lewis's chief contribution to the novel. *Our Mr. Wrenn* also has a robot of business ready for the few deft touches that transformed him into the delicious caricature of Babbitt. The ideas behind the characters and episodes were good, for every attempt blossomed later into the artistry of *Main Street* and its successors, but upon almost every page of the first novel there is the heavy touch of the amateur. In this book Lewis only imperfectly achieves the objectivity that is to become one of his distinctions, his humor is so smart that it reminds one of the ghastly flippancies of O. Henry and Irving Cobb, and through all the story flutters a febrile romanticism that constantly threatens to break out in the white lilacs and the flowing plumes of William Allen White. But crudely amateurish as the book is, it and not *Main Street* began Lewis's career as an author.

Furthermore the other early books by Lewis are not entirely to be disregarded. All of them seem to have autobiographical elements— Mr. Wrenn's trip to England on a cattle boat is founded on a personal experience—and all of them contain a wealth of material for the psychological analyst of Sinclair Lewis. *The Trail of the Hawk* (1915) is a novel, romantic in conception and cumulative effect but quite realistic in its attention to details, that tells the story of a Minnesota boy from youth to maturity. It contains a few very significant pages on the dullness of village life, and it has an outstanding minor character, the village atheist, who was also an economic radical. Early in the book Lewis wrote a sketch of the intellectually debilitating small college, topping off his sketch with a chapel address by the president on evolution, atheism, anarchy, socialism, Bernard Shaw, H. G. Wells, and other like-related subjects. This address is a worthy portent of Babbitt's masterpiece and the tirades of Elmer Gantry and Dr. Pickerbaugh.

Most critics who have taken the trouble to read Lewis's early books hold that *The Job* (1917) is the best of the lot in both its characterization and the handling of the story. It also contains a large number of touches that are obviously autobiographical. The other books of Lewis's early period are *The Innocents* (1917) and *Free Air* (1919).

The Later Novels.—About 1917 Lewis discovered that he had the ability to write facile short stories that would give him popular success and its monetary returns, but he deliberately turned his back on such a career and wrote *Main Street,* knowing that the new book would end his work as the well-paid star of a popular magazine. But *Main Street* surprised every one, including the author. It became the most discussed book of the decade, arousing reverberations that have not yet subsided. Incidentally it contributed a new term to our vocabulary of derogation.

Main Street is primarily a sociological study. The author's interest is so centered on the environment that his plot is fragmentary and his characters are only exhibits in the indictment of the village. Gopher Prairie is indicted on two main counts, economic parasitism and spiritual sloth. In the clatter that arose over the second count, the economic attack was almost overlooked. In fact, it is not stressed by Lewis. *Main Street* was in process of composition for many years—the first outline dates from Lewis's college days—and as the novel progressed, the aim of the author changed. If the book had appeared in 1912, it would have emphasized the economic indictment, but in 1920 the critical emphasis had so shifted that economic questions were outmoded. If all discussion of economics had been omitted from the novel, its effectiveness would have been in no way impaired. Lewis simply attempts to show that the village is an economic waste in that it exploits the farmers whom it dominates through the familiar agencies of social regimentation.

Main Street bears the cicatrices of many literary operations other than the one that almost deleted the economic criticism. We are told on excellent authority that the published work omits many things that were in a late manuscript which would have revealed Lewis very clearly as a social idealist. James Branch Cabell in his *Straws and Prayer-Books* says that he is responsible for the early death of Bea Sorenson, a minor character, whom Lewis desired to make the victor in the struggle with the village environment. She was to find virtues in the town that Carol Kennicott, the protagonist, could never find. In other words she is to be the successful reformer of village ills. Cabell also says that he objected violently and successfully to Lewis's introduction into the book of various suggested remedies for the mental and spiritual lassitude of middle-western villages. It is one of the ironic facts of our recent literary history that Cabell, an arch-romantic, should keep an avowed realist from going to pieces on romantic schemes for social amelioration. The episode is quite destructive to one's faith in Lewis's fundamental realism.

Babbitt (1922), one of the masterpieces of our recent literature, is the realization of Lewis's characteristic devices that were first crudely exhibited in *Our Mr. Wrenn* and *The Trail of the Hawk*. Almost every stroke of characterization and every episode in *Babbitt* succeeds brilliantly. The novel is the richly authenticated story of a business man, the slave of routine and mob-thinking, who tries to hide his stupidity and gloss over his repellent work with stoked-up enthusiasm, forced joviaiity, and blatant optimism. Finally Babbitt revolts from the narrow conventions of his crowd and makes a few awkward gestures toward radicalism. However, his brain was not made to direct thought or action unsupported by the sanction of his group, and he naturally returns to his familiar and comfortable ways, bawling cheerful platitudes to his fellows and lunging into his work with apparent zest. The novel is far more interesting than *Main Street*, and George F. Babbitt is a far better character than is Carol Kennicott. There is relatively little explicit sociology in the book but a vast amount of social satire that is centered on Babbitt as a type of a large group well known in American life. The story is not written in the spirit of realism, for the chief character is the product of selection and comic emphasis rather than of all-inclusive realism. As Babbitt stands he is made to caricature middle-class America. He is industrious, respectable, superficially interested in the church, conventionally moral, unbelievably stupid, and above all exceedingly funny. He is one of the few genuinely humorous characters of recent fiction. The novel as a whole is magnificently successful. With its appearance Lewis's apprentice days were over.

Arrowsmith is a thoughtful, sad story of the difficulties that beset an idealist in an acquisitive society. The romantic idealism that led Lewis to join Helicon Hall and to write the excised social remedies into *Main Street* finds full expression in *Arrowsmith*. And yet the book in its surface details is conscientiously realistic. The novel is specifically a study of the conflict between commercialism and the scientific spirit. The protagonist is a high-minded scientist who is supported by three admirably drawn minor characters. The portrait of Gottlieb is especially well done. The forces of charlatanry are represented by Dr. Pickerbaugh, a mountebank, who is the scientific prototype of Elmer Gantry. He even indulges in public orations in the vernacular. But the main interest of the book lies in Arrowsmith and his friends, and in this group Lewis's idealism finds glowing expression.

Sinclair Lewis is surely one of the most energetic of our literary men, but he must have expended an unusual amount of labor in writing *Arrowsmith*. The author was assisted by a scientist, Dr. Paul de Kruif, who advised with him on technical details, and the two men traveled to the tropics collecting facts. The details thus collected bear the stamp of accuracy, and not the least of Lewis's triumphs is the success that he achieved in writing idealistically in tone and utterly realistically in detail. *Arrowsmith* and *Babbitt* are the best work of the author.

Mantrap (1926) is the weakest novel that Lewis ever wrote. Just why a man, who can bring about the artistic success of *Arrowsmith* and who can command the technical virtuosity apparent in *The Man Who Knew Coolidge*, should write *Mantrap* is a question that must be referred to Lewis's biographer.

Elmer Gantry (1927), a study of a religious hypocrite, is the most violent and bitter work that Lewis has done. Into it he has thrown all his power of vituperation, all his talent for unlovely caricature and satire, and all his journalistic ability. He makes his one big mistake in permitting himself to flame with indignation, but despite this defect the book has great interest. The author must have enjoyed writing it, for the gusto of the vituperative passages could hardly have been simulated.

America has produced many a village Voltaire, but our major novelists have been loath to handle religious questions in a critical spirit, and ministers have usually been above criticism. At one blow Lewis irreparably fractured this gentle tradition. Never since the days of Paine's *Age of Reason* has a religious question received so hostile an examination. It is true that the novel is ostensibly a study of a religious hypocrite, but again and again Lewis pronounces a few vitriolic *obiter dicta* on the church. The effectiveness of this book is vastly impaired by the author's bad temper. If Lewis had taken a lesson from Voltaire in the combining of humor and vituperation, *Elmer Gantry* would have been immensely improved.

The Man Who Knew Coolidge (1928) is a triumph of objective presentation, but it lacks the interest that we have come to expect in

Lewis's works. The book is not a novel; it is only one of Babbitt's monologues expanded to book length. But to write a character sketch through the medium of monologue and never allow the speaker to drop character through 75,000 words of talk is a notable literary feat.

Dodsworth (1929) probably indicates a departure for Lewis. It is not sociological in any sense, nor is it critical. The chief interest is in the study of the chief character who is neither exceptional nor typical. *Dodsworth* has hardly the interest that some of the earlier books have, but it has certain elements that may give it a life beyond that ordinarily possessed by topical and thesis novels.

Lewis as a Novelist.—The chief fault of Sinclair Lewis as a novelist is a poverty of imagination. Over and over he uses the same places, the same incidents, the same literary devices, and, worst of all, the same characters. He hears with unquestionable accuracy, and he sees with uncanny perception, but he has trouble inventing anything. He does not use exactly the same character again and again, but all his major figures have so many traits in common that they may be called only slight modifications of an original. Mr. Wrenn, Carol Kennicott, and George Babbitt are fundamentally alike, and Elmer Gantry has his like in more than one of the rascals in Lewis's novels. Most of the major characters are vaguely unhappy because of repressed desires and futile strivings, and they usually revolt from the environment only to return satisfied or at least acquiescent. Lewis's exposure of ignorance and conceit through the public pronouncement begins with the speech of the college president in *The Trail of the Hawk* and ends with the sustained monologue of Lowell Schmaltz in *The Man Who Knew Coolidge*. The device varies not at all, but the technique shows a steady improvement, though the relatively early oration of Babbitt is immortal. In short, Lewis has learned how to write through constant practice in a very limited field. He has conducted his literary training in public, but the important thing is that he has finally learned how to write with superlative skill. However, his skill should not blind one to the narrowness of his range.

Next to the lack of imagination Lewis's greatest weakness is a violent interest in his themes that make him use his characters as if they were proofs of theses in argumentative dissertations. In his haste to make his points, he sometimes neglects to create convincing characters. This weakness is especially noticeable in his major figures. If Lewis could ever divest himself of intellectual and spiritual interests and write a book composed only of minor figures he might achieve a new type of success, unlimited by topical and geographical interests.

The chief strength of Lewis is his sensitive intelligence. The accuracy with which he puts down what he sees and hears is marvelous. Specifically his greatest contribution to the novel is his handling of the American speech in the mouths of his characters. Furthermore he uses incident very effectively. In his novels, something is always happening; the action is dynamic, and incident succeeds incident almost too energetically. As a creator of character Lewis is good—with qualifications. Some of his figures are only animated theses but others take on the air of verisimilitude. Lewis is said by those who know him to be a talented mimic. This quality appears in his books, for he surpasses most writers in his ability to endow his characters with the superficial aspect of reality. However, he does not penetrate far enough below the surface to get securely into the hearts of his creations. They act and talk like people, but they always lack that final touch of a master that makes the puppet live. In just this failure Lewis may miss the right to be called a supremely great novelist.

But Sinclair Lewis is yet a young man, and the future undoubtedly holds much for him. Prediction as to his future course and an attempt to give him a final estimate are alike dangerous.

In 1930 Lewis received the Nobel Prize, the most famous award in the reach of literary men. He is the only American ever to be so honored, and among English writers only Kipling, Yeats, and Shaw have received the prize. Lewis's honor came, so we are told, not because of any specific novel, but because of his descriptive powers and his ability to create humorous characters. While the award stirred up a considerable amount of adverse criticism, most American critics agreed that the honor was amply deserved. The discussion that followed the announcement of the award tended to bring out the fact that those who objected based their objections upon personal preferences and prejudices rather than upon any judgment of literary art.

SHERWOOD ANDERSON
(1876-1941)

Sherwood Anderson and Sinclair Lewis, the two novelists who are usually associated with the revolt against the village, offer an interesting comparison and contrast. In their personal backgrounds and their reactions to them they are much alike. Both are products of the Middle West, both have watched the processes of social standardization develop until large scale industry has become the dominant element in culture, both hate the stupid repressions that a standardized society inflicts upon its victims, and both bitterly deplore the baffled and frustrated lives that are by-products of a regimented social life and thought. But at that point the similarity stops abruptly, for in their literary aims and methods they are totally unlike. Lewis is primarily a reporter interested in the surface appearance of men and events, and Anderson says that whatever he sees and hears is unimportant. However, it should be remembered that by Anderson's own admission he has learned all the psychoanalysis that he knows by observing people and asking questions. But what goes on in a character's mind is his major interest. Lewis reproduces the surface of life with great fidelity and at times with brilliancy. Anderson gropes awkwardly for the hidden impulse that will explain a whole life. His two difficulties, that of discovering the elusive thing that he is looking for and that of finding words with which to describe it, keep him from becoming a facile writer. He is never brilliant, and indeed he succeeds only occasionally, but his relatively few successes have made him one of the significant figures in contemporary world literature.

Anderson: Novelist and Mystic.—In literary affiliations Anderson is a naturalist in that he accepts the principle of determinism as opposed to the philosophy of free will, but his naturalism differs in the choice of material from that of earlier writers like Crane and Dreiser. The early naturalists were physical. Their concern with environment made them study the effects of economics and politics upon society, and when they came to center their interest upon the actions of the individual, they stated their findings in terms of physics, bio-chemistry, or an objective psychology that never sought to probe into the hidden folds of the mind. The inadequacy of such a procedure is very unsatisfactory to Anderson. He is not content with the objective recording of a stimulus and response. He seeks to penetrate the minds and personalities of his characters searching for hidden facts that will answer his questions. He wants to know why things are as they are, and he feels that he can never know so long as he stands outside and simply watches actions. He wants to creep into the very being of his characters, to live their lives, to share their subconscious minds, and by doing so to effect a mystic union of the one with the many. It is his immense effort to find the undiscoverable that has made him brood moodily over the problems of life, and his failure to find a clear answer to his questioning forces him to express himself in mystical intuitions rather than in the clarity born of factual certainty. Anderson is a tireless seeker, but he has never reached his goal. It may be that there is nothing anywhere that can serve as his goal, but his slow, vaguely directed gropings through the uncharted regions of the unconscious have carried him into hitherto unexplored regions.

Anderson is a true mystic, though in this respect as in every other he is so original that his mysticism cannot be identified with any of the traditional varieties. It is most like that of Whitman, but there is a vast difference between the vague mysticism of *Winesburg, Ohio,* and the buoyant certitude of the mystical passages in *Leaves of Grass.* Anderson wants to feel the mystic identity of mankind, but his failure to find certainty and satisfaction makes him unsure. He yearns for brotherhood as the old man does in "Brothers," one of his most poetic and most significant stories. Like the old man, Anderson never quite reaches the point of equilibrium that is the traditional reward of mysticism. The mystic of Winesburg was born too late into a world too disturbing to allow mystic serenity. A transcendental mystic like Whitman received as his birthright an endowment of unshakable optimism that was founded upon the easy assurance of early romanticism, which in turn had the very tangible frontier to sustain its cheery intuitions. Sherwood Anderson was unfortunate in his birth date. The only vestige of the frontier that he ever knew was a unified society held together by standardized thinking. This condition simply tended to make the old frontier lands accept industrialization with hardly a struggle. Furthermore Anderson was born in the middle of the Dreadful Decade when materialism was triumphant, and his mature life has fallen in the machine age. Such an environment is not an easy one for the mystic. Again, the temper of the modern mind is too skeptical to accept a statement of values that is founded upon so elusive a thing as intuition. With his mysticism attacked upon every side and with his inability to gain the sureness of the scientist, Anderson is thrown into a chronic uncertainty. His final refuge is his intuitive mysticism, and he seems to feel the need of this more than he feels its reality.

Anderson's brooding over the question of life has been compared with that of Dreiser. Such a comparison is not very apt. Both men are looking for answers to their questions, but the questions are not the same. Dreiser is seeking to know the meaning of men's actions in the aggregate; Anderson wants to know why. Dreiser studies cumulative actions in novels of eight hundred pages; Anderson is most successful when he fleetingly glimpses his characters at a significant moment. Dreiser's watchfulness is caused by his desire to get the whole of life into his studies; Anderson's arises from his care to catch his character in a revealing episode.

Both the old gray bearded man and the wicked one puzzle me.
I think and think but cannot understand them.

.   .   .   ○   .   .   .

I keep thinking about the dandified man who laughed all through my story.
If I could understand him I could understand everything.

Anderson's Career.—Anderson was born in Camden, a small Ohio village, where his family had very slight social and financial eminence. The father was a shiftless, boastful harness-maker who contributed little to the family's welfare but who later served as a leading character in his son's first novel, *Windy McPherson's Son.* He also appears in rather thin disguise in some of Anderson's other work. The mother was evidently a resourceful woman of considerable capacity. Three of her sons became well known, Sherwood as a writer and two others as artists. Sherwood's education might charitably be described as desultory, for it was completed in the public schools by the time he was fourteen or fifteen. For a number of years he led a wandering life, making a living by manual labor. In 1898 he joined the army at the outbreak of war with Spain, not because of any interest in the conflict, but because of a desire to escape his unpleasant life. After this experience he moved to Ohio, married, and eventually became a manufacturer of paint. But he was restless and vaguely dissatisfied. One day when he was dictating a letter, he stopped abruptly in the middle of a sentence and left his office never to return again. His great quest had begun. He went to Chicago and for a number of years worked for an advertising agency, all the while experimenting with his writing. His first published work was *Windy McPherson's Son* (1916), a novel that is filled with personal recollections and that to-day the author pronounces very imitative. When he wrote the book, he was under the influence of several writers, notably Dreiser, though the imitation in the novel is more apparent to Anderson than to most readers. However, his intensely original nature makes him displeased with anything that is not altogether his own. *Windy McPherson's Son* is of considerable importance, though the method is far too objective to be typical of the author's later work. The same lack of subjectivity is apparent in *Marching Men* (1917).

In 1919 Anderson reached his true level with *Winesburg, Ohio*, a group of psychological sketches of twenty-four grotesques. Each grotesque is a human character who has been crushed out of resemblance to a psychologically normal person by repressions and the sense of having striven to no avail. In these sketches Anderson for the first time attempts to go far beneath externalities to the psychological basis of personality. As usually is the case with him, some of these pieces are not successful, but in the best of them, "The Teacher," "The Untold Lie," "The Strength of God," "Mother," and "Godliness," the stories of repressed lives and souls sickened with frustrated desires are told with a concentrated intensity of tremendous power.

The Triumph of the Egg is, next to *Winesburg, Ohio*, Anderson's best book. It contains thirteen sketches and two poems in free verse. The book does not have the high average level that the earlier collection possesses, but its best pieces are probably the best that Anderson has done. The finest of the lot are "I Want to Know Why," "Brothers," "The Egg," and "Out of Nowhere into Nothing." The first of these is a soliloquy placed in the mouth of a boy whose first experience in a world of men has filled him with wonder at the gratuitous ugliness and sordidness of life. There is a great deal of Anderson in this soliloquy, as there is in "Brothers," a sketch of an old man whose crazed yearnings for brotherhood make him the symbol of humanity victimized by environment and only half liberated by an imperfectly realized mystical intuition.

The face beseeched me to believe the story the lips were trying to tell. In my mind everything concerning the relationship of men and women became confused, a muddle. . . . The whole story of mankind's loneliness, of the effort to reach out to unattainable beauty tried to get itself expressed from the lips of an old man, crazed with loneliness, who stood by the side of a country road on a foggy morning holding a little dog in his arms.

"The Egg" has been called the epitome of Anderson's grotesques. It is a remarkable story, filled with symbolism that vividly represents man's futile efforts to control life.

One versed in such matters can have no notion of the many and tragic things that can happen to a chicken. It is born out of an egg, lives for a few weeks as a tiny fluffy thing such as you will see pictures of on Easter cards, then become hideously naked, eats quantities of corn and meal bought by the sweat of your father's brow, gets diseases . . . stands looking with stupid eyes at the sun, becomes sick and dies. A few hens and now and then a rooster, intended to serve God's mysterious ends, struggle through to maturity. The hens lay eggs out of which come other chickens and the dreadful cycle is thus made complete. It is all unbelievably complex. Most philosophers must have been raised on chicken farms. . . . Grotesques are born out of eggs as out of people. . . . I awoke at dawn and for a long time looked at the egg that lay on the table. I wondered why eggs had to be and why from the egg came the hen who again laid the egg. The question got into my blood. It has stayed there, I imagine, because I am the son of my father. At any rate, the problem remains unsolved in my mind. And that, I conclude, is but another evidence of the complete and final triumph of the egg—at least so far as my family is concerned.

"Out of Nowhere into Nothing" is a strange, beautiful story of the awakening of love in a young woman and of her mother's reactions to the experience of youth. The story ends on a terrible note of bitterness and disillusion.

Life is dirty . . . There is no love. Life is a lie. It leads to sin, to death and decay.

Anderson's novels are not very successful in their total effect, for his peculiar concentration is hardly susceptible to elaborate treatment. *Many Marriages* (1923) is said to be the favorite of all his books because it contains the most finished example of his subjective method, but the ordinary reader usually finds its psychological explanations too intricate and its symbolism too little mindful of common sense. *Dark Laughter* (1925) is one of the most poetic novels of our time, but it is a very difficult book to grasp. The theme is the familiar one of unrest and escape, but the thread of action is often lost in poetic rhapsodies about the great Mississippi and the half-primitive Negroes who live along its banks. Like D. H. Lawrence, Anderson seems to find in primitive peoples a sense of liberation from the repressions of so-called civilized society. The blacks symbolize the success of a flight that with the restless sons of the pioneer too often ends in a blank wall. To some readers *Dark Laughter* is the least original book that Anderson ever wrote. Portions of it apparently owe much to Lawrence and to James Joyce.

Anderson's Use of Personal Experience.—Anderson has often used personal experiences and recollections in all of his fiction, and in two books he has written a very frank and revealing autobiography. *Tar,* the story of his poverty-stricken childhood in Ohio, contains a vast amount of interesting material for the student of Anderson, but by far the more important of the two books is *A Story-Teller's Story,* a genuinely distinctive account of his career both as business man and as artist. This book reveals Anderson as a mystical dreamer who loathes the standardization of an industrialized society and whose life problem is that of escape from such an environment. In this work the author toys with some idealistic plans for the restoration to mankind of a happiness and satisfaction that seem once to have belonged to the race. Anderson has at heart the ideal of a medieval craftsman, holding that men will be truly happy only when they can again find joy in creative labor. No workman can take pleasure or pride in feeding material to a machine that turns out hundreds of identical products. Working with a machine is an occupation, but it is not an answer to the instinctive craving for creative work. And there is a possibility that craftsmanship may give man spiritual satisfaction in an age of social repression. Anderson's own writing seems to be done in the spirit of the medieval workman. In one place he says about his writing, "I sang as I worked, as in my boyhood I had often seen old craftsmen sing and as I had never heard men sing in factories."

Although Anderson is a Middle Westerner in full revolt against the standardization of his native habitat, he uses a very small amount of specific physical background in his works, and his characters might live anywhere that society exacts a hard price from its members. Sinclair Lewis has written with a sharp eye for localizing detail. His

backgrounds are elaborately middle western, and his people unmistakably spring from the streets of their native towns. Anderson is
so indifferent to what he sees and hears that he has reduced the
background to the requirements of bare necessity, and his characters
are presented as psychological line drawings, considerably distorted.
The characters are not sharply localized. Some of the people in
Winesburg, Ohio, were found, so it is said, in Anderson's boarding
house in Chicago.

However, if one reads Anderson intently, one sees how much he
owes to the Middle West. Spiritually Sherwood Anderson is the reluctant son of a vanished frontier. He sees all about him other
reluctant sons, vaguely discontented, longing to escape from something that they cannot put into words. It is the shift from the old,
physically free frontier to the new, industrialized Middle West that
oppresses men, declares Anderson. They long for spiritual escape
as their forefathers longed for physical freedom. But to-day there
is no public domain of the human spirit. Men have been blocked
and thwarted until their spirits, like animals on tread-mills, can
only strive. They never get anywhere. They cannot escape their
inner selves. Thus in a very definite sense Anderson becomes the
most bitter of the village rebels.

Anderson as a Writer.—Anderson has an almost bare style, unrelieved by any literary tricks and totally guiltless of facility and
smartness. He seeks no rhetorical effects and never calls upon his
readers to admire his cleverness. However uncertain and perplexed
he may become and however great may be his difficulty of saying
exactly what he wants to say, he never attempts to clarify his obscure meaning by the useless expedient of using more words. His
style always retains a strength, honesty, and simplicity that elevate
him to the ranks of genuinely distinguished stylists. In his best
sketches it leaves one feeling that Sherwood Anderson is a strong,
tender man who is telling with utmost honesty and simplicity something that he does not quite understand. His sentences are simple,
homely, and straight-forward. One of the stories begins thus:

Belle Carpenter had a dark skin, grey eyes and thin lips. She was tall
and strong. When black thoughts visited her she grew angry and wished
she were a man and could fight someone with her fists.

Like most mystics, Anderson is at heart a poet. He has published
two volumes in free verse, *Mid-American Chants* and *A New Testa-*

ment, but much of his prose is more poetic in concept and in expression than are these books. A good example of a prose-poem is *Brothers.*

Anderson: Symbolist and Psychologist.—Anderson has so often tried to express the inexpressible and he is so much concerned with the dark repellent aspects of our inner lives that he often writes in symbols. Sometimes the symbolism is clear enough, as, for example, when the egg stands for life or a wall represents a repression or frustration, but his symbolic language is not always so easily understood. Some of the sketches in *The Triumph of the Egg* contain a symbolism that is so original as to be arbitrary, and the occult passages in *Many Marriages* that are accounted alien to common sense owe their dark mystery to symbolism.

Anderson's psychology has aroused a considerable amount of discussion as to its scientific accuracy. The author has repeatedly declared that he is not a scientific psychoanalyst and that the psychology in his writings is the result of personal observations and questions rather than the product of reading books by psychological theorists. He has watched victims of repression beat in vain against the environment, he has observed the soul-sick and the perverse dying of their spiritual maladies, and he has been moved to pity by the timid and fearful who can effect not even a mystical escape. It is greatly to the credit of Anderson's perception that many of the characters in his fiction clearly parallel cases described by the scientific psychoanalysts. In all his observations he has evidently seen nothing in the psychological basis of life that makes him want to abandon the principle of determinism.

Because of Anderson's mysticism and his interest in psychology the village only half holds him, whereas Sinclair Lewis has returned again and again to do battle with the hosts of provincialism. Anderson's characters have in them more than a little of the universal. But he is not quite liberated from the village, nor will he ever be, for he cannot forget that his interesting though pitiable grotesques are made by the repressions of village environment. It is Willa Cather who has gone through the village and completely emerged.

Beyond the Village

WILLA CATHER

(1876-1947)

The novel, for a long while, has been overfurnished. The property man has been so busy on its pages, the importance of material objects and their presentation have been so stressed, that we take it for granted whoever can observe and can write the English language can write a novel. Often the latter qualification is considered unnecessary. . . .

Every one who is an artist knows that his "power of observation" and his "power of description" form but a low part of his equipment. He must have both, to be sure; but he knows that the most trivial of writers often have a very good observation. . . .

The popular superstition that "realism" asserts itself in the cataloging of a great number of material objects, in explaining mechanical processes, the methods of operating manufactures and trades, and in minutely and unsparingly describing physical sensations. But is not realism, more than it is anything else, an attitude of mind on the part of the writer toward his material, a vague definition of the sympathy and candor with which he accepts, rather than chooses, his theme? . . .

The automatic reply to the question is the name of Balzac. . . . In exactly so far as he succeeded in pouring out on his pages that mass of brick and mortar and furniture and proceedings in bankruptcy, in exactly so far he defeated his aim. The things by which he still lives, the types of greed and avarice and ambition and vanity and lost innocence of heart which he created—are as vital today as they were then. But their material surroundings upon which he expended such labor and pains —the eye glides over them. We have had too much of the interior decorator and the "romance of business" since his day. . . .

In this discussion another great name automatically occurs. Tolstoi was almost as great a lover of material things as Balzac. . . . But there is this determining difference; the clothes, the dishes, the moving, haunting interiors of those old Moscow houses, are always so much a part of the emotions of the people that they are perfectly synthesized; they seem to exist, not so much in the author's mind, as in the emotional penumbra of the characters themselves. When it is fused like this, literalness ceases to be literalness—it is a part of the experience.

If the novel is a form of the imaginative art, it cannot be at the same time a vivid and brilliant form of journalism. Out of the teeming, gleaming stream of the present it must select the eternal material of art. . . . The higher processes of art are all processes of simplification. The novelist must learn to write, and then he must unlearn it; just as the modern painter learns to draw, and then learns when utterly to disregard his accomplishment, when to subordinate it to a higher and truer effect. In this direction only, it seems to me, can the novel develop into anything more varied and perfect than all of the many novels that have gone before. . . .

Whatever is felt upon the page without being specifically named there— that, it seems to me, is created. It is the inexplicable presence of the thing not named, of the overtone divined by the ear but not heard by it, the verbal mood, the emotional aura of the fact or the thing or the deed, that gives high quality to the novel or the drama, as well as to poetry itself.

This short statement, by Miss Cather herself, on the art of fiction is the best criticism that has ever been written of the author. She has set a very high aim and the triumphant accomplishment of that aim in her own novels gives Miss Cather a high rank among American novelists both past and present.

Willa Cather, Novelist.—According to her own definition Miss Cather is a realist in that she accepts with candor and deep sympathy the material indigenous to her themes. But she is a realist of the school of Tolstoy or Hardy rather than a veritist who takes an oath to tell the whole truth, omitting nothing at all. She suppresses nothing germane to the subject, but in omitting the irrelevancies that might conceivably crowd into a book like *A Lost Lady* and in gently stressing those facts of artistic significance she manages to create an atmosphere of literal authenticity without recourse to the useless device of cataloging a thousand irrelevant verities. The early novels, *O Pioneers* and *My Antonia,* are written with admirable artistic restraint, but they are only preliminary studies in Miss Cather's characteristic style. Her triumphs of restraint are *A Lost Lady, The Professor's House,* and *Death Comes for the Archbishop.* Each of these books is as stark as a poem by Frost and just as rich in overtones of spiritual beauty and significance. Miss Cather's is a realism washed clean of all superficial and irrelevant aspects of reality. It is founded upon the inner core of being and not upon surface manifestations. And because she has not offered, as Frost says, a great deal of dirt with her potatoes, no one has yet been obtuse enough to doubt their reality.

The success of Miss Cather as a selective realist is all the more remarkable because of the middle-western or western background that she usually chooses. Such backgrounds are rich in distinguishing characteristics, and the amount of supporting material that she could crowd into one of her novels is appalling, but she never allows the richness of her material to beguile her into piling up descriptive detail for its own sake. In some of her stories the rich prairie land of Nebraska is one of the main characters, and she treats it as such, giving only as much detail as is necessary to create an impression of reality. The country is described only in those meaningful aspects that give it significance in the story and that make it a power in the lives of people. If Miss Cather were less restrained, if she were only a brilliant and accurate reporter of surface details, her novels might have been guide-books, histories, statistical abstracts, and sociological studies of Nebraska. But she is a restrained artist, not a literal reporter, she is intimately acquainted with her materials, and she has succeeded at the very difficult task of sharply localizing her novels and, at the same time, of raising them to universal significance.

In Miss Cather's books there is a complete welding of character and background. Some critics have spoken as if they did not consider the background of *A Lost Lady* an important and integral part of the story. It is true that Marian Forrester might have been the same woman in the time of Louis XIV or in the declining days of ancient Rome, but in a congenial background that offered no spiny points of contact, she would have had an utterly different career, and the whole significance of the story would have disappeared. Without the village she would never have been lost. Her very immeasurable distance above the sordid and stupid uniformity of village ways made her a lost lady, and she was doubly lost in her lamentable descent to the level of a clownish, village Don Juan. So completely are character and background fused in *A Lost Lady* that the reader is quite unaware of any line between the two. The book seems to be nothing more than a character study, but one of the chief characters is the spirit of the Nebraska village.

In addition to its restraint, Miss Cather's method is mainly objective, though in her earlier books she had difficulty in combining a deep sympathy and an objective presentation. In *O Pioneers* and especially in *The Song of the Lark* there is often a rather noticeable personal note. In her later books, however, Miss Cather has mastered another difficult task, and *A Lost Lady, The Professor's House*, and *Death Comes for the Archbishop* are as objective as fiction can become without being exclusively in the form of soliloquy or conversation. And yet these books are brimful of human sympathy.

Although her method is objective, Miss Cather has cast around much of her work the reflection of fond reminiscence, that favorite device of Mark Twain. At no time does fondness ever overcome her and force her into sentimentality, but it gives to certain of her books the same quality that it gave to Twain's, the air of familiarity born of intimate knowledge and pleasant associations.

From the standpoint of style and architectonic ability Miss Cather is distinguished among her fellow writers. Her books are well constructed, though she almost completely eschews plot. *My Antonia* owes its unity of impression less to its plot interest than to its larger design realized through detached incidents. However, Miss Cather does not allow a fanatical adherence to form to impede her work of setting forth a story in its spiritual setting. For instance, the narrative of Tom Outland in *The Professor's House* gives that book a "broken back." But it also gives the story of Professor St. Peter a retrospective interlude rich in significance and vocal with spiritual overtones. In style Miss Cather is equally fortunate. She has evidently found conventional grammar, diction, and punctuation not inimical to her work as a writer, for she has attempted no innovations with the avowed aim of making her writing more expressive. Part of her failure to attempt new modes of expression may perhaps be traced to her ability to handle so expertly the English of Fielding, Thackeray, and Hardy. She writes extremely well in that she can tell a story accurately, making fine distinctions of meaning, and at the same time keep her reader from becoming conscious of the writing. This test is the supreme one for narrative style, and Miss Cather passes it triumphantly.

Willa Cather and the Village.—Willa Cather has received a variety of estimates and academic classifications. To many she is distinctly the novelist of the Bohemian and Scandinavian immigrants in rural Nebraska. Such an estimate is misleading, for it utterly disregards all except three of the novels, and even in these three Miss Cather's interest was surely not in the immigrant as a sociological figure. Since *My Antonia* (1918) the author has not used an immigrant as a major figure, if we except the leading characters in *Death Comes for the Archbishop*, and there is none so witless as to think that this book is an "immigrant novel." Again Miss Cather is sometimes accused of dropping a deep interest in transplanted Europeans for a study of other materials, but such a criticism completely disregards the logical continuity of her development as a novelist and the essential unity of her interests. She has not changed in any respect so completely or so rapidly that she cannot be "placed" in our current literature. From *O Pioneers* to *Death Comes for the Archbishop* her work is all of a piece in method and material. Her technical powers have been vastly improved by intelligent practice, and her aims have probably become clearer—certainly they have been more clearly realized—but in no novel has she turned her back upon her early interests.

First and last Miss Cather is interested in the clash of character and environment. Those people who fit into their environment without a struggle do not seem to attract her greatly. From Alexandra Bergson to Archbishop Latour her leading figures are all those of men and women who had to battle with their immediate physical and spiritual surroundings, and in the struggles that inevitably arise in her novels she is apt to stress the value of primitive qualities in her human protagonists. She admires natural strength, directness, and honesty rather than more sophisticated virtues. One of the memorable things about *The Professor's House* is the contrast between Tom Outland, the strong intelligent primitive, who might have been Professor St. Peter's son-in-law, and the trig Lucius Marcellus, who actually was. It is quite possible that an original interest in simple, almost primitive people struggling with their environment made Miss Cather utilize the immigrant in some of her early work.

The environment that Miss Cather first studied and that she has never completely departed from is that of the village. She frequently uses rural settings, but always in the distance one can hear the village chorus passing judgment on people and incidents. The village is in the background of *O Pioneers,* though the book is primarily a rural novel. It takes a more important place in *My Antonia,* rising at times in this story to the position of immediate background. In *A Lost Lady* the village is a powerful element in the sparsely told little drama, and in *The Professor's House* the sons-in-law are both village types. Both are Philistines; one is flashy and successful, the other would like to be. It would require a major operation to separate this group of books from the village background. They are of it just as truly as *Main Street* was born of Gopher Prairie.

But Miss Cather has made few attacks on the village, and her failure to write a book length indictment in terms of Sinclair Lewis has kept many people from associating her with the village school. However, she has said quite enough in her books to let one know just what she thinks of the small town in its least laudable aspects. *The Sculptor's Funeral* is a philippic against the village, placed in the

mouth of the non-conforming lawyer. Mr. Lewis has never written
a more direct or more deadly attack. In no place in this story does
Miss Cather overlook a chance to contrast the great, free, creative
spirit of the sculptor with that of the spiritually pauperized, back-
biting villagers. Furthermore, in *My Antonia,* a book that usually
is spoken of as a romantic idealization of small town and rural life,
these significant words occur:

> They [the houses] were flimsy shelters, most of them poorly built of
> light wood, with spindle porch-posts horribly mutilated by the turning-
> lathe.
> Yet for all their frailness, how much jealousy and envy and unhappi-
> ness some of them managed to contain. The life that went on in them
> seemed to be made up of evasions and negations; shifts to save cooking,
> to save washing and cleaning, devices to propitiate the tongue of gossip.
> This guarded mode of existence was like living under a tyranny. Peo-
> ple's speech, their voices, their very glances, became furtive and repressed.

In *A Lost Lady* Mrs. Beasley, the telephone operator, stands for
the prying, gossiping townspeople, and in the same book Miss Cather
has given a most unflattering picture of village friendliness that is at
heart nothing more than the impertinent intrusion of a curious gang
of busybodies. Marian Forrester fails by descending to the level of
the village rake; Antonia succeeds because she forces reluctant life to
grant her decent terms through the strength of her primitive sense
and courage unbroken by village vulgarity.

But Miss Cather has not stopped with a statement of village faults.
She has refused to be confined geographically by the small town primarily because she declines to be limited by its spiritual range. She
has gone beyond the village at every point, not to idealize Black
Hawk and its thousand prototypes on the western prairies, but to
find in the small town and its tributary farming communities experiences and traits confineless by time or locality. She has given her
novels the appearance of events particularized by a specific background, but by keeping away from this background the easy accre-
tion of details, and by her insistence upon reaching the general
through the specific, she has gone beyond the limitations of locale
to achieve something of the universal. With the eventual disappearance of Gopher Prairie, *Main Street* will have the value and
interest of a sociological study of a society that is past. That is to
say, the book will still be interesting and important, but the fictional
element will not make it so. *My Antonia* can no more be made a

social document by changing custom or manner of life than *Moby Dick* could have been outmoded by the increasing use of petroleum. Upon that probably not far-distant day when the whole human race will be city dwellers, the tragedy of Marian Forrester will be as poignant as it was when the village ruled supreme over middle America. A minor novelist or an enthusiastic reporter would have stopped in the village, but Willa Cather is no minor novelist, and her reportorial ability has been made to serve the purposes of an artist.

Miss Cather's high rank as a novelist is not the result of any accident of public taste or interest. Her development into a fine artist has been by an orderly and logical progression from the promising *Alexander's Bridge* (1912) and *O Pioneers* (1913) to the superlative achievement of *Death Comes for the Archbishop* (1928). She has written book after book with a steadily growing sureness of technique and with an increasingly firm subordination of detail to the design and aim of the story. She is too fully aware of the difficulties that she has overcome in reaching her highest achievements ever to succumb to facile methods or muddied intent. But Miss Cather is more than a novelist of clear aims and sure execution. Her books glow with a placid beauty that is a gift graciously bestowed upon a very few writers, a gift that is never gained through mere application, however rigorous, of the rules of fiction. It is a gift peculiar to soul and heart rather than to mind and hand. The unhurried loveliness of such books as *My Antonia, A Lost Lady,* and *Death Comes for the Archbishop* reminds one of an Indian summer day upon Miss Cather's well-loved western plains when the crisp, cool atmosphere is made luminous by a mellow light that fades in sunset beauties. And in the novels that light is the heart and soul of Willa Cather.

SUGGESTED READINGS

Beach: *Outlook for American Prose*. Chicago. 1926. Anderson, pp. 247-280.
    Anderson receives excellent treatment.
Crowley: *After the Genteel Tradition*. New York. 1937.
    Essays on the leading novelists.
De Voto: *The Literary Fallacy*. Boston. 1944.
    An attack on some of the prominent writers of the 1920's. Sinclair Lewis did not care for this work. The argument between him and Mr. De Voto in the *Saturday Review of Literature* was most amusing.

Hansen: *Midwest Portraits*. New York. 1923.

> A close-up of Sherwood Anderson. Good.

Hartwick: *The Foreground of American Fiction*. New York. 1934.

Hatcher: *Creating the Modern American Novel*. New York. 1935.

Kazin: *On Native Grounds*. New York. 1942.

> Confused and somewhat confusing. One of the best in a field of second-rate books.

Michaud: *The American Novel Today*. New York. 1928.

> Old but sound.

Quinn: *American Fiction*. New York. 1936.

> Many of the judgments are open to question. The chapter on Willa Cather is good.

Whipple: *Spokesmen*. New York. 1928.

> Chapters on Lewis, Anderson, and Cather.

CHAPTER XXVI

THE NEW ROMANCE

Yet more clearly do I perceive that this same man is a maimed god.
. . . He is under penalty condemned to compute eternity with false
weights and to estimate infinity with a yardstick; and he very often does
it. . . .

—There lies the choice which every man must make—or rationally to
accept his own limitations, or stupendously to play the fool and swear that
he is at will omnipotent. . . .

To the problem of living, romance propounds the only possible answer,
which is, not understanding, but escape.

—JAMES BRANCH CABELL in *Beyond Life.*

The Argument of the New Romantics.—Beyond doubt the heaviest
blow ever leveled at human fancy is the rise of science. So long as
the reputed science of earlier centuries was a compound of hope, half-
knowledge, and intuition, it had no very good reason to look upon
its kinsman imagination with toplofty disdain, but when it began to
dominate confidently one field after another of human interests, and
especially when it declared itself the sole custodian of facts beyond
which there is no appeal, then it began to shoulder romance out of
men's lives. And romance is the food upon which imagination lives.
Since that far-distant afternoon when the storm-whipped waters of
an Italian bay closed over the frail abode of an ethereal spirit, the
voices of the scientist and the realistic social critic have been far too
potent in our English-speaking world. Acclaimed by its swarming
devotees as infallible, and with impregnable proof of its infallibility
presented objectively in every laboratory, science has ascended to the
high throne once held by theology. And just as seventeenth century
divines, accounting themselves the authorized spokesmen of the deity,
delivered the unquestionable word of God to their acquiescent followers, so to-day do scientists, hallowed by the possession of Truth,
reveal the facts of the universe by which men must govern their
lives. Secure in their knowledge, scientists have steadily substituted
fact for dream until to-day romantic imagination is a frailty not

willingly possessed by people dedicated to common sense and mindful of their neighbor's respect.

Questionless the assurance that fact has superseded dream would be an illimitable comfort to men, if only the manifest fact had been the concretion of the dream. But this is exactly what the fact has not been. Man wishes to be assured again and again that he is a gallant, theomorphic being of surpassing cleverness and wit, only a very little lower than the angelic choristers whose ranks he will eventually swell. For more generations than are recorded by pictured rock and sun-dried brick man has loved to think of himself as the cynosure of an anthropocentric universe, on terms of intimacy with the most exalted heavenly powers and bank presidents, and attended respectfully by the lower orders of both the celestial and the terrestrial hierarchies. Man's lush imagination has allowed the sufferer to wrest a crumb of comfort even from his tribulations. Just as some convicted criminals enjoy a pleasurable flush of eminence, so we are told, when they rise to receive the death penalty from the august judge, so does man thrill to the thought that his vagrant ways are the objects of special legislation, even though the statute enacted be a bit captious and the penalty a trifle severe. In short, the balm provided by the conceited imagination of man surpasses all spiritual ointments ever prepared for the healing of the abrasions made by reality.

But science with an imperious word disposes of these fancies. Man is informed that his presence upon earth is due to a chance concatenation of impromptu circumstances and that his duration here is dependent upon the impersonal forces of bio-chemistry, societal relationships, and mere chance. And to complete his abject discomfiture he is told that the very globe he inhabits might explode like a bubble and the problematical astronomer on Betelguese would be unaware for many light years that a tenth-rate star had ceased to be. Such are the chastening assurances of scientific fact.

All this in itself would be depressing enough, but there are worse things yet to relate. Science, with true Roman hardness of head, refuses to admit that there are certain things not to be rendered unto Cæsar. When beset by unknown and disheartening forces, man has traditionally resorted to his poets and story-tellers, quite as often as he has gone to the flagon or the rôle of Romeo or his thaumaturgists, to bring surcease of sorrow. Now in these excessively rational days poets and story-tellers have succumbed, along with the rest of us, to the irrefutable argument of fact. Naturalism takes the materials of science, appends thereunto a most despondent interpretation, and writes novels that show man as an automaton in the grip of powers which are not to be moved by orisons, fatted sacrifices, imprecations, or the indifference of despair. Scientific determinism has riveted upon us a collar compared with which the yoke of Calvinistic predestination was light, for the chance that science grudgingly admits into an ordered universe is hardly so comforting in its unintelligence as were the special providences designed to cheer Cotton Mather. Dreiser glooms over the physio-chemical process called man, E. A. Robinson caresses black thoughts too depressing to handle even in refutation, Masters makes the melancholic discovery that the small town has not repealed the physical basis of life, Henry Adams avers that the omnipotent force behind human destiny has no discoverable attribute except strength, and Sherwood Anderson fumbles awkwardly in the mind without finding a scintilla of evidence that free will is more than a pleasantly romantic fallacy. It is all very gloomy.

On the other hand certain potential romantics, somewhat ashamed of their romanticism, passionately aver that earthly life may blossom into the gaudiness of an unregenerate dream, and then these same nascent romantics seize ax, scalpel, crowbar, or the word of truth to lay bare the sorry plight of man which must be fully realized before the world can be made safe for dreams. Obviously a dying man must be comforted by the sight of an autopsy before he can safely be allowed to dream of bliss supernal. Robert Herrick is deeply vexed that city culture wreaks its will upon well-intentioned architects and physicians. Upton Sinclair views with a jaundiced eye the wicked power of capitalism. Sinclair Lewis waxes indignant when he finds that social institutions vaguely discontent Carol Kennicott, George Babbitt, and Elmer Gantry, who unimpeded might develop into estimable personages, as contented as the kine of the sylvan pastures— and just about as interesting. Clearly no dream and no dreamer can endure the vivisections performed by our enthusiastic social critics.

Conceivably there are regions, mythological or geographical, toward which mankind might travel passably happy in the journey even though the goal be forever elusive. The atrabilious Poe found a measure of comfort in the misty, mid-region of Weir. Melville, the black, was tantalized and enchanted by turns with the glimpses that he caught of the island valley of Typee. But these two have had few emulators in the task of discovering chartless domains. Generally the American author is bound to the soil more firmly than ever was a medieval serf. The three-mile limit—recently pronounced too narrow for the legal activities of a puissant nation—is more than sufficiently expansive for our imaginative activities. In fact few of our story-tellers ever stray more than three miles from the place of their nativity. Mrs. Wharton, protesting cogently against our cramping provincialism, removes to France, taking with her the frigid atmosphere of Fifth Avenue during the last glacial epoch, an age that closed with the incursion of the western Goths. By doing so Mrs. Wharton imagines that she has widened her scope. Dreiser always stays within commuting distance of a large city. Anderson never wholly escapes the village, while Lewis finds too many things wrong with Gopher Prairie and Zenith entirely to forsake those places. Only Willa Cather has escaped, and even she more than occasionally casts a backward glance at the doomed village. And when our writers escape regionalism, a feat almost never achieved, rationalism lays a curbing hand upon their fancy. Rather than provide Bohemia with a sea-coast for the convenience of the hard-pressed traveler, our novelists, if they wished to lay a story in that land, would study the *Statesman's Year Book*, *Baedeker*, an encyclopedia, and an atlas of recent date. Then after systematically exploring the country with a personally conducted party of tourists, they would produce a highly documented novel as stimulating to the imagination as the statistical tables of the Bohemian census bureau.

In fine, the combination of science, naturalism, social criticism, and narrow locale has brought our literature to an abjectly low level of imagination. Its Cinderella fancy has deteriorated to a kitchen slattern sitting in an ash-heap and stolidly looking at her dirty hands. Inventiveness is dead. The indispensable dream by which the spirit of man lives is forbidden, and literature has come to be stenographic accounts of long-drawn criminal trials or the secret life histories of itinerant evangelists, written by competent reporters who are equipped with X-ray eyes and dictaphones. Our love stories are concerned with the amours of motormen and clownish bumpkins, our romance of the golden quest takes us through a noisome alley to the village abattoir. It adds but little to the imaginative quality of such a journey to be told in passing that the village garage would be greatly improved in appearance if it were judiciously shielded by sun-flowers. Imaginative literature simply does not exist.

Such were the views of a group who set about the creation of a literature that would "prevaricate tenderly about life." These writers had no intention of challenging any of the findings of science. Such a course would have been suicidal in a world consecrated to the test-tube and the microscope. The new romantics simply disregarded science on the very plausible theory that the more unassailable an unpleasant truth is, the more need of shrugging one's shoulders and politely ignoring it. No writers have ever been more aware of their aims than were the new romantics of the 1920's. To revive and foster the pleasant fiction that man is of supreme importance and that his coming and going are matters of surpassing moment to others than his dependents, to liberate imagination from the rock to which it is so tightly chained, to rescue fancy from the ethic-ridden social critics, to raise a protest against the arrogant domination of realism, in short, to rehabilitate romance was the delightful task of a small group of writers, the first of whom in time and in eminence is James Branch Cabell.

JAMES BRANCH CABELL

(1879-   )

The misfortunes of Cabell at the hands of his critics would be a comic interlude in current literature had they befallen any one other than an artist of the first rank, but there is a genuine danger that the chronic misconception of such a writer will result in giving him a place in American letters that he does not deserve. When Cabell first began to write, laborious critics, busy interpreting serious writers like Churchill, Tarkington, and Irving Bacheller, praised him for his pretty style and dismissed him kindly to the company of those belletrists whose soothing romances were illustrated by Howard Pyle and Harrison Fisher. All this happened in the days when Cabell was a valued contributor to popular magazines.

The arch intelligence and gentle irony of *The Rivet in Grand-father's Neck* made some of the critics wince, and *The Cream of the Jest* caused Cabell's summary expulsion from the ranks of the safely juvenile writers. He was, the arbiters decreed, a grossly irreverent fellow whose low flippancies only proved that he was an awkward imitator of such decorous euphemists as Voltaire and Anatole France. In a word, he was dismissed as a shallow clown of most questionable taste. This attitude persisted until *Jurgen* ceased to be a show piece on the parlor tables of the audacious. Of late we have heard little of Cabell's shallowness and flippancy, but certain ominous hints are abroad that the urbane Virginian is guilty of logical inconsistencies unbecoming a serious thinker. For instance, some have feelingly pointed out that he begins by denying reality and then writes novels that make no attempt to deny such realities as are needed in the process of telling the tales. Thus, it is alleged, he is guilty of muddling his theory and his practice. Logically speaking, he becomes cross-eyed. Such criticism itself is not unacquainted with strabismus. Cabell is an artist, not a philosopher, and if he wishes to reject certain aspects of reality and accept others, we should grant him the freedom of the artist rather than attempt to confine his fancy to logical processes. Let stupid people dispute over his ontology and epistemology, they will find kindred souls in the still stupider ones who find anachronisms in his archæology and somewhat mystifying literary allusions in his more erudite passages. It was unfortunate that critics could see in the early Cabell only a maker of pretty phrases and in the author of *The Cream of the Jest* only a sciolistic jester, but it is doubly unfortunate that any attempt to find in his novels and criticisms any effort toward a consistent metaphysical system.

Cabell's Attitude Toward Life and Literature.—In one respect Cabell is the most consistent of men, for his attitude toward life and literature has never altered. He firmly believes that life is a sorry business, made endurable only by romance, and he holds steadfastly that literature should serve the ends of romance and life by providing the very things that man most desires and least possesses.

Cabell is in perfect agreement with the naturalists who aver that the world is not extraordinarily pleasant. He says explicitly that life is a long gray corridor with a door at the end, but he differs sharply from the naturalists in that he does not use so dismal a thesis as the spine of meaning in any of his books. He grants the thesis without argument long before the beginning of the novel. Down this corridor we pass, says Cabell, millions of us, all so much alike that to distinguish any particularizing features in any one is wellnigh impossible, and yet each of us yearns to be an individual instead of one of a species. Each desires beauty in multifarious forms.

Each longs to feel that importance attaches to every action, and each has a mind to demonstrate his importance by superior wit, cleverness, or physical prowess. And since life stubbornly continues to deny the very boons so ardently desired, it is only by romantic dreaming that man can realize his wishes. "Beauty, and indeed all the fine things which you desiderate in literature—and in your personal experience, I suspect—are nowhere attainable save in imagination," and it is the function of the dream to make man oblivious to the curbing weaknesses of the flesh.

Cabell holds that man's most exalted moments, whether the exaltation come from love, religion, a fine sense of chivalry, or a conviction of surpassing cleverness, are made possible by a romanticization of the drab particles of life into a glittering unity, compact of intelligence, beauty, and desire attained. Without doubt religion magnifies the importance of the individual in the world-scheme, but by doing so it allows man to flatter himself by imagining that his welfare and his desires are the goal toward which all creation labors. Religion simply offers a romantic interpretation of the universe that man is sensible enough to accept. And thus the story goes. All the much-praised finer things of life are sadly lacking in objective proof, but if man is to raise himself above the level of the dust, it must be through the creation of a dream-world filled with these fine, illogical things and the raising of himself to that world through the force of his imagination. It is probably safe to say that in this work romance has its greatest difficulty, not in the creation of beauty out of nothing, but in the credible attribution of cosmic significance to material facts utterly without such significance.

Assuredly romance does not blossom in the minds of the literal-minded. Man creates it out of his romantic exaltations, and then his dislike of seeing it become as transient as the life that it glorifies and his desire to prolong the moment of exaltation lead him to give it permanent form. Thus literature comes into being, not as a polemic to deny that life "is a business of exceeding dullness and of very little worth," but as a beautifully devised story told for the sole purpose of allowing the reader to escape temporarily the annoying inconveniences of reality. Obviously such literature cannot be realistic, for realism seeks to explain the world in a rational manner and to reconcile man to his sorry lot. However, it succeeds in losing itself in so great a maze of facts that it differs from life in no particular. Such literature is worthless, for it simply repeats the sordid facts of which we are already far too cognizant, and "gracefully to prevaricate about life is art's signal function."

To be sure, Cabell does not want the prevarication of romance to go to the extent of denying reality, though some may think that such is his desire. It seems that he would limit his denial of reality to the urbane disregard of inconvenient fact. In *Jurgen* if it became necessary for the hero to take on the incorporeal form of his ghostly grandfather, dead some half-century, the feat was accomplished as easily as that of taking a breath. Yet in Jurgen's loves and hates, in his conversation with mythological personages, and in his naïve admiration of himself as a very clever fellow there is a most convincing reality. And at the very end of the book, Jurgen, the erstwhile incorrigible, who had just romanced through the most charming of journeys upon which he enjoyed all manner of agreeable experiences, climbed down from his eminence as duke, prince, king, emperor, pope, and returned to his respectably obscure business of pawnbroker. And he who had known the love of Guinevere, betrothed to King Arthur, and of Anaïtis, the moon-myth, and of Chloris, the hamadryad, and of Dorothy la Desirée, returned not unwillingly to the dull but efficient housewife whom the prudent pawnbroker had espoused. And as Jurgen came home on the day of his return he looked through the window and saw the portly Lisa busily preparing the supper. "Then terror smote Jurgen, who had faced sorcerers and gods and devils intrepidly," for he had forgotten the butter. But habit prevailed over fear, and the wanderer prepared to face the belligerent Lisa not like a romantic gallant but very much like a hen-pecked pawnbroker, and yet he hung back a little, as a man does, facing a disagreeable experience, who fingers a bit wistfully the shards of a shattered dream. "Then Jurgen sighed and entered his snug home." Surely an allegorical conclusion, whatever the body of the story may mean. After romancing about in contempt of science and its sacred facts, man must return to stolid realities, but the romancing alone makes the fact endurable, and furthermore it places man in that permanently agreeable frame of mind which holds logically enough that anything delightful is rather more than apt to happen to him who keeps undiminished his capacity for dreams.

Thus the Cabellian romance becomes the demiurge, the creator of a new world in which things are fashioned slightly more to human desires than they are under the present inadequate provisions. "Ajax might not have had the strength of ten and Ulysses might not have become invisible at will—but it would be very gratifying if men could do these things." And it is the function of the demiurge to call into being a new cosmos where such phenomena as the strength of Ajax and the limpid transparency of Ulysses are not more remarkable than are rheumatism and respectability among us children of rationalism.

But, some may object, inasmuch as romance tricks man by lulling him into only a transient escape from reality, it does him ultimate harm. Such an objection, if sustained, would give adequate precedent for taking exception to love, chloroform, horse races, circus parades, political campaigns, and all the other anesthetics that give man relief from the pangs of actuality. The sole harm done by romance is to logic, and not to life or to man. Surely only the hypercritic would cavil at a harmless anodyne which makes one pleasantly oblivious to situations that might else be inconveniently answerable to rationalism.

Far from being a harm, it can be demonstrated that romance is a positive good to mankind. Man alone of the animals plays the ape to his dreams, declares Cabell. Evanescent is the vision, but its recollection endures forever. When man plunges as hopefully as he may into the muck of reality, he bears with him constantly the thought of his dream, and it is far from inconceivable that the enduring thought ultimately impels him to seek a life that approximates the fugitive vision. A step farther and romance would become a utilitarian good, but Cabell hastens to explain that art is not a branch of pedagogy and that romance seeks to inculcate no moral truth. Such a denial of ethical interests is very rare among American novelists, for our Puritanism crops out, if nowhere else, in our attitude toward art. With us it is usually not enough that beauty be beautiful. It must teach some lesson, preferably a moral one, and our most atrocious novels are piously glossed over by many critics on the grounds that the authors were animated by laudably ethical intentions. Cabell can see no relationship between ethics and romance. Ethics teaches the art of living in the world on terms dictated by others; romance creates a world of unreality where each can live on his own terms.

Lesser Works of Cabell.—James Branch Cabell bears two names that are familiar to all students of Virginia history, for both the Branches and the Cabells are old and distinguished families on the south bank of the Potomac. Members of both houses have been governors, judges, generals, members of Congress, and prominent men of affairs. Nor have the activities of the Branches and Cabells been confined to Virginia. Their kinsmen have been active throughout the entire South from Maryland to Texas, while some of the scions have carried their family names to distinction in western states. Like a good Virginian of the old stock, Cabell took his degree at William and Mary College in 1898. Before his graduation he taught classes in French and Greek. After two or three years in newspaper work, he has since devoted himself steadily to literature.

For so careful a writer Cabell has produced a large number of books. A list of his writings contains the names of two books of verse, a play, twelve novels, some of which have been revised, five books of short stories, seven volumes of essays, and three works on genealogy. Limitations of space waived, a discussion of Cabell's works is very difficult, for the books are almost impossible to summarize, and seldom do two people agree upon the meaning of any of the works.

Of Cabell's lesser books probably the best are *The Cords of Vanity, Domnei, The Rivet in Grandfather's Neck,* and *The Certain Hour.*

The Cords of Vanity, published first in 1909 and revised in 1920, is a story of picaresque gallantry which gayly relates the continuous love affairs of Robert Townsend from early youth to maturity. Of all of Cabell's works it comes closest to having a "moral," for without doing violence to the facts one can easily detect in the story of Townsend a warning that youthful philandering, if carried far beyond adolescence, is apt to leave one in the thirties hopelessly incapable of true love. The book in its revised form is wonderfully well written. Indeed it is doubtful if any of Cabell's other works surpasses it in beauty of style.

Domnei, published in 1913 as *The Soul of Melicent* and revised under its present title in 1920, is described as a comedy of woman-worship. This book, too, ought to be a bit disturbing to those melancholiacs who see in Cabell only a cynical jester, for it is a story of youthful love sustained and rewarded by unswerving constancy.

The Rivet in Grandfather's Neck (1915) is another gay book, shot with delicious satire upon traditional Virginia chivalry. Specifically it is the story of how a middle-aged grandee, excessively favored in blood and family tradition, but not so blessed with energy and practical sense, married a frivolous, wealthy girl and attempted to hold her shallow affection by vaporing endlessly about his chivalric ideals. This book rather exasperates many people.

The Certain Hour (1916) is a collection of jewel-like stories, each of which relates the experience of a poet at a great moment in his artistic life. These pieces deserve a far wider audience than they seem to have had.

The Major Works.—Cabell has completely divorced himself, in his major works, from the familiar and the contemporary. The complaint that our novelists feel ill at ease when out of sight of their native towns and villages can never be cast at him, for he has created out of his fancy the new kingdom of Poictesme, completely equipped as to cities, provinces, and minor feudal divisions. Externally he has girt it on every side by so well defined geographical neighbors that some place Poictesme in southern France, but such cartographers have overlooked a more likely location in Cabell's fancy. Nor was the creation of the imaginary realm complete when it received geographical definition, for Cabell has endowed it with a full complement of necessary and unnecessary gods, a mythology, a legendary history, and a ruling dynasty which boasted rogues, ruffians, and mighty warriors as numerous and as arrogant as authentic history can cite. But the most famous products of the land of Poictesme are the Dom Manuel cycle and the high legend of Jurgen, tales that Cabell has told in fifteen or sixteen volumes of exquisitely embroidered romance called *The Biography.* And very agreeably the modern descendants of Manuel occasionally resort to this pleasant land of Poictesme when they tire of Litchfield, Virginia.

It is true that some of Cabell's romances are laid in his native state, but the stage management of a highly imaginative work in Virginia might conceivably be somewhat difficult, and besides a few might take as a personal affront every impersonal, recondite allusion. So Cabell invented Poictesme, whose inhabitants seem not to be the least bit squeamish about their social, historical, and mythological legends.

Cabell is probably best understood by reading the following books in the given order: *Beyond Life, Figures of Earth, Jurgen, The High Place, The Cream of the Jest,* and *Straws and Prayer Books.*

Beyond Life (1919) serves as the prologue to the other works. It contains Cabell's philosophy of life and literature interspersed with much gay and penetrating criticism of specific writers. Among the many writers who are discussed are Marlowe, Wycherley, Congreve, Sheridan, Dickens, and a large number of contemporaries. In this book Cabell brilliantly sets forth and defends his theory of literature, and he succeeds in giving it sound historical sanction. *Beyond Life* is a beautiful book, as remarkable for its mental dexterity and acuteness as for its verbal beauty, though as a piece of mere writing it is beyond the reach of any other American stylist.

Figures of Earth (1921), the first part of the Poictesme saga, outwardly relates the story of Dom Manuel, but within it is an ironical allegory of the artist who strives to create beauty out of unpliable stuff. Of course, the dreamer comes at the end to a realization of futility and frustration, but though he fails, his dream has caused him to think of himself in terms of importance. And this reward is something not lightly to be despised.

Jurgen (1919) has already been sufficiently discussed. It is generally conceded to be Cabell's masterpiece, and it seems more clearly than any other novel written in America since *Huckleberry Finn* to bear the promise of relative immortality. Three-fourths of the book is a gorgeous piece of romanticizing far away from the American scene, but toward the end Cabell lashes out with satirical strokes at certain American phenomena that flourished exceedingly during the World War. However, the few topical chapters are magnificently redeemed by the end of the book. In their universal truth and wistful beauty those last pages of *Jurgen* are as immortal as Beethoven's Fifth.

The High Place (1923), very correctly called a comedy of disenchantment, is the story of Florian de Puysange, a member of the great house of Manuel, who undertakes the quest of Melior, a maiden extolled as the perfection of womanhood. Yet when Florian gains his quest, he is speedily disenchanted, for Melior turns out to be intolerably garrulous, and, of course, the young man soon departs on another quest. It would be a very unperceiving person who does not see in this episode the fate of romantic idealists. Next to *Jurgen*, *The High Place* is the best expression of Cabellian irony and philosophical ideas. Indeed the book has so prominent an intellectual cast that it may truly be called the best sustained philosophical novel ever written by an American, though it is true that its rivals are not very numerous. *The High Place*, like *Jurgen*, is crammed with episodic action and minor characters. Many have remarked on the likeness of one of these personages, St. Hoprig, to the cynical intellectuals that Anatole France sometimes uses for his holy men. In passing, it might be said that Cabell seems to owe much to *Penguin Island* and *The Revolt of the Angels*. The close of *The High Place* comes down from the level of the story with a precipitous drop. Like *Jurgen*, it closes on an acknowledgment that futility awaits the romantic dreamer, but this acknowledgment is effected by a prosy device, totally lacking in the poignant truth of Jurgen's homecoming. But for this slip, *The High Place* is written with admirable imaginative and intellectual mastery. To those who like irony and intelligent conversation this novel is one of the most interesting in the Cabellian canon. Others may find it a bit elusive.

The Cream of the Jest (1917) is surely the patent allegory of Cabell himself. The hero, Felix Kennaston, is a modern novelist who is writing an allegorical saga. One day he found in his garden a little metal disk that became his charm, the Sigil of Scoteia, to open dreamland. In this dreamland we see the mind of Kennaston transforming splotchy actualities into romantic beauties. The novel is simply the ideas of *Beyond Life* told in narrative form. "It is only by preserving faith in human dreams that we may, after all, make them come true"—this is the explicit thesis of the book. The jest of the book lies in the belated discovery that the Sigil is only the metallic top of a jar once filled with cold cream. Such are the charms possessed by romantic idealists.

Cabell's Place in Current Literature.—Certain it is that any estimate of Cabell's place in current American letters must be made on a consideration of the author as a literary figure and not as a metaphysician, intent on harmonizing everything in a consistent system of philosophy. But it is equally certain that he is a true philosophical novelist in the sense that Swift, Voltaire, Anatole France, and Samuel Butler are philosophical. Such a term means only that the writer to whom it is applied is interested in ideas rather than in plot, technique, or incident. According to such a definition Cabell is undoubtedly philosophical, "the only philosophical novelist in the United States," he has been aptly called. And of all his intellectual concerns none is more prominent or important than his carefully elaborated theory of romance, though all his characters "toy amorously with ideas."

It is the possession of this theory of romance that differentiates Cabell from the other romantic novelists and poets. He is always fully aware of what he is doing. He knows always that his allegorical epic of desire, laid in Poictesme, is as much a figment of the imagination as are the land itself and the legendary figures of Manuel and Jurgen. He is always the conscious showman exhibiting for a brief moment the pleasant but fictitious pageantry of man's cleverness and overweening importance. But he never makes the mistake of believing the fiction. It is just here that he differs from the other romantics, like Tarkington and White, who seem never to be able to distinguish between the dream and the reality. Such a confusion would be deeply repugnant to the intellectual Cabell who has acquainted us with his contemptuous appraisal of those who confuse fiction and fact.

It goes without saying that Cabell is not widely popular. Frankly, he is simply too good for most readers. He is too intelligent, too disillusioned, too ironical, and his style is far too elaborate and urbane to appeal widely to a people who admire directness and simplicity even when these qualities are achieved by ludicrously infantile methods. One can readily conceive of a society to which he might appeal, but it would be an old-world group, disillusioned to the point of cynicism and deeply interested in ideas as such. But America is too new and its readers are too naïve to appreciate his irony and intelligence. Furthermore Cabell's style is not one to attract readers whose tastes are formed on newspapers. His aversion to the obvious and the banal lead him into indirect, allusive modes of expression. Artificial his style has been called, but it seems to be fitted exactly to the pattern of a complex, highly sophisticated manner of thinking. The vocabulary is scrupulously accurate, but Cabell delights in unfamiliar words that give his prose almost an archaic flavor. Such literary traits do not endear an author to a people whose habitual haste keeps them from deliberateness either in thought or in action and whose quick impatience with words of more than one syllable is a matter of common knowledge.

It is Cabell's irony, urbanity, and air of complete disillusion that set him off from America and off from other American novelists. Indeed in his favoring Poictesme over the banks of the James or the Mississippi and in his preferring Manuel to the jovial Babbitt he states clearly enough his relations to the American scene. A critic of it he cannot be called, for he cares too little about it even to indicate what is wrong, and as for making it over, he positively declines to be interviewed on the subject. But the showman who exhibits the pageant of Manuel takes good care that the glittering plains of Poictesme are quite lacking in many of the qualities so obviously possessed by Gopher Prairie and Zenith.

One can make a plausible case for the contention that Cabell is the finest literary artist among all our contemporary prose writers. None is so little concerned with the topical and the local, not one is so intellectual, and not one is so thoroughly in the current of literary tradition. With the passing of certain phases of American life that may well be transient, many of our most admired novels may lose their pertinency, but it is very difficult to think of a social or political cataclysm that will render obsolete Cabell's comedies of life. Furthermore, Cabell is well equipped with those qualities that the better novelists have traditionally enjoyed, such as inventiveness, the ability to create convincing character, and a flair for illuminating incident. In addition he has his distinctive prose style, carefully wrought into delicate cadences, and attractively flavored with archaic words and constructions. The style may be artificial, as is so often alleged, but it is a wonderfully effective instrument for recording the varying fortunes of the Manuel dynasty, however ill adapted it may be to the use of the monosyllabic reporter. It is probable that the hostile critic can make his most telling attack on Cabell by pointing out the fondness of the novelist for using personified ideas as characters. Such a charge cannot be easily repelled in the case of the minor characters, but Cabell has redeemed himself in creating such life-like major figures as Jurgen and Lisa, Manuel, John Charteris, and many another. Furthermore, those who like the Cabellian romance, with its mixture of fancy and intellectual concerns, will not find it hard to forgive the creator of those abstract qualities and those epitomes of human types that do service as lesser characters in so many of the romances. And not the least agreeable thing about these figures is their inveterate tendency to pause a bit while discoursing pleasantly on various interesting questions of more than immediate import. The pauses are deeply distasteful to the admirers of those romantics who rush their characters breathlessly from one thrilling incident to another. Thus those who like Cabell have no difficulty in finding reasons to justify their admiration for the Poictesme cycle, and one is probably safe in saying that those who do not like him will be hard put to it to find convincing reasons for not including him among the two or three really fine writers now practicing their craft.

And as the ebbing ocean on the beach
Leaves but a bit of evanescent foam,
So beauty passes ever out of reach,
Save to the heart where happiness is home.
There beauty walks, wherever it may be,
And paints the sunset on the quiet sea.

Of all the new romantics Robert Nathan has laid out for himself
the smallest field and has tended it with the greatest care. In the
smallness of his scope and the exquisite finish of his workmanship
Nathan courts comparison with the English poet, A. E. Housman.
Neither strives for cosmic significance in poem or novel, yet each
may have more nearly attained it than have the aspiring artists,
born for miniature work, who insist upon attempting huge themes.

Nathan is a gentle man, a quiet skeptic, who is disturbed at the
growing dogmatism of a world governed by fact and practical considerations. But not even in his objections is he bound to certainty,
for a positive assurance in the rightness of one's views, he finds,
makes one impervious to such virtues as graciousness, benevolence,
sweetness, and moderation. Unlike Cabell, who holds that a forget-
ting of the unpleasant lies in the quest for high adventure, Nathan
finds peace in renunciation and gentleness.

Not one has learned to be happy in poverty or gentle in good fortune. . . . The rich quarrel with the poor, and the poor by way of answer
with rich and poor alike. . . . For happiness is not in owning much, but
in owning little: love and liberty, the work of one's hands, fellowship
and peace.

With such a prevailing cast of thought—it hardly can be called
a philosophy—Nathan writes fantasies, poems, and short novels that
are distinguished by a mellowness of tone and a deep love for quiet
beauty. And most of his work has a faint flavor of cool irony that
gains its cutting piquancy from the unobtrusive contrast of the
actual and the romantic ideal. The novels and fantasies are not
melancholy, such a term is too strong, rather they are wistful commentaries on the failure of men to achieve a peace of heart. To
Nathan that failure constitutes a major tragedy. In the novels
Nathan's personal representative seems always to be a gentle char-

acter who quietly preaches the gospel of contentment. In *Autumn* this character is Mr. Jeminy, the village schoolmaster, in *Jonah* it is Naaman, in *The Puppet Master* it is the master himself, and in *The Fiddler in Barly* it is the fiddler. Much of the charm of these books is created by the gentle shrinking romanticism of these men who eschew alike the High Quest and sordid materialism.

Autumn (1921) is an idyll of village life with the idyllic note supplied by the old schoolmaster rather than by the villagers. Indeed most of the townsfolk are stupid, unimaginative, grasping people who are quite like their fellows in Gopher Prairie. The dull aspirations of the villagers throw into ironic relief the foiled hopes of the gentle schoolmaster. *Autumn* is well named, for the whole book glows with the mellow light and indefinable wistfulness of an October day. *The Puppet Master* (1923) is a pure fantasy in which dolls and their benevolent master are the principal characters. It is a wholly delightful work. *Jonah* (1925) is a free adaptation of the Biblical narrative with sustained overtones of irony. This book in particular has been stupidly misunderstood and misjudged. *The Fiddler in Barly* (1926) uses the scene of *Autumn* as the background for a charming fantasy. *The Bishop's Wife* is a keen little study that seems at times to have its inception in personal satire. Out of the story of the complications of a strange triangle—a bishop, his wife, and an angel—comes the somewhat heartening thought that even an unsatisfactory man is more desirable than an angel. In *There Is Another Heaven* Nathan's delicate but mordant satire reaches its highest pitch in the story of a converted Jew's visit to a distressingly Protestant heaven. It is, however, not heaven that Nathan is satirizing, but a nearer, more familiar land. Evidently a delicate touch and a graceful, pungent wit are not the literary qualities most esteemed by our readers, for this satirical novel has a sophistication and a penetrating intelligence that make it one of the really distinguished works of the last few years, yet it does not seem to have been widely popular.

It is easy to object to a serious consideration of Nathan on the grounds that his lyre is an instrument of only one string. Truly he cannot achieve—at all events he has not sought to achieve—the contrapuntal complexity of *Lord Jim* or the terrific intensity of *Crime and Punishment,* but within a narrow range he gains very charming effects. He too is not a popular writer, probably much less popular than Cabell. The neglect of such a man is deplorable, for not even Frost or Willa Cather better has the power to restore to the commonplace the quiet glow of meaning that is so often tarnished by the fret of everyday experience. In many quarters Nathan is not even a name. A few years ago a serious review of *Jonah* that appeared in a reputedly intelligent weekly of national circulation attributed the authorship of the book to George Jean Nathan, then associate editor of *The American Mercury*. The slight confusion as to authorship was not the only evidence that the review bore of the critic's muddle-mindedness. Despite such critics, those readers who admire a delicacy of touch, a mellow tone, and a quiet deep intelligence in their reading will find in the pages of Robert Nathan some peculiarly beautiful literature that is quite to their liking. And in his later books his satire is second to none that has been written in this country.

DONN BYRNE

(1889-1928)

A few years ago when Donn Byrne's *Messer Marco Polo* appeared serially in a magazine, many critics declared that a new star was rising in American literature. The author's subsequent development did not wholly bear out the predictions of the more enthusiastic critics, but the story of Marco Polo as told by the young Irish-American is one of the most beautiful of our romances, beautiful in its exotic setting and doubly beautiful in its melodious expression.

The trouble with the later books of Donn Byrne seems to lie in the easy grasp of what came to be a formula, and the author succumbed to the facile and the repetitious. Such criticism, however, is not valid when directed against *The Wind That Bloweth* (1922) and *Blind Raftery* (1924). But *Messer Marco Polo* is Byrne's best book and one of the finest works produced by the new romance. It is a story of the far away and long ago told in a naïve, poetic prose that accents the timeless qualities of the tale. Venice in the days of its glory, the legendary cities of middle Asia, the lands of Prester John, the greatness of Kubla Khan, and the loveliness of his daughter Tao-Tuen, little Golden Bells, these are the things that give the story its shimmering, exotic beauty.

To complete his affinity with the writers of the new romance, Byrne shows no sign whatever of believing his own fiction. His best books lie in the shadowy land halfway between fancy and reality, but at no time is there any confusion in the author's mind as to his own whereabouts. The immense realm of the Great Khan and the lands of Prester John are only other names for the kingdom of Poictesme.

One of the most appealing elements in *Messer Marco Polo* is the beautiful style:

> And suddenly at the end of the garden, in the perfumed Asian dusk, there was a beam like moonlight, and into the soft ray of it trod little Golden Bells, with her wee warm face, and her wee warm hands, and her hair dark as a cloud, and her eyes pleading, pleading . . .

Messer Marco Polo was not written with an eye to improving the world, but occasionally the romancer hints that all is not well in the world that he has left behind. "Only let you not be going away from me in my moonlit garden. You will only be turning to trade, Marco Polo, and marrying a woman. Let you stay here in the moonlit garden."

JOSEPH HERGESHEIMER

(1880-   )

Joseph Hergesheimer wrote, we are told on unexceptionable authority, for fourteen years before having a line published, and one is constrained to agree with Cabell that those years are the most important ones in Hergesheimer's literary career, though it is not necessary to follow Cabell's other conclusions. During his apprenticeship Hergesheimer developed a highly wrought style, as a man would who was trying desperately to please editors by the finish of his work. However, his style postures at times so consciously that it drops over into the obviously insincere. One other aspect of his writing must have given him great concern during those fourteen years, and that is his use of background. He was educated in part at the Pennsylvania Academy of Fine Arts, and his training as a painter did not stop with his attempted entrance into literature, for his earliest books and stories show an excessive preoccupation with physical background and costume. Undoubtedly both these traits, a carefully wrought style and a full command of background, are valuable assets to any novelist, but when concern with style comes to be only a frantic search for the unfamiliar word, and when the clothes that a character wears are more important than the character, then these potential assets lose all their value and become actual liabilities.

In his over-striving for background and costume effects, Hergesheimer gives one the very uneasy feeling that he has been a close student—even an obsequious admirer—of the motion picture in the days of its silence. His novels after *Java Head* (1919) betray an increasing fondness for an elaborately contrived, consciously "artistic" background and for striking costume effects, and at the same time his characters become thinner and thinner until they have the cold unreality of certain actors very popular in motion pictures not so long ago. Max Beerbohm neatly impaled Hergesheimer on one piercing witticism, "Poor Mr. Hergesheimer, he does so want to be an artist." And yet despite the cruel appropriateness of such a remark, one hesitates wholly to accept its findings. It is conceivable that Hergesheimer longs to become a popular writer of scenarios that "feature" beautiful heroines, gorgeous costumes, and colorful, exotic backgrounds. *The Bright Shawl* (1922) and *Tampico* (1926) are good examples of novels that depend largely upon background and costumes for their effect. From his latest work, *The Party Dress* (1930), Hergesheimer seems to have omitted everything except the dress and its intimate accessories. One looks in vain for a living character.

But at his best Hergesheimer can be an excellent novelist, and he is at his best when he subordinates freakishness of style and fondness for costume drama to the exigencies of the story in hand. *Three Black Pennys* (1917) and *Java Head* (1919) are his most notable novels. In these two books the author has found occasion to use his talent for etching the outlines of exotic beauty against the background of sordid American life. The best creations of Hergesheimer are the Manchu woman in *Java Head*, who brings to old Salem town an exotic beauty, and the Polish lady, Ludowica Winscomb, in the first part of *Three Black Pennys*. Judged from the standpoint of his chief interests, style and background, *San Cristobal de la Habana* (1920) and *From an Old House* (1925) are excellent pieces of work. In both books the absence of characters and narrative elements leaves the author free to weave endless, colorful strands into his background and to elaborate his style without unduly exasperating the reader.

Of the other novels *Balisand* (1924) is probably the best. It is a costume novel of Virginia when patrician and plebeian were disputing in terms of Jeffersonian democracy for the control of the commonwealth. As a historical novel it is fairly satisfactory, but it has little of the magic evocation of *Java Head* or the first part of *Three Black Pennys*. One novel that has won more than a little praise, *Linda Condon* (1919), sounds like a sketch written by a very talented sophomore and diluted to book length. It undoubtedly has some fine strokes, but they are very far apart, and the intervening narrative is thin to the point of transparency. And when Hergesheimer tries to become intellectual by injecting into his novel a dash of half-understood Freudianism, as he did in *Cytherea* (1922), one positively yearns to have him return at once to his self-imposed task as a purely decorative artist.

All in all, Hergesheimer is not a writer who has justified the high expectations that he raised by his two really fine novels. When he is content with writing well, when he takes his eyes off the background, and when he looks beneath the costume to the heart of the character, then he becomes one of our distinctly good novelists, comparable to so consistent an artist as Cabell. But when he strains for effects that can sound only artificial when achieved, and when he becomes the scenario writer to the extent of seeing a novel in a glittering figure that flits gracefully across an exquisite background, then he becomes a tiresome poseur quite worthy of the epigram pointed by Max Beerbohm.

SUGGESTED READINGS

The best introduction to Cabell is by way of his own *Beyond Life* and *Straws and Prayer-Books*.

Beach: *Outlook for American Prose*. Chicago. 1926. Cabell, pp. 63-80; 87-92; Hergesheimer, pp. 37-41; 112-114.

Mencken: "James Branch Cabell." 1927.

    If he had never done anything else Mencken could claim a considerable degree of critical eminence because of his vigorous defense of Dreiser and Cabell against unintelligent attacks.

Van Doren: *Contemporary American Novelists*. New York. 1923.

    Discusses Cabell and Hergesheimer.

Van Doren: "James Branch Cabell." New York. 1925.

    Not very valuable.

Walpole: "The Art of James Branch Cabell." 1927.

    An English novelist writes an enthusiastic appreciation.

CHAPTER XXVII

THE DRAMA IN AMERICA

It is generally assumed, especially by the younger generation, that American drama dates from Eugene O'Neill's *Beyond the Horizon* (1920) or, at the earliest, from 1910 when we first began to talk about the New Theater and when amateur dramatics became so popular. It is true that the history of American drama shows no masterpieces during the nineteenth century, but the same might be said of the English stage from the passing of Goldsmith and Sheridan to the spectacular rise of Oscar Wilde. However, there was a vast amount of native material in our theaters prior to 1910 that satisfied the patrons and that even to-day stands comparison with the English plays of the same time. But the dearth of masterpieces must be admitted.

There are many reasons why the American stage did not see any very fine native plays until it had been in existence for more than 200 years. In the first place American literature before 1910 was devoted to the novel, poetry, and the short story. Among large numbers of our people the stage was suspected of vague improprieties, much more so than was the novel, and as a result many of our best writers reached maturity with a very slight knowledge of the theater. Furthermore, our early drama was hampered by a slavish devotion to Shakespeare, and the upshot of this situation was the familiar story of Ulysses' bow. In the next place, the drama of the romantic age, while giving full expression to the romantic tendencies of the time, became a vehicle for rhetorical declamation. Character was almost wholly slighted and incident was handled in the most artificial manner. Finally, the precarious rewards of the dramatist until long after the Civil War must have had a tendency to discourage many from writing plays. We know that the unfortunate experience of Robert Montgomery Bird, a very capable dramatist, with the actor-manager, Edwin Forrest, turned one of our best playwrights from the theater to prose fiction.

In general, however, American plays from 1800 to 1890 were

probably quite as good as were the products of the English dramatists. Such works as Mrs. Mowatt's *Fashion,* John Howard Payne's *Charles the Second,* Bird's *Gladiator* and *Broker of Bogota* and Boker's *Francesca da Rimini* are respectable productions for the theater, though they are not great literature.

THE AMERICAN DRAMA TO 1860

The history of our colonial theater was once curtly dismissed as non-existent, but to-day we know that the stage was a recognized part of the cultural life in several of the cities. Theaters were banned in Boston until after the Revolution, but in Philadelphia and New York dramatic performances flourished, and by the end of the eighteenth century both drama and the opera were common in New Orleans. Plays were first produced professionally in this country in 1703, but permanent companies were not organized until some fifty years later. Interest in dramatics seems to have been considerable from the start, and the frequent amateur performances of British soldiers during the Revolution must have added much to the interest already aroused. General Burgoyne and the unfortunate Major André were both devoted to the theater.

The first native dramatist to have his play presented by a professional company was the Philadelphian, Thomas Godfrey (1736-1763). The play was *The Prince of Parthia,* a tragedy in blank verse that shows the unmistakable influence of Shakespeare. The work was not performed until 1767, four years after the author's death. It was revived in 1915 as a curiosity by a group of amateurs in the University of Pennsylvania. Those who saw the performance say that the play is actable, though totally lacking in comic relief.

During the Revolution satires and burlesques held the board in dramatic work, as they did in poetry. After Godfrey the first dramatist of importance was Royall Tyler (1757-1826), soldier, lawyer, and judge, a native of Boston, who presumably saw his first dramatic performance in 1787 in New York where he went on official business. It is said that he wrote his first work, *The Contrast,* in three weeks. This play is a comedy that satirizes the shallowness of fashionable life by contrasting it with unspoiled native sense and dignity. The aim of the play is well indicated by the closing speech of the American colonel, "And I have learned that probity, virtue, honor, though they should not have received the polish of Europe, will secure to an honest American the good graces of his country-woman, and, I hope, the applause of The Public." The chief interest in this play, however, centers in Jonathan, the down-east Yankee servant of Colonel Manly. This character marks the first appearance on the stage of a type that was ever afterwards to enjoy popularity. Tyler also wrote *A Georgia Spec, or Land in the Moon* (1797), which had for its theme speculation in southwestern land. He also wrote a famous novel, *The Algerian Captive* (1797).

William Dunlap (1766-1839) is the most important figure in the theatrical history of his time. He wrote or adapted more than sixty plays, many of the adaptations coming from German originals, and he wrote a history of the American stage that is one of the most valuable sources of our theatrical history. During the Revolution Dunlap saw many amateur performances by British soldiers, and from 1784 to 1789 he resided in England where he frequented the theater. *André*, a patriotic drama in blank verse, is the most accessible of his plays. This work was widely popular.

Several years before Cooper and Hawthorne discovered the literary possibilities in our colonial history, James Nelson Parker (1784-1858) used a colonial setting for his play, *Superstition*. The scene of the drama is New England about 1675. John Howard Payne, who is to-day known as the author of a sentimental song, collaborated with Washington Irving to write *Charles the Second*, a comedy produced at Covent Garden in 1824. Irving's share in this work was not known for a long time. Payne wrote many other plays, most of them melodramas.

In 1839 Nathaniel Parker Willis (1806-1867) wrote *Tortesa the Usurer*, a romantic comedy which was one of the popular plays of its period. Mrs. Mowatt's *Fashion* (1845) was another well-known play of the time. This was a social satire, a form that has always been popular with Americans since the days of Tyler's *Contrast*. *Fashion* was revived in New York a few years ago as a burlesque, but even under that condition and despite the archaic technique, the play showed that it had considerable vitality.

But the greatest names in American drama before the Civil War are those of Richard Montgomery Bird and George Henry Boker, both Philadelphians. From his college days Bird was interested in the drama, and when he was only twenty-four years old, Edwin Forrest accepted his *Pelopidas*. But for some reason the play proved unsatisfactory and the author substituted *The Gladiator*

(1831). This drama gave full expression to the soaring romanticism of the time and offered a fine opportunity for robust acting. It was one of the most successful plays ever produced on the American stage, and it is said to have been the first drama in English that was presented one thousand times during the lifetime of the author. Forrest chose this play to open an important engagement in London when he was to appear almost exclusively in Shakespeare. John McCullough was another great actor who was attracted to this piece. Bird also wrote *The Broker of Bogota* which remained in Forrest's repertoire for thirty years. His tragedy, *Orallossa*, was founded on Pizarro's conquest of Peru. Financial disappointments made Bird turn from the drama to the novel. He received only five thousand dollars for all of his sensationally successful plays, and Forrest is said to have cleared $200,000 on *The Gladiator* alone. Three of Bird's novels, *Nick of the Woods, The Infidel,* and *Calavara* were dramatized, though Bird had nothing to do with the work. The last two deal with the conquest of Mexico by Cortez.

George Henry Boker (1823-1890), a not unjustly neglected man of letters, achieved great success in both poetry and the drama. He was born too late to be caught in the full tide of romanticism and too early to allow development after the Civil War. To-day he is only a name to most people, though his poetry is very much better than is that of contemporaries like Bayard Taylor, and his play, *Francesca da Rimini*, has been placed in the "front rank of verse dramas written in English during the nineteenth century." Produced in 1855 this play has been revived many times. Its last appearance was in the winter of 1901-1902 when it was one of the great successes of the season. Otis Skinner directed this production and played the leading part. During the eighties the play enjoyed its greatest popularity. Boker wrote six other dramas, the most important being *The Betrothal* and *Leonor de Guzman*.

THE DRAMA SINCE 1860

From 1860 to 1900 it seems that the level of American dramatic writing was much lower than it was in the years before the Civil War, though the disappearance of blank verse from the stage and the use of a fairly natural dialogue make the plays of the Gilded Age sound rather less artificial than those of Bird and Boker. But in their stagecraft and in their appeal to unconcealed tricks for dramatic effect, the plays of the seventies and eighties were quite as artificial as anything ever seen prior to the rise of the motion picture. The prime aims of every playwright during that melancholy period of our artistic development seemed to be sentimental tears and melodramatic thrills. So intent were our dramatists on such effects that the dramas of the time were very much like the novels of the fifties when blood and tears very nearly drowned our fiction.

In the years immediately after the Civil War the dramatic trickster ruled the theater. Dion Boucicault (1820-1890), one of the genuinely important names in our theatrical history, discovered the value of clever stage management and the worth of verisimilitude in the setting. Boucicault is said to have had a hand in the writing or adaptation of more than 120 plays, and while none of them is important from the standpoint of dramatic composition, almost every one that he produced marked an advance in the technique of stagecraft. Boucicault was of Irish birth, but he lived in America about thirty-five years, and these years were among his most productive. His best known plays are *London Assurance, The Octoroon, The Shaughraun,* and *Led Astray.* He dramatized many popular novels and adapted many plays by foreign playwrights. For many years he completely dominated the American stage.

Among the plays in which Boucicault had an undefined hand was the famous *Rip Van Winkle* that made Joseph Jefferson internationally famous. Jefferson's contribution to the American stage was an extension of the work of Boucicault, clever stage management and an appeal to humor and sentiment through facile tricks. The dramatist-director of the present most completely in the Boucicault tradition is David Belasco, who is best represented by such plays as *Madame Butterfly, The Return of Peter Grimm,* and *The Girl of the Golden West.*

The chief example in this country of the drama that marked the transition from the inflated, rhetorical poetry of the earlier period and the realism of the present is Steele MacKaye's *Hazel Kirke* (1880), a domestic comedy that achieved huge popularity. The English drama that seems to hold a similar position is Tom Robertson's *Caste* (1867). The progress in dramatic writing that is noticeable in these plays lies in a more accurate observation in the delineation of character and in the handling of incident, a more faithful reporting of the words and acts of people, and an inclination to discard traditional stage situations in favor of situations taken from life. The whole movement was toward a greater realism through the abandonment of obvious affectations. The reticent realism on the stage during the eighties and nineties seems to have been somewhat more popular with theater audiences than was the same element in novels. This was only to be expected, for play-goers are as a class rather more advanced in their tastes and much more sophisticated than are the readers of novels.

But dramatic trickery was to have one excellent fling on the stage before it became numbered with the outmoded conventions of the theater. This fling came largely in the crop of Civil War melo-dramas. The most famous of these plays were *Shenandoah* and *Secret Service*. *Shenandoah* (1888) was the work of Bronson How-ard (1842-1908), the most famous American dramatist of the time. The play handled authentic material in the most romantic and melo-dramatic manner imaginable, using, fittingly enough, for its central episode one of the most spectacular incidents of the Civil War, the famous ride of Sheridan. Readers who are accustomed to the war novels of the present, in many of which there are few or no women characters of importance, will be vastly surprised at the large num-ber of women that managed to intrude into plays like *Shenandoah*. Of course, they are brought in for sentimental purposes, but their presence is disastrous to the realism of such a drama. *Secret Service* (1896) by William Gillette (1855-   ) is a very much more realis-tic play than the preceding, though most of the realism is in the action and not in character or in the broad outline of the work. As many have pointed out, the text of the play, shorn of the stage directions, is quite unexciting, even undramatic, but when the direc-tor utilized the stage tricks of Boucicault, the performance took on the glitter of dramatic excitement. However, *Secret Service* was enormously popular on the stage for a number of years. Other Civil War dramas are Clyde Fitch's *Barbara Frietchie* (1899) and James A. Herne's *Griffith Davenport*. A belated echo of this type of play was had in Augustus Thomas's *Copperhead* (1918).

Other plays by Bronson Howard were *Saratoga, Young Mrs. Winthrop, Old Love Letters,* and *Aristocracy*. Gillette wrote or adapted many plays. Among his best known are *Held by the Enemy*, another Civil War play, *Clarice, Too Much Johnson, All the Comforts of Home*. In the last years of the nineties and the first decade of the new century Gillette was a prominent man in the American theater. His prominence was due to his direction of plays and his acting as much as to his dramatic writing.

David Belasco (1853-   ) carried along the idea of realism in the stage setting until it reached exact verisimilitude, but his importance to the theater is not due to his writing. His most famous plays are *Madame Butterfly* (in collaboration with John Luther Long), *The Girl of the Golden West, May Blossom,* and *The Return of Peter Grimm.*

Clyde Fitch (1865-1909), one of our most prolific playwrights, was the famous American dramatist before 1920. During his short life Fitch wrote or adapted fifty-five plays, more than half of these being original compositions. Of this large number—about three for every year of his productive life—many are naturally far below the author's best work, but all had the merit of being interesting to audiences. Fitch brought to his work an intimate knowledge of the foreign stage in the days when Wilde, Pinero, and Shaw were bringing back English drama to its former high position. However, he was not always fortunate in his foreign interests, for he allowed an admiration for the French well-made play of the Scribe school to affect much of his work just at the time that the Ibsen drama of ideas was ready to possess the world stage. His liking for the Scribe play accounts for the tone of artificiality that his dramas have for the reader of to-day. It also probably accounts for the curiously low valuation that he currently receives from dramatic critics.

Yet Fitch was something of a realist, at least in his natural dialogue and his faithfulness to detail in the recording of incident. It is true that the incidents were artificially juggled about, just as the writer of well-made plays always used them, but in the relation of specific incident Fitch was much more of a realist than were his contemporaries. It is in the broad planning of his plays, in the relation of the incidents to the movement of the drama, that he showed his artificiality.

Fitch did his best work in the field of social satire, but he did not allow his satirical bent to pull him over into the thesis or propaganda play. All his best work has a solid foundation in the shape of a central idea which is not used to prove or disapprove anything. It becomes merely the core of meaning. For instance, *The Truth* (1906), exhibits a zeal as warm as that of Henry Arthur Jones to show the effect of habitual lying upon an otherwise unobjectionable woman. Still the play does not try to prove anything. *The City* (1909) is not a thesis play proving that the city is better or worse than the village; it is simply an attempt to reveal the effect of the metropolis upon country people not strong enough to resist the strain placed upon them by their new environment. Notwithstanding its concern with what came to be known as the battle of the village in our literature, this play does not seem so impressive to the reader to-day as it sounded from the stage twenty years ago.

Among Fitch's other plays may be mentioned *Beau Brummell, Her Great Match, The Woman in the Case, The Girl with Green Eyes, The Girl and the Judge, The Climbers, Nathan Hale,* and *Major André*. The last two are historical tragedies. The huge success of the plays made many think that Fitch was the long-awaited great dramatist of the American stage. His failure to stand the test of time undoubtedly has made those who remember the fate of his reputation rather slow to accept a superlative estimate of Eugene O'Neill.

William Vaughn Moody enjoyed a spectacular success with *The Great Divide* (1906), which critics loudly praised for its convincing realism, but theater-goers of to-day, accustomed to *Anna Christie, What Price Glory,* and *The Cherry Orchard*, respect the work more for its historical significance than for its inherent worth. The play is a contrast of the social conventions of the East and the easy customs of the West. *The Faith Healer* (1909) was not a popular success, though it is quite as effective to read to-day as *The Great Divide*.

In the most distinctive American dramas written before the beginning of the dramatic renaissance about 1910 the most notable quality was not dramatic worth but theatrical effectiveness. The best plays were those that emphasized stage tricks to catch the immediate attention of an audience. Few of the playwrights seemed to be aware that there were any resources open to the dramatist other than those of the trickster. Inveterate imitators, they did everything that older writers had done except put in their plays dramatic situations that would not depend wholly upon surprise or any other trick for their effectiveness. After one hearing the trick loses its power, but real drama remains effective after innumerable hearings. This is the secret that none of our dramatists seemed to have before 1920, and since that date only a few have possessed it.

EUGENE O'NEILL *Playwright*

(1888-   )

Beginning about 1910 the American stage entered upon a period of unprecedented activity and originality. Experimental theaters began their invaluable work, giving opportunities for new writers, allowing the testing of new scenic effects, interesting large crowds of intelligent amateurs in the stage, and tending in general to make the theater less slavishly dependent upon the box-office for direction. A large number of new dramatists arose, any one of whom would have been deemed worthy of highest praise had he appeared at an earlier period. Designers and directors began to study the work of foreigners like Gordon Craig, Reinhardt, and Stanislavsky, and soon theater-goers in this country were familiar with the names of Joseph Urban, Norman-Bel Geddes, Robert Edmund Jones, and Lee Simonson. In the theatrical renaissance the most notable figure is that of Eugene O'Neill, the first American dramatist to win an international reputation.

O'Neill was born in New York City in 1888. He was brought up in the atmosphere of the theater, for his father was James O'Neill, a popular actor, whose greatest success was his performance in *Monte Cristo*. Eugene O'Neill was prepared for college in private schools and entered Princeton in 1906, but he was dropped from the institution before the end of his first year. Then for seven or eight years he led a haphazard, vagabond life that took him into many strange places and that allowed him to meet many queer people. He was the friend of the New York anarchist, Benjamin Tucker, and of other fantastic radicals of the metropolis. After living in New York for some time, he went on an expedition to Honduras looking for gold. He found no gold, but the trip gave him another store of experiences that later were to be used in his writing. The Honduras adventure terminated in a severe attack of tropical fever. O'Neill returned to America and became the assistant manager for Viola Allen's theatrical company on a successful tour of the Middle West with *The White Sister*. One day he read Conrad's *Nigger of the Narcissus* and succumbed at once to the magic power of the novel. Under the spell of Conrad he shipped as an able-bodied seaman on a Norwegian sailing vessel bound for Buenos Aires. He stayed in Argentina for eighteen months, working for various American corporations. From Buenos Aires he voyaged to South Africa and returned to New York by way of Argentina. For a time he was a reporter, and his father gave him a minor rôle in *Monte Cristo,* but he disliked both positions. He frequented the docks of New York, becoming intimately acquainted with a life that he was later to use so effectively in *Anna Christie.* This period was terminated by an attack of tuberculosis. The leisure that he had while recuperating in a sanitarium gave him an opportunity to do his first experimenting in dramatic form. In 1914 he published at his father's expense *Thirst and Other One-Act Plays.* The winter of 1914-1915 he studied dramatic writing at Harvard with Professor George P. Baker, director of the famous course, English 47. His first work to see the stage was produced by the Provincetown Players, an art theater of Provincetown, Massachusetts. In 1916 this group went to New York where they opened with a program of one-act plays in a little theater in MacDougal Street. O'Neill was not given an opportunity in a regular commercial theater until 1920, and even to-day the Theatre Guild produces most of his plays.

Beyond the Horizon, O'Neill's first full length play, won the Pulitzer Award in 1920. He has since received the same prize with *Anna Christie* (1922) and *Strange Interlude* (1928). Since the appearance of *Beyond the Horizon* O'Neill has been the acknowledged leader of American dramatists. His plays have been produced in virtually every theatrical center of the world, and to-day he is as well known on the continent of Europe as he is in his native country.

O'Neill's Early Plays.—After his first book of youthful experiments, *Thirst and Other One-Act Plays,* O'Neill set to work in earnest to perfect his command of the dramatic form. For several years he wrote much but published little, and that little was one-act plays exclusively. In 1919 his second volume appeared. It was called *The Moon of the Caribbees and Six Other Plays of the Sea.* Of the seven one-act plays in the book three are among the best pieces of this type that we have. These three are the title piece, "Bound East for Cardiff," and "Ile." The scene of three of the plays is laid on the British tramp steamer *Glencairn,* and in another piece members of the *Glencairn's* crew are the leading characters. Two characters appear in all four plays, and five are in three of the pieces. This device gives the volume a unity that is ordinarily quite lacking in books of one-act plays.

O'Neill scored his first great success with *Beyond the Horizon,* produced in New York, February 3, 1920. There are grave weaknesses in the play; nevertheless it is one of the author's best and most typical productions. When O'Neill wrote it, he could not handle neatly the mechanism of the long play, and he cut it up into too many acts and scenes and made demands upon the director that were far beyond the limitations of the stage. Despite these defects the play is a tense tragedy of frustration that turns on love, aspiration, jealousy, and mistakes caused by mere chance. Of two brothers one may go to sea and the other stay at home on the New England farm. The wrong choice brings to both the men and to the woman, who loves one of them and marries the other, a deep personal tragedy that none of the characters deserved. The play is one of the grimmest pieces of naturalism on the stage.

Anna Christie (1922) is another realistic drama, but it differs from most of O'Neill's studies of frustration in that the end of the play sees the characters managing to obtain at least a stay of execution from the hand of fate. As some have suggested, *Anna Christie* can hardly be said to have an ending, for the whole piece is too episodic to achieve an effect of finality. But the happy ending, if we can call it such, has given this play a great popular appeal. Its translation into a talking picture with very little revision and "improvement" by the Hollywood adapters was sufficient proof of its popular appeal in its original form. *Anna Christie* is a magic evocation of atmosphere, and in its dramatic intensity it is one of O'Neill's best plays, but if one tries to dissect it for a main thread of meaning, it becomes as elusive as life itself. And that may be one reason for its air of utter reality.

O'Neill's other plays of his early period are *Gold* and *The Straw*, both made out of the stuff of personal experiences.

Later Plays of O'Neill.—Beginning with the early *Emperor Jones* and continuing to the present, O'Neill has shown an increasing desire to transcend the limitations of realism and to write of intangible realities in poetic language that uses symbolism as often as any other device to make itself coherent. The playwright has broadened his imaginative grasp until he has given us his supreme efforts, *The Great God Brown* and *Lazarus Laughed,* two of the finest pieces of imaginative literature of the modern theater. These two plays are as far removed from *Beyond the Horizon* as Dunsany's *Night at an Inn* is from a realistic tragedy of Irish peasant life.

The Emperor Jones marks O'Neill's first break with realism. It is correctly classed as an expressionistic drama because of its throbbing energy and dynamic projection of the central core of consciousness. In eight short episodes this tremendous piece of dramatic composition shows the reversion of a Negro emperor to a primitive black, haunted by atavistic fears and superstitions. The fears range from those of Jones himself to those of the Negro race, but all the dramatic action and the lurking horrors of the jungle are shown through the mind of the principal character.

The Hairy Ape is another piece of expressionism very much like the preceding work. Yank, a stoker on a liner, is the hairy ape of the play. His noisy self-assertive confidence in his own strength, his assurance that he "belongs" as no others do, is the key-note of the opening. "Everyting else dat makes de woild move, somep'n makes it move. It can't move witout somep'n else, see? Den yuh get down to me. I'm at de bottom, get me. . . . I start somep'n and de woild moves. . . . And I'm steel, steel, steel." But Yank's crude confidence in himself is irreparably shattered by the sight of a young girl who is horribly shocked at the hairy ape's appearance and boisterous profanity. Yank starts out to discover if he really belongs, but he finds to his amazed disgust that he does not, until the final scene of crowning brutality, a scene of tremendous symbolism. Then "perhaps the Hairy Ape at last belongs."

All God's Chillun Got Wings (1924) is a brief tragedy of miscegenation in which innocent victims are caught in race hatred and crushed. *Desire Under the Elms* (1925) swings back to the earlier realism. It is a powerful tragedy of passion and avarice brought about by perverted human impulses on an old New England farm. It is a black, repellent play, but it has tremendous power.

The Great God Brown (1925) is one of the finest imaginative productions in our whole literature. It is a symbolical treatment of the deep mysteries of existence in which each of the characters represents some universal phase of human nature. William Brown is the cold materialist so very common in American life. Dion Anthony, the aspiring artist, combines the two impulses of possession and renunciation. His is the sensitive soul unfit for the shock of reality that the materialist creates and totally incapable of reaching the heights to which he aspires. Margaret is the eternal comforting woman, and Cybel is the unfettered power of woman's passion. By the use of masks O'Neill multiplies the effect that he would ordinarily get from the combination of these four symbolic characters and raises the play out of the ruck of immediate time and place, just as in *Strange Interlude* he does the same thing, less successfully, by means of the soliloquy. *The Great God Brown* closes on a note of triumphant exultation that affirms the goodness of life when it is seen in the whole and not in the silhouette. "Blessed are they that weep, for they shall laugh. . . . The laughter of Heaven sows earth with a rain of tears, and out of earth's transfigured birth-pain the laughter of Man returns to bless and play again in innumerable dancing gales of flame upon the knees of God."

This idea of laughter rising above the trivialities of life and death makes the core of meaning in *Lazarus Laughed* (1927). Lazarus has died and has returned to life, and he alone knows that the mystery of death is a piece in the larger planning that admits not the finality of pain and frustration. It is a beautifully idealistic conception, quite in line with the main current of American thought before the Machine Age crushed our idealism. Lazarus is another Walt Whitman, another Thoreau, washed clean, as they were, from fear of life and death and from the cramping limitations of the immediate. But he cannot bring men to accept permanently his heartening assertions, for as soon as he disappears and the sound of his triumphant laughter dies away, then the haunting fear of death and disaster returns. *Lazarus Laughed* is a profoundly beautiful drama that rises through sublimated comedy far above the tragic strain. Esthetically and dramatically it is a true and convincing piece of work. It and *The Great God Brown* stand at the top of O'Neill's works.

The Fountain (1926) is a retelling of the old story of Ponce de León in the general tone of the two preceding plays. It is rather disappointing in the author's inability to achieve the high poetic effects with the same material that he had managed so artistically in his earlier dramas. *Marco Millions* (1927) is another play in much the same spirit, but the obvious element in this drama is a sharp satirization of American hustle and materialistic aspirations. *Strange Interlude* (1928) is one of the unexpected successes of the modern stage. As a piece of writing for the theater it is tremendously long, running to nine acts and requiring about five hours for presentation. The length of the piece was caused by O'Neill's ambition to give to drama the depth and penetrating knowledge of leisurely fiction and by his desire in this particular play to present the lives of a group of people from youth to old age. The drama centers around the crushed aspirations of a young girl, Nina, whose ideal lover was killed in the war. Her neurotic struggle for happiness with the three men who are attracted to her, each of whom symbolizes an aspect of her dead lover, supplies the dramatic material for one of the most interesting plays of our generation. O'Neill gave psychological depth to the play through the use of soliloquy. The complete self-revelations given by each of the characters make the play, more than it would have been, a dramatized symbol of all humanity. The scientist, the idealist, and the materialist, all have essential parts in the struggle of humanity for happiness. Despite the spectacular success of this play and despite its undoubted strength, it has not the significance of *Lazarus Laughed* or *The Great God Brown*.

O'Neill's latest play, *Dynamo* (1929), is a critique of the failure of science to give anything in which we can safely and satisfactorily believe. When it was produced it was not successful, but since it is only the first part of a trilogy, one should not pass an adverse judgment without seeing the other two parts of the group.

O'Neill in American Letters.—Eugene O'Neill is a figure about whom there is critical agreement on one point only. All critics affirm his great importance as a writer of effective plays, and most of them admit that he is a typical and significant interpreter of American life. But at that point agreement ceases. He has been called realist, romantic idealist, naturalist, expressionist, and psychological analyst, and all those who have so diversely classified him can easily gather enough evidence in support of each contention to make plausible cases. The truth is that O'Neill has been all these things that he has been called, and none can say whither the dramatist's next steps will lead. He is a tireless experimenter, working strenuously to express in concentrated form the ideas and aspirations of contemporary life. And it is as such an experimenter that he deserves to be best known. To say that he has frequently changed the dramatic devices by which he expresses his ideas is only half a truth. He has almost as often changed his whole point of view, even to the extent of discarding a philosophy that seemed to be fundamental, in order to interpret the deepest meanings of the life that he sees about him.

In his first plays O'Neill was one with the post-war disillusionists who could believe in nothing and who justified their unbelief by a forthright realism, a crude naturalism, satire, nihilism, or mocking burlesque. The generation that he first represented was hopelessly frustrated spiritually, however great were its physical and intellectual excesses. Psychologically it presented a case of group inversion caused by a morbid sense of futility. The young people who could bear to think brooded endlessly, and always on the problem of failure. Then, as the post-war psychology slowly changed, O'Neill's innate poetry began to find expression, and his plays slowly changed temper until in *Lazarus Laughed* a clear note of affirmation rings out from the stage in the cosmic laughter of him who held in a glance both life and death.

> My foothold is tenon'd and mortis'd in granite,
> I laugh at what you call dissolution,
> And I know the amplitude of time.

For the last decade O'Neill's generation has been interested in life and its fullest and most satisfying expression, not in politics, economics, or questions of social convention or personal morality, the standard subjects of earlier dramatists. And it is the problem of life and its expression that has engaged the attention of O'Neill. But in coming from the heart of a whole generation to speak its inmost fears and dreads, aspirations and ideal triumphs, O'Neill has never settled into provincialism. The New England of *Beyond the Horizon* and *Desire Under the Elms* is not intensely localized, and its people are just as universal as are human beings. Even the sailors of the early one-act plays and Chris Christofferson have about them something more than the air of local color.

O'Neill is at his weakest in the creation of character, but he is an intellectual who is forced to express both the stubborn facts and the ethereal aspirations of life through symbols, and symbolism always tends to weaken the dramatist's conception of highly individualized characters. Anna Christie, of all the major figures, is the least symbolical, the least endowed with universal significance—and the most popular with audiences.

In the narrow sense of the term O'Neill is not a social critic, though running through all his plays there is the implied assertion that modern life is not good. The pressure of society breaks up individual existence and fails utterly to leave any satisfactory substitute, it brings the tragedy of frustration, and it cannot be made to entertain the redeeming fiction of romantic idealism. Social convention almost wrecked Anna Christie's life after the girl had won a first redemption. Shallow materialism receives the brunt of the satire in *Marco Millions*. Nina in *Strange Interlude* is the victim of social convention and a pointless war. In these and many other instances O'Neill is one of our sharpest social critics. But he has not succumbed to the easy way of most critics. He is only slightly concerned with ethics, but he is much interested in the individual right to life and expression. He pays little attention to politics and economics and very much heed to the central core of our discontent. Because of these facts and despite his limitations, he has probably achieved a place in world literature which will be denied to more facile writers who give us highly individualized characters, clearly localized as to time and place.

After a silence of twelve years, O'Neill returned to Broadway in the fall of 1946 with a new play, *The Iceman Cometh*. This work reveals nothing new either in technique or in ideas. Reading it gives one the feeling that it is merely second-rate O'Neill, and a superb production on Broadway failed to conceal this plain fact. His latest play, *A Moon for the Misbegotten,* was tried out in Detroit and was so poorly received that it failed to reach Broadway.

SUGGESTED READINGS

Virtually all surveys of contemporary literature give a section to O'Neill. The following are only a few of many possible references.

Buck: *Directions in Contemporary Literature.* New York. 1942.
Cargill: *Intellectual America.* New York. 1941.
Clark: *Eugene O'Neill.* New York. 1929.
Cowley: *After the Genteel Tradition.* New York. 1937.
Eaton: *The Drama in English.* New York. 1930.
Gassner: *Masters of the Drama.* New York. 1940.
Quinn: *History of American Drama from the Beginning to the Civil War.* New York. 1923.
Quinn: *History of the American Drama from the Civil War to the Present Day.* New York. 1927.
Whipple: *Spokesmen.* New York. 1928.
Winther: *Eugene O'Neill.* New York. 1934.

CHAPTER XXVIII

THE PRESENT CONFUSION

While we are much too near the 1930's to pass accurate judgment on the social and political movements which characterized the first part of that decade, one can say somewhat confidently that the nation during those years moved into new channels. The basis of political power shifted into new hands, governmental functions widened and strengthened, evangelists of a new day bruited solutions for hitherto unknown economic problems, while a horde of new ideas supplied topics for writers and dinner-table debaters. Whether or not America underwent a permanent political and social revolution in the 1930's is still a moot question, though the evidence indicates that the changes wrought during those years were not ephemeral.

Naturally the tone of our literature changed with that of our national life. Proof of this statement need not necessarily be elaborate. Compare typical novels of the 1920's, for example, *Babbitt, A Lost Lady,* and *Dark Laughter,* with *The Grapes of Wrath, The Big Money,* and *For Whom the Bell Tolls.* Even the most imperceptive can see that these two groups of novels are separated by a much more powerfully divisive influence than merely ten or fifteen years of time. All six of the novels mentioned may be considered critical, but in the later ones the tone is wholly unlike that of the earlier works. Steinbeck, Hemingway, and Dos Passos lift the emphasis from individuals and place it on society. To those authors what happens to the individual may be important, but much more important are the economic and political influences and dislocations which affect the individual. Hemingway alone well illustrates the change in the tone of American letters, a fact anyone can see by a comparison of *The Sun Also Rises* (1926) and *For Whom the Bell Tolls* (1940).

The 1930's were notable for the number of new writers who arrived on the scene, but no less notable was the change which came over some of the writers who had firmly established themselves by 1925. Sinclair Lewis made an about-face; Dreiser published no novels between 1925 and his death in 1945; Sherwood Anderson showed more concern with the social order than with fiction; and from 1932 to the present (1949) Eugene O'Neill has been in virtual retirement, though he wrote a number of plays during that time.

Even Willa Cather, that most careful and accurate depicter of American life, has evidently not been immune to the changed temper of the period. After 1931 Miss Cather published only four works of fiction. Four books in sixteen years do not indicate retirement, but they are no sign of vigorous creative activity. It is worthy of mention that the most successful of the three books, *Obscure Destinies,* a volume of three longish stories, was published in 1932, and at least one of the stories, "Neighbor Rosicky," may have been written or at least blocked out considerably earlier. It is also significant that when the volume appeared, it met with a somewhat disappointing reception. Even the critics were perfunctory in their approval. The public in 1932 was looking for sensationalism, either in theme or in treatment. It wanted "hard-boiled" writing, thickly interlarded with words and situations previously absent from American fiction, or it yearned for over-colored sketches of life among the permanently depressed, the abnormal, or the titillatingly vicious denizens of our social jungles. It is all very well to be informed of our more serious social problems. It is even more laudable to desire earnestly that the depressed be elevated, that the abnormal be transformed into uninteresting mediocrities, and that the vicious be made amiable. It would be well, however, for the future of creative writing in this country if the public could distinguish between sociology, the psychology of the unusual, propaganda, and literary art.

For all its chilly reception, *Obscure Destinies* is a work of high distinction, and the first story in the volume, "Neighbor Rosicky" is an undoubted masterpiece, technically worthy a place beside the finest work of Henry James and Edith Wharton. In theme and treatment the novelette reminds one of *My Antonia.* It is a simple sketch of an old Bohemian farmer in Nebraska, a man wedded to his land through long and close association. There is virtually no plot, only the merest thread of a story, but in her ability to fuse landscape and character and to evoke the desired emotional response, Miss Cather showed that she was in full possession of her powers. The fact that the story met with a cool reception in 1932 is evidence that critical judgments were being shouldered aside by other considerations. That fact also offered some little proof that the popular reception of a book in the early 1930's depended at least in part upon the social timeliness of the theme, the flamboyant presentation of that theme, and the political complexion of the author.

In *Lucy Gayheart* (1935) Miss Cather wrote a novel which can hardly be ranked with her great works. It was published in serial form by a popular magazine, and while it was distinctly above the level of most fiction which appears in such magazines, it is far below *My Antonia* and *A Lost Lady*. It is, however, not a bad novel; it is merely slight. To call *Lucy Gayheart* a pot-boiler would be unfair and inaccurate. In writing this novel Miss Cather simply descended to a lower plane than she usually works on. Higher altitude seems to afford a more congenial atmosphere for the delicate and sensitive craftsmanship of the author.

Sapphira and the Slave Girl (1940) has for its background antebellum Virginia. Miss Cather is a native of the Old Dominion, but she was taken to Nebraska at so early an age that she had no chance to develop a feeling for the background of this novel, while the none-too-subtle relationship of master and slave seems to have escaped her entirely. In one of her infrequent comments on her own work Miss Cather has expressed a belief that the best materials for fiction are memories based on the experiences of childhood and youth. *Sapphira and the Slave Girl* must have been based on reports and second-hand recollections. The writing is good, but the characters are not memorable, and the treatment of background fails to invest the setting with that sentient quality so notably a part of "Neighbor Rosicky," *O Pioneers,* and *Death Comes for the Archbishop*.

Miss Cather may have felt during the 1930's that the younger generation was tending to by-pass certain literary criteria to which she had given allegiance. The title of her book of essays, *Not Under Forty* (1936), is not without a hint of asperity. The plain implication is that only the middle-aged and elderly can have an interest in such topics as the technic of the novel, Flaubert's niece, Sarah Orne Jewett, or the integrity of the artist in an indifferent world. In her collected works (1937-1938) Miss Cather changed the title of this volume to *Literary Encounters*. The title piece of the posthumous collection, *The Old Beauty and Others* (1948), is very fine. In it Miss Cather suggests rather than tells the story of a woman's life.

THEODORE DREISER

When Theodore Dreiser died in 1945, he had not published a novel since *An American Tragedy* which had appeared twenty-one years earlier. It was thought that the author had in manuscript the third volume of his trilogy, of which *The Financier* (1912) and *The Titan* (1914) were the other members. This surmise was correct, but the first of Dreiser's manuscripts to be published after his death was not the conclusion of the trilogy but an independent work.

The novel appeared as *The Bulwark*, a title which Dreiser had given to a projected work as early as 1920. Whether or not the book published in 1946 was the same work that he had in mind twenty-six years earlier is a question. The story is about a Quaker family whose younger members failed to live up to the high ideals of the Friends. The chief point of the novel is the careful, though not sentimental, emphasis on the genuine comfort which the central figure found in his way of life. The work is on the whole a surprising performance. In his later years Dreiser repeatedly and defiantly proclaimed his communistic sympathies, and for forty years he had been known as an agnostic. Yet *The Bulwark* contains not a hint of collectivism, and Quakerism is treated tenderly and even admiringly. Dreiser's early themes such as the struggle for existence, determinism, and the use of crass chance are all absent from this novel. As usual Dreiser treats his leading character with immense compassion. *The Bulwark* illustrates many of the defects of its author. The opening chapters are far from sprightly, and some of the sentences are as flat as any that Dreiser ever wrote. In spite of these defects the novel is a most impressive work. When the author finally struggles through his expository section and finds himself in the current of his story, his style, never swift, becomes effective. His characterizations are deliberate, but they create a vividness of impression that many of our more facile writers will never be able to achieve. *The Bulwark* and *So Little Time* are probably the best novels to appear in this country between 1940 and 1948.

The Stoic, the third volume of the "trilogy of desire," appeared in 1948. This unfinished novel shows few of the characteristics which made *The Financier* a notable piece of fiction.

SINCLAIR LEWIS

Of all the debacles in recent American literature, that achieved by Sinclair Lewis is at once the most puzzling and the most deplorable. Before 1932 Lewis made a distinguished and undoubtedly permanent contribution to our national letters, and when he received the Nobel Prize in 1931, most intelligent commentators took the award to mean that an author who was American to the core had established himself as a writer of international significance. Since 1931 the Lewis that we have had is no longer the gay, witty, irreverent writer of the 1920's with a flair for humorous presentation of character and situation. In all the novels published since that year—and there have been some five or six of them—hardly a scene has risen above the level of sprightly mediocrity, while some of the works have dropped to solemn banality.

What happened to Lewis about 1931 is a fascinating question to which no categorical answer can be returned. The Lewis of the 1920's was a satirist and storyteller of uncommon talents who expended enough thought and labor on his material to give his severest strictures an immensely appealing air of spontaneity. He was the irrepressible mocker who aimed his raillery at the culture of the small town, the bustling man of petty affairs, the quack doctor, and the hypocritical minister, to name no more. Did Lewis suddenly run out of material? This is most unlikely. The 1930's offered the satirist a marvelous opportunity. During that decade the United States had an unusual allowance of egregious reformers, raging typhoons of civic virtue, whose characters and careers might well have excited the professional interest of the man who created George Babbitt and Elmer Gantry. In that period the country had more than its usual quota of fantastic schemes to abolish poverty, end international discord, and brighten the somewhat tarnished promise of American life. Distinctly Mr. Lewis cannot complain about the dearth of material.

Perhaps Lewis was overwhelmed by the Nobel Prize. He may have thought that making sport of the solemn and the pretentious was hardly consonant with the dignity of a Nobel Prizeman. The bad boy must reform; he must put behind him childish things. Instead of "destructive criticism" he must evolve something constructive. Proof of the theory is lacking, but proponents of this idea can get some effective ammunition for argument by a comparison of *Elmer Gantry* (1927) and *Ann Vickers* (1932). If the theory be true, the Nobel award dealt American letters a sore blow.

From 1929 to 1932 this country was in a ferment, ideas and ideals were changing, and it may be that Lewis, as sensitive and perceptive as he is, saw that taste was changing, that the audience which had laughed at *Babbitt* wanted a serious discussion, not on what's wrong but on how to make things right. Lewis the satirist became a serious man who talked about the function of the intellectual woman in society, the threat of fascism, the responsibilities of parents, and the not wholly novel theme of middle age and youth locked in the bonds of matrimony. The magnificent recording machine known as Sinclair Lewis became an inexpert dramatizer of platitudinous editorials. The theory that Lewis shifted his approach to his material in response to changing social ideals is not entirely untenable.

Exactly why Lewis shifted is a question that only a biographer can answer, but the fact remains that he changed. *Ann Vickers* is the first melancholy evidence of the change. In this novel Lewis gave a full length portrait of a modern woman, an intellectual, an honor to and a leader of her sex. For many, many pages the author extolled his heroine. She was a great woman. To her came public acclaim and honorary degrees from educational institutions. She was a notable. And yet in all the pages of the novel Ann Vickers never made an intelligent remark and never once even inadvertently performed a sensible act. From her undergraduate days, when she developed a "crush" on one of her instructors, to the close of the book, when she is involved in an affair with a corrupt judge, she acts and talks like an adolescent hyperthyroid. Five years earlier Lewis would have had a most hilarious time with Ann Vickers, but in 1932 oblivious to the comic aspects of his heroine, he recorded all her platitudes and idiotic actions with the naïve admiration of an Elsie Dinsmore.

It Can't Happen Here has for its theme the coming of fascism to the United States. In 1935 the theme was undoubtedly timely, but it afforded the high talent of Lewis no very congenial field for operation. *Cass Timberlane* (1946) is the story of a middle-aged judge who married a young wife. The situation would have given the young Lewis a chance for humorous situations and sharp, swift characterization, but the novel turned out to be a routine performance of no visible merit. In 1926 Lewis refused the Pulitzer Prize on the ground that the award was an effort to make writers "safe, polite, obedient, and sterile." Even if the dire penalty which Lewis envisioned had been attached to the prize, he might as well have accepted the offer.

Regardless of what Lewis does in the future, his position in American literature will remain distinguished, but it must be remembered that he reached that position by writing his novels of the 1920's.

RING LARDNER

(1885-1933)

Ring Lardner during his life was anathema to the teacher of English. His work was usually published in popular magazines to the extreme satisfaction of those who read such periodicals, but not until after his death in 1933 did academic critics in general admit that he was anything more than a facile writer. The academics professed a distaste for his characters. These personages were brutal pugilists, illiterate baseball players, small town practical jokers, ignorant and selfish men dragged in from unusual places. But it could hardly have been his characters that made many disapprove of Lardner. As a matter of fact Lardner's characters are rather high-toned in comparison with those of certain other writers who have won acclaim in academic circles. There is a strong suspicion that teachers reprobated Lardner because of the corrupt English spoken by the personages in his stories.

English teachers consecrate their lives and their most earnest endeavors to the eradication of bad grammar, and one of their favorite arguments for the use of correct speech is the asseveration that good English is swifter, more expressive, and more accurate than corrupt speech. All this is stated cogently, even unctuously, as only a person can argue who is wholly convinced of the truth of his case. It is also stated in utter forgetfulness of *Huckleberry Finn* and passages from *Tom Sawyer*. Mr. Lardner allowed his characters to massacre half a dozen rules of grammar to the paragraph, and yet his stories abound in swift conversation which is clear and altogether delightful in its vivid expressiveness. The dialogue also has a suspicious taint of actuality. In fact, Lardner accurately transcribed the speech habitually used by uncultivated Americans when they are talking naturally without the cramping inhibition imposed by the presence of refined and sensitive listeners. No wonder the devotees of correct grammar became alarmed at Lardner's solecisms, current slang, and garbled pronunciation. Such stories as "Alibi Ike" and "My Roomy" carry portents of disaster to textbook English. The teachers may win, but the victory will not be an easy one.

But if Lardner is to live, his position in literature will not depend upon the facility with which he transcribed the vulgar American dialect. If he lives, he will do so because of the form of his stories, his humor, the vividness of his characterizations, and the totality of effect achieved by his short narratives. Even the detractors of Lardner, when they are willing momentarily to overlook the language, are forced to admit that the man, when judged by the standards just enumerated, takes no low place in the roster of our storytellers. He was not so influential in the development of our literature as Poe, Bret Harte, or Sherwood Anderson. He accepted the conventional mold and used it with great effectiveness.

For years Lardner was a sports writer, specializing in the reporting of baseball games. A good sports writer must be able to tell the story of a game, catch the dramatic high lights, and bring his narrative to a close well within the limit of one thousand words. Writing under such conditions is the best of training for a writer of short stories, and Lardner profited from his experience. The form of his stories satisfies even the capitious. The theme appears casually but early in the story, and once it is stated, Lardner develops it with a Poe-like intensity, never allowing the extraneous to alienate the reader's interest.

Lardner has been accused of selecting his characters from the semi-literate and the moronic, but the assertion that such personages are extraordinary creatures in American life is open to discussion. We may not like the characters of a Lardner story, we may not choose to meet them socially, but the selections included in *Round-Up* prove that the author had a remarkable ability to sketch character in a few swift strokes. Nor did he confine himself to the chief personages of the narrative; minor figures come to life.

All this is achieved with great objectivity. Frequently Lardner employs a narrator who in the telling of the story leaves a clear impression of his own chief traits. "Haircut," for example, has the restraint and objectivity we associate with Robert Frost. This story is a masterpiece. The narrator is a village barber who casually unfolds the necessary details of a sordid story that turns on a brutal practical joke and culminates in murder. The narrative gains immensely from the fact that the barber never senses the brutality and horror of the episode which he is relating.

In addition to his other qualities Lardner has an immense store of American humor in its most characteristic mood and expression. He and Will Rogers were just about the last exponents of that humor which we associate with the frontier. Subtle it is not, but it is penetrating and provocative of laughter.

THE 1920's AND THE LOST GENERATION

In all American history we have had no decade more interesting or more deplorable than the 1920's. It was also enjoyable, provided that one had a sardonic sense of humor and not too much prescience. The decade was like a toboggan ride which ended in a crash. The first World War was accompanied by an emotional outburst which may not have been unique in our history, but which carried ominous portents. The hysteria evoked by the war and so unstintingly encouraged by our leaders, official and unofficial, could hardly be checked by the coming of peace. The sudden reversal of our national policy, the quick and grateful retreat into traditional isolationism, only deflected our frenetic aspirations from idealistic schemes for world betterment. Our emotions were still aroused but undirected. Naturally they found various outlets.

The war brought unreasonable prosperity to certain elements in our society, and the newly rich discovered that their ability to spend surpassed any ambition that might hitherto have been called reasonable. Unfortunately their culture and breeding were insufficient ballast for their cash. Huge sums were poured into sports, so-called recreation, fads, and Babylonian revels. The pent-up profits of war years, dumped into channels of trade, legitimate and illegitimate, infected even ordinarily cautious businessmen with a frenzy for speculative ventures. Consequently the moral tone of the nation suffered a grave deterioration.

Nor was the moral tone of the nation strengthened by the fiasco of prohibition. However noble the experiment may have been, it was conducted under conditions which made success impossible. Hitherto law-abiding citizens either became law violators or silently watched others flout the statutes. Gangsters flourished with brazen audacity. Corrupt officials winked at the illicit traffic in liquor and profited largely through their indifference. Now it must be remembered that defiance of law, corrupt officials, and gangsters were hardly novelties in American life, but the 1920's saw such an outcropping as we had never before known.

After the war the hatred which, during the struggle, had been directed against the Kaiser and Huns in general was directed against other targets. The country suffered a disgraceful wave of intolerance which is still to be felt in our social and political life. The most spectacular and the most publicized of the organizations based on intolerance was the Ku Klux Klan, but this fantastic group was only a symptom of a widespread malady. Intolerance flourished in quarters where the Klan was unknown. Self-appointed literary censors made themselves ridiculous by their attempts to expurgate or ban serious and even important books which were written with no pornographic intent whatever. Editors of high-grade periodicals found that certain issues of their magazines could not be sold in some cities because of local censorship. A play written by an established dramatist on a serious problem was forced to close. The whole episode gave officious busybodies a chance to strut and dictate. While this was distasteful enough, the alarming aspect of this amateur censorship was the fact that it was a symptom of widespread intolerance.

Another hysterical crusade which had its humorous aspects was that directed against radicals. The jailing or deportation of "reds" was a common occurrence, but the timorous public, not content with official action, took the matter into its own unofficial hands. Any one who professed even moderately liberal opinions was in danger of being denounced as an agent of the Bolsheviki, while worthy organizations, religious or cultural in character, were gravely pilloried as subversive influences. For months the country shuddered at every whisper of radicalism. There was a very considerable amount of radical agitation in the United States after the war, and some of the leaders were practitioners of violence, but frequently our efforts to cope with the problem savored more of hysteria than of rationalism.

Looking at these manifestations of intolerance and at the way in which the public reacted to the spectacle, one is forced to conclude that the American people were using censorship and "red baiting" as an outlet for their overwrought emotions.

In sharp contrast to the intolerance of the period towards certain things was our pronounced apathy towards other incidents which should have aroused alarm and reprobation. Scandals erupted in the national government. The major ones were in the Veterans' Bureau and in the administration of the naval oil reserves. While a few of the guilty were punished, others, equally guilty, went free. To a student of American life the important point of this odious affair was not the conviction or the acquittal of the accused. The noteworthy fact was the apathy with which the people as a whole watched the unfolding of the evidence. They were too preoccupied with their business ventures, too engrossed in pleasure, or too interested in some passing fad or fancy to pay any attention. Public indifference in time of national scandal is strong evidence that our moral standards are in a state of disrepair.

As in foreign affairs we had retreated from an emotional internationalism into isolationism, so in domestic policies we lapsed from a mild liberalism into a phlegmatic and unimaginative conservatism. The dominant politicians of both major parties fatuously proclaimed that the country would return to "normalcy." The various administrations watched the witches' dance of speculation and spending with positive complacency. Remedial and precautionary legislation was so effectually blocked that, when the crash came at the end of the decade, the federal government and most of the states had no machinery for handling the debris left by the economic collapse, and, furthermore, there were no blueprints on hand for the construction of such machinery. Naturally the more perceptive and vocal of our citizens found themselves in the unrewarding roles of faultfinders, and among our writers there were more than a few who saw impending disaster.

While the nation was recreant in fulfilling its international duties and phlegmatic in the handling of its domestic problems, the people of the country as a whole showed a febrile zest for sensation. Sensation for the sake of sensation became the order of the day, and one novelty only whetted the appetite for another more exotic and more daring. Mah Jong, an old and quite complicated Chinese game, was imported early in the decade, and within a year it had literally swept over the country. Flagpole sitters attracted the respectful attention that we had hitherto reserved for visiting nobility and Hollywood celebrities. Athletic contests were more and more publicized until a prizefight or championship football game became a mammoth spectacle, attended by thousands, while millions received only slightly diminished thrills by reading lush accounts of the event. Radio blossomed rapidly into an apt purveyor of thrills, and soon any householder could sit in the erstwhile privacy of his living room and hear lively accounts of football games, splendiferous funerals, and noisy political conventions. Tabloid newspapers, coming into full flower, fanned public taste for more and more sensational amusements and diversions, while the motion picture did its expert best not to be outdone by its rivals.

In such an atmosphere women, especially the younger generation, could hardly be expected to live according to the code of manners inherited from earlier times. In the years before the war a woman could not smoke in public without inviting reflections on her audacity or even her moral standards. In the Jazz Age of the 1920's women used so much tobacco that national cigarette advertising was soon "slanted" in the direction of the feminine consumer. Advertising, it should be remembered, is an accurate barometer which is quite sensitive to social changes. During the 1920's women crowded to prizefights, hitherto reserved, in general, for the delectation of men; they found their way into "speakeasies"; they discovered that they had a perfect talent for exciting the reprobation of moralists by indulging in eccentricities of dress, notably short skirts. The "flapper," as the young girl of the period was called, became established as the hallmark of the decade. Now the word flapper is defined as "a young girl or woman whose costume and behavior are characterized by extreme freedom or boldness." The dictionary contains few definitions so explicit and so wholly satisfying. The flapper set at naught the mores sanctified by observance during the age of crinoline, and she demonstrated her new-found freedom by the extreme shortness of her skirt and the extreme breadth of her language. The more literate members of the tribe read and accepted a hodge-podge known as Freudian psychology. That this so-called Freudianism exercised a restraining influence on the manners of young women is distinctly open to doubt. The flapper received fitting literary treatment in such books as *The Plastic Age* and *Flaming Youth*, while on a much higher literary level F. Scott Fitzgerald used her as a figure in many of his stories and novels.

The flapper, as nearly as we can determine from a distance in time of some twenty or twenty-five years, resulted from the emancipation of woman, somewhat too rapidly achieved and carried to ecstatic extremes. At least, many intelligent observers regarded the spectacle as distasteful. Curiously the decade produced no clearly marked masculine counterpart of the flapper. The pre-eminence of women in attracting public attention is probably to be explained by the fact that before the 1920's men lived under fewer restrictions and inhibitions than were imposed on women.

Sensitive and intelligent writers could hardly be expected to produce books which serenely and placidly accepted the social order when they worked in surroundings here briefly set forth. Dreiser, Lewis, Cather, Sherwood Anderson, Hergesheimer, Cabell, Mencken, and O'Neill all did splendid work during the 1920's, and almost without exception they showed, each in his own way, disapproval of the decade. This disapproval ran the gamut of expression from the philippics of Mencken to the gentle and indirect comments of Willa Cather. The time was out of joint, but our literary craftsmen were not bent on setting it right. They tended, directly or indirectly, to point out the dislocation.

The members of the Lost Generation, however, gave the most vivid portrayal of the period. Of the writers who belonged to this group Hemingway and Fitzgerald are the most notable, and they are the ones whose comments and portraits are the most typical and probably the most enduring.

Now it is often asserted that the Lost Generation was the product of World War I. This statement must be diluted with some heavy qualifications. The argument for the oft-repeated assertion rests on the easy assumption that the horrors of war and the unworthy and disappointing peace which followed so embittered and disillusioned our more intelligent young men that they were naturally forced into the state of mind characteristic of the Lost Generation. The argument continues to the effect that only disillusioned idealists could be as bitter as the Lost Generation was. The characteristics of this generation of writers are pretty well known. These young men were marked by a brittle cynicism, a rather self-conscious pose, which imperfectly masked feelings that might easily have found expression in sentimentality. Certain scenes from both *The Sun Also Rises* and *For Whom the Bell Tolls* show that Mr. Hemingway with obvious difficulty repulsed unwelcome sentiment. Usually the repulse was effected by the use of a shattering monosyllable that might or more generally might not be the inevitable weapon. In the second place, the Lost Generation was the sworn enemy of idealism. Naturally it adopted a philosophy of unvarying pessimism. This pessimism was so consistent that one is perhaps justified in questioning its sincerity, for even the most resolute pessimist can usually find a grim pleasure in watching the fulfillment of his dire forebodings.

The Lost Generation reduced life to simple physiological processes, and found a melancholy pleasure not in Byronic and passive contemplation of the obvious but in alcohol and in such exhibitions as the bullfight. This group had once tried to think, it had perhaps indulged in youthful idealisms, but all that was past. Despite the loud and sometimes too strident protests of these sad young men, despite their earnest striving for brutal realism, the suspicious must persist that, in a very true sense, the Lost Generation was as romantic as, for example, Byron. To these writers life was a gory conflict, like the bullfight which to them neatly symbolizes human existence. It should be noted that Hemingway never seems to identify the race of man with the matador. The bull symbolizes man. The animal charges into the ring and for a few minutes wages valorous but futile combat with his artful opponents. At the end the bull is dead. Such is life. If existence ends only in obliteration, the Lost Generation dismisses after-life as a superstition or as figment of naively romantic imagination.

No lengthy argument is required to demonstrate that shallow cynicism, pseudo-mechanistic psychology, irreligion, the anodyne qualities of alcohol, and the momentary diversion of an athletic contest were not discovered by the Lost Generation. All these things were possessions of earlier decades, and the war only accelerated the development of cynicism, irreligion, and pessimism. Without the titanic losses and horror incident to world conflict the Lost Generation would have been just as badly lost, though possibly not so well publicized. When the members of that generation point to war as the cause of their intellectual and spiritual disrepair, one is irresistibly reminded of a graying, rascally ne'er-do-well who in mild alcoholic mood is wont to attribute all his failures and short-comings to an early and unfortunate, though near-forgotten, marriage.

ERNEST HEMINGWAY

(1898-   )

Of all the writers who are usually included in the Lost Generation, Hemingway is at once the most conspicuous and the most important by far, though of late we have seen a justified revival of interest in

the work of F. Scott Fitzgerald. Since the middle 1920's Hemingway
has had a place in American literature. In spite of the marked un-
evenness of his writing, future historians of American letters will
hardly overlook the man. Better than any other writer he caught
the spirit of the decade in *The Sun Also Rises,* and then in 1940 he
published *For Whom the Bell Tolls,* a novel of almost epic qualities,
which clearly reflects the changed mood of the late 1930's. On the
strength of these two novels, the last written when he was only forty-
two years old, Hemingway cannot be denied a place of significance,
perhaps of prominence, in our national letters. Whatever he may do
in the future, and Mr. Hemingway is most unpredictable, his position
is secure.

Hemingway was born in Oak Park, Illinois, July 21, 1898. His
father was a physician. Nothing remarkable is related of his early
years. He participated in athletics and accompanied his father on
hunting trips. These activities later influenced, to a striking degree,
his choice of material for his fiction. As a young boy, just after his
graduation from high school, he had a little experience on a newspaper. While he was still in his teens he enlisted in a volunteer ambulance unit and served in Europe. For a time he was attached to
the Italian army. Hemingway saw the rugged side of war. As an
ambulance man he became acquainted with the horrows of combat
without the excitement of direct participation, while in the Italian
sector he watched war carried on in confusion and disaster.

After the armistice he was foreign correspondent for a Canadian
paper, covering the war between the Turks and the Greeks. While
on this assignment Hemingway saw sights that left indelible impressions which he later recorded in various places. For some time
he lived in Paris as correspondent for a chain of American papers.
During this time he also visited Spain and became well acquainted
with this country and its people.

It is often said that Gertrude Stein influenced him. This statement seems to be open to question or, at least, to elaboration. Miss
Stein may have influenced Hemingway just as any older and powerfully original mind may influence any young writer. She may
have affected his early and experimental work, but the clean-cut objectivity of Hemingway's mature fiction shows slight influence of the
highly subjective and almost irrational Stein. Speaking of *In Our
Time,* an eminent critic mentions Hemingway's "naive and colloquial
accent—partly learned from Sherwood Anderson and Gertrude Stein."

Just exactly what is meant by the phrase "naive and colloquial accent" may not be clear, but if it means a clipped, colloquial dialogue, Anderson and Miss Stein can hardly be accounted inventors of the device. It is to be found in Mark Twain and, to a degree, in Artemus Ward. Anderson and Miss Stein made their contributions by using the clipped colloquial speech to express interior monologues. The one place where Hemingway extensively uses the clipped speech to express the interior monologue is in *Torrents of Spring*, which is usually thought to be a parody of Anderson. It is rather worthy of notice that he prefaced his parody of Anderson with these words from Fielding: "The only source of the true Ridiculous (as it appears to me) is affectation."

Hemingway is one of the few original writers to arise in America since Mark Twain, but, of course, in literary work there is no such thing as simon-pure originality. An original writer is one who gives the effect of novelty by a characteristic mode of expression, or by his point of view, or by his ability to catch the ordinary things of life off guard. The mere use of exotic material does not make a writer original. Hemingway is original, not because he writes of bullfights, Spain, and sudden death in the afternoon. He is original because he has a characteristic point of view which is far from trite, because he expresses himself in no commonplace fashion, and because of the things that he can do with an ordinary incident such as a quail hunt.

Hemingway began his serious literary attempts while he was living in Paris, and some of his early pieces were published in fugitive magazines like *The Little Review*, *The Transatlantic Review*, and *This Quarter*. All of these magazines were then edited in Paris mostly by American expatriates, though *The Little Review* had been founded in Chicago by Margaret Anderson. Before long both the *Atlantic Monthly* and *Scribner's Magazine* published some of the young writer's short stories.

Hemingway's first book was a collection called *In Our Time* (1925). Many of the stories and sketches in this volume are striking, and most of them show the authentic Hemingway touch, but the book is disconcertingly uneven. The volume, however, even in its failure to maintain a high level, is typical of Hemingway's work. *In Our Time* contains fifteen pieces, each with a short introduction which seems to have no relation to the following story. Some of these introductions are exceedingly brief, while none contains more than three hundred words. The subjects are varied: scenes from the war, incidents of the bullring, the execution of political prisoners, and the hanging of a criminal. They remind one of a series of etchings done by a master of line. Dry, totally objective, and superlatively vivid, they are among the finest pieces of writing ever done by the author. The introduction to the first story is typical.

Everybody was drunk. The whole battery was drunk going along the road in the dark. We were going to the Champagne. The lieutenant kept riding his horse out into the fields and saying to him, "I'm drunk, I tell you, mon vieux. Oh, I am so soused." We went along the road all night in the dark and the adjutant kept riding up alongside my kitchen and saying, "You must put it out. It is dangerous. It will be observed." We were fifty kilometers from the front, but the adjutant worried about the fire in my kitchen. It was funny going along that road. That was when I was a kitchen Corporal.

The introduction to the book as a whole is a short but unforgettable sketch of an incident in the war between Greece and Turkey in 1922. Hemingway is usually very fine when he is reporting personal experiences, but that does not mean that he is not good save when he is using first-hand material. The common belief that all of the vivid writing in Hemingway's books is autobiographical has caused many readers to construct a highly colored but wholly fanciful biography of the writer.

Of the longer pieces in this volume, *In Our Time,* probably the best and certainly the most often reprinted is "The Three Day Blow." This story is so lacking in expository material, background, and the chat which other writers usually have with the reader that many find it vague and elusive. Such an opinion is almost certainly mistaken. The story is episodic, at first glance fragmentary, like so much of Hemingway's material, but it still has all the elements of a modern short story. "The Three Day Blow" relates an incident which happened on a camping trip. It abounds in casual, pointless conversation, but the talk sounds natural—inevitable, considering the circumstances. The men were drinking. Into the conversation come overtones of an unhappy love affair. At the end the men take their guns and start out into the hunting field.

"How do you feel?", Nick asked.
"Swell. I've just got a good edge on." Bill was buttoning up his sweater.
"There's no use getting drunk."
"No. We ought to go outdoors."

They stepped out the door. The wind was blowing a gale.

. . . .

None of it was important now. The wind blew it out of his head. Still he could get into town Saturday night. It was a good thing to have in reserve.

There is the authentic Hemingway down to 1937. Life is an inexplicable muddle. Alcohol will help one over the rough spots. It is always a good thing to have in reserve, but the clean winds blowing over the fields and marshes, the whirring flight of the game bird, the sight of something alive which is not human—all these are better. One would hesitate a long time before suggesting that Hemingway, with a different background, physical and spiritual, would have been a brother to Thoreau and W. H. Hudson. But fundamentally there is a bit of similarity. Hemingway looks at nature, however, through the eyes of a sportsman. He is a mighty hunter, and the good hunt ends in the death of the quarry. Death is never far from Hemingway's thoughts even in moments of recreation.

In 1926 Hemingway published his first novel, *The Sun Also Rises*. This brief work represents the author's most successful attempt in the field of sustained fiction. It has superb form—something which cannot be said of the later novels, and naturally it has a stunning impact. The story is that of the Lost Generation, those expatriated Americans who wandered about Europe seeking respite from some rooted foreboding, some vague sense of doom, an inescapable feeling of maladjustment to a life that, at its best, would be unendurable. Although the Americans of the book are in Europe, they would have been just as badly lost in Albany, Grand Rapids, or Seattle as they were in Spain. They are the restless but impotent debris left, they think, by the tide of war. Despite their perfervid efforts to find forgetfulness in alcohol and physical sensation, they can never for a moment shake off their gloomy broodings on their fate, and that fate is to be forced to live and occasionally to think. Living is bad enough, but thinking is intolerable. The woman of the book, Lady Brett, might well attract the objurgations of the moralist, but she is essentially a pathetic figure, pathetic in her loneliness and spiritual desolation. She and her fellows are lost souls, lost in an unwanted world and impotent to change that world or their relations to it. They are not, strictly speaking, immoral; they have only a blank spot where the moral sense should be. They are not irreligious; they are completely anaesthetic to religious suggestion, and they have found no very satisfactory substitute for religion. They are not unintellectual, though they have never taken the trouble to see if they have capacity for reflective thinking. Their thought is mechanical and unconcerned with ideas. To them life is a shadow flecked with mirages of light, and they restlessly pursue the mirages. Happiness is either an opportunity lost somewhere in the past or an impossibility flitting somewhere in the future. At the close of the novel Brett says to Jake, apropos nothing at all, that they could have been happy together. Jake answered, "Yes. Isn't it pretty to think so." On this note of dubiety the book was based, and on that note it ends.

The Sun Also Rises is more than a vivid record of an incident in the life of the Lost Generation. It literally is the Lost Generation. And it is more. It is an excellent novel, neat and compact, filled with sound characterization and superlative dialogue. Some of the effectiveness of the book may be explained by the fact that it was first planned and written as a short story. Then the author expanded the work without diluting it. The short narrative, as we have it, gives the concentrated effect of a short story and, at the same time, the feeling of expansiveness peculiar to the novel.

The Torrents of Spring (1926) is little read. Perhaps that fate is not wholly unmerited. It is 143 pages of parody, a clever caricature of Sherwood Anderson. It may have only slight excuse for living, but it is most amusing. The man who wrote it had read a great deal of Anderson, and he was not too much impressed. In this book the simplicity of *Winesburg, Ohio,* and the incongruities of *Dark Laughter* are broadened into pure burlesque.

Men Without Women (1927) is Hemingway's second collection of short stories. In this volume the author avoids the looseness and episodic quality so apparent in his first collection. The stories, almost without exception, are taut and sinewy. The casual quality is still there, but the over-all effect is more studied. Some of the pieces in this volume are among the best American short stories. "The Killers" and "The Undefeated" are especially fine. Both of these stories have been republished in many anthologies.

"The Killers," though endlessly discussed and studied, remains one of Hemingway's finest productions. The characters are stupid waiters in a cheap restaurant, steel-cold gangsters, and the fellow whom the gunmen are trying to kill. At the end of the story the hunted is lying on a bed in his room, knowing that his end has come, determined to run no more, and merely waiting to get up enough courage to leave the house. Impotent, trapped, doomed, Ole Andreson is the symbol of Man.

The Sun Also Rises had received both popular and critical approval, and the short stories were widely acclaimed, but still many persons insisted upon regarding Hemingway as merely a bright young man who had a flair for treating somewhat exotic subjects. Few considered him as a serious writer of great promise. *A Farewell to Arms* (1929) changed this tentative rating. The novel is in essence the story of a love affair between a young American lieutenant attached to the Italian army and an English nurse. World War I, specifically the fighting in Italy, supplies the background. The writing is spotted. Hemingway tried to avoid sentimentality in the handling of the love story, and he succeeded but at considerable cost. Some of the passages devoted to the principals are so abrupt and jagged that they are as artificial as the long speeches of Elizabethan drama. The best portion of the book is a masterly account of the retreat from Caporetto. This action was a mélange of rout, confusion, and horror. Hemingway was never more effective than in the few chapters which he devoted to this episode. *A Farewell to Arms* may be uneven, but the over-all effect is exceedingly fine. Today the admirers of Hemingway seem to be dividing into two camps, those who like *For Whom the Bell Tolls* and those who prefer *The Sun Also Rises*, but thousands who belonged to the youngest generation of novel readers in 1929 will never forget the impact of *A Farewell to Arms*. Incidentally, it is well to remember that the story of Lieutenant Henry and Catherine Barkley and the account of the Caporetto disaster are not autobiographical.

Death in the Afternoon (1932) is Hemingway's tribute to and exposition of his favorite sport, bull fighting. It is encyclopaedic in its scope, and it is done with immense enthusiasm for the subject. The writing runs from the prolix to the superb, but as a whole the volume is one of Hemingway's major achievements.

The following year saw the appearance of *Winner Take Nothing,* the third volume of short stories. The pieces in the book fall far below those in *Men Without Women*. None of the stories of this volume, save possibly "After the Storm," has the overtones of "The Killers" and "The Undefeated." Hemingway's icy brilliance, his superb command of emotion, the bulletlike impact are all blurred.

Violence, brutality, and death lose their effect when they are employed for their own sake. The blood and violence of this volume are as inartistic as an automobile accident. Hemingway's command of brute force has degenerated into a caricature. Many of the old characteristics remain, but the stories lack direction. That may have been the author's intent, but the pointlessness of life is not too effectively demonstrated by pointless stories.

The Green Hills of Africa (1935) is the attempt to relate the story of a hunting trip in Africa by making use of all the devices of fiction. Hemingway tried "to write an absolutely true book to see whether the shape of a country and the pattern of a month's action can, if truly presented, compete with a work of the imagination." The attempt was an interesting experiment, but it resulted in nothing more than a book on big game hunting.

This work seems to have marked the end of Hemingway's first period, though one must admit that a definite outline of an author who is only fifty years old is impossible, while even tentative suggestions are excessively hazardous. By 1937 the Lost Generation was only a faded historical relic. Its sophomoric pessimism, its neoromantic preoccupation with death, its predilection for physical excitement were all as outmoded as the studied artistry of the Yellow School. The youngest generation, that one which came of age about 1930 had found new interests. The United States was in a whirl of reform, social amelioration, and humanitarian crusades. Writers dutifully followed in the wake of our thinking and actions. Socially minded reviewers unfortunately animadverted upon Hemingway's callous indifference to worthy causes. Evidently these remarks nettled Mr. Hemingway.

A novel, *To Have and Have Not* (1937), was Hemingway's answer to his critics. One is constrained to wish that the critics had kept still. But even if the critics had said nothing, Hemingway was due for a change. He was becoming a bit repetitious in both his material and his effects, and he was far too young and too creative to spend his later years, like Bret Harte, in repeating the kind of work upon which he built his early reputation. Hemingway, figuratively speaking, smote his capacious chest and declared that he too had a social conscience. He was seemingly mistaken. *To Have and Have Not* was literally a disaster. The only thing that it proved was that Hemingway could write a silly novel. The thesis is absurd, and the elaboration of that thesis is far from impressive.

For Whom the Bell Tolls (1940) magnificently atoned for the failure of the preceding novel. The scene is Spain during the late Civil War. The protagonist of the novel is Robert Jordan, a young American university professor, who is fighting on the side of the loyalists. The thesis of the book, memorably stated in the grave accents of John Donne used as a foreword, is that the life and death of Robert Jordan cannot be a matter of indifference to free men everywhere. Whether or not we agree with Hemingway's international thinking or even with his views on the Spanish situation is of no moment. We must admit that the thesis is intelligent and susceptible of artistic treatment, and we must furthermore admit that Hemingway developed his thesis with utmost effect.

Critics disagreed and ordinary readers argued endlessly about this novel. The left-wing critics were offended by the author's chilly attitude toward the communists, while spokesmen for the right-wing felt that the author was irretrievably wrong in his sympathy for the republican faction. The novel is an outgrowth of a particular struggle, a social and political complication, the rights of which are still violently debated. To speak of Hemingway's political views is to open the way to opinions born of prejudice and passion. Literary criticism has little to do with this aspect of *For Whom the Bell Tolls*.

The novel contains some low spots, but these spots are measurably above the high-water marks of numerous other writers. They appear low and flat because of the surrounding terrain. The novel is a thoroughly fine work, well constructed and, in spots, amazingly well written. It is too long to have that sustained tautness of which Hemingway is capable, but as a whole it is most impressive. The dialogue has enough of Spanish flavor that one is always aware that the characters are speaking Spanish, while never does that flavor become obtrusive. Speaking of this aspect of the book, an eminent publisher, whose house did not bring out *For Whom the Bell Tolls*, warmly asserted that the book was as much of a contribution to Spanish literature as to American. This comment may be justified, but one is inclined to suspect that the novel has not had a wide and open circulation in Spain.

The Fifth Column and the First Forty-nine Stories (1938) gives a reader the best possible opportunity to appraise the strength and weakness of Hemingway. *The Fifth Column*, a drama, is only an interesting experiment in a form hitherto untried by the author. The

forty-nine stories include all those written up to 1938. *In Our Time,
Men Without Women,* and *Winner Take Nothing* are republished
along with many others which had appeared only in magazines. This
collection can convince the most sceptical that Hemingway has
enormous power, enough to place him among the world masters of
the story. It may seem foolhardy to put a middle-aged American
in a group which might include such writers as Poe, de Maupassant,
Chekov, Kipling, and Henry James, to name a few from divergent
schools, but here are Hemingway's stories to speak for themselves.
Let the reader peruse them and form his own opinion.

Hemingway is so effective in his stories that one is inclined to
wonder if, decades hence, he will not be esteemed primarily because
of his short pieces. *A Farewell to Arms,* and *For Whom the Bell Tolls*
are both made memorable by their tense episodes of matchless power
and vividness. Many of these incidents might be removed from their
context and republished as short stories with only a bit of exposition
added. This is no adverse criticism of the novels; it is only a comment on Hemingway's undoubted ability to gain his effects with
great economy of space.

Hemingway has moments of weakness. A great flaw is his occasional willingness to relax his hold on his material and allow violence
and blood to run unchecked. He has, however, some other weaknesses which are more irritating than important. One of Hemingway's most obvious traits is his toughness. Now one can make a
fairly convincing argument to the effect that this toughness is assumed. Hemingway may be, perhaps is, a sentimentalist. Many
passages, especially in his novels could easily have been deflected
into sentimentality. At times the temptation must have been almost
irresistible, but Hemingway, like his generation, was so glutted with
idealism and sentimentality during World War I that he is in conscious revolt against the mention of feelings and higher values. The
cruel and insensitive world which Hemingway depicts is never once
alluded to as desirable. The fact may be that he is disgusted with
life simply because it seems to him devoid of values. He has never
indicated a belief in spiritual values—he came nearest in the presentation of Robert Jordan in *For Whom the Bell Tolls*—and to impute to him a credo on the basis of silence would be too hazardous.
Discussion of the point is fruitless. We have the toughness of
Hemingway to reckon with, but the suspicion will not down that it
is in part assumed. When some men are grappling with inexorable

life, they can justify themselves most easily by being tougher than life.

For a rugged and self-sufficient individual, such as Hemingway considers himself, he is unusually sensitive to adverse criticism. This annoying trait is not confined to his personal life and feelings but manifests itself in his literary work. *To Have and Have Not* seems to have been written in answer to critical jibes. When some of his early reviewers foolishly spoke of his predilection for simple declarative sentences, implying that he could write nothing else, he proceeded to show just what he could do. In *Death in the Afternoon* he contrived a few sentences of interminable length, beside which the involved circumlocutions of Henry James are positively simple and easy. Hemingway is so well established and in such command of his characteristic mode of expression that he should be indifferent to criticism. Whether or not he will develop in his natural fashion is another question. He is much too sensitive.

Fortunately Hemingway's merits far outweigh his weaknesses. His power and vividness are beyond question. At his best, especially in the short story, he is a master of form. His objective characterizations carry conviction. His ability as a story-teller, when aroused and kept in hand, gives to his work a tense but strong thread of narrative. In the handling of situation he is superb. No man in American literature has been able to do more with so great an economy of words. His justly admired dialogue is not a stenographic record of a conversation. It is ordinary talk pruned down to the essentials. Thus he maintains verisimilitude while giving to the dialogue great speed and intensity. He has, in short, the technical mastery which a great writer needs.

If Hemingway's reputation, very high at present, fails to expand or to endure, the fault will not lie in his effort to give a lifelike representation of human existence. The fault may lie in his preoccupation with one theme. That theme is death. Hemingway seems to agree with the dictum of Victor Hugo, as reported by Walter Pater: "We are all condemned to death with an indefinite reprieve." Instead of spending their interval, as Pater urged, in art and song, Hemingway's characters spend it seeking sensations that will make them forget momentarily the ultimate day. This neo-romantic dread of death, this insufferable feeling of doom, tends to give Hemingway's work a tone of monotony. To think of the world as only a cell inhabited by the condemned is to narrow one's range.

Life which begins in pain, endures in cruelty, and ends in death is to Hemingway no fit subject for contemplation. One had best not think of it. This point of view is, after all, rather naïve. It reminds of a nurse distracting an infant from its babyish intent by displaying some glittering plaything. If all creative artists had had this idea, how much we would have lost in the fields of tragic art, literature, and music, to say nothing of philosophy. Only when man, fully conscious of his doom, stands up and resists, often for some inchoate reason such as regard for self-respect, does he rise to the dignity of a tragic figure. Hemingway's characters, with the exception of Robert Jordan, are spiritually timorous souls flying from the thoughts of inexorable doom. They are, at best, only pathetic.

At the close of "The Killers" one of the characters says, speaking of Ole Andreson who knows that he is to be killed, "I can't stand to think about his waiting in that room and knowing that he's going to get it." George answered, "Well, you'd better not think about it."

That is Hemingway and that is his greatest weakness.

F. SCOTT FITZGERALD

(1896-1940)

In *The Sun Also Rises* Hemingway gave a picture of that portion of the Lost Generation which went to Europe. F. Scott Fitzgerald took for part of his material the Lost Generation at home. Hemingway wrote of uprooted and aimless young men who wandered about Europe with no thought of revolt. For their part the revolution had been accomplished. What else had been accomplished was uncertain. Spiritually and intellectually too lackadaisical to participate in a revolution, they were the products of revolt, free but unhappy. Fitzgerald took for his early theme the young persons in this country who were in active revolt. They scarcely knew what they were revolting against, but revolution was one way of working off the energy of youth. These young men are not novelties in literary history. They can be found in the Yellow Nineties; they had their prototype in Gautier of the flaming waistcoat; they were brothers to the young men who joyfully hailed the French Revolution. Fitzgerald made the most of a type which he knew very well. As the chronicler of restless youth he is sure of a place as a social historian—a position which he probably did not crave.

There is another aspect of Fitzgerald. In the early 1920's many young persons became convinced that America was devoid of culture and barren of promise. The Puritan background of this country, so the argument ran, made impossible a free and agreeable life. Paris was the mother of modern culture, and in France one could live one's own life without interference. One could at least drink and discuss art. Besides, one could look at James Joyce and Gertrude Stein. As a result of these reflections literally hundreds of young Americans packed up and went to live in France, permanently, they said. The story of these young men who sought happiness abroad, their slow disillusion, their return to this country— this is a part of the material used by Fitzgerald.

Fitzgerald was born in St. Paul, September 24, 1896. After graduation from a Catholic preparatory school, he entered Princeton in 1913. Although he does not seem to have been overly addicted to study, a recently published collection of letters and excerpts from his notebooks seems to indicate that he read widely and that he had a cultivated man's attitude toward literature. It is probably not too much to say that he was the best educated fiction writer of the group linked with him by time and association.

At Princeton he joined the Triangle Club and collaborated on two musical comedies presented by that organization. He left college in 1917 and joined the army. All his service was done in the United States. During the war he worked on a novel which he could not sell. After the armistice he became an advertising writer and in his leisure hours worked on verse, sketches, and fiction. When he was fortunate enough to sell a story for thirty dollars to *The Smart Set*, then under the editorship of Mencken and Nathan, he quit his job, went to St. Paul, and revised his novel. It appeared as *This Side of Paradise* (1920) and achieved a great success. From that time Fitzgerald was a highly paid writer, good enough to win critical approval and sensational enough to be a valued contribution to popular magazines.

Fitzgerald's second novel was *The Beautiful and the Damned* (1922). This was followed three years later by *The Great Gatsby*, the author's major work. The theme of all three novels is literally the jazz age. *This Side of Paradise* is a sprightly—at times brilliant —account of a young man who was not unlike Fitzgerald. The leading character goes through Princeton, the war, and into the malodorous postwar period. To him love was notable for its transience, morality an outmoded inhibition. At the end he is a disillusioned young man of twenty-four. The book is a rather slight but eminently readable social document. It was the first novel to present the flaming youth of the 1920's, and it still is the best.

The Great Gatsby is a more mature work. This novel gives a brief but stunning impression of a society that has money but neither breeding nor the capacity for ordinary decency. In 1937 Fitzgerald, writing to his daughter, spoke a few words about the moneyed but vulgar crowd. The persons to whom he referred were on a higher social level than that frequented by Jay Gatsby, but his attitude toward the two groups was the same.

I have seen the whole racket, and if there is any more disastrous road than that from Park Avenue to the Rue de la Paix and back again, I don't know it. They are homeless people, ashamed of being American, unable to master the culture of another country; ashamed, usually, of their husbands, wives, grandparents, and unable to bring up descendants of whom they could be proud, even if they had the nerve to bear them, ashamed of each other, yet leaning on each other's weakness, a menace to the social order in which they live—oh, why should I go on? You know how I feel about such things.

While this excoriation was written a dozen years after *The Great Gatsby,* and while it refers to another group than that portrayed in the novel, it probably indicates the mood in which Fitzgerald wrote the story of Jay Gatsby and his odious circle.

Fitzgerald's short stories are hard to appraise. They fall between contributions to "slick paper" magazines and art works. They are too polished, too contrived, to bear comparison with Sherwood Anderson's or Hemingway's best, and they are too well written to be ephemeral. In their very polish and glitter they are typical of the period and group to which Fitzgerald belonged. Of the stories "Babylon Revisited" is probably the best, certainly the most frequently reprinted. It is an afterthought, as it were, on the expatriates of the 1920's, those young men who were so sad in their conviction of disillusion. This story, however, was done after the beginning of Fitzgerald's disillusion with disillusion.

In 1934 a novel, *Tender Is the Nght,* appeared. Fitzgerald's admirers seem inclined to place this work in the major canon, but its status is quite dubious. It is not up to *The Great Gatsby*, though its sure touch and subdued tone offered promise of distinguished work in the future. At the time of his death Fitzgerald was working on *The Last Tycoon*, but he passed away before the completion of the novel. The work appeared in unfinished form. The early part is so fine that the book probably would have been the author's best work had he completed it. In 1945 Edmund Wilson, a long-time friend of Fitzgerald, edited *The Crack-Up*, a collection of magazine pieces, letters, and excerpts from the notebooks. This work reveals a well-read man, gifted usually with sound literary judgment and vivid imagination. To persons interested either in Fitzgerald or in literary craftsmanship this is an important volume.

The final status of Fitzgerald in American literature is most indeterminate. It may well be that his life was more significant than his works, though his fiction gives a brilliant account of a period which may or may not seem important to the future. Probably he was too much a part of the circle of which he wrote. Until one of his friends—and he had many—writes a critical biography with full candor and sympathy, to speak of this point is hazardous and tasteless. In a letter written not many years before the end of his life Fitzgerald said that in the preceding fifteen years he had made and spent $400,000. One can be forgiven for wondering if the activities attendant upon the spending of this sum might not conceivably distract an artist from rigid application to his work.

JOHN STEINBECK AND THE SOCIOLOGICAL NOVEL

Since 1932 the sociological novel has tended to fall into two broad categories. First, we have those books which are written in the vein of such older sociological novels as *Uncle Tom's Cabin* and *The Jungle*. In the second group are those works which conform to the Marxist dogma. With very few exceptions the novels in the second group were exceedingly bad. As every college student knows, Marxism rests on dialectical materialism or, as it was formerly called, the economic interpretation of history. To this first doctrine the Marxists add a belief in class struggle and in the eventual dictatorship of the proletariat. The acceptance by a fiction writer of the Marxist doctrine as an interpretation of human history and as a forecast of the future seems to have the unhappy result of forcing the novelist to write according to a formula, and great fiction has seldom been thus written. When the romanticism of the nineteenth century became only a formula, the romantic novel degenerated into a tissue of speciously glittering insincerities. When naturalism became a formula—as it did—the naturalistic novel lost its spontaneity and force. One is perhaps right in saying, though in certain quarters one can never gain forgiveness for saying it, that the Marxist writers have always accepted Marxism as a formula. They have been too self-consciously and belligerently Marxist. Seemingly the fact that Karl Marx arrived at his conclusions through a long and elaborate rational process has impelled the left-wing novelists into a rational presentation of their conclusions through the medium of fiction. Too often the Marxist novelists have failed simply because they were more intent on polemic than on the presentation of human life. Propaganda and fiction sometimes mingle in rather satisfactory fashion, but thus far the Marxists have not hit upon that way.

Probably to the non-Marxist the most unsatisfactory feature of left-wing novels is the presentation of individual character. Since the Marxist considers the group all important, he blurs the impression of individual character in order to emphasize the importance of the larger units of society. Thus far such novelists have not been wholly successful in making social units satisfactory substitutes for individual characters.

Despite the acceptance of the Marxist dogma in the early 1930's by a rather surprising number of authors, most of the fiction writers who self-consciously allied themselves with the left-wing were lacking literary competence. This fact alone would have kept the Marxist novel from reaching a high level of performance. When an aspiring writer of no great skill unblinkingly accepts a formula for the construction of his novels, the results are almost certain to be deplorable. One does not have to look further to find a reasonable explanation for the failure of the radical group on the field of fiction. Marxist novels of the 1930's are significant of a state of mind; they are not notably significant as literary productions.

It is, however, unfair to pass by this group of writers without mentioning the names of two who were emphatically above the level of mediocrity. Albert Halper (1904-   ) published *Union Square, The Foundry,* and *The Chute* in the short space of four years. All of these books show plainly the influence of Marxism, but all are competently written. Halper's credo is that "any writer who considers himself a serious workman must have a message or he is not worth his salt." While one might understandably disagree with the credo, one must admit that Halper's books contain more than a message. They are novels first, and only in a secondary sense are they vehicles of propaganda. Josephine Herbst (1897-   ) is the other left-wing writer who was reasonably successful in blending propaganda and fiction. Her principal works, *Pity is not Enough*, *The Executioner Waits*, and *Rope of Gold*, appeared from 1933 to 1939. From 1940 to 1946 neither Miss Herbst nor Mr. Halper published any long fiction. This fact may be of some little significance.

Although the Marxist novel failed to win wide popularity during the 1930's, the sociological novel of the traditional type achieved immense popular and critical success. During that decade the nation was hag-ridden by a horde of social problems, not one of which was wholly without precedent in American life, but many of which were of unprecedented extent and gravity. Our national social conscience, largely dormant during the 1920's, was awakened. Of all the writers of sociological fiction during the years of depression and partial recovery the most important figure is that of John Steinbeck.

Steinbeck was born at Salinas, California, in 1902. Most of his life has been spent in that area, and nearly all of his better works have a California background. Steinbeck studied at Stanford University, but he did not receive a degree. His first book, *Cup of Gold* (1929), a fictionized biography of Henry Morgan, the buccaneer, showed small promise, as did his next two novels, *The Pastures of Heaven* (1932) and *To a God Unknown* (1933). The failure of these books is probably to be explained by the fact that Steinbeck had not yet hit upon an original theme. This he found for his novel, *Tortilla Flat* (1935), an episodic account of a permanently depressed group near Monterey. In this book he used characters and situations which he understood, and he used them with great effectiveness. The work is deficient in that the theme and the thematic development are slighted, but it presents a series of episodes with admirable vividness. Steinbeck's success dates from the publication of this novel.

In Dubious Battle (1936) centers about a strike. This book is not so good as its predecessor. *Of Mice and Men* (1937) showed Steinbeck once more in possession of characters for whom he had sympathy, and in this book he sounded the theme which is most congenial to him, the desire of a man for a home of his own. Technically this novelette is the best of Steinbeck's works. It is objective in treatment though emphatically not cold. Expository passages, argument, and description are minimized. Dialogue carries the action and thematic development with most satisfying effect.

The Grapes of Wrath (1939) set Steinbeck's mark in popularity. It is the story of a dispossessed family who travel from Oklahoma to California in a dilapidated truck. The thread of the narrative is the account of their experiences on the road and in California. The theme of the book as given in the words of a minor character is, "Place where folks live is them folks. They ain't whole, out there lonely on the road in a piled-up car. They ain't alive no more." This is, of course, a version of the home-seeking theme.

The Grapes of Wrath must be given a high place among American sociological novels. The writing is as good as any that Steinbeck has done, and in places, especially in the speeches of minor characters, it rises to a compelling eloquence. Structurally the novel is on the picaresque model. The action moves rapidly from place to place, and the work contains a very large number of minor characters. The dramatic effect of the novel is impaired by the insertion of many interchapters which serve partly to establish the atmosphere but which, too frequently, are only Steinbeck's vehicle for the expression of his social and economic views. These passages reveal that Steinbeck is a humanitarian, an agrarian—perhaps even a radical agrarian —but they show no Marxist influence. In his social thought Steinbeck is one of the latest outcroppings of that long-established American school which holds that the welfare of society is dependent, at least in part, upon individual ownership of land.

Like most sociological novelists of the past, Steinbeck is more interested in his message and its development in terms of dramatic action than in the delineation of character. He does not, however, try to make the group function as an individual. He presents characters as individuals, but he does not develop them. His characters, in general, are types, and as such they are none too interesting. Certainly they are not complex. The mother is a typical mother; the father is presented with equal simplicity. The two personages of the book who show symptoms of individualization are the grandfather and the renegade preacher, Jim Casy. Casy appears in the book only at intervals, and the grandfather dies soon after the start for California. If the old man had been allowed to stay in

O

the action, he might have deflected interest from the dominant theme. He was too strong and colorful for a sociological novel.

The Moon Is Down, Cannery Row, and *The Wayward Bus,* Steinbeck's latest novels, show an immense drop from the high level set by *The Grapes of Wrath. The Moon Is Down* is a story of Norway under the German occupation. While it was read with approval by thousands of persons, its success can doubtless be attributed to timeliness rather than to literary merit. The other two books are almost surely the product of insufficient planning and hasty writing. The frog hunt in *Cannery Row* is unforgettable, but one episode cannot make a novel. *The Wayward Bus* is totally lacking in the qualities which make for good fiction. The characters are unconvincing, and some of the incidents are wholly incredible. To add to the other and devastating defects of the book, Steinbeck tossed in a liberal quantity of obscure symbolism. The whole effect is most baffling.

THOMAS WOLFE

(1900-1938)

Thomas Wolfe has been acclaimed by his admirers as an unquestioned genius, while his adverse critics have alleged that he was a confused man who expressed himself, somewhat against his will, in the novel. These hostile critics furthermore assert that his novels were long, rambling, confused patchworks which, admirable as they may be in episodic passages, fail to achieve that unity which is the primary aim of sustained fiction. Both these extreme views contain a bit of truth. Those who consider Wolfe a genius can point to passage after passage of vivid and moving prose. Those who fail to see the genius in the exuberant writer can point to any of the novels as illustrations of form sacrificed to exuberance.

The making of a novel seems to be not unlike the building of a house. To build a house one first employs an architect who plans the structure. After that work is done, the builder takes over and executes the plans. In such manner is a novel planned and written. In the making of his blueprints Wolfe was far from a success. In fact, most of his work seems to have been composed extemporaneously without the benefit of plan. But in sheer writing, in the ability to put down words and sentences of wonderfully expressive English, Wolfe has had few superiors in the whole range of American fiction.

In spite of good writing and at times because of the very exuberance of the man, all of his books, with the possible exception of the relatively restrained *Look Homeward, Angel,* fail to achieve that totality of impression which is the ultimate criterion of good fiction.

Most teachers of American literature have doubtless noticed Wolfe's extreme popularity with the younger generation, and many have wondered at it. Perhaps the explanation is to be found in Wolfe's exuberance, in his Elizabethan delight in the use of words, and in the vividness of his episodes. Wolfe was always the boy in his zest for and wonder at the spectacle of life, in his energy and gusto, but he never outgrew his adolescent confusion. His youthful admirers probably like him for his positive qualities and readily forgive his turmoil and undirected strivings.

Wolfe was born in Asheville, North Carolina, October 3, 1900. Those who seek sidelights on the writer's boyhood and youth can gain them from the novels, for Wolfe constantly wrote about himself. He was educated at the University of North Carolina and at Harvard. At the latter institution he received his master's degree. For a short time he traveled abroad and in 1924 he went to New York University where he taught English. Five years later he brought out his first novel, *Look Homeward, Angel.*

Wolfe's manuscripts must literally have been terrifying to publishers because of length, and the first novel was no exception. In its original form it was far too long for publication, but after a painful process of cutting and patching, it came out as the most orderly of his works. The critical success of the book was immediate, though the sales were not particularly good. Sinclair Lewis in his address at Stockholm, when he accepted the Nobel Prize, went out of his way to praise Wolfe. Many persons first heard of the young novelist through the reports of this address. When Wolfe was once established, his fame grew with amazing speed.

Of Time and the River (1935) is the result of herculean literary labors and equally great editorial work. Two huge manuscripts seem to have been compressed into this long novel. One of the manuscripts alone is said to have contained ten or twelve times as many words as the average novel. Only fanatical admirers of Wolfe will deny that this work shows all too clearly the marks of its editorial revisions. In spite of scars and loose structure, it is a compelling piece of fiction, and many of Wolfe's admirers consider it his finest work. During his short life Wolfe published only two other books.

From Death to Morning (1935) is a collection of short stories. The other book, *The Story of a Novel* (1936) is an account of Wolfe's literary methods. It is of extreme importance to all students of Wolfe. In the field of the short story Wolfe scored a surprising success. Vividness of incident and character portrayal are the chief virtues of the stories, and, while his disregard of form marred his novels, he managed to give his short pieces admirable unity. There are critics who feel that Wolfe was distinctly better in the short story than in the novel.

JOHN P. MARQUAND
(1893-   )

Although John Marquand is frequently called the native satirist of Boston, he was born in Wilmington, Delaware. His ancestry, however, is emphatically New England. For example, Margaret Fuller, the high priestess of transcendentalism, was a great-aunt. Marquand was educated at Harvard. He saw service in World War I and later was on the staff of the Boston *Transcript,* the accredited spokesman of the true Bostonian. After a tour of duty in advertising, he began to write short stories for popular magazines, and in a short time he became highly skillful and correspondingly highly paid. This phase of his work culminated in the Mr. Moto stories which for a good many years were a popular feature of the *Saturday Evening Post.*

Marquand's writing of popular stories has operated as both an asset and a liability. Work of this type made him an accomplished technician and gave him a command of a smooth and unobtrusive narrative style. Hence he came to the writing of his important novels with a technical proficiency that few of our novelists possess. On the other hand, certain critics have never been able to forgive him for being a popular writer for the *Saturday Evening Post.* Far too much has been said in derogatory fashion about Marquand's "slickness." In all probability the word would never have been applied to the writer of *The Late George Apley* if the author of that book had not served a most useful apprenticeship as a writer for magazines printed on "slick" paper. Marquand's "slickness," when the opprobrious word is analyzed, seems to mean that the author leaves no loose ends in his narration, that he does not habitually use incident for the sake of incident, and that his characterization is firm and coherent. Technical skill is so rare an accomplishment of the ordinary American novelist that some critics seem not to know how to regard it.

It is a mistake, moreover, to assume that Marquand wrote *The Late George Apley* with no previous training in extended narration. He was already the author of some half-dozen works, several of them in the field of romantic fiction. His first book, *Prince and Boatswain* (1915), done in collaboration with James Morgan, was a collection of sea stories. In 1922 he published *The Unspeakable Gentleman,* a romantic novel which was, in general, pretty favorably reviewed, but it would have taken a most discerning critic to see in this book the hand that later was to write *Wickford Point*.

In 1925 he brought out *Black Cargo,* another romantic work. This is a story of slave-trading days, and it is probably the best book of the author's early period. In the same year Marquand published a biography of the self-styled Lord Timothy Dexter, an incredibly fantastic merchant of Newburyport, Massachusetts. This is a thoroughly successful piece of work. The style harmonizes with the subject, and it well may be that the writing of this book was excellent training for the future biographer of George Apley.

In 1937 *The Late George Apley* appeared. This work is a novel of many aspects. In the first place, it is a delightful parody of the reverential biography in which the biographer accepts, without question and even with approval, all the petty mores, the outgrown traditions, the prejudices, and the formalized society of the subject's immediate environment. This strain is held unbrokenly through the book. The imaginary biographer fails to get the whole point of the novel. But *The Late George Apley* is more than the parody of an official biography. It is social satire of the best type, though the satirical note never becomes obtrusive or strident. Through the use of his fictitious biographer, Marquand maintains an air of complete objectivity. Never does he step forward in his own behalf to point the satire or to make it more apparent to the unperceptive. Never is he unkind to his subject, though George Apley's environment was unbending to the point of cruelty. Apley was the sort of man that he was simply because his environment would not allow him to be anything else. The reader finishes the book with more than a little admiration for Apley and with a tinge of sorrow for the man who was forced by circumstances to order his life in a way that was distinctly neither of his making nor of his choosing. In the hands of another novelist, Dreiser, for example, the conflict, the inner struggle, between the real George Apley and his social milieu could easily have been made into a naturalistic novel of the conventional type. But Marquand gives a comic reading of life, and only those who habitually rate plodding tragedy above light-footed comedy will wish that he had altered his approach to his subject. One might call *The Late George Apley* a naturalistic comedy and support the appellation with some impressive arguments.

When *The Late George Apley* appeared, certain persons who were in a position to know what they were talking about were heard to complain that Mr. Marquand "knew too much." The allegation was possibly true. Further evidence of Marquand's firm grasp of the social background of his novel has recently come to light. A book by Cleveland Amory, *The True Bostonians* (1947), a social history of the Brahmin caste in Boston, sounds as if it might have been written to footnote Marquand's pages.

Naturally a discussion of *The Late George Apley* leads to a mention of *The Last Puritan* by George Santayana. Both books use the same background, though Marquand is interested in social mores, while Santayana is concerned with the intellectual and moralistic aspects of the Brahmin life. Each man knew intimately the background that he used, and both could approach the subject objectively, Marquand by virtue of his characteristic temperament, Santayana, in part, at least, because of his Spanish Catholic antecedents. But at that point comparison leads into contrast. Santayana wrote a philosophical novel on an exceedingly high intellectual level, while Marquand dramatized with comic touch the concepts that Santayana used as the basis for intellectual and moralistic speculation. Marquand's characters are crystallized into clean-cut individuals, while Santayana's remain throughout somewhat nebulous figures involved in the intellectual conversation. Some readers have remarked that every character in the book talks like Santayana. In *The Last Puritan* the dramatic action is exceedingly slight. This is no disparagement of *The Last Puritan*. The book—whether or not it is a novel is of no importance—is a magnificent intellectual creation. It moves one to think, but it seldom arouses emotion. *The Late George Apley* and *The Last Puritan* are totally unlike. They belong to different *genres*.

One of the best things about Marquand's novel is the characters.

Such persons as Apley's father, his Uncle William, his son, and especially Apley himself all belong to the same environment, all typify it, and yet all emerge as individuals and not, strictly speaking, as types. Throughout the book the theme is reiterated. The environment is too strong. Occasional abortive revolutions simply emphasize the strength of the surrounding social structure. Yet because of Marquand's subtle variations on this theme it does not become monotonous. At the close of the book George Apley's son, his youthful rebellion behind him, returns to Boston and picks up where his father left off. The next generation will be like the preceding. The figures of the drama may change, but the environment remains.

After *The Late George Apley* Marquand might have been expected to achieve a resounding anticlimax, but such was not the case. His next novel, *Wickford Point* (1939), is a highly skillful study of a decadent New England family. George Apley is a man caught in a strong but petrified society; the Brill family of *Wickford Point* has an intellectual background, but it has degenerated into a shoddy group which is impotent either to think or to act. *Wickford Point* is a long and somewhat involved book, lacking the crystal clarity and the exquisite sense of direction which characterized *The Late George Apley*, but is a fine group study. The minor characters are extremely good. The figure of Allen Southby, the tweedy, pedantic scholar is a masterly portrait of a pose.

So Little Time (1943) on the surface is the story of Jeffrey Wilson, a successful play doctor on Broadway, but intrinsically it is the story of that generation of Americans which fought World War I and found itself impotently drifting into World War II. Wilson typifies this generation. He has no creative ability, at least, he never took the trouble to develop it, but he is very clever in rewriting the work of others. As an indictment of a whole clever but superficial generation this novel is truly impressive. The narrative, seasoned with satire and irony, is the story of a group whose chief characteristics are intellectual and spiritual impotency, imperfectly concealed by dilettantism. To many members of Jeffrey Wilson's generation the book was most unpleasant. Again Mr. Marquand "knew too much." More than one reader following the story of this truly lost generation, had the strange feeling that he was looking at his own autopsy. While the author constantly emphasizes his dominant theme, the details are far from neglected. Such minor characters as the self-important war correspondent and Wilson's down-at-the-heels brother make brief but memorable appearances. On the whole *So Little Time* is a notable addition to American fiction.

H. M. Pulham, Esq., and *B. F.'s Daughter* are delightful works of fiction, but they fail to reach the high standard set by the three books just discussed.

Point of No Return (1949) is another examination of the malaise that afflicts American businessmen. Marquand's characters, drawn almost always from the upper class, financially speaking, are victimized by their social and economic surroundings. Victimized is probably too strong a word. They are more or less willing victims. In some way, voluntarily or not, they accept the standards of their class. The ambition to get more and spend more is frequently realized, but getting and spending fail to bring satisfaction. The net result is not exactly unhappiness but rather a vague feeling of unrest. *Point of No Return* is written in this vein with humor and sympathy. It adds to Marquand's stature as the foremost social satirist now practicing the art.

Since the death of Miss Cather, Mr. Marquand is probably the most competent technician in the field of American fiction. His style is always clear and flowing, his manipulation of incident is admirably dexterous, and his characterizations are sharp and memorable. He is, in short, an artist, an appellation which can be applied to very few of our novelists, past or present.

JAMES T. FARRELL

(1904-   )

James T. Farrell, though concerned more with individuals than with the epic, comes close to Zola in his preoccupation with evil, using that word in a wide sense. He has been accused, in his own words, "of kicking and tearing civilization to pieces." Some critics cannot see the implication beyond the printed page, but such criticism as that just cited reveals the preternatural ability of some other critics to look beyond the printed page and see the wrong implication. Like Zola, Farrell is a mighty moralist. While some have lamented that the "promise of American life" has become only an ironical phrase, and others have exhorted us to dig down to grass roots or to bring back the frontier or to return to the ebullient optimism of our forebears, Farrell still sees the promise. To him the tragedy is that the promise is not often fulfilled. The promise of youth is still a reality, though a bit tarnished to be sure. It is glimpsed fleetingly, but it is still a reality, even in the crowded streets of the big city. Dreiser pre-empted the title which might have been used for the story of Studs Lonigan. Farrell's American tragedy is the failure of a character to realize our romantic intimations of youth. Environment, aggravated by personal weaknesses, is the villain.

If one is reluctant to detect overtones, the story of Studs Lonigan may perhaps be read as only the detailed biography of a failure. But it is much more. Farrell has written a few lines which may be read as a commentary on this work. He is talking of Mark Twain's two characters, Tom Sawyer and Huckleberry Finn.

Tom and Huck are symbols of the possibilities in human beings. Today they stand as a test not only of ourselves but of the whole of American society. They are, with all their charm, like two accusing figures, with their fingers pointing down the decades of American history. Their very characters seem to ask why—why has this promise not been realized? Why is it so rarely that the man becomes what the boy gave promise of becoming? This is part of their significance as enduring characters in American literature.

The qualities of an author which Farrell thinks praiseworthy are the very qualities which would have received the approval of Zola. In writing a short "revaluation" of *The Brothers Karamazov*, Farrell says, "He [Dostoievsky] wrote with candor, honesty, penetration, and high seriousness." That sentence, better than anything else which has ever been written, expresses Farrell's literary credo, if not always his achievement. Farrell says in another place that the function of literature is to make the reader "more intensely conscious of the problems of life, of the predicaments of people, the possibilities and limitations of living, the diversities of human experience."

In fulfilling his intent, as expressed in the preceding sentence, Farrell is forced to examine the problem of evil. The problems of life, the predicaments of people, the possibilities and especially the limitations of living—all these things turn on evil. Again Farrell is his own best commentator. This time he is talking about Dreiser, a man with whom he has often been compared. "Evil is a problem to him, but he does not treat it in theological terms. To him evil is social; all his novels are concerned with the social history, the social processes of evil." Evil enters into the novels of Farrell simply because it is inherent in the social milieu.

Farrell spends no time telling how to expunge evil. He is no sociological novelist in the ordinary meaning of that term. His task is that of the diagnostician. Like Ibsen, he exposes the malady, and then he is through. The glib patter of the propagandist, the dogmatic answers of the "left-winger" to all questions, the cocksureness of the reformer, all these are absent from Farrell's novels. To call Farrell a naturalist is only to return an easy classroom answer to a difficult question. An old-fashioned naturalist he certainly is not. His works were all composed in the spirit of faith and the hope of ultimate triumph. Certainly Farrell is not a romantic, though in another and earlier age and in a different social and intellectual environment he might have been a towering romantic. Can one say then that Farrell is a short-range naturalist and a long-range romantic? All such answers are merely feats of juggling with words. For all practical purposes it will do to say that Farrell is a realist with faith. To stand on even so simple a characterization one must insist that a realist may have faith. In one of his essays Farrell says: "For we stand convinced that some day there will be built a real City of Man. And that is our ideal, that is our faith, that is our conviction. Get down on your knees, gentlemen, and pray, pray for an artist like Lloyd C. Douglas, only an artist." What Farrell does not say in this passage is that, before the new City of Man can be built, men and women must be made to see the flaws and imperfections of our present abode.

Farrell is a sore trial to many critics and to all classifiers. He is interested in the social background without being sociological. He is a realist with faith, but he never allows his faith to inveigle him into the making of blueprints. He is convinced that most social evils spring from economic factors and that the cure may come only through change, but he never allows himself to become a propagandist. When he writes fiction, his exacting duties as a novelist monopolize his attention.

As a stylist Farrell has received the hearty disapproval of many reviewers. It is true that he writes in a bare, straightforward, almost monotonous style, devoid of ornament and rhetorical devices. Perhaps it is enough to say that an elaborate style would be violently at odds with the materials of his novels. Furthermore, Farrell as a realist is primarily concerned with the impact of his episodes upon the reader. That impact would be softened by the use of a lush style. Imagine *Young Lonigan* written in the rolling periods of a romantic who too often uses grace and rhetorical effects to beguile the reader into the acceptance of the implausible.

Typical of Farrell's work is the *Studs Lonigan* trilogy. The *Danny O'Neill* tetralogy exploits the same material used in the trilogy but in a somewhat different spirit. Aside from his novels, Farrell has written some of the best literary criticism of our time. His critical essays abound in intelligent, if intricate, ideas set forth with immense energy and conviction. Even his adverse critics admit that in this type of writing he has an effective style. His many victims must sincerely deplore his effectiveness. The small volume called *The League of Frightened Philistines* contains some of his most pungent criticism. It is required reading for one who wants to understand Farrell.

CHAPTER XXIX

IN CONCLUSION

When the first edition of this book appeared in 1931, the author opened the last chapter with the statement that "in a guide to American literature like the present one, prophecy has little or no place." Despite that statement, the author named three novelists whose work seemed most promising. The three were Hemingway, Elizabeth Madox Roberts, and O. E. Rölvaag. Subsequent events have more than justified the author's disinclination to display his limited talents for prophetic vision. In 1927 Rölvaag brought out his *Giants in the Earth,* an impressive performance. At that time Rölvaag was fifty-one. No prose writer should be past the climax of his power at that age. Moreover *Giants in the Earth* was so fine that one might feel justified in expecting other sound works from the writer. Unfortunately his subsequent novels fell far short of the mark set by their distinguished predecessor, and Rölvaag died at the early age of fifty-five. He must, therefore, go down in American literature as the author of one first-class work. The same fate befell Elizabeth Madox Roberts. *The Time of Man* was poetic—probably a bit precious—but it was at least a novel and a good one. Later works by Miss Roberts failed to display much except poetic prose. Miss Roberts died in 1941. The career of Hemingway has been briefly discussed.

In short, the history of our letters since 1920 is studded with names of promising writers who, for one reason or another, failed to develop. Today, after a long war and all the dislocations incident to extended conflict, prophecy is even more hazardous than it was in 1931.

It is, however, not quite fitting to close even a hasty survey of our national letters without at least naming some of the recent writers who show great promise. Opinions differ widely as to the promise and achievements of these figures. Certainly one of the most discussed writers of the last quarter-century is John Dos Passos. In 1921 the writer's *Three Soldiers* justly attracted wide attention.

This novel was the work of a disillusioned young man who had gone through the war and emerged with a bitter taste in his mouth. As a picture of army life this book is superb in its vividness and vitality, as the utterance of a disillusioned idealist it went far to establish the critical tone of the 1920's. The book was savagely attacked as a misrepresentation of the American soldier, and its validity is still questioned. It may or not be an accurate social document. That is beside the point. The fact remains that it is a brilliantly written novel whose critical attitude was gladly accepted by thousands of young readers. These young readers were grist to the mill which produced the Lost Generation.

In 1925 Dos Passos brought out *Manhattan Transfer*, a strident attempt to capture the physical and spiritual confusion of a metropolis. Without being experimental in the full sense, it was a novel and striking attempt to do something which had never before been accomplished. The spirit of the big city is implicit in most of Dreiser's work, but *The Financier* and *The Genius* do not try to depict the physical aspects of life in the city. Dos Passos undertook an important and difficult task. His success is not unquestioned. One acidulous critic denounced *Manhattan Transfer* as "an explosion of a bombshell in a cesspool." The context of this pronouncement, coupled with a choice of rather harsh words in the phrase, gives the criticism, in the eyes of some, an unwarranted tone of hostility. Hostile the critic meant to be, but as a matter of fact, the dictum is not beyond acceptance. *Manhattan Transfer* is as explosive as a bomb, and neither the material of the book nor the diction is characterized by an idyllic quality. The novel is distinctly a notable performance, and it may be the author's best work. The book suffers from a lack of focus, and this defect is caused by a lack of concern with artistically significant characters.

Dos Passos then turned to a depiction of the whole American scene from 1900 to approximately 1930. The undertaking was not characterized by excessive modesty. Three novels, published separately and brought together in 1938 under the significant title *U.S.A.*, were the outcome of Dos Passos' work. The aim was to stress the social background of the American people and to indicate the futility of individual struggle in a decadent, rotting civilization. The cause of this decadence is the unlimited spirit of commercialism, the profit motive. At the time when Dos Passos wrote *U.S.A.*, he was politically far to the left, and while these three novels, *1919, 42nd Parallel,* and *The Big Money,* undoubtedly afford the best examples of left-wing fiction in our literature, still the exigencies of such fiction operate strongly against the unquestioned literary success of any work. Even Dos Passos could not find a satisfactory substitute for the individual character of conventional fiction. While the social background receives close and intelligent treatment and while the writing, considered by sections, is lucid, the over-all effect is similar to that which one might get by tossing all the ingredients of an ordinary novel, with the notable exception of the significant protagonist, into a receptacle and stirring with an electric beater.

The most striking things about *U.S.A.* are the technical innovations by which Dos Passos tried to solve the fictional problems of his work. He used the newsreel, the camera eye, and numerous biographical sketches. The newsreel is a combination of headlines, snatches from popular songs, lines from advertisements, and Whitman-like mélanges. The camera eye seems to be the author's more or less conscious musings contemporaneous with the major narrative. The aim of these two innovations seems to be to illuminate the background. The biographical sketches, frequently of real characters, are almost always penetrating and effective. The contribution of the other two devices is most dubious. Typographically speaking, they are striking, and probably for that reason have been accorded more significance than they deserve.

After Dos Passos retreated from his position on the left, he returned to the ordinary novel form and technic. His success has not been notable, but since he is only a little past fifty, speculation on his future is hazardous. He is too young and much too intelligent to be given up as a brilliant promise which faded.

A literary movement of the period between the wars, which did not fulfill the promise envisioned by some of its adherents, was the so-called New Regionalism. It is not unkind to say the New Regionalism was only the old local-color movement adapted to an age of realism and naturalism. During the 1920's, when our fiction was depicting scenes in France and Spain and episodes of life in the newly rich froth of the homeland, many seemed to think that our literature should be firmly rooted in an authentic American background. The movement started out promisingly enough, but soon it deteriorated into a formula for writing. Then it was discovered that a poor writer cannot write a good book even if he goes down to grass roots in the most American portion of the States. Broadly speaking, most of our literature before 1920 was regional, for few writers achieved the continental grasp which Whitman demanded of poets to come. The New Regionalism had little to offer in the way of novelty and less in the way of hope. Marjorie Kinnan Rawlings with *The Yearling* (1938) added a minor classic to our slender stock of such works. This book is sometimes referred to as one of the triumphs of regionalism, but one is forced to say that *The Yearling* is a good novel because it is a soundly planned, well-written, and immensely appealing work of fiction. The use of an exotic background is only a minor contribution to the success of the book.

Among the recent writers of fiction only a few are worthy of notice, but two are exceptionally promising. Robert Penn Warren's *All the King's Men* is an excellent novel. Mr. Warren spent a long apprenticeship in poetry, the short story, and extended fiction before writing this work which presumably deals with the Long regime in Louisiana. He has the requisite technical ability and the knowledge of human nature to become a novelist of the first rank. Only recently (1947) A. B. Guthrie, hitherto unknown, published *The Big Sky,* a story of the Western free trapper of more than one hundred years ago. He had all the material for a flamboyant, sensational novel of Western derring-do, but he did not succumb to the temptation. Mr. Guthrie wrote a novel of great restraint, which, better than any other piece of Western Americana, captures the feeling for the big sky of the mountain region. One novel does not make a significant writer, but a work like *The Big Sky* may be a portent of things to come.

In general the prospect for the novel in this country is none too roseate, and the prospect for the serious young writer is even less attractive. In the past, it is reasonably safe to say, very few novelists of genuine merit, who tried to market their wares, have remained unpublished. Those were the days when a first novel was not an utter publishing failure if it found fifteen hundred buyers. Today production costs have risen to such an extent that few publishers care or even can afford to take a chance on a meritorious manuscript that is certain to appeal only to a small group. To reinforce the publishers' demand for books which can be produced in large quantities, we have the somewhat questionable influence of the book clubs. These organizations offer large sums for books which will not be returned by too many of their huge memberships. Here again the demand seems to be for books which sometimes can hardly be called art products. Furthermore, the astronomical offers of Hollywood for desirable scripts only reinforce the demand for the popular, in the worst sense of that word. As a result the young writer is faced with a real problem. He can write honestly and well and take his slender chances for publication with slender returns, or he can indulge in the sensational exploitation of sex, or martial or marital adventure, or the stoked-up toughness which is the hallmark of Hemingway's imitators. A blown-up historical novel which contains all these elements is sure of a large sale and serious reviews, however meretricious the work. These are only a few of the unpalatable conditions which confront the young writer.

During the 1920's H. L. Mencken was the most intelligent and influential of our critics. Early in the next decade he virtually retired from practice as a critic and devoted himself to other work. His *American Language,* with the two supplements is a vast and well-arranged storehouse of information concerning the varieties of English spoken in the United States. The research that went into the making of these books is appalling even to contemplate. Since Mr. Mencken was the author of these works, they are interesting. In addition to his treatise on our national speech, Mencken has been writing volumes of his autobiography. Thus far three titles have appeared, *Happy Days, Newspaper Days,* and *Heathen Days.* To say that these books are superbly written is faint praise. A glance at a few chapters of *Happy Days* will convince any discriminating reader that the author is a stylist of great skill. Better prose has not been written in this country since the death of Mark Twain.

The three hundred years of our national literature have seen many strange mutations in the constantly shifting color and pattern of the American mind. But despite all vicissitudes of national thought and experience our literature to-day expresses the thinking of the American people, just as it did in the beginning. The dominant interests of our people have always been the dominant interest of our writers, and there is no reason whatever to suppose that changing custom or literary taste will serve to divorce our national mind from our national letters. Prophecy is always dangerous, and it is especially so in the field of literature. Even a diagnosis of current thinking is very hazardous, for one has extreme difficulty in ascertaining which are the significant and which are the insignificant aspects of swirling contemporary life. It may be that our belletristic literature will turn its back upon many of the problems that have been its traditional material, but if it does, we may be very certain that such an action will be caused by the refusal of the American people to consider those questions worthy of serious thought. From John Cotton to Ernest Hemingway our literature has expressed the interests of America, and, if our letters have been able to swing from the extreme theological emphasis of early Puritanism to the disillusioned sophistication of Ernest Hemingway, it is quite within reason to think that American literature can follow any development of our national interests.

INDEX

INDEX

DATE DUE

APR 6	1983		